PAUPER
ANCESTORS

PAUPER ANCESTORS

A GUIDE TO THE RECORDS
CREATED BY THE POOR LAWS
IN ENGLAND AND WALES

DAVID T. HAWKINGS

This book is dedicated to the memory of my friend
the late James (Jim) Stansfeld, whose great-great-grandfather,
Sir James Stansfeld, did so much to help the poor and needy

First published 2011

The History Press
The Mill, Brimscombe Port
Stroud, Gloucestershire, GL5 2QG
www.thehistorypress.co.uk

British Library Cataloguing in Publication Data.
A catalogue record for this book is available from the British Library.

ISBN 978 0 7524 5665 2

Typesetting and origination by The History Press
Printed in Great Britain
Manufacturing managed by Jellyfish Print Solutions Ltd

CONTENTS

CONTENTS

PREFACE

Many years ago my uncle, Thomas Hawkings of Bristol, was told that an old Bristol Corporation building was abandoned and in it were many old books. He decided to investigate but by the time he visited the building it had been demolished; it was a pile of rubble. As he approached the site he saw that someone was loading a number of old books into a van. What treasures were these? Whilst exploring the rubble he found a sheet of pale blue paper with neat handwriting on it. Then another and another and another. He gathered these together. Each sheet was numbered. When assembled together they made a book of 187 pages, though there are only entries up to page 113. There is a name index at the front although letter 'A' is missing. It is a Poor Law Relief Book for the parish of Bedminster, once a parish in north Somerset but now a suburb of Bristol.[1] It is dated 1851 to 1852. In this my uncle noted on page 10, 'Margaret Snook, 70, widow, rec'd 1/6 & 1 L Sergeant Stout. Applies for increase. Refused.' Against her name in the index is written 'Kilmersdon'. Knowing that his paternal grandmother was called Clara Snook before her marriage, my uncle wondered if this Margaret Snook was related to him. Many years later I began to explore the records of the Poor Law Commission, the Poor Law Board and the Local Government Board which are held at The National Archives. To my amazement I found a document dated 1856 referring to this Margaret Snook. She was recorded as 74 years of age, the widow of Thomas Snook. (As other research had later shown, she was indeed related to us.) She had been questioned because she was receiving parish relief. She stated that she was born at Chapple Lizard (Chapelizod) about 3 miles from Dublin. She said, 'I never left that place until I was married to my husband in Galway and I was then nearly thirty years of age'. She said that her husband was born at Kilmarton (Kilmersdon, Somerset). But what was Thomas Snook doing in Ireland? I knew he had been a carpenter and lived in Bristol. Was he perhaps a ship's carpenter and sailed to Ireland? Bristol was, after all, a large port. Alas, there are no known merchant shipping records for Bristol for that early period.

Some time later a friend suggested to me that Thomas Snook might have been in the British Army and served in Ireland. After many extensive searches in the army muster rolls at TNA, I discovered that a Thomas Snook was a private in the 4th Dragoon Guards stationed in Dublin in 1809. But was this the same Thomas Snook who married Margaret in Galway? Then the evidence leapt up at me. The muster roll for the 4th Dragoons for 1818 showed that the regiment was stationed at Cork, and against the name Thomas Snook was written 'at Galway'.[2] (Sadly my uncle died before I had made this discovery.) Were they married in Galway City or County Galway? I have yet to find the details of their marriage. (Working backwards through the army muster rolls, I found that Thomas Snook had earlier served in France and Spain.)

The earliest entry I have found in records of the poor for a member of my family is that of Samuel Cornelius and his son Edward Cornelius. The church warden's accounts for the parish of Wellington, Somerset record, '29th October 1794, Paid Sam. Cornelius to carry his son to Bristol Horsepitle [sic] £1- 1- 0.'[3] Even more surprising was the discovery that the records of the Bristol Royal Infirmary survive.[4] An entry for 24 July 1794 reads: 'Edw. Cornelius age 17, parish: Wellington, recommendor Mr. Maltravers, crurum alcera [ulcers of the leg] discharged Oct. 4th [1794] cured.' (Note that the payment to the father was recorded after his son had returned home, though this might have been due to late entering of the books.)

I also found in the Poor Law Board's records a complaint made by Mary Hawkin(g)s of Wellington, Somerset, in 1855 – a distant relative of mine.[5] She had complained that the District Medical Officer had failed to visit her sick sister, Ann Blackmore, when she had requested him to call. Ann Blackmore was apparently near to death but recovered before the doctor eventually visited her two days later. On enquiry it was recorded that the medical officer had been attending a difficult child birth (see Chapter 9).

My great-gt-gt-gt-grandmother Susan Hawkings was found in the Out Relief Register for Wellington, Somerset, in 1839.[6] It records that she was born in 1760 and was receiving 'Regular Relief', though the amount she received is not stated.

Another member of my family was found in these records.[7] In 1889 Robert Charles Hawkings of Rockwell Green, Wellington, Somerset, with 161 others, signed a petition appealing against the proposed restriction of not being allowed to keep more than four pigs within 150ft of any dwelling house (see Chapter 20).

My latest discovery is a letter dated 1 January 1873 written by the clerk of Wellington Union, Somerset, to John Hawkings at his address in London.[8] (He was a first cousin of my great-grandfather.) Copies of this letter were sent to John's two brothers, Henry, also in London, and Robert Charles Hawkings (mentioned above) in Wellington, Somerset. In this letter the clerk asked for 6d per week to support their mother who also resided in Wellington. Each of these brothers was a successful businessman yet they are recorded in the records of the poor.

What else, I wonder, lies hidden in these records yet to be discovered? There is no doubt that every family will have someone recorded somewhere in these documents. Your ancestor may have been a pauper, being moved from one place to another or on parish relief. He may have been an employee at a workhouse or an inmate. He may have been a guardian of the poor or an overseer; a medical officer or a rate collector. Or maybe he was a working tradesman or a farmer or a landowner, all of whom would have paid into the poor rates and will therefore be on record.

Whoever they were they will be recorded somewhere amongst the mass of documentation of the poor.

David T. Hawkings

Notes

1   This book is now deposited at the Bristol Record Office
2   TNA ref. WO12/634
3   Som. RO ref. D/P/Wel/13/2/1
4   Brist. RO ref. FCH/BRI/3(i)
5   TNA ref. MH12/10494
6   Som. RO ref. D/G/W/136/1/1 & 2
7   TNA ref. MH12/10509
8   Som. RO ref. D/G/W/57/10

ACKNOWLEDGEMENTS

I am particularly grateful to Jeremy Gibson, who, many years ago, suggested to me that I should explore the Ministry of Health records at the Public Record Office (now The National Archives). This suggestion set me on a life-long exploration of records of the poor and Poor Law records.

I have visited many archives throughout the country in order to gather information about the Poor Law system and the treatment of paupers. I wish to thank the following for their help and encouragement over the last twenty-five years: the staff at the Public Record Office, now The National Archives; the archivists and staff at the following record offices: the Berkshire Record Office; the Bristol Record Office; the Devon Record Office at Exeter; and the Plymouth and West Devon Record Office; the Hereford and Worcester Record Offices at both Hereford and Worcester; the Isle of Wight Record Office; the London Metropolitan Archives; the Northamptonshire Record Office; the Oxfordshire Record Office; the Somerset Record Office; the Surrey History Centre; and the Archives Department of the Guildhall Library, London.

Transcripts of documents from Ministry of Health and Department of Education records are reproduced by permission of The National Archives.

My thanks must also go to Roy Overall of the Oxfordshire Health Archives; David Bromwich, Honorary Librarian of the Somerset Archaeological & Natural History Society and late librarian of the local studies library, Taunton; and Jennie Lynch of the Parliamentary Archives, Westminster.

My thanks also go to the following for their assistance and suggestions: Peter Barrett, Geoffrey Baxter, Paul Carter, Irene Coulson, Andrea Duncan, David Janes, Anne and Robin Leamon, Tom Mayberry, Ann Morton, Pauline Pedersen, Julian Pooley, Carol Richmond, Jim Stansfeld, Marion Steel, John Titford, Adrian Webb and Bernard Welchman.

I am also grateful to Simon Hamlet and his staff at The History Press for their able assistance during the production of this book.

ACKNOWLEDGEMENTS

Images of documents and drawings from the following archives are reproduced by permission of the respective county archivists:
Devon Record Office, Exeter
Somerset Record Office, Taunton
Surrey History Centre, Woking

Images of documents from the Somerset Archeaological and Natural History Society's library are reproduced by permission of their honorary librarian.
I am most grateful to John Titford for allowing me to reproduce images of documents from his collection.

ABBREVIATIONS

Brist. RO	Bristol Record Office
Berks. RO	Berkshire Record Office, Reading
Dev. RO (Ex.)	Devon Record Office, Exeter
Dev. RO (Plym.)	Plymouth and West Devon Record Office, Plymouth
Here. RO	Herefordshire Record Office, Hereford
IoW RO	Isle of Wight Record Office, Newport
LGB	Local Government Board
Northants. RO	Northamptonshire Record Office, Northampton
OHA	Oxfordshire Health Archives, Oxford
Ox. RO	Oxfordshire Record Office, Oxford
PLB	Poor Law Board
PLC	Poor Law Commission
PRO	Public Record Office
SANHS	Somerset Archaeology and Natural History Society, Taunton
Som. RO	Somerset Record Office, Taunton
Sur. HC	Surrey History Centre, Woking
TNA	The National Archives, Kew, Surrey

TNA document groups referred to in this book:

ED	Ministry of Education
MH	Ministry of Health
WO	War Office

FOREWORD

It is nearly impossible today to imagine the conditions in Victorian Britain. Poverty was regarded as almost a sin, brought about by the people themselves and was believed to be a sign of low character. Today in this country we accept that it is our duty to help those who lose or cannot find employment and to provide them with the basic necessities of life. We have the good fortune to receive *free* medical care, clean water and sanitation, and education. We accept these things as our right and it is easy to forget the changes brought about by hardworking politicians of the past such as Sir James Stansfeld. '*Free*' is a misnomer because our services today are paid for by those who pay taxes.

It was an uphill struggle by Sir James and like-minded politicians to persuade the moneyed classes that help should be given to poorer people as a right, and not simply as charity. Sir James was deeply influenced in this respect by his religious beliefs and by the Italian politician and reformer Giuseppe Mazzini.

I feel deeply honoured and privileged to be the great-gt-grandson of Sir James, who did so much to help the poor and the repressed in the Victorian era, often at the expense of his own career, specifically with regard to his continued work on the reform of the contagious diseases acts, and on promoting a more prominent role for women in society.

I also feel privileged to be associated with the author David Hawkings. We served as engineering apprentices together, and whereas I continued in engineering, David, after several years, chose also to study social and historic subjects. His books have generated widespread interest and have caused many people to look at their past family history in greater detail. I see this book as a good example of his work and wish him all success.

James Stansfeld

INTRODUCTION

Much has been written by social historians about the development of the system of supporting the poor, known generally as the Poor Laws. Everyone has heard about the harshness of the Victorian workhouses thanks to Dickens' portrayal in his book *Oliver Twist*. Indeed, the workhouse in the early nineteenth century, with such a dreadful reputation, was the last resort for the infirm, the aged and the unemployed. Yet few family historians have explored in any depth the records of the Poor Law, and particularly those held at The National Archives.

Most people must have at least one ancestor who would have been at some time described as a pauper. Many of the most able bodied, skilled and industrious often fell on hard times and thus entered the 'world of pauperism'.

Since the sixteenth century the poor inhabitants of a parish were in some way supported by the more fortunate parishioners; at first by voluntary contributions and later by a statutory poor rate. The parish was, for centuries, the 'social unit' within which communities organised themselves. The church was the centre of religion but it also acted as a meeting place for other activities. Churchwardens were responsible for supporting the parish priest whilst overseers were concerned with the more humanitarian aspects of support in the community. Men were appointed to these posts by ballot. They were unpaid. Women were not eligible until the twentieth century, although the lady of the manor often became involved in charity work in support of the poor, the infirm and the needy.

From the early sixteenth century collections were made parish by parish for the support of the poor. Initially a pauper could only receive help from the parish in which he was born. The laws of settlement were created so that a pauper could only receive support from his *rightful place of settlement*. It was soon apparent that many paupers were not entitled to such help because they were not legally settled in the particular parish in which they were residing and in which the collection had been made. Because of the laws of settlement and the disputes that often arose as to a pauper's *rightful place of settlement*, records of the poor are extensive. Such records contain a wealth of detail for both social and family historians.

The laws of settlement gave a person a legal settlement in a particular place. He could, for example, gain a settlement in a parish by serving an apprenticeship, by renting a house for a specified time or by serving as a parish officer. A child took the place of settlement of its father but an illegitimate child took the place of settlement of its mother, regardless of where it was born. A woman, at her marriage, took the place of settlement of her husband. The rules of settlement are extensive and sometimes difficult to understand because the laws changed from time to time. One rule was often superseded by another.

Provided a man worked and supported himself and his family, he could live wherever he liked and move from one place to another. But it was when he became unemployed and dependent on parish relief that his place of settlement was enquired into. Such a pauper was conveyed to his *rightful place of settlement*, where he was entitled to receive parish support. His place of settlement was often disputed by the receiving parish officers. Why should the parishioners pay to support a pauper if they suspected he was legally settled somewhere else?

Thousands of disputes over settlement were taken to the County Courts of Quarter Sessions. Justices ruled on each case, sometimes quoting the relevant Act of Parliament. The evidence given in these cases can be very enlightening for the family historian. Sometimes witnesses were called on to state what they knew about the pauper, and in doing so all sorts of biographical information was recorded by the clerk of the court.

When seeking to remove a pauper from a parish to his *rightful place of settlement*, a Removal Order was issued requesting the overseers of the pauper's parish to receive him. A Settlement Certificate was also issued which recorded the *rightful place of settlement* of the pauper. Such documents are often to be found with other parish documents, now in county or borough record offices.

The poor of each parish were thus supported by the working population of the parish who paid into the poor rate. An unmarried woman with a child could gain support from her parish. (It appears from the records that often a woman with several bastard children received more financial help than a widow with the same number of children.) A single woman who became pregnant could become a burden on the parish. There are numerous records of such women being 'examined' at court and naming the father of the child 'with which she is now big'. The father was pressed to pay maintenance for the mother and child, with the threat of imprisonment if he failed to do so. Such examinations were usually carried out at the County Court of Quarter Sessions. The records of these courts therefore include such items that are of particular interest to family historians.

At one time farmers were reluctant to pay a fair wage to a labourer knowing that the labourer could often obtain financial support from the overseers of the poor, even when he was working. The farmer was, after all, paying his share into the poor rates. As the system developed more and more parishioners became concerned about the cost of their support of the pauper classes and thus many orders of settlement and removal were challenged.

By the beginning of the nineteenth century the number of unemployed people was growing rapidly. At the end of the Napoleonic Wars thousands of men returned home from the army and navy to find they could not obtain employment. At this time there was also a large increase in the population. The introduction of farm machinery resulted in landowners requiring less farm labourers. This led to many riots, machine breaking and the burning of hayricks. In order to maintain this mass of unemployed people the poor rate was increased and this resulted in much discontent amongst the ratepayers. The country was in crisis and many believed it was heading towards civil war. An enquiry into the situation was initiated and resulted in the Poor Law Report of 1834. Its purpose was 'the attempt by Parliament, with the first industrializing society, to comprehend the condition of the labouring poor and to formulate a policy. It was inspired by the fears of the day, guided by contemporary social philosophy and inhibited by the primitive state of social inquiry.' This resulted in the Poor Law Amendment Act of 1834. This act required the linking together of many parishes to form a *union* of parishes. Theoretically this was to reduce the cost of supporting the poor and therefore reduce the cost to the ratepayer. This indeed was the result, and farmers found themselves able to pay higher wages to their labourers. The creation of the *Unions* had reduced the poor rates by 20 per cent.

The Poor Law Commission was set up at Somerset House, London, in 1834, to organise, control and regulate the Unions. Each Union built its own workhouse where the poor resided and worked at picking oakum, pounding bones into dust for manure and other menial tasks. Some inmates made clothing for themselves and others. The workhouse was deliberately made to be an oppressive place and only the very desperate sought refuge there. Pauperism was seen by many as a 'crime to be suppressed and punished'. The Reverend H.H. Milman wrote to Edwin Chadwick, secretary of the Poor Law Commission: 'The workhouse should be a place of hardship, of coarse fare, of degradation and humility; it should be administered with strictness, with severity, it should be as repulsive as is consistent with humanity.'

A Board of Guardians was established for each Union and staff recruited to supervise and run each workhouse. It was clearly cheaper to run one Union with one workhouse, rather than each parish having its own poorhouse. No thought had been given to the psychological welfare of the inmates. Indeed, as has already been stated, it was argued that the workhouse should be a dreadful place. Those poor souls who had entered the old parish poorhouse were at least in familiar surroundings in their own parish, and could be easily visited by friends and family. By 'centralising' in one Union workhouse many inmates found themselves in strange surroundings many miles from their home parish.

There were many reports of the harsh and brutal treatment of paupers and many people challenged the system. The most notable of them was John Walter, Tory MP for Berkshire and proprietor of *The Times* newspaper. He regularly reported on the appalling treatment meted out to the inmates of workhouses. *The Times* recorded many gruesome events in an attempt to have the system improved. In 1837, when Queen Victoria came to the throne, the harvest failed, many commercial enterprises collapsed and industry was failing. The country faced depression. More than a million people were unemployed. For these the workhouse was the only means of survival and most workhouses became overfilled. Almost every day John Walter wrote in his newspaper of the cruelty to pauper inmates in workhouses. Many were close to starving.

It was the scandal of the Andover Workhouse which tipped the scales. The inmates were so undernourished that they were found to be eating the marrow from bones they had to grind for manure. Unknown to them some of these bones were from human bodies which had been cleared from the church graveyard to allow an extension to be built on to the church. John Walter was horrified and reported the matter to Parliament. At last the government took action which resulted in a complete re-assessment of the workhouse system. In 1847 the Poor Law Commission was abolished and replaced by the Poor Law Board which was controlled by a minister of state. The new system was a great improvement for the paupers. The diet was improved in quality, and clothes and medical treatment were available for the inmates, though by today's standards it would still be considered unacceptable.

And so the Poor Law Board continued to oversee the Unions throughout England and Wales until 1871, when the Local Government Board was established. This new organisation took over the responsibilities of the Poor Law Board. The Local Government Board also became responsible for sanitation, water supplies and drainage, and the maintenance of roads and bridges. These were overseen locally. From this reorganisation developed what we now know as local authorities.

At the formation of the Poor Law Commission the overseers of the poor of each parish continued in their posts within each Union and were supervised by the Union officers. Each Union reported regularly to the Commission and its successors. Often the officers of a Union were unable to resolve a problem and sought advice and guidance from the Commission. In certain circumstances permission was requested from the central authority for the guardians of a Union to undertake a particular task or to authorise payment for an exceptional service. The records of these central organisations therefore contain a wealth of information about the running of the Poor Law Unions, and within these records can often be found much detail about the inmates of workhouses, who are often named. These records also include a detailed record of every person who was recruited to work in each workhouse, from porter and nurse to master and matron (see Chapter 8).

One of the most useful sources for family historians is the records of vaccination. From 1840 children could be vaccinated against smallpox and from 1853 this became compulsory. From 1867 registers of all vaccinations were kept by the local Registrar of Births and Deaths. Each entry not only gives the name of the child, but the place and date of its birth, and the father's name and trade or profession. The date of vaccination is given and the date of death if the child died before vaccination. Apart from not having the mother's name, a vaccination certificate can act as a substitute for a birth certificate. These are freely available for searching at county record offices. Unfortunately, only a small percentage appear to have survived (see Chapter 18).

The documents recording the poor, and those who supported them, are extensive. This book can give only an outline of the mass of records available for research, both at The National Archives and county and borough record offices. It is hoped that it will act as a guide and encourage family historians to research their own families in these records. Whoever they were they will be recorded somewhere. They may have been paupers, but if they were working men, whether tradesmen or farmers, landowners or gentry, they will have paid their taxes and will be found recorded in the tax returns. Many will have been employed at Union workhouses or in lunatic asylums, and others will have been rate collectors, medical officers, guardians of a Union or workhouse inspectors. Some will have been builders or carpenters employed in building and repairing the Union buildings, and others will have been shopkeepers and local manufacturers who supplied food, clothes, bedding and other goods to the workhouse. Every family will be found somewhere in these records.

Each chapter gives some examples of the types of documents to be found in the records created by the Poor Law, both at The National Archives and at county and borough record offices.

Care has been taken with the transcribing of these records. The many peculiarities in the spelling of words are as in the original documents.

The appendices give much useful information:

Appendix 1	This lists the most important Acts of Parliament which relate to settlement and removal, and the control of the poor.
Appendix 2	This lists all the Unions within each county in England and Wales and gives the relevant document piece numbers within the TNA document class MH 12 for each Union. The piece numbers under document class MH 9, which list the staff employed in each Union, are also given.
Appendix 3	This lists the registers of admission (TNA document class MH 94) to lunatic asylums throughout England and Wales. The names of patients are given in these registers.
Appendix 4	This explains and gives examples of use of the old money system (pounds, shillings, pence).
Appendix 5	This lists the web addresses for record offices in England and Wales.

At the time of going to press none of the records referred to in this book are available through the internet. The National Archives, however, is in the process of digitising the records of twenty-two Unions from TNA document class MH 12 for the early period (from 1834). These records will be entered into the main TNA catalogue and the images will be available through TNA documents online service.

The Unions to be covered are:

	MH 12 piece numbers	Dates covered
Axminster, Devon	2096 to 2099	1839 to 1848
Basford, Notts (and Derbys.)	9228 to 9235	1834 to 1845
Berwick, Northumberland (and Co. Durham)	8976 to 8981	1834 to 1852
Bishops Stortford, Hertfordshire	4536 to 4540	1834 to 1852
Blything, Suffolk	11728 to 11735	1834 to 1840

Bromsgrove, Worcestershire (and Warws., Shrop. & Staffs.)	13903 to 13905	1834 to 1842
Cardiff, Glamorgan (and Monmouth)	16246 to 16249	1834 to 1853
Clutton, Somerset	10320 to 10324	1834 to 1853
Keighley, Yorks., West Riding	15158 to 15161	1834 to 1855
Kidderminster, Worcestershire (and Staffs. & Shrops.)	14016 to 14019	1834 to 1849
Liverpool, Lancashire	5966 to 5970	1834 to 1856
Llanfyllin, Montgomery (and Denbighshire)	16546 to 16548	1851 to 1856
Mansfield, Nottinghamshire (and Derbys.)	9356 to 9362	1834 to 1849
Mitford and Launditch, Norfolk	8474 to 8478	1834 to 1849
Newcastle under Lyme, Staffordshire	11363 to 11365	1834 to 1856
Newport Pagnell, Buckinghamshire	487 to 491	1834 to 1855
Reeth, Yorkshire – North Riding	14587 to 14590	1835 to 1871
Rye, Sussex (and Kent)	13076 to 13080	1834 to 1843
Southampton, Hampshire	10997 to 11011	1834 to 1882
Truro, Cornwall	1527 to 1530	1834 to 1849
Tynemouth, Northumberland	9156 to 9159	1834 to 1855
Wolstanton and Burslem, Staffordshire	11196 to 11198	1835 to 1842

Note: Some Unions that were positioned near a county border included one or more parishes in an adjacent county. These counties are given in brackets.

John Walter II, 1776 to 1847. (SANHS Collection)

John Bowen, 1785 to 1854. (Som. RO ref. DD/CLE2)

Sir James Stansfeld, 1820 to 1898. (Courtesy of James Stansfeld)

Mrs Nassau Senior, 1828 to 1877. (Courtesy of James Stansfeld)

CHAPTER 1

FOUR CHAMPIONS
OF THE POOR

John Walter II (1776–1847)

John Walter II was the owner of *The Times* newspaper, taking over from his father in 1803. His father, John Walter I (1739 to 1812), founded the *Daily Universal Register* newspaper in 1785 and changed its name to *The Times* in 1788.

John Walter II was also Tory Member of Parliament for Berkshire and was thus a man of powerful influence. He strongly opposed the Poor Law Amendment Bill of 1834. He saw no reason why a central authority should interfere with well-established local organisations which had been running local Poor Law Relief systems for centuries. He objected to the formation of Poor Law Unions and the building of workhouses nationally. 'To use the poor in a cruel experiment to prove that poverty was caused by idleness; to lock up paupers like criminals just because they were destitute, and even impounding their simplest possessions, was monstrous.'

He spoke against the bill on many occasions and wrote numerous articles in *The Times* decrying the proposed system. But his efforts were all in vain. The government received a majority in favour and the Poor Law Amendment Act was passed on 13 August 1834 by a large majority, and the Poor Law Commission was established at Somerset House, London. The aim was to abolish pauperism.

For eleven years John Walter campaigned against the Poor Law Commission. He objected to the separation of married couples in workhouses and the removal of children from their mothers, the apparent insufficiency of food and the strict discipline. But the public were deaf to his complaints. Indeed, they were pleased with the new system. After all, the rates had fallen by 20 per cent as a result of this reorganisation.

In 1837 the country went into a serious depression. More than a million people were unemployed and the workhouses became overfilled. By 1842 the situation became even worse: 7 per cent of the population was unemployed.

The Andover Workhouse, Hampshire, like most others was an austere and cruel place. The master was an ex-sergeant major and his wife the matron. They treated the inmates like dangerous criminals and ran the establishment like a penal settlement. The master was found to be stealing the inmates' meagre rations and although it was generally known as a dreadful place, the guardians (except one) did not appear to care. The only guardian who showed some concern was Mr Munday, but he failed to persuade his colleagues to improve conditions. He then complained to his Member of Parliament. *The Times* heard of his concerns and sent a reporter to Andover to investigate.

One of the jobs given to inmates in all workhouses was to pound bones into dust which was then used as manure on farm lands. The inmates at Andover Workhouse were so hungry that they chewed the bones and ate the marrow. In order to extend the church at Andover, part of the graveyard had been cleared and so some of the bones being devoured by the paupers were in fact from this clearing; they were human bones!

This was immediately reported in *The Times* and all hell was let loose. There was a government enquiry and at last, in July 1847, after thirteen years, the Poor Law Commission was condemned. The owner of *The Times*, John Walter, was largely responsible for this achievement. He died shortly after this announcement, on 29 July 1847, aged 71 years, knowing that he had at last achieved his goal.

The Poor Law Commission was replaced by the Poor Law Board with the result that the conditions in workhouses were improved and were described at the time as 'the finest in Europe'.

John Bowen (1785–1854)

John Bowen was born in Bridgwater, Somerset, in 1785. He first joined the Royal Navy and was later employed by Trinity House as an engineer in charge of lighthouse construction, much of the time working abroad. He later worked for the East India Company around the coast of India. He returned home to Bridgwater in 1815 and served as an engineer to the Bridgwater Turnpike Trust. He then became a journalist and for two years owned and edited the *Bridgwater Alfred*. By 1820 he had become concerned with the problem of poverty. He became an overseer of the poor in order to 'Root out a disgraceful and fraudulent system so extensive in its ramifications as to render it a most difficult matter to cope with'. It was said that he stood for 'an efficient and thrifty administration of poor relief'. He was very critical of the 'Report of the Poor Law Commission of Inquiry' which he said was 'A nauseous compendium of abuses, improvidence, and crime, without citing a single example of the blessings distributed or the evils averted'. It was generally accepted that the level of poor rates was excessive but he pointed out that the country spent even more on tobacco and snuff. He complained that the design of the new workhouse at Bridgwater would not allow inmates to see out of the windows; the windows were far too high from floor level.

The dietary for the inmates of the Bridgwater Workhouse, as agreed by a committee, was recorded thus:

> A sufficient quantity of wholesome and substantial food and will at the same time keep within the rules laid down by the commissioners that the diet of the able bodied paupers should be so regulated as in no case to exceed in quantity and quality of food the ordinary diet of any class of able-bodied labourers living within the same district.

This can only be described as a scandalous exaggeration, if not a deliberate misleading statement. The diet was in fact far from satisfactory.

Bowen complained vehemently against the new Poor Law system. His complaint, written in a letter dated 9 September 1836, was published in *The Times* newspaper. He thus became a friend of John Walter.

In the summer of 1836 the old Bridgwater Workhouse held ninety-eight inmates, but there were only seven able-bodied women and one able-bodied man, and a few children. The others were aged and infirm. Some of these inmates had been moved from their home parishes up to 10 miles away. There were only forty beds, so that adults had to share two in a bed and up to six children slept in one bed.

The dietary was deliberately made minimal in an attempt to deter paupers from entering the workhouse and thus minimise the cost. It included large amounts of gruel. The breakfast each morning was 8oz of bread for men and 6oz for women, and 1½ pints of gruel each.

Abraham King, the medical officer for the district, wrote:

> On resuming my duties at the workhouse I found that the Board had ordered that oatmeal should be used for the children instead of milk. For some days I watched the results, which was given to the Visiting Committee as producing diarrhoea. Some days after, many of the children became affected with the white mouth, the result of irritation of the stomach and bowels. In this state many were seized with the measles.

The cramped living conditions could only aggravate the situation. It was not until June 1837 that the epidemic had subsided. In that time twenty-seven inmates had died; that is about 25 per cent.

Bowen had continually complained of the ill treatment of the inmates and as a result was elected as a guardian for the Bridgwater Union. After a visit to the workhouse on 21 April 1837 he wrote:

> Found the inmates haggard and emaciated beyond description. The loathsome and heartrending spectacle defied description. A number of persons of all ages suffering intense agony, others involuntarily voiding their faeces, apparently worn out by the operation of the disease. Those who were not yet affected bearing in their countenances the strongest marks of terror and apprehension, and all breathing and absorbing a heavy foetid atmosphere, saturated with the poisonous effluvia of putrid excrements.

By the middle of July 1837 he had seen and heard enough. He resigned from the Board in order to be free to challenge the whole system of poor relief. He demanded an enquiry by the Poor Law Commissioners.

Many of his opponents considered him a 'scandalmonger', but with John Walter he fought on. The Poor Law Commission was eventually replaced by the Poor Law Board in 1847.

John Bowen died on 30 March 1854; he, with others, had succeeded in his mission.

Sir James Stansfeld (1820–98)

James Stansfeld was a deeply religious person and although from a prosperous family (his father was a solicitor and county court judge), he was greatly concerned with the welfare of the working classes. He believed that class distinction should be abolished.

He was educated at University College London and was called to the Bar in 1846. He was elected a Member of Parliament for Halifax in 1859. He held many senior positions in government, including, in 1863, Junior Lord of the Admiralty. In 1866 he became Indian secretary.

He was financial secretary to the Treasury in March 1871 and as the last president of the Poor Law Board he framed the Local Government Act which united the work of the Poor Law Board, the Public Health Department of the Home Office and the Local Government Department. He became the first president of the Local Government Board which was formed in 1871. He held that post until 1874, sacrificing his political ambitions to spend his time fighting for the rights of the poor.

During his time with the Local Government Board he did much to improve the welfare of the poor. He fought tirelessly for equality for women. In 1872, much to the amazement and concern of most Members of Parliament, he appointed a woman, Mrs Nassau Senior, as a Poor Law inspector. He insisted that she should have equal status and equal salary to men in the same office (see page 6). Many women throughout the kingdom applauded James Stansfeld for this action. Numerous letters were published in the press commenting on this appointment. It was Mrs Nassau Senior who began what was described as 'A new era for Poor Law children'. In an article on James Stansfeld, printed in *The Review of Reviews*, dated 15 June 1895, the following appeared:

The author (right) with James Stansfeld (left), the great-great grandson of Sir James Stansfeld. The box between them (and inserted) marked P.L.B. (Poor Law Board) is Sir James Stansfeld's dispatch box which he used when president of the Poor Law Board.

To the Right Honourable James Stansfeld, M.P.,
On the appointment of Mrs Nassau Senior to the office of Inspector under the Local
Government Board Sir, We, the undersigned, believing that the Law of God is one
and indivisible and equally binding upon all, that the one sole duty of Humanity is
the right to the free and responsible fulfilment of duty, that the duty of every human
being is the gradual discovery of the Divine Law, that obedience to the Divine Law
involves the fulfilment by every human being of a threefold duty towards humanity,
the fatherland and the family.

That the human laws and customs which have hitherto restricted Woman to the
fulfilment of the last portion of this duty only are opposed to the design of the Almighty,
who by endowing Woman with special aptitudes and facilities, complementary to the
facilities and aptitudes of man, has assigned to her equally with him the duty of their
full development and employment in the execution of a joint mission on earth, and
acknowledging, that you have been the first English Minister to recognise the great
religious truths indicated above, and that by the appointment of a woman to an office
of public trust and responsibility you have taken the first step towards the practical
realisation of these truths in the political system of our country.

Gladly forward to you this heartfelt expression of our enduring gratitude and esteem.
Harriet Martineau, Ambleside
Kate Amberley, Ravenscroft
Ernestine L. Rose, New York
Emilia Arshurst Venturi
Florence Nightingale, London
Mary Carpenter, Bristol
Lucy Wilson, Leeds
Isabella M. S. Tod, Belfast
Elizabeth Malleson
Josephine E. Butler, Liverpool
Cath. Taylor, Hampstead
Eliz. C. Wolstenholme, London
Mentia Taylor, London
Amelia H. Arnold

James Stansfeld was also known for his opposition to the Prevention of Diseases Acts
of 1866 and 1869. These acts had enforced the examination of prostitutes who plied
their trade in brothels, aimed particularly at the coastal ports where numerous soldiers
and sailors were stationed. The acts authorised the intimate examination of prostitutes,
the aim being to isolate those women who had contracted venereal diseases. Although
this seemed a sensible action, many such women were ill treated and suffered
great indignity when so examined, by force if necessary, and with the aid of the
police. Harriet Martineau wrote: 'Any woman of whom a policeman swears that
he has reason to believe that she is a prostitute is helpless in the administration of the
new law.'

James Stansfeld fought almost continually against these acts. Eventually, in 1886, they were repealed. He had argued that: 'It is a philosophic, a scientific as well as a religious truth that there cannot be dissonance between the laws of nature and the laws of God, and it is therefore inconceivable that the immoral should be also a truly sanitary law.'

In 1895 he retired from politics and was knighted on 5 May that year. He was granted the Grand Cross Order of the Bath. He died on 17 February 1898 at his home at Castle Hill, Rotherfield, Sussex. The following was published in *The Gentlewoman*, on 26 February 1898:

> The death of Sir James Stansfeld removed one of the staunchest supporters of the claims of women to political life. Some of my readers may remember the sensation he caused when at the Poor Law Board by appointing Mrs Nassau Senior, as a Poor Law Inspector, to the horror and dismay of official males. His innovation has been justified by the success of that and similar appointments. He retired from political life at the general election of 1895, when he received an enthusiastic address from the women whose cause he had championed, thanking him for having continually striven for the equality of men and women in all respect before the law.

He did not live to see the parliamentary suffrage given to women, but he had faith in the ultimate success of his efforts.

Mrs Nassau Senior (1828–77)

Mrs Nassau Senior was the first woman to be appointed as a Union inspector. She was born Jane Elizabeth (Jeanie) Hughes, the sister of Thomas Hughes, the author of *Tom Brown's School Days*. She was an amateur singer of some renown and was chosen to sing in the newly built Albert Hall to test its acoustics. She was often invited to perform at dinner parties. She was particularly concerned with the welfare of pauper children and was a co-founder of the British Red Cross.

In 1848 she married Nassau John Senior, the son of Nassau William Senior, an eminent political economist. She had one child, a son Walter, and adopted two other boys. At her home, Elm House in Wandsworth, she made a refuge for the aged, sick and needy, and helped the local poor. She assisted at her local workhouse infirmary and the local industrial school for delinquent girls. She was appalled by the living conditions of the working class in London and actively supported a local project of social housing.

On 28 November 1872, despite being unwell, she attended an interview with James Stansfeld, president of the Local Government Board, and was appointed the first woman civil servant in Britain. Her job as a Poor Law inspector was to investigate the education of pauper girls and report directly to the Local Government Board. James Stansfeld insisted that she should have equal pay and status as men in the same job. Her appointment caused much resentment amongst her male colleagues but James Stansfeld was steadfast; he was determined to support her in every way. As he said: 'Theirs was a meeting of true minds.'

She formed a committee of her women friends and under her guidance they inspected metropolitan workhouse schools with particular concern for the girls' education. She made every effort to follow up those girls who had left school, to check their progress through life. She also visited reformatories, industrial schools and orphanages.

In her report on the education of girls she expressed her concern about mixing together orphans and deserted girls with the children of vagrants. She believed that physically and mentally disabled girls were 'sexually vulnerable'. They needed a 'family structure' in smaller groups, 'more mothering' and 'individual attention'. She realised that there is more to education than learning 'academic facts'. She was outraged by the squalid sanitary conditions in the children's accommodation. She believed their stunted stature, weak eyesight and poor health were directly caused by poor diet. She insisted on the immediate abolition of corporal punishment for girls. To protect them from neglect, seduction and prostitution she proposed legal guardianship until they were 18 years old and the monitoring of them through their employment. She proposed safe housing for them during periods of unemployment. Florence Nightingale referred to her as her 'Dear Senior General of Female Infantry'.

She received much hostile opposition to her report and was pressed by many to withdraw it. Yet despite constant harassment she continued her work and founded a 'safe house' for unemployed girls. In September 1874 her report was finally published to the acclamation of the press.

In October 1874 she nearly died (she had been suffering from uterine cancer for some time), and was forced to resign from her job as a civil servant.

In January 1875 there were several hostile observations published on her report stating that she was 'Irresponsible, too zealous and untruthful'. But she did not submit to such adverse criticism. Always being urged on by James Stansfeld, she wrote in *The Times*: 'I shall fight both for my method and my conclusions.'

James Stansfeld presented the Women's Suffrage Bill in April 1875 but it was defeated. Yet this spurred her on. In 1875, despite being seriously ill, she founded the Metropolitan Association for the Befriending of Young Servants. Once again she received criticism because it was not a Christian-based organisation; it was non-denominational.

In August 1876 she appeared to be recovering from her illness and she looked forward to resuming her public work. Yet by Christmas she had again become weak and exhausted. She died on 24 March 1877, aged 48 years.

CHAPTER 2

PARISH ACCOUNTS

Before and after the creation of the Union system each parish was responsible for the relief and support of its own poor. Such support, both financial and material (food, and sometimes clothing and medical care), is usually to be found recorded in the parish documents either as churchwardens' or overseers' accounts.

Sometimes the cost of enquiring into the *rightful place of settlement* of a pauper and removing him and his family to their home parish may also be recorded in these accounts. Parish accounts are to be found with other parish records in county or borough record offices.

The following are abstracts from some of these records:

**Som. RO ref. D/P/Che.m/13/2/1 Chew Magna, Somerset
Account Book, 1704 to 1728**

April 23d 1716 Disburm[ts] made for the parish of Chew Magna by John Shepperd for the Poor

Paid	£	s	d
Hill, widow		04 – 00	
David Spear		04 – 00	
Hewit, wid.		02 – 00	
Mary Jenkins		05 – 00	
Mary Taylor		01 – 06	
Mary Binny		04 – 00	
Mary Parsons		06 – 00	
Thomas Wade		03 – 00	
[blank]		04 – 00	

Margaret Stone	06 – 00
Grace Stokes	07 – 00
Rebeccah Hewit	03 – 00
Franc. Fear, keeping Hooper's blind	06 – 00
Jane Stone	02 – 00
Richd Redman, keeping Cooke's child	06 – 00
Anne Jenkins	05 – 00
Elizabeth Millar	05 – 00
John Perrin	04 – 00
Prudence Goldstone	04 – 00
Bethia Hooper, keeping Bet. Bouls	08 – 00
Bethia Hooper	02 – 06
Mary Saunders, keeping Bet. Sanson's child	01 – 00
Paid her more keeping Atwood's child	06 – 00
Veale, wid.	02 – 06
Jos. Curtice, keeping Cooke's child	06 – 08
Paid him more keeping Fear's child	04 – 00
Grace Fisher	03 – 00
[blank] Broad, keeping Anne Corey	08 – 00
Richd Hichins	06 – 00
Grace Cooke	05 – 00
Richd Fear & wife	13 – 00
James Tippet, keeping Ric. Balme [?]	09 – 00
	07 – 16 – 02

Som. RO ref. D/P/Che.m/13/2/6 Chew Magna, Somerset
Overseers' Accounts, 1714 to 1779

1771 To Richd Shorton	£	s	d
For 2 papers of powders for Sarah Coxes child	0 –	1 –	0
For ointment for do.	0 –	1 –	0
To a paper of purging powders for Jno. Room	0 –	0 –	4
To 2 papers of do for James Stone	0 –	0 –	8
To 3 ditto for do.	0 –	1 –	0
To a purging potion for Wm Perry	0 –	1 –	0
To bleeding Eln^r Coomer	0 –	0 –	6

[contd]

To 3 papers purging powders for Mary Naish	0 – 1 – 0
To a box of ointment for do.	0 – 0 – 3
To ointment & Turners Ceret for do.	0 – 0 – 9
To 3 doses of purging powders & Ceret for Lit^a Williams	0 – 0 – 9
To a paper of purging powders	0 – 0 – 3
To Tintura Sacra z11 Mary Naish	0 – 2 – 0
To a Composing Draught for Mary Chivers	0 – 1 – 0
To 4 papers of purging powders for S. Smiths children	0 – 1 – 0
To a paper of purging powders for Mary Chivers	0 – 1 – 3
To vitriol for do.	0 – 0 – 3
To a purging potion for do.	0 – 1 – 0
To 4 papers purging powders for S. Smiths children	0 – 1 – 0
To Yellow Bassellican & Turners Ceret for B. Godfrey	0 – 0 – 6
To a large strengthening plaister for R. Radford	0 – 1 – 0
To a paper of purging powders for Eln^r Coomer	0 – 0 – 4
To 3 do. for Betty Harvey	0 – 1 – 0
To a bottle of drops for John Peters	0 – 0 – 8
To a blister plaister & melitot	0 – 1 – 3
To a saline mixture for Eln^r Coomer	0 – 2 – 0
To a purging potion for do.	0 – 1 – 0
To 4 doses of purging powders for M. North	0 – 1 – 0
Allow'd me by the Coroner for attending ye Assizes 4 days when Pashey Williams was tried	2 – 2 – 0
To bleeding S. Weaver	0 – 0 – 6
To an opening mixture with rhubarb	0 – 2 – 0
To a bottle of drops	0 – 0 – 8
carried over to ye other side	£3 – 9 – 11

Dev. RO (Ex.) ref. 3082 add A/PO2 Holcombe Rogus, Devon Account Book, 1792 to 1807

Disbursements					
1791 May 22	The first month's Disbursements by Elias Squire		£	*s*	*d*
	Paid for this book			0 – 4 – 0	
	Gave Samuel Tooze ye cooper in necessity			0 – 15 – 0	

	Gave Jer^m Woodbury over and above his monthly pay	0 – 4 – 0
	Pd. Mrs Eliz. Howett for the cure of Jeffrey Hile's child of a scald leg	0 – 6 – 0
	Pd. for repairing of James Sully's Trusses	0 – 0 – 9
	Mary Needs for tending Daniel Twitchings	0 – 2 – 6
	Expenses in paying the poor	0 – 4 – 0
Received of Thomas Cood 3s which the Overseers had paid towards the burial of his child		
June 19	Shirt and making for Daniel Twitchings and 2 aprons for Edward Gover's child	1 – 1½
	Ann Woodbury in necessity	2 – 0
	Gave Samuel Tooze, the cooper	5 – 0
	Gave Henry Pleace in necessity	2 – 0
Received of Bernard Payne for his son John Payne the balance due to the parish towards the maintenance of Eliz. Yeandall's Base child		7 – 10 – 0
1791 July 17	Gave Richard Martin over and above his monthly pay	1 – 0
	Paid for a shift and a pair of shoes for Eliz. Milton's girl	5 – 3½
	Paid for a pair of shoes for Ann Taylor	3 – 10
Aug. 14	Bed tie and bolster for Daniel Twitchings	8 – 2
	Paid for mending Edward Gower's child's shoes	0 – 9
	Paid for a shift for Henry Woodbury	4 – 1½
	Paid for a pair of shoes for Edward Causey	3 – 4
Sept. 11	Pair of shoes for Susanna Perry	3 – 8
	Shift for Ann Taylor	3 – 7
	Mary Needs for tending Daniel Twitchings	2 – 6
	Jeffrey Hill towards a pair of shoes	3 – 0
	Paid for the burial of Thomasine Stone at Cullompton	9 – 0
Oct. 9	Shirt for Sarah Harrod's boy	2 – 5
	Shoes for Joan Ellis	3 – 9
	" Edwd Gover's boy	2 – 3
	" James Cotterell's boy	3 – 1
Nov. 6	Pair of shoes for Mary Coad cripl.	3 – 9

[contd]

11

Dec. 4	gave Ann Woodbury	2 – 0
	paid for a coat for Henry Woodbury	11 – 3
	paid for repairing James Sully's truss	3 – 0
	pair of shoes for Richard Martin's wife	3 – 9
	Repairing Ann Taylor's shoes	1 – 6
	Richard Payne in necessity	2 – 0
1792 Jan 1st	Thomas Grant's expenses to Bridgewater concerning Samuel Colman's settlement	8 – 0
	Pair of shoes for Mary Colman's son William	3 – 0
	Paid for the burial of Nathan Taylor	9 – 0
	Shirt for Edward Gover	4 – 6
	Coat " "	11 – 4
	Coat for Robert Doyle	11 – 4
	" Jeremiah Woodbury	11 – 4
	Two beds and 2 bolsters for Samuel Colman's family	1 – 0 – 1
	Two blankets for do	17 – 2
	Paid Samuel Coleman & his family for one month	4 – 6 – 0
Jan 29th	Paid Samuel Colman & his family	1 – 17 – 0
	Henry Pleace	1 – 0
Feb 26th	Gave William Frost in necessity	3 – 0
	Susanna Perry over and above her pay	1 – 0
	Coat, Jacket & shift for Ann Taylor	11 – 7
	Paid for Truss for James Sully	12 – 0
	Pd. for a man & horse to go to Honiton for the Coroner	3 – 6
	Expenses concerning the settlement of Samuel Coleman & his family	11 – 15 – 6
1792 March 25th	Mary Southwood for her base child	3 – 0
	Shirt for Wᵐ Ellis 4s – 1½ Shirt for Susanna Perry 3s – 7d	7 – 8½
	Elizabeth Hart	1 – 0
	Jeffrey Hill	2 – 6
	Pair of shoes for Wᵐ Harred	3 – 4
	" " Eliz. Tristram's girl	3 – 4
	Examination of Jane Scott & the examination of Mary Southwood & two vagrants	4 – 0

April 8th	Paid Mr Bridges the surgeon for attending the poor, one year to end of 1792.	6 – 6 – 0
	Alex. Needs, Sarah Ausey, Ann Causey & Sarah Harred for keeping guard over Jane Scott, giving evidence, etc.	7 – 6

Som. RO ref. Q/SR/421 Somerset Quarter Sessions Rolls
Winford and Blagdon, Bill of Costs, Midsummer, 1821
[A rare example found in the Court of Quarter Sessions records of extracts from churchwardens' accounts relating to the cost involved in the examination and appeal against the removal of a pauper.]

The Churchwardens and Overseers of the Poor of the Parish of Winford to Ja[s] W[m] Chadwick

1821		£ s d
May	Attending the Overseers of Winford in consequence of Mary Ann Wyatt being brought to their Parish by an Order of Removal	0 – 6 – 8
	Taking Examination of Pauper	6 – 8
	Journey to Sutton and Winford to examine C. Sage with whom the Pauper was bound as an Apprentice and also W[m] Reed with whom she served as a hired Servant but without consent of Original Master either expressed or implied, the whole day	2 – 2 – 0
	Horse hire and expenses	13 – 9
	Copy Indenture of Apprenticeship	3 – 6
	Subsequence attendance on Farmer James Light with whom Pauper served by consent of Sage to know if he had consented to her Service with Reed, which he declared he had not	6 – 8
29th	Instructions for Appeal against the Order	6 – 8
	Drawing notice of Appeal	6 – 8
	Four fair copies thereof for Service	10 – 0
	Clerk's Journey to Blagdon to serve same	1 – 1 – 0
	Horse hire and Expenses	10 – 6
June 12th	Letter to Mr Whitley to know if he meant to try this appeal	5 – 0
	Postage, Letter in reply offering to refer to Counsel	6

[contd]

	Letter to him in answer refusing reference	5 – 0
22nd	Journey to Wrington to see Mr Whitley and endeavour to settle this Appeal when he said he should recommend Respondents to settle this Appeal by taking back Pauper and paying costs and maintenance to move to quash Order at Sessions but must see Overseer of Blagdon before he could give a final answer & promised I should have an answer by 24th inst. Horsehire &c	2 – 2 – 0
June 28th	Letter to Mr Whitley urging answer or I should prepare for Trial	5 – 0
July 1st	Postage letter in answer agreeing to settle	4
	Preparing undertaking for him to sign and fair copy	3 – 6
	Motion Brief for Counsel to Consent at Sessions that Order be quashed on payment of Costs and maintenance and fair Copy	7 – 0
	Journey to Sessions Coach &c 2 Days including expenses	5 – 5 – 0
	Fee to Counsel	1 – 0 – 0
	Paid entering Appeal	5 – 0
	Court Fees Order quashed	10 – 0
	Drawing Brief – 9 sheets	3 – 0 – 0
		£20 – 3 – 5*

* This is an error and should be £20 – 2s – 5d

Dev. RO (Ex.) ref. 1249A/PO 11 Holne, Devonshire
Receipt and Payment Book, 1836 to 1869

Receipts		
1837 Jan 5	Rec[d] of Richard Hext 13 weeks maintenance of John Bowland a bastard child	0 – 19 – 6
April 19	Paid Doctor Phillips attendance on the Poor from March 25 to Aug. 25, 1836	1 – 3 – 0
1837 Sept 11	Indentures for binding Daniel Bartlett.	
	A horse and expenses for the boy	7 – 0
	do and expenses for self at Totnes	4 – 0

**Dev. RO (Ex.) ref. 3082 add A/PO6 Holcombe Rogus, Devonshire
Overseers' Receipt and Payment Book, 1836 to 1847**

The Churchwardens' and Overseers' of Holcombe Rogus, in an Account from Sept 29th
to Dec 25th 1840

1840 Dec	Paid Mr Tooze's bill for removing Bowerman, his wife and family from Holcombe to Lympstone	18 – 0
Nov 18	Paid relieving officer's bill for journey, horse hire and expenses to Collompton Sessions to prove the chargeability of Ann Gillard	*
	To be submitted to the Board of Guardians	
"	Paid Mr White's fees for Bowerman's Order of Removal, Duplicates of ditto &c	16 – 2
"	Paid Mr White's fees for Gillard's Order of Removal, Duplicates of ditto, Examination of witnesses &c.	1 – 4 – 2
	Overseers' Bill of Expenses paid to witnesses, Summonses &c respecting Gillard's Settlement	1 – 5 – 0
	Overseers' Bill for Coach Hire and Expenses on a Journey to Bristol, Bath, Bradford, Trowbridge &c in search of Wm. Scott who deserted his family	3 – 4 – 6†
1841 March 30th	Paid Relieving Officer for Journey and Expenses to Tiverton to get suspension taken off Maria Carter's Order of Removal	10 – 0
April 1st	Paid Wm. Tooze a bill for removal of Maria Carter from Holcombe to Uffculme	2 – 6
March 30	Paid Fees for Permission to execute Maria Carter's Order of Removal and Duplicate	4 – 6
1842 3 Jan	Fees paid Mr White for Morrell's Order of Removal	18 – 8
19 Jan	Paid a bill for Relief of Giles' 2 children and an Order of Removal	9 – 0
"	Paid at Collompton Examination of William May as to his Settlement	18 – 6
24 Jan	Mr Wood's bill for expenses of horse hire and Turnpike to Tiverton and Wellington respecting Holley's child. His Examination &c.	11 – 1†
24 Jan	Mr Wood's bill, expenses of Jones and Giles and May at Collompton	17 – 6

† These entries have been crossed through

1843 22 March	To cash paid the Relieving Overseer for expenses at Collompton respecting Cottey and Ridgeway Settlement	1 – 18 – 4½
1843		
Receipts	To cash received of the Overseers of Halberton for relief to James Greenwood and family under an Order To cash received of the Overseers of Halberton under an Order of Removal of Wm. Cottey	19 – 1½
10 May	Fees paid Magistrates Clerks at Collompton	16 – 6
	Cash to Elizabeth Carter to take her to Wellington to get her Examination taken	1 – 9
22 June	Paid Overseers of Halberton three weeks relief to Wm. Woodberry and wife	7 – 1½
	Paid Mr White's bill for Holland's Settlement	6 – 0
	To cash Rec^d of Revd W. Wills for one years rent of Church House	5 – 0 – 0
	To cash rec^d of Overseers of Halberton under an Order of Removal of W. Cottey	9 – 6¾
1844 Nov 26	Expenses of horse hire, serving the Overseers of Stogumber with notice of Appeal against the removal of Ann Taylor from the above parish to the parish of Holcombe Rogus	4 – 0
1845 Feb 5	Paid Overseers of Ruishton for the removal of H^y Rowland and family	5 – 13 – 3½
	Conveying the said H^y Rowland, wife and family to the Union	6 – 6
July 16	Journey to Dulverton and Bampton, Horse and Cart hire and expenses of taking Bart Stiles and wife under an Order of Removal	15 – 0
Receipt		
1846	Rec^d of Overseers of Sampford Peverel 3 weeks pay for Geo. Hill	12 – 1½
1846 Feb 16	Relieving Officer's bill of expenses for journeys to Bampton, Taunton and Collompton as to the Settlement of B. Styles, M. Trenchard and Geo. Hill (allowed)	1 – 8 – 6
	Expenses of taking home Geo. Hill and daughter under an Order of Removal	5 – 0

CHAPTER 3

BASTARDY

When an unmarried woman became pregnant she was likely to seek financial relief from the overseers of the poor of her parish. She may also request a place in a workhouse. In order to reduce the financial burden of such women and their bastard children, the woman was expected to name the father of the child. Such enquiries were usually carried out before a justice of the peace at the Court of Quarter Sessions, where the woman was questioned as to the identity of the father. The father was sometimes pressed to marry the woman, though in most cases a reputed father was ordered to pay maintenance for the mother and child until the child reached the age at which it could earn its own living (usually 12 years of age). Records of these examinations will be found in profusion in the records of these courts. Such papers may also be found amongst parish records originally held at parish churches and now in county or borough record offices.

The minutes of the meetings of the Board of Guardians of each Union are often found to include details of unmarried mothers and their bastard children.

The following are some examples:

Som. RO ref. D/P/b lyd 13/5/1 Parish of Bishops Lydeard
Bastardy Orders, 1604 to 1605
[The father of a bastard child is ordered to pay *6d* per week up until the present time and from then on *8d* per week for the maintenance of the child. Both mother and father to confess their offence in church and repent, and if they do not, each to be whipped.]

Somerset. The order sett downe & subscribed by John Francis & Humphrie Windham Esq & by them taken at Lideard Episc. the thirde daie of Januarie in the yeere of the raigne of our Soverayne Lorde James [1604] by the grace of God of England, France & Ireland, king defender of the faith &c the firste & of Scotland the 37th according to the statute made in the 48th yeare of the Raigne of our late Soveraigne ladie queene Elizabeth for a bastarde child begotten & borne out of lawfull matrimony

17

Decon To wit. } To the Church-Wardens and Overseers of the Poor of the Parish of *Cullompton* — in the said County, and to either of them. *These.*

WHereas *Mary Joyce* — of the Parish of *Cullompton aforesaid* Single-Woman, was on or about the *twenty eighth* Day of *May 1765* delivered of a Bastard *Female* Child, within the Parish of *Cullompton* — in the County *aforesaid* which Child is now living and chargeable to the Parish of *Cullompton* — and likely to continue.

And whereas upon Examination of the Cause and Circumstances of the Premises taken upon Oath before Us, and due Consideration being likewise had by Us whose Hands and Seals are hereunto set, Two of his Majesty's Justices of the Peace for the said County, (One being of the Quorum) both living next unto the Limits of the Parish Church of – – – *Cullompton* — aforesaid, do adjudge *Thomas Holland* — of *Cullompton* — to be the Father of the said Bastard *female* 'Child, and for the Relief of the said Parish of *Cullompton* — and also for Provision and Maintenance of the said Bastard Child;

We do this Day, according to the Statutes in that Case made and provided, hereby Order that the said *Thomas Holland* — shall Weekly and every Week from the Birth of the said Bastard *female* Child, and so long as the same shall be chargeable to the said Parish of *Cullompton* — pay unto the Church-Wardens and Overseers of the Poor of the Parish of *Cullompton* the Sum of *Six pence* —

And also shall and will within six Days after Notice of this our Order, pay unto the said Church-Warden and Overseers of the Poor the Sum of *Six Shillings* — towards the Charges the Parish of *Cullompton* — has already been at, for the Maintenance of the said Bastard Child, and obtaining this our Order.

And we do hereby further Order, that the said *Mary Joyce* — — shall Weekly and every Week, for so long Time thereof as the said Bastard Child, shall be chargeable as aforesaid, (in Case she shall not nurse and take Care of the said Child herself) pay unto the Church-Warden and Overseers of the Poor of the said Parish of *Cullompton* — — – — — — for the Time being, the Sum of *five pence* — for and towards the further Maintenance of the said Child.

These are in his Majesty's Name to command you, or some or one of you, with all convenient Speed, to give Notice of this our Order above, unto the reputed Father and Mother therein mentioned, to the End, they and either of them may the better observe and perform the same. Given under our Hands and Seals this *Seventh* —Day of *September* in the Year of our Lord One Thousand Seven Hundred and *Sixty Seven* —

Fran: Drewe

Saml Newte

A Bastardy Order: Mary Joyse, single woman, stating that Thomas Holland of Cullompton, Devon, is the father of her bastard child, 1767. (Dev. RO (Ex.) ref. 2404A/PO210/No 11)

on the bodie of Johan Peeter of Lidearde Episc. aforesaid & of which bastarde childe it fullie appeareth by evidence that Robte Hawkins of Combe Florie, husbandman is the reputed father.

Firstle it is by them ordered that the said Robte Hawkins shall paie for soe many weekes as was betweene the birthe of the said childe & the said thirde daie of Januarye so manye sixe pences that is to saie vi*d* a weeke, and the same to bee paide unto the said Johan, or to the overseers of the poore of Lideard Episc within one monthe after the date hereof for the relief of the said bastard childe.

Secondlie it is ordered that the said Robt Hawkins shall also paie weekelye from the said thirde daie of Januarye until the said childe shalbe able to gett his or her livinge viii*d* & the firste paymt thereof to begin on Sonddie nexte.

Thirdlie it is also ordered that the said viii*d* a weeke appointed to be paide weeklye as aforesaid, shalbee duringe the tyme aforesaid paide upon the Sonddie in everye of the said weekes unto the Churchwardens of Lidearde Epi or to some one of them for the tyme beinge, to the use for the findinge of the said base childe, And that the said viii*d* weeklye soe by him or them received hee or they shall for them paie the same unto the said Johan so longe as she keepeth or findeth the said childe, and if shee shall fortune not finde, keepe, or bringe upp the said childe then the same by hym or them to bee delivered unto suche pson as findeth or keepeth the said base childe.

Fowerthlie it is ordered in like sorte that the said Johan Peeter shall also paie weeklye from the said thirde daie of January until the saide childe shalbee able to gett his or her livinge iiii*d*, for enye suche week wherein the said Johan shall fortune not to finde, keepe or bringe upp the said base childe to paye unto the Churchwardens for the tyme beinge and every of the said iiii*d* to bee paide as aforesaid hee or they receiving the same shall bestow yt towards the findinge & keepinge of the same base childe.

Finallie it is ordered for his and her Corporal punishment wch by vertue of the said Statute is to bee inflicted upon the said Robte & Johan that he & she severalye upon one or several Sondies wch shalbee w'hin two monthes after the date hereof after the firste lesson read in the forenoone in the pishe Church where hee or she dwellethe confesse theire faulte & offence aforesaid hartelye repentinge the same with humble entreating the congregacion then there assembled to praie to god with them that he will forgive the same, with protestinge never to offend in the like again. And if hee or shee shall faile in doing hereof, then it is ordered that hee or she so faylinge herein shall then for his or her corporal punishment bee openlye whipped in such convenient place and at such daie & tyme as by the Justices aforesaid or else by the Justices of the Peace or the greater parte of them that shalbee assembled at the next Quarter Sessions of the Peace within the said Countye to be holden after complainte hereof made, shalbee thoughte meete & convenyente.

    John Francis
    Humfrey Windham
    Robt Kingston

Som. RO ref. Q/SR/48 Somerset Quarter Sessions Rolls
Midsummer, 1624
[The father of a bastard child is ordered to pay 4*d* every Sunday at the parish church for the maintenance of the child.]

Somerset. An Order made and established the xxviith Daie of June in the Yeare of our Lord God 1624 By Sir Henery Berkeley, Knighte and James Farewell Esquire, Two of his Ma^es Justices of the Peace of the said Countie touchinge Richard Lucus a bastard childe borne in Abbas Coombe in the said Countie begotten on the bodie of Amey Lucas of Abbas Coombe aforesaid by James Tynney of the same pishe, woollen weaver.

Imprimus. Wee Order that the said James Tynney the reputed Father his Executors or Administrators shall weekley from tyme to tyme pay over unto the Churchwardens and Overseers of the Poore of the pishe of Abbas Coombe aforesaid for the tyme being the some of Fower pence of Lawful Englishe money for & towards the relief and maintenance of the said childe wch said some of Fower pence wee order to be paid in the South Porche of the pishe Churche of Abbas Coombe aforesaid everie Sunday after thend of morninge prayer and this payment to begin upon the nowe next Sabbath daie and to continue until further Order shalbe taken herein. And the same some of fower pence to be employed by the said Churchwardens & overseers to & for the releife of the same childe.

Wee doe further order that the said Amey Lucas shall for her pte keepe the child her self yf shee shalbe thought fit & able by the said Churchwardens and Overseers to doe the same & to receive the said some of fower pence weekly for the same, of the saide Churchwardens and Overseers for the reliefe of her child as aforesaid.

And wee further Order that both the said Pties viz the reputed father for his pte, & the mother for her pte shall within their duties after such tyme as this Order is made knowne unto them put in sufficient assurance by bond unto the Churchwardens & Overseers of the Poore of Abbas Coombe aforesaid for the discharge of the said pishe & pishoners, of & from the said child and charge thereof.

Wee doe finally Order that the said Amey Lucas for her fault herein upon the next market daie – [torn away] – after the receipt hereof (of or aboute one of the clocke in the afternoone of the same daie) be stripped, her bodie naked from the middle upward and to be whipped aboute the market place, there until her bodie be blodie and allsoe that she be whipped againe the second & last tyme att Abbas Coombe affore said in the open streete there upon the Friday next ensuing aboute one of ye clocke in the afternoone of the same daie until her bodie be bloodie as aforesaid. In witness whereof wee have hereunto sett our hands & seales the day and yeare first above written.

      Henry Berkeley   James Farewell

Wee will and require the Constables of Wyncanton and the Tithingman of Abbas Coombe aforesaid to see the ponishmt executed upon the said Amey Lucas as is expressed in this Order.

Som. RO ref. Q/SR/71/2 Somerset Quarter Sessions Rolls
Epiphany, 1634
[The father of a bastard female child is named at Quarter Sessions and is ordered to pay 12*d* per week for her maintenance.]

Somerset. An Order concerninge the reliefe & maintenance of a base woman childe borne of the body of Emott Brodsherd of Wiveliscombe in the said County made & sett downe by William Frauncis, & William Every esquires, Justices of Peace within the said county the xxxth day of December Ano Dom 1633.

Whereas it appeareth unto us that William Hawkens of Fitzhead in the aforesaid county, husbandman is the reputed father of the said base child and whereas by the Lawe wee are to take course as well for the education & bringinge upp of the said child as for discharge of the said p'ish of Fitzhead wherein the said child was borne and for punishment of the offendors wee doe therefore order & appoint that the said William Hawkens, his Executors or Assignes shall satisfie & pay weekly from the birth of the said base child unto the Churchwardens & Overseers of the poore there for the tyme beinge the sume of twelve pence lawful English money. The said sume to be employed & disposed by them or some of them for reliefe & sustenance of the said base child as they in their discrecons shall thinke convenient & necessarie, wee doe further order & appoint that the said William Hawkens shall wth two sufficient sureties forthwth become bounden unto the said Churchwardens & Overseers of the Poor in some convernient sume of money for the performance of this our Order wee doe further order & appoint that the said Emott Brodsherd shall herselfe nurse & bringe upp the said base child and that this our order shall stand & bee in force until the said William Hawkens, his Executors or Assignes shall take further order for reliefe of the said base child, & discharge of the said pish. Given under our hands att Milverton the day and yeare above said.

Willia Fucey [?]
Willia Fraunces

Som. RO ref. Q/SR/98/1 Somerset Quarter Sessions Rolls
Spring and Midsummer, 1659
[The examination of a woman at Quarter Sessions who is unable to name the father of the child with whom she is pregnant.]

Somerset. The Examination of Ursula Kebby of Venus Sutton [Sutton Mallet] in the County aforesaid, single woman taken before Edward Sealy Esq one of the Justices of the Peace of the said County the 5th of February 1658.

Who upon oath confesseth & sayth that about St James daye last this exam^t travelling towards Bristol mett a stranger neere Banwell in the Highway who alighted from his horse and came to this Examt and carried her on the inside of the hedge and threw her on the ground; and there had the Carnell knowledge of her Body once att wch tyme shee sayth shee was begotten wth child, and that the said stranger is Father of the said child, and sayth that shee knoweth not his name, that hee begate her wth child, nor where he lives, nor never saw him before nor since the tyme he had the carnell knowledge of her Body as aforesaid. And more shee confesseth not.

Edward Sealy

Northants. RO ref. 272P/60
[The reputed father of a male bastard child to pay the lying in expenses, the maintenance of the child up to the age of 7 years, and then to pay for him to become an apprentice – Northamptonshire, 1716.]

Northants. An Order for the Reliefe of the Inhabitants of Potterspury in the County of North'ton for the providing for a Male Bastard Child whereof one Amy Snow was there delivered of.

Whereas Complaint hath been made by the Overseers of the Poore of Potterspury in the said County of Northampton unto us whose names are hereunto subscribed, two of his Majesty's Justices of and for the said County near residing to Potterspury aforesaid (one of us being of the Quorum). That Amy Snow of the said parish of Potterspury, singlewoman, on or about the fifth day of May last past was there delivered of a Male Bastard Child which is likely to become Chargeable to the said parish of Potterspury. And hath also upon her Examination duly taken upon her Oath charged Thomas Rands Jun[r] of Cosgrove in the said County of North'ton, Baker, to be the Father of the said Male Bastard Child.

Wee the said Justices having Examined and heard the said Cause and Circumstances doe find and adjudge the said Thomas Rands Jun[r] to be the reputed Father of the said Male Bastard Child. And doe therefore hereby Order as followeth (that is to say).

First wee doe hereby Order that the said Amy Snow shall keep the said Male Bastard Child until itt shall attaine the Age of Seven Yeares.

Secondly that the said Thomas Rands, Jun[r] upon Notice of this our Order shall pay into the hands of the p'sent Churchwardens and Overseers of the Poore of Potterspury aforesaid the Sume of Twelve shillings & sixpence to reimburse them such sums of money and charges they have expended at & for the Charge of the lying in of the said Amy Snow and in maintaining the said Male Bastard Child to the date of this Order, and also the said Thomas Rands Jun[r] shall pay into the hands of the P'sent Churchwardens & Overseers of the Poore of Potterspury aforesaid and their successors in their said offices for and towards the maintenance of the said Male Bastard Child the sume of One shilling and Six Pence per Week from the date hereof until it shall attaine the Age of Seven yeares if it shall soe long live and be Chargeable to the parish of Potterspury. And that at the End of the said terme of Seven Yeares the said Thomas Rands Jun[r] shall pay to the then Churchwardens and Overseers of the Poore of Potterspury aforesaid the Sume of Five Pounds of lawfull money of Greate Britaine to putt out the said Male Bastard Child as an Apprentice (in Case it be then living). And Lastly wee the said Justices doe hereby further Order that the said Thomas Rands Jun[r] shall forthwith give Sufficient Security to the p'sent Churchwardens & Overseers of the Poore of Potterspury aforesaid for the true performance of this our

Order whereof Notice is forthwith to be given to the said Thomas Rands Junr by delivering to him a true Copy hereof.

Given Our Hands and Seals this Ninth day of June in the Second yeare of the Reign of our Sovereign Lord George by the Grace of God of Greate Britain. Anno Dom 1716.

Fr. Arundell
Edm. Babemans [?]

Dev. RO (Ex.) ref. 2404A/PO209 No 1
[The father of a bastard child, together with his father, accept responsibility for the maintenance of the child – Devonshire, 1769.]

Know all Men by these presents, that we William Vicary of Cullompton in the County of Devon, yeoman and William Vicary the younger of the same place, labourer are held and firmly bound unto Henry Brutton and Whitelock Sydenham, churchwardens and Humphrey Blackmoore, Thomas Heathfield and Thomas Pannell, Overseers of the Poor of the parish of Cullompton aforesaid (in trust for the parishioners of the said parish) in fifty pounds of good and lawful money of Great Britain to be paid to the said Henry Brutton, Whitelock Sydenham, Humphrey Blackmoore, Thomas Heathfield and Thomas Pannell or their certain attorney their Exors, Admonrs or Assigns. To which payment well and truly to be made, we bind ourselves, and each of us, jointly and severally and our each and every of our heirs, Exors and Admonrs firmly by these presents, sealed with our Seals, and dated the Fourteenth day of September in the Ninth year of the Reign of our Sovereign Lord George the Third of Great Britain, France and Ireland, King, defender of the Faith, and so forth and in the year of our Lord one thousand seven hundred and sixty nine.

Whereas Elizabeth Knight of Cullompton aforesaid spinster, before one of his Majesty's Justices of the Peace for the said County of Devon hath sworn that she is great with child and that the above named William Vicary the younger is the father of such child or children she now goeth with. Now the Condition of this obligation is such that if the above bound William Vicary and William Vicary the younger or either of them or either of their heirs, Exors or Admons do and shall from time to time and at all times hereafter, fully and clearly acquit, exonerate and discharge or otherwise well and sufficiently save and keep harmless and indemnify as well the above named Henry Brutton, Whitelock Sydenham, Humphrey Blackmoore, Thomas Heathfield and Thomas Pannell, Churchwardens and Overseers of the Poor of the parish of Cullompton aforesaid and their successors for the time being, and every of them, as also all the inhabitants and parishioners of the said parish of Cullompton which now are or hereafter shall be, for the time being and every of them, of and from all and all manner of expenses, damages, costs and charges whatsoever, which shall in any manner at any time hereafter arise, happen, come, grow or be imposed upon them or any or either of them for or by reason or means of the said Elizabeth Knight being now great with child as aforesaid or for or by reason or means of the birth, maintenance, education and bringing up of such child or children that the said Elizabeth Knight now goeth with, and shall be delivered of, and of and from all actions, suits, troubles, charges, damages and demands whatsoever touching and concerning the same, Then this obligation to be void and of no effect else remain in full force and virtue.

The mark of

Sealed and delivered in the presence of   W V

S. Luscombe   Wm Vicary

William Dansey   The mark of

W V

Wm Vicary the younger

Dev. RO (Ex.) ref. 2404A/PO 209/No 4
[The father of a bastard child pays £100 for the child's upkeep – Devonshire, 1777.]

Know all Men by these presents That I Thomas Courtis of the City of Exeter, corn factor am held and firmly bound unto Henry Brutton and Thomas Parnell, churchwardens of the Parish of Cullompton in the County of Devon and Humphrey Blackmore, William Upcott and Robert Pring, Overseers of the Poor of the said Parish (In Trust for the Parishoners of the same Parish) in the Sum of One Hundred Pounds of lawfull Money of Great Brittain to be paid to their Churchwardens and Overseers or their certain Attorney, Executors, Administrators or Assigns For which Payment well & truly to be made I bind myself my Heirs, Executors and Administrators and every of them firmly by those Presents Sealed with my Seal Dated this Twenty fourth day of February One Thousand Seven Hundred & Seventy Seven.

Wheras Sarah Bliss of Cullompton aforesaid Singlewoman is now with child of a Bastard Child or Children, of which she has declared that the above bounden Thomas Courtis is the true and real Father and the said Thomas Courtis doth acknowledge himself to be the Father of the said Bastard Child or Children of which the said Sarah Bliss is now pregnant. And whereas the said Bastard Child or Children is or are likely when born to be chargeable to the said Parish of Cullompton NOW the CONDITION of this Obligation is such that if the above bounden Thomas Courtis his Heirs Executors or Administrators do and shall from time to time and at all times hereafter fully and clearly indemnify and save harmless as well the above named Churchwardens and Overseers of the Poor of the said Parish and their Successors for the time being, as also all and singular the other Parishoners and Inhabitants of the said Parish which now are or hereafter shall be for the time being, of and from all & all manner of Costs, Taxes, Rates, Assessments, Charges and Expenses whatsoever for or by reason of the Birth, Education and Maintenance of the said Child or Children, and of and from all Actions, Suits, Troubles and other Charges and Demands whatsoever touching or concerning the same Then this present Obligation to be void, or else to remain in full force.

Thos Courtis

Sealed and Delivered   Benjn Durant

in the presence of   Hen^y Purnell

Ox. RO ref. Oxon. QS.Ep.1834/Misc.6
[An order against the father of an illegitimate child – Oxfordshire, 1833.]

To the Court of General Quarter Sessions of the Peace holden at Oxford in and for the said County, the thirtieth Day of December One Thousand Eight Hundred and 33.

Oxfordshire.　　Whereas William Davis is now bound by Recognisance for his
to wit　　　　　personal Appearance at the above mentioned Sessions to answer
　　　　　　　the Complaint of the Churchwardens and Overseers of the Poor of
　　　　　　　the Parish of Bucknell in the said County, for begetting Susannah
　　　　　　　Cracknell of the said Parish, single woman, with Child.

Now we, two of His Majesty's Justices of the Peace acting in and for the said County, do hereby certify that the said William Davis hath this day attended before us and that an order of filiation* hath been made upon him the said William Davis in respect of the said charge.

　　Given under our Hands this thirteenth Day of December 1833.
　　　　Chetwynd　　　　W.L. Browne

* An affiliation order, which was an order of maintenance

Som. RO ref. D/G/W 57/2 Wellington Union, Somerset and Devon
Letter Book, 1836 to 1840
[The master of a workhouse is accused of being the father of the child of an inmate – Somerset, 1838.]

20th December 1838　　　It having been represented to the Board that a young woman, an inmate of the Union Workhouse here, of the name of Mary Stradling is with child, she was called before the Board on Monday last and interrogated as to the father.

　　She alleges that you are the father and that the connexion took place between you at the time you were Master and she an inmate of the Workhouse.

　　The Guardians have in consequence directed me to communicate the circumstances to you and to enquire whether or not you will undertake to maintain the child on its birth. If not I am directed to say that so soon as they are in a position to do so the parish officers of Wellington, to which the woman belongs will make an application to the Court of Quarter Sessions for an Order of Affiliation upon you.

　　If the woman's statement be true I cannot but express my regret that you should have acted so imprudently not only so far as affects yourself but particularly on account of the disquietude it was unnecessarily produced to Mrs Perren and Miss Perren.

Private　　Mr Thomas Perren　　　　　I remain Dear Sir
　　　　　Northleach　　　　　　　　Yours Truly
　　　　　Gloucestershire　　　　　　Wm Rodham

Som. RO ref. D/G/W/8a/3 Wellington Union, Somerset and Devon
Minutes of the meetings of the Board of Guardians, 1839 to 1842
[The fathers of bastard children are recorded in the minutes of the meetings of the Board of Guardians – Somerset, 1840 and 1841.]

25th May 1840
It appearing that Elizabeth White, single woman belonging to the parish of Wiveliscombe was on the 14th day of January last delivered of a female bastard child and that the said child by reasons of its mother being unable to provide for its maintenance did on the 4th day of April last become chargeable to the said parish of Wiveliscombe. The Guardians proceeded to make enquiries as to the father of such child and thereupon found that John Darch of Huish Champflower in the county of Somerset is the father thereof.

Whereupon it was moved by William Hancock, seconded by Mr Joseph Bawdenclarke:- That an application be made to the Justices for an Order upon the said John Darch to re-imburse the Union for the maintenance and support of the said child. Carried.

***

17th November 1841
The Guardians having found that Richard Roberts is the father of the child of Ann Hitchcock; Nicholas Braddick of Clayhidon, butcher, the father of the child of Elizabeth Buttle; Charles Morish of Curry Rivell, sawyer, the father of the child of Ann Stone, and John Davey the younger of Wellington, butcher, the father of the child of Harriet Designey, and notices were signed in duplicate to those parties of the intention of the Guardians to apply to the Magistrates for Orders of Maintenance in each of those cases.

CHAPTER 4

SETTLEMENT EXAMINATIONS, REMOVAL ORDERS AND SETTLEMENT CERTIFICATES

In many cases it was not obvious in which parish a pauper was *rightfully settled*. In such circumstances enquiries were made by the overseers of the poor of the parish in which the pauper had taken up residence. After such enquiries, and once the *rightful place of settlement* was ascertained, a Removal Order was issued and the pauper was conveyed to that place. In a lot of cases paupers were found many miles from their home parish and had to be escorted through one county to another on a direct route until they reached their *place of legal settlement*. In some rare cases documents have been found recording the route by which the pauper travelled.

Documents relating to settlement and removal are often to be found amongst parish records or with Poor Law Union records now usually deposited in county or borough record offices.

Often the churchwardens and overseers of a parish admitted liability for a pauper and issued a certificate stating so (a Settlement Certificate). On many occasions the parish officers challenged the decision to remove a pauper to their parish and such disputes are to be found in the records of the Courts of Quarter Sessions for the county. Settlement examinations were sometimes forwarded to the Poor Law Commission (or later the Poor Law Board) for their observation. Many such decisions were disputed and details were then passed to the Court of King's Bench for a decision.

Enquiries into the place of a pauper's legal settlement are sometimes to be found entered in the minutes of meetings of the Board of Guardians of Poor Law Unions.

The following are examples of Settlement Examinations, Removal Orders and Settlement Certificates:

Brist. RO ref. P/OV/OP/7/3
[A settlement certificate accepting liability for a pauper, 1706.]

Gloucestershire. To the Churchwardens and Overseers of the poore of the parish of Olvestone in the said County and either of them.
Wee whose Hands and Seales are here unto subscribed being the Churchwardens and

Settlement Certificate acknowledging that George Booth is legally settled in St Mary's, Stafford, 1725. (John Titford Collection)

Overseers of the poore of the parish of Almondsbury in the said County doe hereby own and acknowledge Robert Adams, husbandman, and Elizabeth his wife to be inhabitants settled in our said parish of Almondsbury according to Lawe. In witness whereof wee have hereunto sett our hands and seales the six and twentieth day of October in the fourth year of the Reign of our Sovereigne Lady Queene Anne over England. Anno Dom. 1705

> John Holdingham, vic. of Almondsbury
> Will Not, churchwarden
> Nicholas Parish, Church Warden
> Thomas Crany, Overseer
> Edward Fiss, Overseer
> William Hollester, Overseer

Sealed and Delivered by Wm Nick, Nicholas Parnell and Thomas Bracy in the presence of Fra. Freeman, Edward Coules.

Wee whose hands are hereunto subscribed, two of his Majesty's Justices of the peace of the said County of Glouc^r doe hereby approve and allowe of the above written Certificate. As Witnesse our Hands the 24th day of May Anno Dom 1706.

> Rich. Haynes
> Thos. Cannes

Northants. RO Ref. 272P/57/7
[Removal Order to convey a man and his family to their place of settlement, 1716.]

To the Constables of Pottersbury in the County of Northampton & to any of them:

&

To the Churchwardens and Overseers of the Poore of Old Stratford in the Parish of Furtho in the said County of Noth'ton & to any of them.

Whereas Complaint hath been made unto us whose Names are hereunto Subscribed, Two of his Mgties Justices of the Peace of and for the said County of North'ton (One of us being of the Quorum) by the Churchwardens and Overseers of the Poore of Pottersbury aforesaid that John Parrott Dealer in horses & Hannah his wife & Mary their child about two years of age are lately come into their Parish of Pottersbury Endeavouring to gaine a Settlement therein and are likely to become chargeable to their said Parish and whereas it appeared unto us the said Justices upon the Examination of the said John Parrott duely taken upon Oath that about twenty six years ago he was Borne at Old Stratford in the Parish of Furtho aforesaid and it also appearing to us the said Justices upon the said Examination that he the said John Parrott hath done no Act whatever to Gaine a Settlement since his Birth aforesaid and that he the said John Parrott cannot give Security to save, harmless & indemnifyed the said Parish of Pottersbury according to the forme of the Statute in that Case made and Provided.

We doe therefore adjudge that the said John Parrott, Hannah his wife & Mary their child are likely to become chargeable to the said Parish of Pottersbury.

And wee doe hereby in his Majesty's Name require and Command you the Constables and Thirdborowes aforesaid to convey or cause to be conveyed, them the said John Perrott, Hannah his wife & child from Pottersbury aforesaid to Old Stratford in the Parish of Furtho & deliver them to the Churchwardens and Overseers of the Poore there or to some or one of them of the sd parish of Furtho together with this our Order (or a true copy thereof) who are hereby required to receive them and Provide for them according as the law in that Case directs and appoints thereof, faile not att your Perils.

Given under or Hands and Seales this Twentieth day of May in the Second year of the Reign of our Sovereign Lord George King of Great Britain Anno Dom 1717.

Edw. Babemans [?]

S. Fleetwood

Brist. RO ref. P/OV/OP/7/15
[A settlement certificate accepting liability for a pauper, 1728.]

Monmouth   Wee whose hands and Seales are heare unto Sett being Church Wardens and Overseers of the Poor of the Parish of Landeney in the County of Monmouth aforesaid do heareby own and acknowledge William Joanes, Judith his wife and Ann, Isack and Marey three of his children all to be Legally settled in the Parish of Landiney aforesaid.

In Witness Whereof we have hereunto set our hands and seales the 8 day of July in the Second year of the reign of Our Sovereign Lord George ye Second by the Grace of God of Great Britain, France and Ireland King Defender of the faith &c Adominy 1728.

John Harry, churchwarden

John Harry overseer of ye poor

To the Churchwardens and Overseers of the poor of the parish of Olveston in the County of Gloucester or to aney or other of them.

Attested by us Thos Jenkins, James Danes [?]

We whose names are here unto subscribed, Justices of the peace of the said County of Monmouth aforesaid do allow of this Certificate above written Dated the 8 day of June Anno Dom, 1728. John Curre

Were Hebert

Som. RO ref. Q/SR/308/5 No 10 Somerset Quarter Sessions Rolls
Epiphany, 1741
[The examination of a soldier to determine his place of settlement, 1740.]

Somerset To Wit   The Examination of William Russell now a common foott soldier in Major General Handicyde's Regiment of foott and in Captain Walter Devereaux Company now lying in the parish of Shepton Mallett in the County of Somerset taken before me James Strode Esq[r] one of his Maj[tes] Justices of the Peace in and for the said County on Wednesday the Twentyth day of March 1740.

Who upon his Oath saith that he was borne in the parish of Elgine in Scotland and there he lived from his infancy until about eleven years now last past and then he enlisted himself as a soldier in the above said Regiment and Company, and saith he hath lived in the Army ever since and that he was married to Isabelah Hay now Isabelah Russell his wife in the parish Church of Elgin in Scotland aforesaid and that he hath now one son by the sd Isabelah named John of about the age of two years and half old and saith the sd Isabelah his now wife is bigg with child of another child and further saith that the parish of Elgin in Scotland aforesd is the parish of his last Legal Settlement.

	The marke of
Taken & Sworn the day & year	X
above sd before me	William Russell
	James Shodey

Som. RO ref. Q/SR/315/3 Somerset Quarter Sessions Rolls
[Examination of a vagrant who claims to have been born in Flanders, 1747.]

Borough and Town of Taunton in the County of Somerset (to wit)
The examination of Francis Sharp a vagrant taken upon oath before us Two of His Majesty's Justices of the Peace of in and for the said Borough and Town this fourth day of August 1747.

Who upon his Oath saith that he was born at Gwent in Flanders, came over to England at about three years old and was afterwards bound out an apprentice to Thomas Scott a shopkeeper in Shoreditch in the City of London which he believes to be his last Legal Place of Settlement and saith that he with Ann his wife and two children (viz) James about twelve years old and Arthur about five years old have for upwards of one year last past subsisted by begging.

	The mark of
	X
Taken and Sworn the day	Francis Sharp
and year aforesaid before	
J. Hassum [?] Mayor	
Willm Sweeting, clerk	

Dev. RO (Ex.) ref. 2404A/PO202/6 Parish of Cullompton, Devon
[The examination of a woman to determine her place of settlement, 1758.]

Devon to witt   The Examination of Bridgett Moore als [alias] Marsh now residing in the Parish of Cullompton in the said County taken on Oath before Henry Cruwys Esqr one of His Majesty's Justices of the Peace for the said County this 15th Day of May 1758.

Saith that she is the daughter of Robert Moore als Marsh by Catherine his wife and that the s^d Robert Moore als Marsh having served his apprenticeship in the Parish of Plymtree in the said County with one Mr Harwood thereby gained a Settlement there

31

as she is informed and believes, but afterwards marrying with the said Catherine who was born and lived in the village of Poundsford in the said Parish of Cullompton her said father came and lived at Poundsford aforesaid with his said wife and had born there by her, five children of which this examinant was one. And saith that her s^d father supported himself and family there by day labour and that she is now forty years of age and that when she was about thirteen years of age she was bound out an apprentice by her said father to one Richard Mills of Heathallers in the s^d parish of Cullompton. The Officers of the said parish of Plymtree giving her father money to cloath her and that after living about a quarter of a year there she removed with the said master into the parish of Bradninch to an estate called Washbrewhays, there which he had taken at a yearly rent and lived with her said master there about four years, when her said master failed in his credit and ran away upon which this exam^t returned to the said village of Poundsford and there supported herself by daily labour for about 4 or 5 years, and after that went again into the said parish of Bradninch and hired herself with one John Maunder in the said parish and lived with him in his house at fifteen pence a week. About three quarters of a year after which she went into the town of Bradninch and lived there about half a year and supported herself by her daily labour and after the expiration of that time she went to the s^d Mr Maunder and lived with him under the like agreement for the best part th° not a full year without first or last making any express contract for a year, And saith that after that she then returned again into the said parish of Cullompton and hired herself for one year with one Mary Evans but lived with her only about half a year. And after that she went & lived wth Mr John Salter in the said parish of Cullompton for about a quarter of a year without making any agreement but ab^t that time she hired herself with the said Mr Salter for a year at the wages of three pounds and served him the said year and received her wages accordingly and served him some short time afterwards and then left his service and hath done no other Act to gain any settlement elsewhere. And further saith that she is informed and believes that the Churchwardens and Overseers of the Poor of the said parish of Plymptree by their certificate directed to the Churchwardens & Overseers of Cullompton and bearing the 6th of July 1728. Acknowledged the said Robert Moore als Marsh, Catherine Moore als Marsh, This Examinant and Anne and Sarah their three daughters (the other two daughters having been before bound out apprentices) to be Inhabitants Legally Settled within their said parish of Plymtree & obliged themselves to receive them together with any other children by the said Catherine who so ever requested by the Overseers of Cullompton aforesaid and to provide for them. And saith that her said mother who died about ten weeks since had about five years before her death relief from the said parish of Plymtree.

Sworn before me the	The mark of
day & year aforesaid	X
Hen Cruwys	Bridgett Moore als. Marsh

Request by Tiverton Union, Devon, for relief for a sick pauper, John Dunster, whose settlement was in the Taunton Union, Somerset. (Som. RO ref. D/G/Ta/37/2)

Ox. RO ref. PAR/Rotherfield Greys/C/10/8
[Enquiry into a man's rightful place of settlement, 1768.]

Oxfordshire   The Examination of John Day touching his Last legal settlement to wit taken on Oath before us two of his Majesty's Justices of the Peace for the County of Oxford the 11th day of May 1768.

This Examinant saith that he is about twenty eight years of age and that he was born in the parish of North Moore in the County of Oxford, and that he hath lived and served in several services, and saith that about Lady Day 1759 he was hired to [blank]

Pencott of the parish of Stanton Harcourt in the aforesaid county of Oxfordshire, husbandman, to serve him until the Michaelmas following and that he served the full time and received his wages for the same. And saith that at the Michaelmas following he was hired to the said [blank] Pencott to serve him for a year (that is to say from Michaelmas 1759 to Michaelmas 1760) and saith that he served his said master the full year in the aforesaid parish of Stanton Harcourt and received his full wages for the year. And saith that at the Michaelmas following he was hired to John Barrett of the parish of Tilehurst in the county of Berks, husbandman to serve him for a year and saith that he served his said master John Barrett in the aforesaid parish of Tilehurst until within about three weeks of the years service when some disputes arose between this examinant and his master and they agreed to part, and his said master John Barrett deducted out of his years wages five shillings for the time that he did not serve; saith that since that time he hath done no act or deed to gain a settlement in any parish or place but as aforesaid and further saith not.

Sworn before us the day and year first above written

P. Powys

L. Powys

Som. RO ref. D/P/Che.m/13/3/5 Chew Magna, Somerset
Parish Records, 1768
[A Removal Order to convey a woman from Great Marlow, Buckinghamshire, to Chew Magna, Somerset, her place of settlement.]

Bucks to Wit.   To the Constable, Headborough, Tithingman and other officer of the peace of the parish of Great Marlow within the said County to receive and convey. And to the Church Wardens, Chapel Wardens or Overseers of the Poor of the Parish, Place or Precinct of Chew Magna in the County of Somerset or either of them to receive and obey.
Whereas Mary the wife of William Godfrey was on the 17th day of this instant apprehended in the parish of Great Marlow as a Rogue (vide licet) wandring and begging and upon examination of the said Mary Godfrey taken before me William Clayton, Esqr upon Oath (which examination is hereunto annexed*) it doth appear that the place of her last legal Settlement is in the said Parish of Chew Magna in the said County of Somerset. These are therefore to require you the said Constable or other Officer to convey the said Mary Godfrey to the Parish of Bisham in the county of Berks that being the first Place in the next Precinct through which she ought to pass in the direct way to the said Parish of Chew Magna to which she is to be sent and to deliver her to the Constable or other Officer of such place in such next Precinct together with this pass and the Duplicate of the Examination of the said Mary Godfrey taking his Receipt for the same. And the said Mary Godfrey is to be thence carried on in like manner to the said parish of Chew Magna there to be delivered to some Church Warden, Chapel Warden or Overseer of the Poor of the same Parish of Chew Magna to be there provided for according to Law. And you the said Church Warden,

Chapel Warden or Overseer of the Poor are hereby required to receive the said Person and provide for her as aforesaid. Given under my hand and Seal this 19th Day of December in the year of our Lord 1768.　　*Wm Clayton*

* The examination document is not included with these papers

Berks to wit.　To the Constable, Tithingman and other Peace Officers of the Parish of Bisham in the County of Berks or either of them.
Convey the within named vagrant Mary Godfrey to Charnham Street in the County of Wilts, given under my Hand and Seal the nineteenth day of December one thousand seven hundred and sixty eight.　　*Wm East*

Charnham Street in Wilts. Convey the within named vagrant to Bathford in the county of Sumerset. Given under my hand this 22ⁿᵈ day of December 1768.
                                                                                                G. Popham

Som. RO ref. Q/SR/342/1 Somerset Quarter Sessions Rolls
Epiphany, 1774
[The examination of a widow who was born in Germany and whose late husband was from Ireland. She is to be conveyed to Ireland.]

Somerset　　The Examination of Mary Thomson a Rogue and Vagabond, taken on oath before me one of his Majesty's Justices of the Peace, in and for the said County this sixth day of October 1773, who on her Oath saith, That as she has heard and verily believes she was born in Germany and saith that about twenty seven years since she intermarried with her late deceased husband James Thomson who in his lifetime hath often informed her that his legal place of settlement was in the County of Westmay in the Kingdom of Ireland for that he was born there and saith she hath not since intermarried with any other person whosoever and hath done nothing since to her knowledge whereby to gain a settlement and saith that she wandered into the parish of Wellington in the said County where she was apprehended and taken up as a rogue and vagabond.
　　　　　Sworn before me Geo. Atwood　　　　　The mark of　X　Mary Thomson

                                    ***

Somerset　To the Constables, Tythingman, or other Officers of the Peace, of the
　　　　　parish of Wellington in the said County: And also to all Constables, and
　　　　　other Officers whom it may Concern, to Receive and Convey. And to all
　　　　　other Officers of the Peace whom it may concern, to Receive and Obey.
　　Whereas Mary Thomson was Apprehended in the parish of Wellington aforesaid as a Rogue and Vagabond, viz, Wandering and Begging there and upon Examination of the said Mary Thomson taken before me George Atwood Clerk, one of his Majesty's

Justices of the Peace, in and for the County of Somerset aforesaid, upon Oath (which Examination is hereunto annexed), it doth appear that the last Legal Place of Settlement of the said Mary Thomson is in the Kingdom of Ireland.

These are therefore to require You the said Constable, Tythingman, or other Officer of the Peace of the said parish of Wellington to Convey the said Mary Thomson to the City and County of Bristol that being the first place in the next Precinct, through which she ought to pass, in the direct Way to the said Kingdom of Ireland to which she is to be sent, and to deliver her to the Constable or other Officer of such City and County in such next Precinct, together with this Pass, and the Duplicate of the Examination of the said Mary Thomson taking his Receipt for the same.

And the constable or other officer to whom she shall be delivered in the said City and County of Bristol is hereby required to apply to the Justices of the Peace in and for the said City and County for a Warrant to the Master of any Ship or vessel bound for the said Kingdom of Ireland that shall be in the said City and County, to take on board the said ship or vessel her the said Mary Thomson and convey her to such place in the said Kingdom of Ireland.

Som. RO ref. Q/SR/347/3 Somerset Quarter Sessions Rolls
Midsummer, 1779
[The examination of a man who claims he was born in Algiers.]

County of Somerset
The examination of George Hollis, a rogue and vagabond, taken on oath before me, Thomas Horner Esq. one of His Majesty's Justices of the Peace in and for the said County the 9th day of June in the year of our Lord one thousand seven hundred and seventy nine.

Who on his oath saith, That he was born in Algiers in Africa, and is about thirty two years of age, as he hath heard and believes. That he hath been a seafaring man for the greatest part of his life; and about six months since, being on board the *Active* Privateer of Pool, he lost his left arm in an engagement with a French Frigate. That since this misfortune he has supported himself by begging up and down the country, and was yesterday apprehended wandering and begging in the parish of Mells in the said County of Somerset. Saith that he hath done no act to gain a Settlement in England to his knowledge or belief.
Taken and signed the day and year above written, before me.

George Hollis
T. Horner

Brist. RO ref. P/OV/OP/7/41
[The Churchwardens of Michaelston le Pit, Glamorganshire, acknowledging that a pauper is rightfully settled in their parish, 1780.]

To the Church Wardens and Overseers of the Poor of ye Parish of Oulson [Alstone?] In the County of Gloster to every or either of them.

We the Churchwardens and Overseers of the Parish of Michaelston le Pit in the County of Glamorgan hereby certify that we do own and acknowledge Sarah Williams and her two suns (viz) Thomas Williams aged four years & three quarters & John Williams age two years next Chrismas to be all inhabitants Legally settled in our said Parish of Michaelston le Pit, and do promis to serve them into our said Parish whenever they shall be come chargeable.

In witness whereof we ye said churchwardens and overseers of ye Poor Have hereunto respectively set our Hands & seals the 1st day of November 1780.

The mark of
Richard X Jones
Churchwarden & overseer of the poor of ye sd Parish

Witness   John Matthew
           Philip Thomas Rector of the sd Parish

We whose names are here unto subscribed Two of his majesty Justices of the peace for ye County of Glamorgan foresaid do allow of ye above written certificate.

Thomas Pryce
W Haset [?]

Som. RO ref. Q/SR 349/1 Somerset Quarter Sessions Rolls
Epiphany, 1781

[Four merchant seamen who have been captured by the Spanish are returned home and landed at Lyme, Dorset.]

County of Somerset.   The Examination of John Caseate, William Hanman, John Scriving and Daniel Hawley, Rogues and Vagabonds, Taken on Oath before me John Hellier Esquire, one of his Majesty's Justices of the Peace in and for the said County this Second Day of January 1781.

Who saith that he the abovesaid John Caseate, aged about fifty seven or eight years and was born in Ireland and brought up and bread at Chilsey [Chelsea?], William Hanman aged about twenty five years and was born at Sherborne in the County of Dorset but gain his settlement by living as a servant in the Parish of Bow in the County of Middlesex, John Scriving aged about sixteen years and was born at Handbury [Henbury?] in the County of Gloucester, Daniel Hawley aged about fourteen and was born in Whoping [Wapping] in London. And the said John Caseate, William Hanman, John Scriving and Daniel Hawley severally Saith that in August last they entered on board a Letter of Mark called *Admiral Rodney* of Bristol and that the last day of August last they was taken by a Spanish Cutter and Brig and carried into a place called Santon Toney in Spain, and was brought over by the *Avidence Providence* and landed at Lime in the County of Dorset the first day of January 1781 with a Cartail from Croney. And saith that yesterday in the afternoon they was apprehended at Crewkerne in the County of Somerset and this day brought before me by Charles Rendal tythingman of Hinton St. George in the said County.

Sworn before me   The mark   X   of John Caseate
the day and year   The mark   X   of William Hanman
aforesaid   The mark   X   of John Scriving
John Hellier   (signed) Dan[l] Hawley

Som. RO ref. S/SOr Somerset Quarter Sessions Rolls
Rough Order Book, 1780–81
[Vagrants to be whipped and passed to their respective parishes.]

Bridgwater Sessions 10th July 1781
Vagrants.   This Court observing that the Expense of apprehending and removing
vagrants hath of late been greatly increased in this County and being passed without
whipping has principally contributed to such of Expense doth therefore unanimously
recommend it to the Justices that all Vagrants apprehended in future be publickly
whipped (as directed by the Act passed in the 17th Year of the Reign of his late
Majesty King George the second) before they are passed to their respective parish
unless apparently in ill health or incapable of undergoing such Punishment and
doth order that this their Recommendation be inserted in the Publick News Papers.
Rogues and Vagabonds

Som. RO ref. D/P/Che.m./13/3/5 Chew Magna, Somerset
Parish Records, 1786
[A Removal Order to convey a woman from Saint Giles in the Fields, Middlesex,
to her place of settlement which was Chew Magna, Somerset, recording the places
through which she was to travel.]

Middlesex. To the Constables of the Parish of Saint Giles in the Fields in the County
of Middlesex, and also to all Constables and other Officers, whom it may concern to
receive and convey; and to the Church Wardens, Chapel Wardens, or Overseers of the
Poor of the Parish of Chew Magna in the County of Somerset or either of them, to
receive and obey.

     Whereas Sarah Slape hath been apprehended in the said Parish of Saint Giles in
the Fields as a rogue and Vagabond viz there wandering and begging in the open air
and upon Examination of the said Sarah Slape taken before Me upon Oath (which
Examination is hereunto annexed) it doth appear that the said parish of Chew Magna
in the County of Somerset is the place of her last legal Settlement.

     These are therefore to require you the Constables of the said Parish of Saint Giles in
the Fields, to convey the said Sarah Slape to the town of Colnbrook in the County of
Bucks that being the first Parish in the next Precinct through which she ought to pass
in the direct Way to the said Parish of Chew Magna to which she is to be sent. And
deliver her to the Constable or other Officer of the said town of Conlbrook together
with this Pass, and the Duplicate of the Examination of the said Sarah Slape taking
his Receipt for the same. And the said Sarah Slape is to be thence conveyed on in

No. 57.

Norfolk, } To the Churchwardens and Overseers of the Poor of
TO WIT. } the Parish of *Thwaite*
in the said County, and to the Churchwardens and
Overseers of the Poor of the Parish of *Thorpe Market* in the said County

and to each and every of them.

UPON the Complaint of the Churchwardens and Overseers of the Poor of the Parish of *Thwaite* in the said County of Norfolk, unto us whose names are hereunto set and seals affixed, being two of his Majesty's Justices of the Peace acting in and for the said County of Norfolk, and one of us of the Quorum, that *James Hurne Charlotte his wife and Elizabeth their child aged one year and an half*

did lately come to inhabit in the said Parish of *Thwaite* not having gained a legal settlement there, nor produced any certificate owning *them* to be settled elsewhere, and that the said *James Hurne Charlotte his wife and Elizabeth their child*

Wm Blake

are become chargeable to the said Parish of *Thwaite* We the said Justices upon due proof made thereof, as well upon the Examination of the said *James Hurne* upon oath, as otherwise, and likewise upon due consideration had of the premises, do adjudge the same to be true; and we do likewise adjudge, that the lawful settlement of the said *James Hurne Charlotte his wife and Elizabeth their child*

Saml Pitman.

is in the said Parish of *Thorpe Market* in the said County of *Norfolk* We do therefore require you, the said Churchwardens and Overseers of the Poor of the said Parish of *Thwaite* or some or one of you, to convey the said *James Hurne Charlotte his wife and Elizabeth their child*

from and out of your said Parish of *Thwaite* to the said Parish of *Thorpe Market* and *then* to deliver to the said Churchwardens and Overseers of the Poor there, or to some or one of them, together with this our order, or a true copy thereof; and we do also hereby require you, the said Churchwardens and Overseers of the Poor of the said Parish of *Thorpe Market* to receive and provide for *them* as Inhabitants of your Parish.

Given under our Hands and Seals at *Aylsham* the *twenty sixth* Day of *September* in the year of our Lord one thousand, eight hundred, and *twenty six*

Removal Order: for the removal of James Hurne, Charlotte, his wife, and Elizabeth their child, from Thwaite, Norfolk, to Thorpe Market, Norfolk, 1826. (John Titford Collection)

39

like Manner to the said Parish of Chew Magna there to be delivered to some Church Warden, Chapel Warden, or Overseer of the Poor of the same Place, to be there provided for according to Law. And you the said Church Wardens, Chapel Wardens, or Overseers of the Poor are hereby required to receive the said Person and provide for her as aforesaid. Given under my Hand and Seal the 23rd Day of January in the Year of our Lord 1786.   *D. Walker*

      Sarah Slape
Bucks to Witt
To the Constables of Colnbrook in the said County.
Convey the within named vagrant to Maidenhead in the County of Berks.
   Given under my hand this 26th Day of January 1786.
                  J. Broberey [?]

Town of Maidenhead in the County of Berks. To the Constable of the said Town.
Convey the within named vagrant to Charnham Street in the County of Wilts.
   Given under my hand this 27th Day of Jan[y] 1786.
                Wm –?– Mayor

Wilts to Witt
To the Tything man of Charnham Street in the said County.
Convey the within named vagrant to Bathford in the County of Somerset.
   Given under my hand this 2nd of Feb[y] 1786.
                Jas Bolt [?]

Here. RO ref. M61/43/1
[An appeal against a Removal Order, 1812.]

Case. Thomas Bishop aged about 30 years was born as he is informed and believes in the Parish of Bodenham in the county of Hereford where he was put an apprentice (tho' not bound) to Mr South of the Warehouse in the same Parish with whom he lived about 3 years. That he then went to live with a Mr Griffiths of the Court of Maund in the same P'sh where he continued for a year. That he then went to live with Mr Thomas Bascott of the P'sh of Felton as a hired Servant & that he liv[d] there two years & rec[d] 2 years wages but cannot recollect the amount. That then he went to Mr Lawrence of the same P'sh with whom he lived as a hired Servnt one year & recvd his full years wages. That then he went to live with Mr Hill of Hillhampton in the P'sh of Ocle Pitchard as a hired Servant but where he resided but about ½ a year. That then he went to live with Mr Pitt of Ullingswick where he remained for about half a year. That he then hired himself with Mr Pitt for another year which he serv[d] and rec[d] his full year's wages which he believes was 4 Gnas. That he then went to live again with the said Mr Griffiths of Bodenham as a hired Servant for a year which he served & rec'd his years wages accordingly which was 5 Gnas. That from thence he went to Mr Thomas Holders of Docklow where he was hired for a year from May at 6 Gnas, but being drawn to serve in the Militia he ran away about the Hay harvest & did not return until a fortnight before the May following, when, being out of place he was hired from thence for another year at 6 Gnas. That about the latter end of Augt in the same year he was married but continued in his Service till about 3 weeks previous to the expiration of his year. That his Master then asked him if he had any objections to leave his service, as, if he kept him longer it w^d make him a Parishoner of Docklow, that his Master then paid him his wages for the time he served him. That he then took a house in the Parish of Puddlestone where he lived but about 5 weeks and then he returned to Mr Holder's Service where he hired himself for another year at 6 Gnas, but being in the Supplementary Militia he remained there but about a fortnight. That he has a wife and 4 children living and has been relieved by the Officers of Bodenham at different times, his wife having been removed as he is informed by an Order to Bodenham during his absence. You'll please to observe the first removal was from Puddlestone to Bodenham which happen'd about 14 years ago and whilst the pauper was at the Supplementary Militia & that only his wife and one child & upon the examination of the wife alone, when the husband was to be had. This is presumed not to be the best evidence to remove upon. The second removal was previous to the last Sessions of the Husband, Wife & 5 Children from Puddlestone to Docklow and which Order was withdrawn. And now they are removed a third time from Puddlestone to Bodenham.

The Parish of Bodenham are very desirous of appealing to the last Order if you are [of] opinion they have any ground to go upon. You'll please answer the following Questions. First where the removal of the wife and child whilst the Husband was in the Militia will preclude the Officers of Bodenham from appealing to the last Order, or its clear Mr Holder committed a fraud on Bodenham by turning him away previous to his year. This first Order is lost.

Second. Whether the last removal from Puddlestone to Bodenham (being the same Parishes) is not an Abandonment of the first Order and, consequently may appeal. You'll advise Bodenham as fully as you can under the circumstances of the Case.

[Answer] I am of opinion that the officers of Bodenham have no ground for an appeal. The pauper's wife is stated to have been removed to Bodenham; that Order was not appealed to, it is therefore too late to contest that it was made upon insufficient evidence, even supposing the evidence so: An order removing a wife is if unappealed from as conclusive as if the husband himself had been removed with his wife. See Rex v Towchester 11 Const Butt as to the Service with Holder in Docklow I do not think (if that case could be now gone into) that ground is sufficiently apparent to do away the three weeks absence the pauper did not object to the quitting his Service, it was equivalent to his consenting so to do, amounted to a dissolution of the contract. This is within the principle established in Rex v Enverwall & other cases.

Henry Allen

Hereford 24th March 1812

Som. RO ref. Q/SR/402 Somerset Quarter Sessions Rolls
Epiphany, 1816
[The examination of a man who claims to have been born on board a ship.]

Somerset   The examination of Charles Bastone, labourer, aged about 45 years, now residing in the parish of Taunton St. Mary Magdalen in the said County, taken on oath before us, Two of His Majesty's Justices of the Peace, in and for the said County, the 27th Day of August 1814, touching the Place of his last legal Settlement, who upon Oath saith that he hath heard and believes he was born on board a ship at sea. That he hath heard and believes his father's settlement was at Upton Payne [Upton Pyne] in the County of Devon. That examinant never was an apprentice. That he never was in service. That he never rented to the amount of £10 a year. That he never served any parish office nor ever possessed any freehold or other property. That his father was a labouring carpenter and died (when this Examinant was only 10 years old) at Upton Payne aforesaid. That this Examinant believes his father was not so much as 40 years old when he died. That 25 years ago he married his present wife by whom he has two children living with him, Thomas aged 15 and Charles aged ten years.

Chas. X Bastone
mark

Sworn before us   W.Y. Coker
                          Malachi Blake

Another *Examination* taken on 4th November 1815 states that Charles Badstone [sic] gives further information. He stated:- 'that he recollects at about the age of ten or twelve years he lived with his father at Upton Pyne. His father had been at sea but then worked as a sawyer at Upton Pyne and kept house there. That Examinant went to sea leaving his father at Upton Pyne and continued at sea till he was about 17 or 18 years old. That he was employed as a carpenter but never made any agreement otherwise thereby nor ever did any act to his knowledge or belief whereby to gain a Settlement. That his father's name was Charles and his mother's name was Mary. That about thirty years ago he married Dorothy Dodden his first wife who died about three years after. That about 26 years ago he married Mary his present wife by whom he has three children here living with him now who have not acquired a Settlement in their own right (viz) Sarah aged about 20 years, Thomas aged about twelve years and Charles aged about eleven years.'

Som. RO ref. D/G/W/47/1 Wellington Union, Somerset and Devon
Settlement and Removal, Examination by Justices, 1842 to 1846 (1 volume)
[The examination of a man to determine his place of settlement.]

Examination of William Hurtnell, aged 42 years, now residing in Wellington.
'I was born in Clayhidon [Devon]. About the age of 8 yrs my father made an agreement with Mrs Troaks of Clayhidon that I should live with her for my meat & lodging and I lived with her for three years. My father found me in clothes. I then lived 4 yrs with Mr John Blackmore of Deadbur Farm in the parish after which I lived with Mr Gollis

Blackmore for 3 months. I then went to live at Lambrook where I lived for about 5 months when at the Lady day following I went into the parish of West Buckland and made an agreement with Mr Wm Beaden to live [with] him for a year at the wages of four pounds. I lived with him in West Buckland for the year and received my wages, and made an agreement for another year, to be determined by either of us giving one months notice. I lived out the same year with him and received my wages. I then went to Shildon in the County of Devon and lived there with Mr Robert Doble for nearly a year at weekly wages. I then went to Kentisbere, Devon and made an agreement with Mr James Hodge to serve him for a year at the wages of seven pounds. I lived out the whole year and received my wages and soon after married Elizabeth my present wife in the parish of Uffculme in the same county, by whom I have eight children now living, namely Jane aged 18 who was bound an apprentice by the parish of Kentisbere to Mr Frost with whom she now remains. Mary Ann aged 15 who is living with me. William aged 13 who is living with his master Mr Robt Frost in the parish of Kentisbere to whom he was bound by the parish. Thomas aged 9, Susan 7, Elizabeth 5 years, Sarah about two years and John 18 weeks.

his
Wm X Hartnell
mark

Before us J. Clarke
    Wm Burridge   3rd March 1842
William Blackmore Relieving Officer of the parish of Wellington in the county of Somerset, upon his oath saith that William Hartnell and his family are now chargeable to the parish of Wellington.
    Wm Blackmore R.O.

Som. RO ref. D/G/W/47/1 Wellington Union, Somerset and Devon
Settlement and Removal, Examinations by Justices, 1842 to 1846 (1 volume)
[The examination of a prisoner to determine his place of settlement, presumably so that he can be taken there after his release from prison.]

f32 (insert):
Devon to wit. The Examination of John Richards now a prisoner in the Gaol of the
                County of Devon taken on oath before me Sir Warwick Hele Tonkin,
                Knight, one of Her Majesty's Justices of the Peace for the said
                County this twenty fifth day of February 1842.
    Who saith, I was thirty years of age last November. I am the son of Levi Richards and Betty Richards who are now living in the parish of Dunkeswell in the said County. I first recollect myself as a child living with my father and my mother in Dunkeswell aforesaid. I lived with them until I was about nine years of age in Dunkeswell and during this time they repeatedly received relief from the parish of Dunkeswell. I have been with my mother to the Church of Dunkeswell at the Vestry when she has received the pay. I had fifteen brothers and sisters.

[contd]

Poor Law Commission Office,
Somerset House,
February 12th, 1839.

SIR,

THE Poor Law Commissioners, in reference to the frequent enquiries made by Boards of Guardians respecting the desertion of wives and families by their husbands or parents, and the means of punishing the offenders, and the payment of the expences of apprehending and proceeding against them, have considered it desirable to state their views upon the subject, and to direct attention to the following recommendation :—

I.   Every person able, wholly or in part, to maintain himself, or herself, or his or her family, and neglecting to do so, and thereby allowing them to become chargeable, is liable to be punished as a disorderly person under the Vagrant Act, (5 Geo. 4, c. 83, s. 3,) and, on a repetition of the offence, to be punished as a Rogue and Vagabond, (sec. 4).

This provision applies equally to—

1.—Husbands neglecting to maintain their wives.

2.—Fathers neglecting to maintain their children.

3.—Widows neglecting to maintain their children.

and it is the operation of the Poor Law Amendment Act to extend the liability to—

4.—Men, marrying since the passing of this Act, neglecting to maintain their wives' children under 16, (sec. 57).

5.—Women unmarried neglecting to maintain their bastards born since the passing of this Act, (sec. 71).

The above provision applies to the case of a desertion, and is chiefly resorted to when the desertion does not amount to a "running away."

The 4th sec. of the Vagrant Act renders " every person running " away and leaving his wife, or his or her child or children chargeable, or " whereby she or they or any of them shall become chargeable," liable to be punished as a Rogue and Vagabond, and after a conviction for a first offence, to punishment as an incorrigible Rogue.

This provision clearly does not apply to the 4th class of persons above described; but, it is understood to apply to a wife leaving her children in the Workhouse, or otherwise running away, and leaving her children chargeable, or in a condition which eventually renders them chargeable, although her husband be, at the same time, liable to support them.

With

*To the Clerk to the Board
of Guardians.*

Letter from the Poor Law Commission, dated 12 February 1839, setting out the rules regarding the maintenance of dependants and the punishment for those persons who neglect to maintain their families. (Som. RO ref. D/G/Ta/37/2)

2

II. With respect to the expences of the prosecution of offenders under the Vagrant Act, it appears that generally such expences must be paid by the person prosecuting, as in all other cases of prosecution of public offenders, where express provision is not made for the payment of costs out of some public fund.

The only cases in which expences incurred about the apprehension or prosecution of such Offenders can be paid, are—first, where money or effects are found in their possession, in which case such money or effects may be applied towards defraying the expences of apprehension, and of the Offender's maintenance in Gaol (5 Geo. 4, c. 83, s. 8); and—secondly, where an offender may appeal against his conviction, and any person is bound by recognizances to appear at Sessions to support the conviction ; in which case the prosecutor and witnesses may be repaid their reasonable expences, and may be compensated for their loss of time and their trouble at the expence of the County Rates (5 Geo. 4, c. 83, s. 9).

III. These provisions are generally represented as insufficient to induce the Parish Officers and Guardians to take proceedings for the apprehension of persons leaving their families chargeable. The consequent escape of offenders is the subject of frequent complaints.

Under these circumstances, the Commissioners consider it their duty to call the attention of Guardians to the operation of the Poor Law Amendment Act, and of the Regulations relating to the granting of relief by way of loan ; and to suggest, that wherever a wife or family is left chargeable to a Parish, relief may, under the existing Regulations, be administered as a loan to the husband or father, if the latter be able-bodied, and within the ages of 21 and 60.

Relief so granted, will bring into operation the various remedies for recovering of money lent, and especially the attachment of wages, and the summary remedy to compel repayment, given by the 59 Geo. 3, c. 12, sec. 29, on the Summons and Order of two Justices, and by commitment for every default to the House of Correction for a period not exceeding three months.

This course, which affords a remedy to the Parish, and a punishment where the party fails to obey the Justices' Order, appears to the Commissioners to be properly applicable to a large class of the cases referred to, and being for the reimbursement of the Parish, will enable the Parish Officers or Guardians to pay the necessary and reasonable costs of discovering the party liable, and of proceeding against him.

If the Guardians of any Union should desire the regulations for the administration of relief by way of loan to be extended for the above purposes to all persons whatever, females as well as males above the age of 21, the Commissioners, upon application from any Union, will be prepared to issue the necessary Order.

Signed by Order of the Board,

Edwin Chadwick

Secretary.

45

When I was about nine years of age I was bound an apprentice by the parish Officers of Dunkeswell to Mr John Ewins a farmer who then rented an Estate I think called Abbey Wood in the parish of Dunkeswell. I recollect going before the Magistrates in Cullompton when I was bound. Abbey Wood was an Overland Estate and there was no dwelling upon it but Mr Ewins lived about two miles off in the parish of Hemiock. I slept in Dunkeswell the first night or two after I was bound at the House of the Overseer Mr Ellard and he then took me to Mr Ewins in Hemiock with my Indenture. I saw my Master then sign something which they said at the time was my Indenture. Mr Ellard was present. I then left the room and went to work on the Estate in Hemiock. I served the said Mr Ewins about two years working sometimes upon the Estate in Hemiock and sometimes upon the Estate in Dunkeswell, but mostly in Dunkeswell because it was chiefly tillage land, but I always slept in my Master's house in Hemiock aforesaid. When I had served him the first two years my Master wished me to go with his brother Robert Ewins who then lived in the parish of Clayhidon. I went accordingly and served Robert Ewins in Clayhidon aforesaid about two years. At the end of which time my Master, the said John Ewins wished me to go with his brother William Ewins in the parish of Uppottery in the said County and I went with the said William Ewins and served him one year in Uppottery. I then went back to the said John Ewins and served him in Hemiock aforesaid for about one year. I then returned to the said William Ewins in Uppottery and served him there about three years. When I had been with the said William Ewins this second time about one year, my Master the said John Ewins said he would give me up my time and if I liked I might take my own wages and take care of myself. In consequence of this I made an agreement with the said William Ewins for one year at three pounds. I served out that time in Uppottery and them made a fresh agreement with the said William Ewins at higher wages for another year which I also served out and agreed for a third year which I also served except a month. I left in consequence of a quarrel with my Master's son. I was then about eighteen years of age. I left the said William Ewins a month before Lady Day. I then went to Dunkeswell Farm in the parish of Dunkeswell with James Burrows. I agreed with him a month upon a trial which I served. At the end of the month I agreed to serve him out the year at seven pounds the year, I think and served out the year. I then agreed with him for another year and served until Michaelmas.

I entered Mr Burrows service at Lady Day and I was eighteen years old the November previous. When I left Mr Burrows I went out to work at daily labor until Lady Day following. About three weeks after this Lady Day I went into the parish of Sheldon and agreed with Mr Dobles of that parish to serve him at I think two shillings and nine pence per week until the Lady Day following.

I served out this time and left at Lady [Day] which was in the year 1833. I was twenty one years of age the November previous.

I married Mary my present wife in the month of April 1833 at the parish church of Sheldon aforesaid by whom I have now three children living namely Ann aged four years, John aged about two years and Mary aged about six months and they are now living in the parish of Culmstock.

On the fifteenth or sixteenth of November last I took a house of Mr William Corner at the rent of ten pounds a year and to pay all the outs. I occupied this house until the seventeenth of December last when I was brought to the Gaol but my wife and children I believe still occupy the premises. I have paid no rates or taxes.

Before me   The mark of
Warwick Hele Tonkin   X
                                                                 John Richards

Wellington 28th February 1842
The above examination was produced by me Wm Jacobs the Assistant Overseer of Culmstock who was present at the time of its being taken on the 25th instant before Warwick Hele Tonkin, a Magistrate of the County of Devon who signed his name thereunder in my presence.

                                                                 Wm Jacobs
                                                                 Assist. Overseer

Verified before us this
28th February 1842   W.P. Thomas
                         J. Clarke

Ox. RO ref. PAR27/5/1/A/1

[A pauper is unable to work and his son is ordered to pay for his maintenance – Oxfordshire, 1842.]

County of Oxford to wit   Whereas at the Petty Sessions holden at Woodstock for the
                           South Division of Wootton Hundred in the said County
                           before Charles Cottrell Dormer Esquire and the Reverend
                           Thomas Curme two of Her Majesty's Justices of the Peace
for the County aforesaid, a complaint was made by the Churchwardens and Overseers of the Poor of the parish of Begbroke in the County of Oxford that one Robert Neville was then poor and unable to work so as to maintain or support himself and was then chargeable to the said parish, and that one Charles Neville dwelling at Begbroke within the said Division and within the jurisdiction of the said justices, was the son of the said Robert Neville and was of sufficient ability to relieve and maintain the said Robert Neville his father and now at the said mentioned Petty Sessions holden this day at Woodstock for the Division aforesaid we Charles Cottrell Dormer Esquire and the Reverend Thomas Curme, two of Her Majesty's Justices of the Peace for the County aforesaid The said Charles Neville appears before us and having heard the complaint aforesaid does not show any sufficient cause why such an order as aforesaid should not be made in his behalf. Now we the said Charles Cottrell Dormer and Thomas Curme justices as last aforesaid, having duly considered what has now been alleged and proved before us in this behalf do adjudge and determine that the said Robert Neville is poor, old and unable to work so as to maintain or support himself and that he is actually chargeable to the said parish of Begbroke and that the said Charles Neville is the son of the said Robert Neville and is of sufficient ability to relieve and maintain

the said Robert Neville his father and it being proved the said Charles Neville now dwells within the jurisdiction, we do therefore order that the said Charles Neville shall upon notice of this our order, pay or cause to be paid to the Churchwardens and Overseers of the Poor of the said Parish of Begbroke for the time being or to some one of them, weekly and every week from this present time, the sum of one shilling for and towards the relief and maintenance of the said Robert Neville for and during as long a time as the said Robert Neville shall be chargeable to the said parish of Begbroke or until the said Charles Neville shall be lawfully ordered to the contrary.

Given under our hands and seals, at the petty sessions holden at Woodstock for the division aforesaid this ninth day of November in the year of our Lord 1842.

C. Cottrell Dormer
Thomas Curme

TNA ref. MH 12/10215 Bedminster Union, Somerset
[The examination of a woman, details of which were sent to the Poor Law Board.]

Received by the Poor Law Board Jan 13, 1857

City and County of Bristol   The Examination of Sarah Pardy now residing in East Street, in that part of the Parish of Bedminster which is in the said City and County of Bristol, this seventh day of January in the Year of Our Lord, One Thousand Eight Hundred and Fifty seven upon the application and complaint of the Overseers of the Poor of the Parish of Bedminster, partly in the County of Somerset, and Partly in the said City and County of Bristol, unto us that the said Sarah Pardy and her child Alfred aged fifteen years or thereabouts have come to inhabit and are now inhabiting in the said part of the said Parish of Bedminster, which is in the said City and County of Bristol, and in the Bedminster Union, not having gained a legal settlement therein, nor produced any certificate owning them or any of them to be settled elsewhere, but having resided in the said Parish of Bedminster for five years next before the said application and complaint without receiving Parochial Relief therefrom, and that the said Sarah Pardy and her said child are now actually chargeable to the said parish of Bedminster.

Who upon her Oath saith, 'I am the widow of Jonathan Pardy to whom I was married at Yeovil Church, Somerset, about the year 1819. The above named Alfred Pardy is a son of that marriage and was born about the year 1841. My said husband has frequently told me that he was apprenticed to one Nathaniel Sydenham of Yeovil aforesaid, cordwainer and that he served his full time with his master and resided in Yeovil aforesaid and that he had the Indentures of Apprenticeship but he never shewed them to me. I have heard and believe that my father and mother were both natives of Wincanton, Somerset and that I was both born and christened there about 68 years ago. When I can first recollect I was living in that parish and remained there until my parents died. I was then about 13 years of age and was taken to Yeovil by my uncle and lived with him until I was married. I came with my said husband and family to Bedminster about 14 years ago and have continued to reside there without intermission up to this present time. My said husband died in August 1849 and about 3 months before his death I applied for and obtained relief from Bedminster parish which I have ever since continued to receive. To the best of my knowledge, information and belief my said husband never did any other act in his lifetime and I have not done any act since his decease to gain a settlement any where in either of our right.'

Sworn at the Council House in the City
and County of Bristol before us the same   The mark of
having been read over to the said Sarah   X
Pardy and explained to her which she   Sarah Pardy
    appeared to understand
    Daniel Burges
    H. L. Worrall

TNA ref. MH 12/10215 Bedminster Union, Somerset
[The examination of a man, details of which were sent to the Poor Law Board.]

Received by the Poor Law Board Jan 13, 1857

City and County of Bristol   The Examination of William Wookey now residing in East Street in the parish of Bedminster which is in the said City and County of Bristol, laborer and of Henry Hodson of Sargeant Street in the said parish of Bedminster in the said City and County of Bristol, Collector of Borough Rates for the said parish, of and concerning the place of the last legal Settlement of the said William Wookey, Maria his wife and two of their children, taken upon Oath before us, the undersigned, two of Her Majesty's Justices of the Peace in and for the said City and County of Bristol, this eighth day of January in the Year of Our Lord, One Thousand Eight Hundred and Fifty Seven upon the application and complaint of the Overseers of the Poor of the Parish of Bedminster, partly in the County of Somerset, and partly in the said City and County of Bristol, unto us that the said William Wookey, Maria his wife and two of their children have come to inhabit and are now inhabiting in the said part of the said parish of Bedminster, which is in the said City and County of Bristol, and in the Bedminster Union, not having a legal settlement therein, nor produced any certificate owning them or any of them to be settled elsewhere, and having resided in the said Parish of Bedminster for five years next before the said application and complaint without receiving Parochial Relief therefrom, and the said William Wookey, Maria his wife and their two children are now actually chargeable to the said parish of Bedminster.

The said William Wookey upon his Oath saith, 'I was married to my present wife Maria on or about the twenty fifth day of February 1828 at the Old Church in the said parish of Bedminster and have by her five children being namely, Louisa aged 27 years, Eliza aged 21 years, John aged 17 years, Mary Ann aged 15 years and William aged 12 years or severally thereabouts. I was never apprehended nor have I ever done any act to gain a settlement anywhere in my own right. When I can first recollect I was living with my father and mother at the parish of Burrington in the County of

Somerset and remained there until I was about nineteen years of age. I have resided in the parish of Bedminster aforesaid for the last twenty years and upwards without intermission and for twelve years of that time without receiving any Parochial Relief whatever. I am now and for eight years past or thereabouts have been with my said wife and two of my said children wholly chargeable and receiving relief from the said parish of Bedminster.'

William Wookey [signed]

Sworn at the Council House
in the said City and County
of Bristol, before us
   H.L.Worral
   Samuel Burges
The said Henry Hodson upon his Oath saith:-

'On the sixth day of January instant by the direction of the Parish Officers of Bedminster aforesaid, I proceeded to Burrington aforesaid to make enquiries into the place of settlement of the above named William Wookey. I waited on the Incumbent the Revd Mr Bumstey and by him was referred to an old parishoner named Samuel Williams who informed me he was 80 years of age but by reason of rheumatism was unable to come to Bristol to give evidence. He stated that he knew the parents of the said William Wookey who was born in the said parish of Burrington from 45 to 50 years ago. He pointed out the house in which such birth took place. It is in the occupation of one Isaac Howell. I received the same information from one Abraham David there who is nearly 70 years of age and from several other persons. I could find no entry of his baptism in the parish Registry [sic] which the Revd Mr Bumstey accounted for by stating that until about 25 years since it was the custom for persons living near the Brook where the pauper was born which Brook formed the boundary of the parish to take their children to Blagdon church or to Churchill to be baptised, but I had not time to go to those parishes and search the Registers. From the information I obtained at Burrington aforesaid. I have no doubt and verily believe the said William Wookey to have been born in that parish.'

Sworn in the Council House   Henry Hodson [signed]
   in the said City and County
   of Bristol
   Before us   H.L. Worrall
                   Daniel Burges

There were numerous disputes and appeals over the *rightful place of settlement* of an individual pauper or family. Such disputes were often challenged and taken to the Court of Quarter Sessions. Evidence was taken from many people as well as members of the family, and a judgement was made by the justices. Such statements can give a wealth of information about a family. The following is an example.

A family tree compiled from this court case alone is shown on page 51.

Som. RO ref. Q/SR/531 Somerset Quarter Sessions Rolls
Michaelmas, 1843

To the Churchwardens and Overseers of the Poor of the Parish of High Littleton in the County of Somerset, and the Churchwardens and Overseers of the Poor of the Parish of Kilmersdon in the County of Somerset.

Somerset   Whereas Complaint hath been made unto Us, whose Names are hereunto set, and Seals affixed, being two of Her Majesty's Justices of the Peace in and for the County of Somerset aforesaid, (one whereof being of the Quorum) by the Churchwardens and Overseers of the Poor of the said Parish of High Littleton That Thomas Robbins and Margaret his wife and their several children, namely Emma aged about fifteen years, Thomas aged about thirteen years, Martha and Mary (twins) aged about eleven years, Jane now aged about ten years, Rosanna now aged about six years and Fanny now aged about two years, have come to inhabit in the said Parish of High Littleton not having gained a legal Settlement there, nor having produced any Certificate acknowledging them to be settled elsewhere, and are now actually become chargeable to the same; WE, the said Justices, upon the Proof made thereof, as well upon the Examination of the said Thomas Robbins and others upon Oath, as other Circumstances, do adjudge the same to be true, and do also adjudge the Place of the legal Settlement of the said Thomas Robbins and Margaret his wife and their several children, Emma, Thomas, Martha

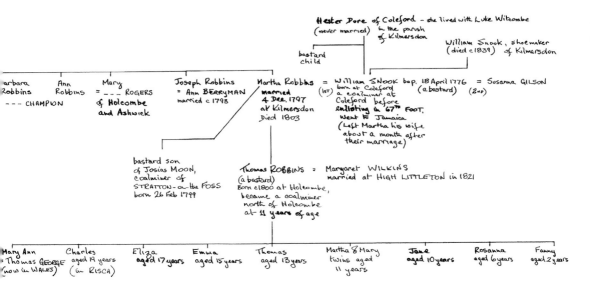

Family tree of the Robbins family drawn up from the settlement enquiry given on pp. 51–58.

and Mary (twins), Jane, Rosanna and Fanny, to be in the Parish of Kilmersdon in the County of Somerset.

THESE are therefore in Her Majesty's Name to require you, the said Churchwardens and Overseers of the Poor of the said Parish of High Littleton or some one of you, or any proper Person or Persons to be employed by you, to remove and convey the said Thomas Robbins and Margaret his wife and their said several children, Emma, Thomas, Martha and Mary (twins), Jane, Rosanna and Fanny from your said Parish of High Littleton to the said Parish of Kilmersdon and there deliver unto the Churchwardens and Overseers of the Poor there, or some or one of them, together with this Order, or a true copy thereof, who are hereby required to receive and provide for them according to Law.

GIVEN under our Hands and Seals, the twenty seventh day of June in the year of our Lord one thousand eight hundred and forty three.

John George Trigg
Wm C. James

County of Somerset.   The Parish of High Littleton in the said County of Somerset.
In the matter of Thomas Robbins a Pauper.
To the Overseers of the Poor of the Parish of Kilmersdon in the County of Somerset.

TAKE NOTICE, that the above named Thomas Robbins has, together with Margaret his wife and their several children, Emma, Thomas, Martha, Mary, Jane, Rosanna and Fanny become chargeable to our said Parish of High Littleton and that an Order of Justices has been duly obtained for their removal to your Parish of Kilmersdon as the place of their last legal settlement, (a Duplicate of which Order, and also a copy of the Examination upon which the same was made, are herewith sent to you): and Take Notice, that unless you appeal against the said Order, and within twenty one days from the date hereof, duly serve Notice of such Appeal, the said Paupers will be removed to your said Parish of Kilmersdon in pursuance of the said Order.

Dated this twenty seventh day of June one thousand eight hundred and forty three.

John Beak

John Blinman

Charles Hall

James Weeks

Churchwardens
and
Overseers of the Poor
of the said parish of High Littleton

COPY

THE EXAMINATION of Thomas Robbins now residing in the Parish of High Littleton in the County of Somerset touching the place of his last legal settlement, taken upon Oath this thirteenth day of June 1843.

Who upon his Oath, saith as follows, viz.

'I am going on 44 years of age and was born in the Parish of Holcombe in this County as I have heard and believe. I have heard I was born in the house of my mother's brother Joseph Robbins. My mother's maiden name was Martha Robbins and I have heard she married William Snook a bastard child of Hester Dore of Coleford in the Parish of

Kilmersdon in this County which said William Snook was a Soldier. I have heard that my mother died in her said brother Joseph's house at Holcombe a few weeks after my birth. I was brought up by my mother's sister Mary Rogers in the neighbourhood of Holcombe and Ashwick in this County until I was about eleven years old when I left that neighbourhood for Timsbury in this County and have worked in the Coal Mines there and elsewhere ever since. I have done no act to gain a settlement in my own right. I have always gone by the name of Thomas Robbins, after my mother's maiden name. In the year 1821 I was married at High Littleton Church to Margaret (Wilkins) my present wife by whom I have now ten children namely Mary Ann, wife of Thomas George in Wales, Charles aged about nineteen years now at Risca, Eliza now aged past seventeen years, Emma aged about fifteen years, Thomas aged about thirteen years, Martha and Mary (twins) aged about eleven years, Jane now aged about ten years, Rosanna now aged about six years and Fanny now aged about two years.'

Taken and Sworn before us Justices of ⎫
the Peace in and for the said County ⎬ Thomas Robbins (signed)
   John George Mogg ⎭
   Wm C James

The Examination of Henry Blinman now residing in the Parish of High Littleton in the County of Somerset touching the place of the last legal Settlement of Thomas Robbins taken upon Oath this thirteenth day of June 1843 who upon his Oath saith as follows, viz.

'I am Assistant Overseer of the Poor of the Parish of high Littleton aforesaid. I now produce two extracts from the Register Books of the Parish of Kilmersdon in this County which extract I have compared with the original Register Books and swear they are verbatim copies of the original entries in such books. The following are true copies of such extracts,' viz.

   Kilmersdon Baptisms 1776
18 April William Snook, natural son of Hester Dore was Baptized.

1797 William Snook of this Parish and Martha Robince of ye same Parish were married in this Church by Banns this 4th day of Dec[r] in the year one thousand seven hundred and ninety seven by me John Graves, vicar

This marriage was solemnized ⎫   Wm Snook X his mark
between us ⎬ Martha Robince X her mark
In the presence of ⎭   Joseph Flower
                 Wm Abraham

Taken and Sworn before us ⎫   Henry Blinman
Justices of the Peace in and ⎬ John George Mogg
for the said County ⎭   Wm C. James

Copy. Examination of Martha Snook in 1799, Pauper's Mother.

Somerset.   The Examination of Martha Snook residing in Holcombe but of the Parish of Kilmersdon, wife of William Snook late of the said Parish of Kilmersdon in the said County, coalminer, taken on oath before me Thomas Samuel Jolliffe, Esquire, one of His Majesty's Justices of the Peace in and for the said County this 12th day of October 1799.

This Examinant on her oath saith, 'That about one year and three quarters ago her husband left her, and he has ever since been serving in the 67th Regiment of Foot, to which he belonged when he married her, that she has never seen him from that time, she believes he is now and has been for some time at Jamaica, that on or about the 26th February last she was delivered of a male bastard child which said bastard child was gotten on her body by Josias Moon of Stratton on the Foss in the same County, coalminer, and that the said bastard child is now living and become chargeable to the said Parish of Kilmersdon.'

The Mark of

X

Martha Snook

Sworn before me the day and year first above written at Holcombe in the said County whither I come by desire of the Parish Officers of Kilmersdon to take the aforesaid Examination and find the above said Martha Snook apparently in the last stage of a deep decline and quite unable to attend at Mells or any distance. From the simple plain account which this poor young woman, who has a very good character given me she has been treated in a most shocking and brutal manner by the aforesaid Josias Moon.

Thos Sam¹ Jolliffe

The Examination of Ann Robbins, widow now residing at Lipyat in the Parish of Kilmersdon in the county of Somerset touching the place of the last legal settlement of Thomas Robbins taken upon Oath this thirteenth day of June 1843, who upon her Oath saith as follows, viz.

'I am now about 71 years old. My maiden name was Berryman. About 50 years ago I married (at Kilmersdon Church) Joseph Robbins who was an elder brother of Martha Robbins the mother of the Pauper Thomas Robbins. I knew said Martha Robbins well. Forty five years ago last December she was married to William Snook, a bastard of Hester Dore of Coleford in the said Parish of Kilmersdon. I was present at the marriage. They went from our house to be married as said Martha Robbins was living with me and my husband at the time. Said William Snook was a soldier on furlough at the time of such marriage. During the existence of the furlough he and his wife Martha from the time of their marriage lived with the said Hester Dore at Coleford, and when said William Snook rejoined his regiment (about a month after the marriage) said Martha Snook his wife returned to our house and lived there and at her sister's Barbara Champions in the neighborhood until her death. She died at our house at Holcombe about forty years ago. About half a year before her death she was confined in our house with the Pauper Thomas Robbins. I was present at the birth. His mother was ill for some time before and after his birth and never nursed him. He was brought up by

Mary Rogers his mother's sister in the neighborhood of Holcombe and Ashwick until he was about eleven years old, when he left that neighborhood for the Coal Works in the North of Holcombe. I never knew that the Pauper went after his mother's maiden name until nine years ago, but it is very much the custom in the neighborhood of Holcombe for children to be called after their mother's maiden name. I don't know where William Snook's regiment lay, nor how many times he came home to his wife on furlough after his marriage to said Martha Robbins. I remember hearing that after the death of said Martha he came to Holcombe and married a woman named Susanna Gilson, who went off with him to his regiment, and neither of them to my knowledge have been in the neighborhood of Holcombe since, and I have never heard whether he is alive or dead. The reputed father of said William Snook was one William Snook a shoemaker of Kilmersdon who died there about four years ago. Said William Snook (the son) was born as I believe at Coleford in the said Parish of Kilmersdon and as I always understood was baptized at the Parish Church of Kilmersdon. He and I were children together living within half a mile of each other for some years. He enlisted a soldier from Coleford. He came home on a furlough to see his mother at Coleford at the time he married Martha Robbins. I knew his mother Hester Dore well. She had another bastard child besides said William Snook by another man. She afterwards lived with a married man named Luke Witcombe and died as I have heard at her house near Coleford several years since. I never knew she lived out of that neighborhood, nor that she ever was married. I believe the Baptismal register extract produced by Mr Henry Blinman refers to the Baptism of said William Snook (the son). The Marriage register extract produced by him refers to the marriage of said William Snook and Martha Robbins. Robbins was heretofore sometimes spelt Robince.'

Sworn before us Justices of the Peace
in and for the said County

John George Moss
Wm C. James

The Examination of John Cary now residing at Coleford in the Parish of Kilmersdon in the County of Somerset touching the place of the last legal Settlement of Thomas Robbins taken upon Oath this 27th day of June 1843 who upon his Oath saith as follows, viz.

'I am now 78 years of age and have lived in the immediate neighborhood of Coleford all my life. I well knew Hester Dore of Coleford before the birth of her bastard son William Snook. I remember his birth at Coleford aforesaid about sixty seven years ago. He was the reputed son of William Snook, shoemaker at Kilmersdon now deceased, and was, as I believe baptized at the Parish Church of Kilmersdon aforesaid. I and said William Snook (the son) when he was young worked together as colliers under ground in the neighborhood of Coleford. He afterwards enlisted a soldier, and left the neighborhood. He came home on a furlough to see his mother at Coleford and married one Martha Robbins. Said Hester Dore had another bastard child, and afterwards lived with a married man named Luke Witcombe, and died at Coleford several years since. She never married to my knowledge.'

Taken and Sworn before us Justices
of the Peace in and for the said County   John Cary (signed)
           John George Moss
           Wm C. James

The Examination of John Dudden now residing in the Parish of High Littleton in the County of Somerset touching the place of the last legal settlement of Thomas Robbins taken upon oath this twenty seventh day of June 1843 who upon his oath saith as follows, viz.

'I am duly appointed Relieving Officer for the District of Clutton Poor Law Union in this County. The Parish of High Littleton aforesaid forms part of such District and Union. The said Pauper Thomas Robbins and his wife and seven youngest children living with him have been chargeable to the said Parish of High Littleton for the last six weeks and are now chargeable thereto.'

Taken and sworn before us Justices   John Dudden
of the Peace in and for this said County
   John George Moss
   Wm C. James

THE PARISH OF High Littleton in the said county of Somerset.
   In the matter of Thomas Robbins a pauper.
To the Overseers of the Poor of the Parish of Kilmersdon in the County of Somerset.
TAKE NOTICE, that the above named Thomas Robbins has, together with Margaret his wife and their several children, Emma, Thomas, Martha, Mary, Jane, Rosanna and Fanny become chargeable to our said Parish of High Littleton and that an Order of Justices has been duly obtained for their removal to your Parish of Kilmersdon as the place of their last legal settlement, (a Duplicate of which Order, and also a copy of the Examination upon which the same was made, are herewith sent to you): take notice, that unless you appeal against the said Order, and within twenty one days from the date hereof, duly serve Notice of such Appeal, the said Paupers will be removed to your said Parish of Kilmersdon in pursuance of the said Order.
Dated this twenty seventh day of June one thousand eight hundred and forty three.
     John Beak   Churchwardens
     John Blinman   and
     Charles Hall   Overseers of the Poor
     James Weeks   of the said Parish of High Littleton

Grounds of Appeal

To the Churchwardens and Overseers of the Poor of the Parish of High Littleton in the County of Somerset. In the matter of an appeal against an order for the removal of Thomas Robbins, Margaret his wife and Emma, Thomas, Martha, Mary, Jane, Rosanna and Fanny their children in which:
   The churchwardens and Overseers of the Poor of the Parish of Kilmersdon in the County of Somerset are the **Appellants**.

And the Churchwardens and Overseers of the Poor of the Parish of High Littleton in the said County are the **Respondents**.

We hereby give you and each of you notice that the grounds of the above appeal are as follows that is to say:-

1. That the Examination on which the said Order of removal was made does not contain any Legal and sufficient evidence that the said Thomas Robbins, Margaret his wife and their several children in the said Order mentioned were or any or either of them were at the time of the making of the said Order settled in our said Parish of Kilmersdon.
2. That the said Examination is bad and insufficient on the face thereof.
3. That it does not appear upon the face of the said Examination that Emma aged fifteen years, Thomas aged thirteen years, Martha and Mary aged eleven years and Jane aged ten years five of the children of the said Thomas Robbins in the said Order mentioned were before and at the time of the making of the said Order unemancipated and Part of the family of the said Thomas Robbins.
4. That it does not appear on the face of the said Examination that the said children, Emma, Thomas, Martha, Mary and Jane had not before and at the time of the making the said Order respectively gained Settlements in their own rights.
5. That the said Examination does not contain any Legal Evidence that William Snook in the said Examination mentioned was born in our said Parish of Kilmersdon or that he was at any time settled in our said Parish of Kilmersdon.
6. That the Evidence set out in the said Examination respecting the Birth of the said William Snook is hearsay and is also founded on conjecture and belief and is uncertain and inadmissible.
7. That the Examination does not contain any Legal evidence that the said William Snook in the said Examination mentioned was a Bastard Child of the said Hester Dore in the said Examination mentioned and that as such Bastard Child he gained a Settlement by birth in our said Parish of Kilmersdon.
8. That the Place called Coleford in the said Examination mentioned is situate in the several Parishes of Kilmersdon, Leigh upon Mendip and Babington and that the said Examination contains no evidence that the said William Snook was born in that part of Coleford which is situate in our Parish of Kilmersdon.
9. That the said William Snook in the said Examination mentioned was not born in our said Parish of Kilmersdon and was not at the time of the birth of the said Thomas Robbins or afterwards settled in our said Parish and that the said Thomas Robbins did not derive a Settlement by Parentage from the said William Snook his supposed father in our said Parish of Kilmersdon.
10. That the said Thomas Robbins was born about 43 years ago in the parish of Holcombe in the County of Somerset and that the said Thomas Robbins, Margaret his wife and their seven children in the said Order mentioned were at the time of the making of the said Order settled in the said Parish of Holcombe.
11. That the name Thomas Robbins in the said Order set out as the name of the Pauper removed by that name is not the right and true name of the said Pauper. That the name of the said Pauper was and is Thomas Snook as appears in and by

the examination on which the said Order was made and that the said Order is bad and defective in not stating and setting out the true name of the said Pauper, his wife and children.

12. That true copies of the Examination on which the said Order was made have not been at any time sent by the Churchwardens and Overseers of the Poor of the Parish of High Littleton or other Proper Officers or Persons to our said Parish of Kilmersdon. That the copy of the Examination of John Cary sent to our said Parish is not a true and correct copy of his evidence as given by him before the Justices who made the said Order. That the said Thomas Robbins, Margaret his wife and their seven children in the said Order mentioned were not at the time of the making of the said Order settled in our said Parish in the manner stated in the Examination.

And Take notice that at the trial of the said appeal we shall rely on all or any one or more of the above grounds of appeal.

Dated this eighteenth day of September in the year of our Lord 1843

Thomas Thatcher
Joseph Holbrook } Churchwardens

Thomas Candy
Richard Ashman } Overseers of the Poor of the parish of Kilmersdon

Served personally John Beak, Charles Hall and Jonas Weeks with true copies of the within notice and left another true copy with the daughter of Mr John Blinman at his dwelling house the 19 day of September 1843.

Joseph French

Som. RO ref. Q/SO/23 Somerset Quarter Sessions Order Book Michaelmas, 1843

[An appeal against an Order of Removal is quashed.]

f143:

Appeals

Kilmersdon Apeals and High Littleton Responds. Upon an Appeal to this Court by the Churchwardens and Overseers of the Poor of the Parish of Kilmersdon in the said County against an Order under the Hands and Seals of John George Mogg and Wm C. James two of Her Majesty's Justices of the Peace in and for the said County made for the Removal of Thomas Robbins and Margaret his wife and their several children namely Emma aged about fifteen years, Thomas aged about thirteen years, Martha and Mary (twins) aged about eleven years, Jane then aged about ten years, Rosanna then aged about six years and Fanny aged about two years from the Parish of High Littleton to the said Parish of Kilmersdon. And upon hearing what is alleged in the Premises by the several Parties concerned their Counsel and proved by them respectively. This Court doth order and adjudge and determine that the said order of Removal be quashed and the same is hereby QUASHED accordingly.

TNA ref. MH 12/10505 Wellington Union, Somerset and Devon
[Enquiry into the place of settlement of a pauper woman and a letter to the Local Government Board regarding this woman who was refused relief.]

Tiverton Union
Charles Marshall Hole (solicitor) Clerk   3rd July 1880
Sir

I am directed by the Guardians of this Union to send to the Local Government Board the enclosed copy of a statement made by a pauper called Elizabeth Dunscombe relative to her application to this Union for relief in consequence of the refusal of the Wellington (Somerset) Union to grant her the same.

By direction of the Guardians of this Union I applied to the Guardians of the Wellington Union to receive the pauper without putting this Union to the expense of an Order of Removal and to repay the expense which had been incurred on her behalf. I enclose a copy of my letter and of the reply.

The Guardians of this Union feel that a pauper has been imposed upon them in a very irregular and unfair manner and hope that the Local Government Board will direct the Guardians of the Wellington Union to comply with the request which has been made.

I have the honor to be,
Sir
Your obedient servant
C.M. Hole
clerk

Tiverton Union

Statement of Elizabeth Dunscombe

Elizabeth Dunscombe, single woman aged 25 states:–

I was born at Milverton, Somerset where my parents still reside and belong. I went to reside with Mr Clarke at Palfreys in Tiverton as his servant on the 4th April 1879. Before that I lived as a servant with Mr Bond at Langford Budville in Somerset. I left Clarke's service on the 4th April 1880 in consequence of being in the family way. I came into Tiverton Town and lived in lodgings there until the 17th April when I went home to my parents at Milverton and lived with them until the 11th May. I had no means of supporting myself and my parents being unable to maintain me, I, on Thursday 6th May went to Wellington and applied to the Board of Guardians for an Order for the Workhouse, stating that I was very near the time of my confinement and wasn't safe for a day. I was refused the Order and was told that I ought to go back to my mother's or to return to Tiverton, that I had no business to come to Milverton but that where I got into trouble I ought to have stayed. After the Board Meeting was over I went to Mr Norman and Mr Ewings two of the Guardians about my case. Mr Ewings told me that I ought to go back to the place where I got into trouble. Mr Norman gave me a note for Mr Flood the R.O. and told me to go to him about an Order for the House. I went to Mr Flood but he said he could not give me one for if he did he should get turned out of his post. I went to Tiverton on the 11th May and applied to

Mr Jarman R.O. for an Order for the Workhouse. He stated that he could only give me a casual Order which I did not accept. I slept in Tiverton that night and next morning I applied to the Master of the Workhouse and was admitted. I was confined about 2½ hours after my admission. I have had 3 children and was confined for the second child in the Workhouse at Wellington having been sent there from Milverton.

(signed) Elizabeth Dunscombe

The Master reports as follows. Elizabeth Dunscombe applied to me about 10 o'clock on the morning of 12th May and stated as above. She also said she was in great pain and believed herself very near confinement. I called the Matron and Nurses attention to the girl and from what they stated I at once sent for Dr Haydon who came and confirmed their opinion that the case was an urgent one. I therefore admitted her under the power given by the 88th Article of the General Orders. The pauper was delivered of a child 2½ hours after her admission in the House.

Som. RO ref. D/G/W/8a/21 Wellington Union, Somerset and Devon
Minutes of the Meetings of the Board of Guardians, 1878 to 1881

[The following refers to the above case. The above statement made by Elizabeth Dunscombe is repeated here. The master's report is also included.]

3 June 1880

Minutes of the Meetings of the Board of Guardians

The minutes continue: 'Moved by Mr Kidner, seconded by Mr Mark White and carried unanimously that the Clerk be instructed to reply to the above letter and state that so far as it affects the Tiverton Union the Guardians of this Union entirely repudiate the Pauper's statement, and furnish them with the following facts …

TNA ref. MH 12/10505 (continued)

[Copy of the letter sent by the Tiverton Board of Guardians to the Wellington Board of Guardians.]

Tiverton Union

Dear Sir,
26th May 1880

Re Dunscombe

I am directed by the Guardians of this Union to send you a copy of a statement made by Elizabeth Dunscombe and read before our meeting yesterday.

She is now well enough to be removed and I am directed to request that you will send me an Order for her admission to your Workhouse with an undertaking to pay all expenses which my Board has been put to on her account. It is clear that the Guardians of your Union and the Relieving Officer could not have understood the case or I am sure she would not have been sent to Tiverton.

Yours faithfully
C.M. Hole
clerk

The Clerk
Wellington Union

Copy Reply

Wellington Union
4th June 1880

Dear Sir,

re Elizabeth Dunscombe

Your letter of the 26th ulto. with the pauper's statement was yesterday read at Board Meeting. So far as it affects you, the Guardians entirely repudiate this woman's statement. On the 6th May last she applied to the Board for an Order for admission to the Workhouse on the ground of pregnancy. The Guardians, on finding that she was residing with her mother at Milverton refused her an Order.

It appears that one of the Guardians casually observed to her in the lobby of the Workhouse after the Board had broken up, that he would advise her to apply to the man who had got her into trouble, with a view to his assisting her. At the time this remark was made he was perfectly ignorant where the man resides. This was all that took place on that day. At the following Board Meeting on the 20th May the mother of the pauper appeared before the Board and brought one of her daughter's illegitimate children who had been previously living with a foster-mother but who had refused any longer to keep the child. The mother stated to the Board that she could not support the child especially as her daughter was about to be confined in her house, and the Board accordingly gave an Order for the admission of the child into the Workhouse. There the matter ended and until the receipt of your letter nothing more was heard of it. This woman had previously had two illegitimate children and the Guardians were strongly of opinion that single women applying for Relief under such circumstances ought to be discouraged and put to personal inconvenience and that the Workhouse should not be made a lying-in Hospital for women of such bad character. With respect to your application for an Order for admission into this Workhouse the Guardians instruct me to say that before they can entertain it, further inquiry will be made respecting the antecedents of the pauper. As her return to the Tiverton Union was not in any way caused by the direction of the Guardians they cannot recognize any payments.

I remain
Yours truly
Robert A. Were
clerk

C.M. Hole, Esq.
Clerk to the Union
Tiverton

[The following notes have been written by the officers of the Local Government Board.]

The Gdns of the Wellington Union deny the statement of the woman that she was told to return to the Tiverton Union, though doubtless the remarks made to her led her to this conclusion. The Board cannot direct the Gdns of Wellington Union to take her back nor can she be sent except under a removal order.   *B*

7 July/80

There is no doubt that Wellington Gdns ought to have admitted this woman as she was near her confinement and belonged to their Union. Now the best thing seems to be that she should be removed to Wellington W.H. under order.

W   9 July 1880

TNA ref. MH 68/306 Bath Union, Somerset
[Appeal against a Removal Order, 1928.]

In the matter of an APPEAL by the CATHERINE UNION against the BATH UNION in respect of the last legal settlement of William Harold Clay, properly William Clay, a Pauper Lunatic.

Whereas by an Order dated the 2nd day of January 1928 made by two of His Majesty's Justices of the Peace for the City of Bath it was adjudged that William Harold Clay, properly William Clay, a Pauper Lunatic aged about 24 years, is chargeable to the Bath Union and that he is not settled in the said Bath Union but in the Catherington Union in the County of Hampshire (Southampton) and for payment by the said Catherington Union to the Bath Union the sums of £2. 13. 5. and £49. 15. 6. for expenses in and about the examination of the said Lunatic and for lodging, maintenance, medicine, clothing and care of the said lunatic respectively.

AND WHEREAS by a Notice dated the 3rd day of February 1928 the said Catherington Union gave notice to the said Bath Union of their intention to appeal to the next General Quarter Sessions against such Order.

Now THEREFORE by arrangement and agreement between the said respective Unions it is mutually agreed that the hearing of such Appeal shall be postponed and the matter of the last legal settlement of the said Pauper Lunatic shall be decided by a reference to the Ministry of Health.

THE UNDERMENTIONED DOCUMENTS are attached hereto:-

A. Notice and Statements of the Grounds of Adjudication.
B. Order of Adjudication of Settlement and for payment of Expenses.
C. Examination as to Settlement.
D. Notice of Appeal against Order.
E. Grounds of Appeal.
F. Certified copy entry of Birth of the Pauper Lunatic.

THE FOLLOWING FACTS ARE AGREED and admitted by the said respective Union.

1. That the said Pauper Lunatic, Clay was born on the 14th January 1903 in the Parish of Catherington in the Catherington Union in the County of Southampton, his parents being Thomas and Charlotte Susannah Clay and that he resided with his mother (his father being absent on Naval Service) at various places in and around Portsmouth until his admission to the Portsmouth Poor Law Institution in about July 1908.

2. That the mother of the said Pauper Lunatic was also admitted to the Portsmouth

Poor Law Institution about July 1908, remaining chargeable until her death in that Institution on 31st December 1909.

3. That Thomas Clay, father of the Lunatic, was resident in Havant Road, Portsmouth, at the time of his wife's death and that he soon afterwards removed to Bitterne, near Southampton, the Pauper lunatic being discharged from Portsmouth Poor Law Institution to the care of his father early in 1910, and residing with him at Bitterne, where he attended the Church of England School until some time in 1910, when the family removed to Ringwood Road, Ferndown, in the parish of Hampreston in the Wimborne and Cranborne Union, the Pauper Lunatic attending School at Hampreston from 24th October 1910 until 9th September 1912, the reason for ceasing to attend being shown as 'Left District'; that the said Thomas Clay was remarried at Ferndown on 25th December 1910 and after leaving Ferndown in the autumn of 1912 resided at Ringwood (Hampshire), Corfe Mullen (Dorsetshire) and near Salisbury (Wiltshire), the pauper Lunatic being resident with his father and step-mother until January 1915 when he was handed over by his father at Sherborne Railway Station to Mr and Mrs Robert James to work as an under Shepherd on Mr Shutters Farm at Silver Lake, Sherborne, Dorset, remaining there from the 29th January 1915 to the 10th February 1917, when he had temporary work for a few months at Bowden Hill, Nr. Milborne Port, being employed by a Mr Cluett; from there he went to work at Bradford Abbas until the 4th May 1918 when he returned to a Mrs Lemon at Silver Lake, remaining there until April of 1919.

4. The Pauper lunatic attained the age of 16 years on 14th January 1919.

5. The whereabouts of the Pauper Lunatic are unknown between the before mentioned date of April 1919 to 27th March 1920, when he enlisted into the Coldstream Guards, and being discharged from that Regiment on 26th May 1920, he returned to Sherborne, and again enlisted, joining the Somerset Light Infantry on 12th July 1920, and being transferred to the Army Reserve on 6th April 1924, when he returned to Sherborne for a short time. In June 1926 he was placed on probation at the Wincanton Quarter Sessions for house-breaking, and in October 1926 he was committed to prison at Bath Quarter Sessions for Arson, and on 31st December 1926 he was discharged from His Majesty's Prison, Birmingham, to the Poor Law Institution, Bath, as a Released Prisoner requiring care (the reason for selecting the Bath Institution being that his offence had been committed in the City of Bath). On 6th January 1927 he was certified as a Lunatic and transferred to the Mental Hospital at Wells, Somerset.

6. Thomas Clay, father of the Pauper lunatic, served in the Royal Navy from 23rd July 1878 until 5th March 1901, enrolled in the Royal Fleet Reserve on 7th December 1901, re-engaged therefrom into the Royal Navy on 6th July 1903, and served until 10th July 1908, again enrolled in the Reserve 11th July 1908 and discharged therefrom 7th March 1913. During his reserve engagement he attended Training annually. On 2nd August 1914 he was called up for War Service, but only served until 21st September 1914. His final period of service from 10th April 1916 to 3rd May 1917.

7. The Guardians of the Catherington Union agree that paragraph three of their Grounds of Appeal is withdrawn as unproved.

8. It is mutually agreed that William Harold Clay, properly William Clay, has acquired no settlement of his own since his birth.

9. THE GUARDIANS OF THE CATHERINGTON UNION by paragraph 4 of their Grounds of Appeal CONTEND that the Pauper Lunatic, William Harold Clay, properly William Clay, takes the settlement of his father, Thomas Clay, which they say is in the Parish of Wednesfield by virtue of his birth therein. The said Thomas Clay states he was born on 8th February 1862 at Wednesfield, Staffordshire, and resided there until the death of his father about 4 years later and afterwards with his mother at Wednesfield and Willenhall, his mother receiving Relief from the Wolverhampton Union. He further states that the date of birth given by him on joining the Navy on 23rd July 1878, namely 8th March 1863 is incorrect; and further that he know of no person who can verify his statement as to his birth.

THE GUARDIANS OF THE BATH UNION CONTEND that the alleged settlement of Thomas Clay cannot be legally proved to be in the Parish of Wednesfield – inasmuch as the evidence of his birth therein rests only on the statement of himself, which statement is contrary to his Naval Record and is borne out by an entry in the Register of Births; and that as before mentioned Thomas Clay further states he knows of no person able to corroborate his statement; that evidence of the identification of the said Thomas Clay is essential before the contention of the CATHERINGTON board can be entertained, and that although exhaustive enquiry has been made, this is not forthcoming; and that the settlement of the Pauper Lunatic is therefore in the place of his own birth settlement.

IN PURSUANCE of their Resolution of 4th April 1928 the COMMON SEAL of the GUARDIANS of the POOR of the BATH UNION was hereunto affixed at a meeting of the Board held on the 16th day of January 1929, by

A A Hunt	Presiding Chairman
C D Butlin	Clerk

The Common Seal of the Guardians of the Catherington Union was hereunto affixed at a meeting of the Board held on Tuesday the 29th January 1929 by

put a seal here
X

W J Borrow	Chairman

In the presence of   E R Longcroft   Clerk

In the matter of William Harold Clay properly William Clay aged about 24 years, a Pauper Lunatic, now confined in one of the County Lunatic Asylums near the City of Wells, in the County of Somerset.

To the Guardians of the Poor of the Catherington Union, in the County of Hampshire.

Take Notice, that the above-named William Harold Clay properly William Clay (hereinafter called the Lunatic) was duly removed to one of the Lunatic Asylums for the County of Somerset, situated near the City of Wells, in the said County, by Order of a Justice of the Peace, on the sixth day of January last past, hath ever since been maintained there at the expense of the Bath Union, in the County of Somerset, and hath ever since been chargeable to the said Bath Union.

That by an Order of Justices bearing the date the second day of January 1928 instant, of which a Duplicate or Copy is hereunto annexed, the last legal settlement of the said Lunatic was adjudged to be the Parish of Catherington in your said Union, and also whereby the Guardians of the Poor of your Union were ordered to pay certain sums of money heretofore expended and paid by the Guardians of the Poor of the said Bath Union, in respect of the said Lunatic, and also to pay a certain sum weekly for his Maintenance in the said Asylum.

And take Notice, that on the Grounds upon which the said Settlement has been adjudged, and the Particulars of the Settlement of the said Lunatic in the said Parish of Catherington in your said Union, and which will be relied on in support thereof, are as follows; that is to say: That the said William Harold Clay properly William Clay was born on 14th January 1903 at Horndean in the said parish of Catherington.

Further particulars.

William Clay is the son of Thomas Clay, whose postal address is Victoria Park Hut, Coates, Barnoldswick near Colne. William Clay has never acquired a settlement other than his birth settlement, having joined the Army at the age of 17 years. Thomas Clay joined the Navy at the age of 15 years and served until July 1908, being then retained on the Fleet Reserve and called up for training annually until mobilised in 1914.

And take Notice, that unless you give Notice of Appeal against the said order within twenty-one days from the sending or delivery hereof, or in case of your application for a copy of the Depositions on which the said order was made within a further period of fourteen days from the sending of such copy, no appeal against the same will afterwards be allowed.

Given under my Hand, this second day of January in the year of our Lord One Thousand Nine Hundred and Twenty eight at the City of Bath in the said County of Somerset.

W.E. Winckworth
Clerk to the Guardians of the Bath Union

It appears from the following that a person who was born abroad and therefore had no place of settlement in England or Wales, when unemployed, could be supported by the parish in which he was resident.

TNA ref. MH 12/10217 Bedminster Union, Somerset
21 September 1864
[A pauper says he was born in Hamburg, Germany.]

Bedminster
21 Sept. 1864

Chargeable Case

Pauper named George Melhurst is 30 years of age and was born as he has heard and believes at Hamburg in Germany. When he was sixteen years of age he went to sea, and has followed the calling of a mariner ever since. About eight months ago he married and took apartments in the said parish of Bedminster, and has resided in such parish ever since and is now ill in the Small Pox. He has never done any act to gain a settlement in England.

Question. Is the pauper exempt from liability to be removed to the place of his settlement.

Answer. A pauper who has no settlement is not rendered irremovable and consequently his relief is not chargeable to the common Fund but to the parish of his residence. [Parish rather than union.]

CHAPTER 5

PAUPER APPRENTICES

Many pauper children (both boys and girls) were placed in indentured apprenticeships, usually from the age of 12 years onwards. Boys were apprenticed to local tradesmen and landowners to learn a trade or 'the art of husbandry'. Girls were often placed in large households to learn housewifery, though sometimes they too undertook trade apprenticeships. In the nineteenth century some schools were established to train girls in household duties. Boys were also able to gain apprenticeships at sea on merchant vessels. Most apprenticeships continued until the apprentice reached the age of 21. Under the terms of the apprenticeship food and clothing, together with accommodation, were usually provided for the apprentice by his master.

> Hurt or damage to his master the apprentice shall not do, consent to or see to be done by others, but to the utmost of his power shall hinder the same, and shall forthwith his said master thereof warn. Taverns or Alehouses he shall not frequent, unless about his Master's business. At dice, cards, tables, bowls or any unlawful games he shall not play. The goods of his master he shall not embezzle or waste, but as a true and faithful apprentice shall demean and behave himself towards his master, his executors, administrators or assigns during the term, and true and just accounts of his master's goods and chattels, and money committed to his charge, or which shall come to his hands, faithfully he shall give at all times when hereunto required by his master.

Local landowners were expected to take on pauper apprentices without payment. This was often carried out on a rota system and any such person who refused to take an apprentice could be fined. In some parishes placement of pauper apprentices was conducted by a type of lottery. The following was found in a church register for the parish of Brompton Ralph, Somerset:

> A Method of binding Poor Children Apprentices in the Parish of Brompton Ralph, in which the Owners or Occupiers of Estates within the said Parish are charged towards the Expense thereof in the same Proportions as to the Poor Rate.

Apprentice indenture for Charles Earle, a poor child of Thwaite, Norfolk, to John Clark of Banningham, Norfolk, dated 4 April 1727. (John Titford Collection)

1. All the Estates in the Parish are distributed into 23 Lots, & every Lot being charged Two Shillings to the Poor Rate, is charged Four Pounds Sixteen Shillings to the Apprentice, that is, a Shilling to the Apprentice for a Farthing to the Poor Rate.

2. The Apprentices are to be appointed to the several Lots as they stand numbered in the annexed scheme in which the turns of taking Apprentices in the old method are preserved, as near as possible.

3. When an apprentice is appointed to a Lot, if the Owners or Occupiers of the Estate therein will not agree amongst themselves to which of them the child shall be bound, the names of the Estates in the Lot shall be put into a hat, and the Apprentice shall go to the Occupier of that Estate which shall be first drawn out of the Hat by any indifferent by-stander, unless such Occupier shall have taken an Apprentice in some other Lot within Four Years before. But a second Apprentice shall not be bound to the Occupier of that Estate, so drawn, until every person in the Lot shall have taken one in turn.

4. Provided always, that no Apprentice shall be bound to the Owner or Occupier of Estates in any Lot which are not rated Four Pence to the Poor, unless he shall choose to take one.
5. If it shall be necessary to bind two or more children at one time, their Names shall be put into a Hat, and the child first drawn by an indifferent Bystander shall be appointed to the Lot standing first in Course to take an Apprentice. The child drawn second, to the Lot second in course; & so on for the Rest.

Brist. RO ref. P/St.MR/OP/1
[Certificate of apprenticeship in blacksmithing, 1667.]

This Indenture made the nine and twentieth day of October in the year of our Lord one thousand six hundred sixty seven According to the Computation of the Church of England. It Witnesseth that the churchwardens and overseers of the poore of the pish of Redcliffe in the Citty of Bristell have thought fitt, and have placed and put forth Sarah Owen as an apprentice unto Robert Peyner and Sarah his wife of the Citty of Bristoll Blacksmith to serve as apprentice and doth covenant to dwell with them from the day of the date of these presents unto the full end and term of seven whole years from hence forth next ensuing fully to be comepleat & ended during all wch term the said apprentice her said Mr [master] and Mrs [mistress] well and truly and faithfully shall serve theyer commandements lawfull and honestly there shall doe. Hurt to her said Master and Mrs shee shall not doe nor consent to be done, the goods of her said Master shee shall not inordinately wast, or them to any body Lend without consent, from her Masters service either by day nor yet by night shee shall not absent herselfe but as a true and faithfull and obedient apprentice ought to doe as well in words as in deeds shee shall carry and behave her selfe during the said Terme, and the fforesaid Robert Peyner and Sarah his wife doth covenant to and with theyer said apprentice during the said Terme to find and p'vide to and for theire said apprentice sufficient meat drinke and appell [apparel] both Linning and woollen, as well in sickness as in health in the sayd Term, And the said Churchwardens John Ford and William Lloyd have payd unto the sayd Robert Peyner and Sarah his wife the sume of twenty shillings in hand x^s at the sealing heareof and tenne shillings more the said Robert Peyner is to receive on the twenty ffourth day of June next ensueing to buy her clothing. And at ye end of the said terme shall give and deliver unto the said apprentice two suits of apparel both linning and woollen one for holy days the other for working days neet and decent for an Apprentice or servant of her degree and calling and shall chastise and use in all due and honest manner & not otherwise.

In Witnesse whereof the pties [parties] above named have heare unto Intesthange-ably [in testimony] put their hands and seales the day and yeare above written.

Sealed and delivered in the   Robert **RP** Peyner
presents of   Henry Perry   his marke
            Mark Castle   Sarah **S** Peyner
                                  her marke

Som. RO ref. Q/SO/12 Somerset Quarter Sessions Order Book
Midsummer, 1750
[An apprentice is discharged from his apprenticeship for misbehaving.]

f 129   Midsummer Sessions, 10th July 1750
Apprentice – Thomas Woodland. It appearing unto this Court that Thomas Woodland, apprentice unto Henry Gibbs of Chilton in this County, Gentleman, is a loose, idle, disorderly apprentice and frequently absconding from his said Master's service. And the said Henry Gibbs having now made application unto this Court to be discharged from his said Apprentice for the causes aforesaid. This Court therefore on the Motion of Mr Bridge doth order that the said Henry Gibbs be forthwith discharged from the said Thomas Woodland his Apprentice and the said Master and Apprentice are hereby discharged from each other accordingly.

Dev. RO (Ex.) ref. 2404A/PO138/20
[Certificate of apprenticeship in husbandry, 1792.]

This Indenture, made the Twenty Second Day of November, in the Thirty third Year of the Reign of our Sovereign Lord George the Third by the Grace of God, of Great Britain, France, and Ireland, King, Defender of the Faith, and so forth, and in the Year of our Lord One Thousand seven Hundred and Ninety Two. Witnesseth That Thomas Pannell and Robert Salter, Church-Wardens of the Parish of Cullompton in the County of Devon AND Henry Bauton, John Hole, Christopher Mountstephen and John Vinicombe, Overseers of the Poor of the said Parish, by and with the consent of his Majesty's Justices of the Peace for the said County, whose Names are hereon subscribed, have put and placed, and by these Presents do put and place Thomas Limpany otherwise Mitchel, a poor Child of the said Parish, Apprentice to John Symes for Mills's Tenement at Mutterton by consent with him to dwell and serve from the Day of the Date of these presents, until the said Apprentice shall accomplish his full Age of Twenty One Years according to the Statute in that Case made and provided. DURING all which Term the said Apprentice his said Master faithfully shall serve in all lawful Business, according to his Power, Wit, and Ability, and honestly, orderly, and obediently, in all things demean and behave himself towards his said Master and all his during the said Term. AND the said John Symes for himself, his Executors, and Administrators, doth Covenant and Grant, to and with the said Church-Wardens and Overseers, and every of them, their and every of their Executors and Administrators, and their and every of their Successors, for the Time being, by these presents, That the said John Symes the said Apprentice in Husbandry affairs shall teach and instruct or cause to be taught and instructed And shall and will during all the Term aforesaid, find, provide, and allow the said Apprentice, meet, competent, and sufficient Meat, Drink, and Apparel, Lodging, Washing and all other things necessary and fit for an Apprentice. AND also shall and will provide for the said Apprentice, that he be not any way a Charge to the said Parish, or Parishoners of the same; but of and from all Charge shall and will save the said Parish and Parishoners harmless and indemnified

Apprenticeship for William Quarry of Kingswinford, Staffordshire, to James Meeson of Dudley, miner. Dated 2 December 1831. (John Titford Collection)

during the said Term. IN WITNESS whereof, the Parties abovesaid to these present Indentures, interchangeably have put their Hands and Seals, the Day and Year above-written.

The Mark of
X
John Symes

We whose Names are subscribed, Justices of the Peace for the County aforesaid, do consent to the putting forth of the abovesaid Thomas Limpany otherwise Mitchell, Apprentice, according to the intent and meaning of the above Indenture.

John Lacocke
Richd Groves

Sealed and delivered in the Presence of
William Bullock

IoW RO ref. Z/HO/M1 Isle of Wight Union, Hampshire
Register of Apprentices, 1802 to 1833

Number 89	
Date of Admission	10 Oct. 1805
Name of Apprentice	Eleanor Harvey
Sex	girl
Age	14
His or Her Parents	Jas. & Eliz.
Their Residence	Carrisbrooke
Name of Persons to whom bound or assigned as the Case may be	Sr R^d Worsley Bt
His or Her Trade	Husbandry
His or Her Residence	Appedairecomb [Appuldurcombe in the parish of Godhill]
Term of the Apprenticeship or Assigment	4 yrs
Overseers Parties to the Indenture or Assignment	Guardians of the Poor
Magistrates Assenting	Sir H^y Worsley Holmes
	7 Jno Delgarno Esq.

TNA ref. MH 12/11768 Bosmere and Claydon Union, Suffolk
[Apprenticeship at Sea, 1851.]

Bosmere and Claydon Union   Board Room, Barham
                                                                    12 Dec 1851

Gentlemen,

I am directed by the Guardians of the Bosmere and Claydon Union to report the following case and to ask your opinion relative to the Indenture.

Joseph Porter aged 13, an orphan inmate of the Workhouse at Barham, chargeable to the Parish of Ashfield is desirous of going to sea. An opportunity has offered which the Board of Guardians deem desirable but as some doubt has arisen with the Guardians respecting the mode of binding to sea.

The Board would feel obliged if you would inform them who are the proper parties to bind this boy and to become a party to the Indenture.

                                        I am
                                 Gentlemen,
                                    J.P. Bray
                                       Clerk

The Poor Law Board

Subject Sea Service

Poor Law Board
London
20 Dec 1851

Bosmere Union

Sir,

I am directed by the Poor Law Board to acknowledge the receipt of your letter of the 12th inst. in which you enquire by direction of the Guardians of the Bosmere Union, who are the proper parties to take the words in the binding Joseph Porter, an orphan inmate of the Workhouse at Barham who is desirous of going to sea.

I am ordered to refer the Guardians to the Statute 7 & 8 Vict. c113 sec 32, from which the Board consider that the Guardians are the proper parties to bind the lad in question.

I am
R.W.J.

Som. RO ref. D/G/W/8a/9 Wellington Union, Somerset and Devon
Minutes of the meetings of the Board of Guardians, 1853 to 1855

[An 11-year-old boy is employed to sweep chimneys contrary to the law.]

28th June 1855
copy of a letter

Honiton
Devon
22nd June 1855

Reply to a poor boy named Joseph Scott

Gentlemen,

A complaint has been laid before me as Mayor of this Borough against a chimney sweeper of Honiton named Dommett for employing a child to sweep chimneys contrary to the Statute 3&4 Vic. cap. 85.

I have had the child before me and examined him; he is very intelligent and tells me he is 11 years of age, but he is a very diminutive urchin and does not look more than 7. He states his name to be Joseph Scott and that up to about two months since he was an inmate of the Union Poor House at Wellington, Somerset where his mother Jane Scott now is; that he can read and write; that about 2 months ago another sweep of this Town named Cross, a relative of Dommett agreed with Mr Dore, the Master of the Wellington Union Workhouse, to take him as a sweep and subsequently transferred him to Dommett with whom he has been working ever since sweeping chimneys. The child does not appear to want food and makes no complaint of ill treatment but he informs me he goes to no School and attends no place of worship on the Sabbath day; his eyes are sore and inflamed from the soot of the chimneys and his knees from climbing.

I have thought it my duty to apprise you of the facts I have learned and to enquire whether in your judgment the Board of Guardians or their Officers should thus get rid of their Paupers and assist in putting them out for purposes which the law declares to be illegal and I have informed the Guardians of the Wellington Union by a letter to their Clerk that I should address your Board on the matter and request you to inform me what is to be done with this poor child in case his mother should be convicted of the offence created by the 3&4 Vic. and should prefer going to Prison to paying the penalty inflicted by that Statute.

TNA ref. MH 12/10460 Taunton Union, Somerset and Devon
[A girl is sent to a training school for servants, 1857.]

Taunton Union
20 Nov. 1857

My Lords and Gentlemen
Sarah Webber

Pauper is aged about ten years of age; deserted by father, an able bodied man, the mother being dead, and is with her brother under order of removal from the City of Norwich to St Mary Magdalen in Taunton, the settlement being admitted.

She is now in The Stanley Home, a training school for servants at Norwich, the Guardians think it desirable to continue her there, and have with that view ordered non resident relief 1/6 per week, the cost of her maintenance at that institution, with your approval.

Reported under Act 6 of the general prohibitory order.
I have the honor to be
My Lords and Gentlemen
Your most obed. servant
John Chorley
clerk
To the Poor Law Board

The following is copied from a printed pamphlet:

The Stanley Home
A Training School for Servants
Peacock Street
St. Saviour's, Norwich

The object of this House is to receive *friendless* girls of *respectable* character, and to fit them for domestic service.

The girls are boarded and clothed, instructed in reading, writing, the four rules of arithmetic, needlework, plain cooking, washing, and general household duties.

It will be seen that the education given is perfectly plain and simple, the primary object being, with the Divine blessing, to train up good and useful servants, who may, hereafter, in their subordinate but important station, become valuable members of society.

Several Members of the Committee meet weekly to superintend the internal management of the Home, and here they desire to acknowledge the valuable assistance received from their worthy Matron, whose kind and judicious conduct in cultivating habits of truthfulness, obedience, and general usefulness, has tended materially to the well-doing of the inmates.

Since the last Report, eight new inmates have been received. Four girls have been placed in service, and these, with one exception, appear to be conducting themselves well. Continued applications are made for others, but most of the sixteen girls now remaining in the Home are too young for service at present, and must, consequently, be maintained for a considerable time before they are duly qualified.

The Committee would therefore, earnestly appeal to the heads of families generally, to co-operate with them in carrying out the objects of this institution. The loss of several subscribers, from death and other causes, and the continued high prices of provisions, oblige them to ask for fresh contributors; and they do so with great confidence, feeling assured there are many in this county and city, who are alive to the importance and the duty of endeavouring to raise the moral character and promote the efficiency of female servants.

The Committee have again to express their grateful acknowledgments to Mr Francis, for his continued kind and gratuitous attention to the girls in illness.

They also beg to thank the kind donors of

> A sack of potatoes
> Some school books
> Sundry articles of clothing, &c., &c.

Any contributions of this kind are extremely valuable.

The Committee Meetings are held on the second Monday of each month at three o'clock.

Committee

Lady Bignold	Mr Charles Evans
Mrs Henry Birkbeck	Mrs S. Foster
Mr John Blake	Mrs John Gurney
Mrs Buck	Mrs Jeffery
Mrs Crosse	Mrs Charles Millard
Miss Ebbetts	Mrs Arthur Upcher

Secretary, Mrs Charles Evans

***

General Account of Receipts and Payments
For the Year ending 31st December 1856

January 1st	£	s	d		£	s	d
Balance in hand	30	6	7	Housekeeping	141	3	1½
Subscriptions	95	19	6	Candles and Soap	6	17	5
Donations	59	6	6	Coals and Kindling	12	8	10
Weekly Payment for Girls	79	14	0	Clothing	22	14	7¾
Earned in the Home	3	16	1	Furniture, House Linen, &c	31	5	5½

	£	s	d		£	s	d
Proceeds of Concert	55	0	0				
Bankers' Interest	1	7	2	Ironmonger	8	5	7
				Bricklayer	2	14	4
				Stationery and Printing	1	13	6
				Rent, Taxes and Salaries	57	7	6
				Incidental Expenses	1	18	2¼
				Balance in Hand	39	1	3
	£325	9	10		£325	9	10

Annual Subscribers for 1856

	£	s	d		£	s	d
Astley, Mrs F.	1	0	0	Gurney, F. Hay	1	0	0
Balls, Miss	0	4	0	Harrison, Miss	1	1	0
Bayning, Lord	2	2	0	Harrison, Miss C.	1	1	0
Bayning, Lady	1	1	0	Harvey, Lady H.	2	2	0
Bignold, Lady	1	1	0	Hamond, Mrs	1	1	0
Birkbeck, Mrs H.	5	0	0	Hotson, Mrs W.C.	0	10	0
Birkbeck, W. Esq.	1	0	0	Hoggart, Mrs	0	10	0
Blake, Mrs J.	1	1	0	Hudson, Miss	1	1	0
Bridgman, Mrs	0	10	6	Huggins and Green, Misses	0	0	80
Buck, Mrs	1	1	0	Jarrold, Mr S.	0	5	0
Buck, Miss	0	10	0	Jarrold, Mr T.	0	5	0
Bugg, Mrs	1	1	0	Jeffery, Mrs	0	10	6
Buxton, Lady	3	3	0	Ladyman, Mr	0	10	0
Caley, Mr	0	10	0	Main, Mrs	0	5	0
Carter, Mrs H.	0	10	6	Martin, Mrs	1	1	0
Chad Scott, Esq.	1	0	0	Millard, Mrs C.	1	1	0
Chapman, Mrs	0	10	0	Morse, Miss	5	0	0
Chamberlain, R., Esq.	[blank]			Mott, Miss	1	0	0
Chitty, Mrs	2	0	0	Mott, Mrs	1	0	0
Cholmondeley, Marchoness of	2	2	0	Mott, Miss I.	2	0	0
Clarke, Mrs E.P.	1	1	0	Norgate, Mr	1	1	0
Clowes, Miss	0	5	0	Ormerod, Mrs	1	0	0
Colyer, Mrs	1	0	0	Pellew, Hon. Mrs	1	0	0
Coaks, R., Esq.	0	10	0	Pitts, Mr (Two years)	0	10	0
Cottingham, L.O., Esq.	[blank]			Pratt, Mr	1	0	0
Crosse, Mrs	0	10	0	Preston, Lady	1	0	0
Cruso, Miss	0	2	6	Proctor, Lady Beauchamp	1	0	0
Cubitt, Mrs W.	1	0	0	Powell, Mr	0	5	0
Cullington, Mrs	0	5	0	Powell, Mrs	0	5	0
Cundall, Mr	0	10	0	Rand, W.F. Esq.	1	1	0
Cunningham, Rev. F	[blank]			Rix, Mrs	0	2	6
Davey, Miss	0	10	0	Scott, Joseph, Esq.	1	0	0

	£	s	d		£	s	d
Dewing, Mrs	0	10	0	Seppings, Mrs	0	5	0
Dewing, Miss	0	10	0	Smyth, Mrs	1	1	0
Evans, Mrs	2	2	0	Springfield, T.O. Esq.	1	1	0
Evans, Mrs H.	1	0	0	Steward, Mrs T.	1	1	0
Evans, Mrs C.	1	1	0	Sultzer, Mrs	1	0	0
Fellowes, Mrs	1	1	0	Tacy, Rev. H.	1	1	0
Field, Mrs	0	10	6	Thompson, Mrs H.K.	1	0	0
Foster, Mrs S.	1	1	0	Unthank, Mrs (Two years)	2	2	0
Gardom, Mrs	1	1	0	Upcher, Mrs Arthur	[blank]		
Graver, Miss	0	5	0	Vincent, Mrs	1	1	0
Gunn, Miss	1	0	0	Webster, Mr	0	5	0
Gurdon, Mrs	1	0	0	Willins, Mrs S.	0	5	0
Gurney, J.H. Esq., M.P.	10	0	0	Wilson, Mrs Herbert	0	10	6
Gurney, Mrs John	[blank]			Wright, Mrs (Close)	2	0	0
Gurney, Miss	2	2	0				

N.B. The Subscriptions left blank had not been received when the Cash Account was made out.

Donations:- 1856

	£	s	d		£	s	d
Arkwright, Mrs	2	2	0	Partridge, Mrs J.	1	0	0
Blyth, Mrs D. Urban		10	0	Preston, Miss	1	0	0
Cadge, Miss		5	0	Preston, Miss A.	1	0	0
Evans, C. Esq.	2	2	0	Proctor, Lady Beauchamp	2	0	0
Fellowes, Mrs (Shottesham)	5	0	0	Redgrave, Mrs		10	0
Foster, Mr		10	0	Sparkes, Miss		10	0
Friend, A.	6	0	0	Stone, James, Esq.	5	0	0
Kett, Mrs	3	0	0	Vincent, Mrs		10	0
Keppel, Lady M.	1	0	0	By the Rev. Dr. Beal	2	2	6
Leicester, Countess of	10	0	0	(collected after a Sermon at Loddon)			
Muskett, Mr C.		5	0	Articles made and sold for the benefit of			
Morse, Miss	5	0	0	the Institution	5	0	0

***

Donations and Subscriptions (the latter being considered due in January) will be thankfully received by the Secretary, or any of the Committee, or they may be paid to 'The Stanley Home Fund' at the Bank of Messrs. Gurney and Co.

Berks. RO ref. G/B 23 Bradfield Union, Berkshire and Oxfordshire
Pauper Service Book
[Paupers put out to service, including some apprentices.]

Pauper's Name	Age	Parish	When Entered Service	Master or Mistress' Name	Place of Abode and Trade or Profession	Remarks
Smith, John	14	Bucklebury	30 Nov. 1875	Mr Johnson	Tailor, South End, Bradfield	
Arlet, Harriet	15	Burghfield	3 Feb. 1876	Mr Brown	Stationer, 261 Brompton Rd, London	
Smith, Richard	15	Basildon	15 Mar. 1876	Mr Smethurst	Fish Merchant, Great Grimsby	
Steptoe, William	14	Bucklebury	29 Apr. 1876	Rev. Thos. Stevens	Bradfield College	Left the College & gone to Mr Balls as a letter carrier
Davis, Louisa	15	Ashampstead	24 May 1877	Mr Deacon	92 London Street, Reading	
Fulbrook, Mary	15	Burghfield	8 Jun. 1877	Mr F. Holmden	Butcher, Theale	
Wheeler, Emma	14	Burghfield	26 Apr. 1877	Mr W. Rhinds	Englefield	
Brooker, Henry	14	Pangbourn	4 Aug. 1877	Mr H. Smethurst	Fish Merchant, Grimsby	This lad went to Mr Cook's but did not stop, conduct bad.
Quelch, Elizabeth	14	Englefield	21 Sep. 1878	Mr I.H.G. Love	Farmer, Bradfield	
Woodley, John Joseph	14	Bucklebury	11 Dec. 1878	Mr Strong	108 Oxford St. Reading	
Goswell, Chas. Henry	14	Aldermaston	23 Jan. 1879	Mr H. Thomas	Tailor, Wickham, Newbury	Apprenticed for 7 years
Allen, Albert William	14	Padworth	17 Dec. 1879	Mr R. Bright	Baker, 71 Weldale St. Reading	Since apprentice to Mr H. Smethurst, fish merchant, Grimsby
Wooders, George	14	Ashampstead	14 Jan. 1880	Mr E. Clarke	Baker, 37 Gt. Knowllys St. Reading	
Parker, Sarah	14	Burghfield	16 May 1880	Mr Richd. Todd	Farmer, Mapledurham	
Henwood, Henry	14	Bradfield	23 Mar. 1880	Mr George Dix	Baker, 29 St. Mary's, Reading	
Cooper, Ernest	13	Beenham	3 Aug. 1881	Mr Killick	Baker, Bradfield	
Holmes, Jemima	14	Bradfield	10 Sep. 1881	Mr J.H.G. Lone	Farmer, Bradfield	
Warner, James	14	Pangbourne	16 Nov. 1881	Mr Thomas Angell	Tailor, Wokingham	Apprenticed
Quelch, Thomas	14	Englefield	28 Dec. 1881	Mr J. Butler	Farmer, Lodge Farm, Padworth	
Nash, John	15	Frilsham	11 Jan. 1882	Mr H. Smethurst	Fish Merchant, Grimsby	Apprentice
Brooker, Alice	13	Pangbourne	25 Mar. 1882	Mr Best	Hotel Keeper, Caversham	
Goswell, Frederick	13	Aldermaston	7 Mar. 1882	Mr Chas. Burton	Baker, Yattendon	
Allen, Mary Ann	13	Padworth	19 Apr. 1882	Mr Hurley	Farmer, Mapledurham	
Wooders, Albert	14	Ashampstead	18 Oct. 1882	Mr C.F. Clarke	Baker, Wokingham	Apprentice for 4 years
Plummer, Thomas	14	Bucklebury	6 Nov. 1882	Mr Thomas	Tailor, Thicket Villa, Wantage	
Willis, Frederick	14	Yattendon	15 Feb. 1883	Mr Thos. Roberts	Boot Maker, 38 Grey Friars Road, Reading	
Marcham, Frederick	13	Streatley	25 Jan. 1883	Mr Hancock	Baker, Burnt Hill, Bradfield	
Wooders, George	15	Ashampstead	14 Mar. 1883	Mr H. Smethurst	Fisherman, Grimsby	
Henwood, Walter	14	Bradfield	17 Feb. 1884	Rev. C.G. Gepp	Bradfield College	Apprentice
Quelch, Edward	13	Englefield	25 Mar. 1884	Mr F. Butler	Farmer, Stratfield Saye	
Woodley, Catherine	13	Bucklebury	21 Jul. 1884	Mr Pargiter	Baker & Grocer, Yattendon	
Franklin, Henry	15	Streatley	23 Jan. 1885	Mr H. Smethurst	Fish Merchant, Grimsby	

CHAPTER 6

UNION RECORDS

All manner of matters were discussed at the meetings of the Board of Guardians of Unions. The minutes of these meetings often include details about workhouse inmates and other paupers. Copies of correspondence to the Poor Law Commissioners and others are also to be found with the workhouse records. Other workhouse records were kept by the Clerk of the Union, e.g. punishment books, births and deaths in the workhouse, workhouse dietary, admission registers, discharge registers, indoor relief registers, etc. The following are some examples:

Berks. RO ref. G/F 1/1 Faringdon Union, Berkshire and Oxfordshire
Minute Book, 1835 to 1836

Tuesday 16th June 1835
At a Meeting of the Guardians of the Union at the Workhouse, Faringdon this day, in pursuance of an adjournment from the 9th instant.
[includes the following]

Resolved

Jane Pike	That the allowance to Jane Pike of Fernham, aged 17, be discontinued, and that she have an order to the Workhouse, if she wants any relief.
Ann Orchard	That the Allowance to Ann Orchard of Fernham be reduced to 2 loaves.
William Smith	That the Allowance to William Smith and his wife of Kingstone Lisle be discontinued and that they be offered the House if they want relief.
Hannah Fuller	That the Allowance to Hannah Fuller of Charney be discontinued for the present.

Elizth Tovey	That the Allowance of relief to Elizabeth Tovey of Coleshill be discontinued unless the Medical Attendant certify that she be unable to work.
Mary Hawkes	That Mary Hawkes of Uffington a widow, aged 80 be allowed 1ˢ/6ᵈ per week and to attend to the past week.
Mary Ann Chivers	On the case of Mary Ann Chivers, living at Challow being reconsidered. That no relief be given.
Widow Stratton	On the application on behalf of the Widow Stratton, 72, parishoner of Longcot being with her daughter at Stanford, who is not able to assist her, and the widow being incapable of doing any thing. That she be allowed 2ˢ/6ᵈ per week.
Thos Gardner	On the application of the wife of Thomas Gardner of Shrivenham aged 44 who was last Tuesday, struck with the lightning for relief, has 5 children, Thomas aged 16, earns 3ˢ/6ᵈ per week, Mary 11, gets her own living and 3 younger ones who earn nothing the wife earned nothing last week. That he be allowed 3ˢ/- for the last week and the like for the present week.
Susannah Collett	That the relief to Susannah Collett of Faringdon, widow be suspended until she satisfy the Board that she has no property. Meetings of the Board That the Members of the Board be separated in 4 divisions so as to secure the attendance of 8 members at the least, weekly in rotation during the present season and that the Clerk do get printed letters to apprise the Members, whose names are on the list for the next Meeting and request their attendance particularly at such Meeting.
Messrs Preedy's Cheese	On examining some cheese 1 cwt. where was received from Messrs Preedy on Friday last, and the same being found to be not sweet and good. That the same be returned to Messrs Preedy.
Jas. Cambray	On the application of James Cambray of Thrupp, aged 72 for relief in consequence of having been too ill to work for several weeks. That he be attended 3ˢ/- per week part in money and part in kind.
John Embling	On the application of John Embling of Littleworth aged 69 for relief, is unable to work, has a family grown up but unable to assist him, lives in a Copyhold House rent free for his life. That he be allowed 2ˢ/6ᵈ per week part in money and part in kind.

Wm. Smarty	On the application of Wm Smart of Littleworth, aged 75, for relief being unable to work, has a wife 70 who works but little, but who is now nursing. That he be allowed 2^s/6^d per week part in money and part in kind.
Richard Higgs	On William Higgs of Longcot attending to make an application for relief for his son Richard Higgs who lives at Little Coxwell and has a wife & 3 children. That the case cannot be heard as no application has been made to the Assistant Overseer.
John Stevens	Mr Hughes having reported the case of John Stevens of Watchfield who is unable to work from rheumatic gout, and who had 2^s/6^d advanced to him last week by way of loan. That the 2^s/6^d advanced be allowed to him for relief and that he have 2^s/6^d for the present week part in money and part in kind.
Buckland Parish	That the Overseers of Buckland be allowed 4^s/6^d for relief offered by them to Thomas Farmer, and that he be allowed to pay to Joseph Pearce the sum of 6^s/- for a Coffin for Charles Farmer and also the sum of 3^s/- to Robert Carter the Clerk for fees.
Richard Batts	That the Assistant Overseer be allowed to pay the funeral expenses of Richard Batts of Longworth amounting to 4^s/1^d.
George Curtis	On taking the case of George Curtis of Uffington (who applied at the last meeting) into consideration. That the Sum of 10^s/- be allowed to him.
Widow Moreton	That the Parish of Ashbury be permitted to afford relief to the Widow Moreton, who resides in the Parish of St. Giles Reading, to the extent of 2^s/9^d per week.
Workhouse Gates	On resuming the subject of the reparations and alterations now in progress at the Workhouse. That the entrance Gates to the Workhouse Yard be Close Gates.

That this Meeting do adjourn to Tuesday the 23rd instant at seven o'clock.

J.F. Cleaver   Chairman

Williton Workhouse, Somerset, 2009. (Now converted into flats.)

Berks. RO ref. G/B 5/1 Bradfield Union, Berkshire and Oxfordshire Letter Book, 1835 to 1841

Bradfield

August 14th 1835

Gentlemen,

You are requested by the Board of Guardians of the above Union to make out the Acct. against John Eustice now in work at Mr Webbs of Calcott, for the support of his child in Tilehurst Workhouse having been left destitute by him from April 7th 1835 to the present period. You are also with the least possible delay to make application for attachment of wages to recover the amount of the said account relying on your immediate attention.

I beg to remain

Your Humble Servt

Thos Beall

Clerk

To The Overseers of Tilehurst

Bradfield Union
Sept. 5th 1835

Sir,

I am directed by the Board of Guardians of the above Union to write to you respecting the Pauper J. Wells who is now receiving relief from the Parish of Bucklebury, the Board do not consider themselves justified in giving relief to Wells without taking possession of his property & from the information recd, it appears that oweing to the Pauper having some time since become weak in his intellect that your Father very kindly managed his affairs and supported him.

Believing you Sir to entertain the same kindly feelings towards Wells as your late respected Father, the Board will feel obliged by your informing them if you will undertake to relieve the Parish, upon the same terms and thus administer to the wants of Wells that the Parish may be compelled to not take possession of his small Property part of which is cultivated by Mr Johnson, but who it appears from his own acknowledgements has paid no rent for a considerable time, having an impression it belongs to the Land he rents of you on the Ground of Wells being supported as before stated. An answer at your convenience will greatly oblige Sir.

Yr most humble Servant
Thos Beall, Clerk

To, Hartley Esq.
Bucklebury

Bradfield Union
Jany 26th 1836

Sir,

I am directed by the board of Guardians of the above Union, to write to you respecting Martha Nokes, belonging to the Parish of Kensington, now under orders of Removal from the Parish of Sulhampstead Abbotts, Berks, in the above Union, she is now an inmate of the Central Workhouse with an infant Child about 3 months old, and if you will acknowledge the Pauper without the Order being executed, I am almost, though not quite, certain that I can procure a situation for her, and she is that kind of a Girl that I think when her Child is out of her arms, she will work and maintain herself and be no further trouble to a Parish unless in case of sickness &c. Should you not approve of the Plan, which is very similar to one a short time since under orders of removal from Kensington to Bucklebury in our Union, she will of course be removed forth with, waiting your reply.

I beg to remain,
Sir,
Your most Obed^t Servt
Thos Beall
Clerk

To The Overseers of Kensington
  Middlesex

Bradfield Union
June 7th 1836

Sir,

  I am directed by this Board of Guardians of the above Union to request the favour of you to be informed if a Ship called the *Dasher* is now in Woolwich Dock. A man of the name of Charles Harding, who formerly belonged to the 28th Regt of Foot, has deserted his wife and family. Wife now confined he has written a Letter stating he is on board *Dasher* at Woolwich Dock and that he has enlisted into the Queen's Service. I am sorry to trouble you but if true that he is there no expense will be spared to bring him to punishment, he is a bad fellow, he left his wife when confined before in great distress.

                    I beg to remain,
                      Sir,
                          Your most Ob[t] Servant,
                              Thos. Beall
                                  Clerk to the Board, Bradfield, Berks

To The Superintendent of Woolwich Dock

Bradfield
near Reading
England
Nov[r] 25th 1836

Sir,

  At the request of your wife Sarah Gardner, I have taken my pen in hand to address you on her behalf, which would have been done long since had she known how and where to direct to you. The day you left England her Sister H[t] took her from the lodgings where you left her and sent the next morning down in the Country to Padworth, she remained with her mother till July since which time she has been with me in the Central Work House, Bradfield and her conduct has been such as to gain and merit the respect of the Guardians of the Union who feel much interested in her behalf. I should inform you without keeping you in suspense that both mother & child are well and that she expects to be confined again daily. I may say hourly yet so anxious is she to hear of you and to be again united that on receipt of a letter from London containing ½ Sovereign dated Oct[r] 2nd 414 Oxford Street with directions to send to J. Gardner her determination whether she would leave England for America she left the Workhouse and went to the place described 414 Oxford Street and could not find any such person as Mr Gardner she therefore returned to the Workhouse at Bradfield and I wrote a letter by order of the Guardians to J. Gardner 414 Oxford Street which brought a letter written by you Oct 9 – 1836 to a Revd Sir but only one half sheet is enclosed to your wife.

The above letter has given her great satisfaction and she is now only waiting a Letter from you to comply with any wish that you may have respecting her. Perhaps when you write you will inform me where your Father is to be found and to what Parish you belong, or rather how you gained your Parish at Mary le Bone, London. She is now about 4s/- pr. week expense to the Parish of Padworth, which Parish must of course be reimbursed or you will be open to the Law for absconding and leaving your wife chargeable to the above Parish this I write by Order of the Board as Clerk to the Guardians of the Bradfield Union, Berks so that you will observe my letter is twofold one part for your wife the other by order as above stated.

I have now read this to your wife who wishes me to add. Esther is doing very nicely and is a very pretty child and she often talks to the child about you, she hopes you will come or send as quick as possible.

I remain,

Y^r Ob^t Servt

Thos Beall

Clerk to the Board & Master of the Central House

To   Mr Gardner

       no.111 Elizth Street

       New York

Berks. RO ref. G/B 25/2 Bradfield Union, Berkshire and Oxfordshire Admission and Discharge Book, 1835 to 1843

Admitted

When Admitted	Name	Age	No.	Trade	Of What Religious Persuasion	By Whose Orders Admitted	Settlement	Observations
1836								
13 Apr.	Wheeler, Eliz.	30	174	Field Work	Ranter	R.O. 2nd Division	Burghfield	Left Tilehurst Poorhouse a short time since
	Wheeler, Will	3½	175	Bastard				
	Appleby, Louisa	28	176	Widow		R.O. 2nd Division	Beenham	Temper so bad her father will not have her at home
	Williams, Adolphus	4	177	Bastard of Louisa Appleby				
	Appleby, Caroline	6mo.	178					

[contd]

14 Apr.	Obsborne, Henry	8	179	Father dead; mother absconded		The Board	Pangbourn	Mother left them a few days since in Reading
	Osborne, Edward	7	180					
25 Apr.	Brown, John	35	181	Pauper		The Guardians	Streatley	
30 Apr.	Eustace, Mary	17	182	Single, left her Service to be married. Is now ill		R.O. 2nd Division	Tilehurst	
6 May	Rogers, Harriett	8	183	Bastard		Overseers	Stratfield Mortimer	Clean
7 May	Woodley, Hannah	15	184	[see page 8, no 88]		The Master	Bucklebury	Left her place with good character. Master failed
1837								
18 Nov.	Drewett, Jane	39	457	Wife, husband transported	Church of England	The Board	Mapledurham	
	Drewett, Charles	8	458	Two children, bastards	Church of England			
	Drewett, Mary	6	459					
20 Nov.	Nokes, Thos.	22	460	Disabled, lame	Church of England	R. Officer 1st Division	Sulh^d Abbotts	
	Beesley, Eliza	13	461	Bastard, mother dead	Church of England	Removed by orders from Winterbourn	Tilehurst	
22 Nov.	Smither, Samuel	24	462	Tailor	Church of England	Overseer of Whitchurch	Whitchurch	Man no work for 7 weeks
	Smither, Mary Ann	25	463	Wife				Wife near confinement
	Smither, Mary Ann	4	464					
24 Nov.	Knott, Eliza	36	465	Widow, field work	Church of England	The Board	Bucklebury	Character not so high as when in the house before
	Knott, Rebecca	9	466					
	Knott, Mary	7	467					
	Knott, Sarah	6	468					
	Knott, Merian	4	469					

25 Nov.	White, Ann	37	470	Husband transported	Ranter	R.O. 2nd Division	Ashampstead	
	White, Rachael	11	471					
	White, Stephen	7	472					
	White, Abraham	3	473					
	White, Jane	3mo.	474					
27 Nov.	Perrin, Mary	14	475	Bastard	Church of England	R.O. 2nd Division	Ufton	
1838								
12 Nov.	Child, Sarah	25	642	Servant, ill	Church of England	R.O. 2nd Division	Bradfield	
14 Nov.	Day, Sarah	24	643	Field work, pregnant	Church of England	R.O. 2nd Division	Aldermaston	Ragged
	Day, Phoebe	17	644	Field work				
19 Nov.	Wheeler, Elizabeth	36	645	Field work, ill	Ranter	The Board	Burghfield	
20 Nov.	Wheeler, William	6	646	Bastard				
21 Nov.	Hemwood, Alice	42	647	Widow, ill	Church of England	R.O. 1st Division	Tilehurst	
	Hemwood, William	5½	648					
	Hemwood, Henry	8mo.	649	ill				
22 Nov.	Wells, Maria	34	650	Widow, lace maker	Church of England	The Board	Whitchurch	
	Wells, Ann	9	651					
	Wells, George	6	652					

Discharged

| When discharged | Name | Time in the House | | Under what circumstances discharged | By whose order | Observations on condition at the time of admission or general character and behaviour in workhouse |
		Days	Weeks			
1836						
28 Jul.	Wheeler, Elizabeth	15	1	By her own desire to go to field work	The Master	Clean, character in the house bad, very dissatisfied & require a very tight rein
	Wheeler, William	15	1			

[contd]

1837						
23 Jan.	Appleby, Louisa	40	5	Gone to reside with her mother at Midgham and work in the paper mill	The Master	Clean but very indolent and bad temper
1836						
23 May	Williams, Adolphus	5	5	Supported by his father	The Master	Clean
1837						
23 Jan	Appleby, Caroline	40	5		The Master	
10 Mar.	Osborne, Henry	47	1	Left with their mother, eldest going to service	The Master	Clean, well behaved. Boys said they had rather remain in the house than leave
	Osborne, Edward	47	1			
1836						
4 Aug.	Brown, John	14	3	Obtained leave of absence and remained out	The Committee	Clean
23 May	Eustace, Mary	12	5	Died		Clean, came to the house in a consumption, a quiet girl and appears very thankful for all she had
1841						
9 May	Rogers, Harriett	261	1	Taken out by her mother	The Master	Clean, good
27 Jul.	Woodley, Hannah	11	3	Gone to service at Mr Ford's, baker at Theale	The Master	Clean and well behaved
1838						
10 Apr.	Drewett, Jane	20	3	Obtained employment for Mr Hutchins	The Master	Clean, good
	Drewett, Charles	20	3			
	Drewett, Mary	20	3			
5 Mar.	Nokes, Thos.	15		Recovered	The Master	Clean, not very good
13 Jul.	Beesley, Eliza	32	1	To live with an aunt		Clean, good
5 Feb.	Smither, Samuel	10	5	Left to obtain work	The Master	Clean, good
	Smither, Mary Ann	10	5			
	Smither, Mary Ann	10	5			
1840						
12 Aug.	Knott, Eliza	89	4	To receive outdoor relief	The Board	Clean, very good

1838						
13 Jul.	Knott, Rebecca	31	4	To reside with her aunt	The Master	Clean, remarkably good
1840						
12 Aug.	Knott, Mary	89	4	With her mother	The Board	Clean, remarkably good
1839						
18 Mar.	Knott, Sarah	69	2	To reside with her aunt	The Master	Clean, good
1840						
12 Aug.	Knott, Merian	89	4	With her mother	The Board	Clean, good
1838						
18 May	White, Ann	24	4	By her own request without any prospect of gaining an honest maintenance	The Master	Very indolent and dissatisfied disposition, a bad woman under the cloak of religion
	White, Rachael	24	4			
	White, Stephen	24	4			
	White, Abraham	24	4			
	White, Jane	24	4			
1837						
11 Dec.	Perrin, Mary	2		Taken out by a relation	The Master	Good and clean
1839						
9 Feb.	Child, Sarah	12	5	Recovered, gone to her situation	The Master	Clean, very good and thankful
1838						
19 Nov.	Day, Sarah		5	Her own request	The Master	Ragged, bad character
	Day, Phoebe		5			
1839						
7 Aug.	Wheeler, Elizabeth	37	2	Her own request to go to harvest	The Master	Very ignorant woman
	Wheeler, William	37	2			
12 Jun.	Hemwood, Alice	29		Recovered	Her own request and the Board	Clean, good
	Hemwood, William	29				
	Hemwood, Henry	8	1	Died	Died	Very ill, recently recovered from small pox prior to entering the house
22 Jul.	Wells, Maria	34	4	Gone out to nurse	The Board	Clean, good
17 Dec.	Wells, Ann	55	5	Left with mother		
	Wells, George	55	5			

Ox. RO ref. PLU7/G/1A1/2 Woodstock Union, Oxfordshire
Minute Book, 1837

At a meeting of the Guardians of the Woodstock Union holden at the Board Room at the Workhouse on Tuesday the 30th day of May 1837

Ordered that Mrs Hubbard be allowed 15s/- for taking care of the children in the Union Workhouse until the arrival of the Schoolmaster & Schoolmistress & that the Treasurer pay the same.

Ordered that the following articles be provided for the use of the School Room and that Mr Chisholme be requested to procure the same.

Viz.   Copy Books, Quills, Ink and Stands, Penknife, Lead Pencils, Indian Rubber, Rulers, Writing Desk.

Ox. RO ref. PLU7/G/1A1/3 Woodstock Union, Oxfordshire
Minute Book, 1839

13th August 1839

Ordered that a Circular Swing be provided for the exercise of the Children in the Workhouse as recommended by Mr Parker the Assist. Poor Law Commissioner and fixed up in the Boys Yard and that the Iron Work be procured from Mr Orbin, Weston House, Norwood, London.

Som. RO ref. D/G/W/8a/3 Wellington Union, Somerset and Devon
Minute Book, 1841

27th September 1841

It appearing that Robert Parkman aged 46 living in Wiveliscombe but belonging to Bishops Lydeard stands in need of a Double Truss. Ord[d] that the clerk write to the Taunton Union and enquire whether that Union will supply it, communicating that the pauper was about three years since supplied with a Single Truss by Bishops Lydeard.

John Keal, aged 50 having a wife aged 45 applied for relief having broken his arm. It appeared that he belongs to the parish of Dymoke in the Newent Union in Gloucestershire.

Ord[d] that the clerk write for confirmation of the relief ordered during his disability.

John Perry aged 79 wholly disabled having a wife aged 77 wholly incapable of taking care of herself through the effects of age and mental imbecility, applied for relief. It appeared that their daughter residing at Uffculme in the Tiverton Union is willing to receive them and to take charge of them, if the Guardians of this Union will grant their relief. The Board ordered them to be relieved with 3[s]/- per week and the clerk was directed to ask sanction of the Poor Law Commissioners to its being granted during a non residence.

DATE 27th September 1841

Ordered that the clerk make up the other Accounts in the Ledger and carry the Balances to the Balance sheet to prove the correctness of the Ledger for the Quarter.

Culmstock	Tapscott, Richard	44	Lumbago	Incapable
	Aplin, Mary	40	Rheumatism	do
	Moon, William	53	Scabies	case for the House
Hemyock	Searle, Elizabeth	53	Rheumatism	Disabled
Ashbrittle	Cotterell, Benjamin	37	Chill	
	Hill, Sarah	19	do	
	Vickery, John	41	do	
Burlescombe	Agland, Richard	41	Gravel	
	Coram, Wm.	66	Hepatitis	
Holcombe	Ridgway, —— [?]	——	Abcess	
Asbrittle	Bowerman, Henry	40	Fever	very ill
	do	7	"	do
	do	4	"	do
Wellington	Keet, John		Fractured Humerus	Sometime disabled
	Gough, William		Hepatitis Disease	Incapable sometime
	Mitchell, Samuel		Disibility some few days	
	Richards, Mark		Rheumatism	Incapable some weeks
Culmstock	Gillard, Jane		Dysentry	Incapable few days
Clayhidon	Samson, Thomas		Cough	Incapable some time
Buckland	Bennett, Thomas		Fall	do
	Marshall, James		Ulcerated leg	do
Holcombe	Norman, Samuel		Chill	do
	Needes, James		Neuralgia & Debility	do
	Jones, William		Rheumatism some long time	
Wilscombe	Wrentmore, John	21	Asthma	Partially incapable
	Poole, George	26	Affection of the heart	do

[contd]

Chipstable	Court, Mary	49	Erysipelas	do
Milverton	Harcombe, Ann		Typhus Fever	Confined to her bed
	Hancock, Sarah		Slow fever	Wholly disabled
Fitzhead	Pring, John		Fever	do
Hillfarance	Greedy, Maria		do	do
	Dyte, William		do	do
	Fox, John & 3 children		Influenza	do
	Fouracre, Betty		Dyspepsia	do
	Tremlett, John		Swelled face	Partially disabled
	Sydenham, John		Fever	Wholly disabled
	Chorley, John		Wound on instep	do
Bathealton	Goldsworthy, John		Rheumatism	do
	Symms, Grace		Dropsey	do
Milverton	Sydenham, James	37	Fever	do
	Gillard, Joan	42		do
Hillfarance	Harris, Robert		[blank]	
Milverton	Owen, Betty		[blank]	

**IoW RO ref. Z/HO/47 Isle of Wight Union
Minute Book, 1843 to 1846 (with index of subjects and names)**

September 13th 1844

Cheque to	R.S. Hearn	£21–0–0
	G.K. Whitmarch	7–0–0
	Robert Ellman	14–0–0
	James Jolliffe	8–0–0
	John Woodford	11–0–0
Cheque to T. Pike	Tailors £3–10–6 } Sundries £2–2–11 }	£5–13–5
Cheque to T. Pike	Lunatic Keeper £1–2–0 } Bricklayer 19–6 } Sundries 17–6 }	£2–19–0

Out Relief
Hannah Thompson
& family
P.E. Turnbull Esq.
} Read the following letter from Peter Evan Turnbull Esq.
one of the Justices acting for the Union of the Isle of Wight

Newport 5th September 1844

My Dear Sir,

As you are Chairman of the Guardians of the Poor, I wish you would be good enough to take into consideration the scale of allowance granted by the Union in cases of temporary illness.

The subject is brought to my notice by the case of a family, that of Hannah Thompson resident at Shide, whose husband has been employed for the last twenty years on Pan Farm, and is now in Winchester Hospital in consequence of an ulceration on the hand. I have no reason to suppose the case in question to have been treated with any peculiar parsimony I assume it therefore, as evincing the extent of relief usually allowed in similar circumstances and I argue on it accordingly, upon general grounds.

What that extent of relief is will be seen from the enclosed Copy of a letter to me from Mr Hearn the clerk of the Guardians. The number of the family residing together, is stated to be seven; their aggregate earnings fourteen shillings per week. It should have been mentioned, (what is known to the Relieving Officer) that, out of this sum, three shillings per week are stopt for rent, leaving a residue of eleven shillings. To this amount, an allowance has been added by the Guardians, during the illness of the husband, of three loaves of bread valued at three shillings, thus making up fourteen shillings in the whole or two shillings per week per head, for the entire supply of the family. I believe I am correct in saying that this sum of two shillings per head is even less than that which is found necessary for the average subsistence of the Inmates of the Union House itself, where a dietary of the greatest economy is adopted, and where aggregation of several hundred paupers admits of economical arrangements being made on a large scale, which are of course impracticable in a peasants cottage. The class of cases, whereof I take that of Hannah Thompson as affording an exemplification involves no question as to the propriety, or impropriety, of out-door relief. The law especially authorises such to be afforded, in food, or money, or both. The applicability of the principles to the particular cases is admitted by the allowance of any relief at all. It becomes therefore, only a question of amount and I think it may be justly submitted to the Guardians, that that amount ought not to be such, as still to leave the family with less degree of means for necessary support than is required in the workhouse itself. It is precisely under such circumstances, whenever they occur. (The exigency temporary, caused by the stroke of providence and the members of a family all doing their utmost towards the common subsistence) that a liberal, and even large allowance seems demanded, on grounds of mere public policy, as well as private consideration, for no other circumstances probably hold out such strong temptations for an incipient deviation into a course of crime, for the relief of unavoidable domestic pressure.

A note in Mr Hearn's letter says 'There has not been any complaint or further application from the woman' and I am told that it is usual to intimate to applicants, that if they find the relief inadequate they may solicit an increase of it. On this point however, no observation seems necessary, as I take for granted that after a Relieving Officer has made his report the amount of relief granted by the board would not be permitted to depend on the greater or less degree of pertinacity on the part of an applicant unless new circumstances should arise. It is on general grounds rather than in reference to a particular case, that I trouble you with this letter and in the hope, that should you concur in the opinions it expresses, you will have the goodness to bring its contents under the consideration of the Board.

With great Truth believe me to remain,

My Dear Sir

Yours very faithfully

Peter Evan Turnbull

To Sir Richard Simeon, Bart.

***

Friday February 24th 1843

Present	Sir Richard Simeon Bt (Chairman)
	Abraham Clarke
	Thomas Cooke
	Henry Percy Gordon
	Richard Hearns Smith
	James Brook
	William Horlock

Apprentices	Elijah Bayley appeared, agreed to take William Salter as an Apprentice. Boy present consents. Father to appear before Justices to consent. Term Full age of 21. Premium £10.
Emigration	Read letter from Mess Carter & Borne for conveying Emigrants to Montreal.
E.W.S. Wilberforce	Remits £10 in lieu of taking Ann Read as an Apprentice in the year 1835.
Average Rates	Let the Churchwardens and Overseers of the several parishes in arrear be summoned before the Justices.
Hester Fox	Write to the Guardians of Portsea Union to make her a similar allowance for relief as they do to their own Paupers.
George Oakford	Whiteparish, Wilts settled there as hiring and service with Mr Box, now 69 years of age; lived with him one year & six months 3–10–0 wages. Wishes to take his daughter Susannah Oakford home.
	Allow him eleven shillings to take her home.

James Burke	14	Wishes to enlist into the 23rd Fuziliers
Charles Osborne	15	The like
John Lock	13	The like
		Guardians consent

94

Mary Ann Jolliffe	May have twelve shillings to take her to her brother in London
George Williams	Applies for discharge. Let him go – give him two loaves
Isaac Cooke	Applies for his discharge – wife & 3 children – give him three loaves
James Plumley	The like – wife & 3 – give him three loaves
John Saunders	The like – wife & 5 – give him four loaves
George Pitt	The like – give him one loaf

Cheque to			
	R.S. Hearn		£25–0–0
	G.K. Whitmarch		£9–0–0
	Robert Ellman		£18–0–0
	James Jolliffe		£12–0–0
	John Woodford		£13–0–0
	Lymington Union		£9–4–1

T. Pike	Tailors	£3–10–6	
	Sundries	£2– 0–5	£5–10–11

T. Pike	Lunatic Hosp^l	1– 2–0	
	Bricklayer	1– 6–6	
	Sundries	10–8	£2–19– 2

R.S. Hearn	Army & Navy Pens^r	£15–0–0

Cornelius Underwood of West Cowes, Pilot to be summond for not maintaining his daughter Emma now in the House of Industry.

June 12. Frederick G – when left home to go to his work left for the children two gallons Bread, Butter & Meat and a sufficiency of Victuals. Mrs Dyer and Mrs Fry (neighbours) stated that the children had plenty to eat. Children make baskets & earned eight pence last week.

Mr H.B. Tuttiett	Application for payment of £1–1–0 for attending the wife of
Surgeon	W. Kingswell of Shanklin in labor, Dec 15/44
Mr T.B. Tuttiett	Application for 10/6d for consultation with Mr Coates
Mr R.M. Wavell	Application for £2–2–0 attending Carney's wife in labor

Nonsettle Poor	Jan 8/45	Treasurers each recd of Wareham & Purbeck Union	1–6–6

***

20th December 1844

The following Tradesmen's Bills having first been examined and found correct. The In Maintenance Account was ordered to be Debited with the same:–

	£	s	d
Mark Morgan – for bread	164	15	10
Stephen Saunders – for Mutton	51	11	5
Henry Blake – for Flour, Barley Meal, Hops, &c	44	9	2
Edward Wey – Barley Meal	7	7	–
John Adams – do	3	8	–
John Duke – Pollard		11	–
Moorman & Son – Malt Tea Sugar Pepper &c	131	18	5
Edward Upward – Pork, Cheese, Treacle, Sugar, Soap, &c	200	18	7
James Warne – Rice, Mop Yarne, &c	10	11	4
John Buckell – Peas	28	–	–
William Drover – Potatoes	74	8	–
Edward Jacob – Milk	18	16	9
Alfred Mew – Wine	1	16	–
Samuel Pring – Brooms, Brushes, Coals, Coke, &c	24	19	10
John Dyer – Coals, Coke, &c	16	4	7
George Hallett – Coals	5	16	–
R.J. Jewell – do	5	14	–
Ab. Clark – do	5	14	–
Eames & Son – do	5	12	9
Timothy Trimen – Clothing	53	14	–
James Wavell – Calico, Canves, Flanel, &c	63	0	5
William Ryder – Calico	20	8	–
Peress & Dallimore – Worsted Check, &c	10	2	–
Messrs Wadmore – Canvas	6	10	6
Charles Dore – Shroud Baize, Thread, &c	5	15	2
James Blake – Straw	9	–	–
Henry Bannister – Line for Bed, Sacking, Yarn	15	12	6
Ann Morris – for Shoes	48	0	9
James George & Son – Leather, &c	8	2	2
William Way & Son – Lees	4	8	–
William Cox – Shaving, &c	5	–	–
Hezekiah Cantelo – for Beef	27	3	–
John Dennison – for Suet	5	6	–
Isaac Alkey – List Slippers	1	18	–

Also. The following Tradesmen's Bills having first been examined and found correct. The Establishment charges were Ordered to be Debited with the same and Credited with Payments.

	£	s	d
Francis Hobbs – Glazing	10	13	6
W.O. Brook – Lead pipe, Plumbing, &c	11	7	7
Thomas Foster – Oil	6	–	
John Cole – Timber	75	5	10
Alexr Lockhart – Bricklayer, &c	11	19	7
William Meech – Bricks & Lime	5	1	7
William Spickernell – Timber	9	18	4
James Dyer – Carpenters Tools	1	18	8
William Biles – Mess Tins, &c	5	2	10
James Ball – Frying Pans, &c	1	0	3
Messrs Cantello – Sundry Ironwork & Mens Trusses	28	13	1
James Ponsford – Ironmongry – Sundry repairs	3	18	7
Isaac Dore – Smiths Work – Shoeing Horse, &c	1	12	3
Thomas Osborn – Coopering	6	5	6
M. & M.A. Morgan – Earthen Ware, &c	1	6	9
John Cheverton – Repairing Chairs, &c	1	5	6
Henry Kingswell – Printing	5	16	6
J.L. & W.T. Gubbins – Stationery	7	10	5
William Upward – do	1	5	6
W.W. Yelf – do		17	10
H.R. Ury – Papering Rooms, &c	3	19	4
Rogers & Cory – Drugs for making Ink		8	2
Frances Eaton – Collar Maker		16	9
George Lock – Carting		10	0
G.H. Ward – for Gravel	2	12	0
Mess. Hearn & Son. Justices C. Fees £1– 0 – 0,			
Misc. £27–17–3	28	17	3

***

97

27th December 1844

Complaint.

Charlotte Sweatman. I have been about 6 months in the Cripple Ward. On Tuesday the 17th all the people in the Ward said its pork was very small. It appeared smaller than usual. Two on that day had mutton, ten to have pork, potatoes, gruel or onion broth, tea and sugar, ½ pint of ale, 1 pint of small beer. Though that day pork had boiled out. Never known any bread sold from that Ward.

People send to Newport for bread & buy it, sometimes I remember cutting the meat that day into 10 pieces.

The Delivery Book produced examined Diet Table had Governor examined. Proved delivery of quantity. Matron examined, proved general procedure.

Resolved unanimously – Complaint not established.

***

Edwin Cave – Governor complains of his refusal to work.

Richard Allen – On Tuesday morning last & on several times previously & since I ordered Cave to do certain work, to break stones. Refused, he said he would not break stones.

Defence. 'I do not know what I was to break stones for.'

Ordered. That he be taken before the Justices tomorrow.

***

27th December 1844

Cornelius Underwood of West Cowes, Pilot, to be summoned for not maintaining his daughter Emma now in the House of Industry.

Complaint of Sarah the wife of Matthew Aldridge of Crocker Street, on behalf of her mother Jane Matthews; made originally to Mr Sayer and by him brought forward – not sufficient Provisions.

Sarah Aldridge. Saturday before last I produced some bread to Mr Sawyer which I received that day from Mrs Matthews my mother in the Cripple Ward. (I went to my mother again on the Tuesday). I had it weighed on the same day, 5½ ozs. Saturday. On the Tuesday I took a piece of pork which my mother gave me that was weighed and weighed one ounce and half. Mother had complained to me that she had not meat or bread enough. It has not cost me less than eighteen pence a week. Mother went out on the 23rd of this month for a week. A great many in the Ward.

Jane Matthews. I have tea 1 oz. every week. ¼ lb sugar, week; butter; half pint of beer every day; no bread. On Saturday there was rice but I did not like it; it was rice and treacle, and a pound of potatoes & salt, & no beer then but beer in the morning. On Tuesday I gave my daughter the pork just after dinner, had tea for breakfast. That was all the pork I had. 1½ oz. I was very ill, therefore I did not eat it. I have never sold any of my allowance but once my bread when I was too ill to eat it. 13 persons in the Ward besides Assistant who does not sleep there. I never has the gruel because I did not like it. Charlotte Sweatman & Mrs Holland put up the food. I know I might have had gruel if I chose. I know I might have had ale if I liked it. I know I might have had beer for supper if I chose but I did not. I gave the daughter the bread because I was ill and could not eat it. The Doctor was attending me. On the Saturday morning I had tea but did not eat any bread. My daughter brought me meat and bread and I gave her my bread. I know I might have had whatever I liked if I had asked the Surgeon.

N.B. Mrs Matthews, widow of a shoemaker who died about 8 years since in Quay Street, Newport, admitted to House in June 1844, has son John a shoemaker in London, says does not know where. Daughter, wife of Joseph Lawrence in London, says does not know where. Daughter, Eliza lives with Mrs Jolliffe at Gafford [?]. Son Wm lives on his own Freehold, Orchard Street, Newport; is a voter for Borough and County. Son Joseph lives at Lymington. Son in law Emanuel [?] ——— lock [?], master shoemaker at Parkhurst Prison, and the above named daughter Mrs Aldridge.

***

Friday January 3rd 1845

Present   Sir R.G. Simeon Bt Cr
    Abraham Clarke
    Joseph Sayer
    John C. Stephens
    Arthur Webb
    Benjamin Hollier
    Robt Jessett
    Thomas Cooke
    Capt Brigstock

Thos Butt	Recvd letter from Clerke to the Guardians of Portsea Union for relief to be given to Thos Butt at Portsea. To be relieved as Portsea Board may think necessary.
Bond Debt	Notice to be given to Churchwardens of Newchurch that £200 part of the sum of £250 secured to them by Bonds of the Guardians will be paid off at Mids^r next.
Lunatic Asylum	Mr Richis applied in writing for the undermentioned Articles for the Asylum. Fire Guard for the Male Infirmary Window Bars 14 pairs of Stockings for Male Patients 12 Shifts Book. Applications & Report – Ordered to be supplied
Gosh's children	A representation having been made by Lieut Wilson respecting Gosh's children of the Forestside, the Relieving Officer was directed to make enquiry therein, and thereon makes the following Reports :–

Visited the abode of Jos Gosh of the Forestside and found his dwellinghouse partly unroofed – Room full of rushes – Not much Bed Clothes – Good Bed and a lot of Rugs for a covering – Children very healthy – Children attend Sunday School and are also instructed by Mrs Fry. Furniture consists of – 2 old chairs – 2 boxes – bedstead & a few plates &c. Gosh is about to take another house, and is at work at Cowes, earns 11ˢ/- per wk – has children, viz. Jane 12, Frederick 9 – when left home to go to his work left for his children two gallons bread, butter and meat and sufficiency of victuals. Mrs Dyer and Mrs Fry (neighbours) state that the children have plenty to eat. Children make baskets and earned eight pence last week.

***

Berks. RO ref. G/N 7/1 Newbury Union, Berkshire
Letter Book, 1847 to 1851

To   The Poor Law Board   Newbury Union
      Somerset House   Oct. 17th 1850
      London

In reply to your letter of the 12th inst. forwarding for the information & consideration of the Guardians of this Union a Copy enclosed of a letter from a Poor person named William Lambdin residing at Newbury. I am directed to say that the Guardians have duly considered the Case of William Lambdin residing at Newbury (but who does not belong to that parish but to some parish in Hampshire) when before them. From his drunken habits the House is in the estimation of the Guardians the best place for him.

***

Som. RO ref. D/G/AX/87/1 Axbridge Union, Somerset
Punishment Book, 1864 to 1905

Date	Name	Offence	Date of Offence	Punishment Inflicted by Master or other Officer	Date of Punishment
1869					
1 Jun.	James Champeny	Positively refusing to work	1 Jun.	Locked up 8 hours	1 Jun.
16 Jul.	Ann Courte	Grose insolence to the Matron	16 Jul.	Locked up from 8 a.m.	
3 Aug.	John Addicott	Stealing onions from Workhouse ground	2 Aug.	Locked up 8 hours	3 Aug.

[contd]

No. of the Case.	N A M E.	O F F E N C E.	Date of Offence.	Punishment inflicted by Master or other Officer.	..	Date of Punishment.	Initials of Clerk.	O
30	Leonard Edward	Refusing to work	1883 4th June	Kept on Bread & Water		1883 4th June	JGR	
31	Young Joseph	Filthy conduct in respect of Lettuce	24th June	Six Stripes with Cane			JGR	
32	Buss Wesley	Filling the salt bowels with broth	9th Novr.	Two stripes with Cane		5th Nov	JGR	
33	Kellyer Samuel	Emptying the salt bowels into the broth	9th Nov	Two stripes with Cane		5th Nov	JGR	
34	Harriet Roper	Throwing about Cups and using Profane & obscene language	5th Nov	Locked up 8 hours		6th Novr	JGR	
35	Harriet Roper	Fighting with Mary Young insolence to the Master and taking Bread	1884 29th Jany	Locked up Eight hours		29th Jany	JGR	
36	Yules Elizth Ann	Assaulting Sophia Radford and also Refusing to work in the Laundry	1885 11th Decr and 11th Decr	Kept on Bread and water for 48 hours		11th Decr 1885	JGR	
37	Yules Elizth Ann	Assaulting Ann Stoner	1886. 6th Feby	Locked up 9 hours		6th Feby 1886	JGR	
38	Jane Groves / Mary Ann Dunston	Persisting in creating a Noise so as to annoy other inmates and also the Officers	10th 11th and 12th May 1886.	Locked up Seven hours		12th May	JGR	
39	Rogers Eliza	Persisting in creating a Noise and striking Mary Ann Dunston	7th and 8th June 1886	Locked up 8 hours		8th June	JGR	
40	Louisa Reed	Persisting in Creating a Noise and making use of Obscene language		Locked up 9 hours		9th Augst 1886	JGR	
41	Eliza Rogers							

Page from the Offence and Punishment Book of Axbridge Workhouse, 1883–86. (Som. RO ref. D/G/Ax/87/1)

4 Aug.	John Addicott	Positively refusing to work	4 Aug.	Locked up 8 hours	4 Aug.
5 Aug.	" "	Again Positively refusing to do any work	5 Aug.	" "	5 Aug.
6 Aug.	" "	Again refusing most positively to do work telling the Master he might lock him up a hundred times if he liked, and he would not work	6 Aug.	8 a.m. to 8 p.m.	6 Aug.
7 Aug.	" "	Again refusing to obey orders to work by the Master	7 Aug.	Locked up from 7 o'clock a.m. until p.m.	7 Aug.
6 Sep.	George Howell	Grose insolence to the Master	6 Sep.	Locked up 7 hours	6 Sep.
20 Sep.	Elizabeth Peddle	Insolence and refusing to work	20 Sep.	Locked up 9 a.m. to 8 p.m.	20 Sep.
21 Oct.	Charles Ridley	Positively refusing to work	21 Oct.	Locked up 8 a.m. to 8 p.m.	21 Oct.
22 Oct.	Charles Ridley	ditto	22 Oct.	ditto	22 Oct.
27 Oct.	William Hall	Swearing and threatening	27 Oct.	Locked up 10 hours	27 Oct.
1870					
21 Aug.	Jane Tilley	Insolence to the Master	6 Aug.	Locked up 8 hours, caned by schoolmaster	6 Aug.

24 Aug 1870 The Schoolmaster caned Harry Lovell, John Plumley, Frederic Vagg and Maurice Brooks, for stealing apples from Mr Day's orchard on 13 Aug

**Som. RO ref. D/G/W 8a/29 Wellington Union, Somerset and Devon
Minute Book, 1853 to 1855**

8th July 1897

The following special report by the District Medical Officer with reference to the case of the crippled child William Brown of Almshayne Ash, Culmstock is read:–

'Not fit to attend school. I fear that he is permanently crippled and that very little can be done medically for him.'

Mr Twose, Relieving Officer, reports that the boy has twice been sent to the Exeter Hospital but that they can do nothing for him.

The boy and his mother appear before the Guardians.

Resolved that the Clerk be instructed to write to Dr. Date and inquire whether in his opinion it would be advisable to send the boy to Dr. Abbot of Taunton whom the Guardians believe is a specialist in such cases.

CHAPTER 7

UNION OFFICIALS AND OTHER LOCAL OFFICERS

Lists of Union officials are to be found in the central correspondence files of the Poor Law Commissioners and their successors in TNA record class MH 12. The correspondence of the General Board of Health, covering the period 1847–71, in TNA record class MH 13 includes lists of other local officials. Union officials can also be found listed in the records of Unions which are held in local record offices. The following are some examples:

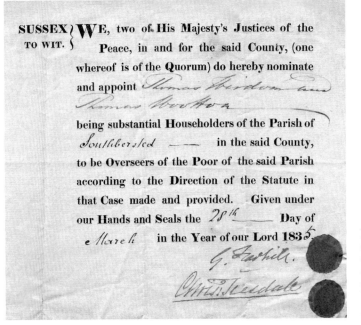

Notice of the appointment of two overseers in the parish of South Bersted, Sussex, 1835. (John Titford Collection)

TNA ref. MH 12/10456 Taunton Union, Somerset and Devon
[From a printed poster, 1846.]

TAUNTON UNION

I do hereby certify that the Election of Guardians of the Poor for the several Parishes in the Taunton Union, was conducted in conformity with the order of the Poor Law Commissioners and that the entries contained in the Schedule hereunder written are true.

Parish	Residence	Calling	Name of Guardian Elected and continued
Angersleigh	Leigh Farm	Yeoman	Bishop, William
Ash Priors	Ash Priors	Yeoman	Melhuish, Matthew
Bagborough, West	Bagborough, West	West Yeoman	Webber, William
Bickenhall	Bickenhall	Tanner	Cozens, Daniel
Bishops Hull	Freathey Cottaged Bishops Hull Mills	Commander RN	Maclean, Wm. Gunston, England, Robert
Bishops Lydeard			[blank]
Cheddon Fitzpaine	Pyrland	Gentleman	Musgrave, John Clitsome
Churchstanton	Churchstanton	Yeoman	Smith, Henry
Coombe Florey	Coombe Florey	Yeoman	Webber, George
Corfe	Corfe	Yeoman	Greenslade, Richd. Norris
Cothelstone			[blank]
Creech St. Michael	Court Barton	Yeoman	Dunning, John
Curland	Curland	Farmer	Grabham, John
Curry, North	Curry, North	Yeoman	Hurman, William
	Knapp	Yeoman	House, William
Durston	Durston	Yeoman	Kidner, William
Halse	Halse	Gentleman	Hancock, John Donne
Hatch Beauchamp	Hatch Villa	Gentleman	Howse, James
Hatch, West	Hatch, West	Yeoman	James, Abraham Rook
Heathfield	Heathfield Farm	Yeoman	Bond, James

[contd]

Kingston	Cutley	Agriculturalist	Gorwyn, J.L.A.
Lydeard St. Lawrence	Whestow	Yeoman	Taylor, John
Monkton, West	Hill Farm	Yeoman	Radford, James
	Hyde Farm	Yeoman	Mogg, Samuel
Norton Fitzwarren	Norton Court	Common Brewer	Hewett, William
Orchard Portman	Orchard Portman	Yeoman	Blandford, Henry
Otterford	Otterford Farm	Yeoman	Wale, John
Pitminster	Fullwood	Farmer	Coram, William
	Sweethay	Farmer	Bicknell, Reuben
Ruishton	Henlade	Yeoman	Ball, Philip Nathaniel
Staple Fitzpaine	Park Farm	Farmer	Burrough, George
Staplegrove			[blank]
Stoke St. Gregory	Mare Green	Yeoman	Hurman, John
Stoke St. Mary	Stoke St. Mary	Yeoman	Maine, John
Taunton St. James	Greenway	Gentleman	Mockridge, John
	Canon Street	Gentleman	King, Henry Daniel
	Lyngford	Gentleman	Gadd, William
	East Reach	Gentleman	Horsey, John Haydon*
	The Priory	Yeoman	Foster, Henry*
Taunton St. Mary	Fore Street	Grocer	Turle, Richard
	Hammet Street	Solicitor	Trenchard, Henry Charles
	Holway	Yeoman	Pring, John
	Holway	Gentleman	Blake, Downing
	Mount Terrace	Gentleman	Stevenson, George*
Thorn Falcon	Thorn Rectory	Clergyman	Harrison, Rev. O.S.*
Thurlbeer			[blank]
Tolland	Tolland	Yeoman	Bishop, William
Trull	Wild Oak	Gentleman	Trenchard, George
Wilton	Wheatleigh Lodge	Gentleman	Stephens, John

* These nominees refused, in writing, to serve the office

Given under my Hand this Ninth day of April, One Thousand Eight Hundred and Forty Six.

John Chorley,

Clerk to the Guardians of the Poor of the Taunton Union

TNA ref. MH 12/4366 Ledbury Union, Herefordshire
[List of Guardians, 1847]

I do hereby certify, that the election of Guardians of the Poor for the several Parishes in the Ledbury Poor Law Union, for the year ending March 25, 1847, was conducted in conformity with the Order of the Poor Law Commissioners, and that the entries contained in the schedule hereunder written are true.

Parish	Name of Person Nominated	Residence	Quality or Calling	Name of Guardian Elected
Ashperton	John Hollings	Verzons, Ashperton	Gentleman	John Hollings
Aylton	George Sexty	Homend St. Ledbury	Gentleman	George Sexty
Bosbury	John Acton	Grainge, Bosbury	Gentleman	John Acton
Bosbury	Thomas Pitt	Stonehouse, Bosbury	Gentleman	Thomas Pitt
Castle Frome	Samuel Smith	Old Birchend, Castle Frome	Farmer	Samuel Smith
Canon Frome	Richard Hooper	Lower House, Canon Frome	Farmer	Richard Hooper
Coddington	Edmund J. Piper	Moorfields, Coddington	Gentleman	Edmund J. Piper
Colwall	Reynolds Peyton	Barton Court, Colwall	Esquire	Reynolds Peyton
Donnington	Rev. John Lander	Rectory, Donnington	Clerk	Rev. John Lander
Eastnor	William Conolly Watson	Bronsil, Eastnor	Gentleman	William Conolly Watson
Eggleton	Francis Hollings	Moor's Court, Eggleton	Yeoman	Francis Hollings
Ledbury	Rev. James G. Watts	Vicarage, Ledbury	Clerk	Rev. James G. Watts

[contd]

Ledbury	Rev. Thomas Dowell	Parsonage, Wellington Heath, Ledbury	Clerk	Rev. Thomas Dowell
"	Francis Higgins	Southend House, Ledbury	Solicitor	Francis Higgins
"	Sidney Gregg	Pegs Farm, Ledbury	Farmer	Sidney Gregg
Little Marcle	William Nutt	Lillands, Little Marcle	Farmer	William Nutt
Mathon	John Jauncey	Hollings Hill, Mathon	Yeoman	John Jauncey
Much Marcle	James Price	Hill Farm, Much Marcle	Farmer	James Price
"	William Smith	Hall Court, Much Marcle	Farmer	William Smith
Munsley	Charles Higgins	Paunceford Court, Munsley	Farmer	Charles Higgins
Parkhold	Thomas Galliers	Pridewood, Parkhold	Solicitor	Thomas Galliers
Pixley	Richard Homes	Poolend	Farmer	Richard Homes
Putley	James Collins	Hatsford, Woolhope	Gentleman	James Collins
Stretton Grandsome	John Hill	New House, Stretton Grandsome	Farmer	John Hill
Tarrington	Henry Poole	Bears Court, Tarrington	Farmer	Henry Poole
Woolhope	Henry William Booth	Hill House, Woolhope	Esquire	Henry William Booth
Yarkhill	James Moore	Monkbury Court, Yarkhill	Farmer	James Moore

Given under my Hand, this twenty seventh day of March, 1847

Jesse Hughes

Clerk to the Guardians of the Poor of the Ledbury Union

TNA ref. MH 13/180 Taunton Borough

[Election of twenty-one members to the local Board of Health, 1849.]

Taunton Borough

I do hereby certify that the election of members of the local board of health for the Borough of Taunton in the County of Somerset was conducted in conformity with the order of the General Board of Health, and that the entries contained in the schedule hereunder written are true.

Name of Candidate	Residence	Quality or Calling	No of votes given for each	Names of the members elected
Smith, Frederick Jeremiah	Silver St. Taunton	Clerk	710	Smith, Frederick Jeremiah
Redfern, William Thomas	St. James St. Taunton	Clerk	472	
Mockridge, John	Greenway, do	Yeoman	928	Mockridge, John
Turle, Richard	Fore St., do	Grocer	574	
Hucklebridge, Thomas	North St., do	Plumber	393	
Turle, John	Fore St., do	Grocer	293	
Herniman, Robert	East Reach, do	Builder	1104	Herniman, Robert
Parsons, Robert	East Reach, do	Tanner	611	Parsons, Robert
Cliffe, Loftus Anthony	Crescent, do	Clerk	187	
Carver, Richard	Wilton, do	Architect	654	Carver, Richard
Atton, Richard William	Fore St., do	Draper	225	
White, John Eales	East St., do	Brewer	967	White, John Eales
Jeboult, James	Fore St., do	China Dealer	643	Jeboult, James
Penny, James	Silver St., do	Esquire	777	Penny, James
Pollard, Samuel	Silver St., do	Surveyor	760	Pollard, Samuel
Balance, Charles	Mount St., do	Silk Manufacturer	296	
Welch, Francis	East St., do	Surgeon	301	
Kinglake, Arthur	Mount St., do	Esquire	400	
Hitchcock, William Pritchard	North St., do	Chemist	430	

[contd]

Cornish, Charles Henry	East St., Taunton	Surgeon	643	Cornish, Charles Henry
Henderson, Joseph Junior	Fore St., Taunton	Mercer	321	
Horsey, John Haydon	East Reach, Taunton	Esquire	552	
Alford, Henry	Mt Elm Cottage, do	Surgeon	410	
Young, John	St. James, do	Gentleman	584	
Stephens, John	Woodbine Cottage, Bishops Hull	Gentleman	600	Stephens, John
King, Henry Daniel	Canon St., St. James', do	Gentleman	922	King, Henry Daniel
Beadon, William	N° 1 Cresent, Taunton	Gentleman	890	Beadon, William
Day, Robert Junʳ	High Street, Taunton	Pawnbroker	178	
Trood, Henry	Tone Bridge, Taunton	Merchant	788	Trood, Henry
Spence, John Ward	Wilton, Taunton	Clerk	138	
Oram, William Ellis	Hourils Court, Taunton	Cooper	692	
Easton, John	Castle Green, Taunton	Land Surveyor	508	
Steven, John	East St., do	Upholder	261	
Rawlinson, William	Mount St., Taunton	Silk Throwster	606	Rawlinson, William
Cornish, Benjamin	High St., Taunton	Cooper	771	Cornish, Benjamin
Reeves, Richard	1 Whitehall, Taunton	Coach Builder	443	
Kallend, James	1 North Town Crescent, do	Gentleman	415	
Goodland, Charles	North Town, Taunton	Coal Merchant	854	Goodland, Charles
Hammett, Benjamin	North St., Taunton	do	495	
Clarke, William	East St., do	Gentleman	94	

Charles, Samuel	East Gate, do	Draper	239		
Powell, James	Victoria St., Taunton	Gentleman	400		
Webber, William	East Reach, do	Builder	566		
Robinson, H^y Eleazer	Tangier, Taunton	Gentleman	209		
Woodford, Francis H^y	Crescent, Taunton	MD	378		
Stone, Richard	North Town, Taunton	Railway Conductor	69		
Shewbrooks, William	South St., Taunton	Builder	854	Shewbrooks, William	
French, Edmund	Tancred St., Taunton	Wool Dealer	336		

Given under my hand this seventeenth day of September
One thousand eight hundred and forty nine.
Henry Badiest [?]
Chairman for conducting the first election

TNA ref. MH 12/4373 Ledbury Union, Herefordshire and Worcestershire
[Printed report.]

STATEMENT

Shewing the amount of Money Expended and the balances due to and from the
SEVERAL PARISHES
in the
LEDBURY POOR-LAW UNION
for the half year ended September 29th 1866
ELECTED GUARDIANS

Parish	Name of Guardian	Residence
Ashperton	Stephen Pitt	Ashperton
Aylton	Jonathan Williams	Aylton
Bosbury	{ Richard Hickman	Bosbury
	{ Alfred J. Borrows	Bosbury
Canon Frome	Francis Pitt	Canon Frome
Castle Frome	Charles Oakey	Castle Frome
Coddington	Henry Edward Vale	Coddington
Colwall	Henry Izard	Colwall
Donnington	John Cummins	Donnington

[contd]

Eastnor	Michael R. Thorold	Eastnor
Eggleton	George Maund	Eggleton
Ledbury	Benjamin Mutlow	Ledbury
	Phillip Baylis	Ledbury
	William Matthews	Ledbury
	William Skittery	Ledbury
Little Marcle	John Sparkman	Little Marcle
Much Marcle	James Powell	Much Marcle
	John Wigmore	Much Marcle
Mathon	Robert A. Swayne	Mathon
	William Dingley	Mathon
Munsley	Edwin Gibbs	Munsley
Parkhold	[blank]	
Pixley	Daniel Pope	Pixley
Putley	William Bengar	Putley
Stretton Grandsome	John Buckle	Ashperton
Tarrington	John Mutlow	Tarrington
Woolhope	Peter Maile	Woolhope
Yarkhill	John Brace Vevers	Yarkhill

The meeting of the Board of Guardians is held every Tuesday at eleven o'clock, at the Board Room, Workhouse, Ledbury.

The Revd. John Hopton, Canon Frome Court,   Chairman
Michael R. Thobold Esq., Bromsil, Eastnor,   Vice-Chairman

MAGISTRATES FOR THE COUNTY OF HEREFORD
EX-OFFICIO GUARDIANS

The Earl Somers, Eastnor Castle
Revd. John Hopton, Canon Frome Court
Captain Jones, Wallhills
Richard Webb, Esq., Donnington Hall
James Martin, Esq., Old Colwall
Thomas Heywood, Esq., Hope End
Rev. Edward Higgins, Bosbury House
Charles W. Henry, Esq., M.D., Haffield
William Money Kyrle, Homme House
Revd. Thomas Bird, Yarkhill
Rev. W. Scarlet Vale, Mathon Lodge
J. Murray Aynsley, Esq., Underdown
Captain Peyton, Barton Court

***

Elected Guardians

Parishes	Names of Guardians	Residences
Ashperton	Stephen Pitt	Ashperton
Aylton	Jonathan Williams	Aylton
Bosbury	{ Richard Hickman	Bosbury
	Alfred J. Burrows	Bosbury
Canon Frome	Francis Pitt	Canon Frome
Castle Frome	Charles Oakey	Castle Frome
Coddington	Henry Edward Vale	Coddington
Colwall	Henry Izard	Colwall
Donnington	John Cummins	Donnington
Eastnor	Michael R. Thorold	Eastnor
Eggleton	George Maund	Eggleton
	{ Benjamin Mutlow	Ledbury
Ledbury	Philip Baylis	Ledbury
	William Matthews	Ledbury
	William Skittery	Ledbury
Little Marcle	John Sparkman	Little Marcle
Much Marcle	{ John Powell	Much Marcle
	John Wigmore	Much Marcle
Mathon	{ Robert A. Swayne	Mathon
	William Dingley	Mathon
Munsley	Edwin Gibbs	Munsley
Pixley	Daniel Pope	Pixley
Putley	William Bengar	Putley
Stretton Grandison	John Brockle	Ashperton
Tarrington	John Mutlow	Tarrington
Woolhope	Peter Maile	Woolhope
Yarkhill	John Brace Vevers	Yarkhill

OFFICERS OF THE UNION

Treasurer	Edward John Webb, Esq., Ledbury
District Auditor	Edward Murrell. Esq., Tewkesbury (salary paid by Government)

	Salary for the half year		
	£	s	d
Chaplain			
The Rev. William J. Morrish, Ledbury	15	0	0
Clerk			
Mr J. Hughes, Ledbury	50	0	0
	plus other payments £20		

[contd]

Workhouse Officers (These officers are provided with rations
  and lodgings)

Mr and Mrs Lloyd, *Master and Matron*	35	0	0
Miss Frankton, *Schoolmistress*	10	0	0
Richard Powles, *Porter*	7	10	0
Ann Johns, *Nurse*	8	0	0

Medical Officers

Mr G.S. Symmons, Ledbury, for the Workhouse	20	0	0
Mr W. Griffin, Ledbury, for Bosbury, Canon Frome, Castle Frome, Coddington, Colwall, Donnington, Eastnor and Mathon	35	0	0
Mr G.S. Symmons, Ledbury, for Ledbury, Ashperton, Aylton, Eggleton, Little Marcle, Much Marcle, Munsley, Parkhold, Pixley, Putley, Stretton Grandison, Tarrington, Woolhope and Yarkhill	92	10	0

Dispenser

Mr E. Allgood, Ledbury	27	10	0

Relieving Officers

Mr W.J. Bailey, Ledbury for Ledbury, Bosbury, Colwall, Coddington, Donnington, Eastnor and Mathon	48	10	0
Mr C.C. Kendrick, Tarrington, for Ashperton, Aylton, Canon Frome, Castle Frome, Eggleton, Little Marcle, Much Marcle, Munsley, Parkhold, Pixley, Putley, Stretton Grandison, Tarrington, Woolhope and Yarkhill	50	0	0

Assistant Relieving Officer (for Tramps)

Mr G. Tanner, Superintendent of Police	2	0	0

Public Vaccinators

Mr W. Griffin, Ledbury	[blank]		
Mr G.S. Symonds, Ledbury	10	0	0
	(other payment)		

Registrars of Births and Deaths

Mr W.J. Bailey, Ledbury (Registration Fees)	11	17	6
	(other payment)		
Mr C.C. Kendrick, Ledbury (Registration Fees)	6	14	3
	(other payment)		

£401 0 0 + £48 11 9

CHAPTER 8

UNION STAFF

Most persons who were employed by Poor Law Unions are recorded in the correspondence files of the Poor Law Commission (1834–47), the Poor Law Board (1847–
71) and the Local Government Board (1871–1900) in TNA document class MH 12.
These take the form of application/appointment forms giving much detail about each
applicant. The records after 1900 do not usually survive. Employees of Unions for the
period 1837 to 1921 (both officers and workhouse staff) are listed in TNA document
class MH 9. They include clerks, chaplains, masters and matrons (these were usually
husband and wife), schoolteachers, industrial teachers, porters, nurses (male and
female), school attendance officers, medical officers, relieving officers, vaccination
officers, overseers and assistant overseers. The relevant references for both MH 12 and
MH 9 for each Union are listed in Appendix 2 of this book.

References to the appointments of staff and sometimes complaints against individuals are also to be found in the correspondence sent to Unions from the central office.

The appointment (and dismissal) of Union staff can also be found in the minutes of
the meetings of the Board of Guardians of the Unions. These records are usually held at
county or borough record offices.

Lists of guardians and overseers are also to be found in both the central correspondence files and in the minutes of meetings and other records kept by the Unions (see
Chapter 7).

Correspondence relating to Poor Law Authorities (TNA document class MH 68),
dating from 1904 to 1933, sometimes includes references to Union staff.

This chapter gives some examples of the records of Union employees:

TNA ref. MH 12/1678 Longtown Union, Cumberland

Appointment of Master

1. State the Christian Name and Surname of the person appointed as Master of the
   Workhouse   *Thomas Lee*
2. His place of Residence immediately previous to his appointment   *Carlisle*

3. His Age   *36*
4. Whether he is married or single   *Married*
5. Whether he has any Children; and if so, whether they are dependent on him, and where it is proposed that they shall reside   *one child dependent on him, in the Workhouse*
    If it is proposed that any of the children shall reside in the Workhouse, the ages and sexes of the children and what sum per week is to be paid to the Guardians by the Master for the maintenance of each child   *A boy, 2 years old*
6. His religious persuasion   *Church of England*
7. His previous Occupations, or Callings   *In the Royal Engineers (Civil Service)*
8. Whether he has been in the Army, Navy, Excise, Police, or other Public Service; and if so, which Service; the cause of his leaving the same; and the Date when he left   *Civil Service, Reduction of the Force, 7th June 1861*
    If he has been in the Police Service whether he produced to the Guardians a Certificate of Good Conduct from the Police Authorities   ————————
9. Whether he has before held any paid Office in any Union or Parish; and if so, what Office, and in what Union or Parish   *No*
    The cause of leaving same   ————————
    And the date when he left   ————————
10. Whether he has ever been bankrupt or insolvent or executed an assignment for the benefit of, or entered into a composition with his creditors; and if so when   *Never*
    If a bankrupt, whether he has obtained his Certificate and what was the Class thereof   ————————
11. Whether he has a competent knowledge of accounts   *Yes*
12. Whether his whole time is given up to the Service of the Union   *Yes*
13. The day on which he was elected by the guardians   *5th August 1861*
14. The date from which his Duties commence   *As soon as he can enter on them*
15. Whether he is to reside in the Workhouse   *Yes*
16. The amount of Salary proposed   *£30*
17. Whether any Rations or other Emoluments are allowed; and if so what   *Yes, Two Rations*
18. Whether he agrees to give the Guardians one Month's amount of Salary, to be deducted from the amount of Salary due at the time of resignation, pursuant to Article 167 of the General Consolidation Order   *Yes, to give notice*
19. The nature and amount of the Security and the names and addresses of Sureties and their occupations   *Bond – £300*
    James Dixon, farmer and joiner
    John Dixon, farmer and grocer
20. What Testimonials the Guardians have received and whether they are satisfied thereby, or otherwise that the person appointed is competent to perform efficiently all the duties of the office of Master   *From the Officers under whose command he has served*
21. The cause of the Vacancy on account of which the appointment is made; if a resignation, the cause thereof, the date on which it took effect, and the name of

the former Officer   *Resignation of James Barton; only holds this office until new Master enters on his duties*

L.B. Hodgson   Signature of clerk
Thomas Lee   Signature of the Officer appointed
Reported to the Poor Law Board   6th August 1861

TNA ref. MH 12/1678 Longtown Union, Cumberland
[Note that the matron here is the wife of the master in the above entry.]

Appointment of Matron

1. State the Christian Name and Surname of the Person appointed as Matron of the Workhouse, in full   *Margaret Lee*
2. Her Place of Residence immediately previous to her appointment   *Carlisle*
3. Her Age   *37 years*
4. Whether she is Married or Single   *Married*
5. Whether she has any Children; and if so, whether they are dependent on her, and where it is proposed that they shall reside   *one child 2 years old dependent on her & her husband: in the workhouse*
6. Her Religious Persuasion   *Church of England*
7. Her previous Occupations or Callings *Daughter of a Farmer, resided with him*
8. Whether she has before held any paid Office in any Union or Parish; and if so, what Office and in what Union or Parish   *None*
    The cause of her leaving the same   ———————
    And the date when she left   ———————
9. Whether her whole time is given up to the Service of the Union   *Yes*
    or, Whether she continues in any other Occupation or Calling   *None*
10. The day on which she was elected by the Guardians   *August 5. 1861*
11. The date from which her duties commence   *12th August 1861*
12. The Amount of Salary proposed   *£10–0–0*
13. Whether any Rations or other Emoluments are allowed; and if so what   *Yes – 1½ rations*
14. If there be no Master of the Workhouse, the nature and amount of the security which she is to give for the due performance of her duties   *Her husband is Master*
15. Whether she agrees to give the Guardians one month's notice previous to resigning her Office, or to forfeit one month's amount of Salary, to be deducted from the amount of Salary due at the time of resignation, pursuant to Article 167 of the General Consolidated Order   *Yes*
16. What testimonials the Guardians have received, and whether they are satisfied thereby or otherwise that the person appointed is competent to perform all the duties of the office of Matron   *Only one relating solely to the Matron. Yes*
17. The cause of the Vacancy on account of which the appointment is made; if a Resignation the cause thereof, the date on which it took effect, and the name of the former Officer   *Resignation of former Master & Matron*

C.B. Hodgson Signature of the Clerk
Margret Lee [sic] Signature of the Officer appointed
Reported to the Poor Law Board for their approval 22nd day of August 1861

TNA ref. MH 12/1021 Nantwich Union, Cheshire

Appointment of Medical Officer

1. State the Christian Name and Surname of the Person appointed as Medical Officer, in full *John Lord*
2. His Place of Residence and Business *Crewe, Cheshire*
3. His Age *34 years*
4. How long has he been in practice as a Medical Man *5 years*
5. Whether he has before held any similar Office; and if so, what Union *No*
6. Whether he is an existing Officer of the Union within the meaning of Article 170 of the Consolidated General Order *No*
7. Whether he is Medical Officer of any other District in this or any other Union; and if so state what District, and what Union *No*
8. State the day on which he was appointed by the Guardians *10th November 1855*
9. State the date from which his Duties commence *10th November 1855*
10. State whether his appointment is permanent *Yes*
  if not, ————
11. State for what period he has been appointed ————
12. Whether a Contract in writing has been entered into with him as Medical Officer *No*
13. State the amount of Salary proposed (exclusive of the Fees allowed by the Consolidated General Order – Articles 177, 182 and 183) *£30 per annum*
14. State whether he has entered into a written Contract for Vaccination within the Union, under the provisions of the Acts 3 & 4 Vict., cap 29 and 16 & 17 Vict., cap 100; and if so, state at what rate *No*
15. State the cause of the Vacancy on account of which the appointment is made: if a Resignation, state the cause and date of such Resignation, and the Name of the former Officer *Mr John Kilshaw Slater having removed out of the Union tendered his resignation to the Board the 15th proximo in consequence thereof*
16. State whether he is qualified according to one of the four modes prescribed by Article 168 of the Consolidated General Order, which are as follow: and if so, state the nature of the Qualification: *No*
 M.D. Edinburgh
 M.R.C.S. London

1. A diploma or degree as surgeon from a Royal College or University in England, Scotland, or Ireland, together with a degree in medicine from a University in England, legally authorized to grant such degree, or together with a diploma or licence of the Royal College of Physicians of London ————

2. A diploma or degree as surgeon from a Royal College or University in England, Scotland, or Ireland, together with a Certificate to practice as an apothecary from the Society of Apothecaries of London. ————

3. A diploma or degree as surgeon from a Royal College or University in England, Scotland, or Ireland, such person having been in actual practice as an apothecary on the first day of August, One Thousand Eight Hundred and Fifteen. ————

4. A warrant or commission as surgeon or assistant-surgeon in Her Majesty's Navy, or as surgeon or assistant-surgeon or apothecary in Her Majesty's Army, or as surgeon or assistant-surgeon in the service of the Honourable East India Company, dated previous to the first day of August, One Thousand Eight Hundred and Twenty-six.

17. State the Names of the Parishes in the District.   *Church Coppenhall, Monks Coppenhall, Crewe, Leighton, Church Minshull, Minshall Vernon, Shavington cum Gresty, Willaston, Wistaston and Woolstanwood.*

18. The Area in Acres   *14,652 acres*

19. The Population   *7551*

20. Whether he resides within the District for which he is appointed   *Yes*

21. If not, the distance he resides therefrom ————

22. Whether there is any other Medical Man resident in the District, and how he is supposed to be qualified.   *Edwin Edwards, L.S.A. London*
                              M.R.S. London
                              William W. Vaughan, L.S.A. London
                              M.R.C.S. London

23. If not, whether there is any Medical Man residing near the District, the distance at which he resides from it, and how he is supposed to be qualified. ————

24. On this side insert a Copy of any special Minute of the Board of Guardians stating the reasons for assigning to any Medical Officer a District exceeding, in respect of Areas of Population, the limits prescribed by Article 159 of the Consolidated General Order; or for appointing any Medical Officer not qualified in one of the four modes required by Article 168 of the Order ————

J. Broadhurst   Signature of the Clerk
John Lord   Signature of the Officer appointed.
Reported to the Poor Law Board for their approval *Thirteenth* day of *November* 1855

TNA ref. MH 12/10225 Bedminster Union, Somerset

Appointment of Nurse

1. State the Christian Name and Surname of the Person appointed as Nurse at the Union Workhouse, in full   *Miss Elizabeth Tooley*
2. Her place of Residence immediately previous to her appointment   *Barnet Union, Herts*
3. Her Age   *35*
4. Whether Married or Single   *Single*
5. Whether she has any children, and if so, whether they are dependent on her, and where it is proposed that they shall reside   ——————
6. Her previous Occupation or Callings   *Assistant Matron at Barnet Union Head Nurse at Bishops Stortford*
7. Whether she has before held any office in any Union or Parish, and if so what office, and in what Union or Parish   *As above*
8. The cause of her leaving the same, and the date at which she left   *Resigned to take the present app^{mt} about the 18th December 1876*
9. The day on which she was elected to her present office   *12th December 1876*
10. The date from which her Duties commence   *12th January 1877*
11. The amount of Salary proposed   *£30 per annum*
12. Whether any Rations or other Emoluments are allowed, and if so what   *With furnished apartment. Rations*
13. Whether she is competent to read and understand correctly the written directions of the Medical Officer, and otherwise to discharge with watchfulness and care, the duties of the office of Nurse   *Yes*
14. The name of the previous Officer, and when, and from what cause she ceased to hold office   *Mrs Kate Yarwood*
    14th November 1876
    Resigned

Henry B. O'Donoghue   Signature of the Clerk
Elizabeth Tooley   Signature of the Person appointed as Nurse

Reported to the Local Government Board for their approval
sixth day of February 1877

TNA ref. MH 12/13433 Nuneaton Union, Warwickshire

Appointment of Collector

1. State the name of the Person appointed as Collector   *John Scrivener*
2. His Place of Residence   *Chilvers Coton*
3. His Age   *Twenty four years*
4. State the Name of the Parish or District for which he is appointed   *Nuneaton*

5. State his previous Occupation, Profession or Callings *Rope Manufacturer*
Whether he has been in the Army, Navy, Excise, Police, or other Public Service, and if so, which service, the cause of his leaving the same, and the period since which he so left *No*
Whether he has kept a Public House, and if so, when *No*
Whether he has before held any Union or Parochial Office, and what *No*
6. Has he ever been Bankrupt or Insolvent? and if so, when? *No*
7. Does he continue in any previous occupation, profession, or calling? *No*
8. Has he a competent knowledge of Accounts? *Yes*
9. State the date from which his duties commence *Immediately*
10. State the amount of remuneration proposed:– (Whether a Poundage is allowed, and the amount) *Poundage after the rate of 7s in the £ for sum not exceeding £10 and 4s in the £ for all large sums*
11. State the nature and amount of the security proposed to be given and the names and addresses of the parties becoming Security *Bound himself and two Sureties in £300 Joseph Scrivener the elder of Nuneaton in the County of Warwick, Rope Manufacturer and Thomas Weston of Bedworth in the said County of Warwick, maltster*
12. Are the Guardians satisfied that he is competent to fulfil the office of Collector, and to perform efficiently the duties required *Yes*
13. State the cause of the Vacancy on account of which the Appointment is made; if a Resignation, state the cause of such Resignation *Resignation caused by Insolvency and a deficiency by a former Collector of Rates*
14. State the authority under which the Appointment is made *Under an order of the Poor Law Commissioners dated 20th April 1846*

John Estlin	Signature of the Clerk
John Scriviner [sic]	Signature of the Officer appointed
Reported to the Poor Law Commissioners	*6th* day of *May* 1846

TNA ref. MH 12/1678 Nantwich Union, Cheshire

Appointment of Schoolmaster

1. State the Christian Name and Surname of the person appointed as Schoolmaster of the Workhouse in full *Thomas Griffiths*
2. His place of Residence immediately previous to his appointment *Burleydam near Nantwich*
3. His Age *21 years*
4. Whether he is Married, and has any, and what children dependent on him *Not married*
5. His Religious Persuasion *Church of England*
6. State his previous Occupations, Professions, or Callings *Schoolmaster*
Whether he has been in the Army, Navy Excise, Police, or other Public Service, And if so, which Service *No*

The cause of him leaving same ——————
And date when he left ——————
7. State whether he has before held any Office in any Union or Parish; and if So, what Office, and in what Union or Parish   *No*
The cause of leaving ——————
And the date he left ——————
8. State whether he has had any Experience in Teaching, or any Training for it; and if so, what   *5 years apprenticeship as a pupil teacher and 1¼ years subsequent experience as master of a mixed annexed school belonging to Lord and Lady Combermere*
9. Whether his whole time is given up to the Service of the Union   *Yes*
or
Whether he continues in any other Occupation Profession or Calling
——————
10. State the day on which he was elected by the Guardians, and the date from which his Duties commence   *Elected 10th November*
Duties commence 15th December
11. Whether he is to reside in the Workhouse   *Yes*
12. The amount of Salary proposed   *£30 per annum*
and
Whether Rations or other Emoluments are Allowed; and if so, what
Board and separate apartments in the Workhouse will be provided
13. State what Testimonials the Guardians have received, and whether they are satisfied thereby or otherwise, that the person appointed is competent to fulfil the Office of Schoolmaster of the Workhouse and to perform efficiently the Duties required by Articles 114, and 212 of the Consolidated General Order. *A Testimonial from the Revd. Roger Kent, Incumbent of Burleydam and Chaplain to Lord Viscount Combermere was received with which the Guardians are satisfied*
14. State the cause of the Vacancy on account of which the appointment is made: If a Resignation, state the cause of such Resignation, and the name of the former Officer, and on what day the Resignation took effect.   *The resignation of Mr Thomas Chesters which took effect on the 24th instant. Mr Chester having obtained a better situation*

    J. Broadhurst   Signature of the Clerk
    Thomas Griffiths   Signature of the Officer appointed
Reported to the Poor Law Board for their approval *1st* December 1855

TNA ref. MH 12/10496 Wellington Union, Somerset and Devon
[Appointment of an industrial teacher to replace the teacher who was found to be 'incompetent to discharge her duties'.]

Appointment of Industrial Teacher

1. State the Christian Name and Surname of the person appointed   *Elizabeth Dart*
2. Her place of Residence immediately previous to her appointment   *Milverton*
3. Her Age   *36 years*
4. Whether Married or Single   *married*
5. Whether she has any Children; and if so whether they are dependent on her, and where it is proposed that they shall reside   *4 children but they are not dependent on her*
6. Her previous Occupation or Calling   *Servant*
7. Whether she has before held any office in any Union or Parish; and if so what office and in what Union or Parish   *No*
8. The cause of her leaving the same   ——————
9. The date when she left   ——————
10. Whether her whole time is given up to the service of the Union   *Yes*
11. The day on which she was elected   *15th September 1859*
12. The Date from which her Duties commence   *29th September* [1859]
13. The amount of Salary proposed   *£15 per annum*
14. Whether any Rations or other Emoluments are allowed; and if so what   *7lbs bread, 3½ lbs cooked meat, 2oz tea, ¾lb sugar, ¾ lb butter, 1lb cheese, 3 pints milk, & vegetables. 7 pints of ale or 3 ½ oz. tea per week*
15. Whether the Guardians are satisfied that she is competent to discharge efficiently the Duties required of her   *Yes*
16. The cause of the Vacancy on account of which the appointment is made; if a Resignation or Dismissal the cause thereof, the name of the former Officer, and the day on which the Resignation took effect   *The resignation of Miss Hellier the former schoolmistress who resigned in consequence of Mr Ruddock, Inspector of Schools reporting that she was incompetent to discharge her duties**

Robert A. Were   Signature of the Clerk
Elizabeth Dart   Signature of the Officer appointed

Reported to the Poor Law Board for their approval *6th* day of *Oct* 1859

*   The report and a letter recording Miss Hellier's incompetence is reproduced here:

TNA ref. MH 12/10496 (continued)

Inspection of Parochial Schools
Form No. XXV.
Refusal of Certificate to Teacher
Wellington Parochial Council School

Committee of Council on Education
Council Office, Downing Street, S.W.
20 May 1859

Madam

The Committee of Council on Education have considered the Report of Joshua Ruddock Esq., H.M. Inspector of Parochial Union Schools, respecting your Examination before him on the 8 day of March 1859, and have caused the papers which you wrote on that occasion to be reviewed.

Their Lordships' estimate of your qualifications is stated below.

Qualifications as shewn by the Papers		
	Religious Knowledge	*Fair*
	Spelling	*Moderate*
	Penmanship	*Good*
	Arithmetic	*Failure*
	Grammar	————
	History	————
	Geography	————
Qualifications as reported by H.M Inspector	Reading	*Good*
	Industrial Skill	————
	State of School	*Not Improved*
	Skill as a Teacher	*Failure*

Their Lordships have not been furnished with any means of judging of your proficiency in those subjects of the foregoing list to which no qualifying word is added.

The Committee of Council on Education, on consideration of the above particulars, have been unable to award you a Certificate.

I have the honor to be your obedient servant,
(signed) T.K. Sandford

To Mrs M.P. Hellier
Mistress of the Wellington Parochial Union School

***

Subject Schoolmistress
Wellington Union (Som)   Poor Law Board
R.A. Were Esq.   Whitehall, S.W.
Clerk to the Guardians of the Wellington Union
Somerset   9th June 1859

Sir,

   I am directed by the Poor Law Board to transmit to you the information of the Guardians of the Wellington Union the accompanying extract from a report of H.M. Inspector of Schools upon the occasion of his last visit to the W.H. of that Union.

   Looking to the unfavourable nature of the Report as to the state of the School and as to the qualifications of Miss Hellier to whom the Committee of Council on Education have been unable to award any Certificate for the current year, the Board think it right to state that as the period mentioned in their letter of the 15th Dec last is about to expire they must decline to assent to Miss Hellier's further continuance in the office of Schoolmistress at the W.H.

      I am
         D Secy

***

Appointment Ind[l] Teacher
Wellington Union (Som)   Poor Law Board
R.A.Were   Whitehall (S.W.)
Clerk to the Guardians of the Wellington Union   15 Oct. 1859

Sir,
I am directed by the Poor Law Board to acknowledge the receipt of your letter of the 8th inst. and to inform you that they see no objection to the appointment of Mrs Eliz[th] Dart to the Office of Industrial Teacher at the W.H. of the Wellington Union.

   The Board approve of the payment of a Salary of £15 per annum to Mrs Dart for the performance of the duties of her Office, and in pursuance of the provisions contained in Article 172 of the General Order of the 24th of July, 1847 they now direct that the said annual Salary of £15 shall be paid to her by the Guardians, according to the terms of the Order applicable to the payment of Salaries in force in the Union.

   The Board also assent to the Industrial Teacher being provided with rations and the other allowances assigned to her by the Guardians.

   The B[d] request that at the expiration of 6 months they may be furnished with a report from the Gd[ns] as to whether the arrangement for the education of the children in the W.H. has been found to work satisfactorily.
No report received
16 May '60
Write for Report 30 May 1860

125

TNA ref. MH 12/10505 Wellington Union, Somerset and Devon

Appointment of Porter

1. State the Christian Name and Surname of the person appointed as Porter of the Workhouse in full   *Charles Dealey*
2. His Place of residence immediately previous to his appointment   *Mantle Street, Wellington*
3. His Age   *46 years*
4. Whether Married or Single   *Single*
5. Whether he has any children dependent on him; and, if so, where it is proposed that they shall reside   [blank]
6. His previous Occupation or Calling   *Shoemaker*
   Whether he has been in the Army, Navy, Excise, Police, or other Public Service, and If so, what Service   *Has served 21 years in the Royal Marines*
   The cause of his leaving the same   *Completion of term of service*
   And the date when he left   *2nd July 1880*
7. Whether he has before held any Office in any other Union or Parish; and if so, what office, and in what Union or Parish   *No*
   The cause of his leaving the same
   And the date when he left
8. Whether his whole time is given up to the Service of the Union   *Yes*
9. The day on which he was elected   *24th August 1882*
10. The date from which his Duties commence   *28th August 1882*
11. The amount of Salary proposed   *£21 per annum*
12. Whether he is to have apartments in the Workhouse, or whether there is a Porter's Lodge separate from the Workhouse in Which he will reside   *Apartments in the Workhouse*
13. Whether any Rations or other Emoluments are allowed; and if so, what   *Rations as follows:–*
    ½ lb loaf sugar, 3½ pints milk, 7lbs bread, 5lbs meat, 1lb flour, ½ lb butter, 5ozs tea, and vegetables (ad lib)
14. Whether he agrees to give the Guardians one month's notice previous to resigning his Office, or to forfeit One month's amount of Salary to be deducted therefrom, pursuant to Article 167 of the General Consolidated Order   *Yes*
15. Whether the Guardians are satisfied by his Testimonials, or otherwise, that he is competent to fulfil the Office of Porter of the Workhouse, and to perform efficiently the duties required by Article 214 of the Order   *Yes*
16. The name of the former Officer   *William Hiscock*
    When he ceased to hold office   *14th July 1882*
    And
    From what cause he ceased to hold office   *Death*

Robert A. Were	Signature of Clerk
Charles Dealey	Signature of Officer appointed

Reported to the Local Government Board for their approval *first* day of *September 1882*

TNA ref. MH 12/10225 Bedminster Union, Somerset

Clevedon Sanitary District
Appointment of Inspector of Nuisances
1. State the Christian Name and Surname of the person appointed, in full
   Henry Taylor
2. His proposed place of Residence, and whether it is within the District
   Chapel Hill, Clevedon
   Within the District
3. His Age   *38 years*
4. His previous Occupation or Calling   *Builder, Clerk of Works and Assistant Surveyor on Town Improvements, Sewerage, Roads, &c – Contractors Engineer and Agent*
5. Whether he is to devote his whole time to the duties of the office of Inspector of Nuisances   *No*
   (a) If not, what other occupation he is to be allowed to follow   *Surveyor to the Authority*
   (b) If he is to hold the Office of Surveyor to the Authority, state the amount of the salary to be assigned to him in that capacity   *Salary as Surveyor £85*
6. Whether he has been in the Army, Navy, Excise, Police, or other Public Service; and if so, which Service, the cause of his leaving the same, and the date when he left   *No*
   If he has been in the Police Service, whether he produced to the Sanitary Authority a Certificate of good conduct from the Police Authorities   ———
7. Whether he has held any Parochial Office; and if so, what Office, and whether he continues therein   *No*
8. Whether he has before held any paid Office in any Sanitary District, Union or Parish; and if so what Office, and in what Sanitary District, Union or Parish; the cause of his leaving the same, and the date when he left   *No*
9. Whether he has ever been Bankrupt or Insolvent, or executed an assignment for the benefit of, or entered into a composition with his creditors; and if so when   *Never*
   If Bankrupt, whether he has obtained an Order of Discharge   ———
10. The Date on which he was elected   *First appointed in September 1873*
    Re-appointed in March 1874 – 1875
    – 19 April 1876 and April 1877
11. The Date from which his Duties commence   *25th March 1877*
12. The period for which the Sanitary Authority propose that his employment should be approved by the Board   *One Year*
13. The amount of Salary proposed   *£80*

14. Whether it is intended to apply for any re-payment in respect of the Salary from the Parliamentary Grant   *Yes*
15. The area of the District in acres   *3000*
16. The population of the District   *4000 (last Census)*
17. Whether he agrees to give the Sanitary Authority one Month's Notice, previous to resigning his Office or to forfeit such sum as may be agreed upon as liquidated damages, pursuant to Section 2, Article 3 of the General Order of the 11th November 1872   *Yes*
18. What Testimonials the Sanitary Authority have received; and whether they are satisfied thereby, or otherwise, that he is competent to perform efficiently all the duties of the Office of Inspector of Nuisances   *From Thos Poyser, Chairman of Commissioners, Burton upon Trent. Messrs I & G Tomlinson, Contractors and Surveyors Derby. W. Goddard, Lane End, Iron Acton Works, Longton. John Stone Wigg, Member of Local Board, Tunbridge Wells. Apsley Smith do. Hon F.G. Molyneaux, Chairman do. W. Brentnall, C.E. Tunbridge Wells John Lawson, C.E. Westminster Jas Mansergh, C.E. do*
   The Local Board are satisfied thereby that he is competent to perform the duties of his office.
19. The cause of the Vacancy on account of which the appointment is made   *No vacancy*
   (a)   If a Resignation the cause thereof, and the day on which it took effect

   (b)   The name of the former Officer   *Original appointment for one year. Re-appointed*

   J. Woodford   Signature of the Clerk
   Henry Taylor   Signature of the Officer appointed
Forwarded to the Local Government Board on the *30th* day of *April* 1877

Here insert a copy of the Resolution passed by the Sanitary Authority appointing or re-appointing, as the case may be, the Inspector of Nuisances, and state what Notice was given of the intention to make the appointment.
Extract from Minutes of Meeting held 18th April.
Moved by Mr Lowle, 'That Mr Henry Taylor be re-elected Inspector of Nuisances for the Year ensuing at the salary of £80.'
Seconded by Mr Middle and carried.
No notice given of the intention to make re-appointment.

TNA ref. MH 12/561 Cambridge Union, Cambridgeshire
[Candidates for situation of Relieving Officer.]

Cambridge Union

At a meeting of the Board of Guardians of this Union held at the Board Room in the Union Workhouse on Wednesday the 10th day of July 1839.

Present   Mr Stevenson Chairman
                 and twenty four other Guardians

The Chairman opened the Testimonials of the following persons as candidates for the situation of Relieving Officer for the First District of this Union viz:

		No. of Votes
1.	Edward Brown	2
2.	----- Banham	none
3.	Jeremiah Rushbrook	none
4.	William Rowton	1
5.	John Corbyn	none
6.	John Race	none
7.	Thomas Legge	1
8.	George Willings	none
9.	Thomas Newman	9
10.	----- Saunderson	none
11.	John Edes	12
12.	John Hazell	none

When the Guardians present votes and the numbers were as appear opposite to the respective names of the candidates and in consequence of none of candidates having an actual majority of votes of those Guardians who were present and Mr Edes and Mr Newman having polled greater number of the votes the Guardians proceeded to a second election between those two individuals when these voted.

To Mr Edes	14
Mr Newman	11
Majority for Mr Edes	3

whereupon the Chairman declared Mr Edes to be duly elected Relieving Officer for the First District in this Union subject to the approval of the Poor Law Commission.

J. Deacon Fetch
Clerk

TNA ref. MH 12/13433 Nuneaton Union, Warwickshire
[Appointment of porter and schoolmistress.]

Poor Law Commission Office
Somerset House
1 Jany 1846

Sir,

I am directed by the Poor Law Commissioners to call your attention to the letter which they addressed to you on the 1st September last on the subject of the appmts of Sarah Wright as Schoolmistress and Joseph Rowe as Porter & Miller at the Nuneaton U^n W.H. and I am to state that the Commissioners are desirous of receiving a Report from the Gns as requested in that letter, as to the mode in which these officers have discharged their duties since their appmt.

    I am, &c.,
    E. C. Secretary

Subject: App^{ts} of Porter & Schoolmistress
Nuneaton Union
John Esther Esqr Poor Law Commission Office
Clerk to the Gns   Somerset House
Nuneaton   10 Feb 1846

Sir,

The Poor Law Commissioners acknowledge the receipt of your letter of the 26th ult° in which you inform them that Joseph Rowe, as Porter, and Sarah Wright, as Schoolmistress of the Nuneaton Un W.H. have conducted themselves to the satisfaction of the Bd of Gdns and the W.H. Master, since their appointment to those situations in August last.

    The Com^{rs} desire to state that they sanction finally the appointments of Joseph Rowe as Porter, and Sarah Wright as Schoolmistress at Salaries of £15 per annum each with rations in the W.H. as proposed by the Gdns.

TNA ref. MH 12/11907 Mutford and Lothingland Union, Suffolk
[Deputy appointed to act for the Registrar in case of illness.]

Mutford & Lothingld Union
Lowestoft Parish

Lowestoft, March 19th 1846

I Samuel Braine,* Registrar of the Lowestoft District do, with the approval of the Poor Law Commissioners for England and Wales given and notified to me on the twenty-seventh day of February 1846, hereby appoint Mr John Barber the younger now dwelling at Lowestoft within the aforesaid District, to act as my Deputy, in case of my illness or unavoidable absence.

Witness my hand this nineteenth day of March 1846.

Sam¹ S. Braine*

Registrar

To the Secretary to the Poor Law Commissioners

* It is not clear whether this is Braine or Brame

TNA ref. MH 12/11907 Mutford and Lothingland Union, Suffolk
[List of overseers.]

Extract from the Minutes of the Quarterly Meeting of the Directors and Acting Guardians of the Mutford and Lothingland Incorporation held at Lowestoft on 1st January 1846

'The Committee appointed at the last Quarterly Meeting for taking into consideration the Question of Relieving Officers &c made their Reports thereon and the same having been read it was moved by Mr A Palmer and seconded by Mr Wᵐ Cleveland and the same was received' (that is to say) :-

Name of Parish	Population	Name of Overseer	Salary	Rate per acre	Duties appertaining to the office
Rushmere	134	Jnᵒ Lydamore	not paid	—	Makes & Collects Rates attends the House & Relieves the Poor
Kessingland	676	Chaˢ Cooper	not paid	—	Do (but must have a paid Overseer at £10 per Annum)
Barnby	296	Wᵐ Algar	7–0–0	2d	Ditto
Mutford	422	Wᵐ Keer	7–10–0	1d	Ditto
Gisleham	260	Wᵐ Neave	6–6–0	¾	Ditto
Pakefield	581	Wᵐ Smith	12–0–0	—	Ditto
Kirtley	467	Jaˢ Peek	5–0–0	1d	Ditto
Carlton Covile	800	M.R. Sharman	10–0–0	⅔d	Ditto
Lowestoft	4837	Hʸ Youngman	not paid	—	Does not make or collect the Rate only relieves the Poor. Average Poor about 175. Serves but one Quarter. Permanent Overseer was paid £80.
Oultons	675	Jnᵒ Osborne	8–0–0	1d	Makes & Collects Rates attends the House & Relieves the Poor
Flixton	23	John Bulton	not paid	—	Ditto
Gunton	77	Robᵗ Baldry	not paid	—	Ditto
Corton	464	Robᵗ Read	1–10–0 or 2–0–0	Subs	Does not make the Rate but collects it & attends the Poor
Blundeston	600	John Lines	8–0–0	5 each Qtr	Ditto
Lound	408	John Rudram	8–0–0	2d	Ditto
Somerleyton	514	J.A. Bowler	10–0–0	—	Ditto
Ashby	53	Wᵐ Bachelor	4–8–0	1d	Ditto

[contd]

Herringfleet	200	Wm Newman	2–10–0	Subs	Ditto
Fritton	230	John Sayer	4–0–0	1d	Ditto
Hopton	250	Wm Smith	8–0–0	1/–	To the Duties of Overseer adds that of Surveyor & Constable without further pay
Bradwell	274	C.W. Crow	10–0–0	1¼	Appointed Assistant Overseer by Law
Belton	465	Ja^s Goldspring	10–0–0	1d	To Duties of Overseer adds the Collection of the Church and Surveyors Rates
Burgh Castle	327	Ja^s Crow	10–0–0	2d	To Duties of Overseer adds making & collecting Church & Surveyors Rates
Gorleston	3820	Ja^s Rivett	60–0–0	1½	Pays £21 for having the Rate made & collected. Appointed Assistant Overseer by Law
Great Yarmouth	680	Ditto	13–0–0	—	Relieves Paupers 3 Miles asunder, is able to do the duties of his Office in 2 days

Total Population	17533	207–14–0
Add for Kessingland		10–0–0
		217–14–0
Formerly paid for Lowestoft		80–0–0
		£297–14–0	Total Cost of Overseers under present system

It would seem therefore that the sum now paid by the several Parishes to Overseers amounts to £207–14–0 and as the Overseers of Kessingland stated that they must return to their old plan of paying £10–0–0 to an Overseer and as the Overseer of Lowestoft was of opinion that the duty of Overseer to that Parish could not be properly discharged by a Tradesman only held the Office one Quarter and that a permanent Overseer would do it better, it would appear proper in estimating the comparative costs of Overseers and Relieving Officers to add their Salaries to those now paid and the cost of present System will stand thus.

Now paid	207 – 14 – 0
Kessingland	10 – 0 – 0
Lowestoft	80 – 0 – 0
	£297 – 14 – 0

And estimating the cost of making and collecting the rates alone at one third of whole sum paid we shall have for relieving the Poor under present System £198–9–0.

We are of opinion that two Relieving Officers could efficiently discharge the duties of the Union and that £80 per Annum each, would be an adequate Salary so that the cost of relieving the Poor would not be increased by their Appointment.

That the 11 Parishes of Rushmere, Kessingland, Barnby, Mutford, Gisleham, Pakefield, Kirtley, Carlton, Lowestoft, Oulton and Flixton containing 9171 Souls and the 13 Parishes of Gunton, Corton, Blundeston, Lound, Somerleyton, Ashby, Herringfleet, Fritton, Hopton, Bradwell, Beton, Burgh Castle and Gorleton with Yarmouth containing 8362 Souls would be a fitting division of the Hundred and the Relieving Officer of each should reside as near as practicable to the centre of his division.

(signed)   T.W. Salmon
Wm Tallent
W.H. Maddison

The said Report having been taken into consideration. It was moved by Mr James Barber and seconded by Mr John Hammond. That it being the Opinion of this meeting that the present System of Relieving the Poor through the Overseers of Parishes has been found to work satisfactorily the Appointment of Relieving Officers is unnecessary.

Mr Charles Cooper moved an amendment seconded by Mr Richard Girling that it is the Opinion of the Meeting that it is advisable that Relieving Officers be appointed.

The Amendment was put and negatived by 15 to 4 and the original Motion was then put and carried.

Som. RO ref. D/G/W/8a/8 Wellington Union, Somerset and Devon Minutes of Meetings (1852 to 1853)

page 11   18th March 1852

The following Application was received for the situation of Schoolmistress at this Union Workhouse in the room of Miss Caroline Windsor, resigned.

Miss Katherine Maria Griffin,

The Asylum for the Protection of Young Females,

Tottenham, London

The Board considered that as the Applicant was only 21 years of age she was too young to have the sole charge of children. The Board therefore thought that it would be advisable again to advertise and directed the Clerk to prepare an Advertisement accordingly.

Applications with Testimonials to be forwarded to the Clerk on or before 10 o'clock on the morning of Thursday the 15 day of April next. The Appointment to take place on the following Thursday and those Candidates whose attendance will be required on that day to be written to. The Duties of the School to commence on Thursday the 29 day of April next. The Advertisement to be inserted twice in the *Times*, *Somerset County Herald*, and the *Western Times* newspapers.

This being the day of the Election of Nurse at the Union Workhouse in the room of Mary Herring, resigned, the Clerk informed the Board that he had not received any application whatever for the situation.

Ordered that the Clerk do re-issue the advertisement by hand bills and cause the same to [be] well circulated around the neighbourhood. Applications for the appointment to be forwarded to the Clerk on or before 10 o'clock on the morning of Thursday the 8 day of April next on which day the appointment will be made. Candidates will be expected to be in personal attendance on the morning of that day.

Note: From the correspondence following the above it appears that no one responded to these advertisements. But on 15 April 1852 it records that Eliza Westcott of Wiveliscombe, aged 22 years, was taken on for a trial period of one month.

TNA ref. MH 12/10459 Taunton Union, Somerset and Devon
[Complaint made against an assistant overseer, 1853.]

To the Honorable Poor Law Commissioners
and
The Board of Guardians of the Taunton Union for Somerset and Devon

Taunton Saint James

March 3rd, 1853

Gentlemen,

I have to acknowledge the receipt of a copy of a letter addressed to the Poor Law Commissioners signed James Kelland complaining of the improper and illegal manner in which the business of the Parish has been for some time conducted by me the Assistant Overseer, and charging me in the strongest terms with having grossly neglected my duty in several particulars.

Without referring either to the character of the person alleging their complaints or the animus by which these allegations are made I will at once proceed to answer without any reservation the statements made by the writer of this letter.

It is first complained that a gross neglect of duty was caused by neglecting to give notice of the last audit according to the 33 Section of an Act passed August 9th 1844 Chap 101, whereby the complainant was prevented from inspecting the Accounts and of objecting to everything contained in the same.

I was not compelled to show the complainants the Book in question the Rate Book of the Parish is open to the inspection of any Rate Payer at any reasonable time but the Receipt and payment Book is not open to the inspection of the Rate Payer except at the time of the Auditor's attendance to audit the Accounts.

I have still further to add in respect of this complaint that in order to avoid even any shadow of complaint or want of courtesy, that I allowed the complainant on two occasions to inspect the Book and to take extracts from it. This will, I hope satisfy you that there was no withholding the Book in question.

It is next complained that the sum of 7s/6d was charged by me as having been paid to a Bill Sticker for affixing to the Church and Chapel Doors, notices of Vestry Meetings, List of Constables, List of Jurors, List of Voters, &c &c. I can only say that it is no part of my duty to do this work and that the payment was authorized by the Churchwardens and Overseers and allowed by the Auditor. This charge of course casts a reflection not only upon the Churchwardens and Overseers but also upon the Auditor.

I am next called upon to show why a larger amount was charged by me for the removal of a pauper of the name of Hallett to a Parish in Dorsetshire than was charged for the same journey during the time the complainant was acting as one of the Overseers. This is easily accounted for in this manner. When the journey was performed by the complainant the horse which was hired of Mr Osmond of this town was compelled by the complainant to go the whole journey to Wootton Fitzpaine a distance of 32 miles and back in one day making together 64 miles over a very hilly country, and the horse was a good deal distressed thereby. Consequently when I went to Mr Osmond again to have a horse of him to go the same journey he refused to allow one of his horses to go the entire journey and would only let us have the use of his horse and Phaeton to go as far as Chard. Consequently when we arrived at Chard I had to hire another conveyance from Chard to Wootton Fitzpaine for which the extra 11s/– over and above the amount paid by the complainant during the time he was in office. When the complainant called upon me to see the books I explained to him the cause of this extra charge and yet he says 'There was nothing peculiar in the latter case to call for additional expense'. I may mention that one of your Relieving Officers (Mr Whitwham) accompanied me on this journey and can vouch for the correctness of this statement.

The complainant next says 'I also found that the expenses of the removal of Mary Slocombe to the Parish of Old Cleeve on the 13th day of November last was not entered in the account audited on the 29th day of the same month contrary to the above named Act Sec 33.

Now the absurdity of this charge is at once apparent, for if I were not to charge the expense of the removal I should have to pay the amount myself, but it will be very apparent why the expense of this removal was not to be found in the account which the complainant saw, it will be known that the Accounts of Overseers are made up half yearly, vizt 25th March and 29th September. The removal spoken of took place on the 13th day of November last, consequently the account of the expense cannot be entered into the Book until the 25th March next. The egregious blunder made by Kelland is caused in this way, the Auditor did not attend to examine our accounts for the half year ending 29th September until the 29th of November last, and the complainant imagined the expense attendant upon an order of removal made on the 13th of November must necessarily be included in our account made up to the 29th September previous simply because the Auditor did not happen to come till the 29th of November.

I next come to the more serious part of the charge made, namely that of want of humanity in conducting the removal of the said Mary Slocombe to her Parish. The complainant proceeds to state that on the 13th Nov' last without the knowledge of the Annual Overseer I obtained an Order for removal of Mary Slocombe. This I deny. Mr Willm Goodland, one of the Overseers being acquainted with the fact by me. I here take the opportunity of showing why this poor woman was removed at all, and by whose instigation this removal was effected. A few days before her removal one of the Overseers informed me that a complaint had been made by the very person who now complains of her removal. That I was doing my duty in allowing the pauper in question to remain chargeable to the Parish inasmuch as he had seen her walking about and perfectly able to be removed. It appears that the pauper was seen by Kelland at the door of the pauper's daughter with whom she was living. This very first time the old woman had come down stairs for several months and he immediately went to one of the Overseers (Mr Woolen) and complained of a remissness on my part in not removing her. Immediately upon hearing of it I took a Medical Man to see the pauper and he reported that she was able to be removed. I then gave the pauper's daughter notice that she would be removed to her Parish (this was several days before the removal actually took place and will sufficiently dispose of the statement made by the complainant that I did not give her sufficient notice) and on Saturday the 13th of November I was ready about 1 o'clock to convey the pauper to her Parish. There was a good deal of demur on the part of the daughter and her husband which was the cause of our not leaving till 3 o'clock. I told them that I had only my duty to perform and must do it, and to oblige the pauper I allowed the daughter to accompany the mother. I hired a close carriage for the pauper and paid all attention I possibly could to her wants. We hoped to have reached Old Cleeve about 7 o'clock, which we conceived would not have been late as the pauper stated she had some relatives at that place. The complainant states that I was accompanied by a male friend. I may state that it has always been a practice to take a person with me in removing paupers in order to be able to rebut anything which may be said, and in this case Mr Thomas Hill, confectioner, a respectable Tradesman of this Town accompanied me. The complainant states that we conducted ourselves in a very unfeeling manner by smoking cigars in the Close Vehicle although it may appear by far too trifling to mention, yet to show how entirely devoid of truth this statement of the case is. I may just say that I rode outside the Vehicle the whole of the way with the exception of two or three miles. I have asked Mr Hill to write me a note to satisfy you about the charge of inhumanity which has been made which I attach to this and is as follows.

[The following letter is written in another hand.]

Dear Sir,

I was much astonished upon hearing from you that a complaint has been made by Mr Kelland of a want of humanity in removing a pauper to her parish. I remember your asking me to accompany you to Blue Anchor on Saturday the 13th of November last. We were ready to start between 1 and 2 o'clock but from some cause which I know not we did not leave till between 2 and 3 o'clock. The pauper and her daughter were inside the vehicle and appeared to be and expressed themselves as being very comfortable. The vehicle was hired of Loynes [?] of this town and the horse he sent was unfit for the journey which was the cause of our not arriving in Blue Anchor till soon after 10 o'clock. I remember very well that you rode outside the vehicle nearly all the way. I was smoking a cigar in the vehicle and frequently so and asked if it was at all offensive. The reply from the woman was 'By no means'. I observed that you paid marked attention in every respect far beyond that which I would have expected you to pay to a pauper and I have no hesitation in saying that Mr Kelland was actuated by a very hard spirit in bringing most unfounded charges against you.

You desire me to say whether we have been to Dulverton or not. In answer I can only say that we neither went nor had any idea of going and that every word of Mr Kelland statement is as false as it well can be.

I have much pleasure in being able to exonerate you from this charge and to add my testimony from what I observed to the considerate manner in which you acted on this occasion.

I am dear Sir,

Yours very truly,

Thos Hill

Taunton

1st March 1853

TNA ref. MH 12/15747 Crickhowell Union, Brecknockshire
[Dismissal of a workhouse master and his proposed replacement, 1841.]

At an Extraordinary Meeting of the Board of Guardians held at the Town Hall, Crickhowell pursuant to notice in pursuant of a Requisition given to the Clerk by two Guardians to take into consideration charges to be preferred against the Master of the Workhouse.   [signed] Edward Davies, Clerk

Present	The Chairman
	The Vice Chairman
	Two Ex-officio Guardians
	Nine elected Guardians

A letter from the Clerk was read calling the attention of the Visiting Committee of the Workhouse to reports in circulation relative to the misconduct of the Master of the Workhouse in taking improper liberties with one of the female inmates and for drunkenness and irregularity.

The Visiting Committee reported to the Board that they had made enquiries into the case by examining the girl Mary Thomas. The Matron and the servant girl submitted the following evidence which the Clerk was ordered to copy into the minutes.

Examinations taken before the Visiting Committee at the Workhouse Thursday October 7th 1841.

Mary Thomas Examined.   I am an inmate of the Llangattock Workhouse. I shall have been here six weeks next Saturday. I am the mother of the child I am now nursing. It is illegitimate and is five months old. On Sunday last I was in the Chapel in the Workhouse when Divine Service was being performed. It commenced at three o'clock in the afternoon. My baby began to cry and disturbed the persons in the Chapel when I was told to go out with it. I went out and went into my own room. I had not been there more than two minutes before Mr Allen the Master came after me, the child was then quiet and there was no other person in the room with us. Allen put his arm around my neck and attempted to put his hand under my clothes. I asked him 'What I should do for shoes for my child'. He said 'You shall have shoes if I shall put my hand'. He then kissed me. A woman whose child had also cried in the Chapel came in to us and nothing further took place. He kissed me on the Friday before that and on the following Tuesday he began to play and tickle in my sides when I went for water into the back kitchen, this was in the evening. I took hold of the mop and told him 'If he would not be quiet I would knock him with the leg of the mop'. He said in answer

'I will put a stick in your brush if you will let me'. I said 'No, I wonder that you, a respectable man should want to do such a thing'.

On Friday last I was sent for into the Master's room when I found the Master, Mrs Mainwaring, Mary the servant and her brother Gabriel Price who was employed to repair the men's clothes. Allen asked me what I had to say against him and I told him in their presence in Welch [Welsh] what I have now told you. He did not contradict me or deny anything. He then opened the door and as I was going out he kicked me. He followed me and opened the door of my room which was opposite and close by and told me if I did not hold my tongue I should have another. I have never spoken to him since. I repeated the conversation that passed between Allen and me to the mistress and the servant on the Monday following and I intended to lay a complaint against him for kicking me as soon as I could get out. I am under an order of removal to Merthyr Cynog and my time is up since last Friday week. What I have said is true every word and I am ready to swear to it. The woman who came into the room to us on Sunday afternoon was Mary Griffiths; she left the House this Morning.

The mark of

X

Mary Thomas

Witness Edward Davies

Mary Arnold Examined.   I am the servant employed at the Workhouse. On Monday week I was washing with Mary Thomas when she told me what had taken place between her and Mr Allen on the Sunday before. I was in the Chapel when her baby began to cry and was requested by the Clergyman to ask her to go out, which she did. She said that as soon as she went into her own room Allen followed her and put his arm around her neck and that he attempted to put his hand under her clothes, that she asked him what she should do for shoes for the child and that he said she should have if he should put his hand. That he kissed her, that another woman who had left the chapel because her child had cried entered the room and nothing further passed. I of course did not hear any part of that conversation as I was in the Chapel the whole time. Mr Allen was not there that afternoon during Divine Service.

I was present on Friday last in Mr Allen's room with Mrs Mainwaring and my brother Gabriel when the girl Mary Thomas was called in. Mr Allen asked her what she had to say against him when she repeated what she told me. He did not contradict her. My back was turned to the door when she went out of the room and I did not see him kick her but I heard him say I will kick you out if you will not go out of my room. I have no reason to think that the girl has told me an untruth. She has always behaved very well since she has been in the House.

The mark of

X

Mary Arnold

Witness Edward Davies

Mrs Mainwaring Examined.   I am the Matron of the Workhouse. The first time I heard of Mr Allen's having taken liberties with Mary Thomas was on Monday week. Mary Arnold and Mary Thomas both told me. I was very much vexed at it and Allen noticed it and asked me what was the matter and if he had done anything to offend me. I said to him 'You know [you] are in a particular situation and that we ought to walk very uprightly' he replied 'Out with it then'. I then repeated to him what I had heard respecting his conduct. He thanked me but said nothing more. On Friday morning following we were at breakfast in his room when Mary Thomas was called in by Allen's desire. A conversation took place in which I did not understand. I saw him kick her as she went out of the room.

This day week (Thursday) he went out to market and did not return until one o'clock in the night when Mary Arnold told me he was tipsy. I was in bed and the servant sat up for him. The day of the meeting of the Board of Guardians (last Monday fortnight) he did not return until past ten o'clock at night when he was tipsy. The following day he went out and returned at twelve at night. I saw him. I sat up for him with the servant and he was then tipsy. He was out again the following day (Wednesday) and did not return until twelve o'clock. I saw him and he was tipsy. I told him there must be some alteration or I must leave as I could not stand it. I intended mentioning it to the Chairman of the Board as soon as I should have an opportunity. After the conversation respecting the girl took place he told me that he never intended staying here, that he never had been contented and that he should go to Van Dieman's Land. He never said so before. The girl has always behaved very well and I have no reason to think that she has told me an untruth. I would not have believed the girl if Allen had not acknowledged it.

signed   Mary Ann Mainwaring

Mr Allen was then called before the Committee and informed of the serious charges that were brought against him. The statements were read to him and he was asked what he had to say in his defence, when he fully admitted the truth what the girl had said and also what Mrs Mainwaring had said as to drunkenness and irregularity.

The foregoing statements having been read over by the Chairman to Mary Thomas, Mary Arnold and Mrs Mainwaring the Board was fully satisfied that the charges were clearly proved and Mr Allen having been called before the Board and questioned as to what he had to say in his defence having admitted the facts alleged against him.

It was unanimously agreed that Mr Allen is no longer entitled to the confidence of the Board and that he be this day discharged.

Ordered that the Clerk do transmit a copy of this day's proceedings to the Poor Law Commissioners.

signed   W.H. Bevan   Chairman

By order of the Board

Edward Davies, clerk

Edward Davies Esq
Clerk to the Guardians
Crickhowel

Poor Law Commission Office
Somerset House
15 October 1841

Dismissal of W.H. Master

Sir,

I am directed by the Poor Law Commissioners to acknowledge the receipt of your letter of the 13th instant on the subject of the misconduct of Mr Allen, the Master of the W.H. of the Crickhowel Union and I am to inform you in reference thereto that the Commrs will immediately issue an order dismissing Mr Allen from his office.

With respect to your enquiry on the subject of appointment of Mr Edward Clinton to fill that office, the Commrs desire to state that they have no information respecting Mr Clinton and therefore can give no opinion at present respecting his competency for the office.

The Commrs in general request that the Master and Matron of a Union W.H. should be husband & wife and although they have consented to occasional deviations from this rule they find that the exceptions confirm their opinion of the expediency of an adherence to it.

I am &c
Secy

MH 12/10225 Bedminster Union, Somerset

[Complaint about a workhouse master, 1877.]

Bedminster Union
Board Meetings every Tuesday, at 10.30 a.m.
Henry O'B. O'Donoghue, clerk
Solicitor, Long Ashton, Bristol
5th June 1877

Sir,

I am directed by the Guardians to acknowledge the receipt of your letter of the 15th May which has received their full consideration and they desire to say that the precise grounds of complaint against Mr James Haydon Stone the Master of the Workhouse are as follows: In consequence of which the Guardians are desirous that he should be called upon to resign his office.

His manner is arrogant both to the Guardians and to the Officers of the house and during the time he has been master there have been numerous complaints originating with him against almost every subordinate Officer of the house and in nearly every case there complaints have resulted in the resignation of the Officers some of whom have been replaced more than once.

He has made use of insulting language on several occasions to different Guardians individually.

He has employed the paid workman and paupers in various unnecessary and expensive work using the materials of the Guardians for his own purposes and use in the Workhouse without the knowledge or sanction of the Guardians.

He has given orders to tradesmen for articles for use in the Workhouse at extravagant prices not sanctioned by the Guardians and has altered orders given to tradesmen without the consent or knowledge of the Guardians.

His conduct has been improper in allowing James Baker the late porter to be absent from the workhouse without leave of the Guardians on various occasions.

The frequency of visitors to the Master who come and stay in the Workhouse as his guests remaining some times at night.

The manifest injury to good discipline in the Workhouse where it is well known that the Master has forfeited the good opinion of the Guardians & has been called to resign his office.

From these reasons and under all the circumstances the Guardians trust that your Board will comply with their almost unanimous request that your Board will call upon Mr J.H. Stone for his resignation the Guardians feel very strongly that it will be absolutely impossible for them with anything like proper efficiency to carry on the management of the Workhouse with the present Master.

The Guardians beg me to request they may be furnished with an answer at as early a date as convenient.

I am Sir,
Your obedient Servant,
Henry O'B. O'Donoghue
clerk

The Secretary
Local Government Board
Whitehall

The following notes have been appended to this letter.
9 June 77
I think that this question as to the substantiating of these charges will be best elucidated by requesting the master, according to the usual course, to submit his explanation of them to the Board.
12 June
1. Send copy to the master and request that he will immediately furnish the Board with an explanation of the charges against him.
2. Acknowledge it and state that in accordance with their usual practice the Board have in the final instance written to the Officer requiring him to furnish them with an immediate explanation of the charges.

MH 12/16131 St Asaph Union, Flintshire and Denbighshire
[Claims against a relieving officer, 1841.]

Board of Guardians meet alternate Thursday

Clerk's Address St. Asaph

Date 18 February 1841

Relating to Claims against Thomas Hughes, late Relieving Officer.

Gentlemen,

The Board of Guardians desire to acknowledge the receipt of your Letter marked 460A and dated 19 ultimo, together with a copy of a letter addressed to them by John Jones of Abergele upon the subject of his claim against Thomas Hughes late Relieving Officer and they beg to state that such has been the confused state of Hughes' Accounts that though he was under the necessity of resigning his appointment more than twelve months ago. The Board has only a few weeks since ascertaining how his Balances stood which may be shortly stated thus.

His debts and liabilities to Relieving Officers and Overseers of distant places for relief allowed to paupers residing out of the Union which the Board have in the infancy of its operation, recognised amounts to £139–14–5.

And the Board having come to the resolution of allowing Hughes to charge in his relief List several Items which were found upon the examination of his books to have been omitted a balance of £109–13–0 appeared in his favour for which amount a Cheque has been issued and which by his consent was lodged with the Clerk to be appropriated to the discharge of the above named liabilities, and which he has effected except about £37 of dubious claims which he believes will be settled for about £18 and if this proves correct it will leave in his hands about £8 beyond the liquidation of the whole of the above claims. This is attributable to the fact of his discovering in the settlement with different parties that Hughes had overpaid them in former accounts together with various other errors. But independent of the former liabilities Hughes appears to have contracted debts while acting as Relieving Officer amounting to Two Hundred and Seventeen pounds and fifteen Shillings and ten pence half penny which may be classed as follows.

	£	s	d
For rent reliefs not paid over to owners of Cottage property	21	18	0
Payment by private persons to paupers	11	14	6
Payments by shopkeepers and other traders and goods obtained from them for paupers together with borrowed money &c, &c.	184	3	4½
	£217	15	10½

In the latter Item of £184 odd is included about £20 incurred for Coals an article which from the distance of the Coal yards from the paupers dwellings and other causes there may be (on the part of the Traders) some excuse for the existence of those liabilities. But the Board of Guardians would especially draw attention of the Commissioners to the fact that they do not consider such claims as that of John Jones' in the least deserving their attention inasmuch as the evil of shopkeeping agency which constitutes a principal vice in the old system of Poor Law management in this country early developed its pernicious tendency in the operation of the Unions and compelled the Guardians after the failure of several expedients to avoid the interested interference of Shopkeepers to come to the following resolution on the 22nd November 1838.

'That in case it be discovered that either of the Relieving Officers do give any relief to any paupers by the payment of Shopkeepers or other trades, Ordered That the Amount of such reliefs be deducted from the Accounts of such Officer or otherwise be debited to him.'

And this determination the Board have every reason to believe was so generally known that John Jones could but be aware of though he continued in common with several other interested parties the agent of the Relieving Officer for the sake of the profit to be made from the paupers' pittance. The Board of Guardians would also desire to impress upon the Commissioners that they have neither directly or indirectly authorized the Reliving Officers of the Union to contract debts of any description (save recognising their account current with Relieving Officers and Overseers for relief to Out paupers as before alluded to) but have uniformly entrusted in their hands such ample balances as would enable them at all times to pay ready money for any articles which it was necessary for them to procure in administering relief in kind. The Board begs also to enclose John Jones' Bill of Account as rendered by himself which confirms the view the Board takes of this matter and evidently shews that the debt was not legitimately contracted by Hughes 'in his Capacity of Officer of the Board' for it will be perceived that £5–10–0 thereof is for money lent and £4–17–6 is stated to be for relief to Thomas Evans a person not in receipt of relief from the Board of Guardians but being employed at the time by Hughes (or his family in his private capacity), And against Hughes states that £9–15–6 is the sum total which he owes John Jones which if correct is less than the above two Items while supposing his claim of £13–0–9 to be due to him, only £2–13–3 appears to have been paid to paupers.

The Commissioners will therefore please to observe that much as the Board of Guardians regret the loss incurred by trading parties they would be very unwilling to contribute to the liquidation of such claims as that of John Jones' while they have no assets of Hughes in hand or any other available funds for such a purpose and the Board hopes that some good will result from this otherwise unpleasant affair, as it will tend to check that species of Shopkeeping Agency of which they have so much reason to complain. But as far as it regards the Sums charged by Hughes for Rent and other reliefs and not paid over by him to the owners of Cottage property and in some few instances to Paupers themselves together with claims for coals furnished to paupers upon tickets from him amounting probably to about £40 the Board of Guardians anxiously desire the discharge of.

And they respectfully beg the Commissioners will give their opinion how far they may be justified in paying off these liabilities and require the repayment of the same from Hughes surety whose Bond for due performance of the duties &c the Bond holds and the party is sufficiently responsible for the amount of the penalty, viz £90.

Signed by order of the Board of Guardians

Tho. K. Robins

Clerk to the Union

TNA ref. MH 12/6370 West Derby Union, Lancashire
[Increase in salary for a workhouse midwife.]

West Derby Union
Clerk, Harris P. Cleaver
14 Clayton Square
Liverpool   18th August 1881

My Lords and Gentlemen

I beg to inform you that at the meeting of the Guardians held yesterday the salary of Hannah Shaw, midwife at the Workhouse at Walton was increased by £5 per annum viz from £25 to £30 per annum, in recognition of her faithful service during her two years of office in the capacity of midwife.

The Guardians had also in view the fact that her duties have materially increased, and they find that a former officer named Sarah Lindsay received a salary of £30 per annum.

I am, my Lords and Gentlemen
Your most obedient servant
Harris P Cleaver
Union Clerk

The Local Government Board

Som. RO ref. D/G/W/8a/29 Wellington Union, Somerset and Devon
Minutes of Meetings of the Board of Guardians, 1897
[Applications for appointment of a porter at the workhouse, and the duties of a nurse.]

17th March 1897

The following applications for the appointment of porter are read:–

W.T. Page	11 Buckwell, Wellington
Fred Hutchings	Pleamore Cross, Wellington
Henry Libby	4 Oakley Terrace, Richmond Road, Taunton
Charles Phillips	1 Long Street, Williton
J. Webber	13 Clarence Street, Taunton
William Harvey	2 Sunny Bank, Cheddon Road, Taunton
William Gibbons	74 Rockwell Green, nr. Wellington
Henry Bradford	7 Victoria Place, High Street, Taunton
George Phillips	The Lift, Ninehead

Resolved that the following Candidates be requested to attend at the next meeting of the Board at twelve o'clock when the appointment will be made.
William Gibbons, Henry Bradford, George Phillips.

Proposed by Mr J. Davey, seconded by the Revd P.P. Broadmead that a salary of £30 per annum be assigned to the appointment of Nurse and the clerk be instructed again

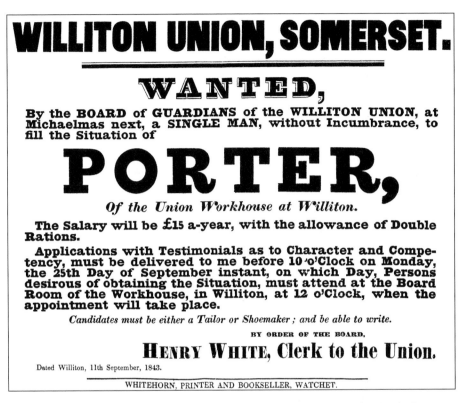

Advertisement for the post of porter at Williton Workhouse, Somerset, dated 11 September 1843. (SANHS Collection)

to advertise for applications from experienced and competent persons at this salary. Such applications to be received at the next meeting of the Board, the appointment to be made on this day four weeks.

8th April 1897

The following Candidates for the appointment of Porter attended before the Board:–

Henry Bradford of 7 Victoria Place, High Street, Taunton

William Gibbons of 74 Rockwell Green, nr Wellington

George Phillips of The Lift, Nynehead

Resolved that Mr William Gibbons be elected Porter at this Union Workhouse at a salary of Twenty pounds per annum, his duties to commence on Monday the 19th day of April.

***

Duties of Nurse

To attend upon the sick in the Sick and Lying-in Wards, and to administer to them all medicines and medical applications according to the directions of the Medical Officer.

To inform the Medical Officer of any defects which may be observed in the arrangements of the sick or Lying-in Ward.

To take care that a light is kept at night in the Sick Ward.

To be responsible for the cleanliness of the patients and the Wards, and see that the body and house linen is regularly changed.

To assist in the distribution of the food at meal times.

To bath and dress all females and young children admitted to the Workhouse and dress out all female Inmates leaving the Workhouse.

To be responsible for the bathing of all female tramps on admission to the Tramp Ward and see them in bed.

To obey the lawfull orders of the Master and Matron and assist them in maintaining the discipline of the House.

TNA ref. MH 68/307 Clutton Union, Somerset
[Resignation of a clerk after more than fifty-one years' service, 1930.]

J. Sumner Dury, clerk

The Union Offices
Temple Cloud, nr Bristol
21st March 1930

Sir,

<u>Clerk's Resignation</u>

I beg to report that I have resigned the office of Clerk to the Clutton Board of Guardians which I have held since May 1895, thus terminating my Poor Law Service of more than 51 years commencing with my appointment at Bristol on 1st November 1878, my resignation taking effect on the thirtieth instant.

Bristol Workhouse had then only two nurses, one of these being past her prime, the Medical Officer came two or three times weekly and the boys were housed in the old prison used for French prisoners of war. I could look out of my sitting room window (I was appointed assistant Schoolmaster without the slightest knowledge of teaching) by standing on a chair and as I was the only assistant, I was actively on duty from 6.30 a.m. until the boys went to sleep in summer about 9 p.m. On rare occasions they went for a walk which was their only opportunity of seeing the world, the wall round their yard being some 20 feet high, but very well fed and clothed.

Being fortunate in getting maximum marks in 8 out of 10 subjects in which I was examined for a Teacher's Certificate, I obtained a certificate (dated 26.1.79) marked 'excellent' against 8 subjects, this entitled me to a grant, most of which was utilised without authority by the 'indoor recipient' (in those days called female pauper) who 'did' my rooms.

After 11 months at Bristol, my Certificate got me a post at the West London Schools, where owing to an inadequate staff, 150 boys were in the lowest standard which was given to me without assistance! My class was seldom below 80, and in my 4th year I passed 100 per cent getting the praise from the Inspector (Mr Holgate), that 'his papers were too easy'.

At these Schools a man (Roberts) who for 6 or 7 years lived in the roof of the dining hall on what food he could appropriate caused much excitement as, during the night, he wandered all over the premises. He was finally discovered during the repair of the roof and got 6 months imprisonment. At this school the children were splendidly fed, clothed, trained in handicraft etc.

From there I went to Bath where owing to horrible neglect, bad food and bad clothes, the boys' hands & feet were simply rotten with chilblains, for their dinner on certain days they had crumbs of cheese left from cutting up the adults' rations, mixed with a good amount of dirt, they wore smocks with little but rags underneath, it was not difficult to improve these conditions although at the expense of some unpleasantness, and the Bath papers made flattering comments on the increased efficiency of the Schools where 100 per cent passed at the annual examination, most of the scholars passing two standards in one year.

Having acquired some knowledge of teaching and knowing nothing whatever of law or accounts, I then became managing Clerk to a Solicitor and Clerk to Clutton Union acting, inter alia, as Deputy Registrar of a County Court. While thus acting, a Chancery Barrister (ignorant of County Court rules) who deputised for Judge Callard, insisted, in spite of my service, in ordering 7 days imprisonment for a witness who neglected to attend, although he had not been served with a subpoena, even had he been, the utmost penalty was a fine! I obeyed the order to enter the judgement but did not exceed instructions by issuing an illegal commitment order.

During my long connection with the officials of the Ministry and its predecessors I have always received the greatest help and assistance from Mr Francis, Mr Turner, Mr Ure, Dr Downes, Dr Rees, Mr Faucett and others at the Central Office, from the Inspectors Lord Courtney, Mr Preston Thomas, Mr Duff and Miss Walton Evans, from the Auditors from Mr Trask (about 1887) Mr Donald Gordon, Mr Lander to Mr Griffiths.

Especially have I been helped during later years when I have had a difficult Board to guide consisting of two diametrically opposed schools of thought in a district gravely distressed by unemployment and where out-door poor increased from 600 to 4600. If I have been a moderating influence, able to assist in preserving harmony and to retain the support of both parties, it has been largely due to the help received from Ministry officials and if I may be permitted to say so, of Mr Francis in particular.

At the first meeting of the Clutton Board I attended (1887) a Relieving Officer (Salmon) reported that unless a certain lady's relief of 1/6d and a loaf was increased to 2/6d she would die as she had absolutely no other income & paid 6d weekly for rent and the Guardians for the parish replied 'Let her die then, she is more good dead than alive.' She had previously maintained herself until nearly 70 years of age hauling coal with a donkey & cart.

I have performed the duties of practically every office under the Poor Law, having actually filled the offices of Clerk, Master, and Schoolmaster. When Master, the Doctor lived 5 miles away and visited about once a week and I often prescribed for colds, indigestion, etc. (there was a stock ward mixture – comforting but harmless). A nurse, who had been a district nurse, moved a sick woman, as she said she could not die under a beam and tied a frog's leg round a young woman's neck to cure epilepsy! I did quite a lot of nursing in those days.

On several occasions when the Chaplain failed I conducted the service and played the organ.

During my half century's service I have tried to do my duty not only in my daily work but at Meetings of the Poor Law Unions Associations of which I am Vice-President, at the Central and other Poor Law Conferences, County Meetings, etc. I trust that in my work I have fulfilled the wishes as well as the Orders of the Central Authority from whom I have always received every help and assistance.

Tempora mutantur et nos mutamur in illis, and that the great change in the personel and system of the Poor Law Administration may prove to be advantageous to the country at large and the poor in particular is the earnest prayer of one who has passed the allotted span of three score years and ten and asks to be allowed to remain.

Always your most obedient servant,

J Sumner Dury

The Secretary
Ministry of Health
Whitehall

CHAPTER 9

CORRESPONDENCE

It is perhaps surprising that paupers were courageous enough to write to the Central Office (the Poor Law Commission or later the Poor Law Board), often complaining about the treatment they had received from their Union authorities. Most of these letters are very well presented and it is likely that they were written by educated people on behalf of the paupers. This is obvious in some cases and the pauper signed at the end of the letter with a cross (X). This chapter includes some examples of these letters, together with letters written from inspectors and clerks of Unions concerning the conduct of staff and the treatment of paupers. Many such letters are found in the correspondence files, document class MH 12, at The National Archives, and transcripts of them may sometimes be found in the minutes of the meetings of the Board of Guardians of the Poor Law Unions, or in their Letter Books.

TNA ref. MH 12/13658 Amesbury Union, Wiltshire
[Help for a deranged old woman, 1837.]

Amesbury Union
R.M.Wilson,   Salisbury Aug 26, 1837
                              Mary Morgan
Gentlemen,
    I have to acknowledge the receipt of your letter of the 10th instant which I have been unable to answer earlier. I find that my letter of the 9th inst. was not strictly correct and I will now give you the facts as I have obtained them from the Relieving Officer and Overseers.
    Mary Morgan, an old woman belonging to the parish of Silchester in the Basingstoke Union [Hampshire] and receiving constant relief from the Guardians of that Union, lived with her daughter in the parish of Winterborne Earls in the Amesbury Union. This daughter was the wife of a labourer and was sent to gaol some time ago for stealing. Whilst she was there Mary Morgan became deranged and cut her throat

with intent to destroy herself. A nurse, proper nourishment and medical relief was immediately obtained for her and information given to the parish officers of Silchester of her situation. By the most unremitting attention her health was restored and she was cured. The parish officer of Winterborne Earls removing her to her own parish as soon as she was able to bear the journey.

The Guardians in affording her necessary relief expended the sum of £2–19–1 and have applied to the Overseers of Silchester for repayment of this money and the Guardians decline sanctioning the same for the reasons detailed in my letter of the 9th instant.

I am Gentlemen
Your Obedient Servt
R.M. Wilson clerk

Aylesbury Union

Poor Law Commission Office
Somerset House
31 Aug. 1837

Case of Mary Morgan a Pauper

Sir,

The Poor Law Commission for England and Wales have to acknowledge the receipt of your Letter of the 26th inst. relative to the refusal of the Guardians of the Basingstoke Union to reimburse the parish of Winterborne Earls the expenses of the Relief given by the guardians of the Amesbury Union in a case of emergency to Mary Morgan a pauper belonging to the Basingstoke Union but resident in Winterborne Earls. The Comm[rs] decline to express their satisfaction at the conduct of the Gdns of the Amesbury Union towards the pauper & they say that the case is one for which there is no remedy, the relief having been ordered by the Gdns of the Basingstoke Union, nor given under an order of removal.

TNA ref. MH 12/13658 Amesbury Union, Wiltshire
[The expense of a pauper's funeral, 1837.]

Amesbury Union
Parish of Wilsford and Lake
Salisbury Nov[r] 16th 1837

Case of Sam[l] Brazier

Sir,

I have forwarded a solemn declaration of Sam[l] Brazier of the above Parish an able bodied male pauper, the expense of the funeral of whose wife was some time since paid by the Parish Officers and on their application to the Relieving Officer to get the same allowed by the Board of Guardians he refused to take the case. It now comes before me as an item in the Overseer's Accounts & as I feel as Auditor some difficulty in deciding whether to allow the charge or not I shall esteem it a particular favor if the Poor Law Commissioners will be good enough to take the subject into consideration and give me their opinion thereon. I have also enclosed a copy of the case & opinion of Mr Merewether procured by the Magistrate who ordered the burial of the deceased.

I am Sir,

Your most Obed Servt

Case

Sam¹ Brazier of the Parish of Wilsford & Lake labourer who had himself a wife & 6 children to support received no Parochial aid but his income was only sufficient, & that barely so to support his family in food & clothing. His wife fell dangerously ill with a Typhus Fever & a Magistrate under the authority of the 54th Sec of the Poor Law Amendment Act ordered Medical Relief from the Surgeon of the Local Union. The wife subsequently died from the fever & an inflammation of the Bowles. The interment as early as possible was absolutely necessary as appears from the following certificate of the Medical Attendant.

'This is to certify that Ann the wife of Sam¹ Brazier has laboured under malignant fever & died from inflammation in the bowels it therefore became necessary to inter her as soon as possible'. signed Charles Pyle

And the Overseer considering the case to come within the words of the above section of the Act as a case of 'Sudden & urgent necessity' (the Husband being destitute of the means to pay the expenses himself) directed that a coffin should be as early as possible provided & the wife interred at the expense of the Parish.

The Overseers considered that he was 'required' to grant such relief on the authority of the above Section of the Act, that such a charge was not at variance with the act or with any Rule of the Commʳˢ but accordant to both in letter and spirit. Read Sections 89 & 98 of the Act & the following Order of Commʳˢ.

'If any Churchwarden or Overseer of the Poor of any Parish or Place in this Union shall in any case of sudden & urgent necessity deem it right that temporary relief to any pauper in Articles of necessity shoᵈ be given out of the Workhouse such Churchwarden or Overseer shall if possible cause the sum to be given by the Relieving Officer for such Parish or Place. But if such Churchwarden or Overseer shall give such relief himself he shall forthwith report the same in writing to such Relieving Officer'.

In this case of 'sudden & urgent necessity' the Overseers expended 18s/– the ordinary allowance of the Board of Guardians for the funeral of a pauper & the facts were made known to the Relieving Officer & the Board.

By the 15th Sec of the Act the Administration of Relief to the Poor is declared to be subject to the direction & control of the Committee who are to make Rules for the purpose but they have no power given them to interfere in any individual case for the purpose of ordering relief.

I am of opinion that this case does not come within the spirit or intention of this Clause nor do the Rules copied in the case apply to it, nor any other of which I am aware or can find in the Commʳˢ Reports. I therefore consider that the Commʳˢ have nothing to do with this matter.

Neither do I find any other part of the act which appears to apply to the subject matter of this case, as it relates only to relief of the Poor & not to such a case as the present.

The 36th Sec uses with respect to the Common Rate for United Parishes the very general Terms 'All expenditure in respect of the Poor' which might apply to such item as this. But it is not stated in the Case whether there is a common Rate for the Union in question or not.

The 52nd Sec. applies only to Relief by money, food or clothing or medicine; & not to the case of a funeral.

The 54th Sec is also confined to Relief & the 56th Sec to Relief given to or on account of the wife & cannot I think be extended to this case; nor the 58th Sec.

The 89th Sec., notwithstanding it refers to all payment &c charged upon the Rates for the Relief of the Poor is still confined to the Provisions of the Act & must therefore I think be limited also to Relief.

There is no objection in this case of any Order of the Justices or Guardians within the 95th Sec. nor any wilful neglect or disobedience of any of the Rules &c within the 98th Section. The omission to give a written report to the Relieving Officer where that person was really not formally informed of the fact cannot be considered as a wilful neglect or disobedience.

It is not stated in the case whether there is an Auditor appointed for this Union under the 46th Sec.; but even if there is I think he would have nothing to do with this Item.

This view of the Act & of the powers of the Commrs I find indirectly confirmed by the 2nd Report of the Comm[rs] for in p122 where there are instances of charges for Funerals allowed as well for Indoor as Outdoor Paupers the former are not carried to the Relief Account but to the Establishment & the others are by a forced implication considered only as Relief. In p536 there is a letter of the Secretary upon the subject which correctly describes this sort of charge as not Relief, but at the same time admits the necessity of the Overseer paying it.

1. I am therefore upon the whole of Opinion that the Board of Guardians have no power to exercise a Judgement upon the Item of Expenditure in question, it not being within the Provisions of the Act.
2. I have in effect answered this question above, for I think this Board of Guardians have nothing to do with the matter.
3. The same answer also applies to the 3rd Section.
4. I am of opinion that the Overseer was under the circumstances bound to inter the corpse as speedily as possible at the expense of the Parish (assuming that the relatives were not capable of doing so), and I think he would have been liable to an Indictment of a serious nature if he had neglected to do so & any fatal consequences would be proveably shewn to have resulted from his neglect.

I do not see from anything stated in the case how the Board of Guardians are to repay the Overseer or from what fund. But I conceive the Overseer is to repay himself & charge it in his accounts & I think no Magistrate will hesitate to allow the Item.

Hen^y Alworth Merewether
Whitehall Place
July 11th 1837

TNA ref. MH 12/10454 Taunton Union, Somerset and Devon
[Confusion over money to be inherited by a pauper from his aunt, 1838.]

To the Poor Law Commission

Gentlemen,

I am directed by the Board of Guardians of this Union to submit for your consideration the following case:–

3 March 1828. Mary Hartnell by her will of this date duly executed and attested after bequeathing as therein mentioned gave to her brother Thos. Hartnell the interest and income of all the residue of her monies, effects and property during his life and at his death give (inter alia) to Thomas Hartnell the younger, son of her said brother fifty pounds. The residue of her effects she gave to her relation Elizabeth Rice and appointed her sole executrix. Thomas Hartnell the legatee for life survived the Testatrix but lately died leaving the said Elizabeth Rice him surviving.

Thomas Hartnell the son is a pauper chargeable to the parish of Halse in this Union and incapable, being an idiot, of giving a discharge to the executrix for his legacy of fifty pounds who retains it and refuses to pay it over until a legal discharge can be obtained.

You will be pleased to advise if, and how, the legacy of fifty pounds can be secured to the Parish Officers to indemnify them costs of the pauper's maintenance who is incapacitated and wholly dependent on the parish for support. If the Parish Officers cannot give a sufficient discharge who is the proper party to do it?

I have the honor to be
Gentlemen
Your Obed^t Servant
John Chorley, Junr
Clerk

24 Feb 1838

***

Appropriation to Parish of Lunatic Pauper's Income

John Chorley, Junr. Esq.
Clerk to the Guardians

Sir,

In reference to your letter dated Feb 24 on the subject of the means of rendering the Lunatic Hartnell's legacy available towards re-imbursing the parish for his support the P.L. Com[rs] for England and Wales desire to state that they know no direct means of attaining that object but the expensive process of an application to the Court of Chancery which in a case like this present appears highly inexplicate. But the Com[rs] see no objection to the Guardians declaring the relief given to the pauper to be a loan, & thus securing to the parish a right of action against his personal representatives, in the event of his death.

Signed &c [sic]

9–3–38

Som. RO ref. D/G/Ta/57/2 Taunton Union, Somerset and Devon
Incoming Correspondence, 1838 to 1839

[Medical officer reporting three of his patients for not following his instructions, and a fourth who was not at home when he called.]

North Curry

Apl. 24 1838

Gentlemen,

I consider it my duty to lay before you the conduct of several of the paupers under my care in this district. I observe their inattention almost daily by which they protract their disorders, impose on me a longer attendance, and of course draw more relief from the rate payers of their parishes. These are not cases of rare occurrence, and I respectfully request you to devise some means to check this evil. Perhaps you would consider it right to order the offending persons to the Workhouse where the Medical regimen could not be neglected. Walter Basket of North Curry who has diseased lungs was ordered to put on a blister Monday week, he had not done so on Sunday last. I have directed Thos Jenkins with ulcerated legs to lay in bed, which he does not comply with. I have directed Roger Beck of Stoke St. Gregory to lay in bed and rest his leg, this is not attended to.

I visited Chas. Wall this day, cold and stormy as it is and notwithstanding he was ordered a blister yesterday which his wife says he put on; he was from home, her excuse was that he was sent for by some farmer near who wanted to see him.

I do not think either of these persons at present able to work.

I remain, Gentlemen

To   Your obedient Servant

The Board of Guardians   Robt Marchant

Taunton Union   Medical Officer 4th District

TNA ref. MH 12/10543 Williton Union, Somerset
[Relief for the family of a mariner, 1841.]

Poor Law Commission Office
Somerset House
26 May 1841

Case of Benjⁿ Chilcott

Sir,

The Poor Law Commissioners acknowledge the Receipt of your Letter of the 19th Instant in which you state to them the particulars of the case of Benjⁿ Chilcott a mariner on board the Guard Ship in Falmouth Harbour having a wife & six children, and you request the sanction of the Com. to an undertaking being given by the Bd of Gd^{ns} of the Williton Union to repay to the Falmouth Union the relief afforded to his family namely three loaves weekly, & the case of the maintenance of one of the children in the Falmouth Workhouse.

I am to state that under the circumstances of this case they are willing to consent that relief should be afforded by the Gd^{ns} of the Williton Union to Benjⁿ Chilcott although residing out of the Union, if the Gd^{ns} sh^d from their enquiry ascertain that the Pauper is settled in one of the parishes of that Union & sh^d then consider such a course desirable.

TNA ref. MH 12/16131 St Asaph Union, Flintshire and Denbighshire
[Dispute over tithes not paid, 1842.]

St. Asaph Union   Denbigh 17th January 1842

Gentlemen,

Some time since the Parish Officers of Abergele forwarded to you a statement of circumstances having reference to the resistance by a John Hughes of Abergele of their claim to the poor's rates charges upon him as the taker or lessee by auction and occupier of the Tithes of several Townships in the Parish of Abergele but the facts being very imperfectly stated it was impossible for you to guide them in regard to the grievance they complained of.

The Tithes of Abergele belong to the Bishop of Saint Asaph as Rector and to The Revd Richard Jackson as Vicar of the Parish. In some Townships the Bishop has the corn and the Vicar the hay; in a few the Bishop has two thirds of the corn and hay and the Vicar the remaining third, and the tithes of some particular districts belong entirely either to one or the other of them. The origin of this arrangement it is unnecessary to observe upon.

It is the practice in Abergele and other parts of North Wales to set the tithes of a Parish by auction subject of course to conditions. The conditions premise the nature of the tithes to be let and that the same were to be let from the 29th of June to the June following and provide for the payment of all Taxes imposed during the year. In cases when the Bishop and Vicar have the corn and hay tithes separately they are let apart. When they own the tithes in different proportions they are let together and each has his separate security for his proportion of the joint letting, and when either party has entire tithes they are let for of course, the benefit of the exclusive owner. On the highest bidder being declared he is considered the taker or lessee and, together with a surety signs a Memorandum to the following effect 'We of &c and C.D. of &c (the latter being surety) have bid for and do take the tithes of the Township of Gwrych at the sum of £60 subject to the foregoing conditions'.

They also sign a promissory note for the sum bid. The memorandum is not usually stamped but the promissory note is. A formal Lease of the tithes is never executed.

On signing the memorandum and promissory note the takers consider themselves to be the Lessees and Occupiers of the tithes for the year commencing the 29th of June and ending the 29th June and act accordingly.

The tithes are generally collected by the takers in kind but sometimes they set to the occupiers of the land they arise from though the latter cases are exceptions to the rule. All rates and taxes have been invariably paid by the takers as tenants for the year, irrespective of the date of the poor rate assessment and even if only a few days from the end of the year, without any claim for a proportion of the rate from their successors under the powers of the 17 Geo. 2 ch 38 sec. 12.

In July 1840 Mr John Hughes took the tithes hay of the Township of Bottegwal Bodwin and in the 'remainder of the Parish' and the Corn tithe of Gwrych, Hendreissa and Abergele for the year commencing the 29th of June 1840 to the 29th June 1841 subject to the usual conditions that the taker should pay all taxes, highway duties and other levies and charges in respect of the said tithes commencing and ending as aforesaid. He signed a memorandum mutatis mutandis [the necessary changes having been made] in the terms of the memorandum above copied and Thomas Williams a surety stands in the place of C.D.

Mr J. Hughes, as had been the previous practice was not called upon to contribute to the last poor's rate charged upon his predecessor, and granted only a few days before his (Hughes') years commenced, under the 17th Geo 2 if applicable.

Mr Hughes has paid all the poor's rates charged in his time up to the 12th day of June 1841; but declines paying more than a proportion of that rate corresponding with his occupation of the tithes to the period elapsing after his occupation and before the next assessment was made upon his successor, the takers under the same circumstances of the tithes, in 1841 claiming the advantage of the 17th Geo. 2.

The disputed assessment is thus headed 'An Assessment for the relief of the poor of the Parish of Abergele in the County of Denbigh and for the purposes chargeable thereon according to Law made this twelfth day of June in the year of our Lord One thousand eight hundred and forty one after the rate of 12 pence in the pound'. This heading is not signed at the foot of it by either the Churchwardens or Overseers, or by any other person nor is the assessment signed at the end by the Parish officers as is usually done after the word 'Assessors' (see vol.4B.J.26 Ed. p131); but the Declaration required by the Commissioners is inserted and duly signed tho' that amounts merely to a certificate of the introduction of certain facts they require to be inserted and does not amount to an assessment of the property referred to.

It is however submitted to your consideration that the requisites to give validity to an assessment under the 43 of Eliz. ch2 are not done away with by the recent enactments or the Commissioners' regulations the latter being merely superadded. The rate thus made has been allowed and published in the usual manner and in those points it is regular. An extract is furnished underneath to show how Mr Hughes was assessed.

Under all the circumstances your advice and opinion is desired for the guidance of the Parish officers on the following points.

1st   Whether the Takers or Lessee entering upon the collection of the tithes in the manner before stated is such an occupation under the written memorandum, for tithes cannot be let verbally as will, under the Laws now [in] force, make him liable to be rated as occupier of the tithes taken by him. The Takers have always been so rated since the tithes have been let by auction.

2nd   Whether the assessment of June 1841, not being signed either under the heading, or, as is more usual under the word Assessors at the end of it, is a valid rate it being regular as respects the allowance and publication? This question is one of great importance and affects many Rates in this part of Wales.

3rd   Whether it is required that the churchwardens and overseers should be together when the Assessment is signed, the making of one being quasi a judicial act? This is also a very important question and is seldom attended to.

4th   Whether, if the rate be valid, must the application of the Overseers to the Magistrates be for a summons against Mr John Hughes for recovery of the rate against him as the party assessed and the overseers legally obtain the warrant of two Magistrates to levy the amount wholly from him or are they bound to enter into the question between Mr J. Hughes and his succeeding occupier of the tithes before a warrant is issued or is the latter question to be a matter of the decision of the magistrates upon the application of Mr J. Hughes for relief as against his succeeding taker or lessee without reference to the Parish Officers?

I have the honor to be

Gentlemen

Your most obedient Servant

T. Edwards

To The Poor Law Commissioners for England and Wales
London

TNA ref. MH 12/3480 Epping Union, Essex
[A clever pauper boy, inmate of a workhouse, to be trained as a schoolmaster, 1845.]

Bury St. Edmunds
9th June 1845

Gentlemen,

Having an official visit to the Epping Workhouse which I paid on the 9th of May instant and whilst giving my attention to the Boys School, I was surprised to hear a little boy of the name of William Evans, who was born in 1838 but unhappily out of wedlock, in Epping Workhouse, where he has ever since remained, his mother having died in it. I was surprised I observed to hear him, when it came to his turn in the class, repeat his verse, a verse from the Psalms in the old Testament without a book, and on enquiry I was still more surprised to learn that he rarely required to use a book from the extraordinary power of his memory more particularly in relation to the Psalms, of which he is stated to have committed forty two to memory for his own gratification.

Calling him out of the class I asked him to repeat to me, if he would, the 18th Psalm which the Boys were then just beginning to read and not only did he at once repeat this psalm of fifty one verses, without the slightest hesitation and without omitting or adding a syllable, but he did not fail to mark by the proper pauses, the occurrence of every stop, and to annunciate every word, (with some pronunciation of accent certainly) but with the most correct emphasis.

On further enquiry I was assured that the rapidity with which he committed portions of Holy Writ to memory was fully equalled by the tenacity of that memory in respect of whatever it had once mastered.

I may also remark that all of knowledge which this child of seven years old has acquired, is referable chiefly if not exclusively, to his own will & exertions. Also till very recently the educational arrangements of the Epping Workhouse have been the reverse of effective.

So greatly gifted a child ought not, I strongly feel to remain dependent for the development of the remarkable faculties which Divine Providence has bestowed upon him, upon an imperfect Workhouse education.

I have therefore prepared a Memorandum (worded sincerely to this report) which I shall shortly address to influential persons in the hope that some one possessed of School patronage and more particularly some Governor of Christs Hospital may thereby be inclined to employ that patronage in opening for such a boy the prospect of a career of much usefulness, perhaps of high distinction is his generation.

In the meanwhile I have taken certain steps which the annexed correspondence with the Epping Board will explain, and I now submit this correspondence for the information and approval of the Commissioners, since although the 6th exception to article 3 of the Probationary order will, as I apprehend, allow of the boy's education at Aubin's without the consent of the Commissioners under Article 6 being first obtained, it would be much more satisfactory both to the Guardians and myself to know that the proposed arrangement has your concurrence.

I heard yesterday that Mr Aubin would receive the boy at 5/– per week, but (in consequence as he states of the District schools) not as an apprentice monitor.

Probably this will not much signify at present, but I shall inform myself why Mr Kay-Shuttleworth's original suggestion cannot now be carried into effect, as I do not understand what the district schools have to do with a boy being an apprentice monitor.

> I have the honor to be,
> Gentlemen,
> Your most obedient Serv[t]
> John Walsham

Copy letter from Sir John Walsham to the Chairman of the Epping Union (respecting the education of William Evans) alluded to in the above report.

Beccles 26th May 1845

My dear Mr Philby,

I have not forgotten since I had the pleasure of going over Epping Workhouse with you to consider how the great faculties with which the little boy William Evans appears to be gifted, could be developed, and I have been in correspondence with Mr Kay-Shuttleworth, the Secretary to the Educational Committee of the Privy Council on the subject who strongly advises that the boy should be sent to Aubin's establishment at Norwood as an apprentice monitor, thence to a normal school to have his education as a Schoolmaster completed.

I take great interest in the well being of this extraordinary little fellow and am prepared, with the concurrence of the Guardians, to show that interest practically by seeing to his being admitted into Aubin's school & receiving attention from the Head Master & Chaplain, & also by eventually contributing some proportion of the sum which may be necessary to give him a years training at a Normal School.

But the expense to the parish of Epping of maintaining William Evans for the ensuing 6 or 7 years at Aubin's will of course considerably exceed that of maintaining him at Epping Workhouse. It will amount in part to 5/– or 6/– a week.

There are however two reasons which I hope & believe will induce the Guardians, & especially those interested in Epping parish, to overlook in this remarkable case the extra cost involved in giving the boy a superior education, viz:–

1st   That the improvement of so wonderful a gift which may be safely anticipated from efficient training might be productive not only of great advantage to the lad himself, but also to Society of which he would probably thus become, under providence, a most useful member.

2nd   That such efficient training until he was about 15 or 16 would, humanly speaking, place him and any family which he may hereafter have, beyond the reach of pauperism, whilst if he should continue in the Workhouse we must look to the chance of his growing up into a mere labourer who and whose children may be continually chargeable to the parish.

I am endeavouring, and shall endeavour to effect some better arrangement as well for the child himself, as for the parish, by getting him for instance, if possible, into Christ's Hospital, but as this is of course very difficult and uncertain I am more anxious to obtain through yourself the consent of your Board to my opening and completing a negotiation with Mr Aubin for the admission of William Evans as an apprentice Monitor at a cost not exceeding 6/– per week. I feel certain they will not have cause to regret putting their hands to so good a work.

I am &c

Copy reply from Epping Board to the
foregoing letter from Sir John Walsham   Epping 31ˢᵗ May 1845

Dear Sir,

Mr Philby introduced to the Board yesterday your letter to him of the 27ᵗʰ instant relative to the little Prodigy William Evans, an inmate of the Union Workhouse and the Guardians present fully concurring in your views, with one voice consented to the proposed allowance of a weekly sum not exceeding 6/– per week, the mode of paying and applying which you will have the Guardians to point out hereafter.

The Guardians presume that your letter to them will justify the Proceeding and that under the circumstances they are not likely to incur the Risqué of Cousure from the Commissioners.

I am also desired to say that the Guardians have great pleasure in assisting you thus far and they feel highly gratified that you take so warm an interest in the Boys Welfare.

I am Sir,
Your most obedᵗ Servᵗ
John Windus

TNA ref. MH 12/10457 Taunton Union, Somerset and Devon
[A petition from a poor starving couple, now in Scotland, 1847.]

23ʳᵈ February 1847

To the Right Honourable Lord John Russell Prime Minister of England
My Lord,

This is the petition of a poor aged starving couple the male petitioner more than seventy years of age and the female seventy four, and both utterly unable to maintain themselves by the labour of their hands. Your petitioners went to the parish of Bishops Lydeard in the county of Somerset in the year 1802. There the petitioner pursued the business of a Plumber, Glazier and Painter in premises rented from the late Sir John and the present Sir Thomas Lethbridge till 1840 paying church rates and King's rates and Poor during the whole period of thirty eight years. During the petitioner's residence in Bishops Lydeard he brought up a family of twelve children three of whom died in infancy, but the remaining nine reached the age of maturity. But it pleases God to take his only son and three of his daughters after a long and lingering illness the expenses of which conjoined with an inability to labour, the result of disease produced by the evil influence of Lead compelled him to relinquish the exercise of his trade and become dependant on his remaining children. As two of his daughters were married and settled in Edinburgh he resolved to proceed thither with his three youngest daughters. On his arrival in Scotland one of his daughters returned while the other two proceeded to Stirling and commenced business as Dressmakers and Milliners and there by unremitting industry supported their parents till the year 1845. But in that year your petitioner's youngest daughter was afflicted with a grievous illness and finding that we should soon want bread at my request the minister of the Episcopal church in Stirling wrote to the Reverend Cecil Smith, one of the Magistrates of Bishops Lydeard an account of our sore distress and to beg some relief from the parish which I had been so long a resident. This appeal was successful and the Inspector of Poor in Stirling was authorised to pay us four shillings and sixpence a week, and on the fourth of August we received the first weekly payment. On the 11th of January of the following year my daughter died, and the health of my remaining daughter being much injured by over fatigue and exertion she was compelled to resign her business and to enter into service also. Thus my Lords your petitioners at their very advanced age were left alone to struggle with the world. At this juncture a gentleman offered us the charge of one of his Park lodges; this we accepted depending on our weekly stipend for our subsistence. But in the month of November of this year we received intimation that our stipend was to be discontinued and thus was our only means of living cut off, for our children however willing to assist us have not the means. My daughter wrote to the Reverend Cecil Smith, and the enclosed note was his answer. Now, My Lord our age and health, even had we the means would effectually prevent us from undertaking the long and fatiguing journey therein proposed. My Lord it is a bold step in a poor old man like myself to address a personage so lofty in station as yourself, but I humbly trust that in consideration of our starving condition you will be pleased to order an inquiry to be made, and our case to be referred to the Poor Law Commissioners. Any information respecting us may be obtained from the Rev[d] Cecil Smith. In the hope that your Lordship will be pleased to cause something to be done for us.

I have the honour to remain,

Your Lordship's very humble petitioner

Samuel Burdge (signed)

Hillside Lodge, Aberdeen, Fifeshire

appended:–

Petition of a poor starving couple Samuel Burge and Sophia Burge now in Scotland.

    Cannot help/against the law

    Can they return to their original parish?

TNA ref. MH 12/10493 Wellington Union, Somerset and Devon

[A pauper woman who has been deserted by her husband, 1851.]

Case   30 May 1851

A pauper by the name of Ann Holland at present an inmate of the Wellington Union Workhouse, was about the year 1833 married to a man called James Holland at Christchurch in the County of Hants. After their marriage they resided in Portsmouth until the latter part of the year 1834 or the beginning of 1835. They then removed from Portsmouth and resided in the parish of Clayhidon [Devonshire] in this Union for a few months only. From Clayhidon they removed to Swansea in Wales where they resided until the year 1843. From Swansea they again removed to the parish of Clayhidon aforesaid where they continued to reside until the year 1847 when the pauper Ann Holland was deserted by her husband. She has not seen or heard anything respecting him since that time. She is 40 years of age and is now chargeable to the parish of Clayhidon.

The Board of Guardians of the Union wish therefore to know whether under these circumstances they can entertain the application for charging her Relief to the Common Charge Fund without proof of the Husband's death.

H^y George Moysey
Chairman
Ja^s Blackmore
Guardian of the parish of Clayhidon

Poor Law Board
Somerset House
17 June 1851

To Wellington Union
R.A. Were Esq.,
Clerk to the Guardians

Sir,

I am directed by the Poor Law Board to acknowledge the receipt of your letter of the 30th ulto forwarding by direction of the Guardians of Wellington Union a joint statement under the 11 & 12 Vict. C.110 S4 of the case of the pauper Ann Holland.

The Board desire now to state that as the husband of this woman has been known to be living till within the last four years there is no legal presumption of his death, and they consider that the pauper is removable and consequently not chargeable to the Common Fund of the Union.

TNA ref. MH 12/10214 Bedminster Union, Somerset
[A woman receiving relief is questioned about her origin, 1853.]

Snook Margaret* 74 years of age, widow of Thomas Snook, he died five years since. I have lived in the Parish of Bedminster since 1818 and never out of the Parish of Bedminster, never rented at £10 per annum or paid taxes, my husband was born as I have heard and believe at Kilmardon [Kilmersdon] near Frome. I was born as I have heard and believe at Chapple Lizard [Chapelizod] about three miles from Dublin. When I can first remember I was living there with my parent [sic] and I never left that place until I was married to my husband in Galway and I was then nearly thirty years of age. Myself or husband have never done any act to gain a Settlement in Bedminster.

Margaret Snook
X
her mark

Witness B.J. Room

***

Another statement follows later:–

Margaret Snook*, 74. Widow of Thomas Snook.

I have lived in Bedminster Parish since 1818 when my husband was one of the Watchmen in the New Gaol & continued so for about 18 years, during that time living as servant to Mr Humphries the Governor at his Farm on the New Cut, he then worked for Mr Hill, Shipbuilder & lived in Apartments at Hanover Place till he died about 5 years ago. My husband was born in Kilmarton, [Kilmersdon] Somerset. I have not received pay since his death in March 1848. We never rented a house in Bedminster during all the above time.

Margaret Snook   X   her mark

I certify that the foregoing is a true statement of the Grounds of Irremovability of the above Pauper so far as I have been able to ascertain the facts.

Dated this 29th day of August 1853

Benjⁿ John Room, Relieving Officer

Gone to Redcliffe

* Ancestor of the author

Som. RO ref. D/G/W/8a/8 Wellington Union, Somerset and Devon
Minutes of the meetings of the Board of Guardians, 1852 to 1853
[The mother of three idiots requests help.]

Tiverton Union   Cruwys Morechard
Aug. 3rd 1853

My Lords & Gentⁿ,

I humbly pray that you will pardon a poor unhappy woman. I am the unfortunate mother of three idiots, me eldest daughter 37, the second daughter 35, my son 22, my husband 75 and myself 63 years of age.

We formerly rented land the amount of nearly £200 per annum in the Parish of Wiveliscombe in the County of Somerset, business failed, we became reduced and were obliged to seek means for a support. In the year 1840 we removed to the Parish of Cruwys Morechard, County of Devon, where my husband laboured in Husbandry, and myself in a School, and here we have remained to the present time. The few pounds we had were expended, and we were obliged to apply to the parish of Wiveliscombe for support for our afflicted family. I have received 2^s/6^d per week for each of them several years but I cannot keep them any longer with that sum, they have such enormous appetites. After 3 years settlement became a law, the parish of Wiveliscombe stopped all relief to my family. An order was made for our Removal. We objected to being removed as we had never asked for any relief for myself or my husband. For the last five years my husband has been as helpless as a child. I have supported him entirely with keeping the Parish School under the Reverend G.T. Cruwys, Rector of the Parish.

It would greatly relieve my mind if you will be pleased to commiserate my distress and inform me if we are liable to be removed from this or any other parish or if we may gain a settlement like other people and if our afflicted family will continue on the parish of Wiveliscombe.

Eliza Wood

P.S. I should have said after the Order of Removal was made, the parish of Wiveliscombe again relieved my family as before.
To the Poor Law Board

The Poor Law Board answered stating, 'they will make enquiry into the circumstances of your case.'

There follows a transcript of a letter from the Tiverton Union dated 23rd August 1853, which states that, Eliza Wood, schoolmistress, has a salary of £16 per annum only with a small fee from each child, amounting to the aggregate of about 1s/6d per week in addition out of which she says £5 per annum for rent. Recommend that the Wellington Board allow 3s/– per week to each of the idiot children.
This was agreed by the Wellington Union.

TNA ref. MH 12/5320 Sevenoaks Union, Kent
[Application by a relieving officer for an increase in salary, 1854.]

Sevenoaks Union
Thomas Carnell clerk   3rd February 1854

Gentlemen,
I am directed by the Guardians of the Sevenoaks Union to communicate to you that having received an application from Mr Jno Wallis the Relieving Officer of the Penshurst District for an increase of his present salary of £75 per annum, they proceeded to take the same into consideration at their weekly meeting held yesterday, when it was unanimously resolved (17 Guardians being present) that such salary be increased to £85 per annum being the amount thereof up to the decease of the late Mr William Young and being the same sum as is paid to the other two Relieving Officers of the Union and I am directed to request your sanction thereof.

I have the honor to remain
Gentlemen
Your most obed. ser^t
Thomas Carnell clerk

The Poor Law Board

TNA ref. MH 12/10459 Taunton Union, Somerset and Devon
[A man who has escaped on the journey to the workhouse, leaving his family.]

Taunton Union   28ᵗʰ July 1854
John Palmer, labourer, has resided in the parish of Durston in the Taunton Union for about 18 years. He married a woman belonging to Durston about 10 or 12 years ago and the issue of such marriage is 7 children, he has lately fallen destitute, unable to maintain his wife & family, and as he was & is an able bodied man he was offered the workhouse which he accepted. An order for which he obtained and started with his wife and family accompanied by the Overseer towards the Union-house. On the road he managed to escape and the wife & children were admitted under the impression that he was coming, however he was ultimately discovered in Wales & brought back, and it has since been found out that he belongs to East Budleigh or Budleigh Salterton in the county of Devon. He has again obtained an order for the Workhouse & was sent there with his wife & family and the Guardian of Durston has applied to the Board to have him fixed on the common fund & the Board were of opinion that the Commissioners should be applied to on the case.

F.W. Fouracre
Guardian
Durston

TNA ref. MH 12/10494 Wellington Union, Somerset and Devon
[Enquiries into the complaint by a woman about the medical officer not attending her sister, 1854. (Includes some details of another complaint about a male pauper who died whilst awaiting a visit from the medical officer.)]

Minutes of Inquiry and Evidence heard and taken in the cases of Ann Blackmore and John Greenslade on Thursday the 7ᵗʰ day of Decʳ 1854.
Immediately in receipt of Mr Pulman's letter of the 5th December 1854.

The Board consider it advisable that before entering upon an inquiry respecting the two cases above complained of, Mr William Reynolds in whose district the Parish of Wellington is situate, and Mary Hawkins* the sister of Ann Blackmore, should be requested to attend before them.

Mr Reynolds being now in attendance, and Mary Hawkins not being yet arrived, the Board first proceeded with the case of John Greenslade.

Mr Dawe Relieving Officer states as follows, 'I gave an order on Thursday last the 30th November for the attendance of Mr Reynolds the District Medical Officer on John Greenslade a pauper aged 70 years, residing at Westford within the Parish of Wellington. The pauper had been under Mr Reynolds care for some time. Mr Reynolds requires the Medical Orders to be renewed every three or four months altho' the patients may not be worse. Did not attend the pauper after giving the order as he was not aware that the pauper was worse than usual.'

* Mary Hawkins is related to the author

Mr William Reynolds states as follows:– 'When the Medical Order was brought to me I received a message from the party who brought it to request that some medicine might be sent to the pauper and that I would call to see him the first time I passed that way. The first urgent message I received was on Saturday last the 2nd December instant. I then was attending a woman called Withyman in her confinement and could not go myself. I however sent my assistant with the usual remedies for Chronic Cough from which the pauper had been suffering for a long time past. On Sunday last between 10 and 11 o'clock in the morning I received a message to say he was no better. I then went to see him and found that he had died about five minutes before I reached his house. I arrived at his house about a quarter past 11 o'clock on that morning, the friends of the deceased expressed themselves sorry that I had not seen him sooner, but were satisfied nothing more could have been done, and that he was worn out. I knew the deceased well and had often attended him. It depends on the message left with a Medical Order whether I call on the patient at once, even if it be a new patient or not. My assistant did not consider the case particularly bad on Saturday when he visited the deceased and gave him ammonia and pectorals, the usual remedies for a complaint of that nature.'

The Board then proceeded with the case of Ann Blackmore.

Mary Hawkins states as follows 'I am a sister of Ann Blackmore. On Monday the 27th November ulto I called at Mr Reynolds' Surgery and saw his assistant, told him that my sister was very ill. I am certain that for the last two months she has not had any attendance or medicine. On Monday the 27th I had some medicine for her, went again to the Surgery on Tuesday (the following day) and saw both Mr Reynolds and his Assistant. Mr Reynolds gave me some different medicine. I did not particularly press Mr Reynolds to call because I knew he was out on a bad case of labour. On Thursday following I sent again to say my sister was worse, more medicine was sent with a promise to call. On Friday I went again and in the afternoon Mr Reynolds called. On Saturday morning I did not think my sister would have lived through the day. Mr Reynolds visited her again on that day and also on Sunday. I told Mr Reynolds' Assistant when I called on Friday afternoon that I thought it very wrong I had not seen Mr Reynolds to speak to him, but I told Mr Reynolds Assistant that my sister might have died for ought they cared. That his Assistant replied that Mr Reynolds had been very much engaged but would no doubt call in the course of the day. The neglect has been talked of to me by Mrs Lock with whom my sister lives.'

Mr Reynolds states as follows:– 'I know nothing of the call of Mary Hawkins on the 27th Nov[r] as stated by her. On the 28th Nov. received a Medical Order to attend Ann Blackmore, said I would call and see her next day. On Tuesday night the whole of Wednesday and Thursday engaged with a woman at Sampford Arundel in a very bad confinement on the last day was obliged to have further assistance from Mr Bridge. On Friday I visited Ann Blackmore and found she was going on very well. I sent her medicine as being an old patient. She was suffering from a cold on the chest.

***

Wellington Union

Wellington, Somerset
22nd December 1854

My Lords & Gentlemen,

I am directed by the Board of Guardians of this Union to Acknowledge the receipt of your letter of the 20th instant informing him of the receipt by you of a communication from the Revd W.W. Pulman, vicar of Wellington, enclosing a copy of a letter addressed by him to this Board complaining of the neglect of the Medical Officer of the parish of Wellington to visit the cases of the poor persons therein referred to, and requesting to be furnished with the observations of the Guardians upon the statements therein contained.

In reply thereto the Guardians have directed me to inform you that immediately on the receipt of the Rev^d Mr Pulman's letter, they instituted an enquiry into the cases complained of, and were satisfied from the evidence produced and the explanations offered by the Medical Officer who was present during the enquiry, that there was no occasion for them to carry the matter further.

I beg to remain,
My Lords & Gentlemen
Your most obedient Servt
Robert A. Were
Clerk

26 Dec 54
Ask for any written minutes of the evidence taken and of enquiry entered into & for any written explanation which the Medical Officer has offered or which he may desire to offer upon the case.
The Poor Law Board
Whitehall
London

***

Poor Law Board
Whitehall
2 Jany 1855

R.A. Were Esq.
Clerk to the Guardians of the Wellington Union
Wellington
Somersetshire

Sir,

I am directed by the Poor Law Board to acknowledge the receipt of your Letter of the 22nd ulto relating to the complaint which has been preferred by the Rev W.W. Pulman against one of the District Medical Officers of the Wellington Union.

167

I am directed to request that the Board may be furnished with the written minutes of the evidence taken and of the enquiry entered into by the Guardians together with any written explanation which the Medical Officer may have offered or which he may desire to offer upon the case.

I am

G.C.L.B.

***

Copy letter from William Reynolds

Wellington Jany 8th 1855

My dear Sir,

In reply to your inquiries I have only to request you will state to the Commissioners my belief that Mr Pulman's charge against me arises from a vindictive feeling in consequence of my resenting very insolent behaviour from him about this time last year, since which he has tried to injure me in every way.

Be kind enough to explain to the Commissioners that my partner Mr Bridge was in Bath the first day Blackmore sent for me, the 2nd he was engaged with me at the confinement mentioned in the minutes of the inquiry before the Board of Guardians.

Yours very truly

Wm Reynolds

R.A. Were, Esq.

***

Mr Gulson

10 Jan^y '55

It appears to me that the facts of this case as set forth in Mr Pulman's letter are admitted by Mr Reynolds.

In the case of Ann Blackmore, Mr Reynolds says he received a Medical Order on Tuesday Novr 28th. He admits he did not go to see her that day but promised to go next day. He did not go till Friday.

He says on Tuesday night & all Wednesday and Friday he was engaged with a confinement but this does not account for his not going to see Ann Blackmore on Tuesday, nor for his omission in not sending a fully qualified substitute to visit for him when he was engaged.

In the case of John Greenslade, it appears that the pauper had been under the care of the M.O. some time but as he requires the Medical Orders to be renewed (which seems quite unnecessary unless a sick pauper has recovered) the R. Officer gave another Order on Thursday Novr 30th which was delivered to the Medical Officer the same day by Mrs Greenslade.

The Medical Officer did not visit or send any one to visit till Saturday Decr 2nd when he sent 'a lad' designated by Mr Reynolds as 'my Assistant'.

On Sunday Decr 3rd he went to the pauper's house & found him dead.

I think it will be best to write to Mr Reynolds, setting out these facts, reminding him that it is his duty to visit the sick paupers when he receives a medical order, in the same way as he would visit a private patient, & that when he is so engaged as to render personal attendance impracticable, it is his duty to provide a fully qualified medical substitute & asking if he desires to offer any further explanation, than that given to the Guardians, of which copy has been received.

Jan 22, 55

Write to the M.O. to the effect that the Bd have received a copy of the depositions.
P.S. I should add that on visiting Ann Blackmore again yesterday the woman she lodges with told me that the Parish doctor, though he said she wanted everything that was nourishing, refused to order her anything saying he would wait till he saw whether it relieved her. Her pay I believe is 1s–6d a week & a loaf.
Act & promise attention then to Mr Gulson

2 Dec 54

***

Copy   Drake's Place
                                                        December 5th, 1854

Gentlemen,

I beg to bring before you as Guardians of the Poor the following facts.

Ann Blackmore of Rockwell Green in this Parish, a middle aged woman, tells me that having an attack of inflammation of the lungs she sent her sister Mary Hawkins on Sunday Nov[r] 27th for the Parish doctor: on Tuesday morning the 28th ult. she sent again to him with an order from the relieving Officer, the doctor neither came nor sent to her and she was I am told delirious that night. On Wednesday she was very ill and was not attended, on Thursday I saw her in a great state of suffering and she sent on that day a third time for the Parish doctor who sent her some powders without seeing her. On Friday Dec[r] 1st at 3p.m. I found she had not been visited and after going to the Relieving Officer's house about it I hear she was at last visited on Friday evening by the Parish doctor as likewise on Saturday and Sunday.

Again, I am told by the widow of John Greenslade of Westford in this Parish that her late husband being very ill last week (and upwards of 70 year of age) on Thursday morning last she herself obtained from the Relieving Officer an order for the Parish doctor to attend her husband and took herself to the doctor's house he said he could not come but sent some medicine, the poor man became worse after taking the medicine and continued very ill. On Saturday morning their neighbour Jane Hurley seeing the state they were in went in (she tells me) to Wellington and told the doctor's apprentice how ill the man was. The doctor did not visit him but his apprentice went to see him. On Sunday morning Jane Hurley informs me that her husband John Hurley went in to the Parish doctor and asked him to come out as John Greenslade was dying, on this the doctor ordered him (he says) out of his surgery and at last between 11 and 12 o'clock that morning he goes to see him for the first time, after he was dead. To my knowledge the Parish doctor had been within five minutes walk of him on the Friday & Saturday when visiting Ann Blackmore as before stated.

Now Gentlemen, I have set these facts before you in my duty to my Parish as I know them not to be solitary cases and in conclusion I beg plainly to say (that I do not wish to be uncourteous by you) that if you as their Guardians are content with such care for our paupers as this, I, as Vicar of this Parish and one of the largest ratepayers in it am far from being satisfied with what I must call such cruel neglect of my poor people and unless an efficient medical officer is for the future provided for this Parish I shall send a copy of this letter with an appeal to them for their interference, to the Commissioners at Somerset House.

I have the honour to be Gentlemen,

Yours very faithfully,

W.W. Pulman

The Chairman & Guardians
of the Wellington Union

P.S. I am told I am mistaken in calling the lad sent to visit the Patient an apprentice and that he is not really so.

Also I have requested the Relieving Officer to be ready to corroborate from his books what I have said as to the times parties to whom the orders were given & lastly I have given the Parish doctor notice that I intended bringing his neglect before you today. Thursday morning.

Note: A full transcript of this letter also appears in the minutes of the Board of Guardians of the Wellington Union at Som. RO ref. D/G/W/8a/9, at the meeting of 7 December 1854.

***

Drake's Place

Wellington

Somerset

December 8th 1854

Gentlemen,

Having laid a letter of which the enclosed is a copy before our Board of Guardians and in vain sought from them redress for my poor people for their neglect and the appointment of an efficient medical officer, I must now beg to bring the cases before you and ask if such a disgraceful state of things is to be permitted under the Poor Law as it now stands, and to beg that you will send down an inspector to make a searching and impartial enquiry into the business. I have not heard that one fact stated in this letter could be disproved by the medical man yesterday and yet the board thought fit not even to reprimand their officer though my poor are allowed to die neglected & unvisited.

I have the honour to be

Gentlemen

Your obedient servant

W.W. Pulman. vicar of Wellington

The Right Honble
The Commissioners of the Poor Law Board

P.S. I should add that on visiting Ann Blackmore again yesterday the woman she lodges with told me that the Parish doctor though he said she wanted everything that was nourishing, refused to order her anything saying he would wait till he saw whether to believe her. Her pay I believe is 1^s/6^d a week & a loaf.
9 Dec 54

***

Subject: Conduct of Medical Officer
Wellington Union
Somerset
Robert A. Were Esq.   Poor Law Board
Clerk to the Guardians   Whitehall
                                                        30 Jany 1855

Sir,

   I am directed by the Poor Law Board to acknowledge the receipt of your letter of the 8th Instant with its enclosures relating to the complaint which has been preferred against Mr William Reynolds, one of the Medical Officers of the Wellington Union, of neglect of duty in the cases of Ann Blackmore and John Greenslade.

   The Board desire me to inform you that they will take into their consideration the evidence which was taken by the Guardians on the occasion of the enquiry which they made into this case & that the Board are in communication with Mr Reynolds upon the subject.

                            I am,
                            C. Sy

***

Subject   Conduct of Medical Officer
Wellington (Somerset) Union   Poor Law Board
                                                             Whitehall
                                                        30 Jany 1855

W. Reynolds, Esq.
Medical Officer
Wellington
Somerset

Sir,

   The P.L.B^d have received from the Gdns of the Wellington Union a copy of the depositions of yourself & Mary Hawkins in the case of the pauper Ann Blackmore, & of yourself & Mr Dawe, Relg. Officer, in the case of the pauper John Greenslade, deceased. Also a copy of your letter to the Clerk to the Guardians of the 8th inst.

The Bd. request that you will inform them whether you are desirous of offering any further explanation with regard to these cases, than that given to the Gns, of which a copy has been received of this Bd.

C

Note: No further correspondence has been found on this case.

TNA ref. MH 12/1412 Launceston Union, Cornwall and Devon
[A soldier's wife applies for help, 1856.]

To the R^t Hon. Lord Viscount Cowdrey
My Lord,

Pray pardon the presumption of a Soldier's wife trespassing on your valuable time by humbly requesting your perusal of the following lines, and to afterwards lay them before the Poor Law Commissioners for their advice and orders.

My name My Lord is Maria Matthews, the wife of John Matthews a private in the 97th Reg^t of Foot, and I have a female child aged 5 months which takes up a great deal of my time to nurse. Notwithstanding which, if I had only some small weekly allowance from the Parish I live in, Launceston, Cornwall, I would do my best to maintain myself and infant. I have no pay from my husband, and I was confined in the Union Workhouse here, and I have applied unto the Board of Guardians for some small Aid to help to support us, but that Aid is denied me, but they say (the Guardians) that I may go into the Union Workhouse and remain there, how far that may be correct, for a Soldier's wife to be sent into the Union Workhouse, and her husband serving Her Most Excellent Majesty and his Country I must leave to your superior Judgement.

Should it be considered my Lord by the Poor Law Board, that I am to lay my situation before the R^t Hon. the Secretary of War, if your Lordship will only so far condescend as to inform me such I will do it immediately on the receipt of your letter.

Your Lordship's great condescension in granting your most humble addresser an answer will cause your Lordship's humble servant as in duty bound for your Lordship Health, Peace, and Happiness to ever Pray.

her
Maria   X   Matthews
mark

At   Mrs Polson's
       Fore Street
       Launceston
       Cornwall
       4th Octr 1856

***

Subject: Individual Case

Launceston Union
Maria Matthews
at Mrs Polsons
Fore Street
Launceston

Poor Law Board
Whitehall
8 October 1856

Maria Matthews,

The Poor Law Board direct me to acknowledge the receipt of your letter of the 4th instant and state that it rests with the Guardians of the Union in which you are residing to decide as to the manner in which they will relieve you if you are destitute.

They are unable to interfere for the purpose of ordering relief in any individual case, being expressly prohibited by law from so doing; and they will send a copy of your letter to the Guardians of the Launceston Union for their consideration.

By order of the Board,
R.U.G.
Secretary

***

Launceston Union
Launceston, 11th Octr 1856

Gentlemen,

In answer to your letter of the 8th inst. no. 37500/56 with reference to the case of Maria Matthews I am directed by the Guardians to say that Maria Matthews came & presented herself for admission being near her confinement & stayed there for some little time after then discharging herself, she has not applied to this Board for Out Relief but met the Relieving Officer on his way to the Board & told him she was coming to ask for Relief which application was not brought before the Guardians being irregular since which time nothing has been heard of her. Her husband has not been out of England but at Bristol ever since he left, & she does not bear a good character having had a bastard child before marriage & the Guardians think under such circumstances the House the most fitting place.

I am Gentlemen
Your Most obt Sert
John Dingley
Clerk

***

The Poor Law Board

Subject: Individual Case
Launceston Union   Poor Law Board
Maria Matthews   Whitehall
at Mrs Polsons
Fore Street   17 Octr 1856
Launceston

The Poor Law Board, having communicated with the Guardians of the Launceston Union, and considered your case, direct me to inform you that they do not think that they can interfere further in the matter.

By Order of the Board,
C
Secretary

TNA ref. MH 12/1412 Launceston Union, Cornwall and Devon
[Guardians of a Union request advice from the Poor Law Board about the place of settlement of a pauper.]

Launceston
25th Octr 1854
Gentlemen,
   May I beg the favor of your opinion in the following case.
   Ann Withers, a pauper aged 71 has been residing in this parish about four years and a half but gained no settlement, the Overseers have obtained an Order of Justices to remove her to Saint Thomas Street the place of her birth, the only evidence produced on obtaining the Order was the woman's own statement stating that her mother pointed out the house to her in which she was born there, & the Magistrates accordingly made an Order.
   The Hamlet of Saint Thomas have given Notice of Appeal stating that paupers husband rented a public house in the parish of Lawhitton about the year 1819 and the will of the Landlord (who is dead) states the rent to be £10 per annum & a cash book of the Landlords is still in existence shewing that he (the Landlord) had received £10 a year from Withers for rent, this evidence has been produced & found since the Order was made, it is the opinion of some that the Will & Cash book cannot be produced as evidence in which case the birth settlement is the only one we can set up. Will you oblige by informing me if these documents are evidence, also if the woman's statement as to her birth is sufficient grounds to withstand the appeal as we are desirous of settling the question without an appeal if possible.
I am, Gentlemen,
Your most ob^t Servt
William Cater
Overseer
The Poor Law Board

Subject: Settlement
Launceston Union
Launceston Parish

Mr William Cater
Overseer
Launceston

Poor Law Board
Whitehall
31 Oct[r] 1856

Sir,

I am directed by the Poor Law Board to acknowledge the receipt of your letter of the 25th Instant, and to state that the Board cannot undertake to express any opinion on the points therein submitted, as it will be for the Justices before whom the appeal may come to determine what evidence they will receive.

If however, the opinion of the Board is desired on the question of the pauper's settlement, the case can be submitted to them in a Joint statement under the 14 & 15 Vict.c.105.s12. The statement of which a blank form* is herewith forwarded for your guidance, should contain precise information as to facts, names and dates, and should be signed by the Gdns or the Overseers of the particular Parishes interested in the matter.

* There is no form with this correspondence

TNA ref. MH 12/10495 Wellington Union, Somerset and Devon
[An unqualified assistant to the medical officer has seduced a girl patient and made her pregnant.]

Drake's Place
Wellington
Somerset
July 24th 1856

Gentlemen,

I beg again to draw your attention to our medical officer & his treatment of our poor.

It appears from a statement made on oath on Tuesday last before S. Dobree, Esq. our resident magistrate that Ann Escott is a young woman, aged about 21, a pauper receiving outdoor relief, diseased & a cripple, unable to walk without a crutch; that she was in the habit of attending at Mr Reynold's surgery (which is I understand detached from his house) to undergo a certain surgical operation; that instead of Mr Reynolds himself performing the operation required, his unqualified medical assistant, Sheppard by name, was in the habit of acting there on a certain occasion about 7 or 8 months since he took advantage of the girl after operating for her & she says forced her however that since that she went on certain occasions to the surgery for the same purpose & had intercourse with him again the result of which is that she is now in the family way & near her time. That he left the Town last Saturday & now finding he has ruined & left her (he having by promises induced her to conceal it up to this time) she

175

has made this statement before our magistrate, J. Dobree, Esq. The Priory, Wellington to whom I must refer you in all particulars.

My object in bringing this case before your notice is to ask whether you permit your medical officers (contrary I understand to the practice of the profession) to entrust delicate surgical operations to their young unqualified medical assistants in their absence & to ask whether you do not consider Mr Reynolds in thus acting in some degree responsible for the ruin of this unhappy girl. I think you will agree with me that this is not a case lightly to be passed over & that if the facts already deposed to be on oath are substantiated after the birth of the child, it becomes you to whom is chiefly intrusted the care of our poor, to take some notice of so horrible a case.

Waiting to learn whether such conduct towards our paupers is in your opinion consistent with the duty of your medical officers. I have the honour to be,

Gentlemen

Your obedient servant,

J.W. Pulman

Vicar of Wellington

The Commissioners
The Poor Law Board

26 July '56

I think it will be best to send the substance of this com^n to Mr Reynolds & ask for his observations & at the same time to refer him to his letter of Feb 19th & to the Board's letter of March 3rd last, and enquire whether since the date of his letter (viz Feb 19. 1856) he has allowed any unqualified assistant to act as his substitute.

N.B If after the correspondence which has taken place on the subject, & especially after the Board's letter of March 3rd, Mr Reynolds has allowed an unqualified assistant to act for him in attending upon pauper patients, (as stated by Mr Pulman) he will have committed a serious offence.

TNA ref. MH 12/10460 Taunton Union, Somerset and Devon

[The wife of a marine applies for non-resident relief to remain at her present place where she can obtain some work.]

Taunton Union

My Lords and Gentlemen,

I am directed by the Board of Guardians of this union to report the following case under Art. 6 of the prohibitory order.

William Hayes is a private in the Plymouth Division of Royal Marines, now absent from his wife and family on actual service.

Harriet his wife and four children of the respective ages of 10, 8, 3 and 1 year in consequence of such absence became chargeable to East Stonehouse and were lately removed to the parish of Pitminster by an order of Magistrates.

The wife has applied to be allowed non resident relief and to return to East Stonehouse alleging that she would be better able to provide for the family there, than at Pitminster, as three of her children would be able to attend the regimental school on payment of ½ only per week each. That she would be sure of two days work weekly at 1/– per day and moreover that her relations, viz mother, sister and brothers reside there.

Ordered 2/6 weekly subject to your approval.

I have the honor to be

My Lords and Gentlemen,

Your most obed. servant

John Chorley

clerk

Taunton

12 May 1858

The Poor Law Board

TNA ref. MH 12/12106 Bermondsey Union, Surrey

[A man who complained to the Poor Law Board about his diet in the workhouse is shown to have been in prison on several occasions.]

Bermondsey Workhouse

Feb. 10th 1862

Sir,

I hope you will pardon the liberty I take in addressing you but having been invalided from Her Majesty's Service of Royal Marines for disease of the heart I am unable to get my own living but am compelled to come into the Workhouse and being unable to eate the house diet the Yardsman spoke to the doctor to give me other food which was half pound of bread with butter and a pint of tea night and morning and a pint of rice milk for dinner and although it is far less than the other diet still I was thankful for it but the master seeing about 20 of the men on that diet he has this day spoken to the doctor and although he knows that I am unable to eat the other food he has taken it from me. Sir it is very hard for a man who has fought for his Queen and Country and disabled in his Country Service to be allowed to die for the common nessarys [sic] of life for there is 5 days per week that I only have one meal per day this the doctor knows for the Yardsman has told him of it hoping you will take my case into consideration.

I Remaine your

Humble Servant

George Button

Board of Guardians

Bermondsey, Surrey

20th February 1862

George Button a pauper inmate of the workhouse was placed 31st January last by the medical officer of the Workhouse on middle diet which by his order was discontinued on the 10th instant.

I am desired by Guardians to forward your Board the accompanying statement of the character of the pauper.

Wm Cornwall, clerk

George Button's committal to Prison from this Workhouse

22 January 1848	Refusing to work – 14 days
15 January 1860	Stealing a canvas frock – one month out of the House
19 October 1860	Felony – Stealing a quantity of lead pipe – 4 cal. months
15 July 1861	Felony – Stealing a barrow – Tried at Surrey Sessions – 6 cal. months
	Discharged 14 January 1862

Received the above statement from the Governor of Wandsworth Prison, 16 Feb.1862

A note appended reads: It is for the Board of Guardians to determine what manner particular persons shall be dieted.

TNA ref. MH 12/10497 Wellington Union, Somerset and Devon
[Relief for a family, the father having returned home after working in Cuba.]

Wellington Somerset
June 27th 1862

Gentlemen,

I am directed by the Churchwardens and Overseers of the Parish to submit to you the following case and to solicit the favor of your Opinion whether or not the circumstances understated are such as constitute a Breach of residence and render the Pauper undernamed and his Family removable.

William Brooks is a Miner, and resided as a Housekeeper with his wife and Family for a period of seven years in the Parish of Whitchurch in the County of Devon.

He continued to reside with them until the month of May 1859, when he entered into an engagement with a London Company to go to the Cobre [copper] Mines in Cuba to work for them for a period of three years, and went there accordingly with a fixed intention of returning to his Family at the end of such three years.

He made a provision with the Company for the maintenance of his Wife and Family. The Company were to allow them £5 per month and did do so until as after mentioned. Brooks remained in Cuba until the 25th of September last when he left and returned to England and arrived at Whitchurch on the 17th November last, and joined his Wife and Family who were then residing and had continued to reside from the time of his departure for Cuba in the same house and premises as he had left them in.

Brooks having had a disagreement with the Manager of the Cuban Mine the advances to the Wife and Family of Brooks were stopped in the Month of August 1861, and they became chargeable to the Parish of Whitchurch, which Parish has obtained an Order for the removal of Brooks, his wife and Family to Wellington on the Ground that his engagement in Cuba notwithstanding it was only for a definite period and his intention to return home at the expiration of that period, was a breach of residence in Whitchurch.

Soliciting the favor of an early reply as we have but a few days to give Notice of Appeal.

I beg to remain Gentlemen,

Your most Obedient & Humble Servant,

James Anning

Assistant Overseer

The Poor Law Board
Whitehall, London

***

Mr James Anning,
Assistant Overseer
Wellington
Somerset

Poor Law Board,
Whitehall, S.W.
9 July 1862

Sir,

I am directed by the Poor Law Board to acknowledge the receipt of your Letter of the 27th ultimo, in which you request their opinion as to the removability of pauper named William Brooks.

As the question is one in which two parishes are jointly interested, the Board consider that they cannot with propriety express an opinion on an ex parte statement of the case. The overseers of the two parishes interested may however, if they think fit agree to submit the case to the Board for their decision under the 14 & 15 Vict c 105 and the agreement should contain a full statement of the facts of the case as mutually agreed upon by the overseers of the respective parishes of Whitchurch and Wellington. A form of agreement can be procured from Messrs King & Co. of no. 90 Fleet Street, London, the authorized Publishers to the Board.

Som. RO ref. D/G/W/8a/14 Wellington Union, Somerset and Devon
Minutes of the Board of Guardians

[A woman is passed from Marylebone Workhouse, London, to Wellington, Somerset, having been deserted by her husband.]

39, Dover Street, W
Dec[r] 13th, 1864

Sir,

I beg to submit to you the following circumstances which have recently come under my notice.

A poor woman with four children was passed some weeks ago from Marylebone Workhouse to Wellington, the parish of her husband who had deserted her. The Guardians called this man before them and ordered him to set aside out of his ample wages, some provision for his family. This he obstinately refused to do declaring that 'He would sooner go to jail,' but offering at the same time to take charge of the two eldest children. The wife then proposed that he should pay her fare back to London give her a small sum to start with and taking the two children himself as he had offered to do. On these terms she said that she would trouble him no further. The Guardians accepted this proposal and fixed 50s/– as the husband's contribution with which sum the poor woman returned to London where after some ineffectual attempts to secure a livelihood she finds herself again reduced to distress.

I shall feel greatly obliged by your informing me whether, under such circumstances the Guardians were justified, first in remitting the proper punishment for desertion (a second offence in this case), and secondly in accepting a compromise like that in question so clearly inadequate to secure any permanent benefit to the wife, who in her simplicity, proposed it.

I should be glad also to know if the acceptance of such a compromise, supposing it justifiable has any legal effect in releasing the husband from further liability on account of his Family.

I have the honor &c

(signed) Townshend

***

39 Dover Street, West

December 24th 1864

Wellington Union

Somerset

Sir,

I reply to Mr. Fleming's letter No. 47132A of the 20th inst. I beg to inform you that the Wellington Union referred to in my letter of the 13th inst. is in Somersetshire.

In connection with the same case I now beg to state that the poor woman in question is again reduced to applying for Parish relief. The application however, must necessarily be made to a London Parish, which will, of course, pass her back to Wellington. Now the Law I am informed, makes it a punishable offence in a Pauper to entail expenses of this kind a second time upon his place of settlement and the question naturally presents itself whether in the case referred to in which this expense is a direct consequence of the injudicious compromise sanctioned by the Guardians this law could in any fairness be applied.

I shall feel greatly obliged by your favouring me with a reply to this question as well as to the others before addressed to you at your early convenience.

I have the honor to be Sir,

Your most obedient Servt

(signed) Townshend

To Rt Hon'ble
C.D. Villiers MP

***

Mr Jas. Anning the Assistant Overseer attends at the request of the Board and in answer to their inquiries states as follows:–

That an Order of Removal dated the 29th July 1864 was received by the Overseers of Wellington from the Parish of St. Marylebone for the removal of William Clarke, his wife and 4 children. That he went to London to make the necessary inquiries respecting the Pauper's Settlement and found that he was residing as a butler in a Gentleman's Service at East Barnet. He accordingly went and saw him and informed him of the Order and that he was liable to be apprehended for deserting his family. The pauper said he would immediately go to Wellington see his wife and make arrangements with her. He did so when the wife made a voluntary proposition to this effect that if he would keep the two elder children and give her 50s/– she would not trouble him again. He agreed to it and has up to the present time supported his two children at Wellington. She received from her husband the 50/– & returned to London and he to his Service and that the Pauper told him that the two younger Children were not born in lawful wedlock and were consequently not his.

Resolved that the Clerk be directed to reply to the same and forward the above statement to the Poor Law Board & inform them that the Guardians were entirely unaware of the above arrangement between the Pauper and his wife which appears to have been entirely voluntary.

[Nothing more has been found about this case.]

TNA ref. MH 12/10498 Wellington Union, Somerset and Devon
[Relief for an ex-criminal and his family.]

Wellington Union
Wellington, Somerset
22nd February 1869

My Lords and Gentlemen,

I am directed by the Guardians of this Union to acknowledge the receipt of your letter of the 12th inst. enclosing for any observations they might desire to make thereon, a copy of a letter received by you from Mr F Flood, a Relieving Officer of this Union.

On perusal of the same, the Guardians observe that Mr Flood has failed to state the facts and circumstances attending the case, which they desire me to furnish you with.

The Pauper, Isaac Hawkins, was sometime since convicted of being concerned in a Burglary at Lord Kensington's in this County, and was sentenced to a term of Imprisonment. During his imprisonment the Pauper's wife and three children, who were then residing at Hillfarrance in this Union, became chargeable to this Union, and were received into this Workhouse. On the Pauper's discharge from Prison he removed his wife and children from the House and took them to the Parish of Heathfield which is within the Taunton Union, and adjoins the Parish of Hillfarrance. He then endeavoured to take a Cottage at Hillfarrance but failed in doing so, his character being so well known. Finding himself thwarted in his endeavours to obtain a Cottage in that Parish, instead of endeavouring to obtain one in some other Parish, he threatened that he and his family would go in and out of the Workhouse, two or three times a week for the sake of annoyance. On the twelfth day of January last he accordingly walked with his wife and Family from Hillfarrance (having lodged there the previous night) to Milverton, where Mr Flood the Relieving Officer resides, which is about 4 miles distant, and applied to him for an order for the admission of himself and family into the Workhouse. The Relieving Officer granted him one, when the Pauper said that his wife and family should not walk, but they should be carried to the Workhouse, and threatened to leave them in the streets of Milverton unless they were conveyed there. The Relieving Officer, in order to get rid of him, was induced to give him an Order upon a Mr Bond of Hillfarrance, for the conveyance of the pauper's wife and children from Hillfarrance to the Workhouse on the following day. At the time however, he gave this order, he was aware that the pauper and his family intended to return to Hillfarrance that same evening (which they did) in order that they might be conveyed from there to the Workhouse on the following day. The distance from Milverton to the Workhouse is 4 miles, and from Hillfarrance to the Workhouse 4 miles. The Pauper and his family therefore walked a distance of about 8 miles for an Order to be conveyed the following day, a distance of 4 miles. They might, on receiving the Order of Admission, have gone at once from Milverton to the Workhouse, the distance being about the same, as his return journey to Hillfarrance. The Pauper is a young powerful, able bodied man, and his wife is a young, able bodied woman. Under the above circumstances the Guardians were of opinion that Mr Flood acted indiscreetly in giving such an Order for the conveyance of these Paupers to the Union House, and consequently disallowed the expense incurred.

I remain
My Lords and Gent[n]
Your most obedient Servant

The Poor Law Board   Robert A Ware
Whitehall   Clerk
London

TNA ref. MH 12/10217 Bedminster Union, Somerset

[Petition from an unfortunate man, who has spent much time in hospital after several accidents, requesting help.]

The Chairman and Board of the Poor Law Commissioners, London

The humble Petition of James Bolt of Dean Lane in the Parish of Bedminster in the County of Somerset, Coal Miner.

Sheweth,

That your Petitioner on the 21st day of January 1835 when following his employment under ground had to blow a Rock, a part of which struck him in the head and fractured his Scull and was taken to the Bristol Infirmary where he lay ill for 17 Months and on his recovery he went to work again until the Month of August 1846 and when decending [sic] into the Pit the rope broke and he was caught by a Cord of Coals which broke his breast bone and three of his Ribs, he was then taken to the Bristol Hospital where he remained 7 months, and on his recovery partially, he went to work for the Dock Company and continued so about 2 years and when he was at work on board one of the said Company's Vessels he had the misfortune to fall down the Hatchway, pitched on his right Shoulder and fractured the bone when he was again taken to the Hospital, and he has lost the use of his Hand and Arm ever since as they are wasting away, and your Petitioner is frequently under the treatment of the Surgeons through bodily afflictions.

That your Petitioner in the year 1852 was obliged to go into the Union Workhouse at Bourton in the Parish of Long Ashton, and there remained about Twelve Months the first time and secondly until the year 1858 when he was discharged and has been allowed Two shillings per week and a loaf of Bread.

That your Petitioner through his affliction is totally incapable of working, is about 65 years of age and has applied frequently to the relieving Officer of the District for further Relief, but he has refused to grant any and stated that your Petitioner must endeavor to do with the Relief he had.

Your Petitioner therefore humbly prays that you will take his distress into your merciful consideration and grant him such further Relief to alleviate his sufferings as you may suggest and think proper to adopt.

And your Petitioner as in duty bound

will ever pray &c

Bedminster

24th January 1866

1. Usual answer
2. Send copy to the Guardians for their consideration

JJ   25th January '66

TNA ref. MH 12/10499 Wellington Union, Somerset and Devon

[Complaint against the schoolmaster of a workhouse who is accused of having a female inmate visit him in his bedroom.]

Wellington Union

Proceedings of a Court of Enquiry held at the Board Room of the Wellington Workhouse on Thursday 14th July 1870 relating to a charge of misconduct, on the part of Mr S. Trim, Schoolmaster at the Workhouse of the Wellington Union.

Mary Winter an inmate, being duly sworn states on the 29th March last I heard the Schoolmaster, Mr Trim, open the gate and I looked out and saw Eliza Bailey going towards the Schoolmaster's bedroom, the top iron gates by the private stairs of Matron's and I went and told the Master. On the 6th April I again saw Eliza Bailey inside the iron gates the Schoolmaster was there. I had seen them there several times before. I saw him through the key hole of the school room. It was about half past seven in the evening.

Q   What hour on 29ᵗʰ March did you see?

A   Near about the same time.

Q   Did you shew yourself from the closet?

A   No. I went down to the Master.

Q   How did you see her out of the closet?

A   I heard the gates open and saw her go through them into the Schoolmaster's bedroom.

Q   Is there any reason why Bailey should not have seen you, as that you should have seen her?

A   She could not have seen me as her back was towards me.

Q   Did you state any thing about seeing Bailey and the Schoolmaster together on 6ᵗʰ April to the Guardians?

A   Yes I did.

Q   Why did you not speak to Eliza Bailey at the time?

A   Because I told the Master and he desired me not to do so.

Q   How soon did you find the Master?

A   Directly.

Q   Can you give any reason for resorting to the closet instead of the keyhole?

A   Because I was not positive it was she.

Q   Did it occur to you to take a witness to the closet?

A   No it did not.

Q   Had there been a fall out after this had occurred?

A   No.

Q   Have you ever been in the lock up upon any occasion?

A   No. I was once at Wiveliscombe.

Q   Upon what charge?

A   My husband that is now lost some money and I was charged with stealing it.

Q   Was it dark when this occurred?

A   It was not very light on 29ᵗʰ March.

The mark   X   of Mary Winter

***

Ruth Bully an inmate, being duly sworn states on the 6ᵗʰ April last I was in the womens' bed room at a little before 7 p.m. I saw Eliza Bailey open the Gates in the Schoolmaster's passage and come out from the Schoolmaster's room and down the stairs and I saw the Schoolmaster go back into his room.

Q   Who was with you?

A   Maria Fowler.

Q   Was Mary Winter with you?

A   No.

Q   How do you know the time?

A   Because it was washing night.

Q   On what days of the week is it washing night?

A   Mondays and Tuesdays.

Q   Did you not on the first examination by the Guardians say that it was the Schoolmaster who opened the gates?

A   Yes it was.

Q   Would not the Schoolmaster's door being open exclude all view from the passage?

A   His door was not open.

Q   Not for any person to go out or come in?

A   Only just wide enough for a person to get in.

Q   Did the Schoolmaster leave it so when he went over and unlocked the gates?

A   No he pushed the door fast.

Q   Did you reveal yourself to the Schoolmaster?

A   No.

Q   Did you knock or announce yourself in any way?

A   No.

Q   Could you not have gone down out of the women's bedroom and gone up the women's stairs and caught them together?

A   She was come down before I was there.

Q   Did you go round for the purpose of going up to them?

A   I did but I was too late.

Q   How long time elapsed before your seeing them together and so going down?

A   Not many minutes.

Q   Did you tell the Master what you had seen?

A   No.

Q   Why not?

A   I told the women in the bedroom.

Q   You are clear it was on a washing day?

A   Yes, as far as I can remember.

Q   Do you know anything about a fall out among the women?

A   Some of them are almost always quarrelling.

Ruth Bully (signed)

***

<u>Sarah Twose</u> Nurse at the Wellington [Workhouse] being duly sworn states Maria Fowler about the beginning of April told me that she saw the Schoolmaster and Eliza Bailey on several occasions upstairs together.

Q   Was not this matter brought before the Guardians by the Schoolmaster and disposed of?

A   I do not know.

Q   Why did you write the letter you addressed to the Guardians?

A   When I found a paper posted against the Surgery door I wrote to know whether it was correct that such a letter should be so posted.

Q   Is it true or false that you are afraid to enter the Schoolmaster's presence he is so fractious?

185

A   I do not know I was particularly afraid only I stopped away.
Q   Did you tell the Master you were obliged to stay away as you were afraid?
A   Yes.
Q   How did you get possession of the paper?
A   I took it out of the Porter's pocket and I shewed it to the Master.
Q   Did you mention it to the Master before writing to the Guardians?
A   Yes.
Q   What women fell out?
A   Spiller and Webber and then they acquainted the Master of what had occurred.
Q   How many years have you been a widow?
A   Ten or eleven.
Q   What is the age of your youngest child?
A   Four years old.

Sarah Twose (signed)

***

Richard Trotman being duly sworn states I am Master of the Wellington Workhouse. In April last Mary Winter told the Matron that she thought something was going on wrong between the Schoolmaster and Eliza Bailey an inmate of the house and to ask if there was any other keys besides those we made use of. The Matron told her not that we were aware of, and she said don't you bring your silly reports here unless you can substantiate them.

Q   Had you any suspicions of any thing going on between the Schoolmaster and Eliza Bailey?
A   I had not but on hearing these reports I went up and saw the woman coming down stairs. I asked her what business she had up there and she said she had been up to see her boy George. This was on the 9th April.
Q   Is it a private stair case?
A   Above the first floor.
Q   Who has charge of the keys at the top of the stairs and the Schoolmaster's room?
A   The Matron, and I the other.
Q   Has the Schoolmaster any key?
A   No.
Q   Did you state that no one could take the key without your's or the Matron's knowledge?
A   I did.
Q   Could a false key be made without taking off the lock?
A   I cannot say.
Q   Had the key ever been lost?
A   No.
Q   Does the Gate make considerable noise in opening the lock?
A   Yes.

Q   Did you give Maria Winter instructions to watch but not to disclose herself?
A   No.

Richard Trotman

***

<u>Samuel Trim</u> (Schoolmaster) simply denies the facts states he has been Schoolmaster for 7½ years. I have never heard any complaint against me. The bell for supper generally rings about 20 minutes after 6 and they come from supper at 20 minutes to 7 and go to bed directly afterwards. I have occupied the same bedroom ever since I have been here. I knew that there was a key hole without a key into the women's ward. I never had the key of the Iron Gates for any purpose.

The Gate makes a great noise to open. No new keys could be made without taking off the lock. If my door were fully open it would extend almost across the passage.

By opening my door it would obstruct the view up the passage. Eliza Bailey was never in my room. Winter or Fowler or Bully never charged me, nor the nurse, nor the Master. I brought the matter voluntarily before the Guardians and they investigated the matter and they disposed of it entirely to my satisfaction the nurses letter brought it up again the following Thursday. The women were making a hearthing for me.

Samuel Trim

***

<u>Maria Berridge</u> being duly sworn states: I am Schoolmistress. I was in the Schoolroom to ask for the Schoolmaster at about ½ past 7 to 8 on 29th March and I sent for him from the Hospital and he came to me. He remained with me until nearly 8 o'clock.

Maria Berridge

***

<u>Robert Clay</u> being duly sworn. I am clerk to Mr Bray. I have known the Schoolmaster for some years. I saw him on the 6th April from ½ past 6 until 8 p.m. and we went together into the town and remained there until 9.

Robert Clay

***

<u>Thomas Williams</u> being duly sworn states. I was an inmate of the hospital in March last. I remember the Schoolmaster coming there on 29th March from ½ past 6 to ¼ to 8 and I remember the Schoolmistress sending for him by one of the boys.

The mark of   X   Thomas Williams

***

187

Wellington Union (Som) Poor Law Board
Subject:– Conduct of Schoolmaster
To Mr Samuel Trim
schoolmaster

Whitehall, S.W.
29th July 1870

Sir,

I am directed by the Poor Law Board to inform you that they have received from their Inspector Col. Ward a Report of the Inquiry recently held by him into the charge of misconduct preferred against you as Schoolmaster at the Workhouse of the Wellington Union, together with a copy of the depositions of the several witnesses who were examined on that occasion.

The Board, having carefully considered the Report and Evidence, direct me to state that, in their opinion, the charge referred to has not been proved, and that you are therefore entitled to an acquittal.

I am &c
A.W. Peel Sec.

TNA ref. MH 12/4015 Clifton Union, Bristol

[A destitute family is admitted to the workhouse.]

C.H. Hunt, clerk
The Workhouse, Fishponds Road, Bristol
10th October 1870

My Lords and Gentlemen

With reference to my letters to you of 29th July last & the 12th ulto & your letter of 10th Septr no. 35752 C.1870 I beg to inform you that the following case has just occurred. James Cordy is a labourer residing in the parish of St. George in this Union, he has a wife & 8 children all under 16 years of age, the man is in regular employ earning 13/– per week, the wife earns nothing. They have rent of 2/– per week to pay. The man is able bodied with the exception that he is ruptured & obliged to wear a Truss.

Fever has attacked the family who are in a dreadfully destitute state & the Guardians have had 3 of the children removed to their Fever Hospital. The eldest James aged 14 is now got so well that it is expected he will be discharged cured next week & perhaps the other 2 children in a fortnight after that but the difficulty again occurs about their clothes. They were brought to the Workhouse almost naked having only a very few rags & those extremely filthy about them, in fact they were all obliged to be wrapped in rugs before they could be put into the Ambulance to be removed & their rags of clothes to be destroyed directly they arrived at the Fever Hospital at the Workhouse.

The Guardians now wish to be favoured with your answer & instructions as asked for in my letter of 29th July as they are at a loss to know what is the correct course for

them to pursue in such cases now that the Auditor is got so extremely particular &
they will therefore feel obliged by your instructions as early as convenient.

I have the honour to be

My Lords & Gentlemen

Your most obedient Servant

C.H. Hunt

To The Poor Law Board
Whitehall
London

TNA ref. MH 12/10466 Taunton Union, Somerset and Devon

[A complaint by an inmate of Taunton Workhouse.]

The Local Government Board
My Lords and Gentlemen,

I, Mary Ann Carrol, an inmate of the Taunton Union Workhouse, wish to make a
complaint of the manner I have been treated while in the above named Workhouse for
the past week, and that during the time mentioned I have been treated in every respect
by the Master contrary to the Rules of the House as regards females. At present I am
suckling an infant that is in ill health, and requires nursing and attendance, but am
unable to attend to it as I ought being separated from it and confined in a separate room
termed the Oakham-shop. How am I to perform the perantal [sic] Duties of a mother
towards my infant child, if, during nearly the whole of the day I am to be took from
it and confined in a separate room, most days locked up by myself, and during work
hours not so much as allowed to suckle it? My Lords and Gentlemen, I also wish to
make a complaint against the Master of the House for unlawfully exceeding his duties.
On reference to the Rules and to one especially, namely Article 134, you will find
what I here state in reference to the master's duties to be correct. It is not in the power
of the Master to punish a woman that is suckling a child, be that woman's child in ill
health or not, by an alteration of diet, or by confinement in a separate room, without
the sanction of the Medical Officer, and the Master has so far exceeded his Duties
and acted contrary to the Article above alluded to, by taking me from my sick child
and placing me in close confinement in the Oakum-shop. My Lords and Gentlemen,
I wish to draw your attention particularly to the following. On days bearing dates the
5th, 6th, 7th, 8th, 9th and 10th I was strictly confined in the Oakum-shop the first four days
during a period of 8 hours, on 9th a period of 9 hours and on Date 10th from 8 o'clock
till half past 12 o'clock. An hour after work hours contrary to the Rules of the House
covering work hours I am even denied the privilege of nursing my own child. I also
wish to state that I think it contrary to the Rules of the House that the male officers
of the House should be in continual attendance upon the female inmates excercising
[sic] those duties required of a Female Officer only, and during the time I have been
so confined I have been attended to both by the Taskmaster and Porter, a duty which
should have been performed by the Matron only, a duty which she has entirely
neglected. I also wish to state I have on three different occasions made application to

the Porter to release me from my confinement to attend to my infant child (it being as I have already stated in ill health) an application which was never granted. My Lords and Gentlemen, I wish to ask you if it is the Rule of the Workhouse, or the duties of a Master of a Workhouse, that a woman should be treated in the manner I have described to be placed in close confinement by herself in a separate Room and not so much as allowed during her confinement to nurse or suckle her own child? I think it myself averse to all the feelings of humanity, and that the Master of this Workhouse has acted in a tyrannical and arbitrary manner, that has exceeded his duties, the Matron neglected hers and the male Officers has performed them in her stead. If I have been treated in this manner as a punishment, I wish to know the offence for which I have been punished, and it's the Duty of the Master in such cases to acquaint the party or parties so offending with their offence and the term of punishment they are to undergo. Before concluding I wish to state that it was my intention on last Board day to make a complaint personally to the Visiting Committee, but as they did not come to the Oakum shop where I was locked up, and being disappointed, I thought it my duty to forward my grievances to the Local Government Board in the manner described.

My Lords and Gentlemen, hoping you will take the above facts into consideration and intercede on my behalf.

Taunton Union	I remain your humble Servant
Feb 12/72	(signed) Mary Ann Carrol

TNA ref. MH 12/3171 Lanchester Union, County Durham

[Permission is sought to remove a child from a workhouse to a Roman Catholic school for poor children.]

To, Local Government Board

Whitehall, London

24th May 1872

Gentlemen,

On the 7th of May 1872 I made an application to you for the removal of Francis Brennan or Brannon from the Workhouse of the Lanchester Union in the county of Durham, to the Roman Catholic Certified Poor Law School at Tudhoe near Durham and had the form returned to me in order; 1st to have the name of the Workhouse at which the child is maintained, inserted. 2nd the other particulars relating to the case correctly set forth. 3rd The Baptismal Certificate of the child stamped. 4th further evidence of the marriage of the parents and of the death of the mother.

I now respectfully renew that application and enclose herewith; 1st The Form with the name of the Workhouse inserted. 2nd as to 'The Other Particulars' referred to I am not aware of any that are required from me beyond those which I have already given but shall be happy to supply them if in my power. On being informed of them. 3rd I send enclosed the Baptismal Certificate of the child stamped. 4th The certificate of the death of the mother, but as to the marriage of the parents, after much trouble and enquiry I have been unable to discover when they were married. I beg however, to refer to three accompanying certificates of the Baptisms of two of the children and of the Death of the mother in all of which the parties are described as man and wife and trust that such undeniable evidence on the point may prove satisfactory to your Honourable Board.

Brooms,	I am Gentlemen
Ludgate	Your Obed[t] Serv[t]
Durham	F. Kearney [Rev. Francis Kearney]

Another document refers to the 'Removal of Francis Brannen or Brennan from the Workhouse of Lanchester Union to the School established at Tudhoe for the reception, maintenance and education of Children of the Roman Catholic religion'.

***

TNA ref. MH 12/5338 Tenterden Union, Kent
[An opium addict's husband has sold all his furniture to pay off his creditors because his wife spends all his income on laudanum (opium).]

30th January 1874

Gentlemen,

The Board of Guardians at their last meeting had several very nice & important cases brought under their notice & as their decision may regulate future cases I was instructed to communicate with you thereon.

The first case is that of Emma Nye the wife of an agricultural labourer living at Appledore. This pauper by her extravagant habits has compelled her husband to sell all his furniture for the benefit of his Creditors & he and his children have gone into lodgings and the wife to the Workhouse. The man while willing to maintain his wife says it is utterly impossible he can live with her as she spends everything she can lays hands on upon laudanum. He is an honest industrial labourer & the Guardians are willing to look favourably on his case at the same time they feel that if they accept maintenance under the 33 sec of 31 & 32 Vict. c122 it is making the Workhouse little better than a Common Lodginghouse.

[A woman whose husband has abused her and been sent to prison for cruelty.]
The next case is that of a woman named Holdstock the wife of a man who has lately returned from prison for cruelty towards her but now earning 15[s]/– per week. The wife and 3 children are in the workhouse. The man says, 'I don't want you to maintain my wife & children if she will come to me, I will do so.' The poor woman in consequence of his drunken habits & violent temper is afraid to do so. The Guardians informed the woman they could not protect her but if the children remained chargeable they should cause her husband to be summoned for the maintenance. This she says would be the means of his taking the children out of the house & depriving her of the care of them which she could not endure. The poor woman is much to be pitied as she is quite willing to work for the children if her earnings could be protected & she has applied to the Magistrates for an order who do not consider her case come[s] within the Act of Parliament.

[A woman who has an incurable disease. Her husband seeks help.]
The last case is that of a labourer named Fagg who has a wife suffering from a very bad internal disease which the Medical Officer pronounces incurable and that the woman may live sometime. The man is an agricultural labourer earning the wages of the neighbourhood but he finds it impossible to provide his wife with the nourishment she requires and the nature of the disease is such that he cannot get nurses for her. Under such circumstances he applies to the Guardians to take her into the Workhouse stating that if they do not he feels he shall have no alternative but to come in with her. The woman is almost one persons entire care.

Will your honorable board be pleased to give the above cases consideration and advise the Guardians how to act under the peculiar circumstances.

	I am
The Local Government Board	Gentlemen
Whitehall	Your obedt servt
S.W.	W.G. Mace
	Clerk

***

The following notes have been added after these letters:
The last mentioned case appears to be within exception 2 to Act of the Gen¹ Out Door Relief Property Order.   M.
The Legal Department   2 Feb 74

Mr Fletcher
As to the first, write as in 53 (Rochford Un.)

Prepare letters. In the 1ˢᵗ & 3ʳᵈ cases as suggested, & in the 2ⁿᵈ state that the Bᵈ can only suggest that the Gdⁿˢ shᵈ cause the Master to be summoned if the family are still chargeable. Ask why the Justices consider that the care of the wife may come within the provision of the Act by which the earnings of married women can be protected.
J.T.   5 Mar 74

TNA ref. MH 12/4018 Clifton Union, Bristol
[Complaint made by a deaf and dumb pauper.]

35 Catherine St.,
Easton
Bristol
Dec 4th 1874

To The Poor Law Board
Gentlemen,
    I am being a deaf and dumb man aged 43 masons labourer and my wife died last Feb. and left me one little daughter. I have taken the liberty to address this note to you,

Gentlemen, & ask you for to give me every assistance in my behalf, if you, Gentlemen, will kindly inquire with the Clifton Union Guardians for me about getting to relieve me out instead of a Workhouse Order, Sir. Gentlemen, I have applied the Guardians three times until again last Friday [sic] for relief but they have refused to assist me and ordered me for a Workhouse, then I would not go, because I don't like to break up a home for my poor daughter's sake. I have not got a friend in the world to help me. I am so tired of the Workhouse but rather work out to get my own bread honestly. I wish the old Guardians had apprenticed me to a trade before they took me back to the Union from the Deaf & Dumb School where I was brought up. They kindly gave me a receipt of 2/6 weekly to help me the little work out. I have had it nearly 20 years but was stopped last year, gentlemen. I don't like to go back to the house again because I go to the Working Men's school 3 times a week to learn & understand the Holy Scriptures. I am so ignorant of the Holy Bible and I don't understand it. I am a poor Bible Scholar. Mr D. Smith their officer told the Guardians that I have had money in the Savings Bank and I was to be seen there. It is a false report. If I had saved a shilling in the pound I might have a right to put a 6d to 1/– in the Penny Bank for to buy clothes &c. I wish the new Guardians would consider very carefully they knew of my affliction. The present Guardians are all fresh and strangers to me. They don't know more of me yet. I am very thankful to the old Guardians for to put me in the Park Row Deaf and Dumb School for 8 years. I am sorry they didn't learn me a trade. I am always miserable because I am unable to speak nor hear. I don't know what to become of me if I don't get relief out. I wish the Guardians w^d assist to relieve me all the winter until I get work gentlemen I send you a certificate of my character & have showed them last Friday.

I am

Gentlemen

Yr most Ob^t Servant

Charles Vale

Deaf & Dumb

P.S. I hope to hear from you & let me know how the guardians get on with you about me gentlemen.

Awaiting the favour of your consideration gentlemen.

[The following letter is attached:]

Church & Philips   Wapping,
Building Contractors   Bristol
                                                   Augt 18th 1874

Gentlemen,

   The bearer Charles Vale who is deaf and dumb has been in our employ for a considerable period & we have always found him attentive to his duties & his home. The only reason for his discharge was no work in that department in which he was employed.

For Messrs Church & Phillips
E. Dyer

Say that subject to the Reg. in force in the Clifton Union it rests with the Guardians to decide in what manner relief where it is needed shall be given, whether in or out of the Workhouse.

The Board cannot direct the Gd[ns] shall allow you out door relief neither can they in fact interfere for the purpose of ordering relief in any individual case.

The Board will however send a copy of your letter to the Gdns for their consideration.

Send copy to Gdns for their consideration and observations.
F.J.
7 Decr/74

[On the flap of the envelope Charles Vale has written:]
'I will not go to the bloody Workhouse with an order from you. If you send me an order for the Dam Workhouse I shall put it into the fire. I would rather go to Jail than Workhouse. I don't care for Buggers who tell you lies of me.'
            Burn the Workhouse note into the fire.
                I shant go.
                    C.Vale

TNA ref. MH 12/8989 Berwick Union, Northumberland and County Durham
[Complaint about the conduct of the master of a workhouse. He is asked to resign.]

27th January 1875

Quarrelsome conduct since October 12, 1874 when he promised better behaviour to the Guardians.

Colville Brown, Medical Officer states. On the 2nd Dec. I had had occasion to speak to the Master about the Dietary. I recommended a change with regard to the Patients on my books and suggested such a change as I thought would give least trouble to the Master. On the following Wednesday I found the Master and Matron in the office. When I went in the Matron complained of the trouble the change would give and the Master said, 'It's all a piece of awkwardness of the Doctor's.' I answered 'Did I not tell you Mr Mitchell, that I would adopt any other plan that would give less trouble'. He pushed the Medical relief Book across the table to me and said, 'I don't do anything in that low dirty underhand way', turning up the books. On the 13th December I was with the Master in the office and having been informed by the nurse that the patients had only got the meat and not the soup on the Wednesday as recommended by me, I asked the Master if such was the case. He said they had got it. He called out to the cook to ask if they had got the soup. I went down to the Hospital to ask the nurse if it was the case that they had not got the soup. She again told me they had not got it. Soon after, while I was in the Hospital, the Master came in and said 'Nurse, did you say they did not get the soup last Wednesday?' She said she had said so. He then addressed me and said, 'I suppose I shall be reported for this in the usual dirty way'.

I had not reported any cases against the Master to the Visiting Committee. I had reported cases of quarrelling to Mr Bone as well as other things I had found fault with. When I give directions about any change in the dietary of a patient I sometimes give it verbally and sometimes it has not been entered in the Medical Relief Book. The Doctors side of the Medical Relief Book has been entirely kept by me since last Spring.

Colville Brown

Sworn before me 15th Jan[y] 1875
  Geo. Culley

Agnes McLeod (Matron) states:– One day since 12th Oct[r] I took a slice of brown bread from the Store. He was very quarrelsome about it and asked me if I did not get my own rations, what right had I there. I took it because I fancied it more than my own rations. I was angry because he found fault with that simple thing, and I said 'I never sold soup'. He answered 'I never sold it either, but at contract price'. He has been more civil since 1st October, but not altogether civil. His conduct does not prevent my doing my duty.

When I said to the Master 'I never sold soup', I was vexed to think he had done such a thing. When I saw the doctor in the Master's Office I said to him 'Oh, Doctor this is an awkward Dietary' I think Mr Mitchell said it was all done for awkwardness to his books. It was awkward because I got no previous notice. The cook and I generally manage the soup. The Master has nothing to do with sending it out.

Agnes McCleod

Sworn before me 15th Jan[y] 1875
  Geo. Culley

Mary Harle, nurse, states:– After the Master asked me on the 13th Dec. whether the patients had got their soup or not and I said 'No' he said it was not his fault, they ought to have had their soup. The Doctor was present and the Master said, 'I'll be to blame about this, as about other things, but it's the Matron's place to look after the soup'.

The Master was very sharp to me about the soup. I did not hear any insolent expression towards the Doctor.

Mary Harle

Sworn before me this 15th Jan[y] 1875
  Geo. Culley

Thomas H. Mitchell, the Master, states:– On the 2nd Dec. in the office the Matron said, 'Oh Doctor you have done this through awkwardness'. I said 'It's a very awkward affair for the books however'. The persons for whom the Doctor had ordered the change of Dietary were scattered through several Wards and I had to go through the book to pick out on the day on which the Doctor found the Matron and me in the office, the dinner had been actually prepared for the changed dietary. On the 13th I expected that the proper patients had got no.3 diet. I did not know there was a mistake till the Doctor informed me. As soon as I heard of it I went first to the kitchen, and then to the Hospital to enquire when I found they had not got their soup. I said this will possibly be another report. The Doctor was in the Hospital at the time but I don't know that he was near us.

   There had been a mistake in the Dietary on one day of the two following weeks.

   I never sold any of the Workhouse soup in my life.

T Mitchell

Sworn before me 15th Jany 1875

   Geo. Culley

Evidence as to character. Andrew Thompson, Chairman of the Board of Guardians, and J.P. of Berwick says 'I have known Mr Mitchell since he was appointed Master of the Workhouse. I have always considered him an exceedingly steady man. I never in my life saw him the worse of drink but his excitable manner might sometimes lead a stranger to think he was. I have always found him most attentive to his duties. Nobody could be more so. I believe he takes a great interest in the happiness of the Inmates of the House and is very careful of the interests of the Guardians.

Andrew Thompson

Sworn before me 15th January 1875

   Geo. Culley

2nd charge. Alleged misconduct with women in the Workhouse.

Withdrawn

[Appended to the above:]

He should not continue to hold his present office.   Asked to resign.

Furthermore the Board find the Matron, Mrs McCleod is inefficient

Matron asked to resign

TNA ref. MH 12/7885 Uxbridge Union, Middlesex

[A destitute family living in squalor.]

Northolt Parish

John Barnett		43
wife	Eliza	34
5 ch.	Maria	11
	Mary	8
	George	7
	Sarah	5
	Thomas	3

This family received continued relief for fourteen weeks. The whole family were in a dirty & most miserable condition, in fact scarcely sufficient clothing to cover their nakedness. The children consequently not being in a fit state to be received into the school.

Barnett was suffering from acute bronchitis, the Medical Officer refusing to certify for his removal to the Workhouse Infirmary; the wife being pregnant (since which time she has been delivered of twins). Mary suffering from inflammation of the lungs. Maria was kept at home to help her mother. After a short time from their first receiving relief the children were cleansed & seen to. George and Sarah then attended school regularly. This case was a difficult one to deal with and owing to the circumstances I had no alternative than to continue the relief ordered by our Board.

Auditor's Report

I do hereby certify that in this account of Mr Arthur James Hanson a Relieving Officer of the Uxbridge Union I have disallowed the sum of fourteen pounds, one shilling and one penny and I do also hereby certify that the sum of fourteen pounds one shilling and one penny is now due from the said Arthur James Hanson.

signed George Gibson
Auditor of the District, which comprises the above named Union

The above sum of £14–1–1 is the amount of relief out of the Workhouse given to certain Paupers with children in the said union during the half year ended Lady-day 1875, and I have disallowed it because no evidence was produced to me at the Audit that the condition upon which alone such relief could be legally continued (contained in the 3rd Section of the 36th & 37th Vict. C.86) had been complied with, or that the children of the said paupers fell within the exceptions set forth in the above mentioned section.

Dated this tenth day of May 1875
Sgd George Gibson
District Auditor

TNA ref. MH 12/4020 Clifton Union, Bristol
[A workhouse inmate requests assistance from the Local Government Board in an attempt to recover his late wife's money and effects, which have been taken unlawfully by his son-in-law.]

Poor Law Commissioners*
Somerset House
London

Clifton Union,
Fishponds Road
Bristol
Septr 21st 1876

Gentlemen,

I beg leave to claim your attention to the following circumstances. I have been an inmate of this Union for some time (being a native of Clifton parish) thro' affliction.

* This is clearly an error as the Poor Law Commissioners had been succeeded by the Local Government Board in 1871

I am in my 67th year. I was married on the 1st June 1837 at St. James's, Piccadilly my wife & self were both servants. My wife died in the 12th day of June 1868, having lived in the Service of the late & present Earl Somers, as Housekeeper at Eastmor Castle for many years & being a place of resort on certain days of the week & sanctioned by his Lordship for visitors did accumulate a certain amount of money. viz over nine hundred pounds. On or about the year 1864 his present Lordship thought proper to allow my wife to retire on a pension of £20 pr annum. I was then & had been living for some time as butler to the earl of Courtown in Ireland. In Septr 1871 I left Ireland, having a number of letters to my wife & receiving no reply. I became anxious to know what was going on, & on my arrival in London I was informed that my wife was dead & had been over two years. My youngest & only daughter living, having married a first cousin who knew of my wife & altho' my wife opposed to the last his marrying of her, I have every reason to believe succeeded in seducing her to force the consent of my wife & so shortened her days as she only lived 6 months after inducing my wife to come & live with them in apartments (or part of their house) all this was kept from me, & rumours was made that I was gone to sea & never heard of & supposed to be dead. Altho' my daughter had received the letters I had written & also 2 books I had sent p^r post with my address one book being *The Gold of Ophir*, & other *The Footprints of St. Paul* they therefore knew where I was & in whose service I was & altho' cards of affectionate remembrance was freely distributed to the Family not one was sent to me or any notice taken of her death. On hearing of my wife's death I hastened to Wales the residence of my daughter, & hearing conflicting stories respecting my wife's death I obtained a certificate from the Medical man who was known to having been employed at her confinement with this very daughter 27 years previous. I afterwards proceeded to the Registrar & there found that the Registry was not certified (Altho' the Medical Man gave a certificate at time of death). It there distinctly states that it was registered by my son in law Evan David who was present at time of her death of which I have a doubt that she died of Diseased Liver & was the wife of George Merrifield formerly a victualler, as the certificate & registry was so opposite I went to Neath & had an interview with the Coroner to know if any Inquest or Post Mortem Examination had taken place who referred me to the Sergeant of Police who remembered it being reported that my wife died rather suddenly & that I was talked of as living in Ireland. Of course all this annoyed me very much & I hesitated & took a lodging for some months feeling something would turn up at length. I made up my mind to call & see my daughter who was not allowed to see me only in presence of her husband. I had 2 interviews in both of which my daughter appeared in great trouble & told me in answer to questions great untruths.

On my return to London my health failed & after spending nearly £100 in Doctors Lodgings &c I obtained admission in the Marylebone Workhouse where I received Medical treatment & was recovering. Thinking my native air would do good I wished to be sent here this was in Winter of 1872. In the Spring following I became worse & was laid up for 18 months not expecting to recover. I did not interfere in the matter.

Thank God I have got over the worst & am now anxious to be no longer a burden on the rates. I hold it is my just right to take possession of my wife's effects & settle with the Guardians for the expense I have incurred. I have no funds to prosecute my claim & the Guardians have no power to advance the means. I have consulted Mr Taddy an Attorney & Proctor & I am advised to administer & citation to follow & have my daughter, & son in Law Examined separately on Oath. My daughter will then tell the truth as it is evidently a conspiracy on the part of my son in Law & family to defraud me & embezzle my late wife's effects.

My son in Law is in a good position being Shipper to the Abor Coal Co. at Porthead, Glamorganshire, he is in possession of several Freehold Houses & from a witness I can produce, my wife's money has been invested in shares of Two vessels registered at Swansea the names of which I have so that the property has not been squandered but comeatable [sic]. Many of her goods &c I have seen in my daughters apartments & I have a list of about £50 worth I am therefore advised by Wm Green, Esqr the late & many years Guardian & Chairman of this Union to forward my Statement to your Honorable Board & solicit your kindness & assistance to enable me to proceed at once with my claim.

> I have the Honor to be,
> Gentlemen
> Your Humble & respectful Servant
> George Merrifield

TNA ref. MH 12/10469 Taunton Union, Somerset and Devon

[A pauper who has refused to obey the Union regulations is sent to prison.]

Committed to Taunton Prison 8th November 1876 for 14 days for refusing to obey the Regulations of the Chard Union.

> Taunton County Prison.

Visiting Justices forward statement by prisoner & extract from Surgeon's Journal
Remission & Letter of discharge 17/11/76
Referred to Local Gov^t B^d 18/11/76
Extract from Surgeon's Journal, 10 November 1876
Frances Evans F 65 General Health Good. Defective right eye. Eyes very irritable from condition of lids, which bear marks of having been granular. She has flat feet and walks slightly lame, states she has been in an Asylum at Dorchester. She is now of sound mind, but of feeble intellect. Her sight ought not to interfere with her performing the ordinary duties of household work, but is so defective as to prevent her gaining a livelihood by her needle. The condition of her feet renders her quite incapable of carrying her baby more than a short distance.

> William Liddon

[contd]

Som. RO ref. D/G/Ch/8a/21 Chard Union, Somerset, and Devon, and Dorset Minutes of the meetings of the Board of Guardians
[Previous case continued.]

18th November 1876
    Frances Evans
    Letters from the Governor of Taunton Prison and Local Government Board read as to this Casual Pauper being prosecuted for refusing to obey certain regulations of the House.
Resolved
    That our Clerk write to the Local Government Board and state that the Guardians gave no special directions for the prosecution in question, but that they considered the prosecution properly instituted when the Medical Officer had given the Master a certificate that the pauper was able bodied.
    That our Clerk take the necessary steps with a view to her removal to her legal place of settlement.

11th December 1876
    Frances Evans and child.   Clerk reports that he was doing what was necessary to obtain Order of Removal Certificate of chargeability signed.

Note: There are three further references to Frances Evans in these minutes but they do not record to where she is to be removed.

TNA ref. MH 12/16681 Pembroke Union, Wales
[Concern about the care of pauper lunatics.]

Pembroke Union
Pembroke, April 17th 1884

My Lords and Gentlemen,
    I am directed by the Board of Guardians of the Pembroke Union to acknowledge the receipt of your letter of the 21st February last having reference to certain paupers mentioned in the Annual Lunatics return as residing alone and requesting to be furnished with further particulars respecting their cases.
    In reply the Guardians direct me to state that in the case of Margaret Cole the neighbours live close by; she is properly attended to and the Guardians do not wish it altered.
    Jane Evans does not reside alone as reported but with her husband. Mary Davies is now no longer a pauper and lives with her husband. George Bowen lives in House, alone, is bedridden, the neighbours who live close by look after him he is attended by a regular nurse. The Guardians consider him properly attended to. Mary Llewhellyn lives in a room to herself in same house as several other paupers. The Guardians consider she is properly taken care of. Margaret Harris lives with a person named James at Newton Hill. Jane Gwyther lives with her parents, she is only 46 years of age instead of 70 as reported. Her mother is aged about 70.

The Guardians are furnished quarterly with a Report of the visits of the Medical Officer to these paupers under the 16 & 17 Vict. Chap 97 Sect. 66.

I am,

My Lords and Gentlemen,

Your obedient servant,

Jno Jones

Clerk

The Local Government Board

Whitehall

London

CHAPTER 10

RATEPAYERS

Amongst parish records there are many ledgers dating from the eighteenth century which list parishioners and the amounts they paid towards the support of the poor of their parish. From Act 17 George 2 Cap. 5 (1743–44) it was a legal requirement for the *poor rates* to be entered into a book and be available for public inspection. The *rate* paid was proportionate to the value of their property. These *rates* were collected by parish *overseers*. Records of these ratepayers can be found in the parish rate books and are now usually held in county or borough record offices. Some pre-date the 1743–44 Act by many years.

From the formation of the Poor Law Unions, following the Act of 1834, the collection of poor rates became the responsibility of the overseers of the poor of each Union, who appointed *collectors* for each parish within their Union. Such records are to be found with the records of each Union. Sometimes lists of ratepayers, and the rates they paid, were sent to the Poor Law Commissioners and their successors. These are to be found at TNA in document class MH 12. (Some ratepayers are also listed in Chapter 17.)

The following are examples of the range of documents which list ratepayers:

Brist. RO ref. P/St.MR/OP/1
Michaelmas, 1716
[List of money payments for the parish of St Mary Redcliffe, Bristol.]

An Assessment made by virtue of a warrant to us Directed on the Lands and Inhabitants of the Parish of St. Mary Redcliff in the City of Bristol, for raising the Sum of Seventy Eight pounds and fifteen shillings for the maintenance of the poor for halfe a year from our Lady Day to Michaelmas 1716.

Persons Names	Real		Personal		Total		
	s	d	s	d	£	s	d
Jon Yeamans pr all his Land	17	0	–	–	–	17	–
Mr Jon Buttle & Company	–	–	14	2	–	14	2

Wid° Shutter	– –	2 6	– 2 6
Sam¹ Purnell	3 6	4 8	– 8 2
Mr Watts's Land, Hospital	6 0	– –	– 6 0
Thoˢ Ewins pr Glass house, ditto	8 0	– –	– 8 0
Benjⁿ Dyer, ditto	4 2	– –	– 4 2
Wid° Barnns, ditto	4 2	– –	– 4 2
Wid° East [?]	4 2	– –	– 4 2
Joⁿ Crocker	6 0	– –	– 6 0
Thoˢ Gatchcombe	8 0	7 6	– 15 6
Joⁿ Pen	6 0	5 0	– 11 0
Mrs Newport	11 10	12 10	1 4 8
Roger Akers Jnr Chequer	12 10	– –	– 12 10
Mr Curr [?]	– –	– –	– – –
Robᵗ Stephens, Coopers Arms	10 0	– –	– 10 0
Henry Bevon	– –	2 6	– 2 6
Joˢ Cooke	4 10	– –	– 4 10
James Powell	3 6	– –	– 3 6
Wᵐ Middle pr all Mr Lane's Land	13 2	10 10	1 4 0
Stepⁿ Clutterbuck per Sugar house	16 0	– –	– 16 0
Mr Jacob Little	8 0	10 0	– 18 0
Roger Dixon	4 0	4 4	– 8 4
Thoˢ Scarlet	3 0	2 6	– 5 6
Mr Jacob Hord	9 6	10 0	– 19 6
Richᵈ Read pr all Barjew's Land	13 10	– –	– 13 10
Joⁿ Cox	14 0	5 0	– 19 0
Joˢ Norman	– –	2 2	– 2 2
Wid° Emery	6 0	– –	– 6 0
Sam¹ Robins	2 6	2 2	– 4 8
James Biggs	10 4	10 0	1 0 4
Thoˢ Rayion, pr Sr Jon Hawkins	6 6	– –	– 6 6
Sam¹ Willcocks	10 10	7 6	– 18 4
Wᵐ Dapwell	5 2	2 6	– 7 8
Roger Williams	3 0	– –	– 3 0
Mr George Whittmoor	12 0	7 6	– 19 6
James Hardin	6 0	2 6	– 8 6
Thoˢ Puxton	9 0	– –	– 9 0

[contd]

Thos Patience	– –	2 6	– 2 6
Mr Wm Barron [?]	6 0	– –	– 6 0
Thos Hort	5 0	– –	– 5 0
Jo^n York	2 0	– –	– 2 0
Giles Tovey pr 2 tenements Hospital	2 6	– –	– 2 6
Wid^o Browne, ditto	1 6	– –	– 1 6
Valentine Saunders 2 tenements ditto	7 4	2 2	– 9 6
James Moggs pr all Mr Bright's	12 0	4 4	– 16 4
John Wilton	8 0	4 4	– 12 4
Enoch Noble	6 0	10 0	– 16 0
Edwd Hooper pr Guideon Noble	– –	– –	– – –
Enoch Noble pr 3 tenements	4 6	– –	– 4 6
Walter Morgan	– –	2 6	– 2 6
Elizabeth Coiney	2 6	2 6	– 5 0

etc., etc.

Northants. RO ref. Northampton All Saints 223P/81

Poor Rates for the parish of All Saints, Northampton 27th Jany 1749 Sheep Street

£ – s		£ – s – d
4 – 10	William Knight	0 – 2 – 3
4 – 10	widow Food	0 – 2 – 6
4 – 0	Thomas Warner on a stable	0 – 2 – 0
5 – 0	Robert Dickenson	0 – 2 – 6
5 – 10	William Atterbury	0 – 2 – 9
8 – 10	Reuben Archer	0 – 4 – 3
7 – 0	Thomas Percival and Garden	0 – 3 – 6
18 – 6	The Worshipful Henry Locock, Esq. and garden	0 – 9 – 0
15 – 0	John Pinchard	0 – 7 – 0
7 – 0	William Payne	0 – 3 – 6
7 – 0	James York	0 – 3 – 6
10 – 0	Sarah Stratford	0 – 5 – 0
20 – 0	Mr William Dicey	0 – 10 – 6
16 – 0	Mr Thomas Brotherton	0 – 10 – 6
16 – 0	Mr Medd	0 – 8 – 0

12 – 0	Mr Ald Merriott	0 – 6 – 0
24 – 0	Mr Robert Ives	0 – 12 – 0
6 – 0	Robert Dicey	0 – 3 – 0
12 – 0	Jos. Duke	0 – 6 – 0
12 – 0	Thos Binyon	0 – 6 – 0
10 – 0	Joseph Churchill	0 – 5 – 0
10 – 0	Thomas Taylor	0 – 5 – 0
9 – 0	Allexander Dance	0 – 4 – 6
2 – 0	Thomas Walkis for a shop	0 – 1 – 0
16 – 0	Mrs Ives	0 – 1 – 0
20 – 0	Ashb. Toll [sic]	0 – 10 – 0
16 – 0	Mr Thomas Bretton, senr	0 – 8 – 0
42 – 0	Mr Joseph Robinson	1 – 1 – 0
7 – 10	Cath. Morris	0 – 3 – 9
5 – 10	Elizabeth Revell	0 – 2 – 9
13 – 0	Job Bartho	0 – 6 – 6
7 – 10	Arthur Lewis	0 – 3 – 9
3 – 0	Glen for his Gate Way	0 – 1 – 6
9 – 0	Francis Cooper	0 – 4 – 6
14 – 0	Thomas Bilson	0 – 7 – 0
1 – 10	Daniel Saunders for a shop	0 – 0 – 9
1 – 0	Ridess	0 – 0 – 6
1 – 0	William Mallard	0 – 0 – 6
9 – 0	Hall	0 – 4 – 6
1 – 0	widow Perkins	0 – 4 – 6
20 – 0	George Bliss	0 – 10 – 0
7 – 0	John Batman	0 – 3 – 6
10 – 0	Benjamin Summerfield	0 – 5 – 0
7 – 0	William Deacon	0 – 3 – 6
10 – 0	Revd. Mr. Gardner	0 – 5 – 0
15 – 0	Henry Lawton, Esq.	– – 7 – 6
20 – 0	Mr. Timothy Rogers not paid pri Bd wrong	0 – 10 – 0
25 – 0	Dr. Kimberly	0 – 17 – 6
24 – 0	Guy Warwick	0 – 12 – 0
6 – 0	Thomas Dunkly	0 – 3 – 0
4 – 0	John Fenn, Junr	0 – 2 – 0

[contd]

10 – 0	Mr Thos Cottone	0 – 5 – 0
7 – 0	widow Smith	0 – 3 – 6
8 – 0	John Odell	0 – 4 – 0
60 – 0	Mr John Page	1 – 10 – 0

Note: There are no headings for the two columns of money. It is assumed that the first column is the rateable value and the last is the rate paid.

Dev. RO (Ex.) ref. 2202 add. 2A/P01 Bishopsteignton, Devon Disbursement Book

Devon, Exminster Hundred – Bishopsteignton
The account of John Coysh, Deputy for Rich[d] Paddon of West Town Estate & Rich[d] Low for his own Estate, churchwardens and Rich[d] Low, Deputy for John Paddons of Cockavon and Thomas Elles for Latte Bickfords Estate, overseers of ye poor of sd parish for alenon [sic] & half Ratts made and given to the saide parish the 31 day of March 1766 and is as follows.

		£ – s – d
	John Lype Esq.	10 – 0 – 6
	for the tythe	6 – 0 – 0
	Wood Barton	5 – 19 – 3¾
	Ash Hill and others	2 – 15 – 5
	pt of Lewworthy	0 – 13 – 10¼
Thos Commyns, Esq., for	pt of Tapleys	0 – 5 – 8
	pt of James Coles	0 – 6 – 6½
	pt of Parrs	0 – 5 – 9
	pt of Jos. Breacher	0 – 8 – 1¾
	East and West Rydons	0 – 6 – 8½
	pt of Trustram Algers	0 – 2 – 10½
	pt of Eastrams	0 – 6 – 10¾
	pt of Rich[d] Algers	0 – 2 – 10½
	Woolgraves	1 – 14 – 6
	Mr Distin, Viccer	0 – 3 – 10
	Mr Eveleigh pt of Edward Geale	0 – 3 – 10
	Greech and others	4 – 13 – 5½
	Thos Woodborne	1 – 18 – 4
	Nic Cove, gent for High Humber	1 – 8 – 8½
	Tho. Bickford	0 – 11 – 6
	pt. of Lewworthy	0 – 2 – 10½
	pt. of Geales	0 – 3 – 10
	Mrs Joanna Comyne for Radway	3 – 5 – 2
	Mr John Ridgley, gent	2 – 6 – 0
	ditto for Franklin Balls	3 – 4¼

ditto for the Acres	1 – 3 – 0
Mrs Jane Narramor	4 – 12 – 5¾
the occupier of Buddel for	11 – 11¾
John Ball, gent	2 – 1 – 8 ¼
ditto pt. of John Geals Land	1 – 9

Som. RO ref. D/P/Durn/13/2/2 Parish of Durston, Somerset

An Assessment for the necessary relief of the Poor and for other purposes in the several Acts of Parliament relating to the poor for the parish of Durston in the County of Somerset made and assessed the 9th Day of March 1832 at 1s in the pound by Thos Hearn and Jas Parkhouse.

Occupier	Premises	Proprietor	£ – s – d
		Revd R. Gray	0 – 0 – 10
Ackland Richd	Cottage and Garden	Self	0 – 16 – 10¼
	House & Land	do	0 – 10 – 3
	Late Savidge	do	0 – 0 – 6
	Part of Dibbles	do	0 – 2 – 3½
Brown Wm	Part of Taylors	Mr Lindon	0 – 16 – 0¼
	Cottons	do	0 – 9 – 6½
	Sealys	do	0 – 13 – 2¼
	Dibbins		[blank]
Buncombe John	Part of Pococks	Self and others	0 – 2 – 4
Brass Wm	Dwellies	Self	0 – 0 – 10
Barrow Wm	Cottage and garden	Self	0 – 1 – 4
Bobbett Mary	Hascoles	Mr Lindon	2 – 11 – 3½
Bond Abraham	Lodge Farm	Mr Richardson	6 – 6 – 9¼
	Lords Mead	do	0 – 4 – 3
Day Wm	Cottage & Garden	Rev R Gray	0 – 1 – 1¾
Elson Jas	2 Cottages & Garden	Seymour Esqr	0 – 1 – 8
Fawn Jerm	Lak Burrows	do	0 – 0 – 10
Greedy Robt	Orchard & Pasture	John Stone	0 – 8 – 5¼
	House & Lands	do	0 – 1 – 8
Godfrey John	Part of Taylors	Self	0 – 5 – 9¼
	do	do	0 – 8 – 5¼
	do	do	0 – 5 – 1
Hatchwell Wm	Cottage & Garden	Seymour Esqr	0 – 0 – 10

[contd]

Hubbard Jos[h]	Cottage & Garden	do	0 – 0 – 10
Harrison Rob[t]	Great Winsaals	Sir John Ackland	0 – 14 – 10
	Reve Plot	Seymour Esq[r]	0 – 0 – 5½
	Lands	Mrs Richardson	2 – 10 – 7½
Tho[s] Hearn	Buckland Farm	Rev R Gray	27 – 12 – 10
	Warren Plot	Slade Esq[r]	0 – 3 – 0
Hearn W[m]	Under Acre	Mrs Smith	0 – 0 – 9
	House & Lands	do	0 – 1 – 8
	Late Dibbles	Cha[s] Elson	0 – 2 – 2½
	Church Lane Gads	Mrs Smith	0 – 14 – 5
House Ja[s]	House & Lands	Self	2 – 3 – 10
	Part of Englands	do	0 – 0 – 10
Hooper Tho[s]	House & Lands	W[m] Trump	0 – 2 – 2½
Kidner Geo.	House & Lands	Mrs Murray	2 – 4 – 3½
	Late Porters	Mrs Richardson	3 – 6 – 2½
	Part of Englands	do	0 – 4 – 2¼
	Part of Lealys	do	0 – 4 – 4¾
Lang Isaac	Lands	Mr Welch	0 – 2 – 3½
Owens Thos	Part of Pococks	Mrs Porter	0 – 7 – 10¼
	House Tenement	do	0 – 4 – 8¼
	Part of Englands	do	0 – 14 – 10½
	do	do	0 – 1 – 10
	do	do	0 – 3 – 1½
Overseers	Poor house	Seymour Esq[r]	0 – 2 – 2½
Parkhouse Ja[s]	Fogload Farm	Mrs Gatcombe	4 – 12 – 1
Parson Cha[s]	Lindon	Lindon	0 – 5 – 5½
Pollard W[m]	Cottage & Garden	Self	0 – 1 – 1¾
Stoodley Benj[n]	Cottage & Garden & Shop	Self	0 – 2 – 2½
Sealy Ja[s]	Cottage & Garden	Geo. Thresher	0 – 1 – 8
Frump W[m]	Late Stodgels	Revd R. Gray	0 – 16 – 1¾
	Taylors	Self	0 – 5 – 8
	Kingstones	do	0 – 1 – 1¾
	Englands	do	0 – 1 – 1½
	Tithes	Revd R. Gray	4 – 4 – 0

	Flageth Chapel	Slade Esqr	0 – 6 – 9¾
	Garden & Ponds	do	0 – 3 – 4¾
	Late Bryants	Self	0 – 7 – 2
Trapnell Jn°	Part of Dibbles	John Gill	0 – 2 – 0
	Part of Englands	John Richards	0 – 3 – 5½
	Murlings Orchard	do	0 – 1 – 5
	House & Garden	do	0 – 1 – 4¼
Trapnell Sarah	Cottage & Garden	Self	0 – 1 – 3
Trot Humphrey	Cottage & Garden	Self	0 – 1 – 4½
Wilkins Rich^d	Cottage & Garden	Self	0 – 3 – 4

1st   Rate   69   16   –
2nd   do   22nd August 1832
3rd   do   14th December 1832
4th   do   13th March 1833

TNA ref. MH 12/1021 Nantwich Union, Cheshire

[List of ratepayers surcharged, 1855.]

List of Rates Surcharged by the Auditor upon a Poor Rate made 21st of April 1855 at 1^s/5^d per £

No	Name of occupier	Name of owner	Rateable value	Amount imposed upon owner instead of occupier		Amount collected		Amount not recoverable		Causes why not recoverable
			£ s	s	d	s	d	s	d	
10	Berrington, William	Dean & Chapter	2 8	2	6	1	8		10	Error in name of owner – partly liable to be rated on only half value
49	Cookson, Elizabeth	Ralph Ardern	3 12	3	10	2	6½	1	3½	Ditto
123	Greenway, John	Rich,d Done	4 –	4	3		2½	4	½	Rate calculated erroneously on ¾s of £4 instead of on 4s
146	Harding, Henry	Maria Crump	1 –	1	5		8½		8½	Error in name of owner – partly liable to be rated on only half value
166	Johnson, John	Dean & Chapter	4	2	10	2		2	8	Rate calculated erroneously ½ of £4 instead of on 4s

[contd]

188	Statham, R.J.	Lord Alvanley		16	1	2½		10½		4	Error in name of owner – partly liable to be rated on only half value
206	Pinnington, Edwin	Jno Arden Esq.	4	16	5	1½	3	5½	1	8	Ditto
308	Young, Charles	Ditto		8	11	4		5½	10	10½	Rate calculated erroneously on full value at £8 instead of 8s
319	Young, Daniel	Dean & Chapter		16	1	2½		10½		4	Error in name of owner – partly liable to be rated on only half value
					£1–13–8½				£1 – 2 – 9		

12 Feb 56   James Cookson
             Richard Cowdock } Overseers of the Township of Tarporley

TNA ref. MH 12/10466 Taunton Union, Somerset and Devon
[List of owners and occupiers of cottages.]

Creech St. Michael
Nr Taunton
April 13th 1872

Honorable Gentlemen,

In reply to your letter of the 10th Inst. respecting the entering of the names of every occupier of a cottage separately I have to say when this Parish was fresh valued by a Committee of the Parishioners in 1864 there was no Field or separate cottage Valuation.

For instance every Farmer in this Parish inhabiting 5 or 6 cottages on his Farm pays the Rate for the whole.

Some others have 3 or 4 cottages and all rated in one sum the owner likewise pays for all without any deduction.

If I am called upon to enter every occupier's name separately and rate every house I shall be obliged to call the Assessment Committee for a Field and Cottage Valuation. The same as when the late William Talley Voicey Esq. was Auditor for this District and also years before.

Trusting this explanation will be satisfactory.
I remain Honorable Gentlemen
Elijah Godfrey
Assistant Overseer

***

Creech St. Michael

Copy of Cottages, Gardens &c as Charges in the valuation made by a Committee of this Parish on the April 12th 1864.

	Description	Measure R – P	Gross £ – s – d	Rateable £ – s – d
Coombe George	3 Cotts & Garden	1 – 6	8 – 0 – 0	6 – 16 – 0
" "	3 " "	1 – 0	8 – 0 – 0	6 – 16 – 0
Dunning Eliza	2 " "	2 – 36	7 – 10 – 0	6 – 7 – 6
Fry William	3 " "	39	5 – 0 – 0	4 – 5 – 0
Heal Levi	2 " " & Orch.	1 – 35	6 – 0 – 0	5 – 8 – 0
Owens William	3 " " "	2 – 10	10 – 0 – 0	8 – 10 – 0
Philpott Ann	4 "	25	12 – 0 – 0	10 – 4 – 0
Page Ann & Ellen (tenants)	3 "	26	19 – 0 – 0	16 – 3 – 0
Radford Frs	4 " & Orch.	1 – 37	12 – 0 – 0	10 – 4 – 0
Sharman Ann	3 " "	1 – 1 – 16	18 – 0 – 0	16 – 4 – 0
Stevens John	2 "	26	6 – 0 – 0	5 – 2 – 0
Trott Ann	2 " "	2 – 24	8 – 0 – 0	7 – 4 – 0
Brass George	4 "	1 – 19	12 – 0 – 0	10 – 4 – 0
Westcombe John	2 "	1 – 30	13 – 0 – 0	11 – 1 – 0
Winslade John	3 " "	1 – 0 – 3	14 – 0 – 0	12 – 12 – 0

This List are Owners of Cottages, Gardens & Orchards, except ones which are marked as Tenant only.

The two first Owners & Occupiers of Large Farms in this parish in addition to the Cotts &c.

Elijah Godfrey
Assistant Overseer

Som. RO ref. Q/SR/389 Somerset Quarter Sessions Rolls
Midsummer, 1813
[An overseer who, at the Court of Quarter Sessions, challenged the amount of his rates.]

To Thomas Martin and Richard Trood, Churchwardens of the Parish of Wellington in the County of Somerset, and to James Blackmore, one of the Overseers of the Poor of the same Parish, and also to Mark Westron, John Snook and William Wensley.

I James Baker of Wellington aforesaid, malster (one of the Overseers of the Poor of the parish aforesaid) do hereby give you and every of you notice that at the next general Quarter Sessions of the Peace to be holden in and for the said County of Somerset I shall enter an appeal against 'An Assessment for the necessary relief of the poor and for the other purposes in the several acts of Parliament mentioned relating to the Poor of Wellington in the County of Somerset' made by you the said Thomas Martin, Richard Trood and James Blackmore on the nineteenth day of June last and allowed by Joseph Guerin and Lawrence Head Luxton, Clerks, two of His Majesty's Justices of the Peace of and for the said County on the twenty first day of the same month.

First   For that I the said James Baker am assessed and charged in and by the said assessment for and in respect of my Stock in Trade in a larger sum than I ought to have been thereby assessed or charged and more in proportion according to the value of my Stock in Trade than the said Richard Trood, John Snook and William Wensley respectively are assessed or charged for their respective rateable property in the said parish and also more in proportion than many other Inhabitants possessing rateable property in the said parish are respectively assessed or charged by the said assessment.

Secondly   For that you the said Richard Trood are not assessed or charged in and by the said assessment in so large a sum as you ought to have been assessed or charged for and in respect of your Stock in Trade as a Tanner.

Thirdly   For that you the said Mark Westron are not assessed or charged by the said assessment for your Stock in Trade as a Tanner in your Tanyard in the parish aforesaid.

Fourthly For that you the said John Snook are not assessed or charged by the said assessment in so large a sum as you ought to have been assessed or charged for and in respect of Park Farm in the parish aforesaid.

Fifthly   For that you the said William Wensley are not assessed or charged by the said assessment in so large a sum as you ought to have been assessed or charged for and in respect of Pinkmore Farm in the parish aforesaid.

Sixthly   For that the Occupiers of divers Dwelling houses and Gardens within the said parish are not by the said assessment assessed or charged with any sum in respect thereof and for that various other persons possessing rateable Property with the said parish are not by the said assessment assessed or rated with any sum for or in respect of such property.

Seventhly Because the said Assessment is not an equal and just assessment on the Inhabitants of the said parish for their respective rateable property in fair proportion according to the respective values thereof.

And take notice also that I shall at the sitting of the said Court of Quarter Sessions or so soon after as Counsel can be heard move that the hearing of the said appeal may be adjourned to their next Quarter Sessions, to give you time to answer the objections above stated to the said Assessment.

Given under my hand the seventh day of July 1813.

James Baker

CHAPTER 11

WORKHOUSE DIETARY

In the early days of workhouses there was much concern voiced about the treatment of the inmates. Thus the Poor Law Board was obliged to take particular interest in the conditions in each workhouse. The food available was inferior; never of sufficient quantity or quality. There were regular visits to every workhouse by inspectors. The Board of Guardians of each Union was also required to report to the Poor Law Board regularly on the conditions and dietary in their establishment. Therefore, there are to be found amongst the Poor Law correspondence (TNA record class MH 12) many reports detailing the dietary in workhouses. Changes to diet were regularly reported.

The following are some examples of the detail they contain:

TNA ref. MH 12/1412 Launceston Union, Cornwall
[Detailed chart of the nutrients contained in the diet of workhouse inmates.]

Amount of Nutriment contained in the Weekly Dietary of Able-bodied Paupers

Substances used in Dietary	Weight of Substances consumed in a Week oz.	Quantity of Nitrogennus Ingredients oz.	Quantity of Substances free from Nitrogen oz.	Quantity of Mineral Matter oz.	Quantity of Carbon oz.
Men					
Bread	111	7.58	54.00	1.68	27.96
Meat	15	3.35	2.15	.07	3.23
Potatoes	36	.50	7.96	.36	4.39
Soup, 3 pts					
Meat	6	1.34	.86	.03	1.29
Flour	1¼	.21	.82	.00	.57

[contd]

Cabbage	1½	.03	.06	.03	.04
Carrots	6	.09	.70	.05	.32
Turnips	9	.18	1.12	.07	.58
Onions	2 ¼				
Pudding 2lbs					
Flour	20	3.40	13.20	.14	9.10
Suet	2 ²⁄₇	.00	2.28	.00	1.80
Milk Broth 10½ pts					
Flour	5¼	.89	3.46	.03	2.39
Milk	31	1.40	2.45	.19	2.15
Meat Broth 6 pts					
Liquor	– –	.60	1.08	.96	.54
Cheese	– –	1.86	1.52	.29	2.21
Proposed Dietary Total		21.43	91.66	3.90	56.57
Present Dietary		22.00	102.53	4.67	62.88
Average of County		24.81	115.69	4.80	63.31
Average of E. & Wales		22.16	93.91	4.01	58.36
Women					
Bread	104	7.10	50.60	1.57	26.20
Meat	12	2.68	1.72	.06	2.59
Potatoes	36	.50	7.96	.36	4.39
Soup, 3pts					
Meat	6	1.34	.86	.03	1.29
Flour	1¼	.21	.82	.00	.57
Cabbage	1½	.03	.06	.03	.04
Carrots	6	.09	.07	.05	.32
Turnips	9	.18	1.12	.07	.58
Onions	2¼				
Pudding 2 lbs					
Flour	20	3.40	13.20	.14	9.10
Suet	2 ²⁄₇	.00	2.28	.00	1.80
Milk Broth 10½ pts					
Flour	5¼	.89	3.46	.03	2.39

Milk	31	1.40	2.45	.19	2.15
Meat Broth 6 pts					
Liquor	– –	.60	1.08	.96	.54
Cheese	6	1.86	1.52	.29	2.21
Proposed Dietary Total		20.28	87.83	3.78	54.17
Present Dietary		20.59	94.72	4.38	58.27
Average of County		23.47	108.82	4.56	59.33
Average of E. & Wales		19.95	89.02	3.63	54.13

27 Sept 56

TNA ref. MH 12/10498 Wellington Union, Somerset and Devon
[Details of amended dietary given to workhouse inmates.]

Milverton, Somerset
13 March 1867

To the right Honorable
        The President and Commissioners of Her Majesty's Poor Law Board
Gentlemen,
                Wellington Union, Somerset
The Guardians of this Union have forwarded or intend to forward to your Honorable
Board, an altered dietary table for the paupers in the Union at Wellington; and a new
dietary table for the pauper children there. And as an official Guardian, a Magistrate
for Somerset, residing in the Union, I beg permission to state for Your Honorable
Board what follows.
    Towards the end of the last January my attention was directed to the dietary by a
public complaint as to it; and on examining the printed table, I found that it had been
in existence, unaltered since 1852. And on enquiry I found that each man was fed with
7 ounces of bread and a pint and half of gruel of oatmeal, water and salt, and each
woman and child between 9 and 16 with 6 ounces of bread and a pint and half of gruel,
every day for breakfast, and the same every day except Sunday for supper: and for
supper on Sundays with the same quantities of bread with 2 ounces of cheese for each
person, thus giving them 13 meals of bread with water gruel every week continuously.
    And for their dinners weekly, on each Sunday and Thursday the same quantities of
bread, with 2½ ounces of cheese for each person. On each of Wednesday and Saturday a
pound of suet pudding for each man, and 14 ounces for each woman and child between
9 and 16: and on each Monday, Tuesday and Friday 2 ounces of meat with vegetables
for each person, being in total 6 ounces of meat weekly: being 2 dinners of bread and

cheese, 2 of pudding, and 3 dinners consisting in all of 6 ounces of meat weekly: and that being the whole of the animal food given to each person, except the cheese, and the pudding. The younger children had the broth or liquor the meat was boiled in.

The printed dietary provided broth instead of gruel for the breakfasts and suppers. The same public complaint stated that instead of 6 ounces only of meat 15 ounces of meat are allowed weekly in the Tiverton Union Workhouse, only 13 miles distant, and 18 ounces at the City Workhouse at Exeter for each person.

On the 7th February last I attended at the Wellington Board and read the complaint to the guardians, and drew attention particularly to the water gruel 13 times a week, and the very small quantity of 6 ounces of meat allowed for each person weekly, and suggested that 12 ounces weekly instead of 6 might be substituted, and I moved that the Wellington dietary should be brought into unison with that of the Exeter City Workhouse 'or otherwise improved'. A committee of inquiry was thus appointed, to meet on 14th February last.

On the 14th February illness prevented me from attending, but I sent a written statement to the Committee suggesting the following alteration in the dietary.

	Breakfast	**Dinner**	**Supper**
Sunday	Bread & Soup	Bread & Cheese	Bread & Soup
Monday	Bread & Gruel	Meat (4 ounces)	Bread & Gruel
Tuesday	Bread & Soup	Suet Pudding	Bread & Gruel
Wednesday	Bread & Soup	Bread & Cheese	Bread & Soup
Thursday	Bread & Gruel	Meat	Bread & Gruel
Friday	Bread & Soup	Suet Pudding	Bread & Gruel
Saturday	Bread & Gruel	Meat	Bread & Gruel

Thus there would be 8 breakfasts and suppers of gruel with bread, and the other 6 of soup with bread.

   3 dinners of meat – 4 ounces each
   2 " of bread and cheese
   2 " of suet pudding, as at present

I now learn that the Board have altered the dietary for men, women and children between 9 and 16 by giving a quart of skimmed milk with 3 quarts of water to each gallon of gruel, but for breakfast only. That they have left the dinners as they were with 6 ounces of meat weekly only, whilst for supper they have taken away an ounce of bread from each person each meal, and substituted for gruel, 2 ounces of cheese three times a week, leaving water gruel for supper 4 times, or gruel 11 times a week continuously. The liquor from the boiling of the meat goes to the children under 9.

I hope I am not wrong in calling the attention of your Honorable Board to these facts, and in believing that your Honorable Board will withhold your sanction from such a dietary for the adult poor of this Union. For growing children between 9 and 16 it seems even more insufficient and improper, and in fact they complain of hunger between meals.

A second dietary, for children below 9 years old has been prepared, and is, I think better than the other, but they too complain of hunger between meals.

As to the children, surely it is of great importance, and an economical point of view, that growing children should not suffer from want of sufficient food, or be kept without food improperly long.

Chas. Rowcliffe

Note: This letter is continued in Chapter 20 (page 397), where the writer is complaining about boys working a water pump.

TNA ref. MH 12/10498 Wellington Union, Somerset and Devon
[Amended dietary chart of food for the workhouse inmates, 1848.]

At a Meeting of the Board of Guardians of the Wellington Union, held on the twentieth day of June 1867, it was resolved that the following amended Dietary Table for the Paupers, of the respective Classes and Sexes hereunder described, in the Workhouse of this Union be submitted for the sanction and approval of the Poor Law Board, pursuant to the General Dietary Order of that Board, dated the 16th of February 1848.

Dietary for the Able-bodied Paupers												
		Breakfast		Dinner							Supper		
		Bread	Gruel (Best Scotch Oatmeal)	Bread	Cheese	Meat	Vegetables	Suet Pudding	Meat Broth	Bread	Cheese	Gruel (Best Scotch Oatmeal)
		ozs	pints	ozs	ozs	ozs	lbs ozs	lbs ozs	pints	ozs	ozs	pints
Sunday	Men	7	1½	7	2½					6	2	
	Women	6	1½	6	2½					5	2	
Monday	Men	7	1½			3	1 4			6		1½
	Women	6	1½			3	1 4			5		1½
Tuesday	Men	7	1½			3	1 4			6		1½
	Women	6	1½			3	1 4			5		1½
Wednesday	Men	7	1½	3				1 0	1	6	2	
	Women	6	1½	2				8	1	5	2	
Thursday	Men	7	1½	7	2½					6		1½
	Women	6	1½	6	2½					5		1½
Friday	Men	7	1½			3	1 4			6	2	
	Women	6	1½			3	1 4			5	2	
Saturday	Men	7	1½	3				1 0	1	6		1½
	Women	6	1½	2				8	1	5		1½

Children between 9 and 16 years of age to be allowed the same diet as Women.
The Sick to be dieted as directed by the Medical Officer.

Hy Gorges Moysey   Presiding Chairman

I consider the allowances in the above amended Dietary to be sufficient.

Wm Reynolds   Medical Officer

The Poor Law Board sanction the above amended Dietary Table 16 Oct 1867

H. Fleming   Secretary

TNA ref. MH 12/10462 Taunton Union, Somerset and Devon
[Roast beef and plum pudding are to be given to the inmates of the workhouse to celebrate the marriage of the Prince of Wales.]

Taunton Union
14th Feby 1863

My Lords and Gentlemen,

The Guardians of this Union being of opinion that the celebration of the marriage of H.R.H. the Prince of Wales the inmates of the Work House should partake in the general festivity on that joyful occasion.

Resolved that application be made to the Poor Law Board for their sanction and permission to regale the inmates of the house on that happy event with the fare usual on the holiday of Christmas, viz – roast beef and plum pudding with ale, and tea for the females and children that the cost thereof be charged to the Union funds through the master's accounts.

Carried unanimously

I have the honor to be my
Lords and Gentlemen
Your most obedient servant
John Chorley
Clerk

To – The Poor Law Board

Answered 19 Feb 1863
The Board will raise no objection to the alteration which the Guardians propose to make in the Dietary of the Workhouse Inmates on the above mentioned occasion.

TNA ref. MH 12/10224 Bedminster Union, Somerset

[An inmate is complaining about the quality of the food.]

The Workhouse
Flax Bourton
Jany 4th 1876

Gentlemen,

I beg to ask you to provide for rations of a better class than hitherto provided. The beef is of a very inferior quality, and my complaint refers to this item of rations provided. In fact sometimes it is hardly digestible and several times I have been unable to partake of it.

I am Gentlemen
Yours Obediently
L. Probert

TNA ref. MH 12/8989 Berwick upon Tweed Union, Northumberland and Durham

[List of food issued weekly for the officers of a workhouse, 7 April 1875.]

Quantity of Provisions to be drawn weekly from the Workhouse Stores for the use of the Officers of the Workhouse and the Master's daughter.

	Meat	Bread	Potatoes	Flour	Oatmeal	Cheese	Bacon	Milk	Butter	Tea	Coffee	Sugar	Barley	Rice
	lbs	lbs	lbs	lbs	lbs	lbs	lbs	pints	lbs	oz.	oz.	lbs	lbs	lbs
Master	4	–	7	7	–	½	½	2	½	4	–	¾	–	¼
Matron	4	–	7	7	–	–	½	3½	½	4	–	1	–	¾
Master's Daughter	1¾	–	3	4	1½	–	–	3½	¼	1	–	¼	–	–
Lunatic Attendant	4	7	7	2	–	½	–	3½	½	2	2	¾	¾	–
Nurse	4	8	7	–	–	½	–	3½	½	2	2	¾	¾	–
Porter	4	8	7	–	2	–	–	3½	½	2	2	¾	–	¾
Totals	21¾	23	38	20	3½	1½	1	19½	2¾	15	6	4¼	1½	1¾

When potatoes are not used 6 ozs of bread instead each day

CHAPTER 12

OUT RELIEF

Many poor people received assistance while still living in their own home, or with a relative or friend, and sometimes relief was granted to paupers even when they were living away from their place of settlement in another parish. This was termed 'out relief' – usually money, with perhaps a loaf of bread and other food and drink. The supply of such foods and drink was referred to as 'relief in kind'. Up until the formation of the Poor Law Unions, records of out relief were kept by parish officers and should therefore be found amongst the parish documents in county or borough record offices. From 1834 onwards, records of out relief were usually recorded by the clerk of the Poor Law Union in which the pauper's parish was situated. In unusual circumstances some cases of out relief were reported to the Poor Law Commission, and its successors, for their approval. Many references to individual cases of out relief are therefore to be found in the correspondence files of these organisations in document class MH 12 at The National Archives.

The following are some examples:

TNA ref. MH 12/10488 Wellington Union, Somerset and Devon

Wellington, Somerset
30 October 1838

'Out door relief to male paupers'

Gentlemen,

I respectfully beg leave to transmit for your sanction the accompanying cases in which this Board have ordered relief.

I have the Honor to be
Gentlemen
Your most obedt & resp. Servt
Wm Rodham, clerk

To   The Poor Law Commissioners
      Somerset House
      London

The following is part of the list of paupers included with the above letter.

Greedy Thomas, Wiveliscombe   46
        wife   35
        children Harriett   9
                 John   7½
                 James   4½
                 Henry   1

The wife and family earn nothing. The man was a weaver but lost his employment in consequence of the decay of Trade at Wiveliscombe. He now works at a Slate Quarry and earns 7/- per week, but has no liquor. An able bodied workman at that employ earns from 9 to 10/- per week. The man is not able at husbandry to earn the wages of an able bodied Husbandman in consequence of his not knowing how to perform the general labor of that class of workman. Has been engaged in quarry work ever since he ceased to weave, about 2 years. The Board have ordered him to be relieved with 1 loaf per week.

Howell, Richmond, Wiveliscome, 40, wife 38, 6 children aged 12, 10, 8, 6, 3, & 6 months. It appears upon further enquiry that this man who works at Stone breaking for roads earns but 6/- per week instead of 9/- as reported to you in the first instance. That he is not competent to do the general work of Husbandry labour. That during summer months he can earn at stone breaking by task work 9/- per week but during the short days in the winter months when he is similarly employed but at daily wages, he only earns 6/- per week.

The Board have ordered him 2/- and 2 loaves with alternative of the Workhouse.

Poor Law Commission
Somerset House
7 Nov. 1838

The Poor Law Commis^rs having carefully considered the cases of the labourers Thomas Greedy and Richmond Howell reported in your letter of 30th ulto, will not undertake to say that relief afforded in these cases is so unnecessary as to justify disallowance but the Commis^rs trust it will not be continued beyond the time when the parties are able to maintain themselves. Meantime the Commis^rs suggest for the consideration of the Gds. the efficiency of receiving one of each of the labourer's children into the Workhouse, instead of the out relief proposed to be given to them.

The Commis^{rs} rely upon the Bd of Gd^{ns} for carrying into effect the principles of the Poor Law Amendment Act, the main object of which is to put an end to relief in aid of wages to able bodied men.

Signed by order of this Bd.
R.B.C.

To The Clerk of the Gd^{ns}
Wellington Union

Som. RO ref. D/G/Ta/8a/4 Taunton Union, Somerset and Devon Minutes of the meetings of the Board of Guardians

6th October 1841
Cases of able bodied men relieved on account of sickness, accident or infirmity during such illness came before the Board, viz.

Parish	Name	Family		Medical Certificate	Relief			
		If Wife	Children under 10		Allowed	In money	In kind	Time if limited
Monkton West	Bradbeer, Saml	1	–	Debility	1/1½	1/-	2	1
	Coles, Robert	1	3	Jane (wife) Inflamed face	–	–	2	1
	Golsworthy, W^m	1	4	George (child) injured thigh	1/1½	–	3	–
	Hill, Henry	–	3	No medical return	–	–	–	
Staplegrove	Reed, W^m	1	2	Lumbago	–	3/-	4	–
Taunton St. Ja^s	Leakey, Robt	1	4	Chill – Sarah (wife) cough	3/3	6/-	6	–
	Hallet, David	1	–	Mary (wife) diseased lungs	Refused			
Taunton St. Mary	Hawkins, Jos. [sic]	1	2	Husband absconded	Workhouse			
	Lake, James	single		No medical return	Workhouse			
	Sampson, Robt	1	2	Betty (wife) pain in side	Pay to be stopped			
	Marsh, W^m	single		Trached (in door)	–	2/6	–	2
Ash Priors	Mantle, Ja^s	1	3	Charlotte (wife) mild fever	–	–	4	–
	Hembrow, John	single		No medical return	–	–	–	–
Bps Lydeard	Davy, Robt	1	4	Hannah (wife) fever	3/- all^d			
	Clement, David	1	2	Inflammation of the leg	–	3/-	4	–

222

Kingston	Parsons, W^m	single		Diseased hip	5/- all^d			
	Vickery, James	1	6	Betsy (wife) child bed	5/-	–	4	4
	Strong, John	1	1	Diarrhea	2/5	2/-	2	–
	Harris, John	1	3	Cut arm	3/7½	2/-	4	–
Ly^d. St. Law.	Pain, W^m	1	2	No medical return child deformed	–	–	2	–
Creech St. Michael	Coleman, John	1	5	Accident – can't work	3/6	5/6	6	–
	Burgess, George	1	4	Man in prison	Workhouse			
	Caswell, W^m.	1	4	Erysipelas	3/6	4/-	–	1
Curry North	Gould, James	1	–	Inflamed Lungs	2/-	2/-	1	–
Stoke St. Gregory	Boobier, Rich^d	1	2	Bowel complaint	2/3	3/-	4	–
	Tulliett, John	1	5	Maria (wife) debility	2/4	–	4	–
Thurlbeer	Gillard, W^m.	1	4	Child birth	5/-	–	4	4
Otterford	Lane, Robt.	1	3	Child birth	Refused			
Trull	Dean, Jo^s.	1	3	do	Refused			
Wilton	Hill, Thomas	1	4	No proper medical return	2/2	–	–	–
	Arberry, Jo^s.	1	2	No medical return	[blank]			
Monkton – West	Richards, James	1	2	Diarrhea	–	1/-	4	–

TNA ref. MH 12/13432 Nuneaton Union, Warwickshire

[Pauper men who applied for relief were sometimes found work as is shown by the following.]

Able bodied men at work at the time of the receipt of the communication from the Poor Law Commission of the 17th Jany 1842.

Kelsey George	3 days work
Wagstaff Thomas	4 do
Slater Richard	3 do
Robinson John	2 do
Suffolk Joseph	2 do
Jelley Robert	6 do
Drakeley Charles	6 do

Board day Wednesday Jan[y] 19th 1842
Application from able bodied men class 8

Nuneaton	14				Houses	8
Astley	1	}	result of application		work	6
Bulkington	3		21		did not attend	4
Chilvers Coton	3				work found	2
						21

Paupers ordered work

Copson Joseph	6 days work
Everitt Joseph	6 do
Marston John	6 do
Enson Thomas	6 do
Hincks Thomas	4 do
Ivens Thomas	6 do

Board day Jany 26th 1842
Applications from Able Bodied Men Class 8

Nuneaton	9				Houses	5
Astley	1	}	results of applications		work at W.H.	4
Weddington	1		16		did not attend	1
Bulkington	1				Refused	5
C. Coton	4				Work found	1
						16

Paupers Ordered to Work

Marston John	5 days work
Copson Joseph	6 do
Ball John	2 do
Hincks Thomas	4 do

Board day February 2nd 1842
Applications from able bodied men Class 8

Nuneaton	4				work at W.H.	6
Bulkington	2	}	results of applications		did not attend	2
C. Coton	3		9		refused	1
						9

TNA ref. MH 12/13432 Nuneaton Union, Warwickshire
[Out relief is given to some able-bodied paupers, but they have to work in a mill.]

Nuneaton Union
John Estlin, clerk
17th June 1842

Gentlemen,

Out Relief

In addition to the list of able bodied paupers forwarded by me on the 15th instant the following have been ordered relief, in work at the Mill to which the Guardians most respectfully request your sanction.

June 9th

William Miller aged 58	2 days work
George Helier, 52, wife & 1 child	2 days work
Thomas Ratcliff, 38, wife & 5 children	6 days work

June 16th

Samuel Allen, 45, wife & 2 children	3 days work
Thomas Critchlow, 42, wife & 5 children	3 " "
William Buckler, 50, wife & 2 children	3 " "
Thomas Atkins, 42, and wife	2 " "
Samuel Wagstaff, 40, wife and 1 child	3 " "
John Davy, 31, wife and 3 children	2 " "
Thomas Petty, 52, wife and 3 children	4 " "
William Smith, 31, wife and 3 children	3 " "

I also forward the weekly statements and am glad to state the Trade of our neighbourhood is in an improving state and the people expect to be better employed soon.

I have the honor to be
Gentlemen
Your very obᵗ Servᵗ
John Estlin

To The Poor Law Commissioners
    London
Recommend these are sanctioned. Mr Estlin's report regarding this neighbourhood confirms my previous actions.   A. Power
                    19 June 1842

Sanction 20th June S.H.

TNA ref. MH 12/13433 Nuneaton Union, Warwickshire
[Out relief is considered for a widow who is living with her daughter.]

Nuneaton Union
John Estlin, clerk
4th Febry 1845

Gentlemen,

Case of Elizabeth Jeffery

An application was made to the Guardians at their last meeting to allow out relief to this pauper who is a widow aged 84 years belonging to the parish of Nuneaton and who wishes to reside with her daughter at Atherstone. The Board seem disposed to grant this request and I was instructed to report the case to you and respectfully to ask your sanction as the Guardians think the old woman will be more comfortable with her daughter than in the Workhouse. I shall be obliged by an answer and have the honor to remain

Gentlemen
Your very obedient Servt
John Estlin

The Poor Law Commissioners
Somerset House
London

Som. RO ref. D/G/W/8a/9 Wellington Union, Somerset and Devon
Minutes of the meetings of the Board of Guardians
[An application for outdoor relief for the family of a pauper who is in a workhouse.]

30th November 1854

Application was made for Outdoor Relief on account of the wife and family of a pauper named Robert Hurford of the parish of Ashbrittle, during the time he is an Inmate of this Union Workhouse.

It appeared that this pauper had his leg broken by the wheel of a cart passing over it. The accident occurred in the parish of Wellington and the pauper, instead of being conveyed to the Hospital at Taunton, was brought into the Workhouse. He has a wife and six children aged respectively 14, 12, 10, 8, 6 and 4 years. The pauper carried on the trade of a thatcher and earned about 10s/- per week. It was represented to the Board that if the pauper's family were obliged to come into the Workhouse he would, in all probability lose his business, whereas if OUT DOOR relief was granted, one of the pauper's sons (who now partly maintains himself) could, with the aid of a journeyman, keep his father's business together.

The Board, considering that under the above circumstances, it would be advisable to grant OUT DOOR relief to the extent of five loaves of bread, directed the Clerk to report the case to the Poor Law Board and obtain their sanction to the same.

Confirmed   Wm Elworthy
Chairman

Dev. RO (Plym.) ref. 1576/41 Plympton St. Mary Union, Devon

[List of persons receiving out relief from an accounts statement. The original also shows those receiving indoor relief.]

The Parochial List and Statement of Account

Plympton St. Mary Union. Parish of Yealmpton

List of Paupers whose Relief is charged against the Parish, together with a Statement of the Amounts respectively credited and debited to the Parish in the Union Accounts, for the Half-Year ending Michaelmas 1857.

Names of the Paupers	If not in the above Parish where	Cause	Amount given to each Pauper during the Half-Year	
			In Money £ – s – d	In Kind £ – s – d
Bowhay Ann	In the Parish	Old age	2 – 0 – 0	– – 17 – 10
Cawse Hannah	"	"	2 – 12 – 0	– – 13 – 3½
Cooper Elizth	"	"	3 – 5 – 0	– – 13 – 3¼
Chapple Sarah	"	Sickness	4 – 9 – 0	2 – 18 – 4¼
Goad John	"	"		3 – 13 – ¾
Husband Jane	"	Old age	2 – 12 – 0	– – 13 – 3¼
Knight Jane	"	"	1 – 6 – 0	– – 13 – 3¼
Kelland Peter	"	"	3 – 5 – 0	– – 13 – 3¼
Miller William	"	"	3 – 6 – 0	– – 7 – 9¼
Maynard Sarah	"	"	2 – 12 – 0	– – 13 – 3¼
Barnes Ann	"	"	2 – 2 – 6	– – 13 – 3¼
Mee William	"	"	– – 13 – 0	– – 13 – 3¼
Penwell Sarah	"	"	3 – 5 – 0	– – 13 – 3¼
Rowse Catherine	"	"	2 – 4 – 6	– – 14 – 5¼
Radcliffe Ann	"	"	3 – 5 – 0	– – 13 – 3¼
Stephen Susan	"	"	2 – 12 – 0	– – 13 – 3¼
Smale Elizth	"	"	3 – 5 – 0	– – 15 – 3¼
Shepherd Ann	Creacombe	"	– – 8 – 0	– – 10 – 2¼
Spurrell Ann	In the Parish	"	1 – 6 – 0	– – 13 – 3¼
Tregillions Mary	"	"	2 – 12 – 6	– – 13 – 3¼
Wyatt John	"	"	3 – 2 – 0	1 – 6 – 6½
Shepherd Agnes	Holbeton	"	1 – 19 – 0	13 – 3¼
Cornish Jane	In the Parish	Sickness	2 – 12 – 0	– – 13 – 3¼
Coyte William	Underwood	"	1 – 6 – 0	1 – 6 – 6½

W.T. Baker Master   *Henry S. Pearce* Relieving Officer

TNA ref. MH 12/10461 Taunton Union, Somerset and Devon
[A Union asks for permission to grant out relief.]

Poor Law Board
Whitehall, S.W.

To John Chorley, Esq.
Clerk to the Guardians of the Taunton Union
28th May 1860

NON-RESIDENT RELIEF

Sir, I am directed by the Poor Law Board to acknowledge the receipt of your letter of the 16ᵗʰ instant respecting the case of Jane Barnstaple, and to state that, under

No	Name of Pauper or Applicant for Relief	Parish to which belonging	Cause of seeking Relief	Residence	Year when Born	If Able or Disabled	Family	Calling
106	Turner, Amelia	Kilmersdon	Old Age	Coleford	1773	dis.		
107	Treasure, Eliza	"	Husband a Mariner	Radstock	–	able	1 child	
108	Weaver, Mary	"	Old Age	Paulton	1760	dis.		
109	Wrintmoon, Mary	"	Afflicted	Coleford	1799	dis.		
110	Witcombe, Sarah	"	Afflicted	"	1785	dis.		
111	Witcombe, Joanna	"	Afflicted	"	1780	"		
112	Willcox, Jnᵒ	"	Afflicted	"	1770	"		Coalminer
113	Willcox, Ruth	"	"	"	1774	able		
114	Witcombe, Honor	"	Old Age	"	1750	dis.		
115	Witcombe, Henry	"	Ruptured	"	1764	dis.		
116	Witcombe, Eliz.	"	–	"	1768	"		Knitter
117	Witcombe, Unice	"	Afflicted	"	1775			"
118	Watts, Betty	"	Old Age	"	1758	"		"
119	Watts, Sarah her daugʳ	"	Illness	"	1791	"		"
120	Willcox, Jemima	"	Widow	"	1789	able	2 childn	
121	Witcombe, Fanny	"	Old Age	"	1758	dis.		
122	Witcombe, Joshua	"	Old Age	"	1761	"		Coalminer
123	Witcombe, Mary	"	Widow	"	1784	able	2 childn	Knitter
124	Yeats, Lucy	"	Widow	Kilmersdon	1764	"		
125	Smith, Caroline	"	Old Age	"	1775	able		Knitter
126	Snook, Martha	"	Widow	"	1795	able	4 childn	
127	Moore, Betty	"	Widow	Coleford	1768	"		
128	James, Eliza	Midsummer Norton	Widow	"	–	–	3 childn	

the circumstances now reported, the Board consider that the case is within the 2nd Exception to Article 3 of the General Prohibitory Order and that it is therefore one which the Guardians of the Taunton Union may, if they think proper, grant non resident relief without the special sanction of this Board.

J. Hunt

Som. RO ref. D/G/F/133/2 Frome Union, Somerset
Frome Workhouse Out Relief Book

If receiving any, and what Temporary Relief	Initials of Presiding Guardian allowing or refusing Relief	Date when allowed or refused, if allowed, for what time	Relief Allowed					Relief Given		Remarks
			Money		Bread			Amount of value		
			s	d	Quantity	s	d	s	d	
1/-	RN	June 28th		6	4lbs		6½	1	½	
1/-		Permanent		6	4lbs		6½	1	½	
1/6			1	6	4lbs		6½	2	½	
2/6			2		4lbs		6½	2	6½	
1/3				9	4lbs		6½	1	3½	
1/3				9	4lbs		6½	1	3½	
2/6			2	6				2	6	
2/-	RN	June 28th	2					2	0	
3/-			3					3	0	
1/-				6	4lbs		6½	1	½	
2/-			2					2		
/6					4lbs		6½		6½	
2/-	RN	June 28th	1		8lbs	1	1	2	1	
1/6			1	6				1	6	
1/-				6	4lbs		6½	1	½	
2/6			1	6	8lbs	1	1	2	½	
1/6			1		4lbs		6½	1	6½	
1/6	GR	July 26th	1	9				1	9	Permanent
4/9			2	9	16lbs	2	2	4	11	
1/3	RN	June 28th		9	4lbs		6½	1	3½	
4/6			2	6	16lbs	2	2	4	8	

[contd]

No	Name of Pauper or Applicant for Relief	Parish to which belonging	Cause of seeking Relief	Residence	Year when Born	If Able or Disabled	Family	Calling
129	Taylor, Rebecca	Kilmersdon	Husband absconded	Kilmersdon	1805	dis.	2 childn	
130	Moore, William	"	Afflicted	Kilmersdon Common	1792	dis.	5 childn	Coalminer
131	Moore, Mary, his wife	"	"	"	1794	able		
132	Ashman, Jane	"	Bastard	"	1836	dis.		
133	Moore, Hester	"	Unable to support herself	Coleford	1786	able	none	Knitter
134	Taylor's, Martha BC	"	Bastard	Kilmersdon Common	1832		Mother	Knitter
135	Coles, Abraham	"	Old & infirm	Kilmersdon	1763	dis.		Coalminer
136	Watts, Martha	"	Old & infirm	Bath	1768	dis.		
137	Button, Mary	"	Bastard	Coleford	1836	able		
138	Yeates, Ann	"	Bastard	Kilmersdon	1834			
139	Plummer, Ann	"	Earnings insufficient	Coleford	1796			Knitter
140	Hill, Harriatt	"	Bastard	Ashwick	1811	able		Dairywoman

If receiving any, and what Temporary Relief	Initials of Presiding Guardian allowing or refusing Relief	Date when allowed or refused, if allowed, for what time	Relief Allowed					Relief Given		Remarks
			Money		Bread			Amount of value		
			s	d	Quantity	s	d	s	d	
2/6	GR	July 19th	2	6	12lbs	12	7½	4	1½	To be increased
5/0	GR	June 14th	2	6	20	2	8½	5	2½	till work is found for him
										till work is found
	GR	June 14th			8lbs	1	1	1	1	To the end of quarter
	WHS	June 28th			4lbs		6½		6½	for one month
1/6	RN	June 28th	1		4lbs		6½	1	6½	
1/6			1	6				1	6	
	GR	June 26th for past week			4lbs					
					8lbs	1	1	1	1	
	RN	June 28th			4lbs		6½		6½	
	GR	July 19th for one week			4lbs				6½	

CHAPTER 13

SICKNESS AND DEATH

There are very few registers recording the treatment given to the sick in workhouse infirmaries but occasionally correspondence (sometimes from an inmate) may shed some light on the medical treatment and behaviour of the medical officer.

Any unusual deaths in the workhouse had to be reported to the central authorities. If a post mortem and inquest followed, these were reported and details can often be found in the central correspondence files, document class MH 12 at The National Archives.

Registers of Deaths survive for many workhouses and will be found in county or borough record offices. The minutes of the meetings of the Board of Guardians of a Union may sometimes record deaths in the workhouse.

The following examples of such correspondence convey what, by today's standards, appears to be very primitive and often harsh treatment of the sick. Some examples from Registers of Deaths, and deaths recorded in the minutes of the meetings of The Board of Guardians of Unions are also included.

TNA ref. MH 12/10455 Taunton Union, Somerset and Devon
[Enquiry into a death when it was found that two death certificates had been issued.]

1841   Death of William Cooke aged 65, labourer who died 8th January 1840 at Silver Street, St. Mary Magdalene, Taunton.
Copies of two entries of Death from the Register Book.
The first entry, dated 11th January 1841, which was reported by Sarah Budd of Silver Street, Taunton, states the death was caused by 'Want of food.'
The second entry, dated 16th January 1841, which was reported by the coroner Richard Pople Cainer, states the cause of death 'Natural death having been some time afflicted with Asthma.'
25th January 1841   An inquest has been carried out on the body of William Cooke.

***

Taunton January 11th 1841

Gentlemen,

Agreeably to directions received from the Registrar General I enclose a copy of the Registration of the Death of William Cooke, who died (according to the declaration of my Informant) from want of Food.

I am Gentlemen,
Your Obedient Servant,
H. Alford
Registrar of Births and Death in the District of Taunton St. Mary Magdalene

**

Poor Law Commission Office
Somerset House
13 January 1841

Sir,

The Poor Law Commission forward to you the accompanying copy of a Letter and Certificate which they have rec'd from the Registrar of Births and Deaths for Taunton St. Mary Magdalene District relating to the death of William Cooke.

The Commissioners request that the Bd. of Gd[ns] of the Taunton Union will make enquiry as to the circumstances of the death of the above mentioned person & will report to them the result of the enquiry.

**

PL Gd[ns]
13 Jan[y] 1841
Death of Wm Cooke

The PL Gd[ns] forward to you herewith the sum of two shillings & sixpence for the certificate you have transmitted to them as to the death of William Cooke.

Som. RO ref. D/G/Ta/8a/3 Taunton Union
Minutes of meetings of the Guardians

3rd February 1841   The Board proceeded to investigate the case of William Cooke, in compliance with a request from the Poor Law Commissioners who as is alleged, died of want of food. The following witnesses were examined. Henry Alford, Sarah Budd, Betty Cooke, Francis Whitwham and James R. Mosse. The further investigation was then adjourned till the next Board day in consequence of Charlotte Cooke, daughter of the deceased being unable to attend from illness.

10th February 1841   The Clerk reported that Charlotte Cooke was still unable to attend the Board to be examined as to the decease of her father in consequence of illness. It was moved by the Chairman, seconded by Mr Musgrave that Messrs

House and Turle be a Committee to examine Charlotte Cooke a witness in the case of William Cooke and that they report to this Board the evidence taken.

The evidence was sent to the Poor Law Commission as a reply to their letter of 14ᵗʰ January.

[There is no detail recorded here of the evidence.]

TNA ref. MH 12/10455 (continued)

Taunton Union
Extracted from the Minute Book

1841, 20 Jan.

The Clerk reported that he had received from the Commissioners a letter relative to the death of William Cook with copy of a letter from Mr Alford, Registrar of Births and Deaths and copy of the registry of death wherein it is stated that William Cook died from 'Want of food.'

The letter from the Commissioners relative to the case of Wm. Cook alleged to have died from want of food was read. The Board after making some investigation into the case directed the Clerk to require the attendance of all necessary witnesses on Wednesday next and adjourned a further hearing of the case until that day.

27 Jan. The Clerk reported that he had called on and required the attendance of the witnesses in the case of William Cooke.

Moved by Mr Marshall, seconded by Mr Sims that the enquiry into the death of Cook the pauper be adjourned until this day week the business of this Board precluding the further consideration of it today. Carried.

1841 3 Feb. The Board then proceeded to investigate the case of William Cook in compliance with a request from the Poor Law Commissioners who as is alleged died from want of food. The following witnesses were examined. Henry Alford, Sarah Budd, Betty Cook, Francis Whitwham and James R. Mosse. The further investigation was then adjourned till the next Board day in consequence of Charlotte Cook, daughter of the deceased being unable to attend from illness.

10 Feb. The Clerk reported that Charlotte Cook was still unable to attend the Board to be examined in the case of her father in consequence of illness it was moved by the Chairman, seconded by Mr Musgrave that Mrssrs House and Turle be a committee to examine Charlotte Cook a witness in the case of William Cook and that they report to this Board the evidence taken. Carried.

Messrs House and Turle the Committee appointed to examine Charlotte Cook reported that they had waited on her and taken her examination in writing which was produced. That they have also taken evidence of Eliza Escott who heard the conversation between Mr Whitwham, Betty Cook and Charlotte Cook which was also produced.

Mr Whitwham was then called in and the statements of Charlotte Cook and Eliza Escott read over to him.

The evidence being now completed the Clerk directed to send copies thereof to the Poor Law Commissioners as a reply to their letter of 14ᵗʰ January last.

Board Room 3 Feb. 1841

Henry Alford – I am Registrar of Births and Deaths. A woman called on me to register the death of William Cook; she said she was present at death. On enquiry as to the cause of death she said 'Why Sir as to that he died of starvation.' I examined her particularly as to the circumstances attending his death; she adhered to the same; said he had been afflicted with asthma many years but had died from want of food. I registered accordingly, and according to my regulations I forwarded a copy of the registration to the Poor Law Commissioners. I did not know the man personally. I did not enquire of any other person. I immediately informed the Clerk of the Union of what I had done as a mere civility to the Board. There has been an inquest held on the case. In consequence I received notice from the Coroner of the cause of death which I now produce.

   Copy. 'I hereby certify that I have this day held an inquest on William Cook late of Silver Street in the parish of Taunton St. Mary Magdalene aged 65 who died on Friday the 8th instant, a natural death having a long time been afflicted with asthma.' Witness my hand this fifteenth day of January 1841.

R.P. Caines of Langport, Coroner.

I registered the death from that information and erased the original entry and have sent to the Poor Law Commissioners a copy of the second registration.

Sarah Budd.   'The Monday fortnight that Wm Cook died the Friday week afterwards Cook's wife came to me and said she thought her husband was near his death. She said by his manner of speaking he called for some bread and water and asked for some. She said she had not any to give him; she did not like to give him cold water as she thought it would hurt him; she had nothing but a few tea leaves in the house which had been boiled down three times before. I desired her to go to Mr Whitwham the Relieving Officer and ask him to give her relief. When she came back she told me that Mr Whitwham could not relieve her on account of her husband not being on the sick list. I was present at his death; I was there about ¼ hour before he died. I went to Mr Alford to have him registered. Mr Alford asked me what he died of; I told him he had an asthma several years; he asked me if he had any other complaints that I knew of. I said no but that he had been in great want.'

Betty Cook.   'My husband desired my daughter to go to Mr Mosse to desire Mr Mosse to come to see him. The Monday that he died the Friday week following. He did not come that day but came the next when Mr Mosse came down I asked him to be so kind as to put my husband on the list to have something of Mr Whitwham. He said it was too late that week because the sick list had been made out for that week; it was between 3 & 4 o'clock in the afternoon. Mr Mosse said he would see what he could do and put him down the Monday after. Before Mr Mosse came to see my husband I had been to Mr Whitwham. I told him what distress I was in and he told me I was to go to Mr Mosse again about 12 o'clock. I went again to Mr Mosse; he was not home. Coming therefrom I met Mr Whitwham. I told him I had been to Mr Mosse who was not home and I said what

235

can I do I have nothing in the house and the dear old soul is most starved to death. He said as Mr Mosse was not home I was to go again to him, and between 2 and 4 in the afternoon Mr Mosse came to see my husband. After Mr Mosse went away I again applied to Mr Whitwham and told him that Mr Mosse had seen my husband. He told me he should go to the Board tomorrow and would give the case in, and told me to come to him on Friday to the pay table. I asked him whatever I was to do till Friday. He again said call again Friday. He did not give me anything then. I went to the pay table Friday; he said has Mr Mosse seen your husband. I said you know he has, as I told you he had on Tuesday. He did not give me anything then. He said I shall give it into the Board next Wednesday. The Monday following I applied to him again having been before to Mr Mosse who gave a note to take to Mr Whitwham. Mrs Whitwham came to the door and said Mr W. was out of town and would not be home till about 5 in the evening. I gave her Mr Mosse's note and she told me to come at 6 o'clock. I was ill and could not go over but on Tuesday morning I went over and saw Mr Whitwham himself. I told him my husband was worse and asked him what I was to do, and Mr Whitwham said if you have not got anything stop, and he gave me a ticket for a lb of mutton and another ticket for a loaf of bread. I received no more from Mr Whitwham till the Friday pay day when he died. My husband died about 6 o'clock in the morning. On the Friday he sent me 2/- and a loaf of bread.

The evidence of the Relieving Officer having been read over in the presence of this witness she said:– 'I deny that part of Mr Whitwham's statement relating to a conversation with me about his attention on my husband; it is not true. I did not say what he has stated, nor did I hear my daughter say so.'

Francis Whitwham, Relieving Officer. 'Mrs Cook came to me on the Tuesday week before her husband died. She wanted to have her name entered for some relief for her husband. I think she said her husband was ill. I told her there was an order from the Board of Guardians to receive no application after Monday but that if her husband was ill she must go to Mr Mosse and he would attend. I then told her if she wished to make application the ensuing week she was to come to me at the pay table Friday. She came and did make application, she did not ask for anything. Between that time and the following Wednesday I visited the man and I found him sitting by the fire. I enquired how he was and told them I would do what I could for them at the Board the following Wednesday but that they never told me or gave me any reason to suppose that they were in the state of destitution she has since stated they were in. The Tuesday morning the wife came to me and said she did not know what to do till Friday. I said if that be the case come inside, I'll give you something. I then gave a note for a lb of mutton and ticket for a loaf of bread. I brought the case before the Board on the Wednesday and 2/- and a half loaf was ordered and 1/- given by me allowed. I heard at the pay table that the man was dead by some one who came from the house and an application was made to me at that time for a coffin. I called on the woman having heard that the man had died from want of food to know whether she meant to impute any blame to me for it. She or her daughter said, 'No not in the least', for as soon as she applied and told what state they were in which was the Tuesday morning I at once said, 'Come in and I will give you something'. The daughter was likewise there and corroborated everything the woman had said. She likewise stated that her husband should say when she came home that some persons were in the habit of saying I was rather hard and did not do as much as I could but he didn't think so, that I had done all in my power for him and felt obliged for it.

The evidence of Charlotte Cook the daughter and Eliza Escott taken by the Committee on the 10th Feb having been read over to the witness he said:–
   'I adhere to my former statement.'

James Robert Mosse.   I am Medical Officer of the Taunton Union. I have many times been called on to see William Cook as he had a long time been afflicted with asthma and given the usual medicines which afforded him relief. I heard of his being ill on the Monday and on the following day I visited him and found him labouring under his old complaint but more severe from the inclemency of the weather. They told me they were poorly off but never made any direct application for relief nor did I ever hear of any until the Monday previous to his death when the usual printed medical certificate was filled out and honoured afterwards by Mr Whitwham. This I know was done as I enquired of the parties the next day that they had had the relief ordered and were thankful. They never murmured to me. The first application was of a Tuesday about ten days previous to Cook's death between 3 & 4 in the afternoon. (Mrs Cook asked me to put her husband on the sick list. I told her I cold not on that week as it had gone into the hands of the Officer but that I would put his name down on my paper tomorrow (Wednesday) the beginning of the new list for the ensuing week. That list would be presented to the Board the week after). I attended him during the week but they never made application for relief to me beyond medicines. The first time they did make application to me for relief was on the Monday previous to his death.

   Evidence taken by the Committee appointed on the 10th February 1841 and
   reported to the Board the same day
Charlotte Cook.   I am 21 years old and lived with my father and mother to the time of his death. A few days after my father's death Mr Whitwham called on my mother and myself to tell us that my father was to have a Coroner's inquest. He said 'do you lay any blame to me?'
I said in my mother's presence 'Oh no Sir how can I lay any blame to you for having my father crowned.' [sic] I returned him 'thanks for coming over to tell us of it'. I never heard my father complain of Mr Whitwham's conduct nor say anything in his favor. Eliza Escott was in the pantry close by me when the conversation between Mr Whitwham and me took place. I deny all Mr Whitwham's statements to the Board of Guardians relative to the above conversation.
Eliza Escott.   I am twenty years old and was in the pantry close by Mr Whitwham, Betty Cook and Charlotte Cook when the above conversation took

place which I declare to be what passed between them. There was nothing said by Mr Whitwham or either of the Cooks at the time except what Charlotte Cook stated.

Taunton Union
Poor Law Commissioners Office
Somerset House
4th March 1841

Death of William Cook

Sir,

The Poor Law Commissioners acknowledge the receipt of your letter of the 12th ult. forwarding to them copies of the statements of witnesses who have been examined by the Board of Guardians of the Taunton Union in the enquiry instituted by them as to the circumstances of the death of William Cook.

The Commissioners observe that the Relieving Officer, Mr Whitwham states as follows. [There then follows a full transcript of his statement.]

The Commissioners request that they may be furnished with an explanation of this evidence and with copies of any regulations of the Board of Guardians as any bye law by which the practice therein adverted to is established. They further request to be informed whether the Relieving Officer is not fully aware that if any one requires before he can duly bring it before the Board of Guardians he has authority to give relief in necessaries and to order medicine relief in the interim.

Yours &c
C. Secy

***

Poor Law Commission Office
Somerset House
10 April 1841

Sir,

The Poor Law Commissioners acknowledge the receipt of your letter of the 11th ult. communicating to them some further information which refers to the circumstances connected with the death of Wm Cook, and having had the whole of the circumstances of the case again under their consideration they desire to state that they consider the deceased was in fact in a state of destitution at the time of the first application on his behalf to the Relieving Officer on the Tuesday week preceding his application. They are of opinion that the Relieving Officer should have visited the case at an earlier period than he did visit it and should have ascertained by enquiry the actual condition of the applicant.

To this extent the Commissioners think that the Relieving Officer's conduct is reprehensible and that he should be admonished to act with greater care in future.

The Commissioners do not charge the R. Officer with any additional neglect. They believe that until the Tuesday before the death of the deceased he regarded the application made on his behalf by his wife as not being for immediate relief in kind, but for relief under the order of the R. Officer in the ordinary way and that his attention was not called to the urgency of the destitution until the Tuesday last adverted to when he immediately gave some relief.

The Commissioners think that Mrs Cook's statement that she complained of want of food on the first Tuesday on which she applied to the Relieving Officer is incorrect and that her complaint was in fact made on the latter Tuesday.

G

Minutes continued:

21st April 1841. The letter from the Poor Law Commissioners relating to the death of William Cooke was read. Mr Whitwham, the Relieving Officer, called before the Board and the contents thereof made known to him. He was admonished accordingly to the purport of the letter to act with great caution in future.

Som. RO ref. D/G/W/8a/3
Minutes of the Board of Guardians of Wellington Union
[Enquiry into the death of a pauper who died shortly after admission to the workhouse.]

17th November 1841
The master of the Workhouse reported that John Burnett, pauper of Sampford Arundel sent into this Workhouse by the relieving officer was admitted in a state of extreme exhaustion on the 17th instant, that the medical officer of the Workhouse was sent for to attend the pauper, that he came and administered such remedies as he considered proper, but that the pauper died in a few hours after his dinner.

The Board deciding the case one in which it was desirable to make enquiry in order to ascertain whether any culpability attached to any one charged with the administration of relief, the following statements are made.

Mr Bidgood Guardian of Sampford Arundel, stated that on the 10th of November Burnett came to the place where the poor were paid. Mr Blackmore, relieving officer, stated that on that day he gave the pauper a ticket of admission to the Workhouse and a loaf of bread, that he was previously in the receipt regularly of 2^s/- and a loaf as outdoor relief.

That on last Wednesday (the 17th) his son went and found that he (Burnett) had been sleeping in linhays and gave him another Ticket of Admission and sent him to the Union Workhouse in a cart.

Mr Southey the Governor stated that he was brought about 3 o'clock on Wednesday to the Workhouse in a cart and was covered over with straw. That every attention was paid to him, and the Medical Officer immediately sent for, who came and considered him in a dying state, that he lived until half past ten o'clock the same night. That he has absconded from the Workhouse wearing away the Union clothes.

The following is the report of the Medical Officer.
'I was sent for on Wednesday afternoon Nov 17th to go to the Union House to see John Burnett, 82 years of age, who was just brought in. Being from home at the time, I did

not go till between five and six that evening. I was accompanied by Mr Southey to see the deceased whom I considered to be in a dying state. I requested that nourishment may be given to him in small quantities and often, but I afterwards heard that he died a few hours after I had seen him. I have no doubt but that death resulted from natural causes.'

TNA ref. MH 12/10543 Williton Union, Somerset
[Death of a Greenwich out-pensioner.]

Williton, Somerset
12 April 1842

Gentlemen,

William Locke, a Greenwich Out Pensioner, died in the Williton Union Workhouse on the 10th ulto having been an inmate there since 20th January 1840.

He had a Pension of £14 per ann. which was assigned to the Guardians under the Provisions of the Act 2 & 3 Vic. C.51.

The Receipts from his pension during this time amounted to £24–10–0 and the cost of his maintenance, clothing and funeral expenses, to £15–14–7 leaving a balance of £8–15–5 in the Hands of the Union due to his Personal Representatives.

The accompanying copy of a Testamentary Paper signed by the Pensioner dated 3rd February 1836 has been presented to the Board on behalf of Susan Wicklen therein named, to whom Locke died indebted in the sum of £1–13–1, but he owed other debts which with Susan Wicklen's claim it is stated will more than cover the balance of £8–15–5 and the Board wish to know whether in your opinion they should pay over the balance of £8–15–5 to Susan Wicklen without requiring her to obtain Probate, which would cost perhaps more than the sum claimed.

I have the honor to be,
Gentlemen
Your most obedient Servt
Henry White
Clerk

TNA ref. MH 12/13432 Nuneaton Union, Warwickshire
[Enquiry into the death of a pauper who has died at his daughter's home.]

Nuneaton Union

John Estlin, Clerk
Nuneaton, 3rd May 1842

Gentlemen,

Death of John Randle

In obedience to your letter of the 25th inst. an enquiry has been made respecting the death of this individual from which it appears that a short time ago Randle was removed from the Nuneaton Union Workhouse to the Parish of Fillongley by order of removal and has since been relieved by that Parish.

Randle afterwards came to Nuneaton Parish and resided with his daughter and was taken ill there. An application was then made to our Relieving Officer for medical assistance and relief and after the Medical Officer had visited the case an order was given to the Relieving Officer for Randle's admission again into the House. The Medical Officer afterwards saw Randle again and finding him worse directed his daughter to come to his surgery for some medicine and a certificate to take to the Relieving Officer to give Randle some temporary out door relief but the daughter never applied either for the medicine or certificate nor was any other application made by Randle or anyone on his behalf either to the Board of Guardians or any of the Officers of the Union for relief or other until his death. It further appears the deceased had children residing near him who were in a situation to render assistance.

I have the honour to be

Gentlemen

Your very ob^t Servt

John Estlin

This explanation appears satisfactory so far as the Union Officers are concerned. Answer & state to the effect. It is not inconceivable this pauper may have suffered privation through the joint effect of the settlement and vagrant laws, which are incompatible with the due advice instruction of relief in such cases. The pauper having returned to the place from which he had been received, could not accept taking the medicine and the food without exposing himself to a criminal prosecution as a vagrant. This state of the law creates some suffering and more scandal & ought to be altered.

A. Power

6 May 1842

TNA ref. MH 12/10494 Wellington Union, Somerset and Devon

[A small child has died in the workhouse.]

January 29th 1855

Mary Hartnell, 4¾ years old, deserted by her mother, left at the door of the Workhouse & admitted 5th February 1853.

This child was born in the Workhouse.

Admitted to the hospital for measles 7th January 1854   Discharged 27th January

Admitted to hospital again 21st April 1854   Discharged 22nd May 1854

Admitted again 20th October, remained there for six weeks and was then out three days and returned to the hospital and continued there till she died on 3rd January 1855.

TNA ref. MH 12/10462 Taunton Union, Somerset and Devon
[Permission is sought to pay the medical officer for removing the tonsils of a pauper.]

Taunton Union

My Lords and Gentlemen,
    Subject to your approval the Board of Guardians of this Union have ordered that
£1–1–0 be paid Mr Samuel Farrant, medical officer, for the removal of tonsils from
Sarah Burgess.
    This was a case of Hypertrophy of both tonsils which rendered their removal
necessary. The operation required great care from the danger of wounding the large
blood vessels and important parts lying close to them.

I have the honor to be My Lords and Gentlemen
your most obedient servant,
John Chorley
clerk

Taunton
9 April 1862
The Poor Law Board

A letter from the Poor Law Board dated 25th April 1862 gave their approval 'in
pursuance of Article 181 of the General Order of 24th July 1847.'

TNA ref. MH 12/10217 Bedminster Union, Somerset
[A woman pauper has a tumour removed from a breast.]

Bedminster Union
5 Oct. 1864

My Lords & Gentlemen,
re Jane Vowles
This poor woman's husband resides at and has frequently been in receipt of parochial
relief from the Parish of Nailsea. She had a tumour in her Breast, and in May last it
was considered advisable to remove it. Mr Adams the Medical Officer for that Parish
performed the operation and he has now sent to the Guardians a Bill claiming Two
Guineas for so doing and subsequent attendance, and which they have agreed to pay
him subject to your approval.
    I am directed by the Guardians to request that you will be pleased to sanction
their paying the same as Mr Adams attended the woman for some time previous and
subsequent to the operation being performed. I enclose herewith the Bill.

I have the honor to be
My Lords and Gentlemen
Your most obedient Servant
Thomas Coles
Clerk.

TNA ref. MH 12/10463 Taunton Union, Somerset and Devon
[Complaint by an inmate for not receiving treatment.]

Letter dated 10th March 1868   Workhouse Taunton
March 13th 1865

Dear Sir,

In reply to the above letter & sent to the Guardians I beg leave to say that I have seen the Medical Officer who still wilfully refuses to afford that attendance my case requires. The water causes severe pain night and day and the swelling only requires to be tapped to render me fit for work. I am not totally unfit for any work and if not attended to shall as stated in my last be ruined for life. I should not have troubled the Poor Law Board if it was not a just and reasonable complaint. All I now ask is that a strict and proper enquiry be made so that the Poor Law Board may arrive at a just conclusion. I am not the only one who complains of the Medical Officer's neglect amongst the paupers of the Workhouse.

Your very humble servant

George R. Spiller.

P.S. Please not address [me] Esqre as the last as you are aware I am only a pauper.

Som. RO ref. D/G/W/8a/15 Wellington Union, Somerset and Devon
Minutes of the meetings of the Board of Guardians

5th December 1867
To the Board of Guardians of the Wellington Union
Gentlemen,

On Monday last the wife of James Salter, a pauper of Clayhidon, was delivered of three children, two of them were dead and the Overseer gave me an Order to bury them which I did by making a coffin sufficiently large to hold both children. After placing them in they were fastened down for burial which was agreed to take place the following day, Tuesday. The grave was dug and at the appointed time I proceeded to the House for the Corpses. On arriving there I found that the third child was also dead and another Carpenter had opened the coffin containing the two children and pushed the third in with them. The coffin was left open and I refused to bury them. The grave is now open. I now ask the Board how I am to proceed in this Case and whether I am to be interfered with in the discharge of my duties.

I remain Gentlemen

Your Obed^t Servt

John Pratt, Contractor

Resolved that the Clerk be directed to inform him that no one has any right to interfere with him in the discharge of his duties but the Guardians request that his Contract with them be at once carried out by burying the children.

TNA ref. MH 12/10468 Taunton Union, Somerset and Devon
[Inquest on the death of a pauper at her home.]

Taunton Union
Henry Charles Trenchard, clerk
19th March 1875

Lords and Gentlemen,
re Betty Parsons

In answer to your letter of the 12th inst. I beg herewith to forward to you a copy deposition taken before the Coroner as requested.

I have the honor to be,
My Lords & Gentlemen,
Your obedient servant
Henry Chas. Trenchard   clerk

Local Government Board

***

Copy of Information of Witnesses severally taken and acknowledged on behalf of our Sovereign Lady the Queen, touching the Death of Betty Parsons at the House known by the sign of the Gore Inn in the parish of Bishops Lydeard on Saturday the sixth Day of February 1875 before William Webber Munckton, Gentleman, one of Her Majesty's Coroners for the said County on view of the Body of the said Person then and there lying dead.

Mary Turner, sworn.   I live near the deceased. She was single; had been a servant. She told me that she was near 86 years of age. She lived by herself in a cottage belonging to the Warre family; she gave a shilling a week for it, and she was kept by the parish. She had 2^s/6^d and a 4lb loaf of bread per week when she received her pay; she made no complaint. I went and paid Mary Dyer's rent to Mr Pavey who takes the rent of the said cottages. (Deceased came whilst I was there and gave Mrs Pavey 2^s/6^d what change she had I don't know. She told me afterwards it was 6d. I left her with Mrs Pavey. About 11 a.m. I saw her again at my house when she told me she had 6d change. Mrs Pavey told me she was behind in her rent. Deceased told me Mr Pavey had told her she owed 2^s/- for rent. This was before she went to pay her rent. She didn't complain of the want of any thing. I didn't think that she wanted for food. If she had, I think she would have gone from house to house to get it. I saw her on Saturday afternoon last, she was lying on her bed. She told me she was very ill; pain in her head. She didn't then complain of want. She didn't wish to have any thing. I asked if she would have a drop of brandy and water she said, 'No, I can't drink it.'

Mary Turner

Ann Burnell sworn.   I reside near deceased. She came to my house on Tuesday morning before she received her pay. She asked me for some hot water to make herself a cup of tea. I did so, and the same when she returned. She found her own tea. She told me she had been to pay her rent and Mrs Pavey had given her back 6d.

I told her that would be short keep till next week. She said, 'I must make ado of it'.

Thursday night I saw her in bed; helped her out of bed. She said she was very ill; didn't say where. I changed her with her daughter-in-law. On Saturday I saw her twice; put brandy and water in her mouth. She was quite sensible. Her daughter-in-law was staying and nursing her. She had coal in house, and there was a large loaf there on Wednesday.

Ann Burnell

***

Mary Parsons sworn.   I am the wife of Abel Parsons the son of deceased. I went to her on Wednesday week in the morning early and found her in bed. I went to see my father, and then returned between 3 and 4 p.m. and found her in bed, she opened the door to me. She said she was very ill; asked why she staid in bed, she said she didn't believe twas so late as it was. She walked upstairs to dress herself and whilst she was doing it I got her a cup of tea, and took it to her when she was in bed again and said she couldn't dress herself. There was a large loaf of bread and some tea & little sugar and a bason of pea soup. There was some coal in house. The house was in a very dirty state, and she had wetted her bed clothes. I staid 'till nine o'clock and went home. The following day I staid 'till nine o'clock and went home. The following day I saw her again. She was near the same. I went to Mr. Pearce the Relieving Officer for an order for the Doctor to see her, but he was gone to the Board. I staid with her that night that is at Jane Burgess going to and fro every half hour and obtained the order the next morning and took it to Dr Dene, and he saw her at once. She had brandy from Mr Pearce as well as some meat in the shape of mutton broth from Mr Matthews. Saturday she was in the same state, but still continued to take in something, the broth and wine. Sunday she died about ½ past nine. Dr Dene saw her about 5 p.m. Saturday. Friday she had some corn flour before I had the mutton broth and sherry wine what she liked to drink. She took in corn flour (a tea cup full) Sunday morning. My husband staid up with her Saturday night and she had a cup of tea about half an hour before she died. I went [to] her then and she was sensible and said she wanted her breakfast, hungry fit to starve. I asked her what I should get her, toast and butter? She said 'No don't want toast and butter.' She refused a biscuit so I said 'I'll go down and get some dinner, she said so do, these were the last words she spoke. I went down and fetched Jane Burge telling her I thought there was an alteration in her. She was present when deceased died. She had no bedding, but her own clothes to cover her. We have always helped her since we have been married for the last twenty years. I gave her a joint of pork about ten days before she died and 6d in money, and Mary Parsons who married another of her sons gave her a small loaf every week and meat and clothes when she asked for it as well as money. I laid her out with Mrs Burge and she appeared to be in good condition. I consider she was not starved. I obtained from Mr Matthews the Vicar, Thursday, some meat broth which she took, and from Mrs Gardiner some corn flour made, and a packet more. Dr Smith sent her a bottle of Sherry wine and a bason of corn flour, egg and brandy beaten up. She took these things.

Mary Parsons

***

Wavell Arundell, sworn. I am Surgeon residing at Bishops Lydeard. I saw the deceased on Friday morning the 29th of last month. She was in bed in a filthy condition; she was locked in. She was badly covered up. Her faeces had all passed from her, and the smell was very bad. Hands & face very cold and a weak intermittent pulse. I asked her what she complained of, she said, 'nothing.' I saw nothing there either to eat and drink. The room down stairs was in a horrible condition. I wrote to Mr Pearce, the relieving officer and told him she was in want of the necessaries of life and begged to call his immediate attention to it. I met him about one p.m. he told me what he had done, and asked me if it were a case for the Workhouse. I said 'Yes' would I give a certificate, I said certainly. On Saturday morning he came to my house and asked me if I would see her during the day as he did not consider that she was fit to be removed. He told me again what he had done for her. If I could do more I advised him to give her some more brandy. I saw her about 5 p.m. she was then considerably weaker. I there saw the son Abel Parsons and his wife. I asked them if I could do any thing for her, if she required any thing. I directed her to go to Mr Pearce for an order for some mutton and brandy. I consider that she died from exhaustion from old age, and want of sufficient nourishment I never saw her before this attendance.

W.A. Dene

***

Henry John Pearce sworn. I am the relieving officer of this district. The deceased has been receiving pay for years. I have paid her regularly for the last twelve. She had lately 2^s/6^d and a four lb loaf. She never complained to me. The 6d was put on the 29th December last. On Friday the 29th January the daughter called telling me that she was very ill, and brought the old yearly ticket and I renew it. It was for the Doctor to attend her at any time. She said she had been up all night with Betty Lock, with her, and they couldn't do it again unless something were provided for them. I directly gave them 2^s/- in money. Soon afterwards I had a note from Mr Dene wishing me to look to the case directly. I saw the deceased between 10 and 11 a.m. and thinking she was very ill I considered it advisable to send her to the Union. I met Mr Dene on my road to Lydeard St. Lawrence between 12 and 1. I told him what I had done, and asked his opinion about taking her to the Workhouse if he would give me a certificate. Between 2 and 3 p.m. I went to see her again and ordered her some brandy by Mr Dene's direction. Spoke to the daughter-in-law in reference to her removal to the Union. She told me 'twas impossible to do so as her clothes were in the wash. I saw her again on the Saturday morning. My impression was she was in a dying state, and I reported the case again to Mr Dene to know what I had better do. The house was very dirty and the daughter-in-law had commenced cleaning it. I threw Chloride of Lime about the house, and then gave her 2^s/6^d and she had a loaf of bread during the [sic] and an order for half a pint of best brandy. I did not go again. I have occasionally visited her house as it is my duty to do & have found the house in a bad state, but I had no authority to interfere with it unless I got an order to send her to the Workhouse which I considered would be very cruel.

W.J. Pearce

W.W. Munckton
Coroner

TNA ref. MH 12/10224 Bedminster Union, Somerset
[Audit made of a medical officer's record keeping.]

Bedminster Union Audit July 27th 1876
Medical Officer's Book for House

Hannah Groves	Admitted to Hospital died their on 4th Oct. no entry made of admission or treatment.
Chas Morgan	Died per admission & discharge on 20th Oct.
3rd week	M.O. states he visited him on the 22nd. No entry made of death. Case brought up again in 4th week.
John North	Admitted to House & Hospital Oct 23rd. Died on 6th of Nov. in Hospital. No entry made by M.O. 3 oz of brandy ordered but not in writing. Master makes the entry. No record of death in M.O.'s book.
John Dyer	Died on 6th Nov.
6th week	Visited on the 12th Entries made by Master in order to make up
9th week	what is given out.
Richd Spurway	Died on 7th Dec. Visited twice after death.
10th week	
Pascall Williams	Died 13th Dec. visited on the 13th & 17th re-entered visited 3
11th week }	times.
12th week }	Ordered milk & brandy.
1st week next Qr	Same occurs again
2nd do	Same again. This man is visited 3 weeks after death and ordered extras.
James Hazell	This man has been in Hospital some time wine ordered & Master
11th week }	enters his name. He died on the 12th. Name entered by M.O.,
12th week }	visited 3 times, wine ordered, same repeated & then masked as dead by Master
	These are a few cases only taken from my notes [sic]

TNA ref. MH 12/10506 Wellington Union, Somerset and Devon
[Enquiry into the death of a 70-year-old man in the workhouse.]

Wellington Union
Wellington, Somerset
21st January 1884

My Lords and Gentlemen,

I am requested by the Guardians of this Union to state the following case and to ask your opinion thereon.

A pauper called George Veals aged 70 years an inmate of this Workhouse, died on the 29th December last. He had been ailing for some time under the care of the Workhouse Medical Officer, who states that he was perfectly aware that the Pauper died from natural causes. On the 31st day of December he made a post-mortem examination of the body without first consulting the Guardians. On being asked by the Guardians for an explanation, he stated that he first went to a sister-in-law, who gave her consent to the examination, and that having obtained such, he considered he was right in making the post-mortem examination in the cause of science. The cause of death was certified to be 'Heart Decease'.

Although under Article 207 of the General Order of the 24th July 1847 it appears that in certain circumstances a Post Mortem examination can be ordered, but as there was no Inquest and the Pauper had been previously ailing, and the Medical Officer had been aware of the nature of his ailment, the Guardians are of opinion that he exceeded his duties in making such an examination without the consent of the Guardians being fist obtained.

They will therefore be glad of your opinion for their guidance.

I remain,
My Lords and Gentlemen
Yours obedient Servant
Robert A. Were
Clerk

The Local Government Board
Whitehall
London S.W.

I think that the M.O. distinctly erred in not obtaining the sanction of the Guardians as well as the consent of the nearest relative. But on the other hand his explanation is perfectly satisfactory from the medical standpoint. The death was due to the progress in a cause from that detected during life of the disease from which he was suffering, and therefore is rightly declared to a natural cause.

F.J.M.
11 Feby 84

***

Wellington
Somerset
Feby 8th 1884

My Lords & Gentlemen,

I beg to state in reference to the Post Mortem made by me upon the body of an inmate of the Wellington Workhouse the following facts which are not wholly in accord with the letter received.

George Veals, aged 70, an inmate suffering from Chronic Bronchitis and Emphysema of very long standing, and broken down by drunkenness, was sent by me into the Hospital suffering from a slight attack of acute rheumatism. After being there a short time (i.e. a few days) he appeared to have become nearly restored to his usual health, when he became unexpectedly worse and shortly expired. I had seen him in the morning and he appeared to me to have nearly recovered from his rheumatism.

With the consent and at the request of the deceased's sister (his only known relative) not sister-in-law, I opened the chest, took out the heart & large vessels, examined them but made no further examination. I found the patient had died from the formation of an ante mortem colorless clot, occupying almost the whole of the aorta & sigmoid valves & strongly adherent, which had been quite unsuspected during the man's life and seemed to have been completed just before his decease, although probably existing for some time.

I must remark that 'the examination was made in the interests of science' were the words of the Chairman of the Board and not mine; the examination was made solely to ascertain the cause of death at the expressed wish of the man's only relative. That the matter could not have been referred to the Board of Guardians as they only meet once a fortnight. That it is true I expressed a belief that the man died from 'Natural Cause' (as I was asked by a member of the Board if I had thought he was poisoned), but from what cause I had been unable to tell, and it appeared to me that the circumstances did not justify an application to the Coroner, whilst the result of the examination disclosed a very rare & unusual form of disease. I may remark that the Board of Guardians has received a communication from me containing all the above facts.

I remain

My Lords & Gentlemen

Your obedient Servant

Engledue Prideaux L.R.C.P. Lond. &c. &c.

Medical Officer to the Wellington Workhouse

R.A. Were, Esq.,
Clerk to the Guardians of the
Wellington Union
Wellington
Somerset

TNA ref. MH 12/10509 Wellington Union, Somerset and Devon
[Enquiry into the death of a pauper – neglect by the medical officer is suspected.]

Wellington Union
Wellington, Somerset
13th September 1890

My Lords and Gentlemen,

I am directed by the Guardians of this Union to inform you that at their meeting held on Thursday Last the 11th instant they had occasion to inquire into the circumstances attending the death of an Indoor Pauper called John Stoate who died in the Workhouse on the 26th August last, when the following Resolution was unanimously passed.

That circumstances connected with the death of John Stoate in the Workhouse on the 26th August 1890, point to a neglect of duty on the part of Mr Engledue Prideaux, the Medical Officer, which together with previous cases of neglect on his part, appear to the Guardians to demand an inquiry by the Local Government Board.

The Guardians are desirous that you will be pleased to cause an inquiry to be instituted.

I remain,
My Lords and Gentlemen
Your obedient Servant
Robert A. Were
Clerk

Local Government Board
Whitehall
London S.W.

***

Wellington Union
Subject Conduct of M.O. of W.H.

Local Government Board
Whitehall, S.W.
25 Sept. 1890

Sir,

I am directed by the Local Government Board to acknowledge the receipt of your Letter of the 13th Inst., in which you request them to institute an enquiry into the proceedings of Mr Engledue Prideaux, the Medical Officer of the Workhouse of the Wellington Union, in connection with the death of John Stoate in the Establishment on the 26th ultimo.

The Board request to be fully informed of the circumstances which have led the Guardians to make this application.

I am &c
C.U.D.
asst. secy

To the Guardians of the Wellington Union,
Somerset

TNA ref. MH 12/9062 Hexham Union, Northumberland

[Suicide in a workhouse.]

Hexham

20th January 1892

Sir,

I am directed by my Guardians to acknowledge the receipt of your letter of the 15th instant enclosing copy of the Deposition taken at the Inquest held upon the body of a woman named Hannah Bell who committed suicide in the Workhouse on the 13th ultimo and in reply to state that the Bath Room where the woman was found drowned is some distance from the official apartments and it was thought that in case of emergency arising it would be advisable that the key should be given to one of the Inmates on the building instead of going to the officials they being such a distance away and which would necessarily cause much delay. The Guardians have now however given instructions that the key shall in future be in the custody of their officials.

I am, Sir,

Your Obedient Servant

Isaac Baty

Clerk

The Secretary

Local Government Board

Whitehall

TNA ref. MH 12/10512 Wellington Union, Somerset and Devon

[A baby is scalded to death.]

Wellington Union Workhouse

Wellington, Somerset

13th May 1899

I have the honor to report that Percy John Tooze, aged 20 months, one of the children resident in the above Workhouse, accidentally fell into a bath containing hot water, in the nursery on the morning of the 10th Inst. was severely scalded about the face, arms and neck and died from the effects of this on the night of the 11th.

An Inquest was held at the Union Workhouse this afternoon and a verdict of death through misadventure was returned.

John Meredith M.D.

Medical Officer

Local Gov[t] Board

Whitehall

Information of Witnesses severally taken and acknowledged on behalf of our Sovereign Lady the Queen touching the death of Percy John Tooze at the Union Workhouse in the Parish of Wellington in the County of Somerset the thirteenth day of May 1890, before Charles Edmund Hagon, Esquire, Deputy of Thomas Foster

251

A page from Return of Deaths, 1871, Chertsey, Surrey. (Sur. HC ref. BG1/63/1)

Barham, Esquire, one of the Coroners of our said Lady the Queen for the said County of Somerset, on view of the Body of the said Person then and there lying dead.

This Informant Sarah Albina Tooze upon her oath saith:

I am a single woman. The body which the Jury have just viewed is that of my son Percy John Tooze who was 20 months old on the 8th inst. I am and have been for the past 4 months an inmate of the Wellington Union Workhouse with the deceased.

At about 6.20 p.m. on Wednesday the 10th inst. I left the Nursery of the Workhouse where I had been all the afternoon with the deceased child to go to the Laundry and left the child in the Nursery. There were several other women and children in the Nursery. Mary Ann Hartnell left the Nursery with me to get some cold water for the bath. When I left the nursery there was a bath in the room with hot water in it. I do not know who drew the water or put it in the bath. My child had been standing by the bath and before I left the room I took him away from it and told him not to go near it again. I also asked one of the inmates named Mapledoram to see he did not go near the bath whilst I ran down stairs. Before I got to the Laundry I heard a child scream. I ran back to the Nursery. I then found the child in the arms of Jemima Mapledoram scalded about the face and arms and was informed he had fallen into the bath. I took the child to the Workhouse Infirmary where he died at 9.30 p.m. on Thursday the 11th instant. It has been the habit of those in the Nursery to draw hot water for the baths first and usually the water is not hot enough to require the addition of cold water. The Matron has however ordered that cold water is always to be put in the bath before the hot and this order was known in the Nursery.

***

This Informant, Mary Ann Hartnell upon her oath saith: I am an inmate of the Wellington Union Workhouse. On Wednesday last the 10th instant Annie Taylor another inmate of the Workhouse drew a bucketful of hot water for the bath in the Nursery. I put the water into the bath and went downstairs for some cold water. There were six infants in the Nursery at the time three of whom could walk. When I left the ward I did not see any children near the bath. I was not out of the nursery long and when I got back I found the deceased child had fallen into the bath and been scalded. It was usual to draw the hot water before the cold. I usually fetched the cold water.

***

This Informant Ann Taylor upon her oath saith: I am an inmate of the Wellington Union Workhouse. On Wednesday last the 10th instant I drew some hot water in a bucket for bathing the children in the Nursery. I drew the water from a tap outside the nursery and left the water in the bucket under the tap. The last witness took it from beneath the tap. I did not go into the Nursery until after the deceased child had been scalded. The rule laid down by the matron is that cold water should be put in the bath first. As a rule cold water is put into the bath first.

***

This deponent Jemima Mapledoram upon her oath saith: I am a single woman and an inmate of the Wellington Union Workhouse. On Wednesday the 10th inst. I was in the Nursery when Sarah Tooze went out of the Nursery. There was a bath in the room containing hot water. I was not asked by Sarah Tooze to look after him. When his mother went out of the room the child was on a rug about the middle of the Nursery. He went towards the bath and I put him back on the rug again I told him to sit there. I went to a cupboard to get some bread and on turning round to see if the child was alright he was by the bath again and as I looked he put his hand in the water and he fell over the edge of the bath. I ran and pulled him out and found he was scalded about the arms and face. The matron has ordered that cold water must always be put in the bath before the hot but it was not done that night. Usually the water is about the right temperature for the bath & does not require the addition of cold water. There are several buckets in and about the bath room.

***

This deponent John Meredith upon his oath saith: I am a Surgeon practising at Wellington and Medical Officer to the Workhouse. On Wednesday the 10th inst. at about 6 o'clock or a few minutes before I was called to the Infirmary of the Workhouse and found the deceased child in the nurse's arms who was dressing some wounds apparently caused by scalds. The child's face, neck, both arms and hands and right foot were severely scalded. The child died on the following day from shock and prostration the result of the scalding.

**Som. RO ref. D/G/Bd/69/1 Bedminster Union, Somerset
Register of Deaths in the Union Workhouse, 1866–1906**
[The following abstract is from a page of this register.]

Date of Death	Name	Age	From what Parish Admitted	Where Buried
1881	(Michaelmas 1881 Continued)			
July 16	William Hancock	52	Bedminster	Bedminster
30	Thomas Patch	68	Winford	Winford
August 4	Thomas Gilmore	62	Pill	Pill
4	Matthew Hill	64	Long Ashton	Long Ashton
14	William Sams	67	Backwell	Backwell
Sept. 3	Elizabeth Latham	40	Clevedon	Clevedon
4	James Merrick	76	Backwell	Backwell
13	Thomas Garrett	16	Bedminster	Bedminster
19	James Parfitt	81	Pill	Pill
23	Lenard Sanford	11 months	Bedminster	Bedminster
25	John Hazel	94	Long Ashton	Long Ashton
28	Ann Newton	70	Clevedon	Clevedon
Oct. 3	George Kent	31	Bedminster	Bedminster
11	Ann Stokes	84	Backwell	Backwell
24	Ann Perry	80	Bedminster	Bedminster
Nov. 6	James Langdon	70	Bedminster	Bedminster
Dec. 7	Eliza Hamilton	81	Bedminster	Bedminster
18	Eliza Fersman	51	Long Ashton	Long Ashton
19	Rosina Quick	17	Bedminster	Bedminster
30	Elizb. Dartch	75	Bedminster	Bedminster
Oct. 3*	John Weaver	76	Dundry	Dundry
10*	John Davis	76	Bedminster	Bedminster
1882				
Jan. 5	Camilla Bees	36	Bedminster	Bedminster
6	John Andrews	76	Bedminster	Bedminster
21	Thomas Hawkins†	66	Bedminster	Bedminster

* Out of chronological order as in the original.
† The author's great-gt-grandfather

TNA ref. MH 12/3174 Lanchester Union, County Durham

[Tabulation summarising the causes and numbers of deaths in Consett District in 1884.]

Diseases	Under Nine Months				Under Five Years					Above Five Years																	
	1	3	6	9	1	2	3	4	5	10	15	20	25	30	35	40	45	50	55	60	65	70	75	80	85	90	
Scarlet Fever	1											1															2
Diphtheria & Croup						1			1																		2
Whooping Cough		1	2		1	1																					5
Diarrhoea						1	1																	1			3
Septicaemia [a]														1						1							2
Puerperal Fever [b]												1															1
Parturition [c]															1												1
Pneumonia & Bronchitis		1	2	4	3	10				1						1		3	1		3					2	31
Phthisis [d]										1	1	1		1	2	1											7
Tubercular Meningitis						1	1	1		1	1																5
Tuberculoses						1	1			2	1								1								6
Peritonitis										1	1		1														3
Malnutrition		4	2	4																							10
Tabes Mesenterica [e]						1																					1
Convulsions	1	1	2	2	2	1																					9
Jaundice	1																										1

[contd]

Diseases	Under Nine Months				Under Five Years											Above Five Years												Total
Debility	4																											4
Spina Bifida	1																											1
Premature Birth	4																											4
Diseases of Heart										1					1		2	2	2	1	2							12
Diseases of Kidney						1	1							1				1										4
Disease of Brain	2											1		1	1	2	1	2	1	3								15
Cancer																	1											1
Stricture of Oesophagus																1												1
Senile Decay																	1	1		1	1							5
Inquest Cases					1							1						1		1								6
Total	11	7	10	11	7	19	4	1	1	6	5	4	2	4	4	3	2	4	5	5	9	6	1	5	4	1	2	142

[a] blood poisoning
[b] due to childbirth
[c] childbirth
[d] wasting disease
[e] disease of intestines

CHAPTER 14

AUDIT AND VISIT REPORTS

The Poor Law Commission and its successors carried out regular inspections of the conditions in Union workhouses and also audited their books. The reports of these visits are preserved in their correspondence files, in document class MH 12 at The National Archives. Sometimes officers of a workhouse also reported on unusual situations. The remarkable detail contained in these reports gives an indication of the thoroughness and dedication with which the visiting inspectors and officers of the Unions carried out their duties.

The following are some examples:

TNA ref. MH 12/561 Cambridge Union, Cambridgeshire
[Inventory of goods in the workhouse.]

Cambridge July 19/39

Gentlemen,

On account of sundry goods charged to the Union which I consider ought not to be allowed I wrote the letter as under to the Board, of which a minute was made 'That the Board of Guardians received the Auditor's letter & think that his remark respecting coals is very just, but as for the goods ordered for use of the Master & Schoolmaster of the Workhouse he has nothing to do with whatever.'

July 17/39

Gentlemen,

It would be as much pleasure to me as to you if the goods as under ordered for the Workhouse & some other items could be allowed out of some other fund than the Poor Rates, but with all deference & respect to you considering myself responsible to the Public, I beg to say that I have not heard of any Union in which the officers have been supplied with more than common necessaries such as I presume two thirds of our Rate Payers are not able to afford for themselves.

It will be seen that I have signed the Quarterly Abstract which I believe is correct on conditions that the Goods ordered for the use of the Master & Schoolmaster are allowed by the Commissioners to whose decision we must refer to.

There is also another item £4-17 charged for a Brass Plate on Super[ts] office door, which property should be charged to the Registrar General's Office, is precisely as the Registrars were obliged to pay for their own sign boards.

In comparing the quantities of coals consumed during the three last quarters, during which time the Union House has been occupied, with the same three quarters of the last year, I find there has been 45 tons (not bushels) consumed more than when the six workhouses were in operation making about £100 a year more, in the consumption of coals only.

The following goods before they can be allowed must be left to the decision of the Commissioners:

2 Handsome blue chamber services	2 doz. white handled knives & forks
1 mahogany chest of drawers and	2 tea trays & 2 bread baskets
1 Japan'd ditto	4 brass chamber candle sticks
2 pair plated candlesticks	1 tea caddy – 2 snuffers & trays
2 dressing tables	3 copper tea kettles
2 dressing glasses	1 oval scoop & 2 coal scoops
1 chimney glass	4 copper saucepans
2 wash hand stands	a doz. blue cups & saucers
2 mahogany dining tables & covers	3 doz. blue plates
2 Pembroke do	2 tea pots & cake plates
carpets & hearth rugs	4 basins & 2 cream jugs
sofa, or hair bottomed settee	a doz. tumblers & 6 jugs
a doz. Windsor chairs & 4 elbows	4 salts & 2 sets of casters
a doz. bedroom chairs	8 blue dishes & 6 baking ditto
1 four post bedstead	4 dishes and covers
1 Japan'd ditto	4 sauce boats

There are also 9 pairs of carvers, 13 sets of table knives and 24 sets of smaller ditto for use of Union.

Gentlemen, If forwarding to you the above statement I am considered going beyond my duty, if so I am very sorry as it is one of the most unpleasant tasks I ever had in my life, but I have been reproved for a supposed error of 2lbs of meat & an ounce of tea I should indeed think I was wanting in my duty if I were to pass the above without your approbation.

Gentlemen
I have the honor to be
Your obedient Servant
Peter Bayes

To The Poor Law Commissioners

TNA ref. MH 12/9920 Market Drayton Union, Shropshire

[Visit report on a workhouse.]

Market Drayton Union

Report of *Aneurin Owen*, Assistant Poor Law Commissioner on the above Union after a visit on the 25th day November 1847

1. Date of last previous visit   *June 29, 1847*
2. Is the Workhouse generally adequate to the wants of the Union, in respect of size and internal arrangements?

    Part of the Workhouse being old and part a new construction, the arrange-ments consequently are defective. It was in contemplation to purchase the Parish land and erect some new buildings, but I understand a difficulty as to the title has arisen.
3. Is the provision for the sick and for infectious cases sufficient? Are the receiving wards in a proper state?

    There are 2 rooms for sick males, 1 holding 8 beds, the other 4 for females, 1 room with 8 beds and 2 with 4 beds in each. Fever cases were placed in some of the rooms apart. There were 13 patients in the 9th week of the September Quarter. On the day of my visit 2 convalescent cases only.
4. Is the Workhouse School well managed?

    I found in School

Boys	<u>*33*</u>
Write in copybooks	*8*
" on slates	*11*
Learn arithmetic	*8*
" arithmetical tables	*11*
Read Testament	*21*

    Learn Tailoring, Knitting, Platting and gardening

Girls	<u>*15*</u>
Write on slates	*5*
Learn arithmetical tables	*3*
Read Testament	*6*

    Learn Sewing, Knitting, platting and household work

    Industrial training very good
5. Are there vagrant wards in the Workhouse, and are they sufficient? Are the arrangements for setting the vagrants to work effective, and is the resolution of the Guardians under 5 & 6 Vict., c.57, Sec.5 duly observed?

    There are 4 sleeping cells holding 15 beds and a large room for 20.
6. Does the visiting committee regularly inspect the Workhouse? Do any of their answers to the queries in the Workhouse regulations suggest the propriety of any interference on the part of the Commissioners?

    The visiting committee visit about once in 3 weeks; the prevalence of fever has caused the attendance to be laxer.

7. Has the maximum number of inmates of the Workhouse, fixed by the Commissioners been constantly observed since your last visit?

    Calculated to hold   *250*
    Largest number ever in   *161*
    Inmates November 25. 1847   *101*

8. Are the proper extracts from the Poor Law Amendment Act, and the Regulations of the Commissioners, hung up in the Workhouse?
    They are.

9. Have all appointments of new offices and changes in salaries and districts since your last visit been reported to the Commissioners?
    They have.

10. Is there any officer whose appointment has been sanctioned provisionally? If so state your opinion?
    The Master has acted occasionally when a Relieving Officer has been unwell, but not lately.

11. Have you any reason to believe that any of the books or accounts prescribed by the Commissioners are not properly kept?
    I believe them to be properly kept.

12. Have you observed any illegal practice or any departure from the Regulations of the Commissioners?
    I have not.

13. Has any marked change taken place in the state of the Workhouse, the number of inmates, or the general condition of the Union, since your last visit?
    There has not.

Aneurin Owen   Assistant Poor Law Commissioner
    Dated the *3rd* day of *December 1847*

TNA ref. MH 12/1021 Nantwich Union, Cheshire

REPORT OF AUDIT
Cheshire and Denbighshire Audit District
A STATEMENT of the AUDITOR
In reference to the Books of the Nantwich Union for the Half-year ended Michaelmas 1855

As to the books required to be kept by the Master of the Workhouse
Mr James Holland

Inventory	No defect
Admission and Discharge Book	No defect
In-Door Relief List	No defect
Abstract of In-Door Relief List	No Defect
Master's Day Book	No Defect
Master's portion of Workhouse Medical Relief Book	No defect

Daily Provisions Consumption Account	No defect
Weekly Provisions Consumption Account	No defect
Provisions Receipt and Consumption Account	No defect
Quarterly Summary of Provisions Received and Consumed	No defect
Quarterly Balance of Provisions Account	No defect
Clothing materials Receipt and Conversion Book	Imperfectly
Clothing Receipt and Expenditure Book	No defect
Clothing Register Book	No defect

Date on which the Audit of the above Books was concluded 16th day of October 1856

   Tho K. Roberts Auditor

   Date 23rd October 1855

AUDIT

Cheshire and Denbigh Audit District

Nantwich Union

James Holland master of the W House   Poor Law Board

of the Nantwich Union   Whitehall

                                                 29 Oct[r] 1855

Sir,

   The Poor Law Board have received a Report from the District Auditor, made after his Audit of the accounts of the Nantwich Union for the Half-year ended the 29th September last, in which he states that the last column of your Clothing materials Receipt & Conversion Book, viz. that headed 'Folio of Clothing Receipts and Expenditure Book &c' had not been used.

                        GCSB

                      ***

                            Nantwich Union

                      Peckforton and Tamporley

                         20th October 1855

My Lords and Gentlemen,

   The District Auditor having disallowed the sum of £4–10–8 charged in the Account of myself and Mr Thomas Dutton as Overseers of the Township of Peckforton for the reasons stated on the other side I beg to appeal to your honorable Board against such disallowance, the payment having been made in ignorance of the law on the subject, and respectfully request that your Board will be pleased to remit the amount in the exercise of your equitable jurisdiction.

   I beg to assure you that I will in future take care to collect enough money to meet the expenses of the Township.

                  I have the honor to be

                    My Lords and Gentlemen

                    Your most obedient Servant

The Poor Law Board   Thomas Dodd

Whitehall   for self and Overseer

London

Cheshire and Denbighshire Audit District
Nantwich Union
Audit for the Half-Year ended Michaelmas 1855
Commenced 12th October   Ended 16th October
I hereby report that at the Audit of the Accounts of this Union, and of the Parishes comprised therein, for the above-named period, I certify the several Sums hereunder set forth to be due from the persons hereunder named.

Date of Certificate	Names and Descriptions of Persons		Particulars	Sums Certified	
1855 Oct 12th	John Jones	Overseers of	Disallowance	0 – 9 – 1	
	James Rutter	Wardle	Correction	4 – 0	0 – 5 – 1
	Wm Hockenhall	Overseers of Tilston	Disallowance	11 – 2½	
	Joseph Sheen	Fearnall	Correction	4 – 0	0 – 7 – 2
	Thomas Barker	Overseers of Henhull	Disallowance	7 – 3 – 9	
	Jno Whitelagg		Balance in favor	2 – 7 – 0	4 – 16 – 9
	Thos Dodd	Overseers of	Disallowance	4 – 10 – 8	
	Thos Dutton	Peckforton	Balance in favor £4 – 3 – 3½ Correction 1 – 4½	4 – 4 – 4	6 – 4
	John Vernon	Overseers of	Surcharge	1 – 1 – 8	1 – 1 – 8
	Wm Shakestaft	Buerton			
	James Unett	Overseers of			
	Wm Harvey	Henllan	do	11 – 6	11 – 6
Oct 13th	Wm Jas Adams	Overseers of			
	Saml Bourn	Dodcote cum Wilkesley	Disallowance	2 – 9 – 1	2 – 9 – 1
	Jno Whittingham	Overseers of	do	8 – 0	
	George Pigott	Batherton	Balance in favor	1 – 16 – 0	
	Samuel Whitmore	Overseers of			
	Thos Parton	Chorlton	Surcharge	3 – 1 – 3	3 – 1 – 3
	Geo. Woolwich	Overseers of	Disallowance	1 – 7 – 0	1 – 7 – 0
	Wm Jones	Alpraham			
	James Cookson	Overseers of	do	4 – 19 – 9	
	Richd Cowdook	Tarporley	Surcharge	1 – 2 – 9	
				6 – 2 – 6	
			Balance in favour	8 – 0 – 2½	

Signed   Tho K. Roberts   District Auditor
The Poor Law Board   22nd day of October 1855

I disallowed in the account of the Overseers of the Township of Peckforton the sum of £4–10–8 charged therein as and for a balance due to the Overseers of the former year Because such Overseers did not receive from their predecessors in Office any Rate or arrears of rate out of which they could repay or reimburse them any money balance which may have been due to them and allowed in their account as the Overseers of the former year, nor has it happened that such preceding Overseers have advanced or expended for the relief or maintenance of the Poor any sum of money which they were able to collect for the purpose during their office.

Stated this 12th day of October 1855

Tho. K. Roberts

District Auditor

Act and state referring to Auditor's report, that
it is necessary that Mr Dulton should sign the appeal.

Subject: Disallowance

Nantwich Union
Peckforton Parish   Poor Law Board
Mr Thomas Dodd   Whitehall
Overseer of the Poor of the   5th Nov. 1855
Township of Peckforton
Nr Tarporley

Sir,

I am directed by the Poor Law Board to acknowledge the receipt of your letter of the 20th ulto, appealing against a disallowance of the sum of £4–10–8 made by Mr Roberts, District Auditor, at his Audit of the a/cts of the Overseers of the Township of Peckforton for the half year ended at Michs last.

From a report which the Auditor has made on the subject of the disallowance the Board observe that the above mentioned sum has been certified to be due from Mr Thomas Dutton as well as from yourself, it is necessary therefore before the Board can interfere in the matter that that gentleman should join with you, under his own signature, in appealing against the Auditor's decision.

TNA ref. MH 12/12395 Kingston Union, Surrey

[Cases of special relief because of severe weather.]

Subject Relief Cases
R.F. Bartrop, Esq   Poor Law Board
Clerk to the Guardians   Whitehall, S.W.
                                                        13 Feb^{ry} 1857

Sir,

I am directed by the poor Law Board to acknowledge the receipt of your letter of the 7th Instant transmitting to them, for their sanction a list of cases in which the Guardians of the Kingston Union have granted out door relief in consequence of the severity of the weather and have set the recipients to work at woodcutting in return for such relief.

I am directed by the Board to state that in the circumstances they sanction the relief which the Guardians have already afforded in these cases. They presume, knowing that as the severity of the weather has ceased the relief has been discontinued.

I am

A.W.J.

Names	Age	No of & Age of Children		Parishes	No of days Work at 9d & one loaf per week
Joseph Roberts	39	2	5 & 2 years	Hampton Wick	4
Harriet wife	25				
Fran⁵ Clarke	53	0		"	3
Martha wife	59				
John Bailey	39	0		"	3
Maria wife	45				
William Noakes	41	2	9 & 2½	"	5
Maria wife	37				
Joseph Hare	61	0		Teddington	3
Mary wife	61				
Thomas Andrews	40	2	10 & 6	Thames Ditton	2
Louisa wife	43				
William Plumbridge	55	0		Hampton	2
Mary wife	30				
John Hedges	24	0		"	2
Eliza wife	33				
James Hedges	43	4	8, 7, 3 & 1½	"	2
Harriett wife	42				
John Bish	43	3	25 (a cripple), 10 & 13	Esher	3
Sarah wife	46				
William Huntingford	43	3	8, 6 & 3	Hampton Wick	3
Elizabeth wife	37				
William Greenway	23	3	12, 5 & 2½	"	3
Nancy wife	36				
Joseph Wells	31	5	10, 8, 6, 4 & 6 months	"	3
Louisa wife	29				

David Wells	42	1	14		"	3
Maria wife	41					
William Christie	26	1	1¾		"	3
Jane wife	23					
William Sale	31	3	7, 3 & 4 months		"	3
Jane wife	31					
Thomas Rawkins	28	1	5 months		"	3
Jane wife	21					
Anthony Lee	64	3	8, 6 & 3 years		"	2
Mary wife	37					

AUDIT

South West Metropolitan District
Kingston Union
R.F. Bartrop Esq
Clerk to the Guardians
of Kingston Union
Kingston-on-Thames

Poor Law Board
Whitehall, SW
18 June 1857

Sir,

I am directed by the Poor Law Board to inform the Guardians of the Kingston Union that they have received a Report from Mr Meymott, District Auditor, made after his audit of the Union Accounts for the half year ended the 25th of March last, in which, in reference to the Application and Report Books of Messrs Fry & Oram Relieving Officers he states as follows Viz. 'The quality of the relief in kind ordered by the Gd^{ns} is not stated, except the bread.'

The Board are desirous of bringing this report under the consideration of the Guardians and they trust that the Guardians will see the importance of causing the quantity of relief in kind which they from time to time order the Pauper applicants to be distinctly specified in the application & Report Books of the Relieving Officers in the manner contemplated by the General Order of Accounts.

J.

TNA ref. MH 12/10496 Wellington Union, Somerset and Devon
[Report on inmates in a workhouse.]

Workhouse

Report of Visit made by the Commissioners in Lunacy,
pursuant to 16 & 17 Vict., cap 96, s.28

County	Union or Parish Workhouse and where situate	Date of Visit	Visiting Commissioners	No of Inmates of unsound mind	
				M	F
Somerset	Wellington W.H. at Wellington	16 June 1860	Mr Procter Dr Nairne	2	2

Total No 4

Medical Officer   Mr John Buncombe
No of Visits   Daily
Lunatics Wards   M ⎫
                                                  F ⎭ None
No Subjected to mechanical Restraints   None

General Observations and Report.
The patients sleep on flock beds. They are bathed once in two months. One of the patients (Jane Baker) sometimes goes out for a few hours, and Lackington's sister takes him out occasionally for a few hours.

All the patients, (except Jane Baker who has tea, and bread and butter for breakfast and tea) have the house diet, which is very poor, comprehending, three meat dinners, each of two ounces of meat only, the other meals consisting of bread and butter. There are no means of restraint in the House and seclusion is in use.

We recommended that the patients should have extra diet and that they should be allowed to take exercise beyond the walls.

The average cost of the inmates per week amounts to two shillings and four pence, and this includes clothing.

NOTE The minutes of the Meetings of the Board of Guardians for the Wellington Union* have entered a transcript of this report in their minutes, and then state:–
'Ordered that the Clerk do reply to the letter of the Poor Law Board and inform that the Guardians had ordered that the recommendations of the Commissioners in Lunacy be carried into effect.'

* Som. RO ref. D/G/W/8a/12

TNA ref. MH 12/4372 Ledbury Union, Herefordshire
[Visit report on a workhouse.]

Ledbury Union
Report by John T. Graves, Esq. Inspector of Poor Laws on the above Union, after a visit on the twenty second day of March 1864

1. Date of last visit   *7th April 1863*
2. Is the Workhouse generally adequate to the wants of the Unions, in respect of size and internal arrangements? *Yes. Holds 180*

3. Is the provision for the sick and for infectious cases sufficient? *Yes. Scarlatina has just appeared among the children*

4. Are the receiving wards in a proper state? *There is one ward, commonly used as a receiving ward which has been found sufficient. Another ward which might be used for the same purpose, if necessary, is now occupied as a store room by bedding*

5. Is the Workhouse School well managed? *I believe pretty well*

   Insert a copy of any entry in the visiting Committee's or other book, made since your last visit by an Inspector of Schools. *No visit by an Inspector of Schools since my last report*

6. What is the number of inmates in the Workhouse not in communion with the Church of England, and what arrangements, if any, exist for affording them the religious consultation and instruction of ministers of their own separate persuasion? *There are 64 paupers in the Workhouse today, all belonging to the Church of England. If any dissenter should be an inmate and desire to see a minister, the minister is sent for*

7. Are the provisions of the 19th Section of the Act of the 4 & 5 Wm. IV.c.76 duly and systematically observed in the management of the Workhouse? *Yes*

8. Are there vagrant wards in the Workhouse, and are they sufficient? *Yes*

   Are the arrangements for setting the vagrants to work effective, and is the resolution of the Guardians under 5 & 6 Vict. c.57, Sec.5 duly observed? *There is no task of work for able bodied male vagrants unless they require breakfast*

9. Does the visiting Committee regularly inspect the Workhouse? *Yes. fairly so*

   Do any of their answers to the queries in the Workhouse regulations suggest the propriety of any interference on the part of the Commissioners? *No*

   Insert a copy of any entry made since your last in the visiting Committee's book, or other report book, by a Commissioner in Lunacy. *No entry by a Commissioner in Lunacy since my last report*

10. Has the maximum number of inmates of the Workhouse, fixed by the Commissioners, been constantly observed since your last visit? *Yes*

11. Are the proper extracts from the Poor Law Amendment Act, and the Regulations of the Commissioners, hung up in the Workhouse? *Yes*

12. Have all appointments of new officers, and changes in salaries and districts, since your last visit, been reported to the Commissioners? *I am so informed*

13. Is there any officer whose appointment has been sanctioned provisionally? If so, state your opinion of his fitness. *No*

14. Have you any reason to believe that any of the books or accounts prescribed by the Commissioners are not properly kept? *No reason*

15. Have you observed any illegal practice, or any departure from the Regulations of the Commissioners? *I have not*

16. State whether the terms of the Contracts for Vaccination are generally fulfilled, and whether there is any defect in the Vaccination arrangements,

upon which you think it desirable that the Board should communicate with the Guardians. *Vaccination. I am informed goes on satisfactorily.*

17.   Has any marked change taken place in the state of the Workhouse, the number of the inmates, or the general condition of the Union, since your last visit? *In this Union there is some increase in pauperism, as compared with the corresponding time of last year.*

John T. Graves   Poor Law Inspector
dated this *25th* day of *March* 1864

TNA ref. MH 12/4015 Clifton Union, Bristol
[Report on lunatics.]

Report of visit made by the Commissioners in Lunacy,
pursuant to 16 & 17 Vict., cap. 96, s.28
Date of Visit   Oct 18, 1870
Visiting Commissioners   Mr Lutwidge
No of Inmates of unsound mind   M   58   F   78

Upon my visit this day Inspected the Lunatic Wards and saw and examined the Inmates, 57 of the male and 77 of the female sex, total 134.

Before I left the Workhouse two or more persons of unsound mind were brought thither viz. Sam[l] Iles, a congenital imbecile, who had before been in the house, and Clara Jenkins of whom nothing previously was known, & who was nearly mute, torpid and apathetic, & was sent by Mr Bernard, the Medical Officer (who accompanied me) to the sick ward for special observation and care until the following morning. She was brought by her father by order of the Relieving Officer, as insane, and was said to have refused food.

In reference to the cases noticed in Mr Wilkes's report of the 19th May 1869, I have to state that Rob[t] King, J. Williams & Eliza Hardwick were duly sent to the County Asylum, & Jane Millard discharged to the care of her friends.

As respects the present inmates the cases of three only appear to me to call for special remark. That of George Batish, a black, seems to be one of questionable insanity. He is very excitable & impatient of confinement, & uses violent gestures & threats, but Mr Bernard was not satisfied that he was insane, & would further watch him.

Charlotte Mary Knool is considered well & about to be discharged.

Jane Huggins is in a state of melancholia, & has during the last two months suffered from epileptic or other fits. Her memory is confused. Her husband died two years ago of brain disease, and she has since lost one of four children. Since her reception a month ago, she has been depressed, and had one fit. Her husband, who was Editor of the Hampshire Chronicle, and a reporter, left her in destitute circumstances. Her case calls for further special observation on the part of the Medical Officer. She very recently threatened, if compelled to wear the shoes given her, that she would hang or drown herself. When I questioned her upon the subject she had no recollection of having said so. I am of opinion that she might derive benefit from care and treatment in the Asylum, to which I recommend that she be sent, if Mr Bernard should, upon due consideration, be satisfied that she is insane.

I have satisfaction in reporting that in accordance with the recommendation of the Commissioners who visited the Workhouse in December 1868, two additional paid attendants (called Under Keepers) have been appointed for each ward, who divided between them the night watch, one before and the other after midnight.

The present staff of Attendants & their salaries are as follows:–

	Male Ward	Female Ward
Headkeeper	£30	£20
2 Underkeepers (each)	£20	£13

The importance of night supervision is enhanced by the number of Epileptics, as many as 20 in the male ward and 24 in the female.

Referring to the recommendations in the last Report I have to state as follows:–

1. During the winter months three blankets are provided for each bed.
2. Linsey dresses have been procured for all the women, of a warm material & very neat pattern. A new & complete stock was about to be distributed within a week after my visit.
3. The handles of the Bath taps have been removed, & Rules, & Thermometers introduced as suggested.
4. The practice of sending Bristol Lunatics to the Court House in the City, with a view to their transmission to the Borough Asylum has, within the last few months, been altogether discontinued. All such Lunatic inmates are now sent by orders of County Justices, to the County Asylum, & none have been subsequently transferred to the Borough Asylum. Two Bristol Lunatics only have, on account of the County Asylum being full, been sent, by order of County Justices, to the Borough Asylum.

It is material to observe that the Ratepayers of Bristol have a direct interest in the adoption of the present practice, in as much as the weekly charge for maintenance at the County Asylum is only 8s/6d whilst that at the Boro' Asylum is 12s/-. There is consequently a strong temptation to send Lunatics, chargeable to Bristol parishes within the Clifton Union, to the Workhouse, instead of directly to the Boro' Asylum. It is the plain duty of the Relieving Officer in the first instance to submit all cases of Bristol Pauper Lunatics to the Boro' Justices.

The patients of both sexes at the time of my visit were free from excitement, and their personal condition generally was satisfactory.

Many of the women were engaged in needle work. In the male ward the making of nets for fruit trees has been introduced. It was considered dangerous, on account of the tools necessarily used, to employ the Lunatics in mat making. Oakham picking also now furnishes occupation for the male patients. Eight work on the land.

The means of amusement have been increased, & there is stated to be a sufficient supply of books and periodicals. A number of dolls & toys were at Xmas last procured for idiot children.

As respects out door exercise I was informed that the Patients of both sexes are taken out in parties of from 16 to 20, for long walks in the country, two or three times a week.

The Bathing arrangements are now satisfactory. The patients are all bathed weekly, on Wednesday or Friday. There is an abundant supply of hot and cold water constantly laid on, and each patient has a fresh bath. This has been the case for twelve months past. The water is pumped up from the brook, for which purpose a new Engine has been ordered.

Special care is bestowed upon the Epileptics who sleep in dormitories appropriated to them wherein, respectively one of the paid Attendants, or a pauper deputy sleeps. Many of their bedsteads have padded heads and sides.

The large, heavy fire guards, to which reference was made at the last visit, are retained, as required for security. I would again suggest the substitution of light high fenders.

The walls of the day rooms in the female ward are painted or colored, and decorated, amongst other means, by paintings, and the rooms present a cheerful aspect. The male day rooms are about to be similarly improved.

I have to report very favourably of the cleanliness and proper order of the day rooms and dormitories, beds and bedding.

About 30 of the male patients, and 40 of the females attend divine service in the Chapel.

The sanitary condition of the workhouse is reported to be good.

Comfortable chairs and settees are still in desideratum in the Wards.

The padded room is imperfectly ventilated & I recommend the introduction of an air brick, near the floor, in the external wall.

TNA ref. MH 12/10224 Bedminster Union, Somerset
[A medical officer's report.]

30 Nov. 1875

Copy of Report made to the Guardians by Mr Wm White Day, Medical Officer of the Workhouse, and enclosed by him in his Workhouse Medical Officer's report Book.

The cases of Scarlet Fever which were sent to the Small Pox & Fever Hospital should not be readmitted to the Workhouse until after a further time has elapsed.

The Guardians at their meeting of Novr 2nd I thought decided this point, and I have directed the Master not to receive them yet into the House. They should be sent to some intermediate house between the Workhouse & Small Pox Hospital before being brought to the Workhouse where another further disinfection should take place.

Before sending the cases of Scarlet Fever (23) which are in the Workhouse into the Schools the same course should be adopted.

There is in the Workhouse the following list of Inspection and Contagious cases at the present time for which there is no proper accommodation for isolation, viz:–

Venereal Case	Contagious
Scarlatina or Scarlet Fever	(infectious & contagious)
Erysipelas	(very infectious)
Ophthalmia	(Contagious & infectious)
Itch Cases	(Contagious)
Chicken Pox	(Infectious & contagious)

N.B. This week there were 6 children 3 of whom, it was a question whether they had not Small Pox. On requesting the master to remove the 3 with rash from the other 3 he said it was quite impossible and the 6 are now together, fortunately it turned out to be chicken pox but it might have been the more serious malady.

The people in the old Infirmary are packed like herrings in a barrel in consequence of two of the wards in the New Infirmary being occupied by the boys recovering from Scarlet Fever, and there is insufficient cubic space.

The House is not large enough for the numbers that are at present, nor for the union. If the House were enlarged proper infectious & contagious wards should be added to the present Infirmary.

Wm White Day

The Visiting Guardians of the day reported:–
That in consequence of Mr Day's report they enquired and were informed by the nurse that the children recently suffering from Scarlet Fever in the Workhouse were convalescent and desiring to get up and in high spirits. As to the people in the old Infirmary they did not complain but said they were comfortable and the visiting Guardians do not believe they are overcrowded.

The children that have had Scarlet fever are in the new Infirmary and the Visiting Guardians have every reason to believe they might be removed from thence into the School being first disinfected the Visiting Guardians taking the whole of the House into consideration believe there is sufficient Cubic space, they find from the blue Book that the house is calculated to contain 420 inmates and at present has less than 320.

This report was received and adopted by the Board of Guardians on the 16th Novr being proposed by the Chairman, seconded by the Vice chairman.

TNA ref. MH 12/10224 Bedminster Union, Somerset

[A schoolmaster's report on the boys' bad behaviour and requesting the use of corporal punishment.]

The Workhouse
Flax Bourton
Jany 4th 1876

To   The Chairman and Board of Guardians of the Bedminster Union
Gentlemen,
After due consideration I beg most respectfully to make the following report.

The average number of boys who have been in attendance during the last week is 45. Out of this number there are two boys whose ages may be reasonably supposed to be 16. Six boys are about the age of fourteen, and eleven boys are about thirteen years of age. Since the first week of Lady Day 1874 up to this present time a period of one year I find by referring to the books that three boys only have been sent out to service or have obtained situations. Out of these three boys who have been sent out one boy has returned from his master, in fact he has had two places in the period mentioned above and is not an inmate of your Workhouse. I urgently appeal to you to take into consideration the desirability of apprenticing the boys out to service. Is it not a serious and deplorable fact that there are no less than 19 boys in your Union School who ought now to be free from the taint of pauperism. Several of these boys have been inmates here for a long period of time, and it appears that no effort has been made to procure them good places under good masters. Had you taken into your consideration the question of apprenticeships I venture to remark that the question of additional buildings would never have had to be considered. Should you think my proposal of apprenticeship to be of any worth, I should be extremely glad to meet a committee of your board, and give them any further information in my power. I might add that I have found that apprenticeship curtailed pauperism to a great extent, as if a boy were legally apprenticed to a master, supposing he had a mother or other friend, the authority of relationship would not be near so great as it is under your present system.

The conduct of the Boys

I am very sorry to have to report to you that the conduct of many of the boys has been very far from satisfactory. In fact the conduct of one boy is very sad, and I have reason to think that he is not the only one. The boy I refer to is Chas. Howell, (brother to the boy who has received the situations mentioned before) and I ask you to take such steps as is most desirable under the circumstances. I myself heard him propose to the old man (who has charge of the boys) to uncover his nakedness. Had I not happened to have overheard these shameful words, the consequences might have been serious. The old man in charge is deaf, and had he been otherwise, and of a bad character, I ask the Guardians to think of the serious consequences that might have ensued. In addition to this the boy openly defies my orders, and on several occasions he has been guilty of indecent behaviour. The boys mentioned below I report to you for constantly disobeying my orders. You will be aware that I have not the power to use corporal punishment unless you give your sanction as to what kind of instrument is to be used. For my part I am somewhat adverse to corporal correction but I find that good words spoken are of no avail, and I therefore appeal to you to aid me to the full extent whatever lies in your power.

Chas. Stowell
Albert Allen
Chas. Wear
Chas. Fortune
Eml. Brookes
Thos Stenner
Jas. Harper

The boys whose ages may be reasonably supposed to be sixteen, I ask that they may be expelled the school. Many of the boys seem to think that they have no business to work, and will look you in the face and tell lies even when I have seen them do wrong every means must be taken to cope with this ill conduct and a great deal lies in your power to prevent the same.

272

Alfred Blackmore	I am Gentlemen
Hy Blackmore	Your obedient Servant
Albert Clapp	C. E. Probert
Joseph Stenner	Schoolmaster
Thos. Clark	

Copy of Report made December 14th 1875

I entered upon my duties as Schoolmaster at this Union Workhouse, and in addition to the various duties set forth in the Consolidated Orders, I find there are several other duties not consistent with the Orders of the L.G. Board that are here required to be performed by me. The apartments are not anything like comfortable, and the furniture is of a very scanty kind, there are not being even sufficient for proper use. I trust however that the Guardians will endeavour to make me comfortable in all respects, and I hope they will lay down such bye-laws for my guidance in addition to the L.G. Board orders as is consistent with the due and proper performance of my various duties. I may further add that so far there is no supervision of the Boys out of Schoolhours. In conclusion I ask you to provide a Schoolmaster's Journal which is of benefit to myself and the Guardians.

C. E. Probert

TNA ref. MH 12/12991 Sevenoaks Union, Kent

[Enquiry into the dismissal of a nurse. The following is a selection only of the statements recorded in this enquiry:]

Report of Enquiry as to administration of Workhouse Infirmary

Sir,

I have the honour to report that on the 12th inst. I held an Enquiry at the Union Workhouse, Sevenoaks with reference to certain charges brought by Nurse Morrel against the Master and Matron. A considerable number of Guardians were present at the Enquiry.

The letter which Nurse Morrel addressed to the Board, was, as it appeared, in exculpation of herself, and the charges made by her against the Master and Matron were by way of showing that she was not to blame for the incident which led to her dismissal by the Guardians. She was nurse at Sevenoaks from the 4th June to the 28th December in the last year. She succeeded a nurse called Fowler and when she left Nurse Fowler returned to the workhouse. The matron, who is highly qualified, acts as superintendent nurse. In November last Mrs Rycroft, one of the Guardians, after a visit to the infirmary, made a report with reference to the state of the wards, the cooking of the beef tea and some other matters which seriously reflected on Nurse Morrel. An extract from the minutes, which I annex will make it apparent why the Guardians decided to terminate her appointment. About the same time a patient called Stevens was moved from one ward [to] another by the direction of Morrel without any previous communication with the superintendent nurse or the Medical Officer. The man died in a few hours, and the other patients then and there made complaint to the Chaplain who at once reported the matter to the Guardians. The Guardians were all of opinion that Morrel was greatly to blame and that the excuse she offered was absolutely untrue. All this explains why statements were made in her letter which would be otherwise unintelligible. Morrel is an undersized and unhappy looking woman who is evidently out of health. During her whole term of office at Sevenoaks she appears to have been on bad terms with everybody, and she kept a diary in which she set down whatever appeared to her to be wrong in the administration of the infirmary; evidently with a view to future use. At her request I summoned the three nurses, Cooper, Flannery and Fowler, but they flatly contradicted her evidence on every material point, and two of them showed the greatest animosity against her. The evidence of the Medical Officer which was given with the utmost fairness, also showed conclusively that she was wrong in her statements. Under these circumstances it is not necessary for me to discuss the charges in any great detail. For the sake of clearness it may be as well to state that besides the superintendent nurse there are the charge nurse who was exempt from night duty, and two other nurses who took night duty alternatively. There are from 50 to 60 inmates in the infirmary a very small proportion of whom are either confined to bed or are suffering from acute illness. There are a certain number of wardsmen and wardswomen who are approved by the Medical Officer under the terms of the Nurses' Order. The cooking is done in the workhouse kitchen with the exception of the beef tea and is sent to the infirmary in bulk where it is cut up by the charge nurse and distributed to the patients under her supervision. The nurses are on fixed rations and do their own cooking, an arrangement which seems to have led to a good deal of ill-feeling among them. The Medical Officer lives about a mile and a half from the workhouse and visits on the average five days a week. The reports in the visitors' book give ample evidence that the Guardians are most regular in their visits and that those visits are not perfunctory. There are three lady Guardians who apparently take a great interest in the infirmary and who were all present at the enquiry; two of them are ladies of good position in the neighbourhood and the third is a representative of the Socialistic Fabian Society in Sevenoaks. In spite of this the three seemed to be quite agreed as to the nature of the charges, a fact which seems to me to be not without significance.

Morrel's evidence as to the want of sufficient linen was contradicted by all the other witnesses, but the matron says: 'Very occasionally, when the washing has been very heavy and the drying difficult, some of the patients have had to wait for two days for their weekly change of sheets.'

Dressings   From Morrel's letter I was under the impression that she alleged that the dressings of the patients were rags, and sometimes coloured rags; apparently what she meant was that the coverings of the dressings which were supplied by the matron were of rags and were insufficient. The Medical Officer states that in all cases he finds the dressings on lin [linen] or tow [hemp], or whatever may be necessary, but he has never observed that the covering rags were insufficient, and that he has no objection to the use of coloured rags for these outside dressings provided that they are clean. The matron says that she occasionally sends down condemned blue and white shirts as rags to the infirmary to be used for poultices.

<u>Hours of Duty</u>   Where there are three nurses only it is hardly practicable to have regular hours of duty, and as the Medical Officer points out, when patients come in late the night nurse is in need of help and the other nurses have to give it. Whether the staff is sufficient or not depends upon whether these occasions are unreasonably frequent; as to the point, the Medical Officer says, 'It would be better if there were definite hours of duty, but the work varies so much that it must at times be heavy, and there are times when the night nurse wants to help. Occasionally cases come in late, and then the other nurses must help. I should say that ordinarily the staff is sufficient, but it would not be sufficient if the nurses has definite hours of duty rigidly adhered to. I am aware of my duty under the Nursing Order with reference to hiring additional nurses.'

<u>Dirty Heads</u>   Morrel says that when she came she noticed several patients with dirty heads and feet. Nurse Fowler, her predecessor, as to this says, 'I left the heads and feet of the patients clean, but I did not find them so when I came back.'

<u>Medical Appliances</u>   Morrel states that the dressing bowls used for surgical purposes were insufficient in number and that when she can the kitchen bowls had to be used for the purpose. She says that she saw them herself so used and that she complained to the Medical Officer. This last statement is denied by Dr Ward, who says that he never heard any complaint as to the bowls until the day of the enquiry. I sent for specimens of all the bowls in use and the facts appear to be these. In Nurse Morrel's time tin enamelled basins were used for washing and so on; in addition some large bowls which were used for poultices alone; brown bowls which were used for making up liniments and other concoctions for the infirmary use and white bowls which were used for the kitchen. It appears from the evidence of the other witnesses that the coloured bowls were purposely bought so that there should be no mixing of the infirmary and kitchen bowls. When Morrel came she made application for additional enamelled bowls for the surgery; six were provided for her and when she left three of them were found still wrapped up in the paper in which they had been sent in. In addition, she asked for porringers, which means flat bowls with handles to them, white in colour, to be used instead of the brown basins, and these were also supplied. No doubt porringers are more modern appliances for the purpose than ordinary brown bowls, but I should not myself say that there was greater risk of brown bowls used for the purposes of the kitchen than white porringers. It appeared to me that Nurse Morrel on being pressed with reference to this matter, said rather more than she meant to say. She alleged that she saw the brown used for kitchen purposes; the other witnesses say they did not see them so used and never received any complaint of their being so used, and there the matter must be allowed to rest. The balance of testimony is largely against Morrel.

Morrel says that the wardsmen frequently came back intoxicated and quarrelsome to the infirmary, and she specifically names an occasion where a wardsman called Bellinger was drunk and threw the tins about. So far as Bellinger is concerned she is corroborated by Nurse Flannery, who says that she saw Bellinger come back drunk and that he was rather nasty to her. The matron also says she heard of the case. The master was called in on the occasion of Bellinger's mis-conduct and Nurse Morrel alleged that he abused her, by which she evidently means that he took the man's part as against her. What the master says in reference to this is, 'I never abused the nurse, and I should not like to swear that Bellinger was drunk. I saw that he and the nurse were quarrelling, so I moved him to the house. I took the view that it was a quarrel with the nurse, but I used no strong language to the nurse.'

It appears to me that Bellinger evidently had had some drink given to him when he was out on a message, and on his return he and the nurse fell out. The master did the only thing he could do in moving the man from the infirmary. The charges of general drunkenness among the wardsmen received no corroboration from any of the witnesses. The Medical Officer says he once saw a wardsman the worse for liquor on Christmas Eve when the people had been going out gathering holly; the man is ordinarily a most useful man. As long as foolish people will give paupers who are sent out on messages liquor, I am afraid that such occurrences will not be un-known, but there is no ground whatever for the charge that wardsmen frequently came back intoxicated to the infirmary; nor did the nurse appear to seriously press her charge that the master was abusive.

Stimulants   The nurse made some observations as to the way that stimulants were distributed to the patients, but she says that no abuse ever arose from it within her knowledge. As a matter of fact the amount of stimulants that is given is very small and there does not seem to be much the matter with the method of distribution.

Beef Tea   There is no doubt that when the beef tea was made in the hospital kitchen it was very bad, apparently because none of the nurses knew how to cook it. Now that it is made in the house and sent over, there is apparently no complaints. It appears to me from the evidence that the matron acting as superintendent nurse should have discovered that none of the nurses at that time in the infirmary either could, or would, cook beef tea and should have made the change somewhat earlier than was made. But I do not attach much importance to this, looking at all the circumstances of the case.

Diets   Morrel says that frequently not enough mutton was sent down from the house to the infirmary and the nurses had to send up for more from the house kitchen; on some occasions no more was to be had and beef or pork was sent down instead, while on two or three occasions there was not meat of any sort and some of the patients had bread and cheese. The facts of the matter seem to be this. Mutton is only used in the infirmary and therefore the supply is not very large and when fresh patients are put on mutton after the orders for the meat have been given the margin is scanty and occasionally the mutton has run out and other meats have been sent to the infirmary. Once when the matron was absent both mutton and other meats had run short in the house and the result was that two nurses on duty gave their meat, which happened to be chops, to the patients and themselves got what they could later on. The master attributes the occasional shortness of mutton to the fact that there was great waste due to careless weighing on the part of the nurses. He says in Nurse Morrel's time the consumption was greater by 20 lbs more than it is now for the same number of patients. Waste may very easily occur even with care. I used to allow myself waste in Nurse Morrel's time; I now allow 7½ lbs for the 6 lb diet. It is quite evident that a nurse can be careless weighing and cutting up waste enough to seriously embarrass the workhouse commissariat, and this fact is well known to nurses who are on bad terms with masters and matrons. This matter is one which righted itself as soon as good feeling was established between the master and matron and the charge nurse.

Nurses Diet   Morrel states that the diet for nurses was very monotonous. The real grievance seems to be that in her time the nurses could not agree among themselves as to who should do the cooking. The food is abundant and apparently the vegetables are given at discretion. Now one nurse has arranged to do the cooking, there is no further complaint.

Case of Stevens and the Fire Escape   It is not necessary to go into the points raised as to the case of Stevens, or as to the use of the Fire Escape by Nurse Morrel. The Guardians believed that Morrel had behaved improperly with reference to the removal of Stevens and that her explanation was obviously untrue; and they were also of opinion that the Fire Escape should not be used as a means of exit for the nurses, but that they should go through the workhouse and the porter's lodge.

Typhoid Case   Morrel states that upon one occasion a case of typhoid was brought into your house and that the nurses were left without proper help. The Medical Officer swears distinctly that he offered to get an extra nurse at once, but that he refrained from doing so because Nurse Morrel said that she did not want one.

Case of Wood   Morrel makes certain statements with regard to the case of a wardsman called Wood who had an epileptic fit and attacked one of the nurses, Cooper. I confess I am unable to quite understand what the grievance is, but apparently the incident alluded to some sort of altercation between the master and Nurse Morrel.

Summary   On review of the whole case I am strongly of opinion that Morrel has failed to prove her charges or indeed to get any corroborative evidence whatever with respect to them from any of the witnesses. I do not say that she has wilfully perjured herself. I think that she is an un-happy cantankerous person who believes that the whole world is against her. Her temper is aggravated by her personal defects and the unhappy habit of keeping a diary, and her grievance at being dismissed by the Guardians worked her into a state of mind which exaggerated every small matter into serious question. She has now got another place and another chance, and I should not be disposed to disturb her in it.

With regard to the administration of the workhouse, it seems to me that the Guardians are fully justified in the confidence that they feel in the master and matron, especially in the latter officer, but I question whether the matron really has enough time to act as superintendent nurse, or whether she is able to take a sufficiently active part in the infirmary administration. Judging from the Medical Officer's evidence, the supply of nurses, although ordinarily sufficient is at times somewhat smaller than it ought to be, and on the whole I thought it right after the enquiry to suggest to the Guardians the consideration of the question as to whether they ought to appoint a superintendent nurse apart from the matron. The matron is quite willing to give up the somewhat thankless office and the Medical Officer has no objection to the appointment. There may be some difficulty in providing proper quarters for the nurses but I am sure that the Guardians will carefully consider the whole question and do what is possible in the matter.

It might be enough for the Board to write to the Guardians and say, that after consideration of my report they are of opinion that the charges made by Nurse Morrel against the master and matron are without foundation, but that they have instructed their inspector to confer with the Guardians with respect to the adequacy of the nursing staff of the workhouse.

I have the honor to be Sir
Your obedient servant
J S Davy

The President of the Local Government Board
December 8th 1898

***

Union Hospital
Sundridge
Nov[r] 23rd 1898

Sir,

Having been asked by the Board to resign my position here as charge nurse I will do so and inform you as soon as possible of the date from which the notice can count.

Faithfully Yours
A.T. Morrell

***

February 16th 1899 – The following letter was received from Nurse Morrell:

Union Infirmary
Cranbrook, Kent
Feb 14th 1899

To the Sevenoaks Board of Guardians
Ladies & Gentlemen

I am pained and surprised beyond expression at hearing that I am charged with taking that which does not belong to me. When I went to Sundridge Infirmary there was scarcely a knife to use. I took out my own & they were in use for a long time. Then some new ones were supplied. I told one of the helpers to clear mine, roll them up and put them in my plate basket. It was not done for some time I think & I was too much worried to bother about it. She must have thought the new ones were mine, I cannot account for the mistake in any other way. Had I had the least idea they had been changed I should soon have put it right as we very much prefer having our own. They belonged to my deceased mother and everything of hers we greatly value.

Re the Tea. That was brought to Sundridge with me. In my previous post the nurses took it in turn to buy extra tea. At Sundridge there was always sufficient so it was never needed.

The Brandy also was brought with me, always keeping a little by me in case of sudden illness, neither ever belonged to anyone but myself, and it, the Brandy, should have been in the Box took away with me.

It is not in the least likely that anyone with dishonest intentions would have left the articles in a Box in Mrs Wilson's care for an indefinite time, again it is absolutely impossible that I should risk forfeiting a life long strictly honest character for such a mean action.

I much regret being unable to personally answer this serious charge but I have been on duty too short a time to get so far.

Trusting this written one will be accepted.

I am yours faithfully,

Ada A. Morrell

***

Moved by Mr Hale

Seconded by Mr Hooker and Resolved unanimously 'That the explanation given by Nurse Morrell be accepted by the Guardians as satisfactory.'

The clerk was directed to inform her accordingly.

I certify that the above are correct extracts from the Minute Books of the Guardians of the Sevenoaks Union extracted this 17th day of April 1899 by me

George Carnell

Clerk to the Guardians

TNA ref. MH 12/15490 Sheffield Union, Yorkshire (West Riding)

[Report on a burial ground, and charges against the clerk for fraudulent book keeping.]

Report of the Attercliffe Burial Board for the year ending March 25th 1884.

The total number of interments during the year have been as follows:–

In the Old Cemetery 260 of which 136 were on the consecrated part and 124 on the unconsecrated part. The receipt for these graves amount to £165–14–3. In the New Cemetery there have been 216 interments 121 on the consecrated portion and 95 on the unconsecrated portion, the fees amounting to £134–8–6. The payments for the purchased graves in both cemeteries amount to £44–2–4 making a total income from these sources of £344–5–1.

Receipts	£ – s – d
from Thos Jessop Esq.	2000 – 0 – 0
Calls upon the Overseers	1100 – 0 – 0
Receipts from graves &c	344 – 5 – 1
The sale of Hay	16 – 0 – 0
Banker's interest & Commission	13 – 5 – 3
Balance owing Sheffield Union Banking Co. on 25th March 1884	96 – 13 – 10
Total	£3570 – 4 – 2

Payments	£ – s – d
By Banker's balance last year	38 – 15 – 9
Interest on Loans	615 – 2 – 7
Repayments of Loans	400 – 0 – 0
Surveyor's & Architect's charges	487 – 6 – 8
Law charges	277 – 16 – 6
Sundry Tradesmen a/cs New Cemetery	246 – 2 – 1
Sexton's and Labourer's wages	134 – 10 – 7
Minister's Fees	86 – 10 – 0
Secretary's Salary	39 – 0 – 0
Printing, Stationery & Stamps	23 – 1 – 8
Rates and Taxes	20 – 16 – 7
Rent of Sexton's House	17 – 12 – 8
Mowing Grass & making Hay	16 – 12 – 0
Banker's Interest & Commission	15 – 12 – 1
Sundries	10 – 0 – 2
Repairs & New Tools	7 – 12 – 1
Balance	1133 – 13 – 2
Total	£3570 – 4 – 2

The last new grave has been dug in the Old Cemetery, but there are a number of lapsed graves, (many of which contain one body only) which have fallen into the Board, and as soon as the books are properly entered up, and the exact locality and the names of the relatives of the persons buried in these graves ascertained, the Board intend to offer them for sale first to the relatives if they can be found, and failing them, to the public.

The Board regret very much to have to report very serious defalcations on the part of their Clerk Mr Saml Wm Kitching.

For months the Board have had to complain and have repeatedly called him to account for the slovenly and dilatory manner in which his duties have been performed, as well as the irregularity with which he has called meetings of the Board.

On the 17th March last a preliminary examination of his accounts showed that no part of the receipts for graves &c amounting to over £300–0–0 had been paid into the Bank. The Board insisted that this money should be forthwith paid into the Bank to their accounts believing at the time that this was the whole of the deficiency and on 19th March the £300–0–0 was paid in the Board have since discovered by relatives of Mr Kitching.

Subsequently examination of the whole accounts by an Accountant revealed a very serious state of things and the clerk was immediately suspended. Not only had he failed to pay a number of accounts for which he had drawn cheques, but he had also drawn cheques twice over for the same accounts, and had also altered the amounts of a number of cheques from that appearing on the counterfoil.

The total deficiency is now ascertained to be £1133–13–2 exclusive of the £300 paid to make up the grave receipts for the year. The matter has caused the Board a vast amount of trouble and anxiety, they are bound to admit that they have not exercised the amount of care and oversight they ought to have done, believing that he was an honest man.

Their easiest course would have been when deficiency was discovered to have prosecuted the clerk. In that case the whole of the money would have been lost to the ratepayers. The Board were not without hope however of getting the whole or at least a greater part of the money back. There is very little doubt but that Mr Kitching had used the ratepayers' money in his private business and as his private estate showed a large surplus they believed it would be available with help from his friends to pay the deficiency and the outcome of the delay has not resulted so satisfactorily as the Board first anticipated but they have had a proposition submitted to them on the matter which they have felt it their duty to submit to the Vestry. It is as follows:–

In addition to the £300 already paid by Mr Kitching's family they agreed to find a further sum of £400 and Mr David Chapman (Mr Kitching's father-in-law) also agrees to do everything that may be necessary to secure to the Board the whole of his interest (by way of dividend) on the estate of Mr Kitching amounting to over £300. The estate shows twenty shillings in the £, if this is realised it will be seen that the family have found and offer over £1000 towards the £1400 deficiency.

This offer is made on condition that no criminal proceedings are taken against Mr Kitching.

The Board are the servants of the Ratepayers and now leave the matter in their hands for a decision and are prepared to carry out the Ratepayers' resolution.

TNA ref. MH 12/15498 Sheffield Union, Yorkshire (West Riding)
[Report on conditions in the workhouse infirmary.]

<table>
<tr><td></td><td>Sheffield Union</td></tr>
<tr><td>Inspection of Workhouse Infirmary</td><td>April 29th 1890</td></tr>
</table>

At the present time the administration of this Infirmary is in the transition stage of a very important change.

The Guardians have I understand to do away with pauper help, with all its attendant evils, in nursing and are remodelling their nursing Staff.

By the alterations which now approach their completion it is intended that there shall be 10 charge nurses (two of whom will be on night duty) 6 assistant nurses and 9 Probationers (5 for day and 4 for night work) and for their accommodation the Guardians have provided a suitable Home.

As head of the Nurses Home with supervision of the Infirmary servants to generally assist the Matron, and to instruct the Probationers an experienced and well trained nurse has been appointed as Assistant Matron. Paid scrubbers are employed for cleaning purposes.

For the guidance of the new Staff carefully considered rules have been framed and when once the new system is in full working order the arrangements for the care of the sick, aged and infirm poor of Sheffield will be on a scale worthy of this important Union. In those matters it is well to move cautiously, but I am strongly of opinion that as soon as the machinery has been fairly tested it will be necessary to entrust to the Assistant Matron greater and more direct control over the nurses than she now appears to possess. I think indeed that under the direction of the Master and Matron as to all domestic matters and of the M.O. as to the medical requirements she should be placed in entire charge of the Sick Wards and nurses. Such an arrangement would strengthen her authority and responsibility in her own proper sphere.

At present she can only deal with any neglect of duty or any irregularity on the part of other nurses or probationers by reporting the same to the Matron and thus be placed in an invidious position and one productive of friction hereafter.

I understand that hitherto some difficulty has been found in filling up the ranks of the new Nursing Staff. Nurses should always in a large Infirmary of this sort be directly subordinate to an Officer herself, thoroughly trained. And it is probable that until the proposed system is altered in this respect there will be found some reluctance on the part of Nurses and Probationers to engage themselves.

At the proper time the Guardians may have to consider whether it will not be well to separate their Infirmary, as in my opinion it should be separated from the rest of the W.H. for administrative purposes.

Two other points which I may mention in connection with nursing arrangements are (1) the need of a night nurse to take charge of the female imbeciles. These are about 80 in number at present, and it certainly appears to me very necessary that there should be a paid officer on night duty to look after them.

Secondly there should be a paid male nurse in charge of the male itch and lock wards. It is obviously inexpedient to entrust the care of these Wards to a female, nor is it safe or in any way advisable that they should continue to be served by an inefficient and irresponsible pauper wardman.

An excellent system of telephonic communication between the various blocks and a central station near to the R.M.O's apartments and in constant charge of an attendant by day and night, is being provided.

A Code of Infirmary Regulations has also been drawn up and recently adopted. These seem to be well devised in general, though No. 11 appears to limit the patients' outdoor exercise undesirably and be incompatible with No.6. No.6 of the bath room regulations would prevent the usual cleansing of macintosh sheets therein, unless the Guardians contemplate making separate provision in this regard. I presume too, that by No.2 of the Bathroom regulations it is not intended that there shall be any interference with the administration of a tepid or cold bath in suitable cases, such as hyperpyrexia, if ordered by the M.O.

There is a well equipped Dispensary in charge of a qualified man, all drugs are supplied by the Guardians and it may be worth consideration whether stimulants, which are practically drugs, should not be served out from here in the same way as any other medicine.

Meanwhile the Guardians have to face the question of Infirmary extension. With a sound administration of the Poor Law and the growth of population the number of sick and aged poor must be a continually increasing quantity, and in a Union such as this the population of which grew at the rate of about 13% for the 10 years preceding last census, while the Main Building may be alternatively filled or emptied by the fluctuations of trade, the Infirmary will necessarily become more and more full as years go on.

At the present time this pressure is urgently felt on the male side. Although the year is now well advanced the Male Infirmary is absolutely full and ordinary male sick have to be placed in the Lock Ward or drafted into huts hastily erected at [the] time of the small pox epidemic and quite unsuitable for permanent hospital use.

On the day of our inspection there were 48 male ordinary sick in these huts, besides 13 children. There were also in the Male Lock Wards 8 non venereal cases, and in the Main Building about a dozen feeble and sick men who should properly be placed in the Infirmary Sick Wards if there were room.

Thus we have at the present time something like 70 adult sick for whom there is not proper accommodation. So that if the Male Infirmary possessed 4 blocks instead of 3 as at present, it would still be overcrowded and it follows that more than one Medical Block is needed to provide the required room.

As a consequence of the congested state of the Male Infirmary classification is very imperfect, children have to be placed with adults, ordinary sick with the venereal, and there is no special ward for the more offensive cases of ulcers, gangrene, cancer and the like.

On the female side (excluding the Maternity Block and Itch and Lock Wards) there were 156 occupants and 26 empty beds – a margin of about 14% probably sufficient for the present.

The immediate question for the Guardians therefore is how to provide the requisite additional accommodation amounting in round figures to nearly 100 beds on the Male Side. There are I believe, several suggestions.

There are 6 large dormitories standing empty in the Main Building, but if the M.B. is to fulfil its legitimate functions in time of labour-stress it is right that there should be when trade is good a large proportion of reserve. The vacant dormitories are none too many for Sheffield and even if it were not so, the M.B. is not fitted for reception of the sick. All experience goes to show that large numbers cannot permanently be lodged with safety under one roof, and the vast unbroken extent of the M.O. here quite precludes its use for Infirmary purposes.

It is suggested that the sheets which were hastily run up during the Small-pox epidemic may now be permanently used, indeed are now used, for ordinary sick, and that Lock and Itch cases might be transferred to the two which at present stand empty.

For such cases whose stay is but short a hut might do, but these huts (ordinary felt roofed, frame work constructions, with 4 quarters, ¾" weather boards & matchboarded) are not adapted for permanent use, even for Lock cases who may have to remain in them for prolonged periods. Wind and weather has already told upon them, they are cold and damp in winter and hot in summer and can only be regarded as temporary experiments designed to meet a temporary emergency and in no way suitable to take the place of a permanent Infirmary. There are objections to their arrangements to the urinals, to the nurses W.C. and to the heating, to which I will not more particularly refer for I think that to patch them up would be in the end a waste of money. For a time however the iron huts near the entrance might perhaps be occasionally used for the separation of children with ephthalmia, ringworm and the like.

Beyond the female end of the Infirmary are two large well built School Blocks. The number of children has lately largely decreased in this W.H. and it may be possible to employ one Block and convert it into a Male Hospital.

I do not enter into the question of what should be done with the displaced children. This would probably be possible and might furnish about 76 beds and a day room for ordinary sick.

The objections apart from the question of providing for the children are that the school dormitories are of inconvenient dimensions 3 of them being only 18' wide, and the other 3, 36' x 32' with wall space insufficient in proportion to floor space.

There is a further objection that this plan would bring males on to the female side and in opposition to the site on which sooner or later a new female block will have to be built.

A better plan, I think, would be to build a new male block for say 70 beds on ground adjacent to the male end of the Infirmary or elsewhere, (I do not more exactly specify this ground because it has not yet been acquired by the Guardians) and perhaps to extend in the direction of the Master's garden the small block of 35 beds now occupied by aged and infirm men.

This need for extension of the Infirmary accommodation is, I believe, recognised by the Guardians and has been impressed upon them by the Inspector of the District who has also directed their attention to other matters which I noted. To these I can only briefly allude.

Many of these matters will, I understand, be shortly amended, such for example as the Charge Nurses duty to keep proper inventories for each block, the provision of properly locked medicine cupboards, and more orderly arrangement of medicine, lotions &c than now prevails. Greater care is needed for the prevention of bedsores of which I found an undue proportion, some of them of serious extent.

There is, I believe, only one full sized water bed available for use. This is quite inadequate; there should be at least half a dozen. An arrangement of hair-mattress over woven-wire bed is found useful in some places for cases tending to bedsores. Funnel sheeting and beds are needed for very wet cases. I did not find sufficient use of proper draw-sheets in several of the Blocks.

The baths are generally awkwardly arranged and, being about 6" higher than necessary add greatly to the labour and difficulty of bathing heavy patients. The wooden casing of the baths and closet apparatus generally should be removed. It only absorbs and harbours filth, prevents immediate recognition of leakage, and favours dry rot. The bath wastes are I believe all properly disconnected, but they should be trapped at outgo from bath, otherwise an offensive current of air passes through them into the Wards. This was very noticeable in the Maternity Block. Waxed floors dry-scrubbed to the Wards would be more wholesome than the ordinary washed boards between the cracks of which dirt and moisture accumulate. Dry scrubbed floors moreover save labour.

There is a general need of pointing, painting and colouring of Wards and their Offices.

The urinals were offensive in some of the Male Blocks notably in the Imbeciles, and non-absorbent floors are needed. The dust sheets in the Imbecile Ward-offices are objectionable. The lifts in these Blocks should be kept locked, and a better pattern of fire-guard provided also a sufficient number of low flapsided bedsteads for epileptics.

I agree with Mr Kennedy that the provision for alternative exit viz by a sash-window into a fire-escape is insufficient for the Imbecile Blocks with their 3 storeys and barred windows.

The difficulty of getting out imbeciles in such a manner at such a time would, I am convinced prove insuperable even if the arrangements worked well in other respects and the rooms which are near the central staircase were not blocked with smoke.

I should recommend the provision of outside iron staircases from the closet lobbies at each end.

A.H.D.   2 May 1890

Appendix
Extract from Infirmary Regulations
Ward Regulations

1. Patients may by permission of the nurse go into the grounds between 10.30a.m. and 12 noon, or between 2 p.m. and 4.45 p.m., or at other times with the approval of the M.O.
6. The doors leading to the grounds to be locked at sunset, after which time no patients may be out.

Bathroom Regulations

2. The temperature of a bath is to be not less than 90° nor above 100° Fahr.

TNA ref. MH 68/126 Grantham Union, Lincolnshire and Leicestershire
[Enquiry into the issuing of tobacco to inmates for extra work carried out in the workhouse and for false accounting.]

Re Tobacco

Sir,

The tobacco was not kept for some considerable period prior to my taking up duty at Grantham.

The Male Attendant Webb gave me his list of names and number of ozs supplied also the Nurse in charge at the Infirmary then Nurse Earl.

I accordingly entered the names in the tobacco a/c and afterwards added all Inmates admitted over 60 and discharged off all Inmates discharged over 60 which is the usual procedure.

The numbers given to the Male Attendant each week were from 45 to 48 and the Nurse from 20 to 24.

The following tobacco I issued personally and I note it is not accounted for on your report as it was given as extras:

Gray	Tramp Fitter, Boiler House Man	2 oz per week
Bond	Messenger	2 " "
Schofield	Boiler House Man	1 " "
Isaacs	Baker	1 " "
Widdowson	Pigman	1 " "

This was given on account of extra work.

The amount given to Webb and the Nurse together with the above figures worked out so far as I can remember in accordance with the total numbers in the Tobacco a/c consequently as I received no complaint I was of the opinion that the Officers issued the Tobacco to the men on the Tobacco a/c.

James H Richards

***

Grantham Union
Union Offices
Grantham
30th September 1924

Sir,

I beg to report for your information that certain irregularities appear to have occurred in the books of the late Master of the Grantham Workhouse, Mr J.H. Richards, and in the discharge of his duties as follows:–

Provisions and Stores   Mutton

On every Friday mutton is specified in the dietary scale for the mid-day meal. On each Friday of the month of March, April and May 1924 the Book contains the following entries:–

Boiled Mutton Issue

	Prepared lbs. oz.		Loss lbs. oz.		Total lbs.
7th March	34	0½	33	15½	68
14th "	34	0½	33	15½	68
21st "	33	14½	32	1½	67
28th "	33	7½	33	8½	67
4th April	33	15½	33	0½	67
11th "	34	2½	34	13½	69
18th "	34	6½	34	9½	69
25th "	33	13	33	3	67
2nd May	33	12	33	4	67
9th "	33	14	34	2	68
16th "	33	13½	33	2½	67
23rd "	33	15	33	1	67

About 50% loss

***

The following is an abstract of a newspaper cutting which is attached to the above statement:–

Grantham Workhouse Inquiry
Tobacco Privilege for Extra Work Done

Former Master and His Books

After lasting nearly four days the inquiry at the Grantham Poor Law Institutions ordered by the Ministry of Health into charges of irregularities preferred by the Grantham Guardians against their late master, Mr J.H. Richards, now of the Hastings Institution, was brought to a close (so far as evidence is concerned) yesterday.

Mr A.M. Lyons (barrister), appearing for Mr Richards said a statement had been made to him that morning by resolution of the House Committee the master of the Grantham Institution for the time being was empowered to give tobacco for any extra work whether that person be on the list or not, and that had been acted upon by this and other masters for many years. Mr Geo. Patman, a member of the Board of Guardians and of the House Committee, was there prepared to give evidence.

Mr Patman was called and he said he was not prepared to say that such a resolution had actually been passed by the House Committee, but to the knowledge of the House Committee the privilege of the master giving tobacco to inmates for extra work had been recognised at the house for many years. The same privilege was in operation at the old workhouse. That privilege came into force before he was a member of the House Committee, and he had been a member a good many years. He had seen tobacco given for work done when he had been present at the distribution. He did not know whether that proceeding was irregular.

Mr O.B. Warren, the present master, was called by the Inspector, who asked him if it was a fact that since he had been at Grantham he considered that he as master was authorised to give tobacco to any inmate at his discretion.

Mr Warren said he did not think he had the authority, but he had done it, and he believed it was established practice throughout the whole Poor-Law service.

Fictitious Entries

Mr Richards was recalled by the Inspector who questioned him in regard to his books. Mr Richards admitted that during March, April and May of this year he had not kept his books according to the regulations.

The Inspector: If you make up the books as you admit you have done, how do you convince the Guardians that there was no waste?

Witness: As far as I possibly know there was no waste and there were no complaints of shortage. I have never had any complaints from the auditor.

The Inspector: Did the auditor know that your entries were fictitious entries?

Witness: No sir. If he had known I certainly would have explained them to him.

EX-MASTER'S DEFENCE

Mr Lyons addressed the inspector on behalf of Mr I Richards. He said there were three charges against his client. First an allegation of irregularities against him in reference to meat. Second. Irregularities in reference to potatoes and tobacco; and the third, a most serious charge against him and Sindall, that they together took part in a fraudulent arrangement to fake accounts, deliberately deliver and accept shortages of meat and pocket the difference. No one could ever conceive that a man like Sindall would say to an absolute stranger as Warren was 'I have been a thief. Come in with me on this occasion and share in the spoil.' Only the strongest evidence and not tittle-tattle could be accreted to confirm that story. What was the evidence brought before that inquiry? He could never conceive evidence so rotten so absolutely unreliable, and so thoroughly faked as the evidence that had been paraded in that case. He could not conceive a more ramshackle case. There had been a parade of most infirm witnesses, the halt, the fame, the blind, and the mentally defective. How could a high officer of the Government accept, in support of a theory of suspicion, the evidence of men who had been certified as mentally defective, men who were lunatics, and semi-lunatics, on a charge tantamount to felony against a man with 18 years unsullied public service. Those making the charge knew they were parading men from the imbecile ward. Had evidence of that nature ever been trotted out in such a case before? It would not have been accepted in an ordinary court. The only thing that had been proved against Richards were the very things he had admitted to the Ministry, and from which he had never attempted to shrink. He had taken the opportunity of giving a more cheerful fare to the inmates when he gave them roast beef instead of boiled mutton, but he ought not to have done it without the sanction of the Guardians. Not a word had been said against it by visiting Guardians one of whom had commented on the fact that the inmates were satisfied and cheerful. He had done wrong but his was a trivial offence, and not nearly the offence for which that inquiry was started. It was something that ought to be excused because it was merely a breach of internal regulations which has done good rather than harm. The wrong he had done by that departure from internal administration, if he had reported it to the Guardians, would never have been considered an official wrong.

This concluded the proceedings. The inspector said he was not absolutely closing the inquiry. He hoped it would not be necessary to call anyone again. If it was, he would give the parties notice. The inquiry was therefore left open until he has seen the Ministry.

CHAPTER 15

ASSISTED MIGRATION TO THE NORTH OF ENGLAND

In the first half of the nineteenth century the manufacturing industries in the north of England expanded rapidly and there was a great shortage of labour there. In the south, however, many family members were unemployed and relied on Poor Law Relief. People in the south were therefore encouraged to move to the north to work and their travel was paid for by the government.

The following letter is recorded in the first report of the Poor Law Commissioner in 1835:

Extracts of a letter from Robert Hyde Greg Esq. to Edwin Chadwick Esq., Secretary to the Poor Law Commissioners

Manchester, September 17, 1834

I have for some time thought of addressing you on the same matter as my friend Ashworth did some time ago; namely, the propriety of opening a communication between our (strange to say) underpeopled districts and the southern overpeopled ones.

It is at this moment a most important suggestion, and deserves to be put into immediate operation.

It must be looked upon as a happy coincidence that at the period of depriving or curtailing perhaps the facilities of gaining a livelihood to the people of one half of England, and causing a fall in their present low wages, and a scramble amongst them for employment, there should exist a difficulty in obtaining labourers at extravagant wages in these northern counties. This fortunate occurrence should be taken advantage of.

But for the operation of the poor laws in binding down the labourers to their respective parishes, in the mode and to the degree I need not attempt to explain to you, of all men, there would have existed a free circulation of labour throughout the country, to the benefit alike of the northern and southern parts. Nothing but the poor laws prevented this circulation, or could prevent it, short of the labourers being reduced again to the state of *adscripti gleboe*.

At this moment our machinery in one mill has been standing for 12 months for hands. In another mill we cannot start our new machinery for the same want. My parlours are without doors, having been sent some time since to be altered, and their progress having been stopped by a meeting of the joiners. The carpenter in the village in which I reside (12 miles from here), cannot get on with my work, having, as he says, been short of men all the year.

The suggestion I would make is this, that some official channel of communication should be opened in two or three of our large towns with your office, or any office, to which the most overcharged parishes might transmit lists of their families. Manufacturers short of labourers, or starting new concerns, might look over the lists and select, as they might require (for a variety of our wants is great), large families or small ones, young children or grown up men or widows, or orphans, &c.

If this could be done I doubt not in a short time, as the thing became known and tried, we should gradually absorb a considerable number of the surplus labourers of the south, and be supplied from there instead of from Ireland.

The English labourers are much preferred to the Irish and justly so. On this subject you will find much evidence procured by Mr. Geo. Cornewall Lewis, who was down here on the part of the Irish Enquiry Commission, with whom I had a good deal of communication upon the subject.

It must be understood at once that we cannot do with refuse population and insubordinate sturdy paupers. We should require fair play. Hard working men or widows, who preferred gaining an honest living to a workhouse, would I am confident, be in demand.

I may add that I think something on a small scale might be attempted soon. We are now in want of labour. Next year will, unless some unforeseen accident occurs, be naturally a year of increase in our manufacture, buildings, &c., and should this prove the case, any farther demand for labour would still further increase the unions, drunkenness, and high wages.

Whilst food is cheap and wages high, the want of education (I do not merely mean the ability to read and write, which few here are without), but education which may effect manners, morals and the proper use of their advantages, is extremely felt and to be deeply deplored. I do hope Government will not allow another session to pass without making some struggle to effect this most desirable object.

***

Such pauper families in the south were indeed encouraged to move to the north of England to obtain employment in factories, and thus relieve the burden on the Poor Law funds in their home parishes. To encourage this migration the Government paid for families and individuals to travel, often by canal, to the north.

A Government report of 1843 lists many of those who were assisted. These migrants came from Bedfordshire, Berkshire, Buckinghamshire, Essex, Suffolk, Kent and Sussex. There are over 800 persons named in this report, often with their ages, and most in family groups. The report also refers to unnamed *single men*.

The year of removal is given with the date of arrival at their destination. The parish 'from whence removed' is also recorded, together with the name and residence of the employer. Their wages are given for the first, second and third year of employment though in some cases these columns have not been filled in.

A page from this report is reproduced on p. 294, entitled 'Labourers' Removal'. It was ordered by the House of Commons to be printed on 12 May 1843 and can be seen at the British Library or the Parliamentary Archives at the Houses of Parliament in London.

The following letter was found in the Poor Law correspondence files at The National Archives:

TNA ref. MH 12/11932 Plomesgate Union, Suffolk
[A letter to *The Times* referring to the migration of paupers.]

Mr Eagle's letter to the Times Newspaper concerning Dr Kay
dated 17th February 1836

To, The Poor Law Commissioners

Gentlemen,

I perceive a letter in the Times Newspaper from Mr William Eagle relating to me.

Mr Eagle states that I strongly recommend migration to Lancashire in an address which I delivered at Mildenhall in Suffolk, and he quotes a discussion which I gave of the condition of the operatives employed in Factory Labour in Manchester in a Pamphlet published some time ago, as proof of my inconsistency.

The pamphlet alluded to, was written to prove that considering the nature and extent of the toil to which the operatives of Manchester were subjected, greater attention ought to be paid to the municipal regulations of the town, and to the domestic improvement and moral culture of the population. It was shown in this slight work that tho' the labour in factories in Manchester was scarce, the state of the huts and dwellings, of the poor, and the improvement of their domestic and moral condition had not received the attention they deserved, but are in fact extremely neglected.

In all these respects I was careful to shew that the country establishments of Lancashire were exceedingly superior to those of the Town of Manchester and I quoted the example of Mr Ashton's Mill at Hyde to prove that such establishments neither injured the moral or physical condition of the population but essentially contributed to the improvement of both.

This is carefully concealed by Mr William Eagle.

I beg to refer the Commissioners to page 311 of their annual report and appendices in which I have said 'Happily these families have chiefly settled in country establishments and now have been brought to the largest seats of the cotton manufacture. The Board will discover by consulting the schedule of mills in which additional horse power will be brought into operation in the course of the next year

291

and a half or two years, that this increase will occur almost entirely in the several towns and country districts a removal to which may be accomplished with far less change in the habits and aspirations of the Southern labourer than if he were carried to the centre of a map of city population, when total change of employment, combined with the sudden transition from agricultural life to become the dweller in the back street of a large town would be a far greater trial to the mind, and to the body than when the change is made to the smaller country towns of the cotton district. Many of the scattered mills are possessed by some of the most enlightened manufacturers of the trade. In these situations minute and systematic attention is paid to the habits and comforts of the workmen employed in the mills. Schools are established in which the children are instructed on the Sundays and on certain of the week evenings, and the masters exercise a legitimate and benevolent influence over manners and morals of these people. Even where the system is less enlightened no more direct and frequent intercourse between master and servant occurs than in larger cities; the cottages are not huddled together in dense masses, and the population is not exposed therefore to the depressing influence which might in large towns impair the health of the southern labourers. The cottages are well built throughout the whole rural cotton district but as they are more frequently the property of the mill owners in the country and in the smaller towns than in the largest seats of the trade they are more generally there provided with those decent comforts and conveniences which have so powerful an influence and the manners, morals and happiness of the working population. It is therefore a fortunate circumstance that the present extraordinary extension of the cotton manufacturers in Lancashire will chiefly occur in country districts, and in the smaller towns, where, besides the great boon of abundant wages there may be offered to the pauperised population of the southern counties, excellent cottages in the country provided with many conveniences and when the immigrants will be placed immediately beneath the observation and moral influence of their master, instead of being at once mixed with the mass of a city population and then not only separated from the influence of the superior classes but subjected to all the deleterious moral and physical agencies which unhappily affect the character of workmen in large towns.

I have never concealed my opinion that the toil of the factories is such as to render great attention to the health and comfort of the operatives necessary. I am now of that opinion and I beg to refer my report to Mr Geo. Gormesall [?] Lewis on the state of the Irish Poor for a further proof of my consistency.

Hard work with abundant wages is however a pleasant exchange from pauperism and starvation. I write in extreme haste being engaged with the Blything Audit, and I have only time to add that Mr Eagle's letter may be explained by the circumstances that he was signally defeated in his attempts to thwart the proceedings of the Commissioners at Mildenhall.

He then attacked me personally in a very un-gentlemanlike manner, and did not provoke me to a personal reply. On the contrary I treated him with the utmost courtesy which was consistent with the defence of the truth and contented myself with putting their several questions to the meeting on all of which he voted alone.

Should the Commissioners request me to reply to his letter, I shall consider it unworthy of notice.

> I have the honor to be
> Gentlemen
> Your obedient servant
> J.P. Kay   17th February 1836

TNA ref. MH 12/11933 Plomesgate Union, Suffolk

[Cost of moving a family by boat from Manchester to Preston – presumably this family had travelled to Manchester from Plomesgate by canal.]

> The Guardians of The Plomesgate Union
> Drs to C.J. Muggeridge
> P.L.C. Migration Agent

John Kerriage
of Rendlesham
and family

Boat from Manchester to Preston	10 – 0	
do for luggage	8 – 0	
Man attending on them at Manchester	3 – 6	
		1 – 1 – 6
Fee ordered to be charged to the Parish		10 – 0
from which the migrants came by the P.L.C.		1 – 11 – 6

Four young men employed	Agency fee 5/-	1 – 0 – 0	
at Preston on Railway	Relief given on arrival	2 – 6	1 – 2 – 6
			£2 – 14 – 0

Preston July 21st 1836

Sir,

I beg to hand you the above account which you will do me the favor of laying before the Board at their next meeting.

> I have the Honor &c
> Chas. J. Muggeridge
> P.L.C. Migration Agent

To W. Enwaur, Esq
  Clk of the Plomesgate Union

LABOURERS' REMOVAL.

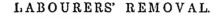

RETURN to an Order of the Honourable The House of Commons,
dated 20 February 1843;—for,

COPIES of an original LETTER addressed to *Edwin Chadwick*, Esq., Secretary to
the Poor Law Commission, by *Robert Hyde Greg*, Esq., dated Manchester,
September 17th, 1834; and of an original LETTER to *Edwin Chadwick*, Esq., by *Henry
Ashworth*, Esq., dated Turton, near Bolton, Lancashire, 2d Month, 13th day, 1835:

COPY of the CORRESPONDENCE relating to, and a RETURN of, the Number of Persons
who were removed from their Parishes in the AGRICULTURAL DISTRICTS into the
MANUFACTURING DISTRICTS, under the Authority and Sanction of the Poor Law
Commissioners; with the Dates and Mode of their Removal, the Names of the
Parishes from which they were taken, and the Names and Residences of the Persons
to whom they were assigned; with a particular Account of the Numbers, Sexes and
Ages in each Family, when they were removed; and also, of the Number of Deaths,
by Accident or otherwise, which have since taken place among them; also, an
Account of those who have been maimed in their Employment; and a Statement of
the Amount of the Wages agreed upon when consigned, with the actual Wages they
received, and also, an Account of their present Residences, Employment and Wages.

(*Mr. Ferrand.*)

Ordered, by The House of Commons, *to be Printed,*
12 *May* 1843.

RETURN RELATIVE TO REMOVAL OF LABOURERS

RETURN of the Number of Persons who were removed from their Parishes in the Agricultural Districts into the Manufacturing Districts, &c.—continued.

NAME of FAMILY.	Ages.	Number in each Family.			Date of Removal.	Mode of Removal from London.	Date of Arrival.	PARISH from whence removed.	Name and Residence of Employer.		Weekly Wages agreed for.		
		Number.	Males.	Females.					Name.	Residence.	1st Year.	2d Year.	3d Year.
					18,6:		1836:				s. d.	s. d.	s. d.
Booth, Mary	47	4	1	3	month not stated	by canal	May	Badingham	Elisha Dickens	Bugsworth	7 -	8 -	10 -
⎯ Edward	20										4 6		7 -
⎯ Sarah	18										4 4	6 5	7 6
⎯ Emmeline	15												
Hobbs, Henry	36	10	not stated	not stated	ditto	not stated	10 May	Astwood	Wm. Cripps, esq.	Newport Pagnell	10 -	10 -	10 -
⎯ Wife	36												
⎯ George	17										5 5	6 6	7 7
⎯ Mary	16										5 -	6 -	6 6
⎯ Edwin	14										4 2	5 3	5 5
⎯ Charlotte	12										6 1	3 1	4 4
⎯ Kazia, and	10										- 1	1 6	3 2
⎯ Three younger	not stated												
Self, James	51	13	ditto	ditto	ditto	by canal	12 May	Brundish	C. Ainsworth & Co.	Bolton	9 -	10 -	11 -
⎯ Wife	46												
⎯ Jane	20										5 6	6 6	6 6
⎯ Emma	18										4 6	5 4	5 5
⎯ James	16										4 6	4 4	4 4
⎯ Peter	15										3 6	3 3	4 3
⎯ Walter	13										3 1	2 1	3 2
⎯ Lydia	10										1 -	1 6	2 -
⎯ Sarah, and	9												
⎯ Four younger	not stated												
Honeyball, Charles	33	10	3	7	ditto	ditto	May	Firmingham	Peter Bould	Ovenden House, Halifax	10 -	10 -	10 -
⎯ Wife	39										5 -	5 6	6 -
⎯ Maria Pel-brow.	17												
⎯ Mary Ann	14										3 6	4 3	4 4
⎯ Elizabeth	12										3 -	3 6	4 -
⎯ Hannah	10												
⎯ Hephzibah	8												
⎯ Aaron	6												
⎯ Zeriah	1												
⎯ Simon	17										5 -	6 -	7 -
Cocksedge, John	40	5	2	3	ditto	not stated	6 May	Pakenham	E. Dickens, esq.	Bugsworth	10 -	11 -	12 -
⎯ Sarah	19										6 -	6 6	7 7
⎯ John	18										4 6	5 6	7 5
⎯ Elizabeth	13										3 -	4 3	5 4
⎯ Anne	11										2 -		4 -

A page from a government report of 1843 listing families who were assisted in moving to manufacturing districts in the north of England.

CHAPTER 16

ASSISTED EMIGRATION

There are detailed records of many destitute families and individuals, and many orphans, who, with their agreement, were given assisted passage to Canada, Australia or New Zealand. There are also records of some rare instances when a pauper was returned to the place abroad from where he had come. The Board of Guardians of a Union funded the travel and sent lists of such families and individuals, with their places of destination, to the Poor Law Commission (and later the Poor Law Board and the Local Government Board) for their approval. Records of these are to be found in the central correspondence files at TNA in document classes MH 12 and MH 68. Requests from the Emigration Department of the Colonial Office for skilled workers to be given assisted emigration to Van Diemen's Land (Tasmania) are to be found in MH 19, together with lists of children sent to Canada.

For half a century or more after the foundation of Australia there was a continuous shortage of young single women. Many immigrant men became 'friendly' with the native women and this must have caused much concern amongst the Aborigines. Much was done to encourage girls and single young women to emigrate to Australia, though this does not appear to have been particularly successful. Very few single girls and young women appear in the records.

The following two letters are copied from the First Annual Report of the Poor Law Board dated 1848:

Emigration of Young Females to Australia.

> Poor Law Board, Somerset House
> November 30, 1848

Sir,

   The Poor Law Board have received a communication from the Colonial Land and Emigration Commissioners proposing to facilitate the emigration, to a limited extent, to Australia, of young females from the English workhouses, provided they be sent out as soon as they are fit for work, and have obtained sufficient education.

The enclosed extracts from the letter will explain to the Guardians the terms on which it is proposed that the emigration should be conducted, and the Board request that the Guardians will take the subject into their consideration and inform them whether the Guardians would be desirous of promoting the emigration of any young females in accordance with the arrangement therein suggested.

A set of forms is sent herewith which will further show the conditions required to be fulfilled and the course that must be pursued in case the emigration is proceeded with.

I am, &c

W.G. Lumley, Assistant Secretary

To: The Clerk to the Board of Guardians

[This letter was presumably sent to every Union.]

Extract from a letter dated 1 August 1848 and addressed by the Colonial Land and Emigration Commissioners to the Poor Law Board:

The Emigration Commissioners would propose to admit as candidates for passages to Australia, girls belonging to the sixth class of paupers (as defined in the workhouse rules of the Poor Law Commissioners) who may have lost their parents and have completed their thirteenth year. Such candidates should be capable of labour and must have been vaccinated or have had the small-pox, and be free from all disease usually considered infectious or contagious. They should also have a sufficient knowledge of reading, writing and arithmetic and the principles of the Christian religion, and have a good character in respect of industry and general behaviour.

If as the Emigration Commissioners are led to suppose the parishes would be willing to provide for persons answering these conditions, the cost of outfit and the expenses of the journey to the port of embarkation, and would contribute the sum of £5 towards the passage of each person embarked, the Emigration Commissioners would be prepared to defray the other expenses attending their conveyance to the colony out of funds applicable to emigration, under the management of the Board.

The Secretary of State will instruct the Governors of New South Wales and South Australia to effect such preliminary arrangements as may be necessary for the reception of these young girls and for placing them with respectable and trustworthy families on their quitting the protection of Government; and also to make such provision by local enactment as may be necessary for their apprenticeship.

It may be here worth while to give the following extract of a report recently received from the surgeon superintendent of the *China* on the disposal of the emigrants by that ship, which show the demand then existing in South Australia for the services of young girls:– 'All the little girls from 12 to 15 years were immediately engaged at from £12 to £13 per annum as nurse girls.'

The following are some examples of records of emigration at The National Archives, and Union records at county record offices:

TNA ref. MH 19/5 Emigration Department
[List of the types of tradesmen required in Van Diemen's Land with the average wages and numbers required.]

Emigration Department
Colonial Office
February, 1836

In consequence of the great demand for Mechanics and Agricultural Labourers in the Australian Colonies, the following Statement (obtained from Returns transmitted from the respective Districts of the Colony to the Governor, and by him forwarded to this Office) shewing the average Wages of Mechanics and others in the Island of Van Diemen's Land, together with the aggregate number of each description required; is laid before the Public for general information. No statement upon this subject has been received from the Governor of New South Wales, but it may be fairly inferred that a corresponding demand for Labour exists in that Colony, and a proportionate remuneration afforded for it:–

Trade or Calling	Average Wages per Diem without Board or Lodgings	Average Wages per Diem with Board or Lodgings	Average Wages per Annum with Board and Lodgings	Total Number Required
	s – d	s – d	£ – s – d	
Bread and Biscuit Bakers	3 – 4½	1 – 11	28 – 6 – 8	11
Butchers	4 – 1	2 – 2	30 – 5 – 8	17
Boat Builders	7 – 1	5 – 0	42 – 0 – 0	8
Brick Makers	6 – 1	4 – 3	45 – 11 – 5	52
Bricklayers	6 – 10½	4 – 8	51 – 10 – 0	43
Blacksmiths	7 – 1	4 – 11½	53 – 8 – 6	28
Bell Hangers	7 – 4	4 – 9	40 – 0 – 0	6
Brass Founders	6 – 6	4 – 6	50 – 0 – 0	1
Brewers and Maltsters	4 – 9	2 – 11	42 – 16 – 0	12
Collar Makers	5 – 8	3 – 6	44 – 5 – 0	7
Confectioners	3 – 9	2 – 6	30 – 0 – 0	3
Chair Makers	7 – 5	5 – 10½	55 – 10 – 0	12
Curriers	5 – 4	2 – 11½	41 – 16 – 0	23
Carpenters	6 – 9	4 – 8	54 – 2 – 6	66
Caulkers	5 – 0	3 – 0	40 – 0 – 0	2
Coopers	6 – 7	4 – 3	59 – 0 – 0	23
Cart Makers	7 – 1	5 – 1	52 – 16 – 8	20
Coach Makers	7 – 3	5 – 0	50 – 0 – 0	11
Compositors	7 – 0	5 – 0	80 – 0 – 0	6
Candle Makers	4 – 6	2 – 6	27 – 10 – 0	6

Cabinet Makers	8 – 0	6 – 1½	58 – 6 – 8	11
Cheese Makers	4 – 0	2 – 6	32 – 10 – 0	11
Coach Spring Makers	8 – 2	5 – 9	60 – 0 – 0	5
Cooks (men)	3 – 5	1 – 10	24 – 8 – 0	40
Cooks (women)	2 – 9	1 – 4½	17 – 3 – 4	60
Colliers	no rate given		15 – 0 – 0	12
Coppersmiths	5 – 9	4 – 0	40 – 0 – 0	1
Cutlers	4 – 6	2 – 6	31 – 0 – 0	3
Dyers	6 – 0	4 – 0	36 – 0 – 0	2
Dairy Women	2 – 6	1 – 2	16 – 8 – 6	68
Distillers	6 – 0	4 – 0	50 – 0 – 0	2
Engineers	10 – 6	8 – 0	57 – 10 – 0	3
Farmers	3 – 10½	2 – 6½	32 – 10 – 0	75
Farriers	8 – 0	6 – 10	90 – 0 – 0	16
Fellmongers	4 – 3	2 – 1	30 – 0 – 0	2
Gardeners	4 – 4½	2 – 4½	29 – 2 – 6	48
Glaziers	6 – 6	4 – 7	45 – 0 – 0	10
Glue Makers	no rate stated			10
Gilders	7 – 0	5 – 0	50 – 0 – 0	1
Gunsmiths	6 – 6	4 – 3	46 – 10 – 0	5
Hairdressers	3 – 9	2 – 3	26 – 13 – 4	6
Harness Makers	5 – 10	4 – 4½	43 – 15 – 0	12
Joiners	7 – 0	4 – 9½	52 – 0 – 0	34
Leather Dressers	5 – 8½	3 – 4	41 – 13 – 4	9
Lime Burners	4 – 8	3 – 1	34 – 16 – 0	21
Locksmiths	5 – 10	3 – 9	42 – 10 – 0	4
Labourers	3 – 10	1 – 6	22 – 10 – 0	139
Millers	4 – 7	2 – 8	43 – 2 – 10	23
Millwrights	7 – 1	4 – 8	66 – 10 – 0	15
Milliners	2 – 6	1 – 3	17 – 10 – 0	14
Milkmen	8 – 2	1 – 7	23 – 0 – 0	8
Nurserymen	4 – 6	2 – 6	33 – 0 – 0	8
Nailers	5 – 0	3 – 6	38 – 15 – 0	13
Painters	6 – 6	4 – 2	44 – 0 – 0	9
Pump Makers	6 – 6	4 – 9	50 – 0 – 0	3
Plough Makers	6 – 10	4 – 10	49 – 10 – 0	15
Potters	5 – 0	3 – 0	45 – 0 – 0	2
Plasterers	6 – 7	5 – 0	62 – 4 – 0	36
Ploughmen	3 – 7	1 – 10	25 – 8 – 8	88
Plumbers	6 – 4	4 – 6	45 – 0 – 0	6

[contd]

Printers and Pressmen	5 – 0	3 – 6	50 – 0 – 0	2
Quarrymen	4 – 9	2 – 9½	29 – 0 – 0	26
Rope Makers	6 – 0	4 – 0	50 – 0 – 0	2
Sadlers	6 – 7	4 – 10	51 – 15 – 0	15
Shoemakers	5 – 3½	3 – 4	40 – 8 – 0	47
Sawyers	6 – 8½	4 – 7	57 – 16 – 0	61
Shipwrights	8 – 0	6 – 0	70 – 0 – 0	4
Stone Masons	6 – 10½	4 – 8	49 – 3 – 4	48
Stone Cutters	7 – 1	4 – 6	45 – 10 – 0	21
Slaters and Shinglers	6 – 7	4 – 6	45 – 0 – 0	22
Shepherds	3 – 3	1 – 7½	25 – 0 – 0	78
Sheep Shearers	6 – 9	5 – 2	- - - - -	66
Sieve Makers	6 – 6	4 – 0	35 – 0 – 0	5
Straw Plaiters	3 – 0	1 – 6	15 – 0 – 0	2
Straw Hat Makers	3 – 0	1 – 6	20 – 0 – 0	
Turners	5 – 3	3 – 0	31 – 0 – 0	8
Tanners	5 – 1	3 – 4	35 – 0 – 0	21
Tailors	5 – 8	3 – 6	42 – 0 – 0	19
Tinplate Workers	5 – 4	3 – 9	54 – 0 – 0	5
Upholsterers	7 – 3	4 – 4	47 – 10 – 0	6
Wheelwrights	6 – 9	4 – 10	56 – 0 – 0	21
Wool Sorters	6 – 0	4 – 6	50 – 0 – 0	14
Wood Splitters	4 – 6	2 – 10	37 – 16 – 4	52
Watch Makers	6 – 6	4 – 6	55 – 0 – 0	11

With a view to enable such Persons, *provided they are of industrious and steady Character*, to emigrate to the Australian Colonies, His Majesty's Government are granting a Bounty of £20 to those who intend taking their Wives and Families with them; but in order to supply the great demand which more immediately exists arrangements have been made, by which a limited number of Families will be conveyed to each of the Australian Colonies, in Ships engaged by the government for that purpose, at a charge of £10 only for a man and his wife, *beyond the aid afforded by Government*. Children under five years old will be charged £5 each, and those above that age £1 for each additional year. Infants under one year will not be charged for.

Government Agents for Emigration have been appointed at London, Liverpool, Bristol, Dublin, Cork, Limerick, Belfast, Sligo, Leith and Greenock, who have been instructed to afford gratuitous information to all persons applying to them, as to the best means of carrying their views of Emigration into effect. Parties, therefore, who may reside in the neighbourhood of these Agents are requested to apply to them either personally (or by letter post-paid), for information on this subject.

All persons desirous of obtaining information upon this object, either for themselves or for others, are requested to apply by Letter only to, J.D. Pinnock, Esq., *The Government Agent General for Emigration* under cover, to the Secretary of State, Colonial Department, London, who is prepared to make the necessary arrangements for the conveyance of Emigrants to any part of the British Colonies.

J. D. Pinnock

Government Agent General for Emigration

TNA ref. MH 12/11932 Plomesagte Union, Suffolk
[List of persons emigrating to Canada, 1836.]

A List of Paupers and their families who have voluntarily agreed to Emigrate to Canada at the expense of the Parish of Kettleburgh in the County of Suffolk at which place they have settlement.

	Age	Amount of relief had during the last year, and description of Paupers
Samuel Smith	38	£5 2s 2d
Mary do his wife	39	Agricultural Laborer
Lydia do child	16	
Elijah do do	15	
Ruth do do	12	
Elisha do do	8	
Moses do do	4	
Aaron do do	3	
Mary do do	1	
Alfred Mayhew	35	£10 14s 0d
Mary do his wife	35	Agricultural Laborer
Henry do child	12	
Maria do do	10	
George do do	8	
Mary Ann do do	6	
Phoebe do do	4	
Robert do do	2	
Alfred do do	1 month	
Joseph Baldry	36	£5 0s 3½d
Susannah child	10	Agricultural Laborer

[contd]

Jeremiah do		8	
Edward do		5	
Mark Groom		39	£5 15s 0½d
Lydia do his wife		37	Agricultural Laborer
Mary Ann do child		16	
George do do		14	
James do do		11	
Ellen do do		8	
Robert do do		5	
Sarah do do		4	
Mark do do		2	
Emma do do		¼	
John Taylor		35	£10 18s 4½d
Letitia do his wife		33	Agricultural Laborer
James do child		14	
Edward do child		12	
Robert do child		9	
Maria do child		7	
Martha do child		5	
Elizabeth do child		1¾	
George Mayhew		19	2s 3½d
Single man			

The relief to the Parish from Emigration of the above Paupers is not to be measured by the money received by them from the rate. Some of them have been employed for the greater part of their time, and all of them are excellent workmen. They are not sent because the Parish has any complaint against them, but because they are willing to go, and will make room for the employment of others. There are at this day 26 able men unemployed and paid from the Rates, and there has been frequently more than that number. The quantity of Land in the Parish is only 1200 Acres.
14th April 1836

Wm Garrett
John Edwards, Guardian
J.B. Pisie
M. Pettit
E. Oxborrow

TNA ref. MH 12/13658 Amesbury Union, Wiltshire
[List of persons emigrating to Canada, 1836.]

A LIST and DESCRIPTION of the PERSONS desirous of EMIGRATING from the Parish of Durrington in the County of Wiltshire

Males	Age	Females	Age	Married	Single	Occupation	Amount of Parish Relief	Where Emigrating to
Samuel Strong	33	Jane Strong	33	Yes		Labourers in Agriculture	2–0–0	Quebec
John Strong	13	Elizabeth Strong	9		Yes			
William Strong	11	Sarah Strong	3		Yes			
Joel Strong	6							
Stephen Strong	0							
James Bishop	35	Christian Bishop	40	Yes		Labourers in Agriculture	1–0–0	Quebec
John Bishop	10	Sarah Bishop	12		Yes			
		Jane Bishop	8		Yes			
Henry Ranger	25	Lucy Ranger	22	Yes		Labourers in Agriculture	2–0–0	Quebec
John Ranger	2							
Edmund "	0							
Thomas Ranger	21	Ann Ranger	23	Yes		Labourers in Agriculture	1–5–0	Quebec
Immanuel Ranger	2							
Edward Ranger	0							
Edward Holloway	39	Letitia Holloway	36	Yes		Labourers in Agriculture	13–0	Quebec
William Holloway	12	Mary Holloway	3					
George Spredbury	25	Ann Spreadbury	22			Labourer in Agriculture	1–0–0	Quebec
		daughter infant	0					
Benjamim Spredbury	21				Yes	Labr in Agric^{re}	2–0–0	Quebec

[contd]

Giles Collins	19				Yes	ditto	0–5–0	ditto
John Maton	20				Yes	ditto	0–5–0	do
Armon Spredbury	19				Yes	do	0–10–0	do
Henry Weeks	30				Yes	do	3–0–0	do

Dated at Durrington
June 25th 1836   Joel Rowden   Churchwarden
                                            John May   Overseer

TNA ref. MH 12/11933 Plomegate Union, Suffolk
[Emigration expenses disallowed, 1836.]

Plomesgate Union
6 Aug. 1836

Brandeston Parish
    At a General Meeting of the Guardians held 10th May 1836 the Parishoners of Brandeston through the Guardians of the Poor of that parish applied for the sanction of the Board of Guardians for the expenditure of not exceeding £21 to be paid by the Relieving Officer for the expenses of emigrating to Canada of Joshua Allum, his wife and 3 children and the expenditure was allowed by the Board the application having been sanctioned by the Inhabitants of the parish generally.
    The family was sent and the expenditure of the sum received £21 was paid by the Relieving Officer and was allowed to him in his account by the Guardians.
    The Auditor has declined to pass the Relieving Officer's account as to the sum on the ground that the expenditure was not previously sanctioned by the Poor Law Commissioners.
    The application to the Guardians and the expenditure allowed by them and made by the Relieving Officer under the impression that the sanction of the Poor Law Commissioners was not required except in cases where money was borrowed, charged upon the rates and to be repaid by Instalments.
    Under the circumstances stated it is presumed that the Poor Law Commissioners will now sanction the expenditure of the money in question being but a very small proportion of the average expenditure of the parish the Relieving Officer having acted under the authority of the Guardians.
    An early answer is requested that the Auditor may pass the Relieving Oficer's account.

(signed) W. Germans [?]
Clerk of the Union pro tem

***

Plomesgate Union
6 Aug. 1836

Framlingham Parish
Emigration Expenses disallowed
This Parish having two pauper families desirous of emigrating to Canada and being willing to bear the expense of such Emigration regular notice was given of a Vestry Meeting to take the matter into consideration. The Meeting was numerously attended and the matter fully discussed when it was determined by a very large majority that these families should be sent out at an expense not exceeding £100 and it was also determined that no money should be borrowed on this account but that the amount expended should be immediately paid.

On the 26th April last the Board of Guardians at their Meeting as appears by the Minute Book resolved 'That the parish of Framlingham should be at liberty to expend not exceeding £100 for the emigration to Canada of Samuel Cousins and family and Thomas Anson and family in all 15 persons, the money expended to be carried to the account of the Out relief of that parish and to be paid by the Relieving Officer.'

These two families were accordingly sent to Canada through the agency of Mr Pennock and the expenses amounting to the sum of £96–3–6 were paid by the Relieving Officer and the expenditure has been allowed to him by the Guardians.

The Auditor has declined to pass the Relieving Officer's Accounts as to the money on the ground that the expenditure was not previously sanctioned by the Poor Law Commissioners.

The money expended does not amount to one seventeenth of the average yearly expenditure of the parish and when the expenditure was allowed by the Guardians and their authority acted upon without the sanction of the Poor Law Commissioners it was under the impression that such sanction was not necessary to authorize expenditure for Emigration except in cases where money was borrowed and charge upon the rates to be paid by Instalments.

Under the circumstances stated it is presumed that the Poor Law Commissioners will now sanction an expenditure of comparatively so small an amount incurred with the consent of a large majority of a Vestry Meeting legally convened and with the recorded allowance of the Board of Guardians.

The Only decision of the Poor Law Commissioners upon this subject is requested that the relieving Officer's account may be passed by the Auditor.

signed W. Germans [?]
Clerk of the Union
pro tem

***

The wives and families of convicts often became reliant on poor relief. Sometimes they were encouraged to join their convict family members by being given assisted passage to Australia. The following is a rare example of a list found in the Poor Law Union records for Taunton Union in 1846:

TNA ref. MH 12/10456 Taunton Union, Somerset and Devon

Table of Wives and Families of transported Convicts now resident in this Union.

Names of Women	Names of Husband	Name of Colony where the Husband is at present	Date and Place of Conviction	No of Children	Age of Children					
					Between 7 and 14		Under 7		Over 14	
					M	F	M	F	M	F
Andrews Sarah	Andrews John	New South Wales	Aug. 1838	4	1	2				1
Blackmore Mary	Blackmore Wm.	Gosport	March 1840, Taunton	6		3			3	
Bussell Sarah	Bussell Hen	Van Diemans Land	Oct 1845, Taunton	5		2	1		1	1
Burford Betty	Burford Joel	Not Known	1839, Exeter	4	1	2				1
Burge Elizabeth	Burge Fras	Van Diemans Land	August 1842, Bridgwater	3	1	1	1			
Cawley Hannah	Cawley Robt	Hobart Town, Van Diemans Land	Jan. 1843, Taunton	5	1	1		1		2
Cook Hannah	Cook Jno	Norfolk Island	Oct 1845, Taunton	5		2		1		2
Chard Mary	Chard Thos	Not known	1840, Exeter	4	2	1	1			
Dunn Sarah	Dunn Sam.	Sydney, New South Wales	about 14 years ago, Exeter	5					3	2
Hake Mary	Hake Willm	Norfolk Island	Aug 1845	4	2		1			1
Keats Ann	Keats W^m	Van Diemans Land	June 1841	5	1	1	1	1		1
Webber Mary	Webber Lazarus	Not known	About 1838	2	1	–	–	–	–	1

The return is not to be delayed for this information, if not readily to be obtained.

Signed the 13th Day of August 1846

John Chorley Clerk to the Guardians

Som. RO ref. D/G/W/57/5 Wellington Union, Somerset and Devon

Outgoing Letter Book, 1846–48

[A child is to be taken to Philadelphia with her aunt. No addressee is given but the following letter is assumed to have been sent to the Poor Law Board.]

Wellington, Somerset
7th July 1847

Gentlemen,

I am directed by the Board of Guardians of this Union to report to you the case of Lydia Thorne aged 8 years, the orphan daughter of Philip and Harriet Thorne, deceased, belonging to, and resident in the parish of Wellington.

She at present resides with and is taken care of by an aunt Susan Thorne who is about to emigrate to Philadelphia in the United States and desirous of taking the Orphan with her. The Guardians are willing to advance the sum of Seven Pounds to assist her, and direct me to solicit your sanction to their doing so although it may not consist [sic] with the Rule you have laid down in reference to the place of destination. I respectfully solicit an early reply as Susan Thorne leaves this place for the port of embarkation on Tuesday next.

I have the honor to be Gentlemen,
Yours Ob^t Serv.
W. Rodham

Som. RO ref. D/G/W/8a/6
Minutes of the Board of Directors of the Wellington Union
[A copy of a letter relating to the last case.]

Poor Law Commission Office
Somerset House
12 July 1847

Wellington Union
Wellington Parish
Sir,

I am directed by the Poor Law Commission to acknowledge the receipt of your letter of the 7th instant requesting the Commissioners sanction to the proposal of the Guardians of the Union to defray the expenses of the Emigration of Lydia Thorne, an orphan aged 8 years, to Philadelphia.

In reference thereto I am to inform you that the Commissioners uniformly decline to sanction the Emigration of poor persons to the United States at the expense of the Poor Rates.

The Commissioners have fully explained their views on this subject in the 8th annual report p38, and in the 11th annual report pages 32 and 33.

The Commissioners therefore are unable to give their sanction to the proceedings proposed to be taken in the case of Lydia Thorne and see no ground for deviating from their universal practice.

I am, Sir. &c

Note: Nothing more has been found of this case.

TNA ref. MH 12/11768 Bosmere and Claydon Union, Suffolk
[People emigrating to Canada, 1850.]

Bosmere and Claydon Union
A List and Description of the Persons who have been assisted by the Guardians to Emigrate, at the period during the Year 1850, under the authority of Orders issued by the Poor Law Board in that year, stating the precise time at which the Persons actually embarked.

Name Males	Age			At the Cost of		Where Emigrated to	Name of Vessel and Date of
	Above 14	Between 7 & 14	Under 7	The Common Fund	The Parish of		
Creasy Joseph	Adult				Framsden	Montreal	Ava
Creasy Frederick	same				same	same	same
Ringe William	same				Michfield	same	same
Sheldrake Howard	same				Stonham Aspel	same	same
Sheldrake Ephrahim	same [sic]		under [sic]		same	same	same
Weeden Edward	same				Helmingham	same	Durham
Haill James	same				same	same	same
Moss Frederick	same				same	same	same
							11th April 1850
Females							
Goldsmith Caroline	Adult				Framsden	same	Ava
Sheldrake Hannah	same				Stonham Aspel	same	same
Sheldrake Susan			under		same	same	same

18th July 1850
J.R. Bragg. Clerk to the Guardians

Som. RO ref. D/G/W/8a/7 Wellington Union, Somerset and Devon
Minutes of the meetings of the Board of Guardians, 1849–52
[Emigration orders for people to Australia.]

26th September 1850
Embarkation Orders for H.M. Colonial Land and Emigration Commissioners granting passage to Adelaide, Australia for:

Ann Tottle } Wellington
Joseph Keates }
Sarah Needs   Holcombe Rogus
Rob.ᵗ Whiteman   Burlescombe

Directing them to proceed to Plymouth, the port of Embarkation and present themselves together with the necessary requisites mentioned in such Order to the Government Emigration Agent, Baltic Wharf, on the 27 inst., they were called in the Board Room and advised as to the importance of their being of good conduct during the voyage and when they gained a place of Servitude to be obedient.

The Clerk was directed to see that some proper person proceeded to Plymouth from the Workhouse with them, the Master undertook to go and return the same evening.

Moved by Mr. Bond, seconded by Mr. Troaks and Resolved unanimously that application be made to the Poor Law Board for their sanction to the Emigration of the above named 4 persons, the Guardians of the several parishes interested having consented thereto.

***

[A woman is given clothing for her passage to Australia.]

28th August 1851

Martha Keats, a single woman belonging to the parish of Wellington in this Union, having obtained from the Government Emigration Commissioners a grant of a free passage as an Emigrant to the Colony of Australia, applied to the Board for the necessary clothing as required by the Government Emigration Commissioners to enable her to proceed there as well as the necessary expenses attending her journey to Plymouth, the Port of embarkation.

Ordered that such application be granted and that the Clerk be directed to write to the Poor Law Board for their approval of the same.

TNA ref. MH 12/12991 Horsham Union, Sussex
[A family emigrating to Canada, 1844.]

Horsham Union
1st June 1844

Gentlemen,

I enclose the Resolution of the Vestry of the Parish of West Grinstead for the Advance of £30 for the Emigration of James Hillman & his family to Montreal. They are desirous of going by the vessel of Messrs Marshall & Co. which will sail from Southampton on the 17th Instant.

I am requested to beg your early answer whether they can embark in this vessel.

I have the Honor to be
Your most obedient Servant
W. Stedman

The Poor Law Commissioners

***

A List and Description of the Persons desirous of **Emigrating** from the Parish of West Grinstead in the County of Sussex

Males	Age	Married or Single	Occupation	Amount of Parish Relief Received during the last year	Where emigrating to
Hillman James	32	Married	Labourer	none	Montreal

Females					
Hillman Fanny	18	Married		2 – 6 – 10½	Montreal
Hillman Sarah	13	Single			do
Hillman Susan	11	do			do
Hillman Ann	9	do			do

It would appear from the following letter that the age of the wife, given in the above tabulation, was questioned:

Horsham

6 June 1844

Gentlemen,

Emigration Expenditure

I beg to acknowledge your letter of the 5th Inst.

The Return of the Description of the Paupers by the Returning Officer states that Fanny Hillman is of the age of 18 years and the wife of James Hillman who was I believe a Widower.

I have the honor to be

Gentlemen

Your most obedient Servant

W. Stedman

The Poor Law Commissioners

TNA ref. MH 12/10211 Bedminster Union, Somerset

[A woman is given assisted passage to return to her native place, St Helena.]

To the Commissioners of the Poor Law Board   received July 6th 1852

Gentlemen,

I hope you will please to pardon the liberty of writing to you. I beg to state I am a native of St. Helena left entirely to the charity of strangers and I am not possessd [sic] of one single relative in England with my health in a very declining state and still continues to get, the climate of England not agreeing with me I had my husband ill 2 years and [missing] months and I wish to get back to my native place but am entirely destitute of the means. There is a Ship going to St. Helena the 20th of this month and has offered to take me for £15, £12 in hand and 3 when I arrive there, and if the W.H. Gentlemen could take my case into their kind consideration and advance me part of the money I intend writing to Government to see if they will advance me the rest. I hope Gentlemen you will please to think of my destitute state and that I am far away from my home entirely dependent upon strangers.

I remain Hon. Gentlemen,

Your Humble Servant,

Sarah Mallett

16 Charlotte St., Coronation Road,

Bedminster, Bristol

Acknowledge and state that the Board will communicate with the Col. Office on her behalf in the first instance. Send copy to Col. Office and refer to the former case in Whitechaple Union. 6 July 1852

Emigration

Poor Law Board

Whitehall

12 July 1852

Mrs Mallett
16 Charlotte Street
Coronation Road
Bedminster
Bristol

Madam,

I am directed by the Poor Law Board, in reference to your letter rec'd on the 6th Instant, relative to your proposed Emigration from the Parish of Bedminster to Saint Helena, of which place you are a native, to state that the Board will, in the first instance communicate with the Secretary of State for the Colonial Department and ascertain whether Government can render you any assistance in the matter.

I am Madam,

C.

***

Poor Law Board

Whitehall

12 July 1852

Sir,

I am directed by the Poor Law Board to enclose herewith for the information of the Secretary of State for the Colonial Department, a copy of a letter which the Board

311

have received from a poor woman named Mallett residing at Bedminster near Bristol who is desirous of returning to St. Helena, of which place she is a native.

The Board in reference thereto request that you will inform them whether the Government are willing to grant Mrs Mallett a passage to St. Helena or to render her any assistance in attaining her object. It appears from the correspondence in this Office that in the year 1849 they granted a passage to St. Helena to a widow named Smith, a native of that island and her family who had been previously residing in the Parish of Christchurch in the Whitechapel Union.

I am &c

C.

***

Colonial Land and Emigration Office

Park Street

Westminster

12 Aug. 1852

My Lord,

I have the honor by direction of the Colonial Land and Emigration Commissioners to inform your Lordships that Sir J. Pakington has referred to this Office your letter to Mr Elliott of the 12th ultimo accompanied by an application from Sarah Mallett to be assisted in procuring a passage to St. Helena of which place she is a native.

In reply I am to state that the Commissioners have no means at their disposal for providing a passage or assistance towards a passage to St. Helena for Mrs Mallett. In regard to the passage said to have been provided in 1849 for W^d Smith, the Commissioners apprehended that there must be some mistake as they are unable to trace in their books any correspondence on the subject or any payments made on such an account and they have never, as far as they can remember, had in their hands any funds belonging to St. Helena.

I have the honor to be

My Lord,

our Lordship's

Most Obedient, Humble Servant

S. Walcott

Secretary

There is another letter dated 17 August 1852, acknowledging receipt of the above letter and referring to it:

***

Downing Street
30th August 1852

My Lord,

I have received and laid before the Secretary Sir John Pakington, your Lordships letter of 17th Inst. relating to the application of Sarah Mallett, a native of St. Helena, for assistance to return.

That under the particulars of the case Sir J. Pakington has authorized the Colonial Agent General, E. Barnard, Esq., 5 Cannon Row, Westminster, to issue £10 being half the cost of a passage to St. Helena, to the Bedminster Union on behalf of the person upon receiving a sufficient certificate that she has been provided with a passage and sailed, but I am at the same time to explain to your Lordship that the Colonial Funds of St. Helena are very limited and that the grant of money made in this case must not be considered as a precedent, since the Revenue of the Island could not defray many such contributions.

I am, my Lord
Your Lordship's most obedient
humble Servant
T. E —— [illegible]

There are three more letters for this case, each dated 7 September 1852. A final letter dated 22 September 1852, from the Bedminster Union to the Poor Law Board, states: '… necessary funds have been raised by private subscription and she is now on her voyage to Saint Helena.'

TNA ref. MH 12/4019 Clifton Union, Bristol
[A workhouse inmate emigrates to New Zealand, 1875.]

Desirous of Emigrating from Clifton Poor Law Union
Sarah Jane Davis, aged 17 years, single, servant. In the Workhouse 152 days. Cost about £4–15–0
To what place Emigrating   New Zealand
This young person has conducted herself very satisfactorily whilst in the Workhouse.
20 March 1875

TNA ref. MH 12/10506 Wellington Union, Somerset and Devon
[Two families emigrating to Canada, 1883.]

28 June 1883   Inmates of Wellington Union
                Poor People wishing to emigrate to Halifax, Nova Scotia

Mary Ann Davis Venting, aged 26 years (deserted by her husband for over 3 years) to Nova Scotia where her parents reside; and her three children.

Sarah Ann	Venting	7 years
Caroline Maud	"	6 "
William George	"	4 "

£6 from the Common Fund of this Union, to be given to assist.

Parish of Milverton

Ann Dyte	40 years
Fred	13 "
Eliza	9 "
Louisa	7 "
George	5 "
Sarah	3 "
Leonard	1 "

   Desirous of emigrating to Hamilton, Canada West
   £13–10–0

Ann Dyte has a father, mother, 3 single brothers and seven sisters all living within a few miles of each other in the neighbourhood of Hamilton, Canada West. Her father and brothers are small farmers.

TNA ref. MH 12/10230 Bedminster Union, Somerset
[Two boys are sent to Canada for adoption, 1886.]

Bedminster union
Henry O'B O'Donohue, clerk,
Solicitor, Long Ashton, Bristol
11th May 1886

Sir,

   I am directed by the Guardians of this Union to transmit to you the enclosed papers showing a resolution as to the emigration of William Missen and William Hawkins passed by the Guardians at a meeting held today.

The boys are going to be adopted by two Farmers at Ontario who wish them sent out at once, and the Board are anxious that they should go by a vessel which sails on Thursday next and I am therefore directed to ask that you will telegraph to me at the Union Offices Flax Bourton tomorrow as early as possible the consent of your Board to the expenditure of the named.

I am Sir
Your obedient Servant
Henry O'B O'Donohue

To the Secretary
Local Government Board
Whitehall
London

TNA ref. MH 12/10231 Bedminster Union, Somerset
[A list of emigrants to Canada, 1887.]

A List and description of the Persons desirous of Emigrating from the Bedminster Union

Names	Ages	If Adults state whether married or single; or if children whether orphans, deserted, etc.	Occupation	Amount of Parochial relief during last year, and its nature	To what place emigrating
William Vaughan Smyth	49	Widower	Clerk	None	Toronto, Canada
Edward Colston Smyth	8	son of above		"	"

Henry O'B. O'Donohue
Clerk to the Guardians
(Received 20 May 1887)

TNA ref. MH 19/11 Children sent to Canada
[The following tabulation is part of a long report dated 3 February 1889.]

Department of Agriculture
List of pauper children reported upon by R. Macpherson
Agent at Kingston

Boys				
Parish from which children were sent	Names	Ages	Names and Addresses of the Persons with whom the children were placed in Canada	Reports of Inspectors
West Ham Union	Samuel Ryall	12	Bruce Kiel, lot 10, in 1st Concession, Kingston Township, Collinshay	Honest and truthful giving full satisfaction. Healthy lad pleased with his place and treatment, will attend school during winter.
Whitechapel Union	Fred Wolhon	12	George W. Tiller, Rossmore P.O. Lot 62 in 1st Con. Ameliasburgh Township	Healthy lad, well cared for, in good home pleased with his place and treatment, will attend school during winter, was in 4th standard.
Stoke on Trent	Herbert S. Hughes	11	Peter Croather, Rossmore P.O. Lot 63 in 1st Con. Ameliasburgh Township	Rather weakly but improving, in good home giving full satisfaction, attending Sunday School, will attend day school, pleased with his place.
St Mary Abbotts, Kensington	Edward Bellow	11	Joseph Langdon, Rossmore P.O. Lot 58 in 2nd Con. Ameliasburgh Township	Self willed but improving. Healthy lad, in good home, generally gives satisfaction, will attend school during winter, pleased with place.
West Derby Union	Henry Clarke	10	Mrs Phillip Ray, widow Belleview P.O. Lot 32, in 2nd Con. Sydney Township	Intelligent lad, in good home, attends day school during winter, was in 3rd standard. Mrs Ray not home.
St Mary Abbotts, Kensington	Henry Boltwood	10	Burley White, Wallbridge, P.O. Lot 23 in 4 Con. Sydney Township	Healthy lad, in good home, giving full satisfaction every way, attends Sabbath School, will attend day school in winter, was in 3rd standard.
West Ham Union	David Fetters	9	George Ostrom, Belleville, P.O. Lot 22 in 1st Con. Sydney Township	In excellent home, giving satisfaction, except the filthy habit (or disease) of wetting the bed nightly, attends Sabbath School, will go to day school if kept.
Liverpool Parish	Ebinezer Busby	17	Marchmont Home, Belleville	Healthy, industrious, intelligent lad, not yet placed.
Stoke on Trent	Joseph Barlow	7	Marchmont Home, Belleville	Apparently healthy child, not yet placed.
Stoke on Trent	Edwᵈ Faulkes	7	Marchmont Home, Belleville	do do do
West Ham	William Coppin	9	do do	Apparently healthy child with Samˡ Bell, Wood P.O. Cardiff, Tp.
Salford Union	George Ingram	9	do do	Apparently healthy child, not yet placed.
Kensington	William Aller	13	do do	Not yet placed, apparently healthy lad.
Stoke on Trent	John H. Phillips	9	do do	do do do

West Derby	Edwd. Champion	6	Marchmont Home, Belleville	do	do	do
Sunderland	Samuel Godfrey	8	do do	do	do	do
West Derby	Henry Gregory	10	do do	do	do	do
West Derby	Henry Jones	7	do do	do	do	do
West Derby	Percy Gosling	13	W.S. Forgey, lot 15, in 2nd Concession Thurlow Tp. Belleview, P.O.	Healthy lad, in good home, well cared for, pleased with his circumstances, not attending school, fairly educated, was in 5th Standard.		
West Ham	William Oudot [?]	11	Jeremiah Buskard, lot 29, in 2nd Con. Thurlow Township, Belleville P.O.	Healthy lad in good home, not always reliable but improving, generally giving satisfaction.		
Whitechapel	Robert Breckle	9	Ridley Cole Blessingham P.O. lot 5 in 4th Con. Tyendmaga Township	Giving full satisfaction. Healthy lad, well cared for in excellent home, attends school, pleased with his circumstances.		
Sunderland	Robert Johnson	11	Albert Pitman, Halsham P.O. lot 7 in 7th Con. Tyendmaga Township	Healthy lad rather dull, generally giving satisfaction, attends Sabbath School, will attend day school in winter, pleased with his situation.		
Sunderland	Robert S. Brown	12	James M. Whiteman, Lonsdale, P.O. lot 37 in 3rd Con. Tyendmaga Township	Healthy lad in good home, giving satisfaction pleased with his situation, will attend school during winter, was in 5th standard.		
Stoke on Trent	Samuel Hollins	13	Samuel Anderson, Albert P.O. lot 35 in 6th Con. Tyendmaga Township	Healthy lad in good home, no fault, pleased with his place and treatment, will go to school during winter, was in 5th standard.		
St Mary Abbotts, Kensington	Jas. H. Powell	10	Robert Garrett, Albert P.O. lot 33 in 6th Concession Tyendmaga Township	Healthy lad tho' not strong, untruthful but of good disposition, fairly educated, pleased with his home, will attend school in winter.		
Liverpool Parish	Richard Thos. Jones	13	Wm. Whiteman, lot 32 in 6th Concession Tyendmaga Township, Albert P.O.	Healthy lad giving full satisfaction, in good home with which he is pleased, attends Sabbath School, will attend day school.		
Stoke on Trent	George Salter	13	Sylvester Dunning, lot 6 in 1st Con. Tyendmaga Shannonville P.O.	Slow in movement generally giving satisfaction in superior home. Pleased with his situation, fairly educated, will attend school.		
West Ham	Percy Coppin	11	Mrs Robert Lawson, widow, Stella P.O. lot 78 in 3rd Con. Amherst Island	Healthy lad, stubborn at times but improving, generally giving satisfaction, in good home, attends Sabbath and day school.		

List of pauper children reported upon by John Smith, agent at Hamilton.

Girls				
West Ham	Florence Stevenson		John Higgins, Shorold	Healthy bright cheerful child, well liked, attends Church, day and Sunday School. Home very good.
Stoke on Trent	Emily Derrington		Mrs Pangman, Dundee	Healthy, Intellect dull, deceitful but honest, very hard to manage. Had a very good home. Returned to Miss Rye.
do	Annie Massey		John McDaniels, Lillys Corners, London (Lindin?)	Healthy intelligent honest good girl. Attends Church and Sunday School.
do	Mary Sherman		Richard Stephens, Chatham	Healthy bright cheerful girl well liked. Attends Church, day and Sunday School. Home very good.
Kensington	Clara East		Leonard Bessie, St. Catherines	Healthy. Removed from R. Johnston Maltin to L. Bessie, thence to Geo. Almas, Boston, Miss Rye having had notice to remove her back to the Home as being unmanageable.
do	Eva Hope		J.J. Wadsworth, Limcoe	Healthy girl has been placed in four different homes and is now with Mr Motherwell, Ashawa who has notified Miss Rye to take her away. She seems to be a disobedient bad unmanageable girl.
Kensington	Louisa Keep		James Chinnie, Chatham	Healthy, honest, bright, good girl, well liked. Attends Church. Home very good.
do	Emily Learkins		Peter Savigney, Port Stanley	Healthy, honest, bright girl, promising character. Attends Church and Sunday School. Home good.
Kensington	Martha Sheet		James Moran, Port Stanley	Suffering from catarrh improving, intellect dull, truthful, honest, good character. Attends Church and Sunday School. Home good.
do	Rose Williams		Richard Willey, Ridgetown	Healthy, good child being too young she was removed to Marie Bunse, Ridgetown. Goes to school. Attends Church and Sunday School. Home very good. Removed to 153 Howland Av., Toronto.
do	Emily Willis		Dr. Comford, St Catherines	Healthy, bright, cheerful, good girl well liked. Attends Church and Sunday School. Home very good.
Salford	Agnes Chambers		Adolphus Pettit, Grimsby	Transferred to James Stevenson, Boyn P.A. Girl healthy, good character. Goes to Church and Sunday School. Home good.

West Derby	Christina Gregory		Isaac Sivarlout, Ridley	Healthy, good girl. Transferred to Mrs Bowen, Thamesville owing to the death of Mrs Sivarlout. Attends Church and Sunday School.
do	Ann Jones		Mrs Julia Stewart, Front Street, Thorold	Healthy, a very good girl and rightly spoken of. Removed to Mrs Mathear Field, a very good home. Attends Church and Sunday School.
do	Emily Jones		Leonard R. Johnson, Prospect Hill, St Catherines	Healthy. A good bright and cheerful girl well liked and now living with Mrs Bassendale Yokahoma Tea Store, St Catherines. Attends Church and Sunday School. Home very good.
do	Jane E. Roberts		David Pew, Southend	Healthy. A very good honest girl well liked. Attends Church and Sunday School. Home very good.
do	Mary E. Jones		Geo. A. Bradt, Amwestbury	Health fair, intellect slightly afflicted, resulting from a blow. A good honest truthful girl trying to do her best and is well liked. Removed to H. Harding, Louth, Dumfries. A good home.
do	Ellen Jones		Edwin Wilson, Ridgetown	Healthy good child goes to Church. Attends day and Sunday School. Home good.

Note: None of the ages of the girls are given in this table.

Som. RO ref. D/G/W/57/12 Wellington Union, Somerset and Devon

[A girl who had emigrated to Canada in 1913 with assistance from Dr Barnardo's Homes was returned home because of ill health and died a year after her return. The following abstracts are selected from this correspondence.]

6th August 1912

Dear Sir,

I am directed by the Guardians to apply for the admission into your Home of a girl named Mary Ann Warren, aged 13 years whom they desire should be received with a view to ultimate emigration. The girl's father is an inmate of the Workhouse here but the girl herself has been boarded-out for some three or four years.

The Guardians are particularly desirous of emigrating her as they wish her removed from the undesirable influence of her friends and relations at Wellington.

I shall be glad to hear from you at your early convenience.

Yours faithfully,

W.S.P. clerk

The Hon. Secretary
Dr Barnardo's Homes
Stepney Causeway
London

319

***

Barnardo's Homes; National Incorporated Association

18 to 26 Stepney Causeway

London E.

9th August 1912

Dear Sir,

I enclose a form for the usual particulars of the girl Mary Ann Warren, but would be glad if you would direct the attention of your Medical Officer, when filling it up to the great strictness of the Canadian Authorities in rejecting cases of eye ailments. Upon receiving the form back from you containing the desired information I will let you know whether we can receive the girl with a view to her emigration.

We desire Poor Law children to be in our care for a probationary period of some 2 months, but as our Party sailing on the 19th prox: will be our last this year we should be willing to entertain this girl's inclusion therein if she could come to us almost forthwith.

Our charges to your Board would be the same as in the case of Bowden & Hitchcock.

Yours faithfully,

A. Fowler

W. Sydney Price, Esq.,
Clerk to Guardians
Wellington
SOM.
[The medical report referred to is not with this correspondence.]

***

Wellington

Somerset

I Mary Ann Warren of Pleamore Cross, Wellington in the county of Somerset, do solemnly and sincerely declare, that of my own free will and consent I am desirous of being emigrated to Canada.

AND I make this solemn declaration, conscientiously believing the same to be true, and by virtue of the Provisions of an Act made and passed in the Fifth and Sixth years of the reign of His late Majesty King William the Fourth intitled 'The Statutary Declaration Act 1835.'

Taken at Wellington in the County of Somerset, before us, two Justices of the Peace for the County of Somerset, this eleventh day of January 1913.

***

25th March 1913

Dear Sir,

Re: Mary Ann Warren

In reply to the enquiry contained in your letter of 20th inst., I write to inform you that the above named girl was included in our Party which sailed for Canada on the 13th inst.

The address in Canada to which she will go in the first place is:–

The Margaret Cox Home for Girls

Peterborough

Ontario

Yours faithfully,

A. Fowler

***

Letter: Barnardo's to Wellington Union.

11th July 1913

Dear Sir,

Re: Mary Ann Warren

In reply to your enquiry, this girl was placed out with Mrs Robt Nicholson, Strathroy P.O. Ontario, and I am pleased to inform you that on the 6th May last one of our Visitors found her well & happy & doing nicely in this home, which was described as an excellent one.

Yours faithfully

A. Fowler

***

Letter: Barnardo's to Wellington Union.

19th October 1914

Dear Sir,

I deeply deplore the necessity to ask your Board to resume their care of the girl Mary Ann Warren, whom we admitted into these Homes & subsequently sent to Canada in 1913 on their behalf. She has developed phthisis, and for this reason has been returned to England, & we are reluctantly compelled to restore her to the care of your Guardians. She reached these offices on Saturday last, and as we have no room in our Sanatorium for her temporary retention, one of our matrons will take her to Wellington tomorrow, Tuesday the 20th inst., & I shall be glad if you will kindly intrust your Workhouse officials to receive her from our matron.

The girl has been in the care of our Authorities in Toronto, & our Medical Officer there has reported the unmistakeable existence of the disease, & has stated that she must have become a charge upon these Homes or upon the State in a short time. He furthermore reported that she was a danger to our Home in Toronto.

321

In these circumstances it was obvious that the girl needed sanatorium treatment but it would have been useless to have applied for this for her in Canada, for under the Immigration laws all cases admitted into Sanatoriums where the patients have not been 3 years in Canada, must be notified to the Immigration Department who immediately order Deportation.

It will thus be seen that our Chief Agent in Canada had no alternative than to send the girl back to this country, & that in taking this step he merely anticipated official deportation.

Again greatly regretting that the girl should have become afflicted with this trouble, & that it should be necessary to ask your Board to take her back into their care; but sincerely hoping that she may derive benefit under appropriate treatment.

Yours faithfully,
A Fowler

***

Letter: Wellington Union to Barnardo's.

20th October 1914

Dear Sir,

re Mary Ann Warren

I am in receipt of your letter and telegram and very much regret that it has been found necessary to return this girl from Canada, the more so as we have just received an order for the removal of her brother who is suffering from the same complaint. It is especially unfortunate as the Guardians have no accommodation for cases of this kind. Can you possibly retain the girl until Friday as my Board are meeting on Thursday and I should like to bring the matter before them and ask their special instructions as to the case.

Yours faithfully,
W.S.P. clerk

***

Letter: Barnardo's to Wellington Union.

20th October 1914

Dear Sir,

I am pleased to inform you that we have been able to avoid what appeared to be the necessity to return the girl Mary Ann Warren to the care of your Board forthwith. We were very loth to take the course contemplated in my letter of yesterday and after consultation between our Chief Medical Officer & the Governor of our Girls' Village Home, a vacancy has been made for this girl in our Sanatorium at the Village, so that we are now in a position to retain her, & give her proper treatment for her disease.

I anticipate that your Board will approve our desire to keep the girl with us in the hope of improving her condition. We have naturally fixed no period for her stay &

your Board will not be unprepared for a request at any time to undertake her custody. If we find it possible to retain her over a considerable period, I will write to you as to her progress.

Yours faithfully,
A. Fowler

[The following is part of a document included:]

Mary Ann Warren   --------   was returned to England per S.S. *Hesperian* on 7 October. The girl was in an advanced stage of tuberculosis.

***

Letter: Barnardo's to Wellington Union.

27th November 1914

The following is a copy of a report by our Chief Medical Officer on the 24th inst. 'The upper part of her L. lung is affected – dullness & small crepitations. There is much clubbing of the fingers.

Her condition is much the same as on her return. Cough very troublesome at night, appetite good.

Prognosis, doubtful yet hopeful.'

Yours faithfully,
A. Fowler

***

Letter: Barnardo's to Wellington Union.

22nd June 1915

Dear Sir,

With reference to your enquiry regarding Mary Ann Warren, the following is a copy of a report by our senior Medical Officer dated 17th inst.

'Has gradually lost strength and flesh. Has a fluctuation temperature from 98° to 103°. Appetite fair. Cough troublesome. Chest gradually getting worse.'

Robert Milne. M.D.

The girl is still at our Sanatorium at our Girls Village Home, Barkingside, Ilford, Essex.

Greatly regretting that I am unable to furnish your Board with more hopeful news.

Yours faithfully,
A. Fowler

Som. RO ref. D/G/W/8a/41
[Concerning the previous case. From the minutes of the meetings of the Board of
Guardians of the Wellington Union.]

Letter from Dr Barnardo's Homes

21st October 1915

Dear Sir,

I am grieved to inform you that the girl Mary Warren whom we emigrated on behalf
of your Board, but who was deported to England a year ago with consumption of the
lungs, died today at the Sanatorium at our Girls' Village Home where she has been, as
you are aware, since her return to this country.

She died 19 – 10 – 15 of Phthisis pulmonalis [tuberculosis of the lungs].

TNA ref. MH 68/342 Salisbury Union, Wiltshire
[Emigration of a boy to Canada, 1928.]

Poor Law Offices
48 Blue Boar Row
Salisbury
18th May 1928

Sir,

<u>William Henry Childs, aged 16</u>

Referring to my letter to you of the 14th April last and your acknowledgement of
the 16th April, I beg to say that I have received a communication from the Overseas
Settlement Department requiring a Form A54 to be completed but I would respectfully
suggest that this is not a case to obtain their approval as the Guardians themselves are
not emigrating this youth. As a matter of fact the Guardians merely decided to make a
grant of £2 towards the expenses incurred by the Church Army, which has been done,
and the boy sailed to Canada in the S.S. *Alamina* on the 27th April last.

The Guardians will, therefore, be glad to receive your sanction to the expenditure of
£2 in order that there will be no difficulty at the Audit.

I am, Sir,
Your obedient Servant.
Ernest Mould

The Secretary
Ministry of Health
Whitehall
London S.W.

A letter dated 31 May 1928 to the guardians of Salisbury Union states that the £2 will be
paid 'subject to the production of a proper voucher to the District Auditor'.

Also filed with the above is the following:

Migration [sic]

At a meeting of the Guardians of the Poor of the Salisbury Union, held at the Board Room on the 11th day of May 1928.

Name of Proposed Migrant	Goldsmith, Leonard William Thomas
Age	21
Married or Single	Single
Occupation	General Labourer
Whether in the Army or Navy Reserve	No

Amount of Parochial Relief during the last year showing the amount each month	In and out of the Poor Law Institution since the 2nd June 1927. Last admitted 24th January and has been an inmate from that date and continues as such.
Name of Migration Society if any	Canadian Government
CHARGES	
Passage Money	£4 – 10 – 0
Outfit	Approximately £3
Railway Fare to Port of Embarkation	£1 – 0 – 10
Railway Fare from Port of Debarkation to final Destination	£3 Landing money
Incidental Expenses, Medical Certificates &c	--------
Total	£11 – 10 – 10

[The following is attached:]

Salisbury Union – Emigration
Consent to Expenditure

Whereas it was resolved at a meeting of the Guardians of the Poor of the Salisbury Union that a certain sum should be paid by them towards the expenses of the Emigration to Canada of Leonard William Thomas Goldsmith.

Now Therefore, the Minister of Health hereby Authorises the said Guardians to expend for the above-mentioned purpose a sum not exceeding Fifteen pounds (£15).

Given under the Official Seal of the Minister of Health this 6th day of June 1928.

Another letter states: '… make arrangements for the man to sail from Southampton on Saturday next, the 9th instant, otherwise the whole arrangements will have to be cancelled.'

Som. RO ref. D/G/W/8a/6 Wellington Union, Somerset and Devon
Minutes of the meetings of the Board of Guardians, 1847–49
[An application for assisted passage to New York is refused.]

At meeting on 19th April 1847
An application was made on behalf of Henry Howse belonging to the parish of
Wiveliscombe, aged 43. Having the following family viz.:– wife Frances aged 26
and children Henry John 17, Frances Mary 15, William 11, Thomas 8, Edmund 6,
Harriet 4, and Charlotte 2, for assistance to enable them to emigrate to New York, and
the Board expressed their willingness to advance £40 to aid him, and the Clerk was
instructed to ask the sanction of the Poor Law Commissioners to their making such
advance.
At meeting on 7th June 1847
[A letter from the Poor Law Commissioners.]

PLC Office
28 May 1847

Wiveliscombe parish – Emigration

Sir,
    I am directed by the Poor Law Commissioners to acknowledge the receipt of your
letter of 21st Instant requesting their sanction to the Guardians of the Wellington
Union expending £40 to assist Henry Howse a pauper of the parish of Wiveliscombe
to emigrate with his family to New York.
    I am directed to state that it is an unvariable rule of practice with the Commissioners
to withhold their sanction to any expenditure from the poor rates for the purpose of
assisting poor persons to emigrate to any part of the United States of America for
the reasons stated in their 8th annual report and therefore to decline to sanction the
proposed expenditure in the present instance.

The letter goes on to state that the 7th & 8th Victoria C101 '… invariably requires that
the parties emigrating shall go to some British Colony.'

CHAPTER 17

EARLY STATE EDUCATION

Up until 1870 the Education Department of the Government had limited powers and was no more than an agency for subsidising voluntary work in the field of education. By the Education Act of 1870 (33 & 34 Vict. cap 75), the Education Department was given statutory powers to improve elementary education. School attendance was made compulsory and children had to attend school up to the age of 10 years. In 1893 this was extended to the age of 11 years; in 1899 to 12 and in 1918 to 14 years of age. In 1947 the school-leaving age was raised to 15 years.

School fees for poor children were paid for by the local Board of Guardians. In 1891 all fees for national schools were abolished.

The records of many national schools survive and are usually deposited at local record offices, though some schools still retain their records. These records include logs kept by headteachers which often name teachers and pupils. The attendance registers are of particular interest to family historians. Not only do they name all pupils but often give their ages and sometimes record the names and addresses of their next of kin.

There are numerous records at The National Archives under the document group ED (Department of Education), recording the early development of education throughout the country. Some of the documents in ED 2 include petitions from ratepayers, and often their signatures are appended to these documents. Document class ED 7 includes returns from parishes giving details of the early schools and often include a record of each teacher in the school. The document class MH 19 also includes some records of early schools.

Document Class ED 2 – Parish Files – 1872 to 1904 (640 boxes)
Document Class ED 7 – Elementary Schools – 1846 to 1924 (172 boxes)
Document Class MH 19 – Correspondence and Papers – 1834 to 1908 (280 boxes)

The following are abstracts from some of these records:

TNA ref. MH 19/22
Central London District School, 1852

Boys 14 years of age and upwards

Name	Age	Occupation	Can read and write
Riley, William	14	Monitor	yes
Tunnard, H^y	14	Shoemaker	"
Hudson, William	14	Monitor	"
Balls, William	14	do	"
Dix, George	14	Tailor	"
Umpeville, John	14	Shoemaker	"
Morton, Luke	14	do	"
English, John	14	do	"
Helham, William	14	———	"
Wade, Charles	15	Farm	"
Watts, James	15	"	"
Hunt, William	15	Tailor	"
Green, Henry	16	Monitor	"
Moren, Thomas	16	"	"
Wood, George	15	Farm	"
Barber, Robt	14	Tailor	"
Davis, George	15	Smith's Shop	"
Hebbard, John	15	Shoemaker	"
Stanton, Joseph	16	Monitor	"
Moore, Thomas	15	Carpenter	"
McDonald, Willm	14	Tailor	"
Turner, Henry	16	Farm	"
Bailey, William	15	Shoemaker	"
Brown, George	14	do	"
Barrett, Daniel	14	———	Read
Simpson, Thos	15	Shoemaker	yes
Cornwall, Willm	15	do	"
McCarthy, Henry	14	Tailor	"
Gossage, John	16	Monitor	"
Gilligan, Thos	16	do	"

Gilligan, John	14	Shoemaker	yes
Bakewell, James	15	Smith's Shop	"
Backthorp, Joseph	15	Tailor	"
Hibbert, Robert	14	do	"
Corp, Campbell	15	Farm	"
Burns, James	14	Tailor	"
Driscoll, Joseph	15	Shoemaker	"
Dennis, Edward	14	Tailor	"
Roberts, Richard	14	Shoemaker	"
Helly, Thos	15	Farm	"
Ingram, Edwd	14	Tailor	"
Oakes, Henry	14	Shoemaker	"
Boorman, Benjn	14	Tailor	"
Callaghan, Thos	14	Shoemaker	"
Johnson, Geo.	14	Tailor	"
Lemon, Charles	16	Smith's Shop	"
Forrester, Fred^k	14	Tailor	"
Fox, William	14	Shoemaker	"
Merriott, James	15	do	"

Girls 14 years of age and upwards

Name	Age	Occupation	Can Read and Write
Bray, Eliza	15	Domestic Work	Yes
Holland, Isabella	14	do	"
Crisp, Eliza	14	do	"
Gibson, Mary	14	do	"
Bailey, Frances	15	do	"
Rabbits, Ann	14	do	"
Wright, Hannah	16	do	"
White, Ann	15	do	Read
Hawkins, Sarah	15	Monitor	Yes
Corbett, Mary Ann	[blank]	Domestic Work	"
Blackman, Ellen	14	do	"
Moul, Catherine	15	do	"
Ford, Isabella	15	do	"

[contd]

Allen, Hannah	14	Domestic Work	"
Finch, Elizth	15	do	"
Trusty, Catherine	15	do	Read
Popkins, Emma	14	do	Yes
Edwards, Christiana	14	Monitor	"
Manley, Elizabeth	14	Domestic Work	No
Flood, Catherine	15	do	Yes
Bryant, Eliza	15	do	"
Henman, Sarah	14	Monitor	"
Carp, Adriana	14	Domestic Work	"
Trainer, Catherine	14	do	"
Waters, Sarah	15	Monitor	"
Yastie, Elizabeth	14	Domestic Work	"
Couling, Charlotte	15	do	"

***

North Surrey District School

Boys from 14 to 16 years of age

Name	Age	Occupation	Can Read and Write
Robert Watson	14	Engineer	Yes
Thos Jefsett	15	Carpenter	Yes
John Usher	15	Out door work	No
Willm Hester	15	Farm	No
Willm Colman	14	Garden	Yes
Edwd Martin	15	Farm	Yes
Wm White	14	Carpenter	Yes
Thos Collard	14	Shoemaker	Scarcely
Wm Crouch	16	Baker	Yes
Edwd Ralph	15	House work	Yes
George West	14	do	Yes
Martin Page	14	Farm	Yes
Fred^k Martin	14	Farm	Yes
Edwd Carpenter	14	Garden	Yes

Ja^s Peckham	14	Shoemaker	Scarcely
Saml Lyward	15	Garden	Yes
Fred^k Stanley	14	Tailor	Yes
Wm Sheppard	15	Carpenter	Yes
James Iles	14	Shoemaker	Yes
Edwin Barnes	15	Farm	No
Alfred Dagwell	16	Out door work	Yes
Wm Moore	15	Tailor	Yes
George Cheeseman	14	Garden	Yes
Saml Dournstow [?] [Downstow?]	15	do	Pretty well
Thos Jones	14	Painter	Yes
Fred^k White	15	Farm	Yes
Henry Howell	14	Shoemaker	Yes
Thos Perry	14	do	Yes
Henry Pearce	14	do	Yes
Thos Chapman	15	Engineer	Yes
Thos Humphreys	15	Shoemaker	Yes
Thos Burchell	15	Carpenter	Yes
Arthur Wright	15	House work	Pretty well
Alfred Fuller	14	Farm	No
James Morton	14	Shoemaker	Yes
Robt Hawkins	14	do	Yes
Henry Warren	14	Farm	Middling
Henry Prate	14	Shoemaker	Yes
George Lake	15	Tailor	Yes
Wm Cuff	14	Out door work	Yes
Chas Chapman	15	Gardner	Yes
Edwd Swaine	15	Tailor	Yes
David Clements	14	Tailor	Yes
Henry Vernon	15	Tailor	Yes
Theophilus Herbert	15	Shoemaker	Yes
Richard Daintree	15	do	Yes
Thos Callon	15	Engineer	Yes
Alfred Benham	15	Out door work	Scarcely
John East	15	Engineer	do

[contd]

Chas Little	14	Baker	Yes
George Knapp	14	Shoemaker	Yes
John Attwood	14	Out door work	Middling
Wm Huggins	15	do	No
John Birt	14	Carpenter	Yes
Alfred Culver	14	Garden	Yes
Wm Day	15	Baker	Yes
John Hammond	14	Farmer	Yes
Saml Wallington	14	Shoemaker	Yes
Joseph Jervis	14	Tailor	Yes
Albert Bell	15	Carpenter	Yes
James Wells	15	Baker	Yes
Edwd Godfrey	14	Shoemaker	Scarcely but improving

Girls above 14 years of age

Name	Age	Occupation	Can read and write
Eliza Ray	16	General House Work	Yes
Sarah Snoxall	15	Teacher	Yes
Elizth Collard	15	General House Work	a little
Eliza Till	15	do	do
Harriet Mee	14	do	Yes
Rebecca Hazell	15	do	Yes
Louisa Denham	14	Farm	a little
Sophia Coleman	14	General House Work	Yes
Matilda Dagwell	14	ditto	a little
Mary Russell	15	do	Yes
Jane Eaves	14	do	Yes
Eliza Spalding	15	Farm	Yes
M.A. Chandler	14	Teacher	Yes
Jane Wild	14	General House Work	a little

Harriet Carey	14	do	Yes
M.A. Arnold	14	do	Yes
Elizth Grant	15	Farm	a little
Ellen Hemans	15	General House Work	Yes
Jane Miller	14	do	a little
M.A. Webster	14	do	Yes
Elizth Baker	14	do	Yes
M.A. Glover	15	Farm	a little
Lucy Humberstone	15	General House Work	Yes
M.A. Davidson	15	do	Yes
Emma Hall	15	Farm	Yes
Amelia Ellis	15	General House Work	Yes

TNA ref. ED 2/391 Treborough, Somerset (undated)

To   The Lords of the Education Department, Whitehall, London
      The Memorial of the undersigned Ratepayers in the Parish of Treborough, Somerset

Sheweth:– **That** a notice has been duly published by order of your Lordships for the formation of a School Board in our said Parish of Treborough, but your memorialists have taken no steps to nominate members of such School Board expecting that a further enquiry will render such a step unnecessary.

    That the population by the last Census was 195. That the next Census will show a considerable decrease, and that the average number of children of School age is about 14.

    That the Parish is surrounded by the undermentioned Schools instructed by Certificated Teachers and within the following distances:–

    Viz.   Leighland School – 1 mile and a half by Road.
            Luxborough School – 1 mile and three quarters by Road.
            Brendon Hill School – 1 mile and a little over.

    That your Memorialists are provided with an excellent School Room and School House built by the late Lord of the Manor, Sir Walter Trevelyan, and that no Certificated Teacher will be content to take charge of such an insignificant number of children.

    That your memorialists with all due respect propose the following solution of the difficulty, namely – A competent infant Teacher shall be provided to instruct the children of the parish up to the age of eight years; and that after that age the children shall be drafted or sent to one or other of the above mentioned Schools for more efficient instruction.

Your Memorialists therefore pray that no School Board may be formed in our said Parish of Treborough and that the above proposed arrangement may be sanctioned by your Lordships.

Signature of Ratepayer	Description
Alfred Gale	Rector
Daniel Badeid [?]	Treborough House, Gentleman
William Pritchard	Villa Treborough, (Guardian)
Charles Dyer	Treborough Farm
John Bishop, Senᵣ	Lower Court Farm
John Bishop, Junᵣ	Higher Court Farm
Eli Vellacott	Chapmans Farm (Overseer and Churchwarden)

TNA ref. ED 2/4

Wobourn Union, County of Bedford
(received April 25th 1872)

Petition

We whose names are hereunto affixed, being Ratepayers in the Parish of Harlington humbly beg your lordships to grant us lease to form a school board for the aforesaid parish:–

George Johnson	(Vicar)
George Pearce	(Esquire)
John W. Fall	(Farmer)
J.F. Eustace	(Farmer)
John Cleaver	(Farmer)
William Asbury	(Publican)
Wᵐ Godfrey	(Farmer)
William Cleaver	(Miller)
John Bonner	(Publican)
Charles Jabbis [?]	(Blacksmith)
Burgess Garsden	(Farmer)
William Horspool	(Gardener)
Jesse Horspool	(Publican)
George Pidden	(Wheelwright)
Phillip Ellis	(Baker)
	Population 546
	Area 1849 [acres?]

Dev. RO (Ex.) ref. 3650C/EFL1 Brixham School, Devon
Log Book, 1862 to 1877 (Indexed – subjects only)

1875 January 22nd
The attendance has greatly improved this week though it is still far from satisfactory, many of the boys attending only half the week. The standard boys have received special attention but the arithmetic is still far from good. The school was visited by G.W. Baddleley, Esq. this morning and also by Rev. G.W. Hickory and Mr W. Bovey. The Annual Inspection by Her Majesty's Inspector took place this morning at 10.40. The following is a list of boys presented for examination with their ages last birthday.

William Spark	8	Edward Clark	8	Samuel Williams	11
Samuel Bully	8	Richard Elliott	8	Henry Tamlieu	10
Silas Pyne	7	Edward Smith	8	Herbert Howis	9
George Drake	7	Alfred Haywood	10	William Bond	10
John Perret	7	Henry Spurdens	8	Russell Gregory	11
James Lake	8	Samuel Colman	9	William Shrives	12
John Banks	7	William Tamlieu	8	Charles Perryman	10
William Crouts	7	William Norris	8	William Cox	9
John Perret	8	Stephen Colman	8	Robert Clark	10
John Slabb	7	William Martin	9	James Banks	10
Frank Cox	8	Henry Howe	9	Arthur Hill	9
Thomas Rolstone	7	George Fowler	9	Samuel Stevens	10
Albert Alward	7	William Loye	9	Henry Bartlett	9
William Sachell	7	William Snell	7	Samuel England	9
Samuel Spurdens	7	Edmund Martin	8	Samuel Helling	9
Edmund Gale	7	Owen Blake	8	John Eales	9
Samuel Tucker	8	John England	8	Charles Jillard	8
Samuel Banks	7	Alfred Wallace	10	William Parsons	10
Henry Osborne	8	Samuel Couch	9	Reeves Spark	10
Frederick Jones	8	George Watts	9	Richard Warren	10
Henry Dodd	7	James Summers	10	Clement Couch	10
William Rouse	8	Charles Cox	10	Charles Lake	11
Alfred Johnson	8	John Taylor	9	Roland Cox	9
Alfred Lee	8	Richard Johnson	12	George Croute	9
Kent Newman	7	James Cumming	9	John Penny	8
etc., etc.					

January 29th   The attendance this week has been very good until today which has been very wet and somewhat interfered with it. The work has been satisfactory, but the order has not been what could be wished.

E. Couch and E. Puddicombe were fifteen minutes late on Wednesday afternoon and the former again on Thursday morning. He was also absent in the afternoon owing to indisposition. The two teachers* [sic] above mentioned behaved this afternoon in a very unseemly manner, whilst at lessons, and at length having refused to continue their lessons put up their books and prepared to leave the school without permission when the master locked the door and detained them until the hour had expired. They left at 5.30pm.

* this is presumably an error for pupils

Dev. RO (Ex.) ref. 2440C/EAL1 Totnes School, Devon
Log Book, 1872 to 1877

1873   **Monday Sept 1st**
Admitted Amelia Polkinghorne, under 7 years of age. Nearly all the older girls can mend now and darn, we shall go on with mending the rest of the week. Admitted Eliza Blacker and her sister Kate, both over 7 years of age. Last week being the Totnes Races nearly all the children were absent. On Tuesday only 5 were present. On Thursday only 5 were present. Although I kept the school open I could not mark for the week.
   Thursday September 18th
Mr Tozer came this afternoon to complain about his little girl. She stayed away on Monday and went to another school without being told to do so. Some other children living in the same passage took her off.
   Monday Sept 22nd
I have been examining the 1st Standard again today. The majority of these children have never been to any school and it seems almost impossible to work them up for a standard.
   Wednesday Sept 24th
Mrs Paige visited the school this afternoon; the little ones were singing.
   Friday Sept 26th
Ellen Weymouth's girls have passed very fairly indeed. Mary Smale's and Emma Toope's are still very backward. I must give Mary Holman some of the 1st Standard girls.
   Monday Oct. 13th
Admitted Beatrice and Florence Heard, both over 7 years of age. Mrs Paige visited this afternoon.
   Monday Oct. 20th
Admitted Clara Jenkins today. This little girl is over 14 years of age. Her mother is a School Mistress about 3 miles from here and she is very anxious that this child should be a teacher. She is very backward, knows nothing at all about grammar and very little about summing. I shall put her into the 1st Class for a few weeks before I take her as a Monitor.
   Wednesday Oct. 22nd
Dismissed this morning at 12.30. No school this afternoon, the room is wanted and the teachers are going to have a good long sewing lesson this afternoon.

Thursday Oct. 23rd

Several of the elder [sic] girls were sent home with bills this morning to pay their school money.

Monday Nov. 24th

Admitted 2 girls today. Rosina Tope, over 9 years of age and Ellen Hill, 10. Neither of these girls can make a letter or a figure. They can read very fairly and have been attending Miss Johnson's school. I have several from that school lately and they can do nothing but read.

Tuesday Nov. 25th

I am afraid I shall not be able to keep R. Tope in the school. She is a very bad girl and on leaving school makes use of dreadful language. I have had 2 complaints already.

Monday Dec. 8th

Annie Polkinhorne, a girl of eleven years of age is staying away mornings. I have sent Mr. Stabb to enquire for her and it appears she has gone to service. I have only a very few girls and many of these I have to send after from day to day.

1874   **Monday Jan. 5th**

Admitted John Hill and Maud Shinner, both under 7

Tuesday March 10th

I have a great many children at school this week. Clara Jenkins is at home ill and Miss Smale is very unwell. I shall have to re-visit her. Ellen Weymouth's coming again on Monday next. She is at home Monday her mother who is ill and she will not even attend after school hours to get the instructions which, according to the book I am bound to give the teachers every day.

Wednesday March 11th

Some of the children are absent this week. They don't pay their school pence and having left back a good sum they are now kept at home. 4 Horrells and 2 Norrishs are among the number.

Wednesday March 18th

A great many of the little children are at home in the measles.

Tuesday April 14th

Admitted James and Florence Norman 4 and 3 years of age, Anna Brown, 5 years of age. Willie Dowell and Alfred Bryant, two little boys in the 5th class, died during the Easter holidays.

Thursday April 16th

A gentleman called today to ask if the children might go to see a panorama tomorrow.

Friday April 17th

All the children came in at 1:45 and left exactly at 4 to go to the panorama.

Monday April 20th

Admitted Bessie and E. Barnes 5 and 3½ years of age. Annie Staines 3¼, Mary J. Tucker, 11 years of age. Some of the little ones are still away in the measles.

***

Summary of Inspector's Report on the School and remarks

'Mixed School – There is an increase in the numbers here since last year, and the Discipline still well maintained. The instruction is satisfactory, except in arithmetic. The infants are well advanced, and the needlework is very good. I must again notice, however, that the children are presented in low standards for their age, and that the number presented above the second standard is far below the average. The lighting and ventilation ought to be improved, and the class rooms fitted up for the Infants.'

'The lighting and ventilation of the Girl's School must be attended to (Article 32(b)) Mr Penwill and L. Mitchell having been returned last year as over six were disqualified by age for further presentation under article 19(b)1.'

M.E. Weymouth (Grammar and Arithmetic)

M. Smale

C.C. Jenkins and M. Holman (Grammar)

Miss Virginia Buttrell	Principal Teacher first division of the First Class
Mary Smale	Pupil Teacher of the Second Year
Mary E. Weymouth	do
Clara C. Jenkins	Pupil Teacher of the First Year
Mary Holman	do

T.H. Edmonds

Clerk to the Totnes School Board

Dev. RO (Ex.) ref. 1075C/EFL1 Bradfield School, Uffulme, Devon Log Book, 1870 to 1902

1870

31st **Oct.** Mrs Walrond opened the school today; gave the children a tea feast.

M.A. Palmer

Mistress

Nov. 1st My whole time today has been occupied in trying [testing] the children. 32 came.

2nd Still examining them one by one – find them very backward in arithmetic notation they have no idea of.

3rd Classed them today in 4 classes.

4th A new girl came this morning. The afternoon is to be devoted to needle-work.

5th School this morning. [This was a Saturday when the school was usually closed.]

7th Have got the children now more orderly than last week.

8th Boys inclined to be rather troublesome.

9th Mrs & Miss Walrond visited the school today.

10th Mr Walrond brought in a gentleman to shew him the school. Gave the children a few words afterwards on politeness.

11th Began teaching the children a school song but found it very difficult work.

Nov. 14th	Mrs Walrond came today and looked at the girls' work.
15th	Have appointed the 4 big girls to do a monitor's work each week in turn.
16th	Miss Walrond gave a singing lesson to all the children.
17th	Punished 3 boys for throwing stones.
18th	Miss Walrond gave a singing lesson – intends doing so twice in the week.
21st	Mr Walrond came in during the afternoon school.
22nd	Find the girls very poor hands at any kind of needlework with the exception of two of the elder ones.
23rd	Taught them how to patch neatly.
24th	Very wet indeed this morning – a few of those who live at a distance came.
25th	Examined the 1st Standard in the Bible History I have been teaching. Found they could not recollect much; it must all be done again.
28th	Mrs & Miss Walrond visited the school this afternoon.
Nov. 29th	A case of theft in the school today but with every exertion the guilty one is not yet found out.
30th	Had to punish 3 of the biggest girls for the perpetual talking.
Dec. 1st	Began today giving the little ones, (those under 6) an idea of putting two & two together.
2nd	Find at the end of the month that the girls of the IIIrd St^d seem to have no idea of notation altho' I have kept them constantly at it.
5th	Had to give the monitor a good scolding for negligence.
6th	Another case of theft – apples stolen from a basket – very much suspect one of the oldest girls but have no proof.
7th	I went out for 2 hours this morning; the Misses Walrond took school.
8th	Began teaching the girls knitting.
9th	Began to teach the girls darning.
12th	Two of the little ones at home with bad colds.
13th	Another case of theft today. I sent for Mrs Walrond who came and examined every child separately, but without success.
Dec 14th	Punished two big girls for quarrelling.
15th	Began teaching the girls to mark.
16th	Find that the scriptures of the past week has either been better taught or the children remember better – answer very good.
19th	Taught 4 Standard subtraction – find them very dull over it.
20th	So wet that several of the small ones are away and several not so well, so that the number is rather thinned out.
21st	Miss Walrond gave singing lesson on Hullah's principle.
22nd	Thrashed Bidgood for swearing and ill-using his little sister. I think there is good in that boy but it requires tact & patience to manage him.
23rd	Today we break up for a fortnight's holiday.

1871

Jan. 9th	Began school again today 4 new scholars.

10th	Very much fear I shall not be able to work IIIrd Standard sufficiently well up in arithmetic by the time of the examination.
Jan. 11th	Put Richd Pearce in the 4th Standard & made all smooth again with the Pines who were kept away from school by some unpleasantness between them and the Neels.
12th	Three of my small children at home on account of illness.
13th	No music lesson today on account of Miss Walrond's absence – intend to explain the collect on Fridays as part of Scriptures lesson began today.
16th	Three of the ten children ill today – several complaining of pain in the head. School their in consequence. [sic]
17th	Ordered the monitor for the week to take the small children for 20 minutes every afternoon to teach them reading whilst I take the 1st Standard, see to the boy's lessons & give the girls needlework.
18th	Fresh instance today of the wildness of the girls; several hats torn by them thro' carelessness.
19th	Miss Walrond & Miss Pitman visited school this morning.

Som. RO ref. A/BPI/2/1 Rockwell Green Infants School
Log Book, 1882–1907
[Rockwell Green is a hamlet in the parish of Wellington, Somerset.]

25th Jany **1883**	Informed the children that the school fees were raised to 1½d for each child in a Family.
9th March	Sent notices to all Parents who still refuse to pay the 1½d School Fee.
March 2nd	Examined 1st Class in the three R's this morning. One half are far in advance of the other. Arithmetic is their best subject. Writing the worst. The Forms [benches] are not suitable for them to sit in for writing. Gave 7 children a farthing each for working [out] a long sum in addition, right first time. Answer 116. The Infant Class has been very noisy all week, the Monitor (E. Vickery) unable to manage them. Many of the children have come to School for several days very dirty & untidy. Sent two home to be washed this morning & cautioned the rest. The boys especially make their needlework dirty & there is no washing apparatus for this Department.
March 5th	E. Hitchcock absent this morning having a bad throat. She came in the afternoon but I sent her home at 3:15 as she was too ill for work.
March 7th	Children very noisy today, weather very cold & snowy. Wellington Fair today but no children stayed away for it as usual. Mrs Dobreè visited & brought me a few Dominoes.
March 9th	Children very troublesome all the week. E. Hitchcock still absent. Sent several boys home to be washed as they came so dirty. The Vicar called this afternoon. Sent Notices to all the Parents who still refuse to pay the 1½d School Fee.

25th April.	Freddy Osmond played truant Monday afternoon to avoid sewing lesson.
May 1st	Freddy Osmond played truant again this afternoon.
May 2nd	I forgave F. Osmond for playing truant, on his promise not to do so again.
May 3rd	F. Osmond again played truant but his Uncle found him & brought him to school at 3 o'clock. I gave him 2 strokes with the cane at his father's request.
Oct. 2nd	Tuesday School closed this afternoon on account of a Circus being in the Town on which account many children were absent this morning.

***

1885

Jany 23rd	Rats are still coming up in the school rooms. Holes mended last Saturday are eaten up again by Monday morning. The noise made by the rats gnawing the floor is often so loud as to frighten the children, and cause work to be stopped.
Feby 2nd	E. Vicary absent to be vaccinated.
April 7th	The rats are again giving great trouble. There are at present four large holes which are covered with slates to prevent the rats coming up. Many of the children are afraid to enter the classroom on account of them.
June 20th	The drains will have to be attended to. The Infant Room is at present infected with rats, no doubt in consequence of their condition.
March 4th	Admitted Ellen Hembrey and Rosa Hawkins.

***

1887

May 23rd	List of children who have made the requisite numbers of attendance viz. 350 to gain a prize. No. of attendances possible 413.

			Age
1.	Frank Stradling	413	6
2.	James Hitchcock	413	6
3.	Ellis Parr	412	6
4.	Mary Jane Perry	412	6
5.	James Bennett	411	5
6.	Alice Baker	411	4
7.	Charles Twose	411	4
8.	Charles Harding	410	5
9.	Emily Troke	410	5

10.	Henry Twose	409	5
11.	Emily Parrott	408	6
12.	Mary Glass	408	6
13.	James Woodbury	408	4
14.	Thomas Jordan	407	6
15.	William Martin	406	4
16.	Walter Perry	406	4
17.	Florence Harding	406	4
18.	John Smith	405	5
19.	Mary House	405	6
20.	William Thorne	403	4
21.	Florence Stradling	403	6
22.	George Stevens	402	6
23.	Mary Scorse	402	6
24.	Thomas Cross	401	6
25.	William Waygood	400	6
26.	William Hembry	400	5
27.	Ellen Stradling	400	6
28.	Herbert Stradling	399	4
29.	Amelia Wright	395	6
30.	Francis Bennett	392	4
31.	Florence Twose	392	6
32.	Charles Barrington	392	5
33.	Florence Blackmore	390	6
34.	William Harding	389	5
35.	Florence Osmond	383	6
36.	John Milton	382	6
37.	Joseph Kelk	385	6
38.	Reginald Alway	378	5
39.	Frederick Grabham	377	6
40.	William Marks	377	4
41.	Charles Tooze	377	4
42.	Thomas Windsor	377	6
43.	Clara Cross	371	5
44.	Mary Sheppard	368	6
45.	William Perry	366	4
46.	Mary Jane Hitchcock	364	6
47.	Elizabeth Parsons	362	5
48.	Albert Hill	360	4
49.	Bertram Venting	360	5
50	William Powell	358	4
51.	John Stevens	357	4
52.	John R. Smith	354	4
53.	Frederick Giles	354	5

TNA ref. ED 2/10 Earley, Berkshire
[A petition from ratepayers for the dissolution of the Earley School Board.]

W.W. Wheeler, Esq.,   Early, 1st June 1888
Clerk of the Wokingham Union

Sir,

    We the undersigned Ratepayers of the Parish of Earley request that you will summon a meeting of the Ratepayers of the said Parish in order to consider the advisability of making application to the Education Department for the dissolution of the Earley School Board as in consequence of the passing of the Reading Corporation Act 1881 by which a larger portion of the Parish of Earley has been incorporated with Reading there is no necessity for the re-election of the Earley School Board.

R. Wills	Thos. Porter
G. Lewendon	Saml. Fawcett
G.B. Wheeler	Thos. Kimble
H.W. Dunlop	J. Allaway
Jas. Craft	Wm. M. Colebrook
Geo. Shackel	Jas. Holder
Henry B. McNair	Robt. Goddard
George John Wait	F.E. Chapman
Joseph George Wyley	Arthur Edward Phillips
Sydney G. Oliver	Mary Helen East
Thomas Green	A.W.A. Webb
Lilian M. Prichard	Capt. R.H. Apthorp
A.E. Prichard	T. Weaver
Sarah Pither	W.G. Burford
George Cane	Thomas Tuggey
Thomas Tanner	T.I. Trower
Wm Nevill his mark X	W.I. Bartlett
Richard Nevill his mark X	G.R. Bloomfield
P. Turner	C. Hill
Thomas Merryfield	Wm. Embling
Joseph Coles	
Oliver Egginton	
Albert Barlow	
Arthur Giles	
Charles Moorcock	
Joseph Deane	
Edward Hobbs	
Ellen Constance Armstrong	
George Fox	
George Fox, Junr	

Robert Parker
Jane Kislingbury
Frederick Cornelius Cook

(Received 5th June 1888. W.W.W.)

TNA ref. ED 2/20

Iver Vicarage
Uxbridge
July 2, 1895

Boys, Girls and Infants National Schools
Iver, Bucks

My Lords,

I have been in bed some time with a poisoned, festered hand, and even now ought not to attend to any business, but I must write to inform you that our Iver School Managers have all the request of our newly formed School Board decided to carry on the Schools to the end of the School year on Nov. 30.

Our Managers decided this at their meeting held on Thursday, June 27.

Our School Board have already had the question of a building site for new schools under consideration and would have got on further with it, had not their time been largely taken up by a threatened Petition against the Election.

The site question will be pressed on with at once. I am writing now to ask on behalf of the School Managers what their position is. The Infants Report of Nov. 30, 1894 stated that no further grant would be given to that Department unless definite steps were taken to provide further enlargement.

Now the School Managers could not take up the question of enlargement in the Spring when we knew a School Board was going to be formed, in fact we gave the Department notice that we must close the Schools on April 30, and owing to delay in School Board Election, this date had to be extended to June 30 and now to November 30.

Our School Managers wish to know their position as to this grant as it is no fault of theirs that the enlargements have not been carried out.

Believe me
Yours sincerely
per pro Septimus Hebert
correspondent for School Managers
and also Chairman of new School Board

The Secretary
Education Department
Whitehall

TNA ref. ED 7/150 Anglesey

Beaumaris New Street Board School
Municipal Borough of Beaumaris
County of Anglesey

Name of Clerk of School Board   Richard Lloyd Humphreys,
7 Stanley Street, Beaumaris

Teachers

Boys or mixed Department under Master

Name	John Edward O'Connor
Exact date of Birth	22nd May 1856
Exact date of entrance upon duty in this School	6th November 1878
Certificated	Yes
Date	Christmas 1876
Class	Second
Whether formerly apprenticed as a Pupil Teacher, and if so, in what School?	Yes. In St. Lukes School, Blackenhall, Wolverhampton
Whether Trained	Yes
Name of Training School	Sactley Training College
Date of Entry	January 1874
Date of Quitting	Christmas 1876
Whether formerly engaged in a School under Inspection, and if so in what School?	Yes, St. Cuthberts Winson Green, Birmingham
Date of Entry	1st June 1877
and Date of Quitting	5th Nov. 1878
	and at Beaumaris Board School
How many Scholars	70

Name	Mary O'Connor
Exact date of Birth	19th August 1853
Exact date of Entrance upon duty in this School	6th November 1878
Certificated	Yes
Date	Christmas 1874
Class	Second

[contd]

345

Whether formerly apprenticed as a Pupil Teacher, and if so, in what School?	Yes, In St. Lukes School, Blackenhall, Wolverhampton
Whether Trained	No
Name of Training School	————
Whether formerly engaged in a School under Inspection, and if so in what School?	Yes. In St. Cuthberts Girls School, Winson Green, Birmingham
Date of Entry	1st July 1877
Date of Quitting	5th November 1878
	and at Beaumaris Board School
How Many Scholars	70

Name	Emilie Taylor
Exact Date of Birth	2nd August 1857
Exact Date of Entrance upon Duty in this School	21st August 1879
Certificated	Yes
Date	Christmas 1878
Class	Second
Whether formerly apprenticed as a Pupil Teacher, and if so, in what School?	Yes, Trinity Wesleyan School, Vine Street, Liverpool
Whether Trained	No
Name of Training School	————
Whether formerly engaged in a School under Inspection, and if so in what School?	Yes, Before obtaining my Certificate at William Henry Street Board School, Liverpool and St. Mathews Church School, Liverpool
Date of entry	22 May 1876
Date of Quitting	31 May 1879
How many Scholars	23

TNA ref. ED 2/20 Linslade, Buckinghamshire

School Board Office
Linslade,
Buckingham
9 Nov. 1875

The Secretary
Education Department
Sir,

The Board regret to be compelled to draw your attention to the results of their endeavours to enforce their Bye-Laws in this Parish, and to ask advice for the future.

The parents of Frederick Woolhead and Francis Bonfield have been frequently summoned before the Board and also before the Magistrates, under Sec. 74 of the Elementary Education Act.

On July 5th ult the case against Woolhead was dismissed to enable the parent to obtain a Certificate under the Agricutural Childrens Act, which could not be obtained, as Fred Woolhead had only made 98 attendances during the preceding year, and has been 18 times since.

The parent, John Woolhead, was summoned again on Oct 4th ult. and the case adjourned for Magistrates to examine the Agricultural Act.

On Nov. 1st the case was dismissed under the Agricutural Act, as being over 12 years of age, no proof of same being required. This lad has been playing truant and idling about the streets and fields setting parent's authority at defiance, often sleeping in a shed, and was not employed in Agricuture or any other labor.

Thomas Bonfield had been absent 12 weeks in succession, idling in fields black berrying or fishing. This case was also dismissed, though the lad was unemployed, and no proof of age was required.

The Board feel it incumbent on them to refrain from spending public money under such circumstances and will be obliged for any instructions which enable them to carry out the provisions of the E.E. Act, as well as the Agricultural Children's Act.

I have enclosed a paragraph cut from today's local paper, bearing on this subject.

I have the honor to be,
Sir,
Your obedient Servant,
W. Carter, Esq.
Clerk to the School Board, Linslade

The following is transcribed from the *Leighton Buzzard Observer* and *Linslade Gazette*, dated Tuesday 9 November 1875:

The Elementary Education and Agricultural Children's Acts

The School Board of Linslade appears to experience much difficulty in enforcing the provisions of the Elementary Education Act, owing to what is considered an undue partiality shown by the magistrates to people in poor circumstances who are summoned before them, and whom they allow to be shielded by overriding clauses in the Agricultural Children's Act of 1873. A month or five weeks ago two men were summoned before Linslade Bench for neglecting to send their children to school. Both of these persons had, we believe, been previously called to account and fined nominal sums, after various excuses had been made on each occasion by mothers of the boys. One of the latter would play truant at one time at another time he was ill; the second lad had been blackberrying, or employed either on a farm or is driving cattle to market, as opportunity offered. In both instances it was stated by the summoning officer that the parents had been requested to attend the Board and give explanations, but that they had treated the request with contempt. One boy had attended school but nine times in three months; the other had been absent for twelve weeks in succession. They were both over twelve years of age, and one, since the date of the summons, was stated by the mother to have attained his thirteenth year, whereby he became free from the operation of the Elementary Education Act. She could not, however, produce a certificate of birth, and the summoning officer said the Board doubted the truth of the statement. The cases had been ordered to stand adjourned from the previous court that the magistrates might have an opportunity of ascertaining whether the Agricultural Children's Act afforded shelter to the boys of the defendants. On Monday last, when the cases were called on again, they decided to dismiss the summonses, on the ground that, by the provisions of the Agricultural Children's Act, the boys, after attaining the age of twelve years, may be allowed to work in agriculture without being called on to produce a certificate of school attendance, provided they are kept constantly in such employment. While not so engaged they must at any intervals, be sent to school until they are thirteen. The parents said they should experience no difficulty in finding constant employment for the boys, and they have consequently succeeded in beating the Board, but, it is said on unfair grounds inasmuch as, although the boys are entitled to the shelter alluded to under the Agricultural Children's Act, it is only on a distinctly specified condition, namely that they shall be *constantly* employed between the ages of twelve and thirteen, whereas in the two cases before the bench on Monday, it was not shown that they were doing other that irregular work, gathering blackberries, playing truant, &c. The School Board is therefore dissatisfied with the action of the justices to whom they attribute a feeling of hostility to compulsion, fearing that a rise in wages must inevitably accompany a strict enforcement of the law. They further point out that the virtual operation of the Agricultural Children's Act enables a boy to leave school altogether at the age of eleven years while the law is thus loosely administered. At that age he may demand a certificate to show that he has made 150 attendances during the past year, and this certificate carrying him away from school for twelve months, he thus reaches the age of twelve, to be altogether exempted from further attendance by the provision of the later act, and as the Board complain whether those provisions are properly satisfied or not. We are given to understand that the circumstances are to be represented and an application in the matter made to the Education Department with a view to overcoming the difficulties which prevent the School Board from enforcing attending at the new schools erected by the parish at so great a cost, and which, moreover, frustrate their endeavours to correct defaulters. The parishioners, too, are generally very wroth that they should have been put to an expense of near upon £2,000 for apparently little or no purpose. We complain in Leighton of inconsistency and extravagance with regard to Highway and Sanitary Boards. Thank Heaven we have no School Board perplexities to harass our minds or affect our pockets, perhaps even to a worse degree.

TNA ref. ED 2/15 Buckingham
Census of children in Buckingham between the ages of 3 and 13
[This document lists all the roads, streets, lanes, etc. in Buckingham, giving the head of each household and the number of children in each. The following examples show entries for Brackley Road and West Street.]

November 17th 1877

Brackley Road		*West Street*	
Mr Kersey	2	Mr Peasnell	0
Mr Collins	3	Mrs Butcher	0
Mr Bartlett	1	Mr Ironmonger	1
Mrs White	0	Mr Hearn	0
Mr Freegard	0	Mrs Bond	0
Mr Jones	0	Mr Simmons	0
Mr Varney	3	Miss Bartlett	0
Mrs Tomlin	0	Mrs Webb	0
Mr Priest	3	Mr Brown	2
Mr Inns (Stowe Lodge)	0	Mr Bradford	2
Mr Inns (Junior)	1	Mr Reynolds	2
Mr Farmer	1	Mr French (B.W. Club)	0
Mrs Graham	1	Mr Timms	1
	15	Mr Major	2
		Mr Cole	0
		Mr French	0
		Mr Lofts	0
		Mr De'Ath	1
		Mr Bennett	0
		Mr Blenkarne	0
		Mr Holt	1
		Miss Kirby	0
		Mrs Mold	0
		Mr Ganderton	2
		Mr Tibbetts	0
		Mr Cherry	0
		Mrs Lynes	0
		Mr Stevens	2
			16

[This list also includes all children in the workhouse.]

The Workhouse

Boys and girls in the Workhouse between the ages of three and thirteen.

John Palmer
Joseph Soton
William Coles
Emanuel Tasker
Walter Perrin
Edward Tarman
Edwin Cadd
George Cadd
Charles Cadd
George Girling
Edwin Hollier
Ellen Tarman
Eliza Tarman
Sarah Holton
Sarah Coles
Martha Coles

TNA ref. ED 2/23 Burnham, Buckinghamshire

Census of children between the ages of 3 and 7 respectively resident in Stoke Gardens and Stoke Road, April 1898. This lists the full names of the children in each household with their ages given as either 3, 4, 5, 6 or 7. The total for Stoke Gardens is 48 children, i.e. 11 children aged 3; 8 children aged 4; 9 children aged 5; 15 children aged 6; and 5 children aged 7. The totals for Stoke Road are 18, 26, 28, 22 and 13 respectively for each age group. Note that the surname of each household is given even when they have no children. The following is part of the list for Stoke Gardens.

Stoke Gardens

		3	4	5	6	7
Isles	Fred Muslin			1		
Timms	Edith	1				
May	(none)					
Rackham	Fred[k]	1				
Jackson	Harry	1				
Pickering	Janet				1	
Snapes	Fred[k] (none)					
Pearce	(none)					
Russell	(none)					
Cox	(none)					

Daws	Eva Rose			1 (RC)*	
King	(none)				
Savage	Ada			1 (RC)*	
Moon	Jane	1			
Moslin	(none)				
Fox	Thomas Henry			1	
Mansell	(none)				
Brooks	(none)				
Pavey	Florrie Nellie	1			
Smith	Charles	1			
	Sarah			1	
Reynolds	Dora	1			
	Victor				1
Knight	(none)				
Trinder	(none)				
Glenfield	(none)				
Blackman	Dorothy	1			
	Alfred			1	

* RC is assumed to indicate that the family follows the Roman Catholic faith

TNA ref. ED 2/5 Little Barford, Bedfordshire

Board of Education

Preliminary Statement

This form is sent in triplicate. One of the copies should be retained by the promoters, one forwarded to the Local Education Authority, and the third returned to the Board of Education, Whitehall, S.W.

Little Barford Church Infant School

*The name here given should be full and distinctive, and should specify the religious denomination, if any, with which the School is connected, as well as the Local Name of the School. This name should be written without alteration at the head of every future communication

Postal Address of School in full	Little Barford, St. Neots
Local Education Authority	Bedfordshire
Minor Local Authority (Borough, Urban District or Rural Parish)	Rural Parish
Correspondent for the Managers	Revd N. Royds
Address in full	Little Barford Rectory, St Neots
Specify the religious denomination, if any, with which the School is connected	Church of England
Give the names and occupations of the Managers	Julius Alington, Gentleman, Lord of the Manor
	Nathaniel Royds Rector of Parish Chas. Edm. Arpinture [?] Gentleman Joseph Warrington Farmer

What is the Weekly Fee proposed to be charged to	Boys	Girls	Infants
	[blank]	[blank]	Nil

Give the exact date of opening of the School	1872
Give the name of the Head Teacher of each Department and the date which he or she took charge:– Infants' School	 Augusta Barnes 1872

Date 16 Nov 1904   *N. Royds* Correspondent for the Managers

TNA ref. ED 2/1
Oxford Diocesan Inspection of Schools

June 13th 1896

Dear Sir,

   I forward you herewith a copy of the Report I have made of my Inspection of your School.

I am, dear Sir,
Your faithful Servant,
Henry Lewis
Diocesan Inspector of Schools
Lydford School

To the Reverand
Dr Camilleri [?]

Examined June 12th 1896

REPORT

This school is doing useful work and the children are taught suitably and carefully by Mrs Hazell.

They are tidy, cheerful and well mannered and are taught to recite hymns and texts very nicely.

The instruction is very rudimentary but appears to me to be very good so far as it goes, and to supply all the reasonable wants of the locality.

The four upper girls did very well for me, in all their work, Rosalina Aldin (prize), Beatrice Eustace, Jane Lay, Mary Barnes.

TNA ref. ED 2/19 Hughendon, Buckinghamshire (undated)

[A petition signed by 216 inhabitants.]

To the Education Department of the Elementary Education Act of 1870, the memorial of the undersigned inhabitants of the parish of Hughendon, being eighteen years of age and upwards, and being out of the sufferage according to the provisions of the Act and being desirous that their views respecting the day schools of their parish should be made known unto you:

Sheweth that they object to public denominational schools as they consider them unjust and imperfect also that they wish the Bible to be read in their schools as they believe it to be the only volume of inspiration, also they beg you will do all in your power to forward their object and your memorialists will ever pray.

William Page, junior	Eliza Tucker*	William Wood	John Lacey
Elizabeth Tucker	Mercy Busby	Ann Kay	Julia Ayers
Jimima Briston	Sarah Waret	Louisa Janes	Eliz. Ayers
Sarah Ann Boreham	Rebecca Smith	Rachel Landers	Lavina Allritt
Ellen Nash	Ellen Boreham	Caroline Charge	Peter Albert Janes
Louisa Briston	Ruth Ward	Elizebeth [sic] Tucker	Mary Janes
Frank Nash	Susan Ward	Eliser Tucker	William L. Janes
Mary Nash	Phebe Page	Ann Tucker	Mary Ann Lacey
Harriet Barnard	Ann Feasey	Isabella Landers	Elizabeth Gott
Caroline Brackley	Sarah Feasey	Louisa Bignoll	Sarah Page
Elizabeth Darvill	John Bestow	Sarah Willis	Sarah Janes
Naomi Taylor	Ann Evans	Ann Janes	Rachael Rodurys [?]
Eliza Tucker*	Phebe Meid	Mary Frott	Charlotte Cape
Joseph Busby	Elizabeth Meid	Sarah Young	etc., etc.
	Ann Wood		

* Two different signatures

CHAPTER 18

VACCINATION AGAINST SMALLPOX

By the Act of 3 & 4 Victoria, cap. 29, 1840, children were to be given the vaccination against smallpox. This became compulsory from 1853 and continued until 1948. Vaccination was free of charge to all. The vaccination had to be administered within six weeks of the child's birth. Under 30 & 31 Victoria, cap. 84, 1867, a Certificate of Vaccination had to be issued. Initially vaccination was organised and applied through the vaccination officers of Poor Law Unions and registers were kept of all vaccinated children. The Vaccination Registers almost duplicate the Registers of Births kept by local registrars. Each certificate records the name, date and place of birth of the child, the father's name and his trade or profession, and additionally gives the date of vaccination of the child. The death of the child is also recorded if it died before vaccination. In addition to the Vaccination Registers, each vaccination officer kept his own Vaccination Officer's Register in which he recorded each child with its date of vaccination and address. These records are to be found with other Poor Law Union records in county or borough record offices, although many do not survive.

The application and appointment documents for the post of vaccination officers are to be found with other Union employee application forms at TNA in document class MH 12 and are listed with other employees in document class MH 9. Other documents relating to vaccination are also found in TNA document class MH 12.

The following are some examples of these records:

TNA ref. MH 12/5675 Burnley Union, Lancashire

CONTRACT FOR VACCINATION

3 & 4 Victoria, c. 29 [1840]
An Act to extend the Practice of Vaccination
Articles of Agreement entered into this twenty seventh day of September One thousand eight hundred and forty nine between John Buck of Colne in the County

Poster dated 10 January 1885, notifying vaccination against smallpox at Dulverton, Somerset. (SANHS Collection)

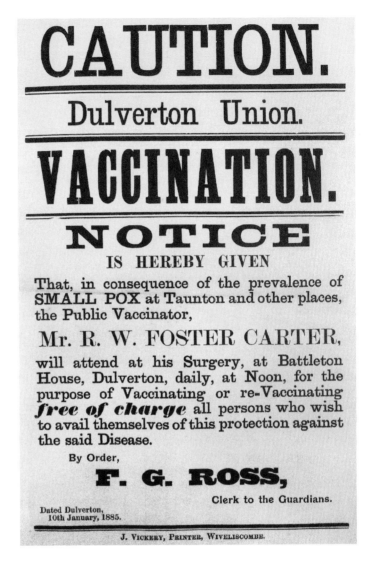

CAUTION.

Dulverton Union.

VACCINATION.

NOTICE

IS HEREBY GIVEN

That, in consequence of the prevalence of **SMALL POX** at Taunton and other places, the Public Vaccinator,

Mr. R. W. FOSTER CARTER,

will attend at his Surgery, at Battleton House, Dulverton, daily, at Noon, for the purpose of Vaccinating or re-Vaccinating *free of charge* all persons who wish to avail themselves of this protection against the said Disease.

By Order,

F. G. ROSS,

Clerk to the Guardians.

Dated Dulverton,
10th January, 1885.

J. VICKERY, PRINTER, WIVELISCOMBE.

of Lancaster, Surgeon of the one Part, and the Guardians of the Poor of the Burnley Union, in the County of Lancaster of the other Part.

It is hereby Agreed, and the said John Buck doth Contract with the Guardians and their successors, that from and after the twenty seventh day of September instant he will vaccinate all persons resident within the said Burnley Union who shall apply to him at times and places mentioned in the Schedule A hereunto annexed, or at such other times and places as the said Guardians shall, with the consent of the Poor Law Commissioners determine.

And that he will, at all times and places, duly Vaccinate all such persons as may be present for the purpose of being Vaccinated, and who may not before have been successfully Vaccinated, and do and perform all such other acts and things as may be necessary for the immediate purpose of causing such Vaccination to be successfully terminated.

And that he will keep two Books to be used respectively on alternate weeks and will immediately after he shall have Vaccinated any Person, so resident as aforesaid, and also immediately after he shall have inspected the progress of Vaccination in any such Person Vaccinated previously by him, make the entries described in the Form I in the Schedule B hereto annexed. And that he will, on the day next before each day of the weekly Meeting of the Board of the said Guardians, deliver to their Clerk, the Book in which he shall have made such entries during the preceding week.

And that in every case in which the result of Vaccination performed by him on any Person shall be successful, he will give to such Person, or to the Parent, Guardian or Nurse of such Person, a Certificate of the fact, in the Form II in the said Schedule B. And that he will also keep a Register in Form III in the said Schedule B of all cases of Small Pox which he shall attend, and will deliver a Copy of the same once every Quarter of the year to the Clerk of the said Guardians, on the twenty fifth day of December, the twenty fifth of March, the twenty fourth day of June and the twenty ninth day of September.

And the said Guardians do, for themselves and their Successors, contract and agree with the said John Buck to pay to the said John Buck his Executors, or Assigns, within one calendar month after the twenty fifth day of December the twenty fifth day of March, the twenty fourth day of June and the twenty ninth day of September respectively; during the subsistence of the Contract, and within one month after its termination, the sum of one shilling for every Person so resident as aforesaid who, not having been previously Vaccinated, shall have been successfully Vaccinated by the said John Buck and with respect to whom the said John Buck shall under Contract have made the Entries, and given the Certificate hereinbefore described.

And it is hereby further agreed between the said John Buck and the said Guardians, that this Contract shall be liable to be put an end to by either of the Parties hereto, on giving Twenty-eight days' Notice to the other Party respectively, of the intention to put an end to the same.

In Witness whereof the said John Buck hath hereunto set his Hand and Seal, and the said Guardians their Common Seal, the day and year first above written.

Signed, sealed and delivered
by the above named John Buck   *John Buck*
in the presence of

Andrew Ainsworth

The Common Seal of the Guardians of the above named Union was hereunto affixed at a Meeting of the Board of Guardians, held on the day of the date hereof, by James Roberts, Chairman of the Board at the said Meeting, in the presence of

Jno Tattersall
Clerk to the Guardians of the said Union

Schedule A

Times and Places of Attendance

Where	When
At the residence of the said John Buck being at Colne	At all such reasonable times during every day except Sunday as the said John Buck shall be at his residence
At the dwelling house of John Mitchell in Trawden	On every Monday in the week from two to three
At the dwelling house of John Elliott in Marsden	On every Tuesday in the week from two to three

TNA ref. MH 12/10211 Bedminster Union, Somerset

[A list of public vaccinators with the number of people vaccinated, 1852.]

Bedminster Union

Names of the whole of the Public Vaccinators of the Union	Vaccination Districts	Year ended 29th September 1852							Observations
		Number and Ages of persons Vaccinated by the Public Vaccinator			Number of such cases Successfully Vaccinated			Number of Registered Births, of all classes during the year including the Workhouse and the whole of the Parishes in the Union	
		Under 1 year	Above 1 year	Total	Under 1 year	Above 1 year	Total		
Thomas Torey Smart	First	139	117	256	135	113	248		Mr Adams – All the cases were successful, some having been revaccinated to produce this result. Mr Allen – There is much more difficulty in getting the people to have their children vaccinated than there used to be.
Henry Joseph Macy	Second, Third and Workhouse	57	17	74	57	17	74		
Thomas Dowling	Fourth	1	5	6	1	5	6		
George Adams	Fifth	36	19	55	36	19	55	1347	
Peter Chester Chadwick	Sixth	–	–	–	–	–	–		
Martin Noble Shipton	Seventh	–	–	–	–	–	–		
George Allen	Eighth	21	48	69	21	45	66		
	Totals	254	206	460	250	199	499*	1347	

* This number has been corrected to 449

[contd]

Dated this seventeenth day of December 1852
Thomas Coles   Clerk to the Guardians

TNA ref. MH 12/1021 Nantwich Union, Cheshire
[A list of public vaccinators with the number of people vaccinated, 1855.]

Nantwich Union

Names of the whole of the Public Vaccinators of the Union	Vaccination Districts	Number and Ages of Persons Vaccinated by the Public Vaccinators			Number of such cases Successfully Vaccinated			Number of Registered Births of all classes, during the Year, including the Workhouse and the whole of the Parishes in the Union	Observations
		Under 1 Year	Above 1 year	Total	Under 1 Year	Above 1 Year	Total		
Richard Baker Bellyse	Audlem	79	46	125	79	46	125		
William Walley	Bunbury	93	4	97	89	4	93		
John Kilshaw Slater	Crewe	273	44	317	261	43	304		
Wm. Edward Wedge Vaughan	Haslington	96	35	131	84	34	118	1324	
Thomas Williamson	Nantwich	247	28	275	203	23	226		
James Henry Rowcliffe	Taporley	79	24	103	74	22	96		Ceased to Vaccinate 21st July
Edward Hancock Rowcliffe	ditto	34	8	42	31	8	39		Commenced to Vaccinate 21st July
William Thomson	Wrenbury	75	7	82	71	7	78		
John Twemlow	Wybunbury	110	23	133	110	23	133		
	Totals	1086	219	1305	1002	210	1212	1324	

It is desired that in all cases the number Vaccinated under one year of age and above that age, be distinguished in the Return   Dated this 24th day of October 1855
(signed) J. Broadbent   Clerk to the Guardians

TNA ref. MH 12/4015 Clifton Union, Bristol
[A report on the vaccination of children against smallpox.]

Mr C.H. Hunt
Clerk of the Clifton Poor Law Union
Fishponds Road
20 April 1871

Sir,

I beg leave to reply to your letter of 17th ult. addressed to two other gentlemen and myself in the matter of the vaccination of this part of the Clifton Union.

Not being in a position to prosecute inquiries into the number of the unvaccinated children in this neighbourhood in order that the names of their parents might be reported to your Board, as suggested in your letter, I took upon myself, individually, to refer to the Medical Officer (lately retired) of the Redland branch of the Clifton Dispensary on the subject, my colleague in the former reference to your Board of the 13th ult, Mr G.M. Stansfeld, having declined to pursue the matter further.

The late Medical Officer of the Redland Branch of the Clifton Dispensary thinks that, on the whole, the Vaccination is well carried out in Redland, but that at the same time, it would be a very good thing to institute a house to house visitation to see if any have escaped vaccination.

The Medical Attendant of the Redland Dispensary for Women and Children states that he has no doubt there are many in this neighbourhood and should Small Pox visit us nothing but a scrutiny of many children in the district would be sufficient to check its progress, and that it would be a very desirable thing to send a sort of deputation, not only into the Quarries, but also amongst the children of the working classes in Lower Redland, among whom are many Welsh settlers, who, he understands, are not particular about obeying the Act.

In every brief and cursory visit paid to the Quarry yesterday, in the company of the first named gentleman, a child of 3 years, a weakly infant of 6 months, and a boy of 7 years old were found without vaccination marks, and an entire family in a somewhat better condition were said to have neglected vaccination. These cases are merely mentioned as indicating the importance, at the present crisis, of an official inquiry.

From information obtained from the office of the Assistant Registrar of the Clifton Sub-District I learn that the Redland Quarry (so called) and its vicinity was the chief seat of the Small Pox outbreak in Clifton in the last Quarter of 1864 and of the renewed outbreak of the disease in the first Quarter of 1865, which appears to have chiefly expended itself in this locality. The attack was spoken of by the inhabitants as 'shocking bad' and the ravages of the disease are said to have been frightful. I beg to subjoin extracts of the Assistant Registrar's Report to the Registrar General. 'Small-pox has been prevalent during the Quarter in this Sub-District. 29 deaths having been registered from that cause. It is now abated, only three deaths having been registered from that disease during the last 3 weeks.' Date 31/12/64.

Second letter. 'Small-pox has again appeared in the Quarry in a more virulent form, about 20 persons. Fresh cases are at present afflicted with that malady; 2 fatal cases there this week. The Local Board of Health have their Inspector and Medical Officer to inspect and report Sanitary conditions thereof, and the matter has been brought before the Guardians.' Date 8/4/65.

I beg further to point out that a house to house visitation is reported to have been pressed by the Board of Health on the Bristol Board of Guardians on the 11th ult. and that on the 22nd ult. a member of that Board reported to have stated publicly in the presence of a Member of the Town Council and several Members of the Bristol Board that there was serious cause to fear that Small-pox would be soon dispersed through the City. They had to look to the fact that a large portion of the population of the city had not been vaccinated, and to the necessity of having some place provided for the accommodation of parties infected with the disease the Public Vaccinator is also reported to have stated that there were a large number of persons still unvaccinated in Bristol, and a great number of persons imperfectly vaccinated. As the Clifton District has been declared by the Registrar General to include many unfavourably conditioned portions of the Municipal population, the above observations may be held to be equally applicable to those portions also.

In the returns of 1864, an abstract of which I beg leave to subjoin, the Clifton Registration District stands the 7th highest in the scale of Small-Pox mortality for that year out of the 632 Registration Districts, and the Bristol Registration District the 15th highest, as follows. In Bristol the vaccination was reported in the 6th Report of Public health for the year 1863 to have been generally very well performed.

Name	Population of 1861	Small Pox Mortality
Dudley	130,000	420
Liverpool	269,000	272
West Derby	225,000	272
Wolverhampton	126,000	244
Birmingham	212,000	232
Porsea Island	94,000	228
Clifton	94,000	180
Walsall	59,000	166
Stourbridge	68,000	157
Sheffield	128,000	152
Prescott	73,000	151
Birkenhead	61,000	133
Islington	155,000	126
West Bromwich	92,000	121
Bristol	66,000	107
Leicester	68,000	104

I beg further leave to subjoin a return of the Small Pox Mortality for both Districts for the last 20 years extracted from the Annual report of the Registrar General.

Years	Bristol	Clifton
1852 – 1860 (total)	266	175
1861	0	1
1862	2	5
1863	29	12
1864	107	180
1865	11	29
1866	0	5
1867	1	0
1868	1	2
1869	0	0
1870	0	2

All which particulars, in corroboration of the application of the 13th ult. I request the favour of your laying before the Board.

I remain &c &c

S. Sneade Brown

110 Pembroke Road
Upper Clifton
April 20, 1871

Dev. RO (Ex.) ref. Totnes PLU 114 Totnes Union, Devonshire
Vaccination Register
[Example of an entry.]

Dartmouth District	
No. in Birth Register	152
When born	6 Dec. 1874
Where born	Kingswear
Name, if any of child	James Edwin
Sex	B[oy]
Name and Surname of the Father, or (if the child be illegitimate) of the Mother	John Lambsin Foster
Rank, Occupation or Profession of Parent	Platelayer
Minutes of Notice given pursuant to 30 and 31 Vict. c84, s.15	
When given	2 Jany 1875
To whom given	Father
Register of Certificate Date of Med. Certificate of Successful Vaccination 30 April 1875 Name of Medical Man by whom the certification is signed R.W. Soper	

A page from the Return of Births, 1871, Chobham, Surrey, with the dates of vaccinations. (Sur. HC ref. BG1/63/1)

Entry from the Officers' Superannuation Register, Wellington Union, Somerset, 1864–97. (Som. RO ref. D/G/W/6/1)

TNA ref. MH 12/16702 Knighton Union, Radnorshire, Herefordshire and Shropshire
[Application for the post of vaccination officer.]

Knighton Union
Presteigne District

Appointment of Vaccination Officer

1.	State the Christian Name and Surname of the Person appointed	*John Hughes*
2.	His age	*44 years*
3.	His Place of Residence, and whether it is within the District assigned to him	*Norton – yes*
4.	His previous Occupation or Calling	*Farmer – Agent*
5.	The Date of his Appointment	*9 October 1884*
6.	The Date from which his duties commence	*22 October 1884*
7.	The fee to be paid for each Certificate of successful Vaccination registered by the Vaccination Officer	*6d for every certificate of successful vaccination duly registered*

8.	Whether it is proposed that he shall devote his whole time to the duties of Vaccination Officer; or, if not, how otherwise he is to be employed.	*Relieving Officer*
9.	The District for which he is to act, and with what Registration District or Districts it coincides*	*Presteigne District coterminous with Presteigne Registration Sub-District*
10.	The Area of the District in acres.	*18000 (estimated)*
11.	The Population of the District according to the last Census.	*2336*
12.	The Total Number of Births Registered in the last Four Quarters, showing the number for each Quarter, in the District for which he is proposed to be employed as Vaccination Officer.	*1st qr 17* *2nd qr 11* *3rd qr 14* *4th qr 17*
		Total *59*
13.	If a Relieving Officer, state:– (a) area, and (b) population of his Relief District; (c) whether the District assigned to him as Vaccination Officer is entirely comprised within his District as Relieving Officer.	*(a) 18,000 (estimate)* *(b) 2,336* *(c) The District is entirely comprised within his out-relief District.*
14.	Also the Number of Persons in his Relief District in receipt of Out-door Relief at the end of the preceding Half-year.	*60*
15.	Enumerate the paid offices, if any, which he has formerly held in any Union or Parish; the dates at which he ceased to hold such offices, and the cause of his ceasing to hold offices.	*None*
16.	The cause of the vacancy on account of which the appointment is made; if a Resignation, the cause thereof, the day on which it took effect, and the name of the former Officer.	*Transfer of Mr Butler to Knighton District*

* It is essential that the Valuation Officer's District should be coterminous with one or more Registration Sub-Districts

Edwin S. Dencey [?]   Signature of the Clerk

               John Hughes   Signature of the Officer appointed
(The Christian Name and Surname being written in full)

Reported to the Local Government Board for their approval *17* day of *Oct 1884*

A Relieving Officer may not be employed to act for a district not entirely comprised within his Relief District.

(This form to be returned without an accompanying Letter)

CHAPTER 19

PAUPER LUNATICS

Many paupers, if they were found to be 'of unsound mind' or others when they became mentally ill, were admitted to lunatic asylums. Those who were permanently 'sub-normal' were described as imbeciles. Others, many of whom were suffering a temporary mental illness, were described as lunatics. All patients were referred to as inmates. The records of many mental asylums survive and contain much enlightening material which records the health and treatment of the inmates. Many of the records are of the inmates themselves, sometimes with a record of the medicines prescribed to them.

The TNA record class MH 94 lists annually, from 1846, all state-aided patients admitted to asylums throughout England and Wales and can be used as a searching aid to locate a particular patient. (These are arranged alphabetically by the first letter only of the surname. The full name of the person is given, together with the name of the asylum and date of admission. The date of discharge, or date of death, is also given.) These also include some private patients. The lists are given in detail in Appendix 3.

The following are some examples of asylum records:

Dev. RO (Ex.) ref 3992F/H21 Wonford Asylum, Exeter, Devonshire
Register of Admissions, 1801–05 (Indexed)

No. 17	Sarah Drake of the parish of Pitminster, County of Somerset, aged 40
Admitted	30th March. In the 2nd Class
Sureties	Thos. Coleman of said parish
	John Prescott of Exeter, waggoner
	Had been ill one month before admission
7th Sept.	After 23 weeks resident went out on trial
7th Dec.	Considered cured, but the Bond was not taken up.

***

No. 542. Name. *Robert Waterman*

ADMITTED. *March 10ᵗʰ 1892.*   BY WHOM EXAMINED. *CJP*

Age	*56*	Epileptic	*no*	Diagnosis	
State	*Single*	Suicidal	*Yes*	Causation :—	
Religion	*Ch. of Eng.*	Dangerous	*no.*	(a) Predisposing	
Occupation	*Confectioner*	Height	*5 feet 8ᵗʰ*	(b) Exciting	
Attack	*1ˢᵗ*	Weight	*171*	(c) (a) or (b)	
Duration	*1 week*	Union			

FRIEND'S ADDRESS. *Elizabeth Passmore 5 Magdalen Street Exeter – Sister*

HISTORY OF CASE

He was manager of a hotel at Exmouth. Has been depressed for over a fortnight. He tried to commit suicide by cutting his throat with a knife, but was prevented from doing anything serious. No history of insanity, Sister died of Phthisis at the age of 25. His sister states that at times he was the worse for drink, but not often. and she attributes his condition to worry in his business as hotel-keeper at Exmouth.

He slept well last night, takes his food, but is depressed and does not associate with the other patients, answers readily if addressed, does not mind being here, does not converse with others, but sits alone. He is in fair health and condition but looks much older than he is. CFPusham.

He continues much the same, as in last note, takes his food and is still unsociable. CFPusham.

Is pleasant in manner if addressed, but sits alone, and does not converse with the other patients is in fair health – CFPusham.

Case book: Digby Mental Hospital, Exeter. Robert Waterman admitted 10 March 1892. (Dev. RO (Ex.) ref. 4034A/UH/2/1)

No. 58	Lieut. Samuel Cuming of the Royal Navy, on half pay, late of Totnes, age 34
	Re-admitted the 9th May 1804. In the 3rd Class
Securities	John Harsey of Exeter
	Geo. Stabback of Exeter

After leaving this house on Trial in September 1803 he went to Lodge with Mr Harvey, and continued well, until about the beginning of May, when it was found necessary to bring him back again.

No. 82   Avice Willis of the parish of Crowcombe county of Somerset, widow
aged 58

Admitted   5th March 1805. In the 2nd Class

Sureties   James Barnard, Esq., Crowcombe Court

John B. Cholwich, Esq., Farringdon House

Had been ill about 3 months before admission

***

No. 84   John Gillett of Bristol, Attorney at Law, aged 35

Admitted   16th April 1805 in the 3rd Class

Sureties   Joseph Sanders Esq., banker

Benjn Wm Johnson, surgeon

Had been ill a short time before admission

After 2$^4/_7$ weeks residence, when found means of eloping, and he is considered as
absent by consent of Friends, the Bond was not taken up.

***

No. 90   Sarah Tucker of Exeter, aged 42

Admitted   2nd July 1805. In the 2nd Class – Came to the house 27th June

Sureties   John Tucker, her husband, watchmaker

Nath. Tucker of Exeter

Had been ill about 5½ years, before admission. In March 1800
was admitted into St. Lukes Hospital in London for 12 months and
discharged uncured.

1806 April 4th After 40 weeks residence she went home on trial.

July 4th   Considered cured but the Bond not taken up.

Dev. RO (Ex.) ref. 3992F/H15/1 Wonford Asylum, Exeter, Devonshire Case Book, 1810–47 (Indexed)

Thomas Carbeth by trade a butcher, single

Admitted   July 12th 1810, aged 39

Was brought to this Hospital from Dr Fox's of Bristol where
he had been some time a patient. His mind has always been very
much impaired. Cannot hold conversation with any person yet not
altogether in a state of Dementia. Sometimes very irritable, is subject
to frequent fits of gout and attacks of epilepsy which leave him weak
for some considerable time after the attacks.

1845 Nov.   Had two abscesses on his foot occasioned by chalk stones which
sloughed, and after some difficulty healed. 29th a severe return of
Epileptic Fit 5, 6, 7. Fits continued. 9, 13, 16, 20, 23, 26 January
1, 3, 6, 9, 11, 13 on the 15th attack of eresypelas [skin infection]

367

of the right leg app. [applied] lotion speritusaen [spirit of arsenic] part affect C.Pil [pilule or pill] Hydrarg [mercury] qr v h s [every 4 hours] 17 Leg much inflamed cont 19 swelling and inflammation of leg decreased cont. mer 21 better 24, 27 in his usual state 31st. Feby 2 some gout 5 weak, 8 better, 10 in his usual state 13, 16, 19, 21 Foot and leg swollen but not inflamed 24 inflamed but not so much swollen. 27 better March 2nd 5, 7, 10, 13, 16, 19, 22, 24, 26, 28.

Aug. 17th	Was this morning attacked with convulsive fits and has fits, six during the day but towards night became 18 better and has passed intolerably without return.
19	No return of fits; bowels moved freely, appears weak.
20	Passed a restless night, takes in but little nourishment is evidently worse than yesterday
21	Another bad night but has taken in some roots.
22	Appears much worse this morning, lays heavy and torpid. Countenance much changed, evidently sinking. 2 pm took a little arrow root but with difficulty. Died 20 minutes to 8pm.

Dev. RO (Ex.) ref. 3992F/H20/2 Wonford Asylum, Exeter, Devonshire Register of Patients, 1853–61 [table opposite]

Sarah Symes, aged 51 years, the first female patient to be admitted to Somerset Lunatic Asylum at Wells, 1848.
(Som. RO ref. DD/X/JENS/7/1)

William Wilkins, aged 60 years, the first male patient to be admitted to Somerset Lunatic Asylum at Wells, 1848.
(Som. RO ref. DD/X/JENS/7/2)

* For more information on Sarah Symes and William Wilkins, see p. 389

Number	191
Date of Admission	10th Aug. 1854
Christian and Surnames at length	Grace Boyle Marshall
Sex and Class	Private/Female
Age	49
Condition as to Marriage	Single
Condition of Life and Previous Occupation	Domestic
Previous Place of Abode	Barnstaple
By Whose Authority Sent	John Boyce Marshall, brother
Dates of Medical Certificate and by whom signed	Richard Budd. M.D. and Charles Henry Heirn, surgeon both of Barnstaple. 9th August 1854
Bodily Condition	Weak and Feverish
Form of Mental Disorder	Melancholia
Supposed Cause of Insanity	Breach of Promise of Marriage
Duration of Existing Attack	2 months
Age on First Attack	49
Date of Discharge or Death	6th October 1855
Discharged	Relieved

***

Number	210
Date of Admission	June 19th, 1855
Christian and Surnames at Length	Joanna Lane
Age	51
Condition of Life and Previous Occupation	Single, Servant
Previous Place of Abode	Barnstaple
By Whose Authority Sent	Richard Blackmore, brother in law
Dates of Medical Certificate and by whom signed	William Land and John William Harris both of Exeter, surgeons, June 19th 1855
Bodily Condition	Very Good
Form of Mental Disorder	Melancholia
Supposed Cause of Insanity	Religion
Duration of First Attack	1 year
Number of Previous Attacks	1
Age at First Attack	48
Date of Discharge or Death	27th Sept. 1856
Discharged	Recovered

Number	213
Date of Admission	1855, August 30th
Christian and Surnames at length	George Row
Age	44
Condition of Life and Previous Occupation	Widowed, Accountant
Previous Place of Abode	Bristol
By Whose Authority Sent	Richard Rowe (brother)
Dates of Medical Certificate and by whom signed	Primrose Lyon, Aug 24th, Stoke Gabriel, and John Tompson Goodnidge, Aug. 28th, Paington, Devon both surgeons
Bodily Condition	Very Good
Form of Medical Disorder	Loss of his wife
Duration of existing attacks	4 weeks
Age at First Attack	44
Date of Discharge or Death	September 24th 1856
Discharged	Not Improved
Observations	Removed at the request of friends

***

Number	230
Date of Admission	5th May 1856
Christian and Surnames at Length	Charlotte Singleton
Age	45
Condition of Life and Previous Occupation	Draper's Wife
By Whose Authority Sent	Charles Singleton, husband
Dates of Medical Certificate and by whom signed	Philip Charles Hayman of Axminster 3rd May 1856, and Charles Hayman of Kilmington, 4th May 1856, both surgeons
Bodily Condition	Thin and Feverish
Disorder	Mania
Supposed Cause of Insanity	Miscarriage after thrown out of a vehicle on her head
Duration of First Attack	1 month
Number of Previous Attacks	5
Age at First Attack	31
Date of Discharge	2nd October 1850
Discharged	Recovered

Discharge certificate for Ann Dunn from St Thomas Hospital for Lunatics, Exeter, 1845. (Dev. RO (Ex.) ref. 3992F/h23/1)

Notice of death of Peter Ougier, who committed suicide at St Thomas Hospital for Lunatics, Exeter, 1845. (Dev. RO (Ex.) ref. 3993F/H23/1)

STATEMENT AS TO DEATH OF LUNATIC.

Name of Patient - · · · · · · *Robert Waterman*

Sex - · · · · · · · *Male*

Age - · · · · · · · *56 years*

Whether married, single, or widowed · · *Single*

Profession or Occupation · · · · · *Confectioner*

His place of abode immediately prior to being } *5 Magdalen Street, Exeter*
placed under care and treatment, if known

Date of Death - · · · · · - *3 August 1892*

Time of Death - · · · · · - *5 P.M.*

Cause of Death and the circumstances attending }
the Death - · · · · · } *Phthisis.*

Duration of the disease of which the patient died - *Some minutes.*

Name or names of any person or persons present }
at the death - · · · · · } *Attendant J. Radford*

Fredk J. Cross.
Clerk of the Exeter Asylum.

R.S. Armiford
Medical Officer of the Exeter Asylum.

Digby Mental Hospital, Exeter. Death of Robert Waterman, 1892. (Dev. RO (Ex.) ref. 4034A/UH/2/1)

Dev. RO (Ex.) ref. 3992F/H22 Wonford Asylum, Exeter, Devonshire
Register of Discharges and Deaths 1845–88

Date of Discharge	Date of Admission	Number in Register of Patients	Christian and Surname at length	Sex M	Sex F	Recovered M	Recovered F	Relieved M	Relieved F	Not Improved M	Not Improved F	Improved M	Improved F	Died M	Died F	Assigned Cause	Age at Death	Observations
29th Sept. 1847	Aug. 1st 1846	17	Eliza Cresswell		1								1					Taken out by her brother
13th Oct. 1847	Aug. 18th 1842	25	Rachel Williams		1										1	Gradual Decay	83	
9th Dec. 1847	Sept. 8th 1847	42	John Howe Snell	1				1										Taken out by his father
20th Jan. 1848	Oct. 29th 1847	44	Harriett Reeve		1		1											Taken out by Mrs Sercombe
26th Jan. 1848	Jan. 27th 1847	30	Elizabeth Battnell		1								1					Taken out by her brother
1st Feb. 1848	Jan. 30th 1847	31	Mary Gould		1								1					Taken out by her husband
1st Feb. 1848	Dec. 14th 1847	48	Charlotte Singleton		1		1											Taken out by Mrs Bastow
29th Feb. 1848	Nov. 2nd 1847	45	William Langdon Hulls	1						1								Taken out by his father
17th Apr. 1848	May 27th 1847	39	Ann Woolcott		1										1	Paralysis	46	
10th May 1848	Feb. 18th 1848	51	Samuel Johnson	1										1		Apoplexy	35	
25th May 1848	Mar. 16th 1848	53	Pakenham Berkley	1		1												
3rd July 1848	Mar. 4th 1848	32	William Hellyer	1		1												Taken out by his mother
14th Aug. 1848	Apr. 19th 1848	56	Elizabeth Sarah Coram Payne		1		1											Taken out by her husband
18th Aug. 1848	Apr. 6th 1848	55	John Shapland	1		1												Taken out by his wife
28th Aug. 1848	May 15th 1848	57	Jane Wiginton		1				1									Taken out by her son-in-law
19th Sept. 1848	Dec. 11th 1847	47	James Henry Topwill	1				1										Taken out by his wife
10th Oct. 1848	Dec. 20th 1847	49	Elizabeth Chappel		1				1									Taken out by Mr Blackmore
19th Oct. 1848	Mar. 21st 1848	54	William Yeo Martin	1				1										Taken out by Mr Organ
19th Oct. 1848	Oct. 13th 1848	66	Joseph Hodges	1						1								
9th Nov. 1848	July 16th 1848	58	Saml Hobson Warren	1										1		Gradual Decay	42	
18th Nov. 1848	Nov. 10th 1847	46	Thomas Wood	1						1								
29th Nov. 1848	Oct. 11th 1848	65	Charles Biggs	1				1										Taken out by his wife

Som. RO ref. Q/ALU/46 Somerset Quarter Sessions Rolls
Maintenance for Pauper Lunatics (1849 to 1868)
[A female prisoner in gaol is found to be insane and is transferred to the county lunatic asylum. Her maintenance is to be paid by the county.]

Somerset to wit   To the Treasurer of the County of Somerset

Whereas Mary Clarke or [alias] May was at the last Gaol Delivery holden for the County of Somerset at Wells the third day of August 1866 convicted of larceny and sentenced to eighteen months imprisonment with hard labour and was confined in the Gaol for the County at Taunton and while so confined appeared to be insane and thereupon Edward Ayshford Sanford, and Henry Gorges Moysey, Esquires, two of the visiting Justices of the County Prison aforesaid where the said Mary Clarke or May was so then imprisoned did enquire with the aid of Francis Henry Woodforde, Physician and Henry Liddon, Surgeon as to the insanity of the said Mary Clarke or May and it was certified by the said Justices, Physician and Surgeon unto the right Honorable Gathorne Hardy, Her Majesty's principal Secretary of State for the Home Department that the said Mary Clarke or May was insane and the said Secretary of State did by Warrant under his hand and seal bearing date the eighteenth day of December last, authorize and direct the Governor of the said Gaol and all others whom it might concern to cause the said Mary Clarke or May to be removed from the said Gaol to the County Lunatic Asylum at Wells in the said County there to remain until further order should be made therein and in pursuance of the said Warrant the said Mary Clarke or May was removed from the said Gaol to the said Lunatic Asylum on the 25th of December last. And whereas William Oakley, Governor of the said Gaol hath this day unto and before William Jeffreys Allen, Clerk and Charles Noel Welman, Esquire, two of Her Majesty's Justices of the Peace for the said County whose names are hereunto set and seals affixed made complaint of the premises and also that the said Mary Clarke or May is still confined in the said Asylum under the said Warrant and insane and that she is a poor person without any means of her own or her relations applicable for or towards her maintenance and that the reasonable charges of inquiring into her insanity amount to the sum of Three Guineas which sum is due to the said William Oakley and that the sum of Eight shillings and ninepence is a reasonable sum to be paid weekly for the maintenance of the said Mary Clarke or May in the said Asylum and that the Treasurer is the proper person to whom the said weekly sum ought to be paid. Now therefore we being two of Her Majesty's Justices of the Peace for the said County of Somerset have enquired into and ascertained by the best legal evidence and information that can be obtained under the circumstances of the personal legal disability of the said Mary Clarke or May that is to say by satisfactory evidence upon Oath the truth of the said allegations in the said recited complaint contained and also that the place of the last legal settlement of the said Mary Clarke or May cannot be ascertained and the pecuniary circumstances of the said Mary Clarke or May and it not appearing that the said Mary Clarke or May is possessed of any property which can be applied to her maintenance do by this our order made in pursuance of an Act passed in the twenty seventh and twenty eight years of the reign of Queen Victoria to amend the Act third and fourth Victoria, Chapter 54 for making further provision for the confinement and maintenance of insane prisoners adjudge that all and singular the premises hereinbefore and in the said recited complaint contained are here and further that the place of the last legal settlement of the said Mary Clarke or May cannot be ascertained. And we the said last mentioned Justices do by this our order made in pursuance and by the authority of the said Order and direct you the said Treasurer to pay unto William Oakley the Governor of the County Gaol aforesaid, the sum of Three Guineas so being the reasonable charges of enquiring as to the insanity of the said Mary Clarke or May and incurred as aforesaid and also to pay unto the said Treasurer weekly and every week the said sum of eight shillings and ninepence or such other sum as shall from time to time be reasonable for the maintenance of the said Mary Clarke or May in the said Asylum in which she is confined during her confinement therein under and by virtue of the said Warrant or until it shall be otherwise ordered according to Law. And we do further order you the said Treasurer to make the first payment of the said weekly sum to the said Treasurer on the first day of February next for the week then following.

Given under our hands and seals the twenty fifth day of January one thousand eight hundred and sixty eight at Taunton in the said County.

(signed) William J. Allen
(signed) C. Noel Welman

**Som. RO ref. D/H/men/17/1/4 Mendip Asylum, Wells, Somerset
Male Case Book, 1862–69 [see table overleaf for an example of an entry]**

Somerset County Lunatic Asylum at Wells, undated. (SANHS Collection)

f311   Case 1529

Sanders Henry, aged 24, single, 2nd attack, duration 10 years.	
Admitted 6 Aug 1866	
Form of Disorder	Epilepsy & mania
Previous History	Parents alive, eldest of 7. 1 male & 6 female. Disposition good, temper hasty, habits industrious, can neither read or write. Church of England. Cabman, Taunton
Present State (Physically)	General health indifferent, pulse 84, tongue clean, skin warm, appetite good, bowels regular, expression vacant, hazel irides [eyes], brown hair.
(Morally)	Conduct dangerous to others, conversation personal, affections natural, propensity to run about naked.
Additional Particulars	Has been under medical treatment for a previous attack 12 months ago.
1866 Aug. 13	In No.3 has had no fits yet, appetite good, sleeps well, quiet. Notice of admission signed for being in lunacy.
Oct. 18	Quiet. In no.1
1867 Jan 6	Had 13 fits by day to the end of last year, quiet, goes out to work.
July 11	Replied to a note from his father.
1868 April 4	In good health, quiet
1869 Jan 1	Works at 'Tree stone' cutting. Has severe fits at times. In good health.
April 6	Is employed with the Mason, quiet and very well except for the fits.
1870 Jan 27	Fits much the same. Health very good. Is industrious. Employed daily with the Mason
1871 Jan 19	Works with the Mason, is very industrious. Fits variable; not very frequent; or severe.
1873 June 30	Continues to work with the Masons. Fits as before. Mentally unchanged.
1874 April 8	Not improved – fits severe.
1875 April 3	Works with the Tree-Stone Mason. Fits still frequent. Bodily health good.
1876 Feb. 9	Violent when suffering from fits. Has just recovered from an attack. Health good.
June 5	Fits are more frequent. In South Wing but out at work with the Stone Cutter.
Sept 12	Fits more frequent. No change. Health good. Works with the mason. In South Wing.
Dec 17	Fits frequent. Mentally unaltered. Health good.
1877 Jan 30	Replied to a note from his father. Just recovering from an attack of epileptic mania.

Sept 16	General health good. Still has fits; no apparent mental improvement.
1878 March 10	In the South Wing; works with the Mason. General health good.
1880 Aug 19	Fits continuous, but attacks of mania are much less frequent. He is at present working with the Masons.
1881 April 3	In good health; no mental change.
Sept 4	Since last report has had one or two outbreaks of epileptic furvor requiring seclusion. Health good.
1882 April 25	Same as last report. Health good.

Note: No further record of Henry Sanders has been found in this case book. He does not appear in the case book before or the case book after the above; neither has he been found in the bundles of discharge papers.

The cost of keeping each pauper in a county lunatic asylum was charged to the Poor Law Union in which the pauper belonged. Thus, if an inmate of an asylum was found to have a legal settlement in another county then the pauper was removed to the asylum in that county.

The following is an example of a pauper lunatic being removed from the Somerset Asylum at Wells to the Oxfordshire Asylum at Littlemore.

Som. RO ref. D/H/Men/23/35 Mendip Asylum, Wells, Somerset
Discharged Patients, 1881

To the Relieving Officer of the Poor of the Oxford Poor Law Incorporation in the County of Oxford.

To the Superintendent of the County Lunatic Asylum at Wells in the County of Somerset and to the Superintendent of the Lunatic Asylum at Littlemore in the County of Oxford.

Whereas one Mary Pike a Pauper Lunatic chargeable to the above Poor Law Incorporation is now confined as a Lunatic in the said Lunatic Asylum at Wells in the County of Somerset and it is desirable that she should be removed from thence to the County Lunatic Asylum at Littlemore in the County of Oxford aforesaid; we therefore the undersigned, being two of the Visitors of the said Asylum at Littlemore in the said County of Oxford and being also two of Her Majesty's Justices of the Peace in and for the said County of Oxford do hereby order you, the said Superintendent of the said Lunatic Asylum at Wells aforesaid to deliver the said Mary Pike to the said Relieving Officer aforesaid upon this Order being presented to you by him and we do hereby order that you the said Relieving Officer do forthwith thereupon remove the said Mary Pike to the said Lunatic Asylum at Littlemore in the County of Oxford and we further order that you the said superintendent of the said Lunatic Asylum at Littlemore do receive the said Mary Pike as a Patient into the said last-mentioned Asylum.

Given under our Hands and Seals this second day of September in the year of our Lord One Thousand Eight Hundred and Eighty Two.

C. ———ish [illegible]
E.W. Harcourt

ORDER FOR THE RECEPTION OF A PAUPER PATIENT

We William Thomas Redfern, M.A. Off. [officiating] Clergyman, Charles Sloman, Relieving Officer, Taunton, the undersigned having called to our Assistance a Surgeon and having personally examined Mary Pike, a Pauper, and being satisfied that the said Mary Pike is a Lunatic, and a proper person to be taken charge of under Care and Treatment hereby direct you to receive the said Mary Pike as a Patient into your Asylum. Subjoined is a statement respecting the said Mary Pike.

Signed   William Thomas Redfern, M.A. Officiating Clergyman of the Parish
of Taunton St. James, Somerset.

Charles Sloman R.O. [Relieving Officer] Taunton.

Dated the 24th Day of April One Thousand Eight Hundred and Eighty Two.

STATEMENT

Name of Patient	Mary Pike
Sex and age	33 years (Female)
Married, Single or Widowed	Single
Condition of Life, and previous occupation (if any)	Domestic Servant
Religious Persuasion	Church of England
Previous Place of Abode	Watchet, Somerset
Whether first Attack	Yes
Age if known on first Attack	32½
When and where previously under Treatment	Nowhere
Duration of existing Attack	6 months
Supposed cause	Not known
Whether subject to Epilepsy	No
Whether Suicidal	Yes
Whether dangerous to others	No
Union to which Lunatic is chargeable	Taunton
Name and Christian Name, and Place of Abode of nearest known Relative of the Patient, and degree of Relationship, if known	Charlotte Pike (mother) Watchet, Somerset.

I certify that, to the best of my knowledge, the above Particulars are correctly stated.

Signed   Chas Sloman

***

MEDICAL CERTIFICATE

I the undersigned Samuel Farrant being a surgeon and being in actual practice as a Surgeon hereby certify, that I, on the 24 day of April 1882 at 15 Denmark Place, Taunton St. James in the County of Somerset personally examined Mary Pike of 15 Denmark Place, Taunton St. James, domestic servant and that the said Mary Pike is a Lunatic and a proper person to be taken charge of and detained under Care and Treatment, and that I have formed this opinion upon the following grounds, viz:–

1. Facts indicating Insanity observed by myself. *Very depressed in spirits, says she wants to die; delusions sees strange things; hears knockings all round the room.*
2. Other Facts (if any) indicating Insanity communicated to me by other.
   Attempted to drown herself on April 23rd by jumping into the river; very excited at times; rushed at a window in night attempting to jump out. Informant Mary Hawkins

    Signed, Name   *Saml Farrant*

    Place of Abode   *North St House, Taunton*

    Dated this 24 Day of April One Thousand Eight Hundred and Eighty Two

***

County of Somerset. Whereas on the twenty fourth day of April last past Mary Pike a Pauper Lunatic then resident in the Parish of Taunton Saint James, in the County of Somerset, and within the Taunton Union, was, pursuant to the Provisions of the Act of Parliament made and passed in the ninth year of the Reign of Her present Majesty Queen Victoria, intitled 'An Act to amend the Laws for the Provision and Regulation of Lunatic Asylums for the Counties and Boroughs, and for the Maintenance and care of Pauper Lunatics in England' duly sent from the Parish aforesaid, to the County Lunatic Asylum for the said County of Somerset, established at Wells, in the said County, and the said Mary Pike has been confined therein as such Pauper Lunatic from the twenty fourth day of April last past, to this day, at the charge of the Common Fund of the said Union, and she now remains resident and confined therein, at such charge, AND WHEREAS the place of the last legal Settlement of the said Mary Pike hath not up to the time of the enquiry now had before us the undersigned Robert Arthur Kinglake and Vincent John Reynolds two of Her Majesty's Justices of the Peace in and for the said County of Somerset, (one of us being of the Quorum) been ascertained according to the Provisions of the Statute in that case made and provided. AND WHEREAS satisfactory Evidence upon Oath as to such Settlement hath now been obtained and produced before us the said Justices according to Law, AND WHEREAS the place of the last legal Settlement of the said Mary Pike is not the said Taunton Union, AND WHEREAS the Guardians of the Poor of the said Taunton Union have this day made Complaint here to us the said Justices, of all and singular the Premises. NOW THEREFORE we the said Justices having pursuant to the Statute in that case provided, enquired into the several Premises, and into the last legal Settlement of the said Mary Pike upon Oath, and the said Complainants on behalf of the said Taunton Union, having now here established before us by satisfactory Evidence upon Oath, according to Law, the truth of all and singular the Premises, and that the said Mary Pike was during all the time aforesaid and now is legally settled in the Parish of St. Mary Magdalen in the said County of Oxford DO BY THIS ORDER adjudge the same to be true, and that the place of the last legal Settlement of the said Mary Pike was at the time of her being so as aforesaid, sent to the said County Lunatic Asylum, and from thence hitherto hath been and still is the Parish of St. Mary Magdalen aforesaid, in the Oxford Union.

Given under our Hands and seals at Taunton, in the said County of Somerset, this Eighth day of July in the year of our Lord One Thousand Eight Hundred and Eighty Two.

(signed) R.A. Kinglake
Vincent J. Reynolds

County of Somerset To the Board of Guardians of the Oxford Union, in the County of Oxford and to their Treasurer, and to the Churchwardens and Overseers of the Poor of the Parish of St. Mary Magdalen in the said County of Oxford.

Whereas on the twenty fourth day of April last past, Mary Pike a Pauper Lunatic then resident in the Parish of Taunton St. James in the said County of Somerset and within the Taunton Union was pursuant to the Provisions of the Act of Parliament made and passed in the ninth year of the Reign of Her present Majesty Queen Victoria, intitled 'An Act to amend the Laws for the Provision and Regulations of Lunatic Asylums for Counties and Boroughs, and for the maintenance and care of Pauper Lunatics in England,' duly sent from the Parish aforesaid, to the County Lunatic Asylum for the said County of Somerset established at Wells in the said County of Somerset, and has been confirmed therein as such Pauper Lunatic, from the twenty fourth day of April last past, to this day, at the charge of the common Fund of the said Taunton Union, and she now remains resident and confined therein at such charge. AND WHEREAS by a certain Order and Adjudication in writing bearing the date this present eighth day of July and hereto annexed under the Hands and Seals of us the undersigned Robert Anthony Kinglake and Vincent John Reynolds, Esquires, two of Her Majesty's Justices of the Peace, in and for the said County of Somerset, we have duly adjudged that the last legal Settlement of the said Pauper Lunatic was at the time of her being so as aforesaid, sent to the said County Lunatic Asylum, and from thence hitherto hath been and still is the Parish of St. Mary Magdalen aforesaid. AND WHEREAS the said Parish of St. Mary Magdalen is one of the Parishes included and comprised in the Oxford Union aforesaid. AND WHEREAS complaint hath been made unto us the said Justices by the Guardians of the Poor of the said Taunton Union that they have been incurred great expense in and about the Examination of the said Mary Pike and in and about her conveyance to the said Asylum, and that they have paid divers Sums of Money to the Treasurer of the said asylum for the Lodging, Maintenance, Medicine, Clothing, and Care of the said Pauper Lunatic in the said Asylum, and the said Guardians of the Poor of the said Taunton Union, now therefore make application to us the said Justices for an Order upon the Treasurer of the Guardians of the Poor of the said Oxford Union, in which the Parish of St. Mary Magdalen is included and comprised as aforesaid for payment to the said Guardians of the Poor of the said Taunton Union, of the amount of the said expenses and of the monies so paid by them to the Treasurer of the said Asylum as aforesaid, and it being now satisfactorily proved to us the said Justices upon oath, that the said Guardians of the Poor of the said Taunton Union, have heretofore and within Twelve Calendar Months next before the making of this Order, paid the following Sums in respect of the said Pauper Lunatic, (that is to say) the sum of two pounds two shillings, being the expenses incurred by the said Taunton Union, in and about the Examination of the said Pauper Lunatic, and the conveying of her to the said Asylum, and also the further sum of seven pounds twelve shillings being the amount of the several sums which by the said Guardians of the Poor of the said Taunton Union, have been hitherto paid to the Treasurer of the said Asylum for the charges of the Lodging, Maintenance, Medicines, Clothing, and Care of the said Pauper Lunatic in the said Asylum. WE DO therefore hereby order you the Treasurer of the Guardians of the Poor of the said Oxford Union, in which said Union the said Parish of Saint Mary Magdalen is situated and comprised and that being the Parish in which the said Pauper Lunatic is adjudged to be settled as aforesaid forthwith to pay to the said Guardians of the Poor of the said Taunton Union, or one of them, the said several sums of two pounds two shillings and seven pounds twelve shillings making in the whole the sum of nine pounds fourteen shillings. AND WE DO also in pursuance of the said Act of Parliament further Order you the said Treasurer of the Guardians of the Poor of the Oxford Union aforesaid, or the said Treasurer for the time being, to pay from time to time on behalf of the said Parish of Saint Mary Magdalen unto the Treasurer for the time being of the said County Lunatic Asylum, all such reasonable charges as may be incurred, and become payable for the future Lodging, Maintenance, Medicines, Clothing and Care of the said Pauper Lunatic in the said Asylum.

Given under our Hands and Seals at Taunton, in the said County of Somerset, this eighth day of July in the year of our Lord One Thousand Eight Hundred and Eighty Two.

R A Kinglake
Vincent J Reynolds

***

OHA ref. L7 A1/6 Littlemore Hospital Admission Registers
Mary Pike, number 4713. Admitted 6th September 1882
[This is a report from Wells Asylum, found at the Oxford Health Archives, repeating all the details given in the statement above with the following addition:]

Indications of insanity at admission. Very depressed in spirits, says she wants to die, delusions sees strange things, hears loud ringing around the room. 'Attempted to drown herself on April 23rd by jumping into the river – very excited at times rushing at windows in night attempting to jump out'. Informant Mary Hawkins. Samuel Tarrant, North St House, Taunton. Wm Thomas Redfern clergyman Taunton St. James. Charles Sloman, Relieving Officer.

OHA ref. L7 A2/2
[The following note was appended to the certificate relating to Mary Pike:]

Somerset & Bath Lunatic Asylum, Wells. Sep 6th 1882. I certify the within to be a true copy of the Order, Statement and Medical Certificate upon which Mary Pike was admitted into the asylum, and I further certify that the said Mary Pike is in a fit state of bodily health to be moved to the Oxford Asylum.
A. Law Wade, MD Medical Superintendent

OHA ref. L8 A1/1/33 Littlemore Case Book

7th Sep.	Fairly well nourished, has imbecilic melancholic expression on her face, head and eyes are natural. No active disease respiratory or vascular organs. Refuses her food and says it is wrong for her to have any.
12th Sep.	Generally sits by herself in a low depressed state and rarely speaks to anyone and it is difficult to get her to answer questions. Sometimes does a little sewing, takes in a little food.
19th Sep.	Is sometimes greatly depressed and sits by herself crying, other times is happy and does needle work.
26th Sep.	Is more cheerful and talks more rationally is very good at needlework, sits by herself when at work.
7th Oct.	Is variable but as a rule is less depressed. Does needlework, prefers to work by herself.
26th Nov.	Not any mental improvement, mopes a good deal.
6th Jan. 1883	Bodily health is fair, is often depressed and cries.
28th Feb.	Discharged; improved.

OHA ref. L7 A1/3 Littlemore Case Book
11th April 1883. Mary Pike – Discharged trial exceeded. Recovered.
[This means she was discharged on trial for an agreed period in which time she was considered well enough to remain discharged.]

A letter from Cicely Burrell, an inmate of Brookwood Asylum, Surrey, asking to see the queen. (Sur. HC ref. 3473/3/2 f240)

Sur. HC ref. 3043/5/9/1/1 Brookwood Asylum, Surrey
Male Case Book, 1867–69

f183

Matthias Petts

Date of Admission	17 March 1868
Previous Place of Abode	Newington Workhouse
Married, Widowed or Single and Age	M 54
Religious Persuasion	Ch of E
Occupation	Clerk, formerly a soldier
Time Insane	Y M D } unknown
Epileptic	No
Suicidal	No
Supposed Cause and Hereditary Predisposition	Intemperance
No. of Attacks	Several
Address of Relatives	Mrs King, 141, High Street, Borough
Brought by	Mr Alfred E. Coombes, R.O. Newington

Page from a Register of Admission: two paupers to Clutton Workhouse, Somerset, 10 January 1875. (Som. RO ref. D/G/Cl/75b/1)

Has been an inmate of the workhouse for irregular periods during the last 14 months, going out for a few days & then returning with evident symptoms of being affected by drink. Generally well conducted. Reported to be dangerous to others & to labor under the delusion that he is dying from the effect of strychnine.

MANIA   State on admission. Quiet, respectful. Replied to all questions without hesitation & on all ordinary topics in a rational manner. Declares that his wife wants to marry again, & with the assistance of another woman has tried to poison him. On the last occasion of his being absent from the Workhouse was taken suddenly & unaccountably ill, due, he believes to something given him by his wife. States that he has been sent to this Asylum owing to spite on the part of the Workhouse Master. Is in fair health of body, somewhat nervous, trembling as though after a recent debauchery, complains of his head. Has some recent venereal sores on his penis, contracted during his last absence from the Workhouse.

March 20 His delusions, as on admission continue. He states he does not sleep at all and has not done so for some time, but the Head and Night Attendants have found him sleeping soundly.

March 22 He complains much of his head being very painful, says he is dying, quite unable to do any work and is melancholic. The delusions remained unaltered.

March 24 The same Rj [prescription] Pot bromide [potassium bromide] igr [one grain] Aqua [water] v.s. [sufficient] zi. [dose 1 drachm] in die sumenda [to be taken each day].

March 28 Has frequently complained of his head-ache, which does not seem to have been benefited by the K.Br. [potassium bromide]. Endeavours to forget the pain by assisting in folding clothes. Fy Ferri et ammon cit [iron and ammonium citrate] gr vi [6 grains] Aqua [water] ziiii [4 drachms] t.d.s. [3 times a day]. He complains of feeling very week and depressed. Sores on penis are now in numbers and soft chanre treated today with initiate of silver, quing zenie oxidi [ointment of silver, zinc oxide] to be applied.

March 31 Is despondent and hypochondrical. The chanres are healing. States he does not sleep, but he really sleeps normally.

June 5 Is better than when last registered was made. He works in the store regularly at his trade as draper, and seems pretty well. He still has a sore on his great toe preventing him from doing much walking.

Sept 24 His toe has now recovered itself. He does not work in the store but prefers working in the ward & especially in the head attendant's room.

Dec 23 Continues in much the same condition mentally, his physical condition is much improved.

1869

Feb 23 Physical condition still improving. He has for some time had extra diet. Is generally quiet & respectful.

April 12 Has continued to assist the Head Attendant in making up his reports &c. Having for a long time past been on extra diet; an egg & a pint of porter daily & his bodily health being good the porter was this day discontinued. On this Med' Sup' visiting at night the dormitory where he slept with a number of invalid patients belonging to the Infirmary Ward, he assaulted the MS with a volley of abuse, using the most gross language intermingled with oaths, and then threatened violence. He was obliged to be removed to another sleeping room.

May 27 Has continued quiet and orderly since the last report employing himself regularly in the office of the head attendant, writing &c. Today was removed to Arlesley Asylum by their head attendant under Transfer Orders signed by two Magistrates of Herts.

Sur. HC ref. 3473/3/1 Holloway Sanatorium, near Egham, Surrey
Female Case Book (with some photographs)
[A sanatorium for the middle classes.]

No. 244	Name of Patient: Emily Ann Valentine
Age	44
Admitted	Sept. 9th 1887
Previous Place of Abode	6, Charlton Park Terrace, Old Charlton
Occupation	None
Married	1
Single	—
Widow	—
Number of Children	8
Age of Youngest Child	1 year 9 months
Duration of Existing Attack	6 months
How many previous attacks?	one
Confined in any Lunatic Asylum	No
Supposed cause of Insanity	Death of near relation
Whether Suicidal	Yes
Has the Patient been of Sober habits?	Yes
Degree of Education	Good
State of Bodily Health	Good
Religious Persuasion	Church of England
Relatives Similarly Afflicted	1 cousin, insanity Uncle, melancholia

1st Medical Certificate
1. Facts indicating Insanity observed by myself.

Says she is very unhappy because she has not done her duty as a wife and a mother that she cannot love her husband or children, that she is tired of herself and took some belladonna with the intention of destroying herself and that she fears doing it again.
2. Other facts (if any) indicating Insanity communicated to me by:
Her husband William Stather Valentine, that she is depressed, has frequently threatened to destroy herself, that she has made two attempts to do so by taking poison within the past few weeks. Shuts herself up in a top room in the house and asked to be left alone and allowed to lie on the floor.

Arthur Rope [?]
Lewisham Hill
Kent

Sept. 18th 1887

2nd Medical Certificate

Relation of informant to patient	Husband
Family History	Insanity &c cousin insane, uncle melancholia Phthisis none Other Diseases —
Acute Rheumatism or Chorea	no
Fits – epileptic or hysterical	no
Fevers, &c	none
Other Diseases	nothing serious
Sober	yes
Number and nature of previous attacks	one of melancholia
Injuries or shocks	none
Time of earliest symptoms	6 months ago
Nature of earliest symptoms	Depression
Progress of case	[blank]
Suicidal or dangerous (facts)	Attempted suicide by drinking Belladonna
Tendency to leave home	none
Hallucinations	[blank]

A woman of medium height, she has dark hair, brown eyes, fresh regular features and a dull & somewhat demure expression. She talks rationally on ordinary topics but she very soon brings the conversation around to her on troubles. She is most melancholic in these times, her eyes filling with tears as she narrates how her husband and children is numbered [sic] how grossly selfish she has been, how painfully stupid she must appear to everyone & how grossly she has managed her domestic affairs. She is convinced that she will never recover and words of hope do not seem to cheer her at all.

14 Sept	Swallowed her gold ring, said she did so as she was worked up into a frenzy & did not know what she was doing, on being searched a screw driver was found in her pocket. An attendant to sit up with her at night.
21 Sept	Somewhat better, not so depressed, does not talk of her suicidal tendencies as she has done freely on former occasions.
5 Oct	Was visited by her husband. Seems to be steadily improving & is as a rule quite bright & cheerful now, & inclined to occupy herself more than formerly.
6 Dec	Has a severe cold and is now suffering from gastritis but is better has required opium & not fomentations. Mentally continues to improve.
24 Dec	Was today discharged recovered by order of her husband.

Dev. RO (Ex.) ref. 4034A/UH/2/1 Digby Mental Hospital, Exeter, Devon Case Book, 1889–92

No. 70	
Name	James Wright
Admitted	9 May '91
Age	39
State	Married
Religion	Ch of Eng
Attack	1st
Duration	3 weeks
Epileptic	No
Suicidal	No
Height	[blank]
Weight	[blank]
Union	Private
Diagnosis	Acute Mania
Causation	Head injury
Friend's Address	James Wright (father) 7, North Street, Crediton
History of Case	see enclosed letter

[A letter has been inserted in this book and reads:]

Crediton
May 10th

Dear Sir,

I send you a few particulars of Mr Wright's case.

On March 28th he had his head cut with a circular saw, (you will see the extent of the wound) going completely through the bone, dura mater and into the substance of the brain, to such an extent that neither my partner, Mr Bell of Exeter or myself thought there was anything but the very faintest chance of his living, he never spoke from the time of the accident until April 10th when he began to speak quite rationally, knew people &c and from what he now said, had evidently noticed and remembered many things said and done by those about him from the time of his accident in this state until April 18th, but from this date did not again speak until April 26th but was quiet and sensible to a certain extent, on April 26th he again began to speak but simply a continual repetition of certain words and sentences with no particular meaning. At first he was fairly quiet and under control, but has gradually become more and more restless and excited. Treatment: The wound was brought together as well as possible, irrigated twice a day with hard colesent water and then dressed with carbolcidt oil. The head being kept cool when necessary by means of a spiral gutta percha cap with continual current of cold water, it has healed in a wonderful manner and we have now, for some time been dressing it with boracic acid ointment. The case is certainly a most interesting one and I should be very glad if you will kindly let me know what you think of the case in a short time. I might say that for a week or two after the accident his temperature kept about 100, and his pulse 120 at times very weak.

Yours very truly,
W. M. Body

[*There is much detail entered in the register about his condition and treatment, and it finally records*:]

Discharged not improved, 6th June 1891
(signed) N.L. Rutherford

Som. RO ref. D/H/Men/17/2/1 Mendip Asylum, Wells, Somerset

Sarah Symes, aged 50 years, admitted 1st March 1848
Domestic servant, unmarried, admitted with chronic mania, eldest of 10 children. First attacked about 6 years ago (about age 44) and has continued insane up to the present period. There is a predisposition to insanity in the family especially on the mother's side, etc., etc.

***

William Wilkins, aged 59, farm labourer, married, admitted 3rd March 1848 with mania. His wife is 63 years old. Been married about 39 years. At marriage wife was 24 and he was 20 years. Married about 1 year at first attack. Has been in Box Asylum [Wiltshire] twice about six months each time.

Sur. HC ref. 6292/27/8 St Ebba's Asylum, Epsom, Surrey
The following is a selection of portrait photographs copied from a female case book.
Full details of each case have not been reproduced here.

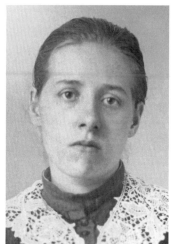

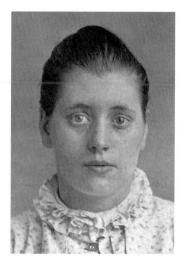

Ellen Lawton
Admitted 8 September 1903
Aged 27

Maud Ponting
Admitted 8 September 1903
Aged 20

Elizabeth Farmer
Admitted 8 September 1903
Aged 23

Mary Feanon
Admitted 8 September 1903
Aged 34

Annie Martin Pescott
Admitted 22 January 1904
Aged 20

Amelia Rebecca Rowland
Admitted 4 February 1904
Aged 40

Sur. HC ref. 6292/27/1 St Ebba's Asylum, Epsom, Surrey
The following is a selection of portrait photographs copied from a male case book.
Full details of each case have not been reproduced here.

William Newcombe
Admitted 25 September 1903
Aged 23

David Crocket
Admitted 25 September 1903
Aged 36

Samuel Sims
Admitted 25 September 1903
Aged 55

Alfred Gilby
Admitted 29 October 1903
Aged 61

Robert Emanuel Hall
Admitted 24 October 1903
Aged 45

William Foot
Admitted 29 October 1903
Aged 71

CHAPTER 20

HEALTH AND SAFETY IN WORKHOUSES AND THE COMMUNITY

Union Buildings and Heating, Sanitary Conditions, Water Supply, Drainage and the Health of the Community

From 1848 to 1856 the Central Board of Health was concerned with the general health of the nation. This organisation came to an end in 1856 when some of its duties and powers were transferred to the Home Office. A branch of the Home Office, known as the Local Government Act Department, became responsible for local bye-laws. The Privy Council took over certain medical functions. The Board of Guardians of each Poor Law Union had powers under the Nuisance Act of 1848 and thus reported on sanitary conditions and other local nuisances to the Poor Law Board. When the Local Government Board was formed in 1871 it took over the responsibilities of the Poor Law Board, the General Register Office, the Local Government Act Department of the Home Office and the Medical Department of the Privy Council. Thus the Local Government Board became responsible for water supplies, drainage and sanitary conditions, and the general health of the residents within each Union. It appears from the correspondence to and from the Poor Law Board that health and safety was of great concern. The overseers of the Poor Law Unions often reported on such matters, not just in workhouses but within the borders of their Unions. The following examples give an indication of the amount of detail to be found in these reports:

TNA ref. MH 12/5320 Sevenoaks Union, Kent
[Letters concerning the health hazard of a cesspit, 1854.]

Thursday
To the Poor Law Commissioners* for England and Wales, and to the General Board of Health, the Memorial of Joseph Bradley, Overseer of the Poor of the parish of Seven Oaks, Kent; sheweth:–

* This is clearly an error and should read 'Board'

That he has for upwards of twelve months past complained of the state of nuisances in this parish, in print, and otherwise.

That no attention being paid to his representations; he, with his fellow parish officers, called a public vestry meeting in July, which was held accordingly, and strong resolutions passed, and communicated to the Board of Guardians of Seven Oaks Union, immediately afterwards.

That these resolutions were not attended to, but same Board of Guardians passed other resolutions at a special meeting on the 6th of October last, and then undertook to form themselves into a sanitary committee, and carry out the orders of the General Board of Health, copies of which orders they forwarded, with their resolutions, to your Memorialist.

That same Board of Guardians have not formed themselves into a Sanitary Committee, and inspected the nuisances in the parish, and have not carried out the Regulations of the Board of Health.

That a nuisance likely to breed fevers and contagious disease now exists in the middle of Seven Oaks town, although your Memorialist has given plain notice for its removal, which was received by same Board of Guardians, on the 9th of February instant, a Copy of which he sends on the other side.

Under the circumstances above stated your Memorialist asks the interference of your Honorable Boards, and hopes that you will see justice done to the poor, and the public.

Joseph Bradley

Seven Oaks, Kent, 11th of February 1854

***

COPY

Seven Oaks, Kent   6th of February 1854

Gentlemen,

As Churchwardens, Overseer, and inhabitants of this town and parish, we hereby give you notice that in a place called the Shambles, there is a foul and offensive cesspool or ash pit, with an accumulation of filth and refuse, all kept so as to be injurious to the health of persons living in the neighbourhood thereof; and we require the law to be enforced so as to cause the complete removal of the above, and have to state that a proper inspection by you of nuisances in our parish is much needed.

We are Gentlemen
Your obedient servants
William Grover, Churchwarden
Joseph Bradley, Overseer

To the Guardians of the Poor of Seven Oaks Union

Som. RO ref. D/G/W/8a/9 Wellington Union, Somerset and Devon
Minutes of the meetings of the Board of Guardians
[Letter concerning the heating system for a workhouse.]

Patent Hot Water Apparatus Manufactory,
6 Francis Street,
Regent Square,
London
6th Nov. 1854

To the Chairman and Board of Guardians of the Wellington Union
Gentlemen,

In accordance with the desire expressed by your Chairman, I have examined the present Heating Apparatus of the Wellington Union.

The Apparatus consists of a Boiler and a series of 4 inch cast iron pipes; the pipes pass through five of the Rooms as follows.

The Dining Room, Women's Day Room, Needle Room, Boy's School Room and the Men's Day Room.

I had not an opportunity of testing the apparatus myself but was informed by Mr Dore that the pipes were never warm enough to be of any use until the middle of the day, and that it required two cwt* of coals to do this.

I am of opinion that the pipes are badly arranged for effecting the object of warming the above Rooms, and also that the Boiler is not large enough to heat the water in the pipes in a reasonable time.

I have taken into consideration the practicability of introducing steam into the pipes, but I am of opinion that there are so many objections to this, it would not be desirable.

I have considered about a new Boiler of larger dimensions for heating the water sooner. This it would be difficult to apply on account of the confined space, and the bad arrangement of the pipes.

Under all the circumstances therefore I should recommend you to apply an Apparatus of small pipes which would effectually accomplish the purpose of warming the Rooms in a reasonable time and with considerable economy of fuel.

I beg to enclose a sketch[†] of the arrangement which I propose for the Furnace and Pipes.

The Furnace to be fixed in the Dining Room as shown on the plan.

The pipes to be carried along the Rooms overhead as indicated by the Blue Lines. This arrangement will place the Furnace under better control and the pipes out of the way of the Inmates and effectually warm the rooms.

My estimate for the new apparatus would be sixty pounds erected complete, for which sum I would execute the work.

With regard to the present Boiler and Pipes it is impossible for me to estimate the value of them if taken up and sold, as the joints may be all broken in removing them. I therefore am sorry that I shall be obliged to decline undertaking their removal as they would be of no value to me.

---

* cwt = a hundred weight = 112lbs   † The sketch and plan do not survive

Perhaps some party in the neighbourhood might find use for the Pipes if taken up and offered for sale, when the true value would be ascertained.

My charge for this Report will be five Guineas which is exclusive of the above estimate.

Waiting your reply, I am Gentlemen,

Your Obedient Servant,

A.M. Perkins

Moved by the Chairman and seconded by Mr Elworthy that the above Report be received and adopted and that Mr Perkins' estimate and tender for erecting complete a new Apparatus for heating the Workhouse for the sum of £60 be accepted.
Carried unanimously

Som. RO ref. D/G/W/8a/10 Wellington Union, Somerset and Devon
Minutes of the meetings of the Board of Guardians
[Report on the cooking, heating, washing and drying apparatus in a workhouse.]

Mr Fraser of London, Engineer, attended at the Board in pursuance of the wish of the Guardians and after having carefully inspected the Workhouse and examined the present Apparatus for Cooking and Drying, he laid before them the following Report and Estimate.

10 Commercial Road

London

Jany 28th 1858

Guardians of the Poor

Wellington Union

Gentlemen,

Agreeably to my promise by your sanction I have gone over your Workhouse to inspect the Cooking, Heating, Washing and Drying Apparatus and having a practical knowledge of the requirements of a Workhouse am willing to give any information in my power on that subject. In the first place allow me respectfully to say, the Cooking and other Apparatus above named are totally unfit for the purpose required. Those parts that are not worn out, require altering to make them effective before you can have a well managed Establishment. At present the Inmates cannot be properly classified having to pass into the Kitchen and Scullery for Hot Water and other requirements which must bring the Inmates away from their respective places and the consumption of fuel alone would soon pay for the outlay. I will now give you a Statement of all I think required with [the] cost of each Item that you may be able to judge whether required or not and will undertake to say that nothing shall be named that is not absolutely required.

Cooking Apparatus for, or equal to 250 Inmates with 4 Cooking boilers, enclosed in substantial casing, copper covers, counter balance weights and cocks and complete; also a substantial Steam Boiler of sufficient capacity for all purposes required, with a

395

separate Hot Water Boiler in the same erection and to be heated by the same Fire with all Cocks, Valves and self acting Gunmetal fittings complete in every respect including

Brickwork and all other expenses.	£180
To convey Hot and Cold Water to the several Stair Cases and Yards, say 13 places in all.	£35
To convey Steam with Hot Water to Women's Washhouse; also to Girls' with all required Cocks, Coppers, Pipes, &c.	£18
To heat Dining Hall, Boys' School, Women's Day Room, Nursery, and Room adjoining, also Girls' School Room	£55
The above item may be done without by keeping present apparatus.	
To supply and fix a complete Drying Closet consisting of six iron poises [sic] inclosed in 5 proofs casing, also Iron Stove to heat the same including all brickwork.	£50

The whole of the work to be best of their several kinds and proper detailed specification sent if required but will hold myself responsible for the well working of the whole Apparatus in every sense of the word both as to value and utility, or not paid for.

I am Gentlemen

Your Obedient Servant

J.W. Fraser

Items		
	Cooking	£180
	Hotwater	35
	Washhouse	18
	7 Smiths	8 – 10
	Heating	55
	Drying Closet	50
		£346 – 10

TNA ref. MH 12/12395 Kingston Union, Surrey
[Construction of a drain.]

Kingston Union | Kingston, Surrey
R.F. Bartrop Clerk | 4 June 1856

My Lords & Gentlemen

Drainage of Union Premises

I am desired to state to you that the guardians have felt themselves obliged to comply with a requisition from the Corporation of Kingston that they should contribute the sum of £40 towards the construction of a twelve inch drain down Coombe Lane from the Union premises to the main sewer in the London Road, for the expenditure of which sum I am to solicit your sanction. The length of drain will be about 550 yards.

You some time since sanctioned the erection of a tank and filter for purifying the drainage, the guardians expecting that the overflow would thereby run away inoffensive, but the experiment has not succeeded, and the guardians have been repeatedly threatened and once proceeded against before Magistrates, for alleged nuisance.

The reasons for the guardians feeling obliged to join in the construction of the proposed drain are, that in the last Session of Parliament a local act was passed to extend the boundaries of the Borough of Kingston, within which the union premises are now included, and in which act are very stringent clauses as to drainage, so that the Corporation has large powers over escapes of sewage such as this, and as the ditches by which the same escapes are by the road side, and are not the property of the guardians, they, the guardians, are by the act under compulsion as to some steps for abating the nuisance.

The yearly cost of Charcoal for the Town is about £20, and I presume that the use of it will be discontinued if you sanction the above outlay of £40, except perhaps an occasional purchase of a small quantity to put into the tank for making manure for the garden.

I have the honor to be

My Lords & Gentlemen
Your most obed^t
R.F. Bartrop

The Poor Law Board
London

TNA ref. MH 12/10498 Wellington Union, Somerset and Devon
[Pumping water from a well. Continuation of a letter written to the Poor Law Board – see also Chapter 11.]

13th March 1867

There is another grave subject of complaint as to the Boys, which it is my duty to bring to the notice of your Honorable Board. There is a horizontal water wheel which they are made to work, for pumping up water from a deep well. It has a central perpendicular shaft with 5 iron arms or rods encircled by an outer iron ring which is only 7 feet 10 inches in diameter. Against each rod 2 boys push the wheel round, within the ring, and one boy inside the other. The outside boy walks round and round, not 3 feet 8 inches from the shaft, and the inner boy at least 14 inches nearer the shaft, and so only 2ft 6 inches from the shaft. One of the Guardians drew my attention to this, as being in fact injurious and stupifying to the boys, whilst other Guardians said the boys liked the work. I asked a boy in the presence of the Master did they like it? The boy's answer was that they did not like it. I asked him why not, and he said it made them very giddy, and it is obvious that even walking where the outer boys walk it inevitably must make them giddy. For the boys in the inner circle it must be extremely injurious. The Master said they work half an hour at a time, two or three times a day.

It appears to me that this engine should be done away with, or very much enlarged and improved.

I now earnestly beg to express my great regret that I should have to trouble your Honorable Board at so much length in calling attention to these details, and that you will allow me to add that I do so solely from an imperative sense of duty to the poor in the Wellington Workhouse and Union. I shall be happy to receive any communication you may be good enough to favour me with.

And I have the honor to remain
Gentlemen
Your obedient humble Servant
Chas Rowcliffe

Mr Gulson

Be good enough to advert to Mr Rowcliffe's letter to that part of it which refers to the employment of the boys in pumping water. You are probably aware of the arrangement to which Mr Rowcliffe objects. Do you think it ought to be continued?

15 April 67

I have not unfrequently [sic] seen the boys at work pumping water & it has not appeared to me to be hard work. I think however that there may be some foundation for the statement made by Mr Rowcliffe as to the confined circle in which the inner boy has to walk in pushing the wheel round, and whether the horizontal wheel used in pumping the water is in future to be worked by the boys or by men I think the wheel should be so enlarged as to make the circle of considerably greater diameter than that within which the inner boy is confined. This might easily be done by the addition of outside rods.

I think it would be well to suggest the enlargement of the circle, and also to state that as far as possible the pumping may in future be done by men & the boys employed on the land attached to the W.H.   C.G. Apl. 16. 67

N.B. I do not think there are enough men in the W.H. able to pump the water required.

Som. RO ref. D/G/W/8a/15 Wellington Union, Somerset and Devon
Minutes of the meetings of the Board of Guardians

[Letter concerning nuisances in the parish of Hemyock, Devon.]

Cullompton
11th Sept. 1867

Hemiock [sic] Nuisances

I have the honor to report for the information of the guardians of Wellington Union that during the past week I have been compelled to serve Notices on the following persons of the above Parish to abate Nuisances in and about their Premises and also to erect proper trapped cesspits viz:–

Mr Jas. Bowerman, Hemyock, owner of two cottages in the occupation of Samuel Moore and Henry Board. Nuisances to be removed forthwith and trapped Cesspit to be erected by the 21st inst.

Mr Jnº Darby, Ottery St. Mary, owner of three Cottages in the occupation of James Pring, John Hine and George Clist. Nuisances to be removed forthwith and trapped Cess Pit to be erected by the 25th inst.

Mr Henry Wood, Hemyock, owner of House and Cottage in the occupation of Thomas Walker and Wm Robins. Nuisances to be removed forthwith and trapped Cesspit to be erected by the 15th inst.

I have further to report for the information of the Guardians that the Hedge Trough in front of Mr Bowerman and Mr Darby's Cottages is in a dirty state, and requires clearing out, the attention of the District Highway Surveyor and the Waywardens of the Parish ought to be called to this matter, and I must say if the water could be carried from the main stream along a trough in front of the cottages named it would add very much to the health and cleanliness of the occupiers.

I have the honor to be, Sir,

Your most obed^t Humble Servt

(signed) R. Collins

Som. RO ref. D/G/W/8a/16 Wellington Union, Somerset and Devon
Minutes of the meetings of the Board of Guardians

[Report on bad sanitary conditions.]

Milverton, 3rd March 1869

To the Wellington Board of Guardians

Gentlemen,

We the undersigned, the deputation appointed by your Board to examine and report as to the sanitary conditions of the Hamlet of Hillcommon in the Parish of Hillfarance having visited and inspected such Hamlet thoroughly, do hereby report that the drainage is insufficient, grievous and most undoubtedly injurious to health.

We are of opinion that an effectual drainage of the Hamlet might be secured at a small cost, as we have had the practical experience of a person on the spot, the particulars of whose calculation we hereafter set forth, in order to shew you the probable cost per rope.*

Having made a House to House inspection we subjoin the list of premises of which we complain.

1. Cottage in the occupation of Edward Long. Offensive smell arising from Privy and Pigstye which are only 10 yards from the Dwellinghouse.
2. Cottage in the occupation of, and owned by John Blake. An open stagnant Drain from Privy. Pigstye close to cottage.
3. Two cottages occupied by Joseph Perrott and James Pugsley. Open drain. Privy with soil exposed, 12 yards from dwelling.
4. Cottage occupied by Ann Hayes. An open Drain with large quantity of filthy matter 5 yards from door of Dwelling. Water from pump sometimes coloured.
5. Two cottages occupied by Charles Cattle and John C. Norman. An open Drain alongside Turnpike Road in front of Dwellings and also one at the rear.
6. Cottage occupied and owned by Samuel Wood. Soil from Pigstye allowed to remain stagnant.
7. Cottage occupied by John Merry. An open Cesspool to Privy adjoining the Dwelling and an open Drain close to road.

[contd]

BATH HOSPITAL.

THE happy effects of the Bath Waters, in relieving various Disorders incident to Mankind, when all other means have proved ineffectual, derive their most ample testimony from the Annals of this Hospital.

The design of this Charity is to enable Poor Persons from distant parts of the UNITED KINGDOM, whose Cases are proper, to obtain the benefit of that Source of Relief which this City affords, and which is not to be found in any other place. The GOVERNORS of this Hospital therefore solicit your Liberality towards the support of so benevolent an Institution.

Patients discharged from MAY 1742, to MAY 1835:

Cured.	Much Better.	Incurable, or No Better.	Improper, or Hectical.	Irregular, or Misbehaviour.	Dead.	Total.
7585	12906	1725	3154	348	589	26307

The PERMANENT Income of the Hospital in Rent and Dividends from Funded Property, is £2097 16 0

Annual Subscriptions last Year 505 0 0

£2602 16 0

The Expenses last Year of a permanent kind were £3449 18s. 8d.; leaving £847 2s. 8d. to be provided for by Collections at the Churches and other Casual Benefactions.

The great Expenses incurred in the late Repairs and Improvements of the Hospital rendered it necessary to sell out £3000 from the Capital Stock in the Consolidated 3 per Cents.

This Expense, however, the GOVERNORS of the Hospital did not hesitate to incur, being satisfied that Public Liberality will never be wanting where real good is accomplished; and they therefore request attention to the following Statement, as the surest test of the efficiency of the measures which have been adopted for rendering this noble Institution as extensively beneficial as possible.

	Patients admitted.		Cured.		Much Better.
Average of Seven Years, antecedent to the late Improvements	329	..	88	..	186
1832. Since the Improvements	449	..	141	..	215
1833. Ditto	452	..	156	..	188
1834. Ditto	449	..	157	..	216
1835. Ditto	511	..	191	..	210

N. B. *The favour of Old Linen will be esteemed an acceptable present, it being much wanted.*

MARY MEYLER, PRINTER, ABBEY CHURCH-YARD, BATH.

Bath Hospital. Summary of the number of patients discharged from May 1742 to May 1835, with details of the cost of running the hospital.

8. Three Cottages occupied by James Hayes (owner), Aaron Hayes and John Chorley. Pigstye and Privy too near the Dwellings.
9. Cottage occupied by James Seaman. Same as No.8.
10. Cottage occupied by James Harris. Stagnant open Cesspool too near Dwellings.
11. Four Cottages occupied by James Waygood, John Slocombe, Wm Hemborrow [sic] and one void. Stagnant open Drain with Privy too near Dwelling.
12. Two Cottages occupied by James Waygood, John Slocombe, Wm Hemburrow [sic], with Pigstyes and Privy too near adjoining premises.

Estimated cost of Labor and Materials per rope*
6 in. piping	1s 10d per rope*
Labour	1s 0
Haulage	5
	3 – 3

Your Committee recommend that under any circumstances the Privies and Pigstyes must be removed before any drainage could be made effectual, the removal of those Privies and Pigstyes to some suitable position be enforced, and covered cesspools used, as by so doing it might obviate further expense of a more extensive system of drainage.

J. King Eagles
J.G. Davis
Wm Bussell

Resolved that the necessary Notices be served upon the Owners of the above mentioned property to abate the Nuisances complained of.

* A rope was a measure used in husbandry for draining or hedging. It was 20ft in length. In walling, a rope was 20ft long by 1ft high. (From *West Somerset Word Book* by Frederick Thomas Elworthy, English Dialect Society, 1875–86)

TNA ref. MH 12/4015 Clifton Union, Bristol
[Request for a steam engine to pump water.]

Clifton Poor Law Union
9th September 1870

My Lords & Gentlemen,

I am directed by the Board of Guardians to ask your permission to their purchasing a Steam Engine required for the purpose of pumping water for the use of the Workhouse & for working the deodorising apparatus, the total expenditure not to exceed £100. The present Engine which has been in use for very many years is completely worn out & in fact was never fit or intended for the work it is now doing. The Guardians will feel obliged if you can conveniently favour them with an answer by next Friday & dispense with their being obliged to comply with the requirement of Art.45 in this case the matter requiring immediate attention.

I am Your Most Obedient Servant,
C.H. Hunt

To The Poor Law Board
Whitehall
London

TNA ref. MH 12/8989 Berwick Union, Northumberland
[Letter highlighting the disgraceful state of water closets, etc.]

Sandgate
Berwick upon Tweed 4th May 1874

To the Urban Sanitary Authority

Gentlemen,

In this my second report I must commence by referring you to many things in my previous one and request that the Authority will come to some determination as to what is to be done, and then to take action thereupon most of the matters that I brought under your notice remain much in the same condition as then, and as Summer is now fast approaching decomposition will go on more rapidly, more noxious exhalations will be given off to the great detriment to health. At present I may congratulate you on the general health in the district under your Authority.

I feel compelled to again bring under your notice the disgraceful state of the Water Closets in various parts and in places where it would be least suspected but in most of these places it arises from the intermittent nature of the Water Supply and this might become the mode of circulating a very large amount of diseases; when the Water is out of the pipes a Vacuum is formed so that whenever the handle of the closet is pulled up an opportunity is afforded for polluted air and Water and in many cases excremental pollution rushing into the pipes to fill the Vacuum and if perchance there should be in the pan any faeces from patients labouring under Cholera Enteric Fever or diseases of a similar nature there could be no more certain method of propagating these diseases to an alarming extent.

To remedy this at once demands the prompt attention of the Authority other closets such as Earth Closets or such like should be constructed in some localities or the pipe supplying the Water Closets should be disconnected from the service pipe of the house which comes always direct from the Main, and Cisterns should be attached to all closets. Where water is used, Gas in the Water pipes is another evil complained of in many houses in the town. It is the practice to turn on the Water tap in the morning (before the Water is turned on) then to apply a light to it and so burn out the gas from the pipe this aught not to exist and it also demands prompt attention.

Sewer Gas. Complaints from this cause are very numerous and some measures require to be adopted to prevent the escape of Sewer Air into houses. I am supported by all Sanitary Authorities when I state that such foul air rushing into houses is one of the most fertile Sources for producing disease and some go further and say that Enteric or Typhoid fever is so bred. In my opinion the more perfectly the drains are trapped it is so much the worse as the foul air which is generated there and bottled up as it were being of such an insidious nature that it will and must escape somewhere so that whenever a house valve is opened or wherever the slightest deficiency exists in any of them there it will enter.

I therefore repeat that I consider this cause is to be remedied or modified to a large extent by the thorough ventilation of the sewers. This is a matter of the utmost importance and in my opinion it would best be done by the introduction of the down spouts from the spouted houses into the drains or otherwise by means of ventilating pipes placed in proper situations care being taken that the exit of the foul air is made to avoid the upper windows of the houses where they are attached this would afford a constant exit for these obnoxious accumulations.

Sanitary matters requiring attention

Water supply to be kept free from contamination.

Drainage and Sewage require careful attention.

Sanitary Conditions of Streets, Courts and Back Yards requiring a larger amount of surface Cleanliness.

With the Inspector during the quarter I have visited the Slaughter Houses, Backhouses and Common Lodging Houses and found all of them in a very fair condition not having occasion to report any of them.

Tweedmouth and Spittal have also been carefully inspected and things there are generally in a better state of Cleanliness, if I except the gutters or channels in Tweedmouth in the main street leading from the Bridge to the High Toll Gate and I find that the rakings of the Streets in both places are allowed to remain for too long a period before they are carted away.

Deaths during the Quarter 82 – arranged as follows:

Brain	10	Croup	4
Heart	8	Abdomen	2
Chest	18	Diarrhoea	2
Phthisis	8	Diphtheria	2
Marasmus	3	Delirium Tremens	1
Fever	6	Hooping Cough	2
Necrocis	1	Suicide	1
Childbirth	1	Old Age & Dibility	13

69 coresponding [sic] number same quarter last year.
Number of Births during the quarter
93 Births   44 Boys, 49 Girls
                     1 Boy, 4 Girls Illigitimate [sic]

98 Coresponding [sic] number same quarter last year.

I[n] conclusion I may mention that the fever I alluded to as prevailing in my last report has considerably abated and as I stated at the time it was not of a virulent type as only 6 deaths from that cause have been registered during the quarter.

I have the honor to remain

Gentlemen

Yours Truly

Robert Carr Fluker

Med. Officer of Health

TNA ref. MH 12/10229 Article in *The Local Government Chronicle*, 9 August 1884
[A lady keeping a large number of cats and dogs in her house is causing an offensive smell.]

The Countess and Her Cats

At the July quarter sessions of the peace for the hearing of appeals against the convictions on orders made by metropolitan police-court magistrates, at the Guildhall, Broad Sanctuary, the Dowager Countess Mary de la Torre, who carried a large bundle of legal papers, appealed against a decision of the justices of the Kensington Division, dated 3rd June, 1884, whereby she was ordered to discontinue keeping thirty-three cats and dogs, and other animals. Mr Poland and Mr Burnie appeared for the respondent justices; Mr Kisch appeared for the Countess. Mr Poland said the order against the appellant had been made by two justices of the county under the Nuisances Removal Act. The appellant had not been convicted and fined. The neighbours had for a long time past been suffering from the most intolerable nuisance, formerly at the house adjoining (no. 38), and latterly at the present house. It was of such an abominable nature that the inhabitants of the neighbourhood wished it at once put an end to, and an order made by the justices maintained. Every indulgence had been given to this lady, who formerly occupied the house next door (No. 39), where a similar nuisance took place. On June 14th, Mr Sheil, the police magistrate, made an order against the appellant to stop the nuisance; but she evaded it by removing next door, where of course, the order made in respect of No. 39 ceased to be operative, and fresh proceedings were obliged to be taken against her. The inhabitants hoped then that after that warning this lady would cease to annoy them for the future. She was cautioned and warned over and over again, but she still persisted in this nuisance. Inspector Whitefoot stated that he visited the appellant's house, but before he got near it he noticed a most abominable stench. On visiting the premises he found in the front kitchen three puppies, in the back kitchen six cats, on the first floor eleven cats, one or two on the stairs, and some fowls in a room at the top of the house; and several witnesses having been called as to the serious character of the nuisance, the appellant was then cross-examined. She said her husband was the Count de la Torre, and was a Minister at Rome. She was a great student of natural history, and could pass an examination as a doctor, but her father was opposed to it. She had taken an interest in cats all her life, from feelings of humanity, and because she was writing a book on natural history. Her object was to find homes for cats. People brought stray cats to her, and she had placed seventy-seven cats in different houses in less than nine months. She looked upon it as a labour of love and an act of mercy to rescue stray cats. She provided bamboo chairs in the drawing-room for some of the cats when they had kittens, and that she called the 'nursery.' By the Court: She had several very valuable cats worth £100 each, and had taken several prizes. She had two Manx cats which were considered perfect. She had been annoyed by boys throwing stones at her house and breaking her windows. After some further evidence Mr Kisch addressed the Bench and said that his client had shown a great deal of sincerity in her care of cats, which she looked upon as a Christian duty, and pointed out discrepancies in the evidence as to the number of the cats and the degree of offence caused by their being kept by her. The Assistant-Judge, in giving the decision of the Bench, said they entertained no doubt about keeping so large a number of animals being a nuisance injurious to health, and as the appellant seemed obstinately bent on resisting the order of the magistrates, it would be the duty of the local authority to enforce forthwith in the most effectual manner. The order was confirmed, with costs.

TNA ref. MH 12/15840 Cardigan Union, Cardiganshire and Pembrokeshire, Wales
[A dilapidated building.]

St. Dogmaels Vicarage
Cardigan S.W.
Nov 27. 1886

Dear Sir,

Kindly permit me to ask what is the best course for me and the Churchwardens to adopt under the following circumstances.

Previous to the year 1849, the Vestry meetings of this parish were held in the gallery of the parish Church, but about the middle of 1849 the old building being in a very dilapidated state was pulled down, and a new Church treble its size (will seat 540) erected instead at the cost of £2,760, not by a Church Rate but by voluntary contributions.

From the year 1849 to 1862 the parish vestries were held in an old Chapel in the centre of the village, and from 1862 to this day they have been held in a private house called 'Angel Inn' (a shop) but as we have only one room at our disposal we find it rather small (11 feet by 10).

Such being the case, it has occurred to one or two of my parishioners that there is no place so convenient and roomy as the Nave and Chancel of my Church. The Vestry proper is only 7 feet by 6 with heavy furniture for keeping the vestments &c, so that no more than four or five persons can even stand in it.

But the Churchwardens and myself have declined to grant their demand as our Church going people feel very strongly upon the point. Besides there is no need of leaving our present room as the shopkeeper is prepared to remove the partition and add another room to the one which we have already, at the annual rent of one pound, the two rooms converted into one will be large enough for all practical purposes. But the question we wish to decide is, will the Vestry be legal if held in a private house i.e. where it has been held for the last 24 years? And further is it essential to validity of a Vestry Meeting that it should be held in a Church?

Your kind reply will be deemed a favour
Believe me yours faithfully
Thos Jones

The Secretary
Local Government Board

***

[Answer] Say that if the Vestry Act was put in force in the parish & the consent of the Board obtained to the provision of the room referred to as the Vestry Room for the parish, Vestry Meetings could legally be convened to be held therein.

Add that if an appl[n] be made to the Board, with the consent of the Vestry, to put the Act in force & for the Board's consent to the provision of a room for use as a Vestry Room, they will be prepared to consider it.

Add usual instructions (Draft to me) 29 Nov 86

The Meeting for obtaining the consent of the Vestry to the Appl[n] could be convened to be held in the Vestry of the Church & the meeting once commenced therein could at once be adjourned to a more convenient place. 30 Nov 86

TNA ref. MH 12/10231 Bedminster Union, Somerset
[Report on the number of deaths.]

Report for the Urban Sanitary District of Clevedon for the year 1887.

The Medical Officer of the Clevedon Urban Sanitary District respectfully begs to apologize for the late return of his Annual Report, the delay has been occasioned by ill health.

The accompanying forms A & B have been compiled according to the instructions and as every care has been taken to collect the material from the various sources indicated it is hoped that they will be found correct.

The total number of deaths registered is considerably below the average, the number is 69, as against 87 for 1886 it is to be noted that of the 69 deaths, the large proportion of 27 occurred over the age of 60, this fact may be taken as an indication of the longevity of the inhabitants.

Table B will show that an outbreak of Scarlatina occurred during the year. This outbreak commenced at the end of January and was of an alarming nature it was marked by two important points.

1st   The Definite History of the origin of the Infection.

2nd   The rapid suppression following proper means of Isolation.

The History of the origin is as follows. About the middle of January the juvenile members of a local church choir were taken into Bristol to see the Pantomime. About six days after the treat, a boy who had been with the party had a mild attack of Scarlatina. Taking into consideration the period between the visit and the appearance of the illness and the fact of the prevalence of Scarlatina in Bristol at the time, there can be little doubt that this boy caught the infliction in Bristol. The lad's illness was of so slight a nature that no medical assistance was called in and after being confined to the house for a few days he returned to his duties as a choir-boy and also attended school with the result that in a few days several cases occurred amongst the choir boys and school children and this outbreak led to the discovery that this boy had been ill and on examination his skin was found in a state of desquamation. From the nature of the outbreak the Medical Officer of Health anticipated a rapid spread of the disease. A special meeting of the Sanitary Authority was at once summoned and in the absence of any right accommodation for cases of infectious disease the Committee of the Provident Dispensary gave up their building for temporary use as a Fever Hospital with the fortunate result of the outbreak being rapidly checked. The day after the means of isolation was provided three fresh cases occurred in three new and different centres being all poor and crowded parts of the town, these cases were at once removed to the temporary Hospital and no fresh cases occurred in either of the districts from which they were taken. It is much to be regretted that notwithstanding this striking proof of the prompt isolation there should be strong opposition on the part of some members of the Sanitary Authority to a scheme for the establishment of a permanent Fever Hospital of sufficient size to meet the requirement of the district. A scheme which the Medical Officer has used every means in his power to advance hitherto with definite success.

The rather high number of cases of diarrhoea seen in Table B, occurred during the hot months and were most probably due to the long continued drought and heat and to the unusual abundance & cheapness of stone-fruit.

Of the 3 cases of enteric fever, one owed origin to the drinking of contaminated water from a well whilst on a visit to a country house near Devizes. Another case occurred in a lodging house and was due to serious sanitary defects which were at once remedied, the 3rd case was admitted to the Cottage Hospital from a small old-fashioned & damp cottage and was caused by inhaling sewer gas from an untrapped drain. This cottage is unfit for habitation and is about to be pulled down. During the past year the Inspector of Nuisances has been engaged upon a house-to-house inspection which has led to very valuable results, he reports that people generally, especially the lodging house keepers, are becoming more alive to the sanitary state of these houses and are gradually substituting modern sanitary appliances in place of old-fashioned and defective ones as a proof of this statement. It may be mentioned that within the 3 last months of the year 50 houses were supplied with washout pan closets with a 2 gallon flush tank each.

The sewers have been frequently examined and regularly flushed both by the Automatic tanks and the river. Several improvements have been made in the drainage system.

The slaughter houses have been regularly inspected. During the coming year several improvements will be made and increased accommodation is to be provided.

Amongst the chief sanitary work of the year ranks the Inspection of the Dairies, Cow sheds & Milk Shops, necessary improvements & alterations have been carried out and all the premises in this district are now in satisfactory order.

Notwithstanding the long continued drought the water supply of Clevedon has remained throughout the year plentiful and of excellent quality on account of the rapid increase of houses & population the water Company have recently increased their plant in order to meet the extra demand.

George Price Pizly

Medical Officer of Health

Clevedon

Somerset

May 9th 1888

Mr Longe

12th June 88

TNA ref. MH 12/10509 Wellington Union, Somerset and Devon

[Undated petition regarding the keeping of pigs near houses. Received by the Local Government Board, 9 December 1889.]

To The Local Government Board and the Wellington (Somerset) Local Board

We the undersigned Farmers, Pigdealers and Residents of the Parish of Wellington, Somerset would respectfully call the attention of your Boards to the following objections to the proposed Bye Law No.2 of the Wellington (Somerset) Local Board.

1. Such Bye Law would prohibit the keeping of more than four pigs within 150 feet of any dwelling house without any reference whatever either to the position and surrounding circumstances of the premises or to the drainage or sanitary condition thereof.
2. That pigs are and it has been proved by experience can be kept within such distance without causing any nuisance or annoyance to the neighbouring occupiers.

3. That the Board has already full powers of dealing with all cases in which a nuisance is caused and by the existing Bye Laws the keeping of pigs within 60 feet of any dwelling house is totally prohibited.

4. That the proposed Bye Law would press most injuriously and unfairly upon persons now keeping more than four pigs within such a distance of 150 feet. Such persons would if the proposed Bye Law be adopted be compelled to remove at great expenses buildings erected in conformity with plans duly approved by the Local Board and thoroughly drained and maintained in proper sanitary condition to their satisfaction.

5. In the case of Heap v The Burnley Union Rural Sanitary Authority it was held that a Bye Law made by the Defendant Authority who had obtained the powers of an Urban Authority forbidding the keeping of swine within 50 feet of a dwelling house was unreasonable and not enforceable and it is contended that the circumstances to which the proposed Bye Law would apply are practically those of a Rural and not of an Urban District.

6. It is also pointed out that while the proposed Bye Law would, very properly, not prohibit the keeping by 10 adjoining occupiers of pigs within a space very little more than 60 feet from their dwelling houses yet that it would prohibit the keeping of the same number of pigs under exactly the same conditions if it happened that such pigs were owned by one person instead of ten.

Your Petitioners therefore contend that the proposed Bye Law is unnecessary and unreasonable and would pray that the same be not confirmed.

John Bird	Westford House, Wellington	Edward Stradling	Rockwell Green
Samuel Bishop	Ro Green	William Smith	Rockwell Green
Charles Baker		William Baker	Rockwell Green
Thomas Hitchcock	Rockwell Green	Thomas Powell	Rockwell Green
William Always	Rockwell Green	Joseph House	Rockwell Green
Charles Twose	Rockwell Green	G.G. Hartnell	Rockwell Green
William Martin	Rockwell Green	Robert Slade	Rockwell Green
William Milton	Rockwell Green	Edward Wright	Rockwell Green
Edward Milton	Rockwell Green	James Baker, Junr	134 Rockwell Green
Henary [sic] Harding	Rockwell Green	Robert Baker	Higher Westford
William Woodbury	Rockwell Green	Albert Fouracre	Rockwell Green
Daniel Woodbury	Rockwell Green	Charley Shattock	Rockwell Green
William Couch	Rockwell Green	Thomas Cross	Rockwell Green
John Pyne	Rockwell Green	James Parr	Rockwell Green
Allen J. Milton	Rockwell Green	Henry Powell	Rockwell Green
Mark Baker	Rockwell Green	James Bowerman	Rockwell Green
Albert Blackmore	Rockwell Green	Thomas Marks	Rockwell Green

John Coram	Rockwell Green	Edward Stephens	Rockwell Green
William Blackmore	Rockwell Green	Joseph Baker	Rockwell Green
James Curtis	Rockwell Green	John Doel	22, Rockwell Green
James Ackland		William Cutler	Westford
Robert Wright	Rockwell Green	Abner Cutler	Westford
Charles Spiller	Rockwell Green	Joseph Poole	Westford
Racherd [sic] Thorne	Rockwell Green	William Maunder	Westford
Samuel Browing	Rockwell Green	William Hill	Westford
Frank Stradling	Rockwell Green	Edwin Twooze	Westford
Frederick Selwood	Rockwell Green	James Austin	Westford
James Taylor	Lower Westford	W.J. Timewell	Rockwell Green
Richard Ridgway	Westford	Mark Selwood	Westford Cottage
Tom Hutchings	Westford Cottage	Joseph Baker	Pumping Station
James Baker	Rockwell Green	William Hitchcock	Rockwell Green
Charles Baker	160 Rockwell Green	Robt C. Hawkings*	R. Green

[The foregoing list of sixty-four signatures is part of a petition, the total number of signatures being 162.]

    * Related to the author

TNA ref. MH 12/15021 Halifax Union, Yorkshire (West Riding)
[Letter regarding sewage and storm water.]

Sowerby Bridge Local Board of Health

Clerk's Office
Commercial Bank Chambers
Crown Street
Halifax 11th Novr 1891

Dear Sir,

Sewage & Storm Water

    We are obliged by the receipt of your letter of the 10th inst. in reference to the flow of storm water & sewage from the adjoining Districts.

    We shall be glad if you will kindly state what further information you require as we have endeavoured to bring about an arrangement with the adjoining Local Board & they decline to come to any agreement as to dealing with the sewage & storm water but insist on sending them into the Sowerby Bridge Local Board District which lies lower down the valley that the other Districts complained of.

    The matter is becoming very serious & it cannot be to the interests of the respective Districts that the Sowerby Bridge Local Board should stop up all their drains at the extreme boundaries of their districts, and thus prevent the sewage & storm water coming within their district, & thereby create a public nuisance.

If you will say what further information you require we shall be pleased to do what we can to supply the same.

We are Sir

Yours truly

Godfrey Rhodes Evans

The Assistant Secretary

Local Government Board

Whitehall

S.W.

TNA ref. MH 12/16651 Haverfordwest Union, Pembrokeshire, Wales

[Water supply for the parish of Llangwm.]

Llangwn

Report on an inquiry with reference to an application from the Rural District Council of Haverfordwest in the County of Pembrokeshire for the sanction to borrow £210 for works of Water Supply for the Parish of Llangwn.

Haverfordwest

Llangum

16 March 1896

To The Right Honorable Henry Chaplin, MP

The President of the Local Government Board

Sir,

I have the honor to report that I held this Inquiry at the National School, Llangum on Wednesday the 26th of February 1896.

There were present:–

Mr. J. James, (Clerk to the Rural District Council)

Dr. Griffiths, (Medical Officer of Health to the Rural District Council)

Mr. J.F. Francis, (Sanitary Inspector to the Rural District Council)

Mr. Summons, (Surveyor to the Rural District Council)

Mr. Eaton Evans, (Agent for the Hook Estate)

Mr. Allen, (Tennant of Nash Farm)

Mr. Roberts, (Managing Partner Hook Colliery Co.)

Mr. T. Griffiths, (Clerk to the Parish Council, Llangum)

Messrs. Davies, Wm. Childs, (Parochial Councillors, Llangum)

The Revd. D.D. Timothy, (Rector, Llangum)

The Revd. J. Jones, (Independent Minister, Llangum and District Counciller)

Messrs. Bryant, Wm. Morgan, R. John, T. Davies, Wm. John, Wm. Evans, Reed, Jas. Edwards, Jas. Jones, D. Davies, Geo. John Palmer, R. Jones, Robt. Peters, Pawlett, Simlett and others (Parochial Electors).

The Clerk proved the posting of the notice.

The returns of the contributory place are:–

410

Population of the whole Parish	946
Population to be supplied with water when the proposed works are completed	314
No. of houses to be supplied with water	79
Annual Assessable Value of the whole Parish	£2006
Outstanding loans	Nil

The application was opposed by the Parish Council. They were represented by their Clerk Mr Griffiths. The aim of the opposition will be dealt with at the latter end of this Report.

The resolution, to apply to the Local Government Board for sanction to borrow £210, was passed by the Rural District Council of Haverfordwest on the 11th of December 1896. A copy will be found on the file with 153208/95.

HISTORY AND GENERAL EXPLANATION

This application to supply so much of the village of Hook, in the Parish of Llangum, as has not already a water supply.

The village, the inhabitants of which consist principally of miners and their families, is situated on the anthracite coal formation and on the west side of the tidal reach of the river Cleddaw, about 5 miles south of Haverfordwest.

Part of the village has already been supplied with water by a standpipe at the point A plan No.1 about 200 yards South of West Hook.

The supply was brought in 1890 to this point from a source at Pitt Stone by means of a 2" wrought iron galvanized pipe. At the same time a force pump was fixed at the source at Pitt Stone and a 1½" rising main laid to supply North Nash Farm. At North Nash Farm a cistern containing 900 gallons was erected.

The total cost of the work to bring the water to the stand pipe at A plan No.1 and to North Nash Farm, amounted to about £210. Towards this expense the late Mr. Harcourt Powell, the then owner of the Surface on the North and North East of Nash Lake and of Hook Colliery, contributed £125, leaving a balance of £85 to be paid by the Authority.

The source supply at Pitt Stone and the land on the South and South West of Nash Lake is the property of Mr J.F. Lort-Phillips.

A grant in fee of the right to take water from the spring and well at Pitt Stone, and also the right to lay down pipes, to construct a reservoir and to execute other works, were given to the Rural Sanitary Authority on the 22nd August 1887.

The ground on the North and North East of Nash Lake, formerly the property of the late Mr Harcourt Powell, is now the property of his trustees.

Most of the people in the village of Hook, except those at a great distance, at present fetch the water for drinking purposes, from the standpost A. The most distant dwellings in the village from the standpost at A plan No.1 are East Hook Farm, 2248 yards and Middle Hook 1313 yards.

Some years ago, before the water was in 1888, laid on to the standpost at A, fever was very prevalent in the village of Hook. Since that date, (1888), very few cases have occurred and none in the immediate vicinity of the standpost A. In the more distant parts of Hook, especially at and near to east Hook Farm, fever has been and is prevalent. The Medical Officer attributes this fever to the bad supply of water in that part of the district, which supply is taken from dip wells.

At East Hook Farm the well is situated about 50 feet from the Farm Yard and at a lower level and there is no doubt but that the well is contaminated. The water from this well has been analysed and condemned by the County analyst for Pembrokeshire.

The Medical Officer believes the supply of water to cows, whose milk is used for dairy purposes, is polluted.

In a spot about ¼ mile from East Hook, there was at the time of the Inquiry, a case of enteric fever. I examined the water supply to this house and found it was a dip well taking surface drainage. The Medical Officer considers the well the cause of the trouble.

The Medical Officer said the Death Rate was low and the Parish was generally healthy.

THE PROJECT

It is proposed to extend the present water supply by laying galvanized wrought iron pipes 1½" in diameter from the existing standpost at A to the point B.

A cross piece will be inserted in the main at B and a ¾" pipe laid eastward to C where a standpost will be erected to supply the neighbourhood of East Hook; a ¾" pipe northward to D where a standpost will be erected to supply the neighbourhood in the North part of the district; and another ¾" pipe Southward to E where a standpost will be erected to supply the neighbourhood of Middle Hook. (see plan No.1)

The source of supply will be [the] same as heretofore, viz: that at Pitt Stone.

The Medical Officer stated that the water from this source at Pitt Stone is good, as proved by analysis and experience.

On October 4th 1895 the Surveyor gauged the spring at Pitt Stone and found the discharge was 1200 gallons per hour. The spring rises from a trap dyke about ¼ mile broad which divides the coal measures from the old red Sandstone. [Inserted later]: – 'Since this report was written the Surveyor has sent me a geological section which I have put with the file. He has also sent two 25" Ordnance Maps.'

The Section (Plan No.2) commences at the existing standpost A, so it is well to mention that the source of supply, at Pitt Stone, is 2825 feet above the top of the brickwork of the fountain at A or at a reduced level of 178.25. This level and the levels on the section have not been reduced to Ordnance Datum.

The trustees of the late Mr Harcourt Powell are practically the owners of the whole of the estate which will be benefited by the scheme. It will be seen in referring to the plan (Plan No.1) that the pipes for the proposed extension will be laid across the private property of the trustees for the whole distance. Neither the trustees nor tenants will charge anything for compensation as the property of the trustees will improve by the scheme and land being generally poor will not be damaged to any extent.

The trustees have not given but will give an agreement to allow the pipes to be carried across their property without charge. Mr Eaton Evans (the Solicitor and agent for the trustees) said he thought the agreement might give permission in perpetuity; but he could not say anything off-hand.

Mr Roberts (the managing partner of Hook Colliery and the tenant of East Hook Farm) stated at the Inquiry that he had no objection to the pipe going through his land. He considered the supply was necessary. He pays on a rateable value of £540.

The present and future supply are shown in the subjoined table.

	Houses	Population
Supplied already from present standpost at A	37	137
To be supplied from extension pipes	42	177
Totals	79	314

OPPOSITION

The Parish is divided naturally into two parts by Nash Lake. That part of the Parish on the South Side has a rateable value of £1187

That part of the Parish on the North side has a rateable value of 817

Total £2004

It is the part of the Parish on the North side of Nash Lake which is now in want of water. Mr Lort Phillips, the owner of the land on the South side of Nash Lake has already supplied the majority of his tenants with water. These tenants of Mr. Lort Phillips, who are so supplied, object to pay for the supply of water to the tenants of the trustees of the late Mr Harcourt Powell. The Parish further object to the laying of a special pipe from B to C, a distance of 700 yards, for the supply of one farm and one cottage at East Hook.

Generally it may be stated that there is a considerable feeling of dissatisfaction throughout the Parish, outside the village of Hook, as the people contend the landlord should carry out the work.

Remarks

The whole scheme is so small that it is a mere toy. It is not proposed to take any water into the houses. All water will have to be fetched from the existing standpost at A and the proposed standposts at C, D and E.

The pipes are so small that I believe that if it was attempted to draw water from all the taps at one time it would be impossible to obtain any from the one in the worst situation.

If any extension is to be carried out I am of opinion

1st   That 3" pipes should be substituted for the present 2" pipes between the source and the existing standpost at A.

2nd   That the pipe between the existing standpost at A and the cross at B should be at least 2" in diameter.

3rd   That neither of the branches to C, D, E, from B should be less than 1¾" in diameter.

It would however be better if the 3" pipes were continued to B, and there were no pipes less than 2" in diameter. If the branch pipe to East Hook Farm BC were struck out of the scheme I do not think there would be much opposition. I am inclined to think that this branch should not be struck out, as besides the Farm and the Cottage adjoining the inhabitants of other cottages might find the standpost at East Hook more convenient than D or E. But the route and terminus might be altered.

In any case I consider that sanction should be deferred until the Authority amend the scheme as suggested.

At the same time the Authority should be warned to take great care that the present source does not become polluted as it is situated on the side of a dirty road.

I have the honour to be, Sir,
Your obedient Servant,
G William Willcocks

RECOMMENDATION

That sanction be deferred until the Authority amend the scheme as suggested on page 7 of my report and make some agreement for passing through private land.

At the same time the Board might warn the Authority that the present source is likely to become polluted unless care is taken to keep it pure as it is situated on the side of a dirty road.

G.W. Willcocks
16 March 1896

TNA ref. MH 12/20 Ampthill Union, Bedfordshire

[An article on water divining, 1897. From *The Cheltenham Examiner*, 24 March 1897.]

The following article was printed in a pamphlet and filed with the records of the Local Government Board in 1897.

WATER DIVINING EXPERIENCE

by G.H. Ward-Humpreys, Esq.,
L.R.C.P. Lond., M.R.C.S., F.R.M.S., Cheltenham

The subject of water-divining, or the power supposed to be possessed by the hazel twig in indicating the presence of water near at hand, is not only of scientific interest but of great commercial importance. So far as can be seen, it is likely to continue to be of scientific interest, in that up to the present, no one has been able to suggest even a plausible explanation of the causes which indulge the twig to move, as it undoubtedly does, in the hands of some persons, when carried over running water hidden from the sight. That it is of commercial value is now thoroughly established; and in the current number of *Pearson's Magazine* there is an account of recent experiments, and also photographs of seven professors of the art, who find sufficient demand for their services to provide them with an ample means of livelihood.

I had been greatly interested in the experiment at Hatherley, and this interest was further stimulated by the article in *Pearson's*. It was with singular pleasure, therefore, that I found myself about a week ago staying at a large country house, where I met Mr

Gataker, one of the best known of water-diviners. It was evening when we first met, and at the dinner-table conversation naturally turned to the subject of divining. Various theories were propounded, and nearly everybody had suggestions and explanations to offer, except the professor himself. One could not help being struck with the candour with which Mr Gataker spoke of his powers. He was unable to explain them, nor was he able very clearly to describe the sensations which had for five or six years led him successfully to diagnose the presence of springs in almost every part of the country. His visit here was an evidence of the accuracy of his divinations, for the year previously he had succeeded in finding several springs which had enabled our host to construct a series of lakes in his park, one being of considerable size. There seemed no doubt about it – but for myself, the spirit of Thomas Didymus was strong within me.

Early the next morning we sallied forth, I taking care to arm myself with what I thought would be an impenetrable cuirass of scepticism. I confess that I listened with something like amusement to the simple and business-like statements of the expert, who appeared to be certain of finding water, if water there was, as ever was a huntsman of finding a fox when about to try some noted covert.

But the reader may ask, if water had already been found in such abundance, where was the necessity for further prospecting? The fact was that the lakes had grown to a size which made our host anxious that other supplementary springs should be discovered, lest in a hot summer the lakes should become dry or appreciably diminished in area. A brisk walk of about twenty minutes brought us to the large piece of water, on the far side of which there was a hill rising with a gentle slope to about 150 feet. Part of this was covered with shrubs and saplings, and in a slight depression on one side the hazel and blackthorn grew luxuriantly. The night before, Mr. Gataker had expressed the belief that I was likely to possess the power of divination; and he was now very anxious for me to try my luck at once. He cut several twigs and armed me with one, and then, taking me down to the side of the lake where water already was pouring in, he suggested I should walk across the covered-in stream. This I did, three or four times in succession, holding the twig, but I was conscious of nothing, nor did I see any movement of the twig. He then, however, laid his hands upon the back of mine, and he walking backwards in front of me, we together crossed over the flowing water. Immediately the V-shaped twig turned completely round in my grip. Perhaps it is unnecessary to say anything about the astonishment with which I regarded this extraordinary movement of the inanimate twig. But what happened afterwards was even more remarkable, for, on going round to unbroken ground upon the other side of the lake, at one spot I felt the twig, which I was carrying with its point downwards, so turn in my hand that the point was raised through an angle of 90 degrees. Enquiries elicited the fact that this spot was exactly over a stream which had been found twelve months ago. But even now I was not convinced, though I could not believe that the others were deceiving me, I thought it possible that I might be deceiving myself. So I suggested that I might be blindfolded, led some distance from the spot where I was then standing, and then should be guided in such a direction that I must cross the line of the same stream. This was done and I started my walk at a distance which I afterwards found to be about 65 yards away. Walking then in the direction I have indicated, I suddenly became aware that the twig was commencing to move. This tendency became stronger at every step. I cast to the right and to the left, and finally guided by the stronger movement of the twig, walked some fifteen yards to the left of my original path and then stopped, the twig having now moved through an angle of 180 degrees. My companions, who had hitherto been silent, were greatly amused as the sceptic, who found, when able to see, that he had stopped about three feet away from a peg which had been put in to mark the site of one of Mr. Gataker's springs. After this scepticism vanished.

So much then, for my own experience. What followed was an answer to the question, as to whether this power is latent in the twig or inherent in the agent who carries it. Mr Gataker proceeded to prospect himself, evidently concentrating his attention by definite effort upon the work to be done. Spreading out his hands rigidly in front of him and about three feet from the surface of the ground, he walked first in one direction and then in another, till, suddenly running quickly and then stopping, he declared that water would be found underneath. In answer to the question, how deep it would be, he replied, 'About eighteen feet'. He acted similarly in two other places, and although steps could not immediately be taken to confirm his statements, our host's experience led him to fully accept their accuracy. Indeed, it would have been difficult not to have done so, with the lakes right in front of one, owing their existence to the correctness of the divination of the year before.

On the homeward journey, or course, both professor and pupil had much to say on what was to the latter a newly-found power. The question rose uppermost was that to which allusion has been made; namely, is the twig the author of the movement, or merely the indicator or needle, as it were, which acted upon by some nervous force from the holder, is but the interpreter of this power? Mr Gataker certainly took this view, and the fact that, by long training and practice, he had developed the faculty of interpreting for himself the sensation which the presence of water caused him to feel, necessarily controlled his opinion on the subject. In illustration of the 'indicator' theory, the needle of the old-fashioned telegraph instrument may be taken as an example. Unconnected as it is with the coils of wire behind, the needle moves either to the right or left in response to the impulses communicated to it by the current passing one way or the other through the coil. The twig, it would appear, acts very much in the same way. And it is worthy of notice that the material of which the divining rod is made does not seem to affect the success of the experiment. The twigs on this occasion were indifferently blackthorn or hazel, and in *Pearson's* a photograph is given of a similarly used rod, made of aluminium. Probably a considerable number of people possess the faculty, but like all others, it can be developed and increased by practice. Indeed the mere possession of the power would be of comparatively little value, when put in competition with an expert. Merely to indicate that water exists underneath the ground upon which one stands, is a very different thing from being able to say, as Mr Gataker undoubtedly can, that at so-or-so many feet below the surface will be found a stream or spring yielding so-or-so many gallons of water per minute; and it is of course, this development of the power, which is of the special commercial utility. I need not attempt to cover all the points of the subject, so well set forth in the magazine article. One aspect however, remains to be noticed. It was explained by Mr Gataker that concentration of purpose was essential to success. He would not be conscious of these impulses, although in all probability they would still exist, if, for instance, he were merely taking a country walk, with his thoughts upon other matters, just as a man walking through a grove, if intent upon some absorbing theme, would be oblivious to the warbling even of a nightingale.

TNA ref. MH 12/16650 Haverfordwest Union, Pembrokeshire, Wales
[An analysis of water.]

Dr Frankland's Report   Water Analysis Laboratory

The Yews
Reigate
June 15th 1895

Dear Sir,

Herewith I enclose results of an analysis of a sample of water collected on the 30th ult and sent by you for examination on behalf of the Haverfordwest Urban Sanitary Authority.

This water possesses an extremely high degree of organic purity and is in every respect of most excellent quality for dietetic and all domestic purposes. It is one of the very best waters that I have ever examined.

The water is very soft and therefore well adapted for washing and for steam purposes,

I am
Yours very truly
E. Frankland

Charles Brigstocke, Esq.
Medical Officer of Health

I certify the above to be a true copy of the original.

H Davies
Town Clerk
Haverfordwest
27 Feb[y] 1896

CHAPTER 21

OFFICIAL REPORTS

At the formation of the Poor Law Commission in 1834 and the Poor Law Board in 1846, annual reports were published at the end of each year by these organisations. These reports include much detail about the setting up and running of the Unions, and rules and regulations appear from time to time. The duties of Union officers and workhouse employees are detailed. There are many reports from visiting Union inspectors and within these reports there are often references to named paupers and other persons.

The following are some examples from these reports:

The First Annual Report of the Poor Law Commission, 1835

Orders and Regulations issued by the Poor Law Commission for England and Wales, *for the Guidance and Government of the Boards of Guardians of Unions.*

Windsor Union
To all to whom these presents shall come. We, the Poor Law Commissioners for England and Wales, send Greeting.

Whereas, in pursuance of the powers given to us in and by an Act passed in the fourth and fifth years of the reign of His present Majesty King William the Fourth, intitled, 'An Act for the Amendment and better Administration of the Laws relating to the Poor in England and Wales,' We, the Poor Law Commissioners for England and Wales, appointed under the said Act, did, by an order under our hands and seal, bearing date [blank] day of this instant August, order and declare that the parishes and places named in the margin of the said order, which are situated in the counties of Berks and Surrey, being the same which are now named in the margin at the front of this page*, should, on the seventh day of September next, be, and thenceforth, should remain united for the administration of the laws for the relief of the poor; and further, that on the eighth day of September next, and in the manner therein mentioned, the said parishes and places should respectively elect a guardian or guardians for the said Union.

And whereas by the said Act it is provided, that the Poor Law Commissioners shall prescribe the duties of guardians, and shall also, as and when they shall see fit, direct the guardians of any Union to appoint such paid officers, with such qualifications as the said Commissioners shall think necessary, for the superintending or assisting in the administration of the relief and employment of the poor, either within or out of a workhouse, and for examining and auditing, allowing or disallowing of accounts in such Union, and otherwise carrying the provisions of the said Act into execution. And the said Commissioners are thereby empowered to define and specify and direct the execution of the respective duties, and determine the continuance in office or dismissal of such paid officers, and the amount and nature of the security to be given by, and regulate the amount of salaries payable to such officers respectively, and the time and mode of payment thereof.

* New Windsor with Dedworth, Old Windsor, Clewer, Sunninghill, all in the county of Berks; Egham, Thorpe, both in the county of Surrey

There then follows in great detail the method of recording the minutes of the weekly meetings of the Board of Guardians, the appointments of clerk, treasurer and relieving officers. The duties of the clerk and relieving officers are given together with the duties of churchwardens and overseers of the poor.

Admission of Paupers to the Workhouse

I   Paupers are to be admitted into the workhouse in any one of the following modes, and in no other; viz:–
By an order of the Board of Guardians, signified in writing by their clerk.
By a provisional order in writing, signed by an overseer, churchwarden or relieving officer.
By the master of the workhouse, without any such order, in case of any sudden or urgent necessity.

II   No pauper shall be admitted under any written order as above mentioned, if the same bear date more than six days before the pauper presents it, and claims to be admitted.

III   If a pauper be admitted by the provisional order of an overseer, churchwarden or relieving officer, or by the master of the workhouse, in a case of sudden and urgent necessity, the admission of such pauper shall be brought before the Board of Guardians at their next weekly meeting, who shall decide on the propriety of the pauper's continuing in the workhouse or otherwise, and order accordingly.

IV   As soon as a pauper is admitted, he or she shall be placed in the probationary ward, and shall there remain until examined by the medical officer of the workhouse.

V   If the medical officer, upon such examination, pronounces the pauper to be labouring under any disease of body or mind, the pauper shall be placed either in the sick ward, or the ward for lunatics and idiots not dangerous, as the medical officer shall direct.

Names.	Office.	Salary per Annum.
		£. s. d.
Rev. H. C. Brice	Chaplain	70 0 0
Josias Downing	Master	250 0 0
Elizabeth Duncan	Matron	80 10 0
John Brady	Apothecary	210 0 0
Charles Morgan	House-steward	150 0 0
John Hemmons	Visitor and inspector of the out-poor	150 0 0
John & Elizabeth Cotsell	Steward and matron of the Stapleton Asylum	85 0 0
Thomas South	Clerk in the counting-house	100 0 0
James Moody	Do.	78 0 0
William Powell	Do.	39 0 0
Stephen Thos. Crocker	Clerk in the Tax-office	100 0 0
William Merrick	Do.	78 0 0
John Pritchard	Do.	62 8 0
William Dwelly	Officer	78 0 0
George W. Clark	Dispenser	52 0 0
		1,582 18 0

Names.	Office.	Wages per Week.
		£. s. d.
James Howell	Constable employed to convey paupers to their places of settlement, &c. &c.	0 14 0
Daniel Sexton	Do.	0 12 0
William Brock	Gate-keepers and porters at St. Peter's Hospital	0 14 0
Thomas Carter		0 14 0
Robert Thomas		0 12 0
John Taylor	Gate-keeper at Stapleton Asylum	0 8 0
Thomas Holloway	Superintendent of the oakum shop	1 5 0
Thomas Davis	Schoolmaster	1 2 0
Elizabeth Williams	Schoolmistress	0 18 0
Elizabeth Piggins	Superintendent of the knitting shop	0 10 0
		7 9 0
		or £387 8s. per annum.

SCHEDULE B.

List of Paid Paupers in St. Peter's Hospital on the 8th day of September, 1842.

Wards.	Names.	Occupation.	Wages per Week.
			£. s. d.
1	Ann Oliver	Nurse	0 0 6
2	Mary Tamplin	Do.	0 1 0
	Mary Moore	Hall servant	0 1 0
	Mary Hall	Cook	0 1 0
	Ann Cotterell	Assistant do	0 0 3
	Sarah Strong	Head washer	0 1 6
	Ann Phillips	Washer	0 1 0
	Mary Kingdown	Do.	0 1 0
	Ann Edwards	Do.	0 0 6
	Bridget Bryan	Do.	0 0 3
	Eliza Hollister	Do.	0 0 6

Wards.	Names.	Occupation.	Wages per Week.
			£. s. d.
3	Mary Chilcott	Nurse	0 1 0
	Ann Brown	Deputy do.	0 0 2
	Mary Barlow	Laundress	0 1 0
	Phœbe Shepstone	Do.	0 0 9
	Eliza Fennel	Do.	0 0 2
Lying-in-Ward	Mary Patrick	Nurse	0 1 6
	Mary Aslop	Deputy do.	0 0 6
	Mary Dudley	Errand woman	0 0 6
Surgery Ward.	Jane Chidzey	Nurse	0 1 0
	Caroline Fisher	Deputy do.	0 0 6
	Mary Cowlisham	Teacher	0 0 6
6	Ann Hopwood	Nurse	0 1 0
	Mary Hussey	Deputy do.	0 0 2
7	Elizabeth Mitchell	Nurse	0 1 0
	Susan Mitchell	Deputy do.	0 0 6
	Elizabeth Nash	Nurse	0 1 0
	Mary Green	Deputy do.	0 0 6
8	Ann Brooke	Nurse	0 1 0
	Sarah Swinson	Deputy do.	0 0 6
	Eliza Aylesbury	Schoolmistress	0 1 0
Medical Ward.	Ann Stafford	Nurse	0 1 0
	Mary-Ann Robins	Deputy do.	0 0 6
11	Elizabeth Adremson	Nurse	0 1 0
	Ann Butcher	Deputy do.	0 0 6
	Ann Rees	Dispensary	0 0 6
Lunatic . 1	Ann Bowden	Nurse	0 1 6
	Mary Parker	Deputy do.	0 0 6
	Mary Coombe	Nurse	0 1 6
Lunatic . 2	Jane Davis	Deputy do.	0 1 0
	Mary Hussey	Nurse	0 1 6
Lunatic . 3	Mary Sarah	Deputy do.	0 1 0
	Joanna Marshall	Nurse	0 1 0
Foul Ward	Mary Bees	Deputy do.	0 0 6
	Hannah Masters	Seamstress, &c.	0 0 6
	Mary Abbott	Mistress of the workshop.	0 1 0
	Ann May	Workshop	0 0 6
	Ann Beale	Do.	0 0 6
	Mary Bennett	Do.	0 0 6
	Sarah Hooper	Do.	0 0 6
	Rhoda Hopkins	Do.	0 0 6
	Mary Holt	Do.	0 0 4
18	Thomas Staddon	Nurse, &c.	0 1 2
Lunatic	George Fowler	Nurse	0 2 6
	Jethro Dawe	Deputy do.	0 1 0
	Robert Liscombe	Deputy do.	0 1 0
23	John Edwards	Nurse	0 1 0
	Maria Jarrott	Deputy do.	0 0 6
	William Blackburn	Porter	0 1 0
	William Corin	Nurse	0 0 3
	John Harding	Ostler	0 1 6
	Henry Hookey	Painter, &c.	0 1 6
24	Enoch Summers	Nurse	0 1 0
	Mary Endicott	Deputy do.	0 0 6
	Richard Barry	Carpenter	0 1 6
	William Arnold	Window cleaner	0 0 9
	Thomas Green	Undertaker	0 2 0
	William Palmer	Brewer's deputy	0 0 6

Three tables from the Poor Law Commissioners' Ninth Annual Report, 1843, listing: A. Paid officers of the Corporation of the Poor, Bristol; B. Paid paupers in St Peter's Hospital, Bristol; C. Paid paupers in the asylum at Stapleton, Bristol.

VI If the medical officer pronounces the pauper to be free from disease, the pauper shall be placed in that part of the workhouse assigned to the class to which he or she may belong, and shall thereafter be treated according to the regulations hereinafter contained.

VII Before removal from the probationary ward the pauper shall be thoroughly cleansed, and shall be clothed in the workhouse dress; and the clothes which he or she wore upon admission shall be purified, and deposited in a place to be appropriated for that purpose, to be restored to the pauper on leaving the workhouse, or else to be used by the pauper as the Board of Guardians shall direct.

VIII   The clothing of the paupers shall be made of such materials as the Board of Guardians shall determine, and shall, so far as possible, be made by the paupers in the workhouse.

Classification of Paupers

IX   The in-door paupers shall be classed as follows
1. Aged or infirm men.
2. Able-bodied men, and youths above 13.
3. Youths and boys above seven years old and under 13.
4. Aged or infirm women.
5. Able-bodied women and girls above 16.
6. Girls above seven years of age and under 16.
7. Children under seven years of age.

X   To each class shall be assigned by the Board of Guardians that apartment or separate building which may be best fitted for the reception of such class, and which shall respectively remain, without communication, unless as is hereinafter provided.

XI   Provided Firstly. If the workhouse shall not be of such capacity and arrangement as to admit all the classes above specified, it shall, so far as it is capable, and as it may thereafter be rendered capable, be applied for the reception of the several classes in the following order:— Firstly for paupers of the second and fifth classes; secondly for paupers of the third, sixth and seventh classes; and lastly for paupers of the first and fourth classes.

Secondly. If for any special reason it shall at any time appear to the majority of the Board of Guardians, to be desirable to suspend the above rule on behalf of any married couple, being paupers of the first or fourth classes the guardians shall be at liberty to agree to a resolution to that effect. Such resolution, and the special reasons for which they deem the suspension of the order to be desirable, shall be duly entered in the minute book and a copy of the same shall be transmitted to the Poor Law Commissioners for their consent and approval without which the said resolution shall be of no effect.

Thirdly. Any paupers of the fifth or sixth class may be taken out of their respective classes and employed as assistants to the nurses in any of the sick wards or in the care of infants, or as assistants in the household work for any of the classes except the second and third classes, and may be so employed, either constantly or occasionally.

Fourthly. Any pauper of the fourth class whom the master may deem fit to perform any of the duties of nurse or of assistant to the matron may be so employed in the wards of the fourth, fifth, sixth or seventh classes; and any pauper of the first class, who may by the master be deemed fit may be placed in the ward of the third class to aid in their management and superintend their behaviour.

Fifthly. The children of the seventh class shall be placed either in a ward by themselves, or in such of the wards appropriated to the female paupers as the Board of Guardians shall direct. The mothers of such children to be permitted to have access to them at all reasonable times. With the foregoing exceptions no pauper of one class shall be allowed to enter the wards or yards appropriated to any other class.

XII   The paupers of the several establishments comprised in the Union shall be employed in any work which may be needed and of which they may be capable, for the use of any or all of the establishments within the Union, or in any other way the Board of Guardians may direct.

Discipline and Diet

XIII   All the paupers in the workhouse, except the sick, aged and infirm, and the young children, shall rise, be set to work, leave off work, and go to bed, at the times mentioned in the accompanying table, Form A [see p. 424], and shall be allowed such intervals for their meals as therein are stated; and these several times shall be notified by ringing a bell, and during the time of meals, silence, order and decorum shall be maintained.

XIV   Half an hour after the bell shall have been rung for rising, the names shall be called over in the several wards provided for the second, third, fifth and sixth classes, when every pauper belonging to the ward must be present to answer his or her name and to be inspected by the master or matron.

XV   No pauper of the second, third, fifth or sixth classes shall be allowed to go or to remain in his or her sleeping room, either in the time hereby allotted for work, or in the intervals allowed for meals, except by permission of the master.

XVI   As regards aged and infirm persons and children, the master and matron of the workhouse shall (subject to the directions of the Board of Guardians) fix such hours of rising and going to bed, and such occupation and employment as may be suitable to their respective ages and conditions.

XVII   The meals for the aged and infirm, the sick and children, shall be provided at such times and in such manner as the Board of Guardians may direct.

XVIII   The boys and girls who are inmates of the workhouse shall for three of the working hours at least, every day, be respectively instructed in reading, writing, and in the principles of the Christian religion; and such other instructions shall be imparted to them as are calculated to train them in the habits of usefulness, industry and virtue.

XIX   The diet of the paupers shall be so regulated as in no case to exceed in quantity and quality of food, the ordinary diet of the able-bodied labourers living within the same district.

XX   No pauper shall be allowed to have or use any wine, beer or other spirituous or fermented liquors, unless by the direction in writing of the medical officer, who may also order for any individual pauper such change of diet as he shall deem necessary; and the master shall report such allowance or changes of diet so made to the next meeting of Guardians, who may sanction, alter or disallow the same at their discretion.

XXI No pauper shall be allowed to work on his own whilst an inmate of the workhouse; the Union which supports him being entitled to the full produce of his labour.

XXII Any pauper may quit the workhouse, upon giving the master three hours previous notice of his wish to do so; but no able-bodied pauper having a family shall quit the house without taking the whole of such family with him or her, unless the Board of Guardians shall otherwise direct; nor shall any pauper, after so quitting the house, be again received into the house, unless in one of the modes prescribed in Rule I for the admission of paupers.

XXIII No person shall be allowed to visit any pauper in the workhouse, except by permission of the master, and subject to such conditions and restrictions as the Board of Guardians may direct; provided that the interview shall always take place in the presence of the master or matron, and in a room separate from the other inmates of the workhouse, unless in case of sickness; provided also that any licensed minister of the religious persuasion of any inmate of such workhouse, at all times in the day, on request of such inmate may visit such workhouse for the purpose of affording religious assistance to such inmate and also at all reasonable times for the purpose of instructing his child or children in the principles of their religion; such religious assistance and such instruction being strictly confined to inmates who are of the religious persuasion of such licensed minister and to the children of such inmates; and not so given as to interfere with the good order and discipline of the other inmates of the establishment.

XXIV No work except the usual household work and cooking, shall be performed by the paupers on Sunday.

XXV Divine service shall be performed every Sunday in the workhouse, at which all the paupers shall attend, except the sick and the young children, and such as are too infirm to do so, and except also those paupers who may object so to attend, on account of their professing religious principles differing from those of the Church of England.

XXVI Any pauper, who shall neglect to observe such of the foregoing rules as are applicable to him or her; Or who shall make any noise when silence is ordered; Or use obscene or profane language; Or by word or deed, insult or revile any other pauper in the workhouse; Or who shall not duly cleanse his or her person; Or neglect or refuse to work; Or pretend sickness; Or who shall wilfully waste or spoil any provisions, or stock, or tools or materials for work; Or wilfully damage any property whatsoever belonging to the Union; Or disobey any of the legal orders of the master or matron or other superintendent; Shall be deemed disorderly, and shall be placed in apartments provided for such offenders or shall be distinguished in dress, and placed upon such diet as the Board of Guardians shall prescribe.

XXVII Any pauper who shall within seven days, repeat one of the offences specified in Rule XXVI or commit a second of the offences specified in Rule XXVI or who shall by word or deed insult or revile the master or matron, or any officer of the Union; Or who shall be guilty of any act of drunkenness or indecency shall be deemed to be refractory and shall be punished by such confinement and alteration of diet as the Board of Guardians shall direct by any regulation for that purpose; but no pauper shall be confined under this rule for any misbehaviour or offence, for a longer period than 24 hours, or for such further space of time as may be necessary in order to have such pauper carried before a justice of the peace, to be dealt with according to law.

Duties of Workhouse Staff

There then follows instructions to visiting committees and a detailed account of the duties of the master, the matron, the chaplain, the schoolmaster and schoolmistress, the medical officer and the porter.

Format of Forms to be used in the Workhouse

The design and format of the various forms to be kept by the workhouse are shown, together with instructions to the clerk and other Union officers on how to record the minutes of meetings.

Detailed reports of the many visiting inspectors of the Unions, and evidences collected from local people, give much detail about local conditions.

(A.)

	Hour of Rising.	Interval for Breakfast.	Time for setting to Work.	Interval for Dinner.	Time for leaving off Work.	Interval for Supper.	Time for going to Bed.
From 25 March to 29 September .	6 o'clock.	From ½ past 6to7.	7 o'clock.	From 12 to 1.	6 o'clock.	6 to 7.	8.
From 29 September to 25 March .	7 o'clock.	From ½ past 7 to8.	8 o'clock.	From 12 to 1.	6 o'clock.	6 to 7.	8.

(B.)

ADMITTED.														DISCHARGED.									
When admitted.	Name.	Age.	Number.	Folio in Pauper Description Book.	Description, Occupation, Trade, or Profession.	Of what Religious Persuasion.	By whose Order Admitted.	Settlement.	General observations.	Numbers admitted.				When discharged.	Name.	Time in the House.		Under what circumstances discharged.	By whose Order.	Observations on Condition at the time of Admission, or on General Character and Behaviour in Workhouse.	Numbers Discharged.			
										Men.	Women.	Boys.	Girls.	Total.			Weeks.	Days.				Men.	Women.	Boys.	Girls.	Total.

A page from the Poor Law Commissioners' First Annual Report, 1835, giving the daily timetable for inmates. It also gives a table showing the type of records to be kept of each inmate.

Bastardy

The following is a small part of a report on the Unions in Buckinghamshire:

Evidence of Mr James Edmonds, overseer of Chalfont St. Peter's Parish Says:- Up to the passing of the present Poor Law Amendment Bill we had in our parish nine bastards born within the last five years; no year passed without one or two coming upon the parish. The new Bill and particularly the bastardy clauses were talked of before it passed. In the last year we have not had one bastard and I have not heard that any of our poor people, single women are pregnant. I attribute the change to the effect of the new Bill which has put a stop to the trade, for it was a perfect trade of bastardy. In point of expense I have no doubt we shall save money by being in the union.

Employment of Paupers

I had one man in my parish; I offered him a place of 9s a week. He refused it and told me he could get as much from the overseers for doing nothing. Since [the formation of] the Union this man has found work in the parish at 10s as a constant man.

Evidence of Mr John Clarke, farmer of Bledlow, Buckinghamshire

The last year, that is the year before the new Act, there were eight eighteen-penny rates amounting altogether to nearly £2000. There was at this time a great surplus of labour and a great number of men, fifty I suppose, doing nothing except lying on the roads. Their general habits were very dissipated, arising from a long system of mismanagement in the weekly pay being given without labour. In fact the relief from the poor-rate was more desirable than independent labour. The men were very insolent and disorderly; we had no control over them. I have known many instances, many have come under my own knowledge, where a labourer has acted ill for the very purpose of getting discharged. He would then come to the overseer and say he had no work. The overseer then relieved him. The reason why he preferred parish relief is simply this, that he received as much money from the parish in a state of idleness, as for work when with a master. My labourers had to work from six o'clock in the morning till four in the evening, whilst the pauper had nothing to do but go to the road at any hour he pleased, employing his time principally in his own garden, and many of them getting fuel from the adjoining wood and selling it, thereby obtaining a larger weekly income than the independent labourer.

How is it that, with such a state of things, you could obtain any labourers?

There were some very few old labourers, aged people, who had passed their youth under a different system and still felt a shame in being paupers. These old men do more work than the generality of the young men, and always were employed. We were obliged to pick out of the others, those who were best characters, and do the best we could with this labour. It is a very common thing for men if we found any fault, to tell us that they did not care whether we kept them or not, for they could get as much on the parish and not work for it, and a burthen of wood in addition. It was a common expression among the farmers, when the men behaved ill, to say that he only wanted his discharge to get upon the parish; and one farmer, a Mr Billing, being angry with his man, refused to turn him away as a punishment, to prevent him going on the

ENGLAND.

County.	Name of School.	Name of Teacher.	Certificate.	Class.	Salary.
					£ s. d.
BEDFORD	Ampthill	Lucy A. Powell	Competency	3	24 15 0
	Bedford	Benjamin Spence	Competency	3	33 0 0
	„	Sarah E. Burnham	Competency	3	28 0 0
	Biggleswade	Susan Ashford	Probation	1	21 5 0
	Leighton Buzzard	John Wickstead	Competency	3	28 5 0
	„ „	Mary A. Wickstead	Probation	2	19 18 0
	Woburn	Sarah Punchard	Probation	2	19 0 0
BERKS	Abingdon	Richard Percy	Competency	2	31 0 0
	„	Elizabeth Brown	Probation	1	19 15 0
	Bradfield	Thomas Blyth	Competency	1	33 15 0
	„	Ann Ragless	Probation	1	22 12 0
	Cookham	Elizabeth Painter	Probation	3	16 0 0
	Easthampstead	George Gibbons	Probation	1	24 10 0
	Farringdon	Benjamin Kirk	Competency	1	34 0 0
	„	Julia Prince Long	Probation	2	20 0 0
	Hungerford	William Hutton	Competency	2	31 10 0
	„	Mary Jane Reynolds	Probation	1	22 15 0
	Newbury	James Dury	Competency	2	35 0 0
	„	Mary Bufoy Dukes	Competency	3	28 0 0
	Wallingford	William Glendinning	Probation	2	23 15 0
	Wantage	James Chivers	Competency	2	30 15 0
	„	Jane Davis	Competency	2	26 15 0
	Windsor	William Henry Holmes	Competency	1	36 0 0
	„	Catherine Eliza Puleston	Probation	1	22 12 0
	Reading and Wokingham District	Brice Bennett	Competency	3	35 0 0
		Eliza Davis	Probation	2	20 0 0
BUCKINGHAM	Amersham	John Bettsworth	Probation	1	24 7 0
	„	Elizabeth A. Eaton	Probation	2	20 0 0
	Aylesbury	Thomas Grace	Probation	1	23 15 0
	„	Elizabeth Roberts	Competency	3	27 5 0
	Buckingham	Rose Roberts	Probation	1	19 3 0
	„	Philip Taplin	Competency	2	30 15 0
	Eton	Benjamin Hall	Competency	2	32 5 0
	„	Mary Anne Major	Probation	2	20 0 0
	Newport Pagnell	Richard Bodley	Probation	3	20 0 0
	„ „	Sarah E. Lord	Probation	1	20 1 0
	Winslow	Anne M. Pybus	Probation	1	21 2 0
	Wycombe	Charles Maine	None.	—	—
	„	Elizabeth Maine	None.	—	—
CAMBRIDGE	Cambridge	Henry Gee	Competency	3	35 0 0
	„	Elizabeth Chapman	Probation	3	16 0 0
	Caxton & Arrington	Margaret Stempson	Probation	1	20 10 0
	Chesterton	Robert Bennett	Competency	2	33 15 0
	„	Ellen Miller	Probation	2	19 15 0
	Linton	Joseph Housden	Probation	2	24 10 0
	„	Ann Green	Probation	2	19 9 0
	Newmarket	William Andrews	Probation	1	28 8 0
	„	Emma Andrews	Permission	—	12 0 0
	North Witchford	Wright Lissett	Permission	—	15 0 0
	„ „	Lucy Taylor	Probation	1	21 8 0
	Wisbeach	Mary Bland	Competency	3	28 0 0
	„	Francis Slipper	Probation	1	29 9 0

The first page (of thirteen) from the Poor Law Board's Annual Report, 1854, listing, county by county, the name of each teacher in each Union, with salary.

parish. We could find no remedy for this evil; we could find no work and the ultimate effects of the whole system would have been, in a very short time, to have driven every farmer from the parish, and have left it like Cholesbury, perfectly pauperised. The land in a very few years would have maintained the paupers and must have been given up; indeed some land had been given up, the farmer not being able to bear the burthen of the poor-rate. We had a poor house in our parish into which the aged and infirm were put but none of the able-bodied. We did not know how to manage it; we found that the smallness of the parish would not warrant any expense and the magistrates constantly gave orders for relief out of the house and always objected to able-bodied men being sent there; so that the house instead of being a benefit has been an injury.

Have the evils of which you complain been removed or lessoned; are the industry and conduct of the labourers improved?

Yes, they are very materially; we have much lessened the numbers of the paupers. Shortly after the new Bill several of the paupers who had applied to the magistrates, finding that the power to order relief was taken away, applied to the Commissioners, when the very next day Mr Gilbert came into the parish to inquire into the state and condition of the parish, and to advise us generally how to act. We told him that nothing could induce the paupers to leave the parish to find work and that even at the rail-road at Tring, about fifteen miles distant, where work was to be had, none could be prevailed on to go. In accordance with Mr Gilbert's advice, who told us that the first course to be adopted was some system that would make independent labour more desirable than the pauper relief, and that he advised spade husbandry as the employment, and payment should be partly in kind. We immediately set aside several pieces of ground to employ the men on. We gave them the land to dig by the pole,* half in kind and half in money. The men grumbled and were very discontented.

* A pole was 30¼ square yards which is equal to 25.3 square metres

Work in the North of England

Mr Gilbert constantly visited the parish and advised us to proceed, which he did and soon found that the men became even more civil and did all they could to find work. They applied to us at the vestry to give them work. Several came to our homes, and having ascertained that the men were really anxious to be employed, the Commissioners offered them work in the north of England, near Manchester. Several large families who had never gone out of their parish before, and whom we could never prevail on to go out and look for work, even at the railway, immediately offered to go, and the result has been that eighty-three persons, including children, who had before been all supported by the parish, went down into comfortable situations and with the exception of five or six of the worst characters, who have returned, all remain in full work. Most of the families were engaged for three years certain, some of them at 30s a week for the first year, 35s for the second year, and 40s for the third year.

Many letters have been received from the paupers who have gone, conveying the most satisfactory reports. One of the men, John Stevens, whom I last saw at his home

Counties.	Parishes.	Amount authorized to be raised or borrowed.	Males.			Females.			Total Number of Emigrants.	To what part Emigrated.
			Adult Persons above 14 Years of Age.	Children between 7 and 14 Years of Age.	Children under 7 Years of Age.	Adult Persons above 14 Years of Age.	Children between 7 and 14 Years of Age.	Children under 7 Years of Age.		
		£. s. d.								
Bedford ..	Cheddington...	12 0 0	2	.	.	.	.	.	2	New South Wales.
,, ..	Cople.......	10 0 0	.	.	.	.	.	.	.	
,, ..	Cranfield	50 0 0	.	.	.	.	.	.	.	
,, ..	Dowlish Wake ..	*	3	.	.	5	.	.	8	Ditto.
,, ..	Egginton	12 0 0	.	.	.	.	.	.	.	
,, ..	Flitwick......	75 0 0	1	.	.	1	.	.	2	Ditto.
,, ..	Harlington....	30 0 0	.	.	.	.	.	.	.	
,, ..	Hawnes	*	6	4	5	5	2	4	26	Cape of Good Hope.
,, ..	Leighton Buzzard	15 0 0	.	.	.	1	.	.	1	New South Wales.
,, ..	Marston Moretaine	10 0 0	.	1	.	2	.	.	3	Van Diemen's Land.
,, ..	Milton Bryant ..	40 0 0	1	3	2	4	.	.	10	New South Wales.
,, ..	Polton	25 0 0	.	.	.	.	.	.	.	
,, ..	Pulloxhill	22 0 0	6	2	.	7	2	3	20	South Australia.
,, ..	Steppingley ...	20 0 0	.	.	.	.	.	.	.	
,, ..	Toddington ...	*	2	.	.	.	.	.	2	New South Wales.
,, ..	Woburn	100 0 0	.	.	.	.	.	.	.	
Berks ...	Brightwell	*	7	.	1	2	2	1	13	Canada.
,, ...	Newbury . ..	42 0 0	2	1	.	3	1	.	7	South Australia.
,, ...	St. Mary-the-More	3 10 0	.	.	.	.	.	.	.	
,, ...	Welford	15 0 0	.	.	.	.	.	.	.	
Buckingham	Amersham.....	100 0 0	.	.	.	.	.	.	.	
,,	Beaconfield ...	10 0 0	.	.	.	.	.	.	.	
,,	Bierton	3 0 0	.	.	.	.	.	.	.	
,,	Brill	180 0 0	.	.	.	.	.	.	.	
,,	Buckingham ...	100 0 0	2	1	2	3	1	.	9	Canada.
,,	Chalfont, St. Peter	25 0 0	1	.	.	1	.	.	2	South Australia.
,,	Chesham	100 0 0	.	.	.	.	.	.	.	
,,	Claydon, East .	35 0 0	.	.	.	.	.	.	.	
,,	Coleshill	10 0 0	.	.	.	.	.	.	.	
,,	Cuddington ...	*	1	.	.	.	.	.	1	Ditto.
,,	Hornton.....	10 0 0	.	.	.	.	.	.	.	
,,	Iver.......	36 0 0	.	.	.	.	.	.	.	
,,	Langley Marsh..	10 0 0	.	.	.	.	.	.	.	
,,	Loughton	*	1	.	.	2	.	1	4	Ditto.
,,	Ludgershall ...	40 0 0	.	.	.	.	.	.	.	
,,	Marston, North .	60 0 0	.	.	.	.	.	.	.	
,,	Mentmore....	40 0 0	4	1	.	2	.	1	8	Ditto.
,,	Mursley.....	12 0 6	2	.	.	1	.	1	4	Ditto.
,,	Penn.......	30 0 0	1	.	.	.	.	.	1	Ditto.
,,	Steeple Claydon .	60 0 0	2	.	3	2	.	2	9	Canada.
,,	Soulbury	40 0 0	.	.	.	.	.	.	.	
,,	Stone	14 0 0	2	1	1	5	2	1	12	New South Wales.
,,	Stewkley	30 0 0	1	1	1	1	1	1	6	South Australia.
,,	Stoke Mandeville	20 0 0	1	.	1	1	.	1	4	Ditto.
,,	Taplow	10 0 0	.	.	.	.	.	.	.	
,,	Wing	50 0 0	4	.	1	1	.	.	6	Ditto.
,,	Wingrave	20 0 0	3	.	.	2	.	2	7	Ditto.
,,	Winslow.....	* {	1	.	.	1	.	2	4	New South Wales.
		{	1	1	.	1	3	2	8	South Australia.
Cambridge.	Bottisham	12 0 0	.	.	.	.	.	.	.	
,,	St. Mary-the-Less	*	1	1	1	1	1	.	5	Ditto.
,,	Tydd, St. Giles..	30 0 0	.	.	.	.	.	.	.	
,,	Upwell	17 10 0	1	.	.	.	.	.	1	Ditto.
,,	Wisbeach, St.Mary	50 0 0	.	.	.	.	.	.	.	
,,	Wisbeach, St.Peter	100 0 0	1	2	1	1	1	1	7	Ditto.
	Carried forward	1,736 0 6	60	19	19	55	16	23	192	

* Vide Report I.

The first page (of five) from the Poor Law Board's Annual Report, 1849, listing the numbers of persons from each parish who have emigrated.

at Quarry Bank, pointing to his house and furniture, expressed his strongest thanks for the change he had experienced and made use of this extraordinary expression, 'That all the horses in Buckinghamshire should not draw him back again.'

Four hundred and fifty-five pounds, after paying the expense of the men to Manchester will have been saved in this parish since the month of November last, and in the whole year will be one half less than before.

Paupers who remained in the south

Many who remained are now maintaining themselves and the amount now paid weekly in the parish is so much reduced, and that the reduction continuing to increase to such an extent the character and conduct of the labourers are so much improved, that all apprehension of pauperism is removed and great confidence felt, that as regards the able-bodied the parish will totally be dispauperized.

The paupers that remain upon the parish being relieved partly in kind is productive of much good, one of the most beneficial parts of the system. The wives and families that before were left almost in a state of starvation, while the husband spent the money at the beer-shop, obtain now a fair subsistence. The custom of the beer-shops diminishes and the good order and sobriety consequent upon the new system apparent. The men cannot sell their bread because everyone has a supply, and the mode of payment prevents the possibility of the family being left as they often previously were, without sustenance. The bread payment is disliked by the disorderly pauper and acts also as an inducement on him to find work.

Do you find any other effect from the payment in kind?

Yes; I do find that the little tradesmen, who had formerly an interest in the increase of pauperism, now persuade the paupers to find work; formerly the more paupers the more money the little tradesman made; but now that a contractor supplies the bread, the less pauperism and the more independent labour the more to the shopkeepers. One of these shopkeepers called and remonstrated with me, that all the men were not employed; and I know that he and others do all they can to prevent the men being paupers and encourage their becoming independent labourers.

What is your opinion, as a farmer and employer, of the effect of granting no relief in aid of wages, except in kind?

My opinion is, that the relief in kind is judiciously substituted for money. If all relief in aid of wages were withdrawn I have no doubt farmers would give higher wages; for instance I have thrashing to do, or hay to cut, or any other work. I must have men and if the parish would pay part I should feel it unnecessary to give out of my pocket so large a sum; but if the parish gives nothing I must pay the man full wages and get from him a good full day's work; and as the men get independent and the rates get lower the wages will get higher.

If I have the free use on Saturday night of £5, instead of paying it to the overseer I shall be able to lay this out in labour on my land in the next week; whilst the labourer was half pauper and half labourer, he was like a man with two masters and could do justice to neither; but now he feels that he is wholly a labourer, he works hard and willingly. My 8s wages will purchase for me labour sufficient to produce 10s worth of crop, but with a pauper my 5s paid will be a loss; for all the labour such a man will do won't be worth half-a-crown. With independent labourers the more I have in moderation the more I make; but for the paupers the more I have the more I lose. I will employ as many of the former and as few of the latter as I can. Ten independent labourers would do more good than five; while of paupers five would be more desirable than ten.

Evidence was also given by:–

The Rev. Charles Turner of Wendover, J.P. and member of the Board of Guardians of the Wycombe Union.

James George Tatem, Esquire, Chairman of the Board of Guardians.

Mr Samuel Clarke of Chenies, Overseer.

James Gilbert of Risborough, victualler and millwright and Overseer last year.

James Stratton of Risborough, farmer and Overseer for the present year.

Daniel Smith, Relieving Officer of the Amersham Union.

Mr Thomas Brickwell, surgeon of the Amersham Union.

Benjamin Quartermain Simons, Master of Aylesbury Workhouse.

PARISH OF BARKWAY.

LIST of Able-bodied Males who have applied to the Parish for Work or Relief since last Harvest.

The Number of Days during which each Man has been on the Parish. (The first Column is for the first Week in September, the next for the next Week, and so on up to the present time.)

NAME	Age	Wife living	No. of Children in each Family under 14	Allowance for a whole Week (s. d.)	September	October	November	December	January	February	March	April
Philip Jackson	80	yes	.	6 6	6 6 6 6	6 6 6 6	6 6 6 6	6 6 6 6	6 6 6 6	6 6 6 6	6 6 6 6	6 6
Lott Watson	65	yes	.	5 6	6 6 6 6	6 6 6 6	6 6 6 6	6 6 6 6	6 6 6 6	6 6 6 6	6 6 6 6	6 6
Joseph Sharp	60	yes	4	8 .	6 .	. . .	. . . .	. . . .	6 6 4	. . .	. . .	. 5
William Johnson	45	yes	5	8 .	5 5	. .	. . . .	. . . .	. . .	. . .	. . .	. .
William Searle	50	no	.	3 .	5 1	. .	. . . .	. . . .	. . .	6 6 3	. . .	. .
William Edwards	70	yes	1	5 6	4 6 6 6	6 6 6 6	6 6 6 5	. . . .	6 .	. . .	. . .	. .
Edward Dockril	18	.	.	3 .	4 3	. .	. . . .	. . . .	. . .	. . .	. . .	. .
Thomas Nunn	45	yes	3	7 .	2 .	. .	. . . .	. . . .	. . .	6 . 6	. 1 2 4	. .
Thomas Nunn	18	.	.	3 .	2 .	. .	. . . .	. 6 6	. . .	6 6 . 6 6	. 3 .	. 4 1
John Wright	35	yes	5	8 .	5 .	. .	. . . .	. . . .	6 4 6 6 6 6	6 6 6 1	. . .	. .
Napier Guiver	50	yes	2	7 .	6 6 6 6	6 6 6 6	6 6 6 6	6 . . .	. . .	. . 5 6	6 6 6 6	6 6
Joseph Dradge	60	.	.	3 .	6 .	. 6 6 6	6 6 6 4 5	4 6 6 6 6 6 6 6	. 6	6 6 6 6	6 6 6 6	6 2 . 6
James Dale	22	yes	1	6 .	. .	. .	. . . .	. 3 5 6	. . 4	3 . 4	. . .	. 3 6 6
William Head	18	.	.	3 .	. .	. .	. . . .	3 3 4 6	. 6 4	. . .	. . .	. .
John Pitty	40	yes	1	5 6	. .	. .	. . . .	6 6 6 5 1 4 4 3	6 2 . 5 1	. . .	. . .	. .
James Edwards	50	yes	4	8 .	. .	. .	. . . .	2 . .	6 3 6 .	6 6 .	6 .	. .
James Searle	25	yes	1	6 .	. .	. .	. . . .	. 2 6 6 5 3 6 5	. 6 6 6 5 .	. 2 3 6	6 2 3	. .
Samuel Bunyan	22	yes	3	7 6	. .	. .	. . . .	. 6 6 6	. . .	. 3 6 6	6 6 6 6	6 .
John Grapes	60	yes	.	5 6	. .	. .	. . . .	. 6 . 6	. . .	. . .	. . .	. .
Richard Hart	18	.	.	3 .	. .	. .	. . . .	6 6 6 1	. . .	. . .	. . .	. .
George Watson	25	yes	3	6 .	. .	. .	. . . .	6 . . 6 6	. 5 . 1	. . .	. . .	. .
James Joiner	26	yes	2	6 .	. .	. .	. . . .	. 6	. 6 . 6 6 6	. 6 . 6 6 3 6	. .	6 6
James Bunyan	19	.	.	3 .	. .	. .	. . . .	. .	6 6 6 . .	. . 6 .	6 6	6 6
William Wright	22	yes	1	6 .	. .	. .	. . . .	. 2 6	. . . 6	. 2 . 6	. .	. .
Henry Cotton	15	.	.	2 .	. .	. .	. . . .	. 3 3 6 4 4	. . . .	. .	. .
John Sharp	65	.	.	3 .	. .	. .	. . . .	. 6 4	. . .	. 3 6	. .	. .
Joseph Young	23	yes	.	5 6	. .	. .	. . . .	. 6 4 6	6 . 6	6 6	. .	. .
Samuel Sharp	20	yes	.	5 6	. .	. .	. . . .	. 5 6	6 . 6 6	. .	. .
Thomas Belsham	74	.	.	3 .	. .	. .	. . . .	3 .	. . .	. .	. .
Thomas Cotton	17	.	.	3 .	. .	. .	. . . .	4 6 6 6 6	. 6 6	. .
James Warren	43	yes	5	9 .	. .	. .	. . . .	5 5 4 5	6 .	. .
William Evans	65	.	.	3 .	. .	. .	. . . .	4 .	5 6	. .
Jonathan Franklin	18	.	.	3 .	. .	. .	. . . .	6 6 6 6 5	6 5 5 6
James Warren, jun.	18	.	.	3 .	. .	. .	. . . .	6 6 6 .	6 . 2 . 6
William Pittey	43	yes	3	8 .	. .	. .	. . . .	. 5 6 6 .	5 6 6 .
Joseph Bull	45	yes	2	6 .	. .	. .	. . . .	. 6 6 6 6 6	6 6
William Watson	26	yes	1	5 6	. .	. .	. . . .	. 6 6 4 3	. .
William Watson	25	yes	3	8 .	. .	. .	. . . .	. 3	. .
William Sharp, jun.	12	.	.	3 .	. .	. .	. . . .	. 6 6 . 6 .
John Watson	25	yes	1	6 .	. .	. .	. . . .	. 5 6 6	6 6
William Watson	65	yes	.	5 6	. .	. .	. . . .	. 5 . 6 6 6
James Cotton	25	yes	.	5 6	. .	. .	. . . .	. 6 6 6
John Smith	40	yes	.	5 6	. .	. .	. . . .	6 6 6 6
George Guiver	35	yes	.	5 6	. .	. .	. . . .	. 6 3 6
John Parker	38	yes	3	7 .	. .	. .	. . . .	. 6 . 6

A table from the Poor Law Commissioners' First Annual Report, 1835, listing the able-bodied men who have applied for work or relief in the parish of Barkway, Hertfordshire.

Name of the Father or Mother, or of the Immigrant, if single.	Previous Occupation.	Place whence they Migrated.	Condition:— Widow, Widower, Orphan, Found-ling, Bastard, Deserted, Child, or Wife.	Place where Settled.	Name of present Employers.	Number of Family.	Age of Father.	Age of Mother.	Age of Immigrant.	Weekly Earnings from Wages or Parish Allowance, or both, before their Immigration.							Present Weekly Earnings of the Family.								Weekly Earnings, Second Year.	Weekly Earnings, Third Year.	Future Prospects.
										Father.	Mother.	First Child.	Second.	Third.	Fourth.	Fifth.	TOTAL.	Father.	Mother.	First Child.	Second.	Third.	Fourth.	Fifth.	Sixth.	TOTAL.			
Jesse Neal ⎱ live together	paper-mill	Bledlow, Bucks	deserted.	Turton, near Bolton	H. & E. Ashworth	1		16									2 6									6 6	7 6	9 0	41 in third year.
Tho. Neal	in workhouse	ditto	deserted.	ditto	ditto	1		14																		5 6		8 0
Geo. Allen	labourer	ditto		ditto	ditto	9	35		9 0	3 0						19 0	12 0	3 0	2 6	2 0				19 6	21 0	24 0
Joseph Shepherd.	ditto	ditto		Egerton, near Bolton	ditto	9	50		4 0		2 0	2 6	0 9	16 3	12 0	9 0	6 6	5 0	4 6	2 6	2 0	41	31 6	6 46	0 53 0	
Joseph Stevens.	parish	ditto		ditto	ditto	9	40		7 0	2 6	2 0			11 6	12 0	7 6	3 6	3 0	2 6		28 6	33 0
James Fryer	labourer	ditto		ditto	ditto	10	36		8 0	2s. 6d.	1 0	2 6	14 0	13 6	5 0	4 0	2 6	2 0		27	0 30	0 34 6
George Grimsall.	none	ditto		ditto	ditto			18												7 0	8 6
James Arnott	,,	ditto		ditto	ditto			15												6 0	6 9	7 9
Samuel Blick	labourer	Prince's Risborough, Bucks.		Stayley Bridge	Harrison & Brothers	10	41		8 0	2 0	2 6	2 0	14 6	12 0	11 0	8 0	3 0	2 0	36 0	
William Bayley	parish	ditto		ditto	ditto	10	43	5 6	1 6	1 6	1 6	1 6	6 3	16 0	12 0	7 0	7 0	7 0	5 0	4 6	42 6	
Mary Mines	washerwoman	ditto	widow.	ditto	ditto	5	52	2 4	1 6	0 2	6 2	0	9 10	3 0	8 0	8 0	5 0	3 0	27 0
James Blick	parish	ditto		ditto	ditto	3	24	5 6					5 6	12 0				12 0
John Hickman	ditto	ditto		ditto	Bayley and Brothers	7	42	8 0					8 0	14 0	3 6	3 6	lodgers. 4 6	25 6
William Wootton	labourer	ditto		ditto	ditto	7	44	6 0	2 6	0 10			9 4	14 0	7 0	6 6	2 4	29 10
Ditto	ditto	ditto		ditto	ditto	3	24	5 0						14 0	6 3		20 3
George Stephens.	ditto	ditto		ditto	ditto	8	40	7 0	1 0	0 0	6		10 6	14 7	6 0	3 6	0	27 5
Joseph Rance	parish	ditto		ditto	ditto	6	34	6 0		1 6			8 6	14 0	2 0	0 3	6	21 6
John Dean	labourer	ditto	orphan.	ditto	ditto	1	18	18					7 0				12 0
William Hives	workhouse	ditto		ditto	ditto	1	17	17									12 0
Philip Peddor	labourer	Cranfield,Beds.		Mellor, Derbyshire	Mr. Clayton.	8	43	7 0	1 0	1 6	2 6	2 6	0 10	15 4	19 0	5 0	1 0	5 0	4 6	2 6	30 0
Thomas Clarke	ditto	ditto		ditto	ditto	7	39	7 0	1 0				9 0	12 0	4 6	3 0	19 6
William Rogers	ditto	ditto		ditto	ditto	3	37	5 0	0 4	1 0			6 4	12 0	4 6	3 0	19 6
Thomas Wright	ditto	ditto		ditto	ditto	6	32	7 0	1 0	1 6			9 6	13 0	4 6	4 6	21 0
William Smith	parish	Prince's Risborough, Bucks.		Heywood	Cleggs & Hall	6	53	52	5 0	1 0	rent.			6 0	14 0	3 0	3 0	3 0	12 0	35 0	0 42	0 45 6
William Clarke	ditto	ditto		ditto	ditto	12	45	46	8 0	1 6	8	0 2	6 0	6	15 6	10 0	4 0	4 0	6 0	3 0	3 0	30 0	0 42	0 53 0	63 0
																£9 16 1									£28 2 6			

A table from the Poor Law Commissioners' First Annual Report, 1835, listing the families who have migrated from Buckinghamshire, and giving the places 'where settled' in the north of England.

Mr Joseph Fleet, Vestry Clerk of the parish of Iver.

John Miller, Relieving Officer of Amersham Union.

Mr Edmund Mason of Slough in the parish of Upton-cum-Chalvey.

William Lowndes of Chesham, Esquire, JP and Guardian *ex-officio* of the Amersham Union.

Benjamin Fuller of Chesham, a County Magistrate and a Member of the Board of Guardians of the Amersham Union.

William Weedon of Chesham, yeoman, Guardian for Chesham.

John Gomm, Master of Chesham Workhouse.

This report also contains much detail about the migration of paupers from the south of England to the north. Many paupers are named.

Migration to the North of England

The following is one of many reports on named individuals:

Egerton near Bolton, Lancashire, 13 miles from Manchester

Messrs H. and E. Ashworth

Families

Joseph Shepperd, aged 50, from Bledlow (Bucks). Wife dead 12 months ago; family of eight children; has been 13 weeks here. Earned 7s per week at Bledlow as a farmer's labourer, or received this sum from the parish in which latter case he worked upon the roads.

Joseph aged 19 was employed by a farmer at 4s per week, and when not thus employed received 2s 6d per week from the parish.

James aged 18, lived with a farmer and received board and lodging and £2 a year for his work. None of his earnings assisted the family.

Thomas aged 16, had 3s per week in harvest and at other times was at home with his father and earned 1s 6d.

George aged 15, worked in a paper mill and earned 2s to 2s 6d per week.

Eliza age 11, earned at the lace-pillow at school from 6d to 9d per week.

None of the other children earned any thing. The wages of the family, taking every thing into consideration, did not, when they were in employ exceed 16s 3d, but Shepherd thinks the average was much lower; he says about 12s per week.

Paid 1s per week for a thatched cottage with a garden. He was greatly favoured by his landlord in having a cottage at so low a rent. He was able to afford but little for clothing and when he came here the family were in tatters. He was glad to conceal his nakedness beneath the smock-frock.

The family now earn £2 1s 6d per week (their wages having recently been raised by Messrs Ashworth for good conduct and skill).

	1st year	2nd year	3rd year
The father earns, as labourer	12s 0d	12s 0d	12s 0d
Joseph in factory	9s 0d	12s 0d	15s 0d
James ditto	6s 6d	7s 6d	8s 6d
Thomas ditto	5s 0d	6s 0d	7s 0d
George ditto	4s 6d	5s 6d	6s 6d
Eliza ditto	2s 6d	3s 0d	4s 0d
Eden ditto	2s 0d	2s 6d	3s 0d

The children when they were in Bucks, were scattered about in the farm-houses; they are now gathered under his own roof; he has bought good clothes for them and for himself; has an excellent cottage for which he pays 2s per week; has been exceedingly well treated by his employers and by the workmen.

Messrs Ashworth have already raised the earnings of his family 6s beyond the contract made with them because they have proved so docile and skilful. It is probable they will earn 10s beyond the contract in the second year, or 46s, and 53s in the third.

Other families named in this report include:–

George Allen, aged 35, from Bledlow

Jesse Neal, aged 16 an orphan by Allen, from Bledlow

Joseph Stevens, aged 40, from Bedlow

James Fryer, aged 39, from Bledlow

A table from the Poor Law Commissioners' First Annual Report, 1835, listing the names of 119 families with their weekly wages earned in 1833, employed by Thomas Ashton of Hyde, Cheshire.

NAMES.	No. of Family.	Average Weekly Earnings. £ s. d.	NAMES.	No. of Family.	Average Weekly Earnings. £ s. d.
			Brought forward	52	17 3 4
Armitage, Thomas	7	2 15 0	Bagshaw, Samuel	2	1 8 8
Ashton, William	4	1 18 4	Broadhurst, Aaron	8	1 10 0
Ashley, John	5	1 5 0	Broadbent, Samuel	2	2 5 0
Ainsworth, John	8	2 1 8	Broadbent, Thomas	8	2 15 0
Arundale, Joseph	9	2 16 8	Britnor, Enoch	10	2 1 8
Barker, John	6	2 5 0	Bussey, John	8	2 0 4
Booth, John and Matthew (two families)	13	4 1 8	Barnes, Henry	4	1 3 4
Bradley, Joseph	8	2 5 0	Beeley, John	7	4 5 0
Bredbury, William	2	1 5 0	Murray, Hugh	8	2 10 0
Barlow, James	11	3 16 8	Newton, William	9	2 10 0
Bramwell, George	7	2 8 4	Newton, Samuel	4	1 10 0
Beard, Thomas	8	3 3 4	Newton, Charles	6	1 18 4
Broadbent, John	8	2 15 0	Nuttall, James	6	4 10 0
Brown, George	8	2 6 8	North, John	11	4 15 0
Brogdent, James	5	1 10 0	Owen, James and Thos. (two families)	10	3 0 0
Beardsell, Joseph	9	2 11 8	Ormerod, Thomas	8	2 18 4
Bent, Betty	7	1 15 0	Oldham, Charles	9	2 11 8
Crinnion, Henry	6	1 8 4	Peel, Richard	5	1 11 8
Chapman, Matthew	6	1 6 8	Platt, Robert	11	2 0 0
Crawshaw, Richard	6	2 13 4	Penny, William	5	2 5 0
Crompton, Isaac	8	3 1 8	Pendlebury, John	12	3 0 0
Dobson, James	6	1 11 8	Ryley, Joseph	11	2 13 4
Darlington, Ralph	10	3 1 8	Roscoe, Thomas	5	1 6 8
Draper, Noah	12	3 10 0	Ravenscroft, Nancy	5	1 6 8
Darnley, Ann	3	1 5 0	Redfern, John	9	5 8 4
Ecroyde, Abram	8	2 11 8	Redfern, Josiah	3	1 8 8
Foster, John	6	1 19 8	Redfern, James	5	1 18 4
Foulstone, Joseph	8	3 0 0	Rowbotham, Joseph	5	2 15 0
Foster, Joseph	6	2 10 0	Rayner, John	8	2 16 8
Fletcher, George	7	2 16 8	Rayner, Joseph	6	2 16 8
Flitcroft, James	8	2 15 0	Rayner, Robert	9	3 6 8
Grainger, John	9	2 11 8	Sedgewick, John	8	2 16 8
Hall, John	11	5 11 8	Smith, John	5	2 13 4
Harrison, Thomas	15	3 3 4	Seville, George	6	2 8 4
Hibbert, John	5	0 18 4	Slater, James	4	1 7 0
Heathcote, Matthew	5	1 13 0	Schofield, Jacob	6	1 13 4
Heelis, George	7	1 10 0	Seddon, Robert	6	1 16 8
Hoyle, John	11	2 8 4	Schofield, John	10	3 6 8
Hague, William	4	1 11 8	Slater, John	4	1 0 0
Hunt, James	3	2 3 4	Simpson, Henry	10	3 15 0
Hadfield, Edward	7	2 0 0	Thomas, Solomon	8	1 13 4
Hollins, Josiah	6	2 8 4	Taylor, Worsley	10	3 8 4
Hartley, Richard	3	1 18 4	Taylor, Joseph	8	1 10 0
Hegginbotham, Jane	9	3 6 8	Tempest, Joseph	8	3 11 8
Hargreaves, John	9	1 16 8	Taylor, James	6	2 13 4
Higginbotham, Alice	9	1 18 4	Wragg, Adam	11	3 10 0
Jackson, William and Thos. (two families)	6	3 10 0	Walker, James	13	3 10 0
Kidd, Henry	5	0 15 0	Wynne, Patrick	7	2 6 8
Kerfoot, John	6	2 0 0	Whiteley, Jeremiah	7	1 15 0
Kershaw, William	9	1 18 4	White, George	8	3 1 8
Leaver, Robert	10	2 10 0	Whittaker, Thomas	7	2 1 8
Leigh, David, sen.	8	6 5 0	Williams, Thomas	4	1 5 0
Leigh, David, jun.	3	2 6 8	Whitehead, Samuel	9	2 18 4
Leech, John and Wm. (two families)	16	4 8 4	Wyatt, Thomas	8	3 18 4
Mellor, George and Jonathan (two families)	15	5 11 8	Watson, Gabriel	7	2 13 4
Mottram, John	8	3 15 0	Wilde, James	7	1 11 8
			Wilde, Richard	3	1 15 0
			Yates, George	2	2 1 8
Carried forward	473	160 0 0	Total Weekly Average in 12 Weeks, ending as above	835	286 19 0

County.	Union.	Chairman.	Vice-Chairman.	Clerk.	Auditor.
ENGLAND.					
Bedford	Ampthill	H. M. Musgrave	T. W. Overman	George Robinson	Charles Austin
,,	Bedford	C. L. Higgins	Captain Bell, R.N.	Samuel Wing	D.G.Adey (Asst.-Com.)
,,	Biggleswade	C. Barnett	R. Lindsell	Edward Argles	William Smith
,,	Leighton Buzzard	Rev. W. B. Wroth	S. Reeve	Joseph Woodman	J. P. Kipling
,,	Luton	Marquis of Bute	H. B. Morris	T. E. Austin	Charles Austin
,,	Woburn	George Pearse	T. Bennett	W. Cole	R. A. Reddall
Berks	Abingdon	Rev. N. Dodson	J. C. Neale	R. Ellis	W. Graham
,,	Bradfield	Wm. Stephens	M. G. Thoyts	Thomas Beall	J. S. Pidgeon
,,	Cookham	Charles Sawyer	E. G. C. East	W. J. Ward	James Smith
,,	Easthampstead	Sir H.W.Rooke, K.C.H.	Col. T. Kenah	Charles Cave	W. Mellish
,,	Faringdon	Viscount Barrington	Geo. Dyke	John Haines	R. W. Crowdy
,,	Hungerford	G. H. Cherry	W. H. Halcomb	W. Rowland	James Julfs
,,	Newbury	W. Mount	B. Hawkins	John Tanner	G. Barnes
,,	Reading	C. Blundy	T. Havell	T. G. Curties	John Fowler
,,	Wallingford	F. J. Skilliard	W. Toovey	Hedges and Son	H. T. Birkett
,,	Wantage	B. Wroughton	R. Sherwood	W. Ormond	J. Brooks
,,	Windsor	T. H. Ward	G. Kimberley	W. C. Long	T. W. Martin
,,	Wokingham	H. Clive	R. J. T. Perkin	J. R. Wheeler	John Bryan
Bucks	Amersham	W. T. Drake	John Rolfe	Thomas Marshall	J. Charseey
,,	Amesbury	Rev. G. P. Lowther	R. Hughes	R. M. Wilson	W. D. Whitmarsh, jun.
,,	Aylesbury	G. G. Pigott	John Dell	Acton Tindal	T. S. Chapman
,,	Buckingham	Sir H. Verney	J. Loveridge	Thomas Hearn	J. W. Cowley
,,	Eton	John Bent	G. J. Penn	C. P. Barrett	John Charsley
,,	Newport Pagnell	W. Swabey	Henry Lucas	W. Powell	John Garrard
,,	Winslow	Sir T. F. Fremantle, Bt.	John Hale	D. T. Willis	J. W. Cowley
,,	Wycombe	J. G. Tatem	James Grace	Chas. Harman	John Parker

The first page of a table from the Poor Law Commissioners' Third Annual Report, 1837, listing all the Unions in England and Wales and giving the names of chairmen, vice-chairmen, clerks and auditors of each Union.

Samuel Blick, aged 39, from Prince's Risborough

William Bayley, aged 43, from Prince's Risborough

Mary Mines, aged 52, from Prince's Risborough

James Blick, aged 24, son-in-law of Mary Mines

James Hickman, aged 32, from Prince's Risborough

William Wootton, aged 44, from Prince's Risborough

William Wooton, aged 24, from Prince's Risborough

George Stevens, aged 40, from Prince's Risborough

Joseph Rance, aged 34, from Prince's Risborough

John Dean, aged 18, from Prince's Risborough

James Curtis, aged 29, from Prince's Risborough

Philip Pedder, aged 39, from Cranfield, Bedfordshire

Thomas Clarke, aged 39, from Cranfield, Bedfordshire

William Rogers, aged 37, from Cranfield, Bedfordshire

Thomas Wright, aged 32, from Cranfield, Bedfordshire

Ninth Annual Report of the Poor Law Commissioners, 1843

Pauper Lunatics

The Poor Law Act of last session 5 & 6 Vict. c.57, s.6 provided that the returns of lunatics, which, under County Lunatic Asylum Act, 9 Geo. IV c.40 were to be made

	Number Indicted for Murder of Bastard Children.	Pleaded Guilty.	Capitally Convicted.	Found Guilty of Concealment of the Birth.	Acquitted on the Ground of Insanity.	Inquisition quashed for want of Formality.	Not Guilty.
1730	1	..	..	..	..	..	1
1731							
1732	1	..	1				
1733							
1734	1	..	1				
1735	1	..	1				
1736	2	..	1	..	..	..	1
1737							
1738	1	..	..	..	..	..	1
1739							
1740	1	..	..	..	..	..	1
1750	1	..	..	..	..	..	1
1760	3	..	1	..	..	..	2
1770	2	..	..	..	..	..	2
1780	2	..	..	..	..	..	2
1790							
1800	2	..	..	..	..	..	2
1801	2	..	..	..	..	..	2
1802	1	..	..	..	..	..	1
1803	1	..	..	..	..	..	1
1804	2	..	..	1	..	..	1
1805	1	..	..	1			
1806							
1807							
1808	1	..	..	1			
1809	2	..	..	2			
1810							
1811							
1812	1	..	..	..	..	..	1
1813							
1814							
1815	1	..	..	..	..	..	1
1816	1	..	..	..	..	..	1
1817	4	..	1	1	..	..	2
1818	1	..	..	..	..	..	1
1819							
1820							
1821	1	..	..	..	..	..	1
1822	2	..	..	..	1	..	1
1823	2	..	..	..	..	..	2
1824							
1825	2	..	..	..	..	1	1
1826	1	..	..	..	..	..	1
1827	1	..	..	..	..	..	1
1828							
1829	2	..	..	2			
1830	1	..	..	1			
1831	2	..	..	1	..	..	1
1832							
1833	1	..	..	1			
1834	1	..	..	..	..	..	1
1835	3	..	..	..	1	..	2
1836	4	1	1	1	..	..	1
1837	1	..	..	..	..	..	1
Total	60 Indicted.	1 Pleaded Guilty.	7 Capitally Convicted.	12 Guilty of Concealment.	2 Insane.	1 Want of Formality.	37 Not Guilty.

A table from the Poor Law Commissioners' Fourth Annual Report, 1838, listing the number of females indicted at the Old Bailey for infanticide, from 1730 to 1837.

Number of Lunatics and Idiots chargeable to Parishes in each Union, in the month of August, 1842.

COUNTIES.	Population in 1841.	Number of Lunatics and Idiots.										Grand Total Lunatics and Idiots.	Proportion per Cent. to Population.	Where maintained.												
		Lunatics.			Idiots.			Total.						In County Lunatic Asylum.			In Licensed House.			In Union Workhouse.			With their Friends or elsewhere.		
		M.	F.	Total.	M.	F.	Total.	M.	F.	Total.				M.	F.	Total.	M.	F.	Total.	M.	F.	Total.	M.	F.	Total.

A table from the Poor Law Commissioners' Ninth Annual Report, 1843, listing county by county the number of pauper lunatics and idiots chargeable in 1842.

to the clerk of the peace by the overseers of separate parishes, should be made by the clerk of the Guardians for each Union, and that a duplicate of every return should be sent to the Commissioners. This enactment will enable us to present an annual return of pauper lunatics, exhibiting all material facts relating to this afflicted class of person. We subjoin in the Appendix an elaborate table, showing the results of the very complete returns which have been made to us under this clause. We have likewise added an account abstracted from answers to some inquiries which were transmitted to the directors of the several county lunatic asylums in England. From this account it will be seen that only 16 counties in England have provided lunatic asylums under the 9 Geo. IV c.40, and that there is no county lunatic asylum in Wales. Even of the 16 lunatic asylums in the English counties, four are stated in the answers transmitted to us, to be insufficient for the wants of the county. From these facts it is we think, apparent that the present legal provision for pauper lunatics is inadequate.

Second Annual Report of the Poor Law Board, 1849

Vagrancy

Report of Andrew Doyle, Esq., Poor Law Inspector, on the subject of Vagrancy in the several Unions in his District, which comprises the Counties of Salop [Shropshire], Anglesey, Carnarvon, Denbigh, Flint, Merioneth, Montgomery, and the eight Unions in Cheshire.

Sir,

In compliance with the instructions of the Board, that I should communicate the result of any measures adopted in this district for the repression of vagrancy, I have the honour to inform you that immediately after the Circular of August 4, 1848, was issued I took occasion to bring it under the consideration of the Guardians of the different Unions the increasing pressure of vagrancy was then severely felt, and I found amongst the Guardians a general disposition to avail themselves of the remedies suggested in the circular of the Board.

Of a number of communications received by me in reply to inquiries which I made immediately after the circular has been issued, I select the following letter from Mr Kemp, the master of Wrexham Workhouse, as containing, I think, a not exaggerated statement of the character of the evil which had attracted the attention of the Board:–

For a length of time we were in the practice of giving the tramps their supper and lodgings without any return being asked in the shape of work; but the breakfast in the morning was withheld until some little was done in the way of acknowledgement. At some times they had the option of going away without breakfast, if they preferred that to working. The number of vagrants continuing to increase, the Board of Guardians passed a resolution embodying a labour test by which the tramps were to have their breakfast at the usual hour (at the same time as the other inmates of the house), and be detained for three hours and a half thereafter to work at the mill or break stones. When this alteration became known *on the road*, it for a short time operated in reducing the number, but not until gang after gang had been sent to gaol for refusing to work.

The magistrates in their places at the Board complained of the expense to the county of those wholesale committals, and as this resistance to the labour test on the part of the tramps appeared more to arise from the fact of their being turned out on the road in the middle of the day and with a comparatively empty stomach, having had their breakfast four hours previous, than to the mere labour test itself, it was ordered that they be put to work immediately after rising, and have their breakfast three hours and a half after, so that they thus left the house about 10 o'clock, A.M., having just had a tolerable meal, and were in a comfortable plight for the day. The consequence of the above alteration was, as you will readily conceive, an almost immediate increase in the number of tramps. In about three weeks the number rose from about 70 to 120 per week. On this becoming apparent, the matter was again reported to the Board who instantly placed the order on its original footing, viz., that they (the tramps) be set to work three hours and a half *after breakfast*. This was, as before, resisted, but on the parties finding that the Bench and the Board were both determined to carry it out they submitted, and for months we had no trouble on account of their refusing to work. As these parties appeared, as it were, to have taken our terms and their numbers began again to increase the Board again took the whole question into full consideration, and after due deliberation it was determined to refuse to the *systematic* vagrants, at the same time the officers were instructed to use their best discretion to prevent any *casual poor person from suffering,* and hence acting on this order in the spirit of good faith, while we (I mean the paid officers) have refused relief to any of the vagrant fraternity (for a fraternity they are, and are easily distinguished as such), we have given relief as usual to the other poor travellers who appeared to be on a *bona fide* errand.

I then Sir, as a matter of opinion hold that the last course above referred to is the best, and decidedly think that vagrants as a class deserve but little pity, and ought rather to be under the cognisance of the police than the poor law officers. They are for the most part, if not criminals, at least on the verge of crime. The greater portion of them have never done a week's work consecutively in their lives, and, if they can help it, never intend to do one. From many who have been taken ill on their journey and had, for a time to remain in the house, I have ascertained that they have, since shortly after the passing of the New Poor Law, passed their time circling from Union to Union, and either begged or stole to eke out an existence. On one I found a written list of all the workhouses for several counties round, and had those marked off for more frequent visitation, which he deemed the best. I have personally examined many who began a life of vagrancy at about 12 years of age and from the facilities afforded by workhouse relief have continued ever since in the same pursuit, outcast from society, knowing no home, counting all men their enemies and thus educating themselves for the most flagrant crimes, and are ready on a day's notice without remorse, to concentrate themselves for mischief in any part of the country.

About three months ago two, who had passed the night at this Union, were committed for setting fire to a stack of hay, and another for the same offence last week. One who has often visited here was lately committed for an attempt at highway robbery, and another is now lying in Ruthin Gaol, under a sentence of transportation for theft.

In giving these parties relief, then, in the way we have done, I really think we are aiding them in their criminal career, as it afforded them a comfortable leisure to mature their plans and go, without the care of providing for themselves, in quest of adventure. By the refusal of relief they are only put a little more to their shifts, and must either betake themselves to honest pursuits or show themselves in their true colours, and, consequently, be absorbed through the law.

The statements of Mr. Kemp were corroborated generally by the officers of other Unions and I, therefore, adopt his letter as exhibiting fairly enough the character of the evil with which the Guardians of several Unions of this district had to contend.

The measures adopted by the different Unions in this district for the repression of this evil were generally in strict accordance with the suggestions contained in the Circular of the 4th of August 1848. I shall now submit to the Board in detail, but as succinctly as possible, a statement of the results of those measures.

There then follows reports from the following:–
Chester Incorporation, Congleton Union, Wirral Union, Bridgnorth Union, Church Stretton Union, Cleobury Mortimer Union, Clun Union, Ellesmere Union, Ludlow Union, Madeley Union, Markey Drayton Union, Newport (Salop) Union, Shiffnall Union, Shrewsbury Incorporation, and Whitchurch Incorporation.

Seventh Annual Report of the Poor Law Board, 1854
[The following is part of a very long and detailed report:]

Parochial Union Schools
From Mr Jelinger C. Symons' General Report for 1854

South-East Salop District School
It appears to me that there can be but one opinion as to the desirability of removing children very early from adult pauper influence, under which they would be sure to imbibe the bad habits and vices of their parents and others of the same class, with whom they are daily brought into contact; but if so removed and associated with children of their own age, under good teaching and training, they are as innocent, and will remain so, as any better class, and it is fair to assume that a large percentage of them will turn out well in after-life. When I look at the accompanying list of men and women who were once children in this school, and who have kept up occasional intercourse by visit or letter, sometimes by a sudden and vigorous seizure of the hand in the street, when, with hearts bursting with gratitude they have made themselves known to me and declared that 'Their being sent to this school was the best thing that ever happened to them.' I think I am justified in coming to this conclusion. I beg distinctly to say that this is not a *picked* list but one made from memory of those I have present knowledge of; had not the books which I had in use previous to the formation of this district been recalled by the Bridgnorth Union, I should no doubt have been able to show a much larger one. Nor have the results since the formation of this into a district school, in October 1851, been less satisfactory. I can point to a girl whose first place was to nurse the child of a working farm bailiff; her second place is with

Third Annual Report of the Poor Law Board, 1850

A table from the Poor Law Board's Third Annual Report, 1850, listing, county by county, the poor rates receipt and expenditure for the year ending Lady Day 1850.

a shopkeeper of an adjoining parish, where she only keeps their books, but actually carries on the whole of their correspondence. To a boy who, fourteen months ago took his first place at 5s per week (out of which he had to board, lodge and clothe himself), raising himself gradually from that low sum to 6s., 8s., 10s., and 15s., till on January 18, he writes me, 'I am getting on first-rate in my new place, and have now 18s per week.' To a girl whose first place was at a farm-house where she remained two years, her second in a baronet's family near Stourport. To a boy in a gentleman's stables of whom the coachman told me 'He could trust him to put a pair of horses to, or take them out, as well as he could himself.' To another, a page at Dudmaston Hall; also a girl in the same gentleman's family, and many others, some to trades and others in service whom no doubt time will show to be good and useful people.

There is one thing in particular that strikes me as very remarkable and that is, that not only those who are grown up, but those who are still mere children, have a strong dislike to the term 'workhouse', and when the difference between this school and a workhouse has been pointed out to them there is an evident feeling of satisfaction, which I think promises well.

(signed) H. Garland

Persons who had left the School before it became a District School and of whom I have a present knowledge:

Benjamin Blunt	A farm labourer near Ludlow
Charles Edwards	Brush maker, New Jersey, America
John Edwards	With his brother
John Rowley	Postman, Wolverhampton
George Rowley	Works for a corn dealer, Birmingham
Phoebe Gritton	Married, in good circumstances
Sarah Gritton	Married to a butcher in Staffordshire
Mary Gritton	Married to a publican, able to retire any day
Mary A. Langford	Servant in a gentleman's family, London
Mary A. Reed	ditto in Birmingham
Eliza Reed	ditto ditto was once servant here
Elizabeth Harris	ditto at a farm near Bridgnorth has had only two places in six years
Elizabeth Bytheway	ditto ditto near the Cley Hills
Fanny Maisfield	ditto near the Cley Hills
Ann Bishton	married, near Kidderminster
Maria Biggs	Nursemaid in gentleman's family, Birmingham
Emma Smallman	Married, residing at Bridgnorth
Jane Smallman	ditto ditto
Ann Smallman	Servant at farm near Bridgnorth
Jane Thomas	Married, near Bridgnorth
Martha Thomas	Servant in Birmingham
Sarah Morris	Married, near the Cley Hills

Caroline Morris	Dairymaid, near Corve Dale
Eliza Morris	Married a farm labourer
William Wood	With his uncle in Birmingham
Elizabeth Good	Dairymaid and cook
William Good	Farm labourer
Michael Fazey	Currier, Wolverhampton
John Carter	Plane maker, Birmingham
Richard Carter	Soldier at Preston
Adah Carter	Drowned by accident
Joseph Crowther	Engineer to a water company
John Crowther	ditto ditto
Ellen Crowther	Domestic servant, Wolverhampton
James Davis	Farm labourer, near Stottesden
John Tailor	Shoemaker, near Oldbury, Worcestershire
Isaac Tailor	Farm labourer, near Alveley
Eliza Tailor	With her brother John, who finds her work
Thomas Bennet	Bricklayer
John Devenport	Servant to an auctioneer, Worcester, *very respectable*
Emma Devenport	Domestic servant, near Wolverhampton, *very respectable*
Samuel Jones	Foreman of a large establishment, Birmingham
John Nevitt	Private in the Royal Marines
Henry Hayward	Apprenticed to a broker, Stourbridge
Henry Lewis	Shoe maker, Wolverhampton
William Hitchcock	ditto Bridgnorth
George Ellis	Baker, Wolverhampton
William Fewtrill	Farm servant, wagoner
Sarah Salmon	ditto near Bridgnorth
William Moore	Bricklayer's labourer, Bridgnorth
Valantine Bishton	Gentleman's footman
William Rowley	Shoemaker, Bridgnorth
Frederick Pulley	Medical assistant, in France
James Fewtrill	Hostler, Bridgnorth
Ezekiel Tipton	Labourer, not very respectable
Edward Law	Carpet weaver, Kidderminster
John Broom	Collier, near Wolverhampton
Sarah Davis	Farm servant, near Church Stretton
Mary Justone	Domestic servant, Kingswinford
Ann Bowden	Married to a farm labourer
Mary Hall	Works at carpet factory, Bridgnorth
Jane Dalaway	Married
Hannah Pearce	Dress maker, near Bridgnorth, *very respectable*
Sarah Pearce	ditto ditto ditto
Jane Pearce	ditto ditto ditto

Mary Painter	Married, in London
Fanny Poutney	ditto to farm labourer, near Alveley
John Walter	Huckster, or dealer in fruit, game, &c.
Eliza Tomkins	Schoolmistress, Gloucestershire

BIBLIOGRAPHY

The History and Development of Poor Laws and the Support of the Poor in England and Wales

Anstruthers, Ian, *The Scandal of the Andover Workhouse*, Alan Sutton, 1984

Ashcroft, P.F. and Preston Thomas, H., *English Poor Law System*, 1888

Ayres, G.E., *Social Conditions and Welfare Legislation 1800–1930*, Macmillan, 1988

Booth, Charles, *The Aged Poor in England and Wales*, London, 1894

———, *Life and Labour of the People in London*, London, 1902

Bosanquet, H., *Social Work in London 1869 to 1912, A History of the Charity Organization Society*, 1914

Bowen, John, *The Bridgwater Case*, John Hatchard & Son, 1839

Brundage, Anthony, *The Making of the New Poor Law, 1832–39*, Hutchinson, 1978

Cambers, George F., *Digest of Cases Relating to Poor Law Matters*, Knight & Co., London, 1896

Cannan, G., *History of Local Rates in England*, 1927

Chambers, Jill, *Buckinghamshire Machine Breakers*, 2nd Edn, 1998

Chance, W., *Children under the Poor Law*, 1897

Checkland, S.G. & E.O.A., *The Poor Law Report of 1834*, Penguin, 1974

Chillcott, Charles, *The Poor Law and the Clutton Union*, Radstock & District Museum Society, 1996

Chinn, Carl, *Poverty Amidst Prosperity*, Manchester University Press, 1995

Cole, Anne, *Poor Law Documents Before 1834*, The Allen Group, 1993

Cole, John, *Down Poorhouse Lane*, Littleborough, 1984

Cowherd, R., *Political Economists and the Poor Laws*, Athens, Georgia, 1977

Crowther, M.A., *The Workhouse System 1834–1929*, Batsford, London, 1981

Davenport-Hill, Florence, *Children of the State*, Macmillan & Co. Ltd, 1889

———, *Children of the State*, 2nd Edn, 1889

———, *Children of the State: The Training of Juvenile Paupers*, London, 1868

Davey, Herbert, *The Poor Law Acts, 1894 to 1908*, Hadden, Best & Co., 1909

———, *Poor Law Settlement and Removal*, 3rd Edn, 1925

Digby, Anne, *The Rural Pauper Palaces*, Routledge & Kegan Paul, 1978

———, *Pauper Palaces*, Routledge & Kegan Paul, 1978

———, *The Poor Law in Nineteenth Century England and Wales*, The Historical Association Gen. Series, 1982

Driver, Felix, *Power and Pauperism, the Workhouse System 1838–1884*, Cambridge, 1993

Durmsday, W.H., *The Workhouse Officers' Handbook*, Hadden, Best & Co., 1907

———, *Local Government Law and Legislation*, Hadden, Best & Co., 1912

Eden, F.M., *The State of the Poor*, 1797

Edsall, Nicholas, *The Anti-Poor Law Movement 1834–44*, Manchester University Press, 1971

Engels, Frederick, *The Condition of the Working-Class in England in 1844*, George Allen & Unwin, 5th Edn, 1943

Fawcett, Henry, *Pauperism: Its Causes and Remedies*, Macmillan, 1871

Fenton, E. Pitts, *Model Rules, Regulations and Duties for Poor Law Officials*, Chas. Knight & Co. Ltd, (undated)

Finer, S.E., *The Life and Times of Sir Edwin Chadwick*, London, 1952

Fletcher, G.S., *The London Dickens Knew*, London, 1970

Fraser, Derek, *The New Poor Law in the Nineteenth Century*, Macmillan, 1976

———, *The Evolution of the British Welfare State*, Basingstoke, 1984

Frazer, W.M., *A History of English Public Health, 1834–1939*, London, 1950

Freeman, Albert C., *The Planning of Poor Law Buildings and Mortuaries*, St Brides Press Ltd, London, (undated)

Fuller, S.D., *Charity and the Poor Laws*, London, 1901

Gaunt, W., *English Rural Life in the Eighteenth Century*, 1925

Glen, W.C., *The Poor Law Orders*, Knight & Co., 1898

Gray, F., *The Tramp, His Meaning and Being*, 1931

Griffiths, Ken, *Workhouse – Brief Glimpses of the Poor Law and Life inside Clutton Union House*, Fiducia Press, 2005

Haw, G., *From Workhouse to Westminster: The Life Story of Will Crooks M.P.*, 1907

Higginbotham, Peter, *The Workhouse Cookbook*, The History Press, 2008

Hurley, Jack, *Rattle His Bones*, privately published, 1996 (Copy at Somerset Local History Library)

Jenner-Fust, H., *Poor Law Orders*, King & Son, 1907

Jennings, W. Ivor, *The Poor Law Code and the Law of Unemployment Assistance*, Chas. Knight & Co. Ltd, 1936

Jones, Kathleen, *Lunacy, Law and Conscience, 1744–1845*, Routledge and Kegan Paul, 1955

Knott, John, *Popular Opposition to the 1834 Poor Law*, London, 1986

Leach, R.A., *Pauper Children; Their Education and Training*, Manchester University Press, 1890

Leonard, E.M., *Early History of English Poor Relief*, Cambridge University Press, 1900

Levy, Leon S., *Nassau W. Senior, 1790–1864*, Newton Abbott, 1970

Lewis, R.A., *Edwin Chadwick and the Public Health Movement, 1832–1854*, London, 1952

Little, J. Brooke, *The Poor Law Statutes*, Shaw & Sons and Butterworth & Co., 1902

Longmate, Norman, *The Workhouse*, Temple Smith, London, 1974

Mackay, T.A., *The English Poor*, John Murray, 1889

———, *A History of the English Poor Law from 1834 to the Present Time*, John Murray, London, 1899

Marshall, Dorothy, *The English Poor in the Eighteenth Century*, George Routledge and Sons, 1926

Marshall, J.D., *The Old Poor Law, 1795–1834*, Macmillan, 1968

Maude, W.C., *Settlement and Removal*, Poor Law Publications Ltd, London, 3rd Edn, 1922

McCord, N., *The Implimentation of the 1834 Poor Law Amendment Act on Tyneside*, International Review of Social History, 1969

Melling, Elizabeth, *Kentish Sources. IV The Poor*, Kent County Council, 1964

Nicholas, C. Edsall, *The Anti-Poor Law Movement, 1834–1844*, Manchester, 1971

Nicholls, Sir George, *History of the English Poor Law*, P.S. King & Son & Mackay, Thos., 1904

Nolan, M., *Treatise of the Laws for the Relief and Settlement of the Poor*, 1808

Novak, Tony, *Poverty and the State: An Historical Sociology*, Milton Keynes, 1988

Oxley, G.W., *Poor Relief in England and Wales, 1602–1834*, David & Charles, 1974

Pashley, Robert, *Pauperism and Poor Laws*, Longman & Co., 1852

Percival, Tom, *Poor Law Children*, Shaw & Sons, 1911

Poynter, J.R., *Society and Pauperism: English Ideas on Poor Relief, 1795 to 1834*, Routledge & Kegan Paul, 1967

Pratt, John Tidd, *The Act for the Amendment and better Administration of the Law relating to the Poor, in England and Wales*, B. Fellows, 1834

Preston-Thomas, H., *The Work and Play of a Government Inspector*, 1909

Probyn, J.W., *Local Government and Taxation in the United Kingdom*, 1882

Reid, Andy, *The Union Workhouse*, Phillimore, 1994

Ribton-Turner, C.J., *A History of Vagrants and Vagrancy, and Beggars and Begging*, 1887

Richardson, John, *The Local Historian's Encyclopedia*, Historial Pubs, 1977

Rogers, J., *Reminiscences of a Workhouse Medical Officer*, 1889

Rose, M.E., *The English Poor Law 1780–1930*, David & Charles, 1971

———, *The Relief of Poverty 1834–1914*, Macmillan, 1972

———, *The Poor and the City: the English Poor Law in its Urban Context, 1834–1914*, Leicester, 1985

Sargent, W.L., *Economy of the Labouring Classes*, London, 1857

Scull, Andrew T., *Museums of Madness, the Social Organization of Insanity in Nineteenth Century England*, London, 1982

Slack, Paul, *Poverty and Policy in Tudor and Stuart England*, London, 1988

Smellie, K.B., *A History of Local Government*, London, 1968

Smith, F.B., *The People's Health, 1830–1910*, London, 1979

Stallard, J.H., *London Pauperism among Christians and Jews*, London, 1867

Tate, W.E., *The Parish Chest*, Phillimore, 1983

Taylor, Geoffrey, *The Problem of Poverty, 1660–1834*, London, 1969

Thane, Pat, *The Foundation of the Welfare State*, London, 1985

Treble, J.H., *Urban Poverty in Britain, 1830 to 1914*, London, 1983

Twining, L., *Workhouses and Pauperism*, 1898

Vorspan, R., *Vagrancy and the New Poor Law in late Victorian and Edwardian England*, English Historical Review, 1977

Webb, S. and B., *The Parish and the County*, Longmans, Green and Co., 1906

———, *English Local Government: English Poor Law History*, London, 1927

———, *English Poor Law Policy*, Cass, 1963

———, *English Poor Law History, Part I: The Old Poor Law*, Cass reprint, 1963

———, *English Poor Law History, Part II: The Last Hundred Years*, 2 vols, Cass reprint, 1963

Whitbread, Samuel, Substance of a Speech on the Poor Laws: Delivered to the House of Commons on Thursday 19 February 1807, J. Ridgway, 1807

White, John Meadows, *Remarks on the Poor Law Amendment Act as it affects Unions, or Parishes under the Government of Guardians or Select Vestries*, B. Fellows, 1834

Williams, Karel, *From Pauperism to Poverty*, London, 1981

Wohl, Anthony, *Endangered Lives: Public Health in Victorian Britain*, London, 1983

Wood, Peter, *Poverty and the Workhouse in Victorian Britain*, Stroud, 1991

Wythen Baxter, G.R., *The Book of the Bastile*, 1841

Young, G.M., *Early Victorian England, 1830–1865*, London, 1934

Reference Books for Family Historians Which Relate to the Poor Law

Baker, W.H., *Guide to Monmouthshire Record Office*, 1959

Bartlet, Eileen and Hillier, Angela, *Bastardy Cases – Bullingdon Petty Sessions* [Oxfordshire], The Eureka Partnership, 2004

Berkshire Records Office, *Guide to the Records of the New Poor Law and its successors in Berkshire, 1835 to 1948*, Berks Record Office, 1984

Bristol City Council, *The Poor Law in Bristol*, A handlist of records held at Bristol Record Office

Cole, Anne, *Poor Law Documents before 1834*, Federation of Family History Societies, 2nd Edn, 1996

Colwell, Stella, *Family Roots. Discovering the Past in the Public Record Office*, Weidenfeld and Nicolson, 1991

Cox, J.C., *Churchwardens' Accounts*, 1913

Dyer, T.F. Thistleton, *Old English Social Life as told by Parish Registers*, 1898

Fitzhugh, Terrick V.H., *The Dictionary of Genealogy*, Alpha Books, 1985

Gibson, Jeremy and others, *Poor Law Union Records* (in 4 parts), Federation of Family History Societies, 1993

Holdsworth, W.A., *The Handy Book of Parish Law*, (reprint) Wiltshire Family History Society, 1995

King, J.E., *Somerset Parochial Documents*, Somerset County Council, 1938
Munckton, Thelma, *Somerset Paupers, Unremembered Lives*, Wincanton Press, 1994
Smith, Joshua Toulmin, *The Parish*, 2nd Edn, 1857
Tate, W.E., *The Parish Chest*, Phillimore, 3rd Edn, 1883
Trotter, Eleanor, *Seventeenth Century Life in the Country Parish*, 1919
Webb, Adrian James, *An Index to Somerset Settlement Cases in Quarter Sessions, 1607 to 1700*, Harry Galloway Publishing, 1997

APPENDIX 1

ACTS OF PARLIAMENT RELATING TO THE POOR LAW

The following lists the most important Acts of Parliament from the sixteenth to the twentieth century which relate to the relief and governing of the poor:

22 Hen. VIII cap. 12 1530–31	A beggar must have a licence to beg.
27 Hen. VIII cap. 25 1535–36	Parishes to collect alms on Sundays to provide for the impotent poor. Children between the ages of 5 and 13 years who are begging or in idleness to be placed to masters in husbandry or other craft, to be taught. If any such children between the ages of 12 and 16 years refuse they are to be whipped with rods.
1 Edw. VI cap. 3 1547	Relief of the impotent poor by the charitable disposition of parishioners.
3&4 Ed. VI cap. 16 1549–50	Pauper children to be given apprenticeships.
5&6 Ed. VI cap. 2 1551–52	Officials to be appointed in every parish for the collection of alms from all householders for the relief of the Poor.
5 Eliz. I cap. 3 1562–63	If any parishioner refuses to contribute to the parish funds for the poor, the Justices of the Peace at Quarter Sessions can tax him and imprison him if he still refuses.
5 Eliz. I cap. 4 1562–63	Every householder may take any person above the age of 10 years and under 18 years as an apprentice to serve as the parties can agree. No trader shall take any apprentice or servant unless the apprentice or servant be his son. Every cloth-worker, fuller, shearman, weaver, tailor or shoemaker, who shall have three apprentices shall keep one journeyman, and for every other apprentice above three, one other journeyman, on pain of £10. An apprenticeship can only be created by an indenture. Justices are authorised to grant warrants to apprehend apprentices or servants who shall abscond from service, and to imprison them until they demean themselves properly. Owners of ships, householders using the trade of fishing, cannonries and shipwrights may take apprentices being above 7 years of age. No person shall exercise any art, mystery or manual occupation in England and Wales, except he shall have been brought up there in seven years at least as an apprentice, nor set any person on work in such art, mystery or manual occupation, except such person shall have been an apprentice as aforesaid.

5 Eliz. I cap. 4 1562–63	A pauper child may become an apprentice.
5 Eliz. I cap. 29 & 30	Authorised Justices to raise taxes.
14 Eliz. I cap. 5 1572	Begging licences abolished. Overseers of the Poor to be appointed by Justices of the Peace in addition to the elected collectors of taxes for the relief of the poor. [This replaced the collection of voluntary contributions.]
18 Eliz. I cap. 2 1575–76	A woman with an illegitimate child which is likely to become chargeable to the parish, to be examined to establish the name of the father. The father then to make payments to support the child. Default of payment will result in a prison sentence.
18 Eliz. I cap. 3 1577–78	Justices may make order for the maintenance of a bastard child by charging the mother or reputed father a weekly payment.
31 Eliz. I cap. 18 1588–89	No cottage must be built unless four acres of land is allotted to it; and the keeping of lodgers prohibited. [The purpose of this act was to reduce rural poverty by preventing over-population of villages where employment was restricted by the availability of land.]
35 Eliz. I cap. 4 1592–93	Rates imposed for county funds to provide disability pensions for soldiers and sailors.
39 Eliz. I cap. 3 1596–97	Appointment of overseers for every parish to provide for the poor who cannot support themselves. Overseers to provide accounts annually to Justices.
39 Eliz. I cap. 4 1596–97	Vagrants to be punished by whipping and sent back to the place where they belonged.
39 Eliz. I cap. 5 1596–97	Private charities encouraged to provide workhouses for the poor. [Some charitable foundations did establish workhouses but these did not survive for long.]
43 Eliz. I cap. 2 1601	Overseers of the poor to be appointed annually to raise and distribute relief to the poor with the consent of two or more justices. Justices and magistrates neglecting to appoint overseers shall forfeit £5 to the poor. The place of legal settlement assumed to be the pauper's place of birth or in which parish he has dwelt for at least three previous years consecutively. Overseers empowered to bind poor children of their parish from the age of 7 years to apprenticeships anywhere they see convenient. A boy apprentice to continue until he reaches the age of 24 years. A girl apprentice to complete the apprenticeship when she reaches the age of 21 years, or at marriage. The father and grandfather, and the mother and grandmother of any poor, old, blind, lame and impotent person, or other persons not able to work shall relieve and maintain every such poor person. [A Jew was not liable to maintain a daughter under 43 Eliz. I cap. 2 and therefore, where an order was made for a Jew to maintain an only daughter whom he had turned out of doors for embracing Christianity, it was quashed.]
1 James I cap. 17 1603–04	No hatter or felt-maker shall retain more than two apprentices at the same time, nor those for any less term than seven years on pain of £5, except the apprentice be his own son bound for seven years and the term not to expire till he be 21 years old.
7 James I cap. 4 1609	Persons running away from their families and leaving them on the parish are incorrigible rogues – such persons shall be sent to the House of Correction. [Giving birth to an illegitimate child became an offence if the child became chargeable to a parish.]

13&14 Chas II cap. 12 1662	Overseers empowered to remove any person who is likely to become chargeable to their parish, to their rightful place of settlement. Persons who reside for forty days upon a tenement of yearly value of £10 shall not be removed. A reward to be paid to local officials to implement the law against vagrants.
1 James II cap. 17 1685	Forty days shall run from the day written notice is given to the overseers for the removal of a pauper after which time the pauper cannot be removed. [This act gave the authorities time to identify a pauper and draw up a Removal Order. Before this act many paupers were not removable because they had remained in a parish for more than forty days before being identified.]
3&4 Wm. & Mary cap. 11 1692	Justices to authorise all relief except in a case of emergency. Books to be kept in every parish, and a register of those receiving relief, which can be examined by parishioners. No soldier, seaman, shipwright or other artificer in the King's service shall have any settlement in any parish until after his dismission [sic]. Settlement may be gained by apprenticeship. If any person inhabiting in any parish shall for himself, and on his own account be charged with and pay his share towards the public taxes or levies of the said parish, he shall thereby gain a settlement. A person who – on his own account executes any public office – shall thereby gain a settlement. If an unmarried person not having a child or children shall be lawfully hired into any parish or town for one year, such service shall be deemed a good settlement therein.
3 Wm. & Mary cap. 18 1692	Notice of a removal to be read out in church and entered in the overseer's account book.
7&8 Wm. III cap. 32 1696	Town parishes can unite to create a more efficient system, thus making financial savings. To be run by professional staff.
8&9 Wm. III cap. 30 1697	Paupers receiving relief to wear a P and the first letter of the parish, upon the shoulder of the right sleeve, in blue or red cloth. The penalty for not doing so is either to have his relief suspended or to be whipped at the House of Correction and kept to hard labour up to 21 days. [This was repealed in 1810 by 50 Geo. III cap. 52.] Any person entering a parish shall bring a certificate [which identifies their place of settlement]. Foreigners having no place of settlement cannot be removed from the place in which they land from abroad. If a foreigner marry and have children and they become paupers before the father has acquired a place of settlement such children shall take the settlement of their mother. An unmarried person hired to serve for a year as a servant will gain a settlement in the parish of employment.
9 Wm. III cap. 11 1697	No certificated person shall be capable of gaining a legal settlement by hiring and service. No certificated person shall be capable of gaining a settlement by apprenticeship.
11 Wm. III cap. 18 1699	The expense of removing vagrants to be paid for from county funds and not by individual parishes.
12 Anne cap. 18 1713	If any person shall be hired a servant to, or with a certificated person, such person, by being hired by or serving such certificated person as a servant, shall not gain any settlement.
13 Anne cap. 26 1714	Rogues and vagabonds to be examined to determine their rightful place of settlement before justices of the peace. The records to be kept with the records of the County Quarter Sessions. Vagrants to be returned to their place of settlement.

9 Geo. I cap. 7 1722	Churchwardens and overseers, with the consent of the majority of the parishioners or inhabitants in vestry for that purpose assembled, upon the usual notice thereof first given, may purchase or hire any house or houses in the parish and contract with any person for the maintaining of their poor.
3 Geo. II cap. 29 1730	Overseers of a parish removing a pauper to another parish to be reimbursed for the cost of the removal by the receiving parish.
6 Geo. II cap. 31 1732	The reputed father of a bastard child to be committed to gaol if he does not indemnify the parish from the cost of maintaining the child.
17 Geo. II cap. 3 1743	Churchwardens to give notice in the church of the rate of relief to the poor.
17 Geo. II cap. 5 1743	Rates raised for poor relief to be entered into a book for public inspection. Bastards born on the street where the mother is wandering and begging shall not be settled where born, but shall have the mother's settlement.
17 Geo. II cap. 38 1743	Allows appeals to Quarter Sessions against poor rates. All persons who run away and leave their wives and children whereby they become chargeable to any parish or place, shall be declared rogues and vagabonds.
22 Geo. II cap. 44 1748	Officers, marines and soldiers who have been at any time employed in His Majesty's service since 11th June 1727, and have not since deserted the said service shall not be removed from any parish or place in Great Britain or Ireland in which they shall set up and exercise any such trades as are within the 5 Eliz. I cap. 4.
26 Geo. II cap. 107 1752	No sergeant, corporal or drummer of militia, nor any private from his enrolment to his discharge shall be compelled to serve as a peace or parish officer. [But not officers of the militia.]
2 Geo. III cap. 22 1761	Parishes to keep a register of all children born in the workhouse.
3 Geo. III cap. 8 1762	All officers, marines, soldiers &c., may exercise trades without having served apprenticeships.
13 Geo. III cap. 82 1772	No bastard born in a hospital shall be legally settled in the parish in which the hospital is situated. Such child shall have the settlement of the mother. Parish officers of the mother's place of settlement shall have authority to apprehend the reputed father of such bastard child.
13 Geo. III cap. 84 1772	No person renting the tolls of turnpikes and residing in any tollhouse belonging to the trustees shall hereby gain a settlement.
18 Geo. III cap. 47 1777	Apprenticeship for boys reduced to a period of 7 years or until he reaches the age of 21 years.
19 Geo. III cap. 72 1778	A substitute in militia whose family becomes chargeable – order of relief of such family – overseers in which parish they shall serve to reimburse the parish in which the family is relieved.
22 Geo. III cap. 83 1781	[Gilbert's Act] Parishes allowed to form themselves into unions for the better management of the poor. These to be supervised by a committee of local gentry. The able bodied to be provided with employment outside the workhouse. Indoor relief to be confined to the impotent poor. Children under 7 years of age to be allowed to remain with their parents, and orphan children to be boarded out.

24 Geo. III cap. 6 1783	Officers, marines, and soldiers, who have personally served since 1st April 1763 and also their wives and children, shall not be removed from any parish or place in which they shall set up and exercise any trade until they become chargeable.
26 Geo. III cap. 107 1785	As 24 Geo. III cap. 6 above and to include militia men who are married.
28 Geo. III cap. 48 1787	A boy of 8 years old, with the consent of parents, can be an apprentice to a chimney sweep.
32 Geo. III cap. 44 1792	Justices may order vagrants to be conveyed by masters of Houses of Correction. The Sessions shall fix the rate to be allowed for passing vagrants.
32 Geo. III cap. 57 1792	If the master or mistress of an apprentice dies during the apprenticeship, the apprentice to be maintained by the executors for not longer than three months. The apprentice can then serve another master.
33 Geo. III cap. 8 1792	The family of a militia man who was 'ordered to march' to be given support.
35 Geo. III cap. 101 1795	No persons can be removed from a parish until he applies for relief and therefore becomes chargeable.
36 Geo. III cap. 23 1795	Justices authorised to grant emergency out door relief.
42 Geo. III cap. 46 1802	[This refers to 43 Eliz. I cap. 2 – Apprentices] Every parish which binds out poor children as apprentices to keep a book recording all the apprentices with the name and residence of the master or mistress.
43 Geo. III cap. 58 1802–03	A woman who conceals the birth of a bastard child can be prosecuted.
48 Geo. III cap. 96 1808	Justices shall by warrant remove into an asylum lunatic paupers, and the parish chargeable shall pay the asylum a weekly allowance for them.
50 Geo. III cap. 52 1810	The act of 8 & 9 Wm. III which required all paupers to wear a badge indicating their parish on their right shoulder, is repealed.
55 Geo. III cap. 137 1815	Inmates of workhouses who abscond with workhouse clothes, tools, utensils, etc., to be punished with imprisonment.
56 Geo. III cap. 139 1816	A child not to be bound an apprentice until he reaches the age of 9 years.
59 Geo. III cap. 12 1819	Authorises the election of parish standing committees and the appointment of paid officers. Loans permitted to Greenwich and Chelsea Pensioners for the support of their families. The loans are recoverable quarterly. Parishes may provide land for the employment of the poor which must not exceed 20 acres. This act also authorises the provision of allotments for the poor at the parish expense to encourage the poor towards self sufficiency and thus reduce the rates. Justices are empowered to order payment of the wages of a seamen, whose family, during his absence, has become chargeable, for the indemnity of parishes. Owners of all houses, apartments and dwellings, which are let to occupiers at a rent; not exceeding £20, nor less than £6 by the year for any less term than one year – shall be assessed to the Rates for Relief of the Poor. [i.e. The owner not the occupier to pay the rates on the property in these circumstances.]

9 Geo. IV cap. 31 1828	A woman that is delivered of a bastard child which dies and secretly disposes of the body of the child shall be liable to imprisonment.
2&3 Wm. IV cap. 96 1831–32	Permits roundsmen [unemployed labourers] to be sent to work on farms in their parish and their wages to be paid wholly by the parish, or jointly by the parish and farmer, or wholly by the farmer.
4&5 Wm. IV cap. 76 1834	The Poor Law Amendment Act. The creation of Poor Law Unions throughout England and Wales by uniting parishes. A workhouse to be built in each union. The Poor Law Commission was established in London. [From 1834 the laws relating to the poor are known as the New Poor Law. The period before this is known as the Old Poor Law.]
3&4 Vict. cap. 29 1840	Children to be vaccinated against smallpox.
7&8 Vict. cap. 101 1844	Guardians of Unions can apply money raised or borrowed, for the expense of the emigration of paupers within their union. Paupers who die in a workhouse are to be buried in the parish to which they were chargeable in their lifetime.
9&10 Vict. cap. 66 1846	Persons who have continually resided in a parish for 5 years cannot be removed to their place of settlement.
24&25 Vict. cap. 66 1861	Persons who have continually resided in a parish for 3 years cannot be removed to their place of settlement.
30&31 Vict. cap. 84 1867	A certificate of vaccination to be issued for all children vaccinated against smallpox.
33&34 Vict. cap. 75 1870	The Education Department given powers to improve elementary education.

1846	The Poor Law Board replaced the Poor Law Commission.
1871	The Local Government Board was formed and took over the responsibilities of the Poor Law Board, together with responsibility for sanitation, bridges and highways, water supplies and drainage.
1919	The administration of the Poor Law was transferred to the Ministry of Health.
1930	County councils formed Public Assistance Committees which took over the functions of Poor Law Guardians.
1948	National Assistance provided for the needy.

APPENDIX 2

LISTS OF POOR LAW UNIONS IN ENGLAND AND WALES

The National Archives references to the correspondence files are given under MH 12. These files commence in 1834 and run to 1900. There are some missing records for a small number of unions and gaps in the dates of others. Most of the later records (from 1900) were destroyed in the Second World War. Poor Law Union staff are recorded in Registers of Paid Officers under MH 9 (1837–1921).

England	MH 12	MH 9
Bedfordshire	Piece No	Piece No
Ampthill	1 to 20	1
Bedford	21 to 54	2
Biggleswade	55 to 76	2
Leighton Buzzard	77 to 95	10
Luton	96 to 125	10
Woburn	126 to 138	19
Berkshire		
Abingdon	139 to 161	1
Bradfield	162 to 180	3
Cookham (renamed Maidenhead in 1899)	181 to 200	11
Easthampstead	201 to 216	6
Faringdon	217 to 233	7
Hungerford	234 to 251	9
Maidenhead *see* Cookham		
Newbury	252 to 274	12
Reading	275 to 296	14
Wallingford	297 to 317	18
Wantage	318 to 334	18

[contd]

Windsor	335 to 361	19
Wokingham	362 to 379	19
Buckinghamshire		
Amersham	380 to 404	1
Aylesbury	405 to 435	1
Buckingham	436 to 456	3
Eton	457 to 486	6
Newport Pagnell	487 to 511	12
Winslow	512 to 524	19
Wycombe	525 to 558	19
Cambridgeshire		
Cambridge	559 to 597	4
Caxton	598 to 614	4
Chesterton	615 to 645	4
Ely	646 to 666	6
Linton	667 to 683	10
Newmarket	684 to 713	12
North Witchford	714 to 730	12
Whittlesey	731 to 740	18
Wisbech (or Wisbeach)	741 to 769	19
Cheshire		
Altrincham (became Bucklow in 1895)	770 to 820	1
Birkenhead	821 to 876	2
Chester (founded in 1762)	900 to 933	4
Congleton	934 to 967	5
Great Boughton (Tarvin from 1871)	877 to 899	3
Macclesfield	968 to 1,012	11
Nantwich	1,013 to 1,058	12
Northwich	1,059 to 1,102	12
Runcorn	1,103 to 1,137	14
Stockport	1,138 to 1,199	16
Wirral	1,200 to 1,244	19
Cornwall		
Bodmin	1,274 to 1,298	3
Camelford	1,299 to 1,312	4
Falmouth	1,337 to 1,363	7
Helston	1,384 to 1,406	8
Launceston	1,407 to 1,428	10

Liskeard	1,429 to 1,452	10
Penzance	1,453 to 1,485	13
Redruth	1,486 to 1,515	14
St Austell	1,245 to 1,273	1
St Columb Major	1,313 to 1,336	5
St Germans	1,364 to 1,383	7
Isles of Scilly	none	
Stratton	1,516 to 1,526	16
Truro	1,527 to 1,556	17
Cumberland		
Alston with Garrigill	1,557 to 1,564	1
Bootle	1,565 to 1,580	3
Brampton	1,581 to 1,592	3
Carlisle	1,593 to 1,623	4
Cockermouth	1,624 to 1,674	5
Longtown	1,675 to 1,683	10
Penrith	1,684 to 1,705	13
Whitehaven	1,706 to 1,747	18
Wigton	1,748 to 1,771	19
Derbyshire		
Ashbourne	1,772 to 1,798	1
Bakewell	1,799 to 1,839	2
Belper	1,840 to 1,890	2
Chapel en le Frith	1,891 to 1,919	4
Chesterfield	1,920 to 1,983	4
Derby	1,984 to 2,020	6
Glossop	2,021 to 2,039	7
Hayfield	2,040 to 2,059	8
Shardlow	2,060 to 2,094	15
Devonshire		
Axminster	2,095 to 2,123	1
Barnstaple	2,124 to 2,165	2
Bideford	2,166 to 2,192	2
Crediton	2,193 to 2,216	5
Devonport (from 1898) *see* Stoke Damerel		
Exeter (founded in 1697)	2,238 to 2,257	6
Holsworthy	2,258 to 2,272	8
Honiton	2,273 to 2,299	9

[contd]

Kingsbridge	2,300 to 2,327	9
South Molton	2,493 to 2,516	15
Newton Abbott	2,328 to 2,393	12
Okehampton	2,394 to 2,419	12
Plymouth	2,420 to 2,462	13
Plympton St Mary	2,463 to 2,492	13
St Thomas (Exeter)	2,567 to 2,604	17
Stoke Damerel	2,517 to 2,535	6 and 16
East Stonehouse	2,217 to 2,237	6
Tavistock	2,540 to 2,565	17
Tiverton	2,605 to 2,635	17
Torrington	2,636 to 2,655	17
Totnes	2,656 to 2,704	17
Dorsetshire		
Beaminster	2,705 to 2,723	2
Blandford	2,724 to 2,743	2
Bridport	2,744 to 2,763	3
Cerne Abbas	2,764 to 2,776	4
Dorchester	2,777 to 2,796	6
Poole	2,797 to 2,818	13
Shaftesbury	2,819 to 2,829	15
Sherborne	2,830 to 2,845	15
Sturminster Newton	2,846 to 2,860	16
Wareham and Purbeck	2,861 to 2,884	18
Weymouth	2,885 to 2,910	18
Wimborne and Cranborne	2,911 to 2,927	19
County Durham		
Bishop Auckland	2,928 to 2,967	1
Chester le Street	2,968 to 2,988	4
Darlington	2,989 to 3,017	6
Durham	3,018 to 3,051	6
Easington	3,052 to 3,067	6
Gateshead	3,068 to 3,118	7
Hartlepool	3,119 to 3,146	8
Houghton le Spring	3,147 to 3,164	9
Lanchester	3,165 to 3,187	10
Sedgefield	3,188 to 3,200	15
South Shields	3,201 to 3,240	15

Stockton	3,241 to 3,267	16
Sunderland	3,268 to 3,312	16
Teesdale	3,313 to 3,332	17
Weardale	3,333 to 3,346	18
Essex		
Billericay	3,347 to 3,373	2
Braintree	3,374 to 3,395	3
Chelmsford	3,396 to 3,427	4
Colchester	3,428 to 3,455	5
Dunmow	3,456 to 3,477	6
Epping	3,478 to 3,511	6
Halstead	3,512 to 3,531	8
Lexden and Winstree	3,532 to 3,554	10
Maldon	3,555 to 3,579	11
Ongar	3,580 to 3,600	12
Orsett	3,601 to 3,623	12
Rochford (includes Southend)	3,624 to 3,660	14
Romford	3,661 to 3,705	14
Saffron Walden	3,706 to 3,727	15
Tendring	3,728 to 3,768	17
West Ham	3,769 to 3,861	18 and 20
Witham (*see* Braintree)	none	19
Gloucestershire (including the City of Bristol)		
Bristol: Barton Regis	4,025 to 4,053	3
Clifton	4,000 to 4,024	3
Cheltenham	3,912 to 3,961	4
Chipping Sodbury	3,962 to 3,979	5
Cirencester	3,980 to 3,999	5
Dursley	4,054 to 4,071	6
Gloucester	4,073 to 4,107	7
Newent	4,114 to 4,130	12
Northleach	4,134 to 4,144	12
Stow on the Wold	4,145 to 4,163	16
Stroud	4,164 to 4,195	16
Tetbury	4,196 to 4,204	17
Tewkesbury	4,205 to 4,223	17
Thornbury	4,224 to 4,235	17
Westbury on Severn	4,236 to 4,261	18

[contd]

Wheatenhurst	4,262 to 4,270	18
Winchcombe	4,271 to 4,284	9
Hampshire		
Alresford	10,613 to 10,624	1
Alton	10,625 to 10,644	1
Alverstoke (founded in 1799)	10,645 to 10,660	1
Andover	10,661 to 10,668	1
Basingstoke	10,669 to 10,700	2
Bournemouth and Christchurch (to 1900)	10,710 to 10,750	5
Catherington	10,701 to 10,709	4
Droxford	10,751 to 10,766	6
Fareham	10,767 to 10,789	7
Farnborough (founded in 1794)	10,790 to 10,791	7
Fordingbridge	10,792 to 10,803	7
Hartley Wintney	10,804 to 10,819	8
Havant	10,820 to 10,844	8
Hursley	10,845 to 10,852	9
Isle of Wight (founded in 1770)	11,084 to 11,144	19
Kingsclere	10,853 to 10,864	9
Lymington	10,865 to 10,884	10
New Forest	10,885 to 10,895	8
Petersfield	10,896 to 10,915	13
Portsea/Portsmouth	10,916 to 10,970	13
Ringwood	10,971 to 10,982	14
Romsey	10,983 to 10,996	14
South Stoneham	11,035 to 11,056	15
Southampton (founded in 1772)	10,997 to 11,025	15
Stockbridge	11,063 to 11,073	16
Whitchurch	11,074 to 11,083	18
Winchester	11,168 to 11,195	19
Herefordshire		
Bromyard	4,285 to 4,307	3
Dore	4,308 to 4,322	6
Hereford	4,323 to 4,347	8
Kington	4,348 to 4,363	9
Ledbury	4,364 to 4,384	10
Leominster	4,385 to 4,404	10
Ross	4,405 to 4,427	14

Weobley	4,428 to 4,440	18
Hertfordshire		
Barnet	4,466 to 4,517	2
Berkhampstead	4,518 to 4,535	2
Bishops Stortford	4,536 to 4,556	2
Buntingford	4,557 to 4,565	3
Hatfield	4,566 to 4,575	8
Hemel Hempstead	4,576 to 4,590	8
Hertford	4,591 to 4,611	8
Hitchin	4,612 to 4,638	8
Royston	4,639 to 4,659	14
St Albans	4,441 to 4,465	1
Ware	4,660 to 4,678	18
Watford	4,679 to 4,708	18
Welwyn	4,709 to 4,715	18
Huntingdonshire		
Huntingdon	4,716 to 4,741	9
St Ives	4,742 to 4,763	9
St Neots	4,764 to 4,782	12
Kent		
Blean	4,818 to 4,840	2
Bridge	4,841 to 4,854	3
Bromley	4,855 to 4,886	3
Canterbury (founded in 1771)	4,897 to 4,910	4
Cranbrook	4,911 to 4,922	5
Dartford	4,923 to 4,954	6
Dover	4,955 to 4,987	6
East Ashford	4,783 to 4,797	1
Eastry	4,988 to 5,018	6
Elham	5,019 to 5,053	6
Faversham	5,054 to 5,074	7
Gravesend and Milton	5,075 to 5,090	7
Greenwich	5,091 to 5,133	7
Hollingbourne	5,134 to 5,156	8
Hoo	5,157 to 5,165	9
Lewisham	5,166 to 5,194	10
Maidstone	5,195 to 5,225	11
Malling	5,226 to 5,248	11

[contd]

Medway	5,249 to 5,278	11
Milton	5,279 to 5,292	11
North Aylesford (Strood from 1884)	5,293 to 5,305	16
Romney Marsh	5,306 to 5,314	14
Sevenoaks	5,315 to 5,327	15
Sheppey	5,328 to 5,332	15
Tenterden	5,333 to 5,342	17
Thanet	5,343 to 5,371	17
Tonbridge	5,372 to 5,387	17
West Ashford	4,798 to 4,817	1
Woolwich	5,388 to 5,412	37
Lancashire		
Ashton-under-Lyne	5,413 to 5,474	1
Barrow-in-Furness (founded in 1872)	5,475 to 5,485	3
Barton-upon-Irwell	5,486 to 5,528	2
Blackburn	5,529 to 5,592	2
Bolton	5,593 to 5,655	3
Burnley	5,673 to 5,710	3
Bury	5,730 to 5,737	3
Caton (became part of Lunedale in 1869)	none	4 and 10
Chorley	5,738 to 5,742	5
Chorlton	5,743 to 5,751	5 and 20
Clitheroe	5,752 to 5,765	5
Fylde	5,766 to 5,824	7
Garstang	5,825 to 5,839	7
Haslingden	5,840 to 5,878	8
Lancaster	5,889 to 5,925	10
Leigh	5,926 to 5,965	10
Liverpool	5,966 to 6,032	10 and 20
Lunesdale (founded in 1869)	6,033 to 6,038	10
Manchester	6,039 to 6,093	11 and 20
Oldham	none	12
Ormskirk	none	12
Prescot	6,094 to 6,111	13
Preston	6,112 to 6,146	13
Prestwich	6,147 to 6,175	13
Rochdale	6,176 to 6,219	14
Salford	6,220 to 6,271	15

Todmorton	6,272 to 6,298	17
Toxteth Park	6,299 to 6,319	17
Ulverston	6,320 to 6,349	17
Warrington	6,350 to 6,366	18
West Derby	6,367 to 6,377	18
Wigan	6,378 to 6,386	19
Leicestershire		
Ashby de la Zouch	6,387 to 6,397	1
Barrow-upon-Soar	6,398 to 6,412	2
Billesdon	6,413 to 6,420	2
Blaby	6,421 to 6,442	2
Hinckley	6,443 to 6,467	8
Leicester	6,468 to 6,510	10
Loughborough	6,523 to 6,543	10
Lutterworth	6,544 to 6,565	10
Market Bosworth	6,566 to 6,580	11
Market Harborough	6,581 to 6,608	11
Melton Mowbray	6,609 to 6,628	11
Lincolnshire		
Boston	6,629 to 6,656	3
Bourne	6,657 to 6,676	3
Caistor (renamed Grimsby in 1890)	6,677 to 6,706	4 and 7
Gainsborough	6,707 to 6,717	7
Glanford Brigg	6,718 to 6,724	7
Grantham	6,725 to 6,731	7
Holbeach	none	8
Horncastle	none	9
Lincoln	6,732 to 6,737	10
Louth	6,738 to 6,762	10
Sleaford	6,763 to 6,780	15
Spalding	6,781 to 6,796	16
Spilsby	6,797 to 6,816	16
Stamford	6,820 to 6,842	16
London and Middlesex		
City of London	*746 to 781*	*10*
Bethnal Green	6,843 to 6,899	1
Brentford	6,900 to 6,958	3
Chelsea	6,988 to 7,019	4

[contd]

Edmonton	7,025 to 7,071	6
Fulham	7,078 to 7,100	7
Hackney	7,154 to 7,199	8
Hammersmith	7,220 to 7,221	none
Hampstead	7,203 to 7,217	8
Hendon	7,222 to 7,266	8
Holborn	7,286 to 7,361	8
Holborn (Clerkenwell)	7,022 to 7,024	5
Holborn (St Giles in the Fields and St George Bloomsbury)	7,137 to 7,152	7
Islington	7,366 to 7,407	9
Kensington	7,437 to 7,459	9
Limehouse	none	none
Mile End	7,530 to 7,562	11
Paddington	7,564 to 7,589	13
Poplar (founded in 1889)	7,681 to 7,713	13
Shoreditch	7,718 to 7,762	15
Southwark	none	7
St Marylebone	7,485 to 7,529	11
St Pancras	7,593 to 7,680	13
St George Hanover Square	7,127 to 7,136	7
St George in the East	7,103 to 7,126	7
St Martin in the Fields	7,483 to 7,484	11
Staines	7,767 to 7,797	16
Stepney	7,798 to 7,833	16
Strand	7,834 to 7,874	16
Uxbridge	7,875 to 7,911	17
Westminster	7,412 to 7,436	none
Whitechapel	7,912 to 7,957	18
Willesden	7,958 to 7,963	19
Norfolk		
Aylsham	8,185 to 8,207	1
Blofield	8,208 to 8,223	2
Brinton (founded in 1738)	none	3
Depwade	8,224 to 8,248	6
Docking	8,249 to 8,267	6
Downham	8,268 to 8,292	6
Erpington	8,293 to 8,317	6
East and West Flegg	8,340 to 8,355	7

Forehoe	8,356 to 8,374	7
Freebridge Lynn	8,375 to 8,391	9
Guiltcross	8,393 to 8,413	7
Henstead	8,415 to 8,428	8
King's Lynn	8,429 to 8,450	9
Loddon and Clavering	8,455 to 8,473	9
Mitford and Launditch	8,474 to 8,501	11
Norwich	8,502 to 8,530	12
St Faith's (founded in 1805)	8,325 to 8,339	9
Swaffham	8,639 to 8,653	16
Thetford	8,555 to 8,577	17
Tunstead and Happing (renamed Smallburgh in 1870)	8,578 to 8,595	17
Walsingham	8,596 to 8,615	18
Wayland	8,616 to 8,629	18
Yarmouth	8,630 to 8,663	19
Northamptonshire		
Brackley	8,671 to 8,688	3
Brixworth	8,689 to 8,710	3
Daventry	8,711 to 8,730	6
Hardingstone	8,731 to 8,748	8
Kettering	8,749 to 8,779	9
Northampton	8,780 to 8,808	12
Oundle	8,809 to 8,827	12
Peterborough	8,828 to 8,860	13
Potterspury	16,727 to 16,741	13
Thrapston	8,861 to 8,878	17
Towcester	8,879 to 8,897	17
Wellingborough	8,898 to 8,926	18
Northumberland		
Alnwick	8,927 to 8,953	1
Belford	8,954 to 8,963	2
Bellingham	8,964 to 8,975	2
Berwick	8,976 to 9,001	2
Castle Ward	9,002 to 9,019	4
Glendale	9,020 to 9,031	7
Haltwhistle	9,032 to 9,039	8
Hexham	9,040 to 9,070	8
Morpeth	9,071 to 9,095	11

[contd]

Newcastle-upon-Tyne	9,096 to 9,135	12
Rothbury	9,144 to 9,155	14
Tynemouth	9,156 to 9,227	17
Nottinghamshire		
Basford	9,228 to 9,293	2
Bingham	9,315 to 9,332	2
East Retford	9,333 to 9,355	6
Mansfield	9,356 to 9,398	11
Newark	9,411 to 9,438	12
Nottingham	9,444 to 9,499	12
Radford	9,511 to 9,523	14
Southwell	9,524 to 9,548	15
Worksop	9,549 to 9,576	19
Oxfordshire		
Banbury	9,577 to 9,613	2
Bicester	9,614 to 9,636	2
Chipping Norton	9,637 to 9,657	5
Headington	9,658 to 9,680	8
Henley	9,681 to 9,705	8
Oxford	9,706 to 9,731	12
Thame	9,732 to 9,752	17
Witney	9,753 to 9,774	19
Woodstock	9,775 to 9,792	19
Rutland		
Oakham	9,793 to 9,805	12
Uppingham	9,806 to 9,821	17
Shropshire		
Atcham	9,822 to 9,849	1
Bridgnorth	9,850 to 9,868	3
Church Stretton	9,869 to 9,881	5
Cleobury Mortimer	9,882 to 9,895	5
Clun	9,896 to 9,917	5
Ellesmere	9,935 to 9,953	6
Ludlow	9,954 to 9,980	10
Madeley	9,981 to 10,001	11
Market Drayton	9,918 to 9,934	6
Newport	10,002 to 10,018	12
Oswestry	10,019 to 10,039	12

Shifnal	10,040 to 10,052	15
Shrewsbury (founded in 1784)	10,053 to 10,058	15
Wellington	10,059 to 10,084	18
Wem	10,085 to 10,100	18
Whitchurch (founded in 1792)	10,101 to 10,117	18
Somersetshire		
Axbridge	10,118 to 10,157	1
Bath	10,158 to 10,203	2
Bedminster (renamed Long Ashton in 1899)	10,204 to 10,242	2
Bridgwater	10,243 to 10,284	3
Chard	10,285 to 10,319	4
Clutton	10,320 to 10,345	5
Dulverton	10,346 to 10,357	6
Frome	10,358 to 10,376	6
Keynsham	10,377 to 10,405	9
Langport	10,406 to 10,426	10
Shepton Mallet	10,427 to 10,451	15
Taunton	10,452 to 10,486	17
Wellington	10,487 to 10,514	18
Wells	10,515 to 10,541	18
Williton	10,542 to 10,566	19
Wincanton	10,567 to 10,585	19
Yeovil	10,586 to 10,612	19
Staffordshire		
Burton upon Trent	11,232 to 11,275	3
Cannock	11,389 to 11,412	4
Cheadle	11,276 to 11,296	4
Dudley	13,958 to 13,996	6
Leek	11,297 to 11,329	10
Lichfield	11,330 to 11,362	10
Newcastle under Lyme	11,363 to 11,383	12
Seisdon	11,413 to 11,427	15
Stafford	11,428 to 11,457	16
Stoke on Trent	11,458 to 11,508	16
Stone	11,509 to 11,531	16
Tamworth	11,532 to 11,558	17
Uttoxeter	11,559 to 11,577	17
Walsall	11,578 to 11,6124	17

[contd]

West Bromwich	11,625 to 11,673	18
Wolstanton and Burslem (to 1922)	11,196 to 11,231	19
Wolverhampton	11,674 to 11,727	19
Suffolk		
Blything	11,728 to 11,761	2
Bosmere and Claydon	11,762 to 11,779	3
Bury St Edmunds	11,780 to 11,792	3
Cosford (founded in 1779)	11,793 to 11,812	5
Hartismere	11,813 to 11,836	8
Hoxne	11,837 to 11,854	9
Ipswich	11,855 to 11,888	9
Mildenhall	11,889 to 11,905	11
Mutford and Lothingland (founded in 1763)	11,906 to 11,931	11
Plomesgate	11,932 to 11,953	13
Risbridge	11,954 to 11,978	14
Samford	11,979 to 11,990	15
Stow	11,991 to 12,013	16
Sudbury	12,014 to 12,041	16
Thingoe	12,042 to 12,062	17
Wangford	12,063 to 12,076	18
Woodbridge	12,078 to 12,101	19
Surrey		
Ash	none	1
Bermondsey	12,102 to 12,107	2
Camberwell	12,108 to 12,142	4
Chertsey	12,143 to 12,166	4
Croydon	12,167 to 12,218	5
Dorking	12,219 to 12,234	6
Epsom	12,235 to 12,269	6
Farnham	12,270 to 12,299	7
Godstone	12,314 to 12,331	7
Guildford	12,332 to 12,369	7
Hambledon	12,370 to 12,388	8
Kingston on Thames	12,389 to 12,455	9
Lambeth	12,456 to 12,519	10
Newington	12,520 to 12,527	12
Reigate	12,575 to 12,596	14
Richmond	12,597 to 12,631	14

Rotherhithe	12,632 to 12,638	14
St Olave	12,528 to 12,574	12
St Saviour	12,639 to 12,688	15
Wandsworth and Clapham	12,689 to 12,745	9
Sussex		
Arundel	12,746 only	1
Battle	12,747 to 12,768	2
Brighton (founded in 1810)	12,769 to 12,799	3
Chailey	12,800 to 12,812	4
Chichester	12,813 to 12,828	5
Cuckfield	12,829 to 12,853	5
Eastbourne	12,854 to 12,885	6
East Grinstead	12,886 to 12,904	18
East Preston (founded in 1791)	12,905 to 12,930	6
Hailsham	12,931 to 12,949	8
Hastings	12,950 to 12,988	8
Horsham	12,989 to 13,014	9
Lewes	13,015 to 13,027	10
Midhurst	13,028 to 13,045	11
Newhaven	13,046 to 13,059	12
Petworth	13,060 to 13,075	13
Rye	13,076 to 13,098	14
Steyning	13,099 to 13,126	16
Sutton (founded in 1791)	13,127 only	16
Thakenham	13,128 to 13,137	17
Ticehurst	13,138 to 13,156	17
Uckfield	13,157 to 13,175	17
Westbourne	13,176 to 13,188	18
West Firle	13,189 to 13,197	18
Westhampnett	13,198 to 13,217	18
Warwickshire		
Alcester	13,218 to 13,231	1
Aston	13,232 to 13,269	1
Atherstone	13,270 to 13,285	1
Birmingham (founded in 1783)	13,286 to 13,276	2 and 20
Coventry	13,377 to 13,402	5
Foleshill	13,403 to 13,418	7
Meriden	13,419 to 13,431	11

[contd]

Nuneaton	13,432 to 13,447	12
Rugby	13,448 to 13,475	14
Solihull	13,476 to 13,491	15
Southam	13,492 to 13,507	15
Stratford upon Avon	13,508 to 13,529	16
Warwick	13,530 to 13,560	18
Westmorland		
East Ward	13,561 to 13,580	6
Kendal	13,581 to 13,624	9
West Ward	13,625 to 13,638	18
Wiltshire		
Alderbury (1836 to 1895 – renamed Salisbury in 1895)	13,639 to 13,657	15
Amesbury	13,658 to 13,667	1
Bradford (renamed Bradford upon Avon in 1895)	13,668 to 13,685	3
Calne	13,686 to 13,698	4
Chippenham	13,699 to 13,718	5
Cricklade and Wootton Bassett	13,719 to 13,734	5
Devizes	13,735 to 13,750	6
Highworth and Swindon (renamed Swindon and Highworth in 1889)	13,751 to 13,775	16
Malmesbury	13,776 to 13,788	11
Marlborough	13,789 to 13,799	11
Melksham (renamed Trowbridge and Melksham in 1898)	13,800 to 13,818	11
Mere	13,819 to 13,829	13
Pewsey	13,830 to 13,843	14
Salisbury (see also Alderbury)	13,844 to 13,848	1
Tisbury	13,849 to 13,862	17
Warminster	13,863 to 13,880	18
Westbury and Whorwellsdown	13,881 to 13,891	18
Wilton	13,892 to 13,902	19
Worcestershire		
Bromsgrove	13,903 to 13,929	3
Droitwich	13,930 to 13,957	6
Dudley	13,958 to 13,996	6
Evesham	13,997 to 14,015	6
Kidderminster	14,016 to 14,038	9
Kings Norton	14,039 to 14,078	9
Martley	14,079 to 14,102	11

Pershore	14,103 to 14,114	13
Shipton on Stour	14,115 to 14,133	15
Stourbridge	14,134 to 14,167	16
Tenbury	14,168 to 14,178	17
Upton on Severn	14,179 to 14,201	17
Worcester	14,202 to 14,231	19
Yorkshire		
East Riding		
Beverley	14,232 to 14,255	2
Bridlington	14,256 to 14,271	3
Driffield	14,272 to 14,290	6
Howden	14,291 to 14,305	9
Kingston upon Hull	14,306 to 14,329	9
Malton (and North Riding)	14,513 to 14,530	11
Patrington	14,333 to 14,343	13
Pocklington	14,344 to 14,357	13
Scarborough (and North Riding)	14,610 to 14,628	15
Sculcoates (and North Riding)	14,358 to 14,383	15
Selby (and West Riding)	15,430 to 15,445	15
Skirlaugh	14,384 to 14,395	15
York (and North Riding and West Riding)	14,396 to 14,427	19
West Riding		
Barnsley	14,674 to 14,704	2
Barwick	15,548 to 15,549	2
Bradford	14,720 to 14,767	3
Bramley	14,707 to 14,719	3
Carlton	15,286 to 15,288	4
Dewsbury	14,830 to 14,882	82
Doncaster	14,903 to 14,937	6
Ecclesall Bierlow	14,938 to 14,953	6
Goole	14,954 to 14,973	7
Great Ouseburn (and North Riding)	15,275 to 15,285	12
Great Preston	15,350 to 15,367	13
Halifax	14,974 to 15,029	8
Hemsworth	15,041 to 15,055	8
Holbeck	15,056 to 15,062	8
Huddersfield	15,063 to 15,134	9
Hunslet	15,141 to 15,157	9

[contd]

Keighley	15,158 to 15,200	9
Knaresborough	15,201 to 15,223	9
Leeds	15,224 to 15,270	10
North Bierley	14,768 to 14,829	12
Otley	none	12
Pateley Bridge	15,289 to 15,303	13
Penistone	15,304 to 15,320	13
Pontefract	15,321 to 15,349	13
Ripon (and North Riding)	none	14
Rotherham	15,368 to 15,408	14
Saddleworth	15,409 to 15,418	15
Sedbergh	15,419 to 15,429	15
Selby (and East Riding)	15,430 to 15,446	15
Settle	15,447 to 15,464	15
Sheffield	15,465 to 15,511	15
Skipton	15,512 to 15,535	15
Tadcaster	15,536 to 15,549	17
Thorne	15,550 to 15,565	17
Todmorden	6,272 to 6,298	17
Wakefield	15,566 to 15,615	18
Wetherby	15,616 to 15,626	18
Wharfedale	15,627 to 15,654	18
Wortley	15,655 to 15,672	19
York (and East and West Ridings)	14,396 to 14,427	19
North Riding		
Aysgarth	14,428 to 14,435	1
Bainbridge	none	none
Bedale	14,444 to 14,453	2
Doncaster (and West Riding)	14,903 to 14,931	6
Easingwold	14,436 to 14,443	6
Guisborough	14,454 to 14,482	7
Helmsley	14,483 to 14,493	8
Kirby Moorside	14,494 to 14,501	9
Leyburn	14,502 to 14,512	10
Malton (and East Riding)	14,513 to 14,532	11
Middlesbrough	14,533 to 14,559	11
Northallerton	14,560 to 14,574	12
Great Ouseburn (and West Riding)	15,275 to 15,285	12
Pickering	14,575 to 14,586	13

Reeth	14,587 to 14,594	14
Richmond	14,595 to 14,609	14
Ripon (and West Riding)	none	14
Scarborough (and East Riding)	14,610 to 14,630	15
Sculcoates (and East Riding)	14,358 to 14,382	15
Stokesley	14,631 to 14,638	16
Thirsk	14,639 to 14,655	17
Whitby	14,656 to 14,673	18
York (and East and West Ridings)	14,396 to 14,425	19

Wales		
Anglesey		
Anglesey	15,673 to 15,690	1
Bangor and Beaumaris	15,964 to 15,997	2
Holyhead	15,691 to 15,706	8
Breconshire		
Brecknock	15,707 to 15,733	3
Builth	15,734 to 15,746	3
Crickhowell	15,747 to 15,768	5
Hay	15,769 to 15,782	8
Caernarvonshire		
Caernarvon	15,998 to 16,022	4
Conwy	16,023 to 16,051	5
Pwllheli	16,052 to 16,074	13
Cardiganshire		
Aberaeron	15,783 to 15,795	1
Aberystwyth	15,796 to 15,816	1
Cardigan	15,817 to 15,844	4
Lampeter	15,845 to 15,857	10
Newcastle Emlyn	15,949 to 15,962	12
Tregaron	15,858 to 15,871	17
Carmarthenshire		
Carmarthen	15,872 to 15,896	9
Llandeilo Fawr	15,922 to 15,936	10
Llandovery	15,937 to 15,948	10
Llanelly	15,897 to 15,920	10
Denbighshire		
Llanrwst	16,075 to 16,086	10
Ruthin	16,987 to 16,103	14

[contd]

Wrexham	16,104 to 16,130	19
Flintshire		
Hawarden	16,165 to 16,175	8
Holywell	16,176 to 16,208	8
St Asaph	16,131 to 16,164	1
Glamorgan		
Bridgend and Cowbridge	16,209 to 16,245	3
Cardiff	16,246 to 16,312	4
Gower	16,313 to 16,325	7
Merthyr Tydfil	16,326 to 16,353	11
Neath	16,354 to 16,392	12
Ponterdewe	16,426 to 16,436	13
Pontypridd	16,393 to 16,418	13
Swansea	16,437 to 16,477	16
Merioneth		
Bala	16,478 to 16,485	2
Corwen	16,486 to 16,502	5
Dolgellau	16,503 to 16,521	6
Festiniog	16,522 to 16,542	7
Monmouthshire		
Abergavenny	7,964 to 7,991	1
Bedwellty	7,992 to 8,030	2
Chepstow	8,031 to 8,058	4
Monmouth	8,059 to 8,085	11
Newport	8,086 to 8,151	12
Pontypool	8,152 to 8,184	13
Montgomeryshire		
Forden (later Montgomery and Welshpool)	16,580 to 16,596	7
Llanfyllin	16,543 to 16,563	10
Machynlleth	16,564 to 16,579	11
Newtown and Llanidloes	16,597 to 16,618	12
Pembrokeshire		
Haverfordwest	16,619 to 16,651	8
Narberth	16,652 to 16,666	12
Pembroke	16,667 to 16,689	13
Radnorshire		
Knighton	16,690 to 16,708	9
Presteigne	16,709 to 16,714	13
Rhayader	16,715 to 16,726	14

APPENDIX 3

REGISTERS OF ADMISSIONS TO LUNATIC ASYLUMS

This series is held at The National Archives in Document Class MH 94. The following lists have been arranged in date order. Note that some documents have been numbered out of sequence.

Admission Registers

Piece number	Dates	Piece number	Dates	Piece number	Dates
Metropolitan Licensed Houses		16	1855 to 1858	30	1891
1	1846 to 1847	17	1859 to 1861	31	1892
2	1848 to 1850	18	1861 to 1864	87*	1893
3	1851 to 1848	19	1864 to 1866	32	1894
4	1859 to 1875	20	1867 to 1869	88*	1895
5	1876 to 1885	21	1869 to 1871	89*	1896
6	1886 to 1900	22	1872 to 1874	33	1897
Provincial Licensed Houses		23	1874 to 1876	34	1898
7	1846 to 1847	24	1877 to 1878	35	1899
8	1848 to 1850	25	1879 to 1880	36	1900
9	1850 to 1857	26	1881 to 1882	37	1901
10	1857 to 1879	27	1883 to 1884	38	1902
11	1880 to 1900	83*	1885	90*	1903
County Asylums and Hospitals		84*	1886	39	1904
12	1846 to 1847	85*	1887	40	1905
13	1847 to 1849	86*	1888	41	1906
14	1849 to 1851	28	1889	42	1907
15	1851 to 1855	29	1890	43	1908

* Numbered out of date order

[contd]

475

Piece number	Dates	Piece number	Dates	Piece number	Dates
44	1909	66	1931	96	1953
45	1910	67	1932	97	1954
46	1911	68	1933	98	1955
47	1912	69	1934	99	1956
48	1913	70	1935	100	1957
49	1914	71	1936	101	1958
50	1915	72	1937	102	1959
51	1916	73	1938	103	1960
52	1917	74	1939	*Private Patients in County Asylums and Hospitals*	
53	1918	75	1940		
54	1919	76	1941	105	1883 to 1899
55	1920	77	1942	106	1890 to 1900
56	1921	78	1943	107	1916 to 1917 (records of formalities)
57	1922	79	1944		
58	1923	80	1945		
59	1924	81	1946	108	1901 to 1908
60	1925	82	1947	109	1909 to 1916
61	1926	91	1948	110	1917 to 1923
62	1927	92	1949	111	1923 to 1928
63	1928	93	1950	112	1929 to 1934
64	1929	94	1951	113	1935 to 1947
65	1930	95	1952	114	1948 to 1960

APPENDIX 4

THE OLD MONETARY SYSTEM

4 farthings = 1 penny (*d*)
12 pennies (*d*) = 1 shilling (*s*)
20 shillings (*s*) = 1 pound (£)
1 pound (£) and 1 shilling (*s*) = 1 guinea

Name	Value	Description
Farthing	¼*d*	Coin – made of copper and later bronze
Ha'penny	½*d*	Coin – made of copper and later bronze
Penny	1*d*	Coin – made of copper and later bronze
Thrupenny piece *or* thrupenny bit *or* thrupence	3*d*	Coin – made of silver and in 1937 a twelve-sided brass coin
Sixpence	6*d*	Coin – made of silver
Shilling	1*s*	Coin – made of silver
Florin	2*s*	Coin – made of silver
Half-crown	2*s* 6*d*	Coin – made of silver
Crown	5*s*	Coin – made of silver
Guinea*	£1 1*s*	Coin – made of gold (taken out of circulation in 1813 but the term 'guinea' continued in use)
Half-guinea*	10*s* 6*d*	Coin – made of gold
Sovereign	£1	Coin – made of gold
Half-sovereign	10*s*	Coin – made of gold
Two-pound coin	£2	Coin – made of gold
Ten-shilling note	10*s*	Paper note
Pound note	£1	Paper note
Five-pound note	£5	Paper note

* Many dealers, particularly those dealing in farm livestock and horses, usually dealt in guineas and not pounds. Jewellers often priced their products in guineas

Notes

A number of bronze or copper coins were known collectively as 'coppers'.

A number of silver coins were known collectively as 'silver'.

Gold coins were withdrawn from general circulation in 1920.

Examples of Written and Spoken Costs

£1–19s–6½d } 'one pound, nineteen shillings and sixpence ha'penny'
or £1–19– 6½ } *or* 'one pound nineteen and sixpence ha'penny'

£5–17s } 'five pounds and seventeen shillings'
or £5 – 17 } *or* 'five pounds seventeen'

5½d   'five and a half pennies' but spoken as 'five pence ha'penny'
2¾d   'two and three-quarter pennies' but spoken as 'tuppence three farthings'

12s–11d } 'twelve shillings and eleven pence'
or 12/11 } also spoken as 'twelve and eleven pence' *or* 'twelve and eleven'

15s – 2d } 'fifteen shillings and tuppence'
or 15/2 } also spoken as 'fifteen and tuppence' *or* 'fifteen and two'

17s – 6d } 'seventeen shillings and six pence'
or 17/6 } *or* 'seventeen and sixpence' *or* 'seventeen and six'

11½d   'eleven pence ha'penny'*

* The term 'eleven and a half pence' was never used

5s/11½ *or* 5/11½   'five shillings and eleven pence ha'penny'
                          but spoken as 'five and eleven pence ha'penny'

¼d   a farthing*
½d   a halfpenny or ha'penny
¾d   three farthings*

* The terms 'a quarter of a penny' or 'three quarters of a penny' were never used

Slang Monetary Terms:

Pony	£25	Gen	1s
Nicker	£1	tanner	6d
Quid	£1	tester	
Half a bar	}	teston	} 6d
Half a sheet	} 10s (£½)	testoon	}
Half a nicker	}	bob	1s
Dollar	5s	three ha'pence	1½d
Half a dollar	2s 6d	(three half pennies)	

APPENDIX 5

WEBSITES FOR RECORD OFFICES IN ENGLAND AND WALES

England

Bedfordshire	www.bedfordshire.gov.uk/CommunityAndLiving/ ArchivesAndRecordOffice/ArchivesAndRecordOffice.aspx
Berkshire	www.berkshirerecordoffice.org.uk/
Buckinghamshire	www.buckscc.gov.uk/archives
Cambridgeshire	www.cambridgeshire.gov.uk/archives
Cornwall	www.cornwall.gov.uk/default.aspx?page=1729
Cumbria: Carlisle and Whitehaven	www.cumbria.gov.uk/archives
Derbyshire	www.derbyshire.gov.uk/leisure/record_office/
Devon: Barnstaple and Exeter	www.devon.gov.uk/index/councildemocracy/record_office.htm
Plymouth	www.plymouth.gov.uk/archives
Dorset	www.dorsetforyou.com/archives
Durham	www.durham.gov.uk/recordoffice
Essex: Chelmsford, Colchester and Southend	www.essexcc.gov.uk/vip8/ecc/ECCWebsite/dis/gui.jsp?sectionO id=168&channelOid=13813&guideOid=14802
Gloucestershire: Gloucester	www.gloucestershire.gov.uk/archives
Bristol	www.bristol.gov.uk/recordoffice
Hampshire: Winchester	www.hants.gov.uk/archives
Isle of Wight	www.iwight.com/library/record_office
Portsmouth	www.portsmouthrecordsoffice.co.uk/
Southampton	www.southampton.gov.uk/s-leisure/artsheritage/history/archives/
Herefordshire	www.herefordshire.gov.uk/leisure/archives/3584.asp
Hertfordshire	www.hertsdirect.org/libsleisure/heritage1/HALS/

Huntingdonshire	www.cambridgeshire.gov.uk/archives
Kent: Maidstone	www.kent.gov.uk/archives
Dover (East Kent) Strood	www.medway.gov.uk/index/leisure/archives/28228.htm
Lancashire: Preston	www3.lancashire.gov.uk/corporate/atoz/a_to_z/service.asp?u_id=1202&tab=1
Wigan	www.wlct.org/Culture/Heritage/arc_coll.htm
Manchester	www.gmcro.co.uk/Sources/index.html
Liverpool	www.liverpool.gov.uk/Leisure_and_culture/Libraries_and_archives/Catalogues_archive_and_local_history/index.asp
Leicestershire and Rutland	www.leics.gov.uk/record_office.htm
Lincolnshire: Lincoln	www.lincolnshire.gov.uk/archives
Grimsby	www.nelincs.gov.uk/community-people-and-living/records-and-archives/
London: London Metropolitan Archives	www.cityoflondon.gov.uk/lma
Guildhall Library	ihr.sas.ac.uk/gh/
City of Westminster Archives	www.westminster.gov.uk/archives
The National Archives	www.nationalarchives.gov.uk
Norfolk	www.archives.norfolk.gov.uk/
Northampton	www.northamptonshire.gov.uk/en/councilservices/Community/ro/Pages/Records.aspx
Northumberland: Newcastle upon Tyne	www.tyneandweararchives.org.uk/
Nottinghamshire	www.nottinghamshire.gov.uk/archives
Oxfordshire	www.darkarchivist.com/
Shropshire	www.shropshire.gov.uk/archives.nsf
Somerset: Taunton	www.somerset.gov.uk/archives
Bath	www.batharchives.co.uk
Staffordshire: Dudley	www.dudley.gov.uk/archives
Stafford and Lichfield	www.staffordshire.gov.uk/archives
Walsall	www.walsall.gov.uk/index/leisure_and_culture/local_history_centre/local_history_centre_services/local_history_centre_archives.htm
Wolverhampton	www.wolverhampton.gov.uk/leisure_culture/libraries/archives
Suffolk: Ipswich and Bury St Edmunds	www.suffolk.gov.uk/archives
Surrey	www.surreycc.gov.uk/surreyhistoryservice

Sussex, East: Lewes	www.eastsussex.gov.uk/leisureandtourism/ localandfamilyhistory/esro/collections/esccarchive.htm
West: Chichester	www.westsussex.gov.uk/record-office
Warwickshire: Birmingham	www.birmingham.gov.uk/archives
Warwick	www.warwickshire.gov.uk/countyrecordoffice
Westmorland	www.cumbria.gov.uk/archives
Wiltshire	www.wiltshire.gov.uk/archives
Worcestershire	www.worcestershire.gov.uk/records
Yorkshire: York City Archives	www.york.gov.uk/leisure/Libraries/archives/
East Riding: Beverley	www.eastriding.gov.uk/cs/culture-and-information/archives/ summary-of-collections/?secat=6634
North Riding: Northallerton	www.northyorks.gov.uk/index.aspx?articleid=3134
West Riding: Bradford and Calderdale	www.archives.wyjs.org.uk/

Wales

National Library of Wales	www.llgc.org.uk/
Anglesey	www.anglesey.gov.uk/archives
Brecknockshire (Brecon) *see* Powys	
Caernarfon (Caernarvonshire)	www.gwynedd.gov.uk/archives
Ceredigion (Cardiganshire)	www.archifdy-ceredigion.org.uk/
Carmarthenshire	www.carmarthenshire.gov.uk/English/education/archives/Pages/ Home.aspx
Denbighshire	www.denbighshire.gov.uk/archives
Flintshire	www.archivesnetworkwales.info/
Glamorgan: Cardiff	www.glamro.gov.uk/
Swansea	www.swansea.gov.uk/index.cfm?articleid=406/
Meirionnydd (Merioneth)	www.gwynedd.gov.uk/archives
Montgomeryshire *see* Powys	
Monmouthshire	www.archiveswales.org.uk/
Pembrokeshire	www.pembrokeshire.gov.uk/content.asp?nav=107,1447&parent_ directory_id=646
Powys (Brecknock, Montgomeryshire and Radnorshire)	www.powys.gov.uk/index.php?id=647&L=0&
Radnorshire *see* Powys	

INDEX OF PLACE NAMES
AND SHIPS

Note: Place names are given in the modern spelling. Ships' names are given in italics.

INDEX OF PERSONAL NAMES